D0198918

WESTERN CIVILIZATION TO 1648

Diane W. Darst, Ph.D.

An American BookWorks Corporation Project

McGraw-Hill Publishing Company

New York   St. Louis   San Francisco   Auckland   Bogotá   Caracas   Hamburg
Lisbon   London   Madrid   Mexico   Milan   Montreal   New Delhi   Oklahoma City
Paris   San Juan   São Paulo   Singapore   Sydney   Tokyo   Toronto

With love to David, Elizabeth and David Jr.

Diane W. Darst received her M.A. and Ph.D. degrees in modern European cultural and intellectual history from Columbia University, working under Jacques Barzun. She has taught survey courses in modern European history at Dowling College, New York.

Editor, James Casada, Ph.D., Winthrop College, Rock Hill, SC

Review Editor, Jay Pascal Anglin, The University of Southern Mississippi, Hattiesburg, MI

The maps were executed by Jean Paul Tremblay, Francis & Shaw, Inc., Dyno Lowenstein, and Vantage Art, Inc.

Western Civilization to 1648

Copyright © 1990 by McGraw-Hill, Inc. All rights reserved. Printed in the United States of America. Except as permitted under the Copyright Act of 1976, no part of this publication may be reproduced or distributed in any form or by any means, or stored in a data base or retrieval system, without the prior written permission of the publisher.

1 2 3 4 5 6 7 8 9 10 11 12 13 14 15 16 17 18 19 20 FGR FGR 8 9 2 1 0 9

ISBN 0-07-015395-7

Library of Congress Cataloging-in-Publication Data

Darst, Diane W.
      Western civilization to 1648 / Diane W. Darst.
          p.   cm. — (McGraw-Hill college review books)
      "An American BookWorks Corporation project."
      ISBN 0-07-015395-7
        1. Civilization, Occidental.   I. Title.   II. Series.
CB245.D35   1990   89-13260
909'.09821— dc20   CIP

Map Acknowledgments

The maps on pages 19, 41, 78, 213, 251, 343, 389, 434, and 535 were reproduced from John B. Harrison, Richard E. Sullivan, and Dennis Sherman, *A Short History of Western Civilization*, 7th ed., McGraw-Hill, New York, 1990. The maps on pages 99, 162, 284, and 552 were reproduced from the 6th edition, 1985.

Preface

The study of Western civilization sheds light on the forces that have shaped our Western world. It traces the development of key Western ideas, institutions, and socioeconomic conditions and notes their interaction with non-Western cultures where relevant. A knowledge of Western civilization is essential to all educated human beings for it offers a chronological framework upon which to organize information from many areas of study and it heightens our appreciation for the rich and diverse heritage of the West.

This volume provides a clear and concise account of the main developments in Western civilization from prehistory to 1648. It is designed to serve either as a self-contained classroom text or as a review guide used in conjunction with assigned texts. Although it is primarily intended for college students enrolled in introductory courses in Western civilization and European history, it will also be of value to secondary school students and teachers, university students in other courses, and anyone seeking greater understanding of the growth of Western civilization.

A number of features have been provided to enhance the reader's comprehension and retention of historical material. First, each chapter begins with an overview and ends with a summary. Second, time lines preceding every chapter set forth in chronological order the main occurrences of each period. Third, a system of clearly related headings and subheadings helps the reader locate, review, and remember important themes. Fourth, strategically placed maps impart visual understanding of historical circumstances and how they have changed over time. Additional comprehensive maps are available in paperback form in the *Rand McNally Atlas of European History*, the *Penguin Atlas of Ancient History*, and the *Penguin Atlas of Medieval History*. Fifth, extensive lists of recommended readings at the end of each chapter direct interested readers to standard works and the latest research about topics covered. An additional selection of primary sources that refers to the entire book is the *University of Chicago Readings in Western Civilization*.

Acknowledgments

This book has been both a pleasure and a challenge, and there are many people whose support and efforts have helped me bring it to fruition and to whom I offer my heartfelt thanks. At McGraw-Hill, Tom Dembofsky first conceived of the idea for a McGraw-Hill Review Book series in the humanities and enlisted my aid. More recently, John Carleo has been most cooperative and efficient in expediting publication. Jeanne Flagg has served as a sympathetic and helpful sponsoring editor. I am also indebted to outside editors, Nancy Cone for her careful reading of the text and for providing clear and concise subheadings and Dr. James Casada for his work in shortening the manuscript and his contributions to Chapter 15.

At Connecticut College, Dr. Edward Cranz and Dr. Helen Mulvey first introduced me to the subtleties and insights of the historical discipline. In writing this book, I have been inspired by Dr. Jacques Barzun, my doctoral adviser at Columbia University. His many works set a superlative example of history that is well-written and of broad appeal.

My greatest debt of gratitude goes to my family. My parents, Mr. and Mrs. E. Robert Wassman, created a happy environment in which love of learning and the desire for excellence could grow. They have remained close and caring parents, always quick to offer help when needed. My children, Elizabeth and David, are my greatest joy. I thank them for their interest in my work and for all the wonderful fun we have together. My deepest appreciation goes to my husband, David, for always encouraging me to take challenges and then providing the love, advice, and assistance necessary to see them through. In so many ways, this book would not have been possible without him.

D. W. D.
Greenwich, CT
August 1989

Contents

Maps

CHAPTER 1

Introduction and Prehistory

Time Line

c. 3 to 4 million years ago	First hominids
c. 2 million to 10,000 B.C.	Paleolithic culture; first tool-making
c. 93,000 B.C.	Modern *Homo sapiens* appears
c. 11,000 B.C.	End of Ice Age
c. 10,000 B.C.	Mesolithic culture
c. 8000–6000 B.C.	Emergence of Neolithic culture
c. 6500–5500 B.C.	First pottery

c. 3000 B.C.   Neolithic period ends; rise of urban civilizations

---

History, as its name implies, is the story of past human experience. Unlike literature, however, it bases its account of the past on factual evidence that has been critically analyzed. History begins at the moment, traditionally dated about 5200 years ago, when people started to keep written records. Because much of what occurred was either not written down or was destroyed, our picture of human experience in the past can never be complete. It tends to focus on the great individuals, great ideas, and great events that stand out for their uniqueness or their ability to effect change. Yet historians today are ever mindful of the broader scope of history. They examine the underlying cultural assumptions and long-term social and economic trends that contribute to the course of human events.

In seeking to explain the causes of past thoughts and actions, the study of history helps people to think critically and to perceive patterns and relationships. These skills are crucial to dealing with the present and making choices for the future.

Prehistory is the study of human life before writing was invented. It relies primarily on information provided by fossil and material remains. The term prehistory encompasses the period from approximately 3 million years ago to 3500 B.C., although new evidence suggests that written record keeping may date from as early as 10 thousand years ago.

The Earth's Origin

It is impossible to say for certain how old the earth is or how it was created. Using radioactive dating techniques, geologists have determined that the earth's oldest stratum dates from about 4.2 billion years ago. That would make the earth somewhere between 4.5 and 5 billion years old.

Scientists today believe that the Universe was created about 15 billion years ago in a tremendous explosion of energy, the "Big Bang." Ten billion years elapsed before our solar system came into being. The most widely accepted theory suggests that it was formed by the gravitational condensation of a vast cloud of interstellar gasses and dust into discrete bodies.

The origin of life is equally obscure. Evidence suggests that life began approximately 4 billion years ago in shallow pools of organic liquid on the earth's surface. Within them, single-celled organisms (such as bacteria) were formed. Over billions of years, life evolved from simple to more complex. The appearance of oxygen-producing plants created an environment in which animal life could exist.

Geological Eras

By analyzing the earth's strata, geologists have divided its history into five eras. The geological timetable shown in Table 1.1 coordinates with the development of life from its earliest forms to the present.

Table 1.1
Evolutionary Timetable of the Development of Life

1. Precambrian Era: 4.6 billion to 570 million years ago

   First fossils found (one-celled organisms) date to around 3.4 billion years ago; multicellular organisms appear 700 million years ago.

2. Paleozoic Era: 570 to 225 million years ago

   More abundant plant and animal life including shellfish, crabs, worms, and various fish. At end of era, first amphibians and land plants indicate beginning of move out of oceans and onto land.

3. Mesozoic Era: 225 to 65 million years ago

   Era of great reptiles of which dinosaurs were the largest. Mammals first appear at the end of the era and eventually supplant the reptiles.

4. Cenozoic Era: 65 million years ago to the present

   A. Tertiary Period

Paleocene Epoch: 65 to 54 million years ago

Appearance of first primates.

Eocene Epoch: 54 to 38 million years ago

First primates: ancestors of tarsiers and lemurs.

Oligocene Epoch: 38 to 26 million years ago

Appearance of monkeys and their evolution along several lines.

Miocene Epoch: 26 to 7 million years ago

Appearance of anthropoid apes and their spread across continents.

Pliocene Epoch: 7 to 2.5 million years ago

Development of first hominids.

B. Quaternary Period

Pleistocene Epoch: 2.5 million to 10,000 years ago

Era of four great glacial advances that created the earth's landscape as we now know it and during which time *Homo sapiens* evolved.

Holocene Epoch: 10,000 years ago to the present

Epoch from the New Stone Age to recent times during which humans developed as social beings and producers of culture.

Human Evolution

Our Ape Ancestors

Since the nineteenth century, increasing evidence has pointed to the evolution of human beings from an extinct, apelike ancestor. Obvious anatomical and molecular similarities place humans, apes, and monkeys in the same family of primates. By examining, dating, and comparing fossils, it is possible to construct a probable theory of evolution from the simplest primates to humans. In plotting this development, paleontologists focus attention on several significant events: the change from tree-dwelling to ground-dwelling, the assumption of an erect posture and two-legged (bipedal) locomotion, the development of the thumb, the disappearance of huge canine teeth, the increase in body and brain size, numerous other skeletal changes, and the ability to make tools.

An evolutionary tree of our primate ancestors is summarized in Table 1.2.

Table 1.2
Evolutionary Tree of Some of Our Primate Ancestors

50 million years ago: Existence of earliest primates (small, lemurlike creatures who dwelt in trees and ate insects). Humanlike traits include fingernails, a rudimentary thumb, and changes that favor sight over smell.

35 million years ago: Line leading to apes splits off from those leading to present-day monkeys.

28 million years ago: Division between tree-dwelling and grounddwelling apes.

20 million years ago: Dryopithecus, fossil genus of extinct ancestor of both humans and modern apes. Larger brain, stereoscopic vision. Teeth still apelike.

14 million years ago: Ramapithecus, possibly the earliest hominid, but may be related to the orangutan. Most likely still a tree-dwelling fruit and nut eater, but teeth are less apelike.

9 to 4 million years ago: Gap in fossil record just when hominid line separated permanently from that of the apes. Hominids learn to walk upright, a change that frees hands to be used for carrying food and for manipulation.

The Emergence of *Homo Sapiens*

True humans, as opposed to humanlike creatures (hominids), appear with the development of the genus *Homo* approximately 2 million years ago. There are two schools of thought as to where our earliest human ancestors arose. One holds that modern humans first appeared simultaneously in different places in Africa, Asia, and Europe. The more widely accepted view posits an African site of origin with later spread to the rest of the world. The latter theory is bolstered by evidence from molecular biologists; they have shown that every living person is descended from one "African Eve" who lived between 100,000 and 200,000 years ago.

Scholars disagree over whether certain fossils belong in the direct line of descent or whether they represent different forms that became extinct. A simplified arrangement of our possible evolutionary path is shown in Figure 1.1.

The Development of Culture

The earliest humans had no culture. They spent their short lives wandering in search of food. Their main objectives were survival and reproduction. They had no shelter, no fire, no tools, no agriculture, no domesticated animals, no social, political, or religious organizations, and no art. They did possess, however, the mental and physical attributes that slowly, over hundreds of thousands of years, would make all the above possible. The ability to create culture in the most elementary sense of fashioning tools, communicating by means of symbolic language, and living in society distinguishes humans from other creatures. Not even the ape is able to make the simplest advances of Paleolithic culture.

Paleolithic Culture

The earliest human cultures—Paleolithic, Mesolithic, and Neolithic—derive the second part of their names from the Greek word *lithos* for stone, the type of material used for their tools and weapons. The increased complexity of Paleolithic culture as time passes reflects the evolution of human beings from apelike creatures to true *Homo sapiens*.

Tool Making

During the Paleolithic period (the Old Stone Age), human beings made their first recognizable tools by striking pieces of rock against other stones to create pebble tools. There are three stages of tool making in this period: utilization, fashioning, and standardization.

Utilization Stage. Some time around 2 million years ago during the

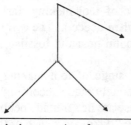

Australopithecus afarensis
3 to 4 million years old. First known hominid; 500 cc brain; walked on two legs; vegetarian; fossil "Lucy" 3.5 feet tall.

3 million years ago. Two emerging human-like species:

Australopithecus africanus
2.5 million years old. May be an ancestor of *Homo* or the same as *Australopithecus afarensis* or on a line with *A. boisei* or *A. robustus*.

A. boisei   A. robustus
1.8 million years old. 500 cc brain; vegetarian; new evidence suggests manual dexterity; branch died out 1.2 million years ago.

Homo habilis
2 million years old. First tool-maker; used pebble tools; 650-700 cc brain; 4 feet tall; fully erect; probably ate meat; teeth small and square; well-developed thumb.

Homo erectus
1.6 million to 400,000 years old. 900-1,000 cc brain; 5 to 6 feet tall; fully erect; meat-eater; hunter; protruding jaws and brow ridges; first to use fire; made stone tools such as hand axe; migrated out of Africa to Asia (fossils: Peking Man and Java Man, 700,000 B.C.) and to Europe (fossil: Heidelberg Man, 500,000 B.C.).

Homo sapiens (archaic)
400,000 to 30,000 B.C.. 1300-1600 cc brain; reduced jaws and brow ridges; heightened forehead; made elaborate tools; skillful hunter and fisherman.

Homo neanderthalensis
125,000 to 30,000 B.C. 1,450 cc brain; stooped posture; larger jaw, base of nose, and teeth than modern man; used fire; lived in caves; made clothes and stone tools; not a direct ancestor of modern humans; became extinct.

Homo sapiens (modern)
93,000 B.C. to the present. Anatomically similar to modern humans.

Fig. 1.1 Possible Evolutionary Path of *Homo Sapiens*

Pleistocene epoch, *Australopithecus* may have used the most primitive form of tool, the *eolith*. These hominids could have simply picked up any rock in order to perform the task at hand. We cannot, of course, know for certain if the rocks found at Australopithecine sites were used as tools since these are indistinguishable from other rocks.

Fashioning Stage. The next stage of tool making, fashioning, encompasses tools made haphazardly when needed. The early pebble tools are of this type and have been found near the fossils of *Homo habilis*.

Standardization Stage. The third stage of tool making, standardization, occurs when tools are deliberately made according to a set pattern and preserved for later use. These are better made pebble tools with sharp cutting edges and tools of the "flake" type such as the hand ax. The latter are pointed and have two sharp faces that facilitate cutting, chopping, scraping, and digging. These tools were first used by *Homo erectus*. With *Homo neanderthalensis*, the range of standardized tools increased and specialized tools and weapons such as stone-tipped spears and bone needles began to be used. *Homo sapiens* made an even greater variety of new tools to meet specific needs. These included blade tools, tool-making tools, harpoons, and bows.

Method of Food Procurement

During the Old Stone Age, people were food gatherers and hunters. They subsisted on the fruit, berries, and nuts they could collect, and, increasingly, on the animals and fish they could kill. Hunting forced them to live a nomadic life. They found shelter in caves or manmade tents. Their social organization was probably that of an extended family or clan.

Religion and Art

Old Stone Age humans appear to have practiced a rudimentary religion based on the worship of fertility goddesses and the animistic belief that spirits inhabited all things in nature. Paleolithic people created the first art in the form of statues, paintings and personal ornaments. The cave paintings of the late Paleolithic period suggest they engaged in ritualistic practices. Recent research attributes a higher level of cognitive capacity and cultural complexity to late Paleolithic humans than had previously been recognized.

Use of Fire

The harsh environment of the four great Ice Ages forced people and animals to retreat south. During this time, humans learned to use fire for light, heat and cooking. Life changed little over thousands of years, but progress, though slow, was made. By 10,000 B.C. the stage was set for a major breakthrough.

Mesolithic Culture

The Mesolithic period refers to a transitional stage of human culture varying according to location but centering around 10,000 B.C. During this period some new elements were grafted onto an essentially Paleolithic culture.

Semisedentary Life

In Mesolithic times, people tended to live near lakes, rivers, or seacoasts where fish, especially shellfish, were plentiful. This afforded a more sedentary existence. The dog was probably domesticated at this time.

Climatic Changes

Once the last Ice Age ended, around 11,000 B.C., changing weather patterns led to the appearance of lush forests in some places and barren deserts in others, as well as to the extinction of the great mammals Paleolithic peoples hunted. Humans necessarily adapted to this changed environment.

New Inventions

The characteristic tool of Mesolithic culture was the microlith, a small, delicate instrument. Those who lived in forests discovered how to chop wood, use the bow and arrow, and make skis, sleds, and canoes.

New Food Source

Another consequence of the end of the last glacial phase was the growth of vegetation. It is possible that some Mesolithic peoples in the

Near East began eating cereal grains derived from wild grasses, a practice that would lead them to the next stage of cultural development.

Neolithic Culture

Five main characteristics set Neolithic culture apart from earlier cultures and together represent a significant advance in human cultural evolution.

Food Production

First and foremost, Neolithic people became food producers. They discovered how to grow their own food, mainly wheat and barley. This momentous discovery took place first in the Near East between 8000 and 6000 B.C. and spread throughout Eurasia and Africa during the next several thousand years. The ability to cultivate grains was probably aided by climatic and environmental changes that followed upon the end of the last Ice Age.

Domestication of Animals

A second feature of Neolithic culture, the domestication of animals, enhanced the quality of primitive life. Coupled with the production of food, these features created revolutionary changes in the human condition. The keeping of sheep, goats, cattle, and pigs assured a steady supply of meat and milk. Wool and animal hairs could be woven into more practical and adaptable types of clothing. Later, draught animals such as the ox and the horse provided a means of transportation and nonhuman power resources. The dog aided humans in hunting and tending flocks as well as offering companionship.

Settlement in Villages

The Neolithic "revolution" contributed greatly to the next major characteristic of Neolithic culture—that of settlement in villages. Unlike hunting, farming necessitates living in one place. Thus for the first time people could build permanent homes for themselves. This led to the growth of village communities in which almost all of the members were engaged in the sowing and reaping of crops. Social organization changed from a matriarchy to a patriarchy at this time.

Pottery Making

The more settled and stable nature of Neolithic life opened up a whole new range of cultural activity. Between 6500 and 5500 B.C. humans baked the first clay vessels. This pottery was often decorated and served a variety of practical purposes.

Advances in Tool Making

The New Stone Age witnessed a noticeable improvement in the type and quality of tools produced. This stage of tool making is often summed up as the use of polished stone tools. Neolithic people learned how to drill holes in stone. They made axes, chisels, and even sickles with which to cut grain. Their tools were also better crafted; they displayed a more finished surface, were more carefully shaped, and were made of materials better suited to their function. Even at this stage, tools are the best indicators of cultural progress.

Transition to Riverine Civilization

The Neolithic period ends with the rise of urban civilizations beginning c. 3000 B.C. On the banks of great rivers in the Near East, Egypt, India, and slightly later, China, Neolithic villages grew slowly into cities. The soil along riverbanks is well irrigated and thus fertile, insuring abundant harvests and making possible a food surplus. An excess of food enables a community to feed more people and frees some of them to work at other occupations. The differentiated functions of its inhabitants as well as its larger size distinguishes a city from a village. This new stage of development is called the Bronze Age after the material from which its tools and weapons were made.

The advent of civilization at this time is associated with three major breakthroughs: the emergence of urban life, the ability to deal with metals to the point of producing bronze, and the invention of a system of writing. From this moment on, prehistory is at an end and recorded history begins.

Homo sapiens is neither the strongest nor the swiftest nor the best physically equipped of all creatures, yet it has managed not only to survive but to flourish. This remarkable evolution is thanks in part to the very fact that our species was not perfectly suited to survive in a specific environment but rather was forced to make do with what it had. This ability to improvise has made humans the most adaptable of all beings and therefore the most able to control their environment.

Our hominid ancestors possessed several physical and mental traits—notably an erect posture, stereoscopic vision, a powerful thumb, and an enlarged brain—which set them apart from other creatures and enhanced their ability to improvise. The story of human evolution and the creation of culture is told in the development of these traits as well as a few others.

Recommended Reading

George O. Abell, *Drama of the Universe* (1978).

François Bordes, *The Old Stone Age* (1968).

R. Braidwood, *Prehistoric Man* (1975).

J. Bronowski, *The Ascent of Man* (1973).

Christopher Dawson, *The Age of the Gods: A Study in the Origins of Culture in Prehistoric Europe and the Ancient Near East* (1928).

John Gowlett, *Ascent to Civilization: The Archaeology of Early Man* (1984).

Stephen Jay Gould, *Ever Since Darwin* (1977).

Stephen Jay Gould, *The Panda's Thumb* (1980).

John Gribbin and Jeremy Cherfas, *The Monkey Puzzle: Reshaping the Evolutionary Tree* (1982).

Stephen W. Hawking, *A Brief History of Time* (1988).

R. Jastrow, *Red Giants and White Dwarfs: the Evolution of Stars, Planets and Life* (1967).

Donald C. Johanson and Maitland A. Edey, *Lucy: the Beginnings of Humankind* (1981).

Mary Leakey, *Disclosing the Past* (1984).

Richard Leakey, *One Life* (1983).

Richard Leakey and Roger Lewin, *Origins* (1977).

Alexander Marshack, *The Roots of Civilization* (1972).

Jonathan Miller and Borin Van Loon, *Darwin for Beginners* (1982).

T. Douglas Price and James A. Brown, eds., *Prehistoric Hunter-Gatherers: The Emergence of Cultural Complexity* (1985).

Kevin Reilly, *The West and the World* (1980).

Steven M. Stanley, *The New Evolutionary Timetable: Fossils, Genes and the Origin of Species* (1981).

L.S. Stavrianos, *Man's Past and Present* (1975).

CHAPTER 2

First Civilizations: The Ancient Near East

Time Line

c. 3500–3000 B.C.   Urban civilization present in Sumer; Sumerians develop an early system of writing

c. 3500 B.C.   Discovery of bronze; beginning of Bronze Age

Oldest extant potter's wheel

c. 3400 B.C.   Two distinct kingdoms emerge in Egypt

c. 3100 B.C.   King Menes unites Egypt

c. 2700–2200 B.C.   Egyptian Old Kingdom; Pyramid Age

c. 2340 B.C.	Akkadians under Sargon I conquer Sumer
c. 2060–1950 B.C.	Neo-Sumerian period at Ur
c. 2050–1800 B.C.	Egyptian Middle Kingdom
c. 1800 B.C.	Biblical Abraham moves to Canaan; God's First Covenant with Israelites
c. 2000 B.C.	*Epic of Gilgamesh* compiled
c. 1750 B.C.	Babylonian Kingdom established by Amorites
c. 1595 B.C.	Hittites sack Babylon
c. 1570 B.C.	Ahmose I founds Eighteenth Dynasty and begins New Kingdom
c. 1400–1200 B.C.	Hittite Empire
c. 1379–1362 B.C.	Akhenaton proclaims worship of one god, Aton
c. 1320 B.C.	Rameses I founds Nineteenth Dynasty; last period of Egyptian imperial greatness
c. 1200 B.C.	Movement of "Sea Peoples"; beginning of Iron Age
c. 1000 B.C.	David proclaimed king of Israel
c. 922 B.C.	Solomon dies and Israel divided
c. 884–612 B.C.	Height of Assyrian Empire
c. 800 B.C.	Carthage founded
586 B.C.	Fall of Jerusalem; Babylonian Captivity
546 B.C.	Cyrus the Great of Persia defeats Lydians
331 B.C.	Alexander the Great ends Persian Empire

The roots of Western civilization lie in the ancient Near East. The earliest known civilizations grew up along the banks of the Tigris, Euphrates and Nile rivers over 5000 years ago. Their more advanced development went unrivaled in the ancient world for almost a millennium, although the discovery in 1975 of a major center of urban civilization in northern Syria, the Kingdom of Ebla, has led scholars to revise their opinion of Syria as a peripheral region in the third millennium B.C. Around 2000 B.C., other Near Eastern peoples began to enter history's stage. The civilizations that flourished in the Fertile Crescent (an arc of arable land encompassing Mesopotamia, Syria, and Palestine) and in Egypt, Asia Minor, and Persia between 3000 and 500 B.C. made enormous contributions to the development of human knowledge.

Mesopotamia

The transition from a Neolithic to an urban culture first took place in Mesopotamia, "the region between the rivers." The fertile valley between the Tigris and Euphrates rivers allowed for a food surplus substantial enough to support a diverse urban population. Since c. 7000 B.C., Neolithic peoples had inhabited the area.

Sumer

Sometime during the fifth millennium, a new people of obscure origins, the Sumerians, appeared in the lower part of the valley. They spoke a tongue unrelated to any other known language. Around 4300 B.C. (during the Al Ubaid stage of early Sumerian culture), the Mesopotamians were still Neolithic farmers who worshipped at small shrines. Sometime between 3500 and 3000 B.C., an urban civilization called the Uruk culture emerged in Sumer. It was characterized by the use of bronze tools and weapons; the development of a system of writing; the evolution of new political, social and economic forms; and the presence of a temple-centered religion.

The Use of Bronze

The discovery of bronze marks an important step toward civilization. By c. 4500 B.C., some Neolithic peoples had learned how to extract copper in order to fashion metal tools and weapons that were clearly superior to stone ones. Sometime around 3500 B.C., metal workers in the Middle East discovered that when tin was added to copper, the resultant alloy, bronze, was stronger and more desirable.   The Sumerians took advantage of the superior properties of bronze and became adept at smelting and casting it.

System of Writing

Perhaps the most important characteristic of civilized life, the art of writing, was also present in Sumer by 3000 B.C. The Sumerians' nonalphabetic system of writing appeared later than the Chinese did and evolved through three stages: pictograph, ideogram and phonetic sign. At first its symbols represented pictures of things, but during the third millennium B.C., the symbols came to stand for sounds as well as pictures. This truly phonetic script was later common to most people in the ancient Near East. The complex system consisted of over 350 characters and is called cuneiform (from the Latin *cuneus* for wedge) after the wedge-shaped impressions made by pressing a reed pen into soft clay tablets.

Government

Although Sumer dominated lower Mesopotamia during the third millennium B.C., it was never able to unify the region successfully. Rather there were approximately a dozen city-states, each with its own ruler, or *lugal,* and its own city god. These city-states were constantly fighting one another for supremacy. At first, government was in the hands of elders, but eventually this system gave way to monarchy. An all-powerful king exerted the social and economic controls necessary to organize the increasingly more complex life of cities and the needed engineering projects for controlling the rivers. He was considered an agent of the gods but not a god himself and ruled for his people's well-being.

The Temple

Sumerian life revolved around the temple. The king as chief priest directed his people to build a ziggurat, a terraced tower with a sanctuary at the top. There the priests appealed to the gods for protection against the floods that periodically ravaged the land. Every individual was part of his city's temple community, which was referred to as "the people of the local deity." The temple owned much of the land, and rented it to the people in return for a portion of the crop. Surplus crops were then stored in the temple's own granaries in case of famine or were redistributed. Control of the surplus enabled the temple to employ most of the specialized craftsmen and scribes. In fact, writing may have been invented in order to keep track of the temple's possessions.

Social Classes

Urban life fostered specialization of labor and the creation of three social classes: nobles (large landowners) and priests, commoners, and serfs and slaves. The vast majority of the people worked on the rented and common lands or maintained the irrigation system. Nonetheless, commerce and trade gained in importance as Sumerians exchanged agricultural surpluses for wood, metals, and other natural resources they lacked.

Technology

Urban life fostered technological and cultural advances. The Sumerians created an all-important network of canals, dams and dikes which attempted to control the river's flooding and irrigate the land. They invented ox-drawn plows and wheeled vehicles. The oldest known potter's wheel (c. 3500 B.C.) and sailboat (c. 3250 B.C.) are both found in Mesopotamia. Using baked clay bricks, the Sumerians constructed the arch and vault. The ziggurat was their most impressive architectural creation.

Religion

Sumerian art and literature were essentially religious in nature. The Sumerian religion held that humans existed to serve the gods and that failure to do so resulted in punishment. All of life was contained in the divine order of things. Every natural phenomenon had its own god who lived a very human life. Enlil, the storm god, was important because he was responsible for the floods which so terrorized the Sumerians. The Biblical story of Noah's Ark echoes an earlier Mesopotamian flood myth. Since humans occupied a low position in the hierarchy, they had to be careful not to offend the gods. Thus they used literature and art to curry favor with their deities. A powerful

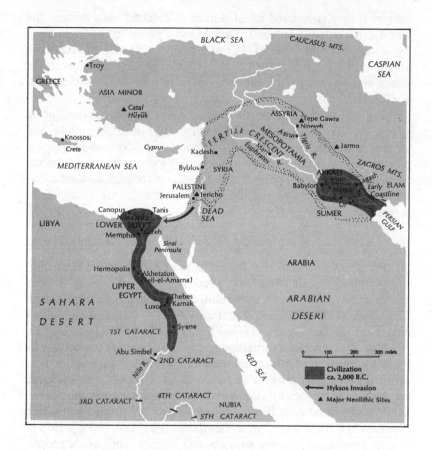

Early Mesopotamia and Ancient Egypt

priesthood was charged with maintaining good relations with the deities through magic, ritual and divination. The Sumerians did not hope for immortality. Their view of an afterlife was vague and dreary.

Akkad

The period of Sumerian supremacy in Mesopotamia ended with the rise of their neighbors to the north, the Semitic Akkadians. Under

Sargon I, they conquered all of Sumer c. 2340 B.C. and created the world's first empire. Sargon I made Akkad's power felt as far away as Syria and Anatolia. One of Akkad's major rivals was the powerful kingdom of Ebla in northern Syria. The discovery of its extensive palace archives has greatly enriched our knowledge of the world's first civilizations.

The period of Akkadian supremacy was a prosperous one during which the Akkadians adopted the superior Sumerian culture and blended it with the Semitic. Still, Mesopotamia's exposed geographic position and its rich land made it susceptible to frequent raids from the north and east. In c. 2180 B.C., the Akkadian empire succumbed to the attacks of a barbarian people, the Guti, from the Zagros mountains of present-day Iran.

Ur

For about a century after the collapse of Akkad, chaos reigned in most of Mesopotamia. Then in c. 2060 B.C., the third dynasty of Ur, a Sumerian city-state, drove out the Guti and reunited Sumer and Akkad. The *lugals* of Ur established a centralized government, bringing other city-states and the priesthood under tight control; the king was deified.

The most notable contribution of the neo-Sumerian period was its system of justice. Ur-Nammu, the third dynasty's founder, is now credited with being the world's first law-giver. His laws are remarkable for their stress on social justice and their attempt to protect the poor.

The large and magnificent city of Ur was destroyed by invading Elamites in c. 1950 B.C. Again Mesopotamia experienced a period of foreign domination, internal struggle, and hardship until a new people, the Semitic Amorites, established a strong kingdom in Babylonia c. 1750 B.C.

Babylonia

Babylonia's best known and most talented king, Hammurabi (c. 1792–1750 B.C.), set up his capital at Babylon and brought most of Mesopotamia under his sway. He reestablished a strong central government and closely regulated the economy.

Code of Hammurabi

Hammurabi issued the earliest major written law code in existence today. The 3200–line code, found at Susa in 1901, called for just treatment of his people, but also imposed harshly retributive punishments on transgressors. Hammurabi's codification was neither complete nor absolutely binding in the courts. Yet it was an important step forward in conducting government and social relations according to a clearly stated set of laws. Its notions of crime and punishment reveal a cultural mentality very different from our own. For example, a commoner was punished more severely for harming a noble than for committing the same crime against another commoner or slave. If a person accused another of a serious capital offense and could not prove his charges, he was put to death.

Epic of Gilgamesh

Babylonian culture drew inspiration from earlier Sumerian civilization. Much of its religion and literature was derived from Sumerian myths. The Babylonian *Epic of Gilgamesh* (composed c. 2000 B.C.) about a king of Uruk who failed in his search for immortality reflects the pessimistic outlook of Mesopotamian civilization as a whole.

Mathematics and Astronomy

The Babylonians were probably the best mathematicians of the ancient world until the Greeks. Building on Sumerian foundations, they devised tables for multiplication, division, square and cube roots; solved quadratic equations; had an equivalent for zero; knew the place value of numbers; and discovered the theorem for computing the angles of a right triangle before Pythagoras. From the Babylonians' use of 60 as a base number, the West inherited its division of the circle into 360 degrees, the hour into 60 minutes, and the year into 12 months.

The Babylonians were also keen observers of the universe. They devised a lunar calendar of seven-day weeks based on the five visible planets as well as on the sun and moon. They used their astronomical data, however, exclusively for religious purposes.

Foreign Invasions

Hammurabi's successors found it increasingly difficult to stave off foreign attacks and to preserve political unity. In c. 1595 B.C. the Hittites sacked Babylon and ruled briefly until in c. 1530 B.C. the kingdom fell to the Kassites, Indo-European nomads from Iran who introduced the horse and chariot to the region. From then until its resurgence under the Assyrian Empire beginning c. 1100 B.C., Mesopotamia sank into a dark age.

Egypt

Geography played an important part in shaping Egyptian civilization. The Nile River dominated the landscape, as it still does today, and dictated the rhythms of Egyptian life. The river's annual summer flooding watered a narrow ribbon of land on its banks and supplied it with fresh alluvial soil. By the fifth millennium neolithic peoples had learned to till the rich soil in accordance with the Nile's precise rise and fall. The river's impassability beyond the first cataract for many centuries and the surrounding desert isolated Egypt from invading forces, while easy navigability facilitated water travel within the kingdom. These conditions helped Egypt to create a brilliant civilization of astonishing continuity that lasted for over three thousand years.

The Predynastic Period

Egyptian civilization began to emerge during the fourth millennium. There is evidence that Egypt had contact with Sumerian civilization and may have received an influx of Mesopotamian peoples at this time. Egyptians during the predynastic period made copper tools, reclaimed sections of the northern marshland, began large-scale irrigation projects, and probably invented a system of writing.

As in Mesopotamia, the task of controlling the river's overflow and installing irrigation systems necessitated a common effort that in turn called for a more highly organized society. Around 3400 B.C., two distinct kingdoms emerged: Lower Egypt, a region approximately 150 miles in length encompassing the broad delta of marshy land where the Nile empties into the Mediterranean, and Upper Egypt, consisting of the thin ribbon of arable land that extends southward along both sides of the river for about 525 miles. Outside of these areas Egypt is virtually a desert and many parts are uninhabited even today.

The Archaic Period

According to legend, King Menes of Upper Egypt unified the two kingdoms c. 3100 B.C. and founded Egypt's first dynasty. The first two dynasties (c. 3100–2700 B.C.) are known as the Archaic or Early Historical Period. Although evidence about them is slight, they must have witnessed the rapid development of Egypt as a civilization. The use of the potter's wheel in Egypt and the invention of the earliest known solar calendar of 365 days probably date from this period.

The Old Kingdom

Our knowledge of Egypt increases greatly with the advent of the Old Kingdom, a period that includes Dynasties III through VI (c. 2700–2200 B.C.), during which all the major characteristics of Egyptian civilization are present.

The Egyptian King

For most of Egypt's ancient history, political power resided in an absolute monarch. The Egyptian king, who was probably not called a pharaoh until the New Kingdom, was considered a god, hence his lofty inaccessibility. He owned all the land, controlled the irrigation systems, levied taxes, made the laws, and exercised supreme authority in all political, economic, and spiritual matters. He ruled this theocratic state with the aid of a vizier, who was assisted by royally appointed governors, numerous lesser officials, and a body of priests.

Mummification

The king's divinity assured his immortality. Mummification was first practiced under the Old Kingdom. This elaborate process of embalming and wrapping the corpse arose from the belief that the king's body must be preserved so that his soul, which was released by death, would have a home when it revisited our world. Statues and wall paintings of the pharaoh were also included in his tomb as an abode for his soul should the mummification process fail.

The Pyramids

The Old Kingdom is also known as the Pyramid Age. During this time, the Egyptians built monumental pyramids, or tombs, to house the mummified bodies of the king and his family. Because Egyptians believed that life after death would be like their earthly life in every way, they included in their tombs all the material possessions they would need in the next world. Although only the king was at this time to have an afterlife, his immortality reassured the Egyptians that their civilization would survive. This belief helps to explain how the king was able to accomplish such gigantic building projects without revolt.

Egyptian Gods

The Egyptians worshipped not only their king but also an astonishing number of overlapping and sometimes contradictory gods who represented forces of nature and who were often depicted in animal form. Religious concerns dominated all aspects of Egyptian life. During the Old Kingdom, Re, the sun god, gained supremacy, and the priesthood of Re became very powerful. The Egyptians were the first civilization to believe in an agreeable life after death, although under the Old Kingdom this privilege was reserved for the king alone.

Egyptian Society

Egyptian society was divided into classes, but the boundaries between them were fluid. The vast number of people, however, worked the land, paid taxes in kind, and labored on royal projects. Women were especially well off in Egypt. They could buy, sell and inherit property. Succession to the throne descended from both the mother and the father. Kings often married their sisters in order to assure the continuation of their lines.

Crafts and Learning

Industry and commerce thrived during most of Egypt's ancient history. The Egyptians were expert craftsmen with a refined sense of beauty. As mathematicians, the Egyptians were less advanced than the Mesopotamians, although the pyramids show their practical knowledge of geometry. The earliest known medical treatise dates from the Old Kingdom, but because they lacked scientific understanding, the Egyptians attributed the causes of disease and its treatment to divine punishment for one's transgressions.

Egyptian Writing

Egyptian writing is known as hieroglyphics. At first these hieroglyphs ("sacred signs") were purely pictorial, but at some point signs for each consonantal sound were invented so that the script could be read phonetically. The Egyptians wrote on papyri, rolls of writing material made from the pith of the abundant papyrus plant. Thanks to Egypt's dry climate, many thousands of these have survived and are the most valuable source of information about ancient Egypt. Although the Egyptians produced no great epic comparable to the Babylonian *Gilgamesh*, they did create a variety of literary forms.

Decline of the Old Kingdom

The Old Kingdom (as symbolized by the Great Pyramid at Giza) reached its cultural apex under the Fourth Dynasty. By the end of this dynasty and in the ones that followed, art, commerce, and trade continued to prosper, but the king's centralized power gradually declined. The priests of Re insisted upon greater privileges while the provincial governors forced the king to recognize their offices as hereditary. This undermining of royal authority led to the collapse of the Old Kingdom.

The First Intermediate Period

The years from 2200 to 2050 B.C. constitute a period of disorder and distress in Egyptian history. Civil wars raged and the country fell prey to invasions. The lower class especially suffered from the breakdown of justice. Finally, under the Eleventh Dynasty, a ruler from the south restored unity and order and moved the capital to Thebes.

The Middle Kingdom

The kings of the Middle Kingdom (2050–1800 B.C.) reasserted their absolute authority. Although provincial governorships remained hereditary, each change required the king's approval. The vitality of the Middle Kingdom is best seen in its new irrigation and drainage projects and in its extension of cultural and economic influence as far as Palestine and Syria. Bronze probably came into use in Egypt during this time. The Egyptians also pushed their border up to the second cataract of the Nile by defeating the Nubians to the south.

Religion and Society

The most significant changes occurred in the realm of religion. The prominence of Thebes led to the ascendancy of its city god, Amun, who was merged with Re and worshipped as Egypt's national deity, Amun-Re.

The Egyptians came to believe that a happy afterlife was within the reach of everyone. Osiris, the dying and rising fertility god whose rebirth held out the hope of immortality for all, was transformed into the judge of those who could enter the "Field of the Blessed." Moral behavior and good deeds became the criteria for salvation. In general, the lot of the masses improved under the Middle Kingdom.

Decline of the Middle Kingdom

Towards the end of the Twelfth Dynasty, a series of incompetent kings slowly lost control of the country. The Hyksos, a foreign people, infiltrated Egypt, conquered the Delta, and eventually subjugated the rest of the land.

The Second Intermediate Period

Little is known about the Hyksos or their rule in Egypt. They were probably Semitic nomads from Asia, and most likely they occupied the throne at the time Joseph brought the Hebrews to Egypt. The Hyksos' Semitic origin helps to explain their promotion of Joseph to high office. The Hyksos introduced the horse, chariot, and compound bow into Egypt.

The Egyptians hated their barbarian conquerors, who refused to honor native religion and customs. Thus a movement of resistance centered at Thebes slowly gained strength and, under the leadership of Ahmose I, succeeded in expelling the Hyksos.

The New Kingdom

Ahmose I and Ahmose II

Ahmose I founded the Eighteenth Dynasty in 1570 B.C. and set about restoring a strong national government and a loyal bureaucracy. Ahmose's son, Ahmose II, continued strong centralist rule and made it possible for his successors to conquer much of the ancient Near East without domestic dissension and disunity.

Thutmose I

Under Thutmose I (1526–1508 B.C.) the New Kingdom began to earn its name as the Empire. Thutmose's army pushed Egypt's border up to the fourth cataract of the Nile in the south and reached as far north as the bend of the Euphrates River in northern Syria.

Thutmose III

Egypt's greatest military conqueror and one of its most able administrators was Thutmose III. The twenty-year-old son of Thutmose II and his concubine inherited the throne in 1504 B.C., but he was displaced by his father's wife, Hatshepsut, Egypt's only female "king," and did not actually reign until 1482 B.C. Thutmose III was an aggressive nationalist who launched seventeen campaigns in Asia. He defeated the petty princes who joined to eliminate Egyptian influence in Syria and Palestine and fought against Kadesh and the Kingdom of Mitanni in northernmost Mesopotamia. Thutmost III died in 1450 B.C.

Amenhotep III—The Golden Age

After reigns by two competent but unremarkable kings, the New Kingdom attained its greatest fame under Amenhotep III (1417–1379 B.C.) His reign has been viewed as a "Golden Age" partially because of the pharaoh's skill in publicizing himself. At this time, the New Kingdom spanned the Near East from Nubia and Sudan in the south to Palestine and Syria in the north. Amenhotep III conducted diplomatic relations with the Kassites, the Assyrians, the Mitanni Kingdom in Mesopotamia, and the Hittites of Asia Minor. At the beginning of the fourteenth century, Egypt was the wealthiest kingdom in the Near East. Its agriculture, commerce, and crafts thrived although slavery also increased. Its influence extended as far as Cyprus and Crete. Its palaces, temples, obelisks, and tomb paintings were of high quality. The literature of the New Kingdom, such as the magic spells of The *Book of the Dead*, hymns to the sun, and tales of adventure, was equally distinctive.

Akhenaton (Amenhotep IV) and the Sun God

A major disruption in Egyptian culture occurred during the reign of Amenhotep III's successor. In his efforts to reform Egyptian religion and to reduce the wealth and power of the priests of Amon at Karnak, Amenhotep IV proclaimed the sole worship of Aton, a solar deity related to Re and represented by the sun's disk. He closed the temples of all the other gods, founded a new capital city, Akhetaton, and changed his name to Akhenaton. During this Amarna Revolution, Egyptian art became more naturalistic and personalized. Because Akhenaton devoted himself entirely to the veneration of his universal god, he neglected the affairs of state, allowed his army to grow weak and corrupt, and ignored requests for aid against invaders from local rulers in southern Syria, who thus turned against the Empire. By the time of his death in 1362 B.C., Egypt had lost most of its foreign territories.

Tutankhamun

The boy-king, Tutankhamun, whose small but dazzling tomb was discovered intact in 1922, slowly abandoned all of Akhenaton's innovations and restored the old order. A later pharaoh attempted to efface all references to Atonist rule.

Rameses I and Rameses II

The pharaohs of the Nineteenth Dynasty, founded by Rameses I in c. 1320 B.C., sought to recapture Egypt's lost empire. Under Rameses II (c. 1304–1237 B.C.), Egypt experienced its last period of national greatness. Rameses II held Palestine firmly but was frustrated in his efforts to reconquer Syria from the Hittites. After several bloody but indecisive battles, the two nations agreed c. 1284 B.C. to a treaty of nonaggression. (See page 29.)

The Decline of Egypt

The revived empire of Rameses II proved short-lived. Towards the end of the thirteenth century, Egypt was invaded several times by new migratory hordes, the "Sea Peoples," who disrupted the entire Fertile Crescent. Although Egypt successfully defended its borders, it lost its empire and was badly weakened internally. Priests and local governors again undermined royal authority. A period of decline set in from which the ancient Egyptian civilization never recovered. In 1085 B.C. the New Kingdom ended with the division of Egypt into northern and southern kingdoms. The once great nation came under the control of the Libyans in 940 B.C., the Nubians in 745 B.C., the Assyrians in 671 B.C., the Persians in 525 B.C., and Alexander the Great in 332 B.C.

The Hittites

The Hittites were an Indo-European people who entered Asia Minor sometime around 2000 B.C. By 1700 B.C. they had formed a unified kingdom and ruled over the native population. The Hittites were a warlike nation. Around 1600 B.C. they sacked Babylon but were unable to hold onto their Mesopotamian conquests. Later, between 1400 and 1200 B.C., the Hittites established an empire in the Anatolian peninsula that rivaled the great valley civilizations.

The Hittite Empire

The Hittite empire reached its height under King Suppiluliumas (1380–1340 B.C.). A contemporary of Akhenaton, he took advantage of the pharaoh's preoccupation with religious concerns to conquer the Mitanni and extend Hittite control over the city-states of northern Syria. Under later pharaohs, the Egyptians engaged the Hittites in a prolonged struggle over Syria. Finally c. 1284 B.C., the two nations agreed to cease their war by signing the only nonaggression pact known in the ancient Near East. The pact established spheres of influence and included a pledge that each empire aid the other during emergencies. It was sealed by the marriage of a Hittite princess to the pharaoh. The Hittite empire fell in the wake of the onslaught of "Sea Peoples" c. 1200 B.C. From then until 800 B.C., Asia Minor ceased to play a role in Near Eastern affairs.

Hittite Culture

Hittite culture blended Indo-European, native Anatolian, and Mesopotamian elements. Its chief contribution, aside from its use of iron, is that it passed on its rich Mesopotamian inheritance to the later inhabitants of Asia Minor, the Phrygians and Lydians, who in turn spread it to the Greeks.

Government

Hittite government differed from Mesopotamian and Egyptian models in that initially the king was merely the strongest noble, probably chosen by the other nobles to look after military, civil, and religious matters. The king granted vast estates to the nobility in exchange for their military service. Sometime around 1500 B.C., however, kingship was made hereditary. From King Suppiluliumas's time forward, the king was deified at death and ruled as an absolute monarch.

Religion and Society

Hittite social structure is interesting for two reasons: (1) an essentially Indo-European nobility ruled over but was somewhat detached from the masses who were primarily indigenous Anatolians; and (2) women took an active part in social and religious life. The Hittites worshipped a diverse pantheon of gods drawn from Egypt, Mesopotamia, and Asia Minor as well as their own Indo-European deities. The Hittite system of laws is noteworthy for its relatively lenient punishments in contrast to the Code of Hammurabi.

The Use of Iron

The Hittites were one of the first people to produce iron weapons and tools. The ancient world knew of raw iron from meteorites, but the technique of smelting was not made practicable until the Hittites. The Hittites mined their rich deposits of iron ore, yet even they seem to have preferred to work in copper and bronze.

Literature

The Hittites spoke an Indo-European tongue that they wrote in cuneiform script adopted from the Sumerians. With Mycenaean Greek, it is the earliest example of a written Indo-European language. Hittite literature is at its most original in its official histories, which display a keen appreciation for the role of human motivation.

Art and Architecture

The Hittites especially excelled at carving stone reliefs, working in metals, and constructing impressive fortifications with huge gateways guarded by fierce stone animals.

The Small States of Syria and Palestine

The close of the thirteenth century B.C. marks a turning point in Near Eastern civilization. By 1200 B.C. the use of iron implements had spread throughout the Near East, bringing the Bronze Age to an end. At the same time, the invading "Sea Peoples" brought instability and dislocation and contributed substantially to the collapse of the Egyptian and Hittite empires. Mesopotamia was likewise in decline. This temporary respite from the domination of great powers allowed the smaller states of Syria and Palestine to flourish. Among them, the most important were the Canaanites (who came slightly earlier), the Phoenicians, the Arameans, the Philistines, and the Israelites.

The Canaanites

The Canaanites were a mixed Semitic people who gave their name to the whole region of what was later known as Syria to the north, Phoenicia in the middle, and Palestine to the south. Canaan had been inhabited since Paleolithic times and was the site of a very early Neolithic culture at Jericho. Its position at the crossroads of the Near East made it subject to frequent invasions as well as peaceful infiltrations. The city-states of Canaan experienced their period of greatest prosperity between 1400 and 1200 B.C. After the latter date foreign invasions plunged most of them into chaos.

Culture

Canaanite culture was more advanced than the Bible depicts it. The Canaanites were good potters and builders. They produced an exceptionally rich body of literature and wrote in cuneiform, hieroglyphics, or their own alphabet—one of the earliest known. Their poetry and myths were primarily religious, and some Old Testament stories are now thought to be Canaanite in origin.

Religion

The Canaanites' chief deity was El. The storm god Baal was a dying and rising fertility god associated with the life-giving autumn rains. The Canaanites believed that the soil's renewed fecundity depended on sexual intercourse between Baal and his partner, Astarte. To ensure this, the Canaanites imitated the gods in acts of sacred prostitution. The Baal cult also practiced child sacrifice. Although the Israelite prophets vehemently denounced this religious primitivism, the people of Israel were often tempted to turn to Baal for success in agriculture.

The Phoenicians

Some of the Canaanites who were uprooted by the migratory "Sea Peoples" settled in an area along the Mediterranean coast that the Greeks later called Phoenicia (modern Lebanon). The Phoenicians left their mark on history in several ways.

Trade

Although the Phoenician confederation of city-states was too small to be a great political or military power, its commercial presence was felt from Syria to the Straits of Gibraltar. The Phoenicians were expert mariners and established trading colonies along the Mediterranean coasts. The most famous of these was Carthage, founded just before 800 B.C. Carthage later became a great commercial empire in its own right and a rival to the Greeks and Romans.

Alphabet

As sailors, the Phoenicians disseminated Near Eastern knowledge to the rest of the Mediterranean world. Their most important legacy to the West was their alphabet, itself a perfection of an earlier Canaanite one, that contained twenty-two symbols for consonantal sounds. The Phoenician alphabet, modified later by the Greeks, who added vowels, is a direct ancestor of our own. By simplifying writing, it facilitated the expansion of literary culture.

Decline of Phoenicia

In the sixth century B.C. Phoenicia was absorbed into the Persian empire and gradually lost its cultural originality. At about the same time, the Greeks challenged their supremacy on the sea.

The Arameans

The Arameans occupied a position in overland trade analogous to that of the Phoenicians on the sea. A Semitic people, the Arameans lived in Syria east of the Phoenicians. Their kingdom centered around its most important city, Damascus, at the head of the caravan routes through the desert. From this strategic location the Arameans were able to control much of the Fertile Crescent's inland trade. By the early seventh century B.C., Aramaic served as the international language of the Near East and was spoken by Jesus. The Arameans came under the domination of the successive great empires of the Near East and Mediterranean, yet they retained their commercial influence and prosperity for many centuries.

The Philistines

Palestine derived its name from the Philistines, one of the invading "Sea Peoples" who settled along the coast in southern Canaan some time during the twelfth century B.C. A century later their use of iron weapons and the close-knit political organization of their confederacy made them a formidable force in the area and Israel's major adversary. Although the word "philistine" today connotes an insensitive, materialistic person, the ancient Philistines were a highly cultivated commercial nation.

The Israelites

Of all the ancient Near Eastern civilizations, the Israelites contributed most directly to our Western heritage. Their Holy Scriptures comprise the Old Testament in the Christian Bible. The Bible has probably had the single greatest influence on the religion, ethics, and literature of the West. Judaism, Christianity, and Islam are all rooted in its ideas. The Old Testament has a very personal meaning for the Jews because it recounts the story of their experiences from the patriarch Abraham down to the state reestablished after the return of the Jews from exile in Babylonia. This narrative history was first communicated orally and then written down over a period of a thousand years. Although the Old Testament contains many myths, legends, and embellishments, archaeological findings have confirmed its basic historical authenticity.

Early Hebrew History

According to the Old Testament, Abraham, the founder of the Hebrew people, came from "Ur of the Chaldeans" in Sumer. He was probably the patriarch of a nomadic tribe that worshipped a clan god. The Bible stories of the Creation, Fall, expulsion from Eden, Flood, and Tower of Babel all echo earlier Mesopotamian myths, thus lending support to the account of the Hebrews' Mesopotamian origins, though Hebrews probably include both Semitic and non-Semitic peoples. Around 1800 B.C., Abraham and his family migrated from Ur to Haran, where the god Yahweh appeared to the childless Abraham and told him to move again to Canaan (Palestine) where he would make a great nation of Abraham's descendants. This was Yahweh's first covenant with his Chosen People and was symbolized by circumcision. Thus Abraham entered into a unique personal relationship with one god whom he promised to worship in return for God's guardianship. The Hebrews who settled in Canaan became known as the Israelites. Abraham and his progeny lived peacefully, mingling with the native Canaanites.

The Mosaic Covenant

Around 1700 B.C. Abraham's grandson, Jacob, and his family, perhaps motivated by a scarcity of food, led a group of Hebrews to Egypt, where they prospered under the mild rule of the Semitic Hyksos. After the Egyptians expelled these foreign rulers, however, the Hebrews were enslaved. Perhaps at the time of Rameses II a new leader, Moses, arose to conduct them out of Egypt. The Egyptian Exodus and forty years of wandering in the desert constituted a period of great trial for the Hebrews, but also one in which their cohesiveness as a people and their knowledge of their unique relationship with God were strengthened. The covenant between God and the Hebrews was reaffirmed. God presented Moses with the Ten Commandments and other laws that set down what God expected of his Chosen People. He again promised to deliver the Hebrews to a "land flowing with milk and honey."

The Period of the Judges

Although Moses led his people to within sight of the Promised Land of Canaan, it was left to his successors to conquer the land. This was probably accomplished slowly by infiltration and drawn-out struggle, although modern research supports the Biblical account of Joshua's stunning victory at Jericho. During this period, the Israelites were organized into twelve tribes each headed by clan leaders called Judges who were responsible for waging wars and interpreting the legal code which grew out of the Mosaic laws. Contact with the more easy-going life of the Canaanites lured many Israelites away from strict adherence to these laws.

The Israelite Monarchy

Beginning in the twelfth century B.C., a new foe confronted the Hebrews in Canaan. The Philistines' expansion throughout the land threatened the Israelites because, as autonomous tribes, they lacked the political unification necessary for effective action against a highly organized opponent. Thus the people called for a king to lead them.

Saul. Israel's first monarch, Saul (c. 1020–1000 B.C.), won some impressive victories, but met with opposition among his own people. The prophet Samuel, who had anointed Saul, warned against the dangers of monarchy and defended the old tribal confederacy. Meanwhile the young shepherd boy David gained immense popularity as a soldier and musician at Saul's expense. The despondent Saul killed himself after being badly defeated by the Philistines.

David. David was proclaimed king c. 1000 B.C. Ruling for forty years, he forged Israel into a great nation that encompassed almost all of Syria and Palestine. He led his reorganized professional army to victory, ending the Philistine threat forever. He established Israel's first capital at Jerusalem and replaced the loose confederation of tribes with a strong central government in the hands of the king.

Solomon. David's successor, Solomon (c. 960–922 B.C.), continued his father's policies. Every man was required to serve in the army, pay taxes, and labor on Solomon's gigantic building projects such as the temple and palace in Jerusalem. His reign epitomized Israel's wealth and glory. The arts thrived under his patronage. Yet heavy taxes, forced labor, and corrupt government fostered discontent. The north especially resented the preeminence of the south. After Solomon's death in 922 B.C., the empire split into two kingdoms, Israel in the north and Judah in the south.

The Prophetic Age

A prolonged time of troubles descended upon the Israelites after the division of their nation. During this period prophets arose who denounced Israel's sins and called it back to the purity of its earlier faith. They interpreted the tragedies that befell the divided kingdom as an expression of divine will.

Fall of Israel. In 721 B.C. the Assyrians conquered Samaria, the capital of Israel, and deported thousands of Israelites to the region of Persia. These became the Ten Lost Tribes of Israel.

Exile of Judeans. Judah struggled on independently for over a century, but in 586 B.C. its capital, Jerusalem, fell to the Chaldeans. During the Babylonian Captivity that followed, many Jews (so called from their kingdom, Judah) were dispersed throughout Egypt and Babylonia. Even in exile, the Jews retained their faith in God and held fast to their traditions, laws, and nationalism.

Return to Jerusalem and Later History

With the ascendancy of the Persian Empire, the Jews were permitted to return to Jerusalem in 538 B.C. and to rebuild their temple, but they were later conquered by Alexander the Great and then by Rome. With the exception of the brief time following the Maccabean revolt (167–128 B.C.), the Jews would not enjoy political independence again until the twentieth century. However, during the post-Exilic Diaspora, the Jews were scattered throughout Europe, Asia, and Africa, and their religious understanding and sense of identity were further deepened.

The Hebrew Religion

In contrast to the polytheism of their Near Eastern neighbors, the Israelites worshipped only one god, a supreme being who created heaven and earth. Unlike other deities of the Fertile Crescent, Israel's god did not personify an aspect of nature, have a female consort, or act human. He was absolutely transcendent, a pure being who could not be named, seen, or worshipped in any image or likeness. Even his name, Yahweh, translates both as "I am who I am" and "he who causes to be." This very abstract concept of a god transcendent to nature represented a bold departure from the idol worship and anthropomorphism of other ancient religions and made possible the development of modern Western science.

The Israelites transformed the meaning of religion as well. For them its purpose was not to coerce or appease nature gods by means of ritual, magic, or myths. Rather its essence became God's relation to humanity, especially to the Israelites, his Chosen People. Yahweh is a god of history who reveals his divine will in the course of human events. Although there is an unbridgeable gulf between the creator and his creatures, God has made a covenant with Israel to protect it in exchange for its absolute loyalty. The religious person is one who is devoted to God alone and is obedient to his laws. According to the Book of Isaiah, God has made "a new covenant" between himself and each individual. He will save not only the Israelites but all humanity for he is now considered the universal creator and redeemer while all other gods are idols.

The Assyrians

From the ninth through the seventh centuries B.C., Assyria was the undisputed master of the Fertile Crescent. Its most prominent trait was its militarism. The roots of the Assyrian state go back to the middle of the third millennium when a group of Semitic peoples founded the city of Ashur on the Tigris River north of Akkad. For centuries other Near Eastern civilizations overshadowed Ashur, but gradually Assyrian power grew. By the thirteenth century it had already begun to menace its neighbors.

The Assyrian Empire

The power vacuum that followed the invasion of the "Sea Peoples" worked to Assyria's advantage. As a result, Tiglath-Pileser I (ruled 1114–1076 B.C.) stopped the encroachments of the Urartu state to the north and waged campaigns against Babylonia and northern Syria. By means of calculated terroristic policies, a superb army and efficient administration, he succeeded in eliciting hostages and tribute from the conquered states; but the empire did not long endure.

Conquests of Ashurnasirpal II

Assyria's real period of greatness began in the ninth century with Ashurnasirpal II. He conquered Urartu to the north, several Aramean cities to the west, and parts of Syria. Ashurnasirpal II's success as an empire builder is attributed to his energetic personality, his willingness to use cruelty to intimidate his subjects, and his capabilities as an administrator.

Height of the Empire

Another strong ruler, Tiglath-Pileser III (ruled 744–727 B.C.), reasserted Assyrian hegemony over Syria after a period of weakness, and conquered Babylonia. The Assyrian Empire attained its zenith under its next four kings. Sargon II (ruled 721–705 B.C.) completed the subjugation of Israel while his successor, Sennacherib, fought with Judah. Both kings had to battle constantly to maintain their wide-reaching empire.

Decline of the Empire

Esarhaddon foolishly conquered Egypt in 671 B.C., thus adding to the burdens of the already overextended domains. Egypt successfully revolted in 662 B.C. during the reign of Ashurbanipal, a learned king who won no major battles but who advanced Assyria culturally. His fabulous library at Nineveh contained ancient works from all over Mesopotamia. Its excavation has provided scholars with invaluable source materials for the study of antiquity. The problems of overseeing such a large realm increased in magnitude after Ashurbanipal's death. In 612 B.C., the Assyrian Empire fell to a coalition of Chaldeans and Medes.

Assyrian Art and Architecture

Assyrian culture adapted Sumerian and Babylonian forms to suit its own distinctive nature. The Assyrians were especially innovative artists and architects. Their large and splendid palaces were made of mud bricks like those in Mesopotamia but were supplemented with large stone slabs that lined the gateways and most important lower walls. On these stones the Assyrians carved magnificent bas-reliefs depicting military conflicts or royal hunts. The scenes were meant to narrate Assyrian victories and are therefore executed in precise detail. This historical purpose differentiates Assyrian from Egyptian or Mesopotamian art.

The Chaldeans (New Babylonians)

With the fall of Assyria, control of Mesopotamia passed to the Chaldeans, a Semitic people who had lived in the southern portion of Mesopotamia since 1000 B.C. King Nabopolassar declared Chaldean independence from Assyria after Ashurbanipal's death in 626 B.C., and, fourteen years later he joined the Medes to bring down Nineveh. The spoils of victory gave the Chaldeans hegemony over Mesopotamia, Syria, and Egypt.

The New Babylonian Empire

While short-lived, the Chaldean, or New Babylonian (Neo-Babylonian), Empire experienced its period of greatest glory under Nabopolassar's son, Nebuchadnezzar, who ruled from 605–586 B.C. During his reign, Babylon with its famous Ishtar Gate and "Hanging Gardens" emerged as the most splendid city of the ancient world. Babylonian cultural forms enjoyed a renaissance. The Chaldeans were noted astronomers, although their observations were made in the service of astrology, not science. The priestly class wielded tremendous power over affairs of state, especially after Nebuchadnezzar's death.

The New Empire's Decline

The Chaldeans were never able to hold their empire together as tightly as the Assyrians. In 600 B.C. the Egyptians repulsed Nebuchadnezzar's attempt to bring them under further control. Perhaps inspired by this example of resistance, the king of Judah declared his independence from Babylon. Nebuchadnezzar besieged and took Jerusalem, deporting the king and a large part of the population. Eleven years later, when the Jews again rebelled, he razed the city and spread destruction throughout the land. After Nebuchadnezzar, several weak kings were incapable of opposing the steadily growing Persian Empire. In 538 B.C., Cyrus the Great captured Babylon, thus bringing the Chaldean Empire to an end.

The Persians

The Medes

Sometime around 1500 B.C., a group of nomadic Aryan peoples migrated to the Iranian plateau, an area east of Mesopotamia, from southern Russia and Turkistan. Among the most prominent were the Medes who settled to the north and Persians to the south. Both spoke closely related Indo-European languages and lived simple pastoral lives. For many centuries the Medes were the more important of the two. With the ascendancy of Cyrus to the Persian throne in 559 B.C., however, Median supremacy was quickly terminated. Cyrus captured the Median capital of Ecbatana in 550 B.C. and turned the Medes into Persia's vassals.

The Persian Empire

Cyrus the Great

The creation of the Persian Empire was essentially the work of Cyrus the Great. After subduing the Medes, he rapidly brought the rest of the Near East under Persian domination. In 546 B.C. in Asia Minor he defeated the Lydians, whose king, Croesus, was reputedly the wealthiest man in the ancient world, and who are credited with inventing the system of coinage. Cyrus then annexed the Greek cities on the coast of Asia Minor. Turning east, he extended control over his neighbors as far as the borders of India. In 538 B.C. Babylon fell easily to his

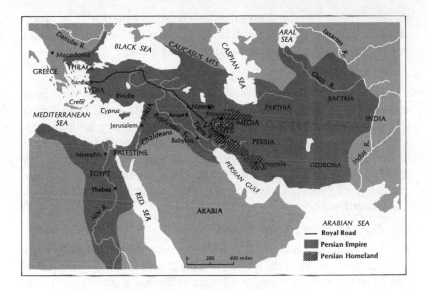

The Persian Empire, c. 500

army, making Persia the master of most of Mesopotamia. Cyrus allowed the Jews to return to Palestine, where the Persians ruled with a light hand. In general, Cyrus was liked by his subject peoples because he respected the traditions and religion of each region.

Darius the Great

Cyrus's son, Cambyses II, conquered Egypt and parts of the African coast to the west by 525 B.C., but was slain on his way home from Egypt three years later. Confusion over the succession created the opportunity for the rise of Darius I, the Great, who ruled from 521 to 486 B.C. The twenty-eight-year-old Darius, who was distantly related to the king, removed the usurper and assumed the throne himself. After putting down revolts within the empire, he went on to become one of Persia's most outstanding rulers. Darius was particularly adept at administering his vast realm by means of satraps (governors). He was also an able soldier whose campaigns extended the empire up to the Danube in the northwest and to India in the east. Darius met with considerably less success in his conflicts with the Greeks, against whom he launched wars (known as the Persian Wars) that lasted on and off for fifty years. Darius's last expedition ended disastrously after the battle of Marathon in 490 B.C., but his successors continued the fighting.

Persian Culture

Darius was a great patron of the arts and his palace at Persepolis epitomized the monumental style of Persian architecture. The religion of the Persians at this time mixed old deities with a new faith derived from the teachings of the native prophet Zoroaster (c. 600 B.C.) Zoroastrianism was the first religion to posit a separate principle of evil at work in the world and thus the necessity of moral choice as the grounds for salvation. It influenced the development of both Judaism and Christianity.

The End of the Persian Empire

The century-and-a-half following Darius's death was marked by the growth of power of the satraps and the bloody disputes that accompanied every change of ruler. Persia remained a great power, but internal decay had set in. In 331 B.C. Alexander the Great of Macedonia brought the Persian Empire to an end.

The world's earliest known civilizations arose in Mesopotamia and Egypt around 3300 B.C. Located along rivers, both developed methods of irrigation that enabled them to control flooding, achieve a food surplus, and thus support a diversified urban population. The Sumerians founded one of the earliest systems of writing and created the world's first literature. They made tools out of bronze and invented wheeled vehicles, animal-drawn plows, sailboats, and the potter's wheel. Later Mesopotamian states inherited much of their culture from Sumer. Egyptian civilization was noted for its remarkable longevity and continuity over time. Its monumental architecture expressed the Egyptian's belief in the king's divinity and the everlasting nature of their civilization.

During the second millennium B.C., the Israelites developed a radically new monotheistic religion. Its conception of god as an unconditioned, transcendent being who alone is sacred and its notion of the working out of God's will in history represent significant contributions

to Western thought. Between the ninth and the fourth centuries B.C.,
*Assyria and Persia successively assembled the two largest empires in
the ancient Near East at that time. The Persians ultimately came into
conflict with the Greeks, the next people to occupy center stage in the
story of Western civilization.*

Recommended Reading

Bernhard W. Anderson, *Understanding the Old Testament* (1957).

James H. Breasted, *Development of Religion and Thought in Ancient Egypt*
(1986).

Giovanni Castelli, *The First Civilizatons* (1985).

L. Finkelstein, ed., *The Jews: Their History, Culture and Religion* (1960).

Henri Frankfort, *Ancient Egyptian Religion* (1948).

Henri Frankfort, *The Art and Architecture of the Ancient Orient* (1971).

Henri Frankfort, *Before Philosophy* (1946).

Sir Alan Gardiner, *Egypt of the Pharaohs* (1966).

John Gardner and John Maier, trans., *Gilgamesh* (1984).

Michael Grant, *The History of Ancient Isreal* (1984).

O.R. Gurney, *The Hittites* (1961).

W.W. Hallo and W.K. Simpson, *The Ancient Near East: A History* (1971).

Richard Mansfield Haywood, *Ancient Greece and the Near East* (1964).

J.A. Hexter, *The Judeo-Christian Tradition* (1966).

Michael Hoffman, *Egypt Before the Pharaohs, the Prehistoric Foundations of
Egyptian Civilization* (1979).

Warner Hutchinson, *Ancient Egypt* (1978).

Samuel Noah Kramer, *History Begins at Sumer* (1981).

Samuel Noah Kramer, ed., *Mythologies of the Ancient World* (1961).

Samuel Noah Kramer, *The Sumerians, Their History, Culture and Character*
(1963).

Samuel Noah Kramer, *Sumerian Mythology* (1972).

Elizabeth Lansing, *The Sumerians, Inventors and Builders* (1972).

James Mellaart, *The Earliest Civilizations of the Near East* (1966).

Barbara Mertz, *Red Land, Black Land: Daily Life in Ancient Egypt* (1978).

Barbara Mertz, *Temples, Tombs and Hieroglyphs* (1978).

P.R.S. Moorey, *Ur "of the Chaldees" : A Revised and Updated Edition of Sir Leonard Woolley's Excavations at Ur* (1982).

Hans J. Nissen, *The Early History of the Ancient Near East* (1988).

A.T. Olmstead, *History of Assyria* (1923).

A.T. Olmstead, *History of the Persian Empire* (1948).

A. Leo Oppenheim, *Letters from Mesopotamia* (1967).

H.M. Orlinsky, *Ancient Israel* (1960).

James B. Pritchard, ed., *The Ancient Near East: An Anthology of Texts and Pictures* (1958).

Douglas B. Redford, *Akhenaten, The Heretic King* (1983).

C. Redmond, *The Rise of Civilization: From Early Farmers to Urban Society in the Ancient Near East* (1978).

G. Roux, *Ancient Iraq* (1976).

Peter Stearns, ed., *Documents in World History* (1988).

J.E. Manship White, *Ancient Egypt: Its Culture and History* (1970).

J.A. Wilson, *The Culture of Ancient Egypt* (1956).

CHAPTER 3

Early Greece to 478 B.C.

Time Line

c. 3000 B.C.	Beginning of Minoan civilization on Crete
c. 2000 B.C.	Mycenaean civilization established on Greek mainland
c. 1750–1450 B.C.	Use of Linear A script by Minoans
c. 1600–1400 B.C.	Zenith of Minoan culture
c. 1450 B.C.	Minoans begin use of Linear B script (i.e., early Greek)
c. 1450 B.C.	Fall of Knossos to the Mycenaeans
c. 1200 B.C.	Supposed date of Trojan war
c. 1100 B.C.	Mycenaean civilization ends

c. 1100–800 B.C.	Greek Dark Age
c. 850–750 B.C.	Homeric epics composed
c. 800 B.C.	Rise of the *polis*
776 B.C.	Traditional date of first Olympic Games
c. 650–450 B.C.	Archaic Age of Greek culture
c. 620 B.C.	Draco appointed to publish Athenian laws
594 B.C.	Solon given emergency powers in Athens
561 B.C.	Pisistratus seizes power in Athens
c. 530 B.C.	Red-figure style of pottery invented
508 B.C.	Reforms of Cleisthenes
499 B.C.	Ionian Greeks revolt against Persia
490 B.C.	Athens defeats Persia at Battle of Marathon
480 B.C.	Xerxes invades Greece
479 B.C.	Greeks defeat Persians at Battle of Plataea

Of all the ancient peoples, the Greeks exerted the greatest influence on Western civilization. They laid the foundations of Western art, architecture, literature, philosophy, science, mathematics, and democracy. Their spirit of rational inquiry and high regard for the individual represented a new and significant departure for intellectual history. The creativity and originality of Greek culture are foreshadowed in the earlier Aegean civilizations of Crete and Mycenaean Greece that flourished in the third and second millennia B.C. Although these first advanced cultures to develop in Europe were destroyed by 1100 B.C., they left a substantial legacy for Hellenic civilization.

Aegean Civilizations

The Minoans

About 3000 B.C., a wave of peoples from somewhere in Asia Minor, Syria, and Palestine migrated westward to the Aegean Islands and mainland Greece. These people brought with them the beginnings of a Bronze Age civilization which took root throughout Greece.

Sir Arthur Evans, the English archaeologist who excavated the major Cretan city of Knossos in 1898, named this civilization "Minoan" after the legendary King Minos. Evans divided Minoan history into three periods according to the sequence of different pottery styles found at Knossos: Early Minoan (c. 3000–2200 B.C.); Middle Minoan (c. 2200–1500 B.C.); and Late Minoan (c. 1500–1000 B.C.). The Minoans were not Greeks since they did not speak the Greek language, but they did strongly influence the first true Greeks, the Mycenaeans, who established a civilization on the mainland beginning c. 2000 B.C.

Crete

The first of the Minoan settlements to develop into an advanced culture was located on the island of Crete. The geographical position of Crete naturally favored the development of maritime trade. Cretan ships sailed on long voyages to ports in Egypt and the Near East and established trading outposts throughout the Mediterranean. As the ancient Greek historian Thucydides maintained, the Minoan fleet probably ruled the Aegean sea lanes at one time. Contact with other lands undoubtedly stimulated the growth of Minoan civilization. Egyptian influence on Crete was especially prevalent in the years following 2100 B.C., yet the Minoans created a highly distinctive and personal culture which, in its fundamental attitudes, bore little resemblance to other ancient Near Eastern civilizations.

Society

The Minoans used the wealth accumulated from active trading in olive oil, wine, metalware, pottery, and other goods to fashion a life of elegance, beauty, and leisure. The huge, ornate Palace of Minos at Knossos, built and rebuilt over five centuries beginning c. 2000 B.C., featured many amenities such as frescoed walls, running water, and flush toilets. Women wore jewelry, makeup, and a revealing style of dress. Their position in society appears to have been higher than in any of the ancient Near Eastern civilizations.

Dancing, games, and sports were especially popular with the Cretans. The famous acrobatic feat of grabbing a bull's horns and back-flipping onto his haunches depicted in Minoan wall painting was probably performed in connection with a religious ritual, but was certainly so dangerous that it may not have been widely practiced, if at all.

Art

Nowhere is the creative energy of the Minoans more evident than in their art. Minoan wall paintings, colorfully decorated pottery, and statuettes are highly appealing in their spontaneity, delicacy, animation, and feeling for nature.

Religion

While not enough is known about Cretan religion to describe it with certainty, the absence of temple remains and the recovery of numerous terra cotta statuettes of elegant, bare-breasted women, sometimes holding snakes, suggests that the Minoans worshipped some fertility goddess at open-air shrines or in their homes and palaces. The bull appears to have occupied a significant place in Minoan religion. Unlike other Near Eastern peoples, the Minoans were not dominated by a powerful class of priests nor did they, as far as we know, seek in religion the promise of an afterlife. Enjoyment of this world was the hallmark of Minoan culture.

Monarchy

The Minoans were ruled by a king who probably also performed religious functions. His name, Minos, may have been more an official title than a family name. It is uncertain whether the king at Knossos held sovereignty over all Cretan cities, several of which also possessed large palaces. He does appear to have had a monopoly over trade, with a large bureaucracy to keep track of it.

Writing

As in Mesopotamia and Egypt, writing was most likely invented at

Knossos in order to record possessions and keep accounts. The Minoans first developed a form of hieroglyphic writing, but between c. 1750 and 1400 B.C., they used an undeciphered syllabic script, which Evans named Linear A. Around 1450 B.C., a new script, Linear B, which has now been shown to be an archaic form of Greek, appeared at Knossos.

Decline of Minoan Civilization

Minoan culture reached its zenith between 1600 and 1400 B.C., yet within this time archaeological evidence reveals that the Palace of Minos was mysteriously destroyed several times. Who or what caused these catastrophes is still a matter of great scholarly debate. One popular theory attributes the devastation to the effects of a volcanic eruption on a neighboring island. Whatever their origins, these dislocations seem to have weakened the Minoans to such an extent that around 1450 B.C. Knossos fell easily to a Mycenaean invasion. After 1400 B.C., when a final disaster befell the Palace of Minos, cultural supremacy shifted from Crete to the Greek mainland.

The Mycenaeans

The first civilization on mainland Greece is called the Mycenaean after its most important settlement, Mycenae, in the Peloponnesus. The Mycenaeans were the first inhabitants of Greece to speak the Indo-European language, Greek. Descended from a group of Indo-Europeans who arrived in Greece, probably from the north, shortly after 2000 B.C., these newcomers settled down at numerous locations and slowly absorbed the native population. For the next four centuries they lived the simple, agricultural existence of an early Bronze Age society. Then, around 1600 B.C., as indicated by archaeological evidence, there was a marked rise in Mycenaean wealth and power. A set of extraordinary royal graves and the first remains of a palace, which were found in 1876 by an amateur German archaeologist, Heinrich Schliemann, date from this period.

Trade

Like that of the Minoans with whom they competed for control of the Mediterranean, Mycenaean wealth was based on trade. In the period between 1500 and 1400 B.C., when Knossos came into their possession, the prosperity of the Mycenaeans increased even more. During their age of greatest affluence, from 1400 to 1200 B.C., the Mycenaeans were undisputed leaders of the Greek world.

Society

Our picture of Mycenaean society is extremely sketchy. Mycenae was probably ruled by a king who seems to have employed a large number of craftsmen, scribes, merchants, and others to tend to his needs and oversee trade. Mycenae was not a real city as Knossos was, but rather a heavily fortified palace that overlooked a few homes of the well-to-do commercial class. The majority of the population worked the land and lived in small villages spread throughout the countryside.

Writing

Mycenae's role as an administrative and economic center is clear from the remains of tablets inscribed in the Mycenaeans' Linear B script which were found at the palace. These tablets recorded goods stored in the palace storerooms, wages paid to various craftsmen, and taxes collected in kind from the people. There is no evidence, however, that Mycenaean writing was ever used for literary purposes.

Art and Religion

Much of Mycenaean culture reveals the imprint of contact with the Minoans, but Mycenaean architecture seems more Near Eastern in inspiration. The Mycenaeans constructed an impressive palace, and, around 1300 B.C., the greatest of the Mycenaean beehive (*tholos*) tombs was built. Schliemann gave this large tomb, whose inner room measured fifty feet in diameter and forty-five feet in height, the rather fanciful name of the Treasury of Atreus, after Agamemnon's father. *Tholos* tombs were in fact used exclusively for burial and may have had sealed entrances. These conical-shaped tombs appear to be unique to the Mycenaeans. The care with which the Mycenaeans buried their dead suggests an Egyptian influence, although in other respects Mycenaean religion resembles more that of Crete than of Egypt; some of their gods, such as Zeus, Poseidon, Artemis, and Dionysus, would be important in later Greek religion.

Decline of the Mycenaean Civilization

Beginning in the late thirteenth century B.C., Mycenaean trade gradually dwindled in the face of Phoenician competition and because the "Sea Peoples" made sailing unsafe. Mycenaean civilization drew to an end around 1100 B.C., when the palace at Mycenae was attacked by the Dorian Greeks and destroyed by fire.

Troy

According to Homer, the Mycenaeans fought the people of Troy in a war which began soon after 1200 B.C.

The Iliad

In the *Iliad*, Homer relates how the Trojan prince Paris abducted Helen, the wife of King Menelaus of Sparta, and refused to return her. This led to war between the Greeks and the Trojans, who were led by Agamemnon and Hector, respectively. Many of the great heroes of Greek mythology, such as Achilles, Ajax, Odysseus, and Diomedes, took part. After a decade of fighting, the Greeks finally captured and sacked Troy by a ruse: they hid their soldiers within a hollow wooden horse which the gullible Trojans took within their walls.

Schliemann's Discovery

Heinrich Schliemann had read the *Iliad* as a child and believed in the essential truth of Homer's account. After earning a fortune in business, he set out in 1870 to find the legendary city of Troy. Excavating at present-day Hissarlik, in Turkey, he discovered the remains of an ancient city which he proclaimed to have been Troy. Schliemann's city was in fact much older, dating from the second layer of habitation c. 2200 B.C. Archaeologists have since uncovered nine layers of consecutive habitation at Troy, with the seventh layer, known as Troy VIIA, corresponding to the Troy that existed from 1250 to 1200 B.C.

The Trojan War in History

The discovery of a Trojan city destroyed at the time that Homer placed the Trojan War lends credence to the story, though other Near Eastern peoples may have been responsible for the destruction. Some historians question the existence of a Trojan War. Nevertheless, the

Mycenaeans might have been tempted to launch an expedition against Troy. Mycenaean pottery found at Troy confirms that the two cities traded with each other. Troy was obviously wealthy. Its situation near the Dardanelles (the straits which separate the Aegean from the Sea of Marmara and the Black Sea) afforded the opportunity to control the land and sea trade between Europe and Asia. Thus Troy may have fallen victim either to a Greek piratical raid or to a commercial war with the Mycenaeans. While much of Homer's epic is myth, it seems to contain an element of truth which enables us to include the Trojan War as a legitimate part of early Greek history.

The Greek Dark Age

The period between the fall of Mycenaean civilization and the beginning of classical Greece (from roughly 1100 to 800 B.C.) is called the Greek Dark Age because Greek culture appears to have suffered a major setback. These 300 years are especially difficult to characterize because archaeological evidence is so scanty. Numerous signs do, however, point to a real cultural weakening at this time.

The Dorian Invasion

Greek tradition informs us of an invasion by the Dorians, a new wave of Indo-Europeans who spoke the Doric dialect, a particular way of pronouncing Greek. Around 1200 B.C., for unknown reasons, the Dorians and other tribes allied with them began moving southward, destroying Mycenaean centers as they went. They scattered themselves throughout the Greek isles and even parts of Asia Minor, but the majority of them settled in the Peloponnesus at sites such as Corinth, Argos, and Sparta. The Spartans of classical Greece were of Dorian descent.

Destruction of Mycenaean Culture

The Dorian invasion completed the destruction of the already declining Mycenaean culture. Long distance trade virtually disappeared. The most significant indication of the disruptive effects the invasion had on earlier Greek culture is the apparent loss of the ability to write. No Linear B tablets dated much later than 1200 B.C. have been unearthed. Linear B script would have been unintelligible to the classical Greeks, who based their own writing system on the easier alphabet borrowed from the Phoenicians.

Geometric Pottery

While the Greek Dark Age was in many ways a period of cultural decline, it was also one of transition. The break with Mycenaean culture cleared the way for the artistic, political, and intellectual innovations of Hellenic Greece. This is evident in the Geometric pottery style that developed at this time. This first characteristically Greek style in the fine arts with its abstract linear patterns and simple geometric forms marked a definite change from the curvilinear and naturalistic designs of Mycenaean pottery.

Coastal Settlements

The Greek Dark Age saw the movement of Mycenaean refugees into Athens and Ionia and along the Aegean coast of Asia Minor some time between 1000 and 900 B.C. Although never able to penetrate the interior of Anatolia, they established along the coast and on nearby islands cities which would become famous as centers of flourishing Greek culture in the late seventh century B.C.

The Homeric Epics

The epic poems attributed to Homer, the *Iliad* and the *Odyssey*, are two of the greatest masterpieces in Western literature as well as two of its most fascinating puzzles.

Authorship

Some scholars view the Homeric epics as a collection of sagas transmitted orally during the Dark Age in a rather imperfectly stitched together mosaic. Tradition, however, weighs in favor of Homer's principal authorship even though the *Odyssey* was probably composed nearly 50 years after the *Iliad,* and is strikingly dissimilar in tone and vocabulary. The classical Greeks always spoke of Homer as the creator of both epics and esteemed him as their greatest poet. Yet they disagreed on his place and date of birth. At present, many scholars accept that the poet was born in Ionia sometime during the eighth century or a little earlier.

Dates

Homer composed his epics orally following the tradition of oral poets who wove their heroic tales from fragments of ancient sagas. The Homeric epics were most likely composed between 850 and 750 B.C. They remained unwritten until decades after that, when some unknown scribe set them down in an augmented form. The epics contain material, however, that is much older than the eighth century, perhaps reaching back to the Mycenaean Age that the poems purport to describe.

The Odyssey

Whereas the *Iliad* is a tragedy, the *Odyssey* is a tale of the adventures that befall the Greek hero, Odysseus, as he struggles for ten years to return home after the Trojan War. The story ends happily. Odysseus rids his house of his wife's predatory suitors and is reunited with the faithful Penelope.

Homer's Achievement

In both epics Homer conveys a sense of the heroic ideals and fixed code of behavior that animated early Greek life in a warrior society. The poems inspired almost all later classical Greek literature. Homer's lasting greatness lies in his deep understanding of human nature. His sympathetic and believable presentation of his characters' personalities and problems make the *Iliad* and *Odyssey* timeless reservoirs of knowledge about humankind.

The Greek Renaissance

Greece awoke from its Dark Age to produce a new and brilliant civilization. For reasons that still are poorly understood, prosperity and confidence gradually returned to the Greeks soon after 800 B.C.

The Restoration of Foreign Contacts

An early sign of this rebirth was the renewal of overseas commerce.

Trade brought the Greeks back in touch with the Near Eastern world. Between 725 and 650 B.C. the geometric style of Greek pottery was replaced by a new orientalizing style whose curvilinear forms, exotic beasts and expressive human forms reveal an Eastern influence. At about the same time, the Greeks launched an impressive colonizing movement that spread outposts of Greek civilization throughout the Mediterranean.

The Alphabet

An important consequence of Greek contacts abroad was the adoption of the Phoenician alphabet around 800 B.C. By augmenting its consonants with vowels to accommodate certain uniquely Greek sounds, the Greeks acquired a simple but efficacious alphabet that allowed them to produce a literature of stunning originality. One version of this alphabet passed on to a Greek colony in southern Italy. From there it was transmitted to the Etruscans, the Romans, and on to the modern West.

Dawn of the Greek Historic Age

Another example of the renewed creativity of renaissance Greece is the development at this time of the *polis*, or city-state, as an essentially Greek unit of government. According to tradition, the first Olympic Games took place in 776 B.C. The ancient Greeks used this date as the starting point of their chronology and thus it symbolizes the birth of the historic age of Greek civilization. With the resumption of trade and communications and in possession of the art of writing, the Greeks went on with renewed vigor to produce a culture whose brilliance shines down to the present day.

The Colonizing Movement

The tremendous movement of Greek colonial expansion occurred in response to the pressures of overpopulation. Greece's rough mountainous terrain and poor soil were inadequate for its growing population. Many poorer farmers migrated to more fertile areas of the Mediterranean in order to satisfy their hunger for land. Others settled in the new areas in hopes of engaging in trade or improving their social status.

The revived familiarity with the sea and the spirit of daring of the new age helped make the venture possible.

The Founding and Organization of Colonies

The Greeks founded their colonies not as the collective efforts of individuals or small families but as prearranged communities under the auspices of a mother city, or *metropolis*. Although the new colonies often retained strong economic and emotional bonds with their mother cities, they were not politically subservient to them. Each colony formed a new and independent Greek city-state, and some of them, notably Syracuse, soon outstripped their mother cities in importance. By 600 B.C. Greek settlements had been planted all along the shores of the Black Sea and the Mediterranean, even as far west as Spain. Byzantium (modern Istanbul), Naples, Marseilles, and Cadiz all started as Greek colonies.

Effects of Colonizing

The colonizing movement had several important results. It eased for a time at least the social tensions that plagued the mainland. It also stimulated Greek trade and brought increased prosperity to the city-states. The colonies furnished such raw materials as iron and grain in return for the mainland's finished products, especially pottery and woolen goods. The adoption of the Lydian system of coinage around 650 B.C. facilitated this exchange. By 500 B.C. the Greeks had become masters of the Mediterranean trade. Besides bringing the Greeks prosperity, colonization put them in contact with new peoples and new ideas while it also spread Greek culture, which was widely assimilated and eventually passed to the modern West.

Greek Religion

Perhaps the most remarkable characteristic of Greek religion was its naturalness. The Greek gods were perceived in human form. Although superior beings endowed with immortality, they were all too human in their passions, petty rivalries, and meddling in worldly affairs. In time, however, the growing influence of philosophic thought redirected later Greek religion to more rational concerns.

Origin of Deities

The Greek deities personified the forces of nature as well as abstract concepts such as love (Aphrodite) and wisdom (Athena). They derived from Minoan, Mycenaean, Egyptian, Near Eastern, and Indo-European sources. Zeus, father of the gods who ruled from Mount Olympus, was the sky god of the Indo-Europeans who invaded Greece c. 2000 B.C. His marriage to Hera, a fertility goddess of the Neolithic inhabitants of Greece, symbolized the union of the two cultures.

Characteristics

Greek religion differed dramatically from other Near Eastern religions, especially that of Israel. Greek religion prescribed no code of ethical behavior and established no fixed way of worship. It was devoid of sacred writings and its priestly offices possessed no political power and were not the exclusive domain of any one caste. The Greek gods were neither remote not transcendental powers, but rather they were worldly beings who by turn could be cruel or affectionate towards mortals. Greek religion had little sense of sin and no notion of divine responsibility for humanity's redemption.

Divine Contact with Humans

The Olympians did, however, oversee human affairs, help their favorites, and punish those who offended them. Divination played an important role in Greek belief as a means of revealing divine wisdom. The Greeks also visited places where they thought the gods spoke directly to humanity. The most famous of these was Delphi, northwest of Athens. There a local peasant woman worked herself into a trance during which she supposedly expressed the prophecies of Apollo, god of light, prophecy, medicine, music, and poetry. The priests of Delphi then translated her incoherent ravings into ambiguous but generally moderate counsels.

Civic Deities

With the rise of the *polis*, the Greek gods assumed added importance as civic deities. While still worshipping all the gods, each city-state had a founding deity to whom it looked for special treatment, protection from disease and destruction, and increased prosperity. The

Athenians, for example, built the Parthenon to Athena and had festivals and made offerings to keep her favor.

Olympic Games. The Olympic games held at Olympia in the western Peloponnesus illustrate well the intimate association of religious and civic life. These celebrations of human prowess were in fact a form of worship for the Greeks. Dedicated to Zeus, the games attracted citizens from all over the Greek world. Solemnized by a day of sacrifices, they underlined the joyous, natural, and worldly quality of Greek religion.

Cults

Two other aspects of Greek religion, the cults of Demeter and Dionysus, gained in importance as the civil strife of the fifth century B.C. called into question the efficacy of the Olympian patron gods.

Demeter. Demeter, the earth mother and goddess of grain, was worshipped in secret ceremonies at Eleusis near Athens. She and her daughter Persephone, who according to myth was forced to spend half the year in the underworld, fall into the category of dying and rising gods. The Eleusinian Mysteries, which only initiates to the cult could witness, probably reenacted the story of Persephone's abduction and release in connection with the seasonal death and rebirth of vegetation. Participation in the cult seems to have held out the hope of immortality to its members.

Dionysus. The cult of Dionysus also offered the promise of something better—in this case the release from care and responsibility in drunken, orgiastic festivals. Dionysus was god of wine and fertility about whom many contradictory legends exist. In general, he epitomizes the emotional, instinctive, and creative sides of human nature, in contrast to Apollo, who represents that which is rational, moderate, and orderly.

The Pre-Socratic Philosophers

The Greeks were the first people whose speculations about the nature of humankind and the universe merit the title of philosophy. Although the Mesopotamians and the Egyptians attained an impressive level of practical knowledge about the world, they did not analyze or systematize their findings. Beginning around 600 B.C. in the city of

Miletus and elsewhere in Ionia, there arose a group of thinkers who sought to explain the origin and nature of the physical world without recourse to religion or myth. The philosophers of the Milesian school came to view the universe as composed of one primal element from which issued the origin and destruction of all things.

Thales

For Thales (c. 640– c. 545 B.C.), the first recorded philosopher of the West, water was the primary substance from which all else was derived. Thales' reasoning, while perhaps influenced by the Babylonian myth of the world's creation from water, reflects his observation that water exists in three states: liquid, solid, and vapor. He believed that water could also change to other forms in less readily visible fashion.

Anaximander and Anaximenes

Anaximander (c. 611– c. 547 B.C.), who may have studied with Thales, proposed a more generalized concept of the basic stuff of the universe which he called the "boundless" (*apeiron*). Anaximander's notion of the "boundless" is vague and difficult, but it presages the modern theory of the indestructibility of matter. Some of Anaximander's comments on human development from fish also prefigure later evolutionary theories. Another Milesian, Anaximenes, who contended that air was the primary substance, foreshadows the evolution of an atomic theory.

Heraclitus

The great philosopher Heraclitus of Ephesus, who lived between c. 535 and c. 475 B.C., put forth as the explanatory first principle yet another element, fire, which, while retaining its eternal identity, is able to be transformed into changing substances. Fire symbolized change within permanence. Heraclitus believed that behind its apparent fixity, the universe was in continual flux as expressed by the saying that one can never step twice into the same river. Yet there was one unchanging reality, which Heraclitus called the *logos*, or law, by which the universe is ordered and which human beings could comprehend with the "thinking faculty." This idea of an orderly universe (*cosmos*) that is understandable to human reason is crucial to all later Greek thought.

Pythagoras

Another important early Greek philosopher, Pythagoras of Samos (c. 560– c. 480 B.C.), founded a secret brotherhood whose cardinal beliefs were the transmigration of souls and an abstruse theory of numbers. Pythagoras is said to have begun with the discovery that musical harmony is expressed in terms of mathematical ratios; that is, on a vibrating string, harmonious notes correspond to the exact division of the string by whole numbers. From this he concluded that number was the basic principle of the universe. The Pythagoreans held that all things, even moral concepts, were essentially mathematical relationships. The significance of Pythagorean beliefs in the development of Western thought lies in their finding that natural phenomena can be dealt with in abstract, mathematical terms. Because of their interest in numbers, the Pythagoreans made important contributions to the study of mathematics. The Pythagorean theorem that the square of the hypotenuse of a right triangle is equal to the sum of the squares of the other two sides (which the Egyptians knew empirically) was proved by the Pythagoreans to be a general rule.

Early Greek Literature and Art

Hesiod

The writings of the epic poet Hesiod, who is believed to have lived on mainland Greece during the eighth century B.C., signal a new departure in Greek thought and literature. While continuing in the language of Homer, Hesiod's poetry reflected his own times and concerns as a common man in an age of oligarchy. In *Works and Days*, the poet offered practical advice to the small farmer and defended him against the injustices of the noble landlords. Hesiod's writings championed a new set of values for Greek civilization. Whereas Homer had praised the aristocratic virtues of a bygone heroic age and portrayed the gods as capricious, Hesiod urged the values of moderation, social justice, righteousness, and hard work, which all people could pursue. He charged Zeus with the responsibility of upholding justice and punishing excess. Likewise, in *Theogony*, a genealogy of the gods drawn from numerous myths, Hesiod stressed Zeus's role in imposing a just order on humanity and the gods.

Lyric Poets

The trend towards greater realism and more personal expression, which is hinted in Hesiod, became evident in the lyric poets of the Archaic Age from c. 650 to c. 450 B.C. In contrast to older epic poetry, this new form placed greater emphasis on individual feelings and experiences. The seventh century B.C. poet Archilochus, whom the ancients credited with the invention of iambic meter, was the first Greek to write openly and engagingly about his own adventures and disappointments. In the early sixth century B.C., Sappho of Lesbos composed passionate yet simple verses about the pains and pleasures of her love for other women. She stands as the first great woman poet and perhaps the best writer of early Greek lyric poetry. Several generations later, Pindar of Thebes (518–438 B.C.) won renown for his victory odes.

Sculpture and Architecture

The Archaic Age is also associated with a particular artistic style. Prior to the seventh century B.C., all Greek buildings and sculptures were made of wood. Renewed contact with Egypt probably introduced the revolutionary new technique of working in stone. From roughly 660 to 480 B.C., Greek statues were frequently of nude young males called *kouroi* or draped female figures called *korai*. Both were idealized types, not real portraits, and were created according to very strict conventions. The *kouros* (singular), for example, usually stands rigidly erect with his left leg advanced, his fists clenched, and a slight smile on his lips. This highly formalized stance reveals an acquaintance with Egyptian models. Yet even at this time, Greek sculpture displays a freshness and vitality that distinguishes it from Near Eastern art. In architecture the Greeks worked out the elements and proportions of the Doric order during this period.

Vase Painting

The Archaic Age was the great era of Greek vase painting. The transitional Orientalizing style gave way to the broad-ranging Archaic style with its vigorous and exquisitely rendered scenes from mythology or daily life. By the mid-sixth century B.C., artists began to sign their finest works, indicating a new awareness of the role of personality in art. The black-figure style of pottery was invented at the beginning of the Archaic Age. In it, the design is painted in black on a reddish clay background. Around 530 B.C., a new red-figure technique in which the figures are left the color of the clay and the background is filled in in black allowed for even greater mastery of detail and subtlety of effect.

The Polis, 800–500 B.C.

The *polis*, or city-state, emerged as the distinctive Greek form of social and political organization some time after 800 B.C.

The Origin of the Polis

In the beginning, the *polis* was an elevated, fortified citadel to which the neighboring countryside retreated in times of distress. Eventually this center grew into a real city, and the *polis* came to refer to a politically independent city-state which encompassed a "high city," or *acropolis*, and its surrounding area. The *polis's* modest size, which rarely exceeded 500 square miles, perfectly suited Greece's segmented geography and fostered a strong sense of identity among its inhabitants.

Cycles of Government

While the political evolution of the several hundred Greek *poleis* varied according to time and place, most of them underwent a similar pattern of development from monarchy to oligarchy to tyranny to democracy and back to oligarchy.

Monarchy

In Homeric times, Greece was divided into numerous tribes composed of families and clans and ruled by kings who were merely first among equals. A council of nobles and a popular assembly existed to check monarchical abuse. The *polis* first appeared in Ionia, perhaps because the disruptive effects of migration weakened the old tribal structure and the exigencies of defense argued for a single fortified government center.

Oligarchy

By 800 B.C. the Ionians seem to have transferred political power from the king to the *polis*, whose government organization was in the hands of the aristocracy. The *polis* gained at the expense of the tribes as well, assuming a number of the latter's religious and military duties. These changes from monarchy to oligarchy and from clan to *polis* occurred on the Greek mainland somewhat later.

During the Age of Oligarchy, from the mid-eighth to the mid-seventh century B.C., the nobility expanded their agricultural holdings at the expense of the poorer farmers. The dearth of good lands created widespread popular discontent, which was mitigated to some extent by the founding of colonies. The rise of a middle class of entrepreneurs, merchants, and prosperous farmers contributed to the mounting social tensions.

Tyranny

After 650 B.C., more and more *poleis* resorted to tyrants in order to resolve their economic and social conflicts. Tyranny in the original Greek sense of the word referred simply to one-man rule and did not possess the evil connotations that it does today. Greek tyrants were usually wealthy and talented men who rose to power by championing the lower and middle classes against the aristocracy.

Democracy

Rarely were a tyrant's progeny able to retain political power. In fact, once the power of the nobility had been broken, a tyrant was no longer needed. Instead, a revived popular assembly usually took over. During the fifth century, with Athens showing the way, many *poleis* gradually reformed their constitutions to institute democratic government, or direct rule by the citizens. Athenian democracy was a limited one, however, because women, slaves, and resident aliens were ineligible to become citizens. Nonetheless, it was for many centuries the most advanced example of its kind, with an electorate essentially that of the mid-nineteenth century United States.

Return to Oligarchy

By the end of the fourth century, democracy had proved itself equally unable to stop the internecine warfare that marred Greek history. Thus many *poleis* freely chose or were compelled to return to tyranny or oligarchy.

Sparta

The city-state of Sparta in the Peloponnesus was founded by the invading Dorian Greeks.

Unique Features of Sparta

From its beginnings Sparta differed from most other Greek *poleis*. Rather than expanding through trade and colonization, Sparta turned against its neighbors, subjugating Laconia and Messenia around 735–715 B.C. The threat of rebellion by its conquered population forced the Spartans to stress military discipline above all else. The Spartan *polis* was composed of five agricultural villages joined together. It never developed into an urban center, nor does it seem to have been fortified. Sparta also evolved a unique political system. While most other *poleis* rid themselves of kings and slowly moved towards democracy, Sparta retained the institution of kingship and established a system of government that remained virtually static.

Government

Early in its history, Sparta reformed its political constitution in order to eliminate tribal rivalries and to tighten control by the ruling Dorians, who comprised a distinct minority amidst a hostile populace. The reforms associated with the name of the legendary lawmaker Lycurgus provided Sparta a system of government that was essentially oligarchic, although some historians describe it as a limited democracy. Aristotle called Sparta's constitution "mixed": its kings represented monarchy, its council represented oligarchy, and its assembly represented democracy.

At its top stood two kings, hereditary relics of an age when Sparta was probably ruled by two rival families. Although the kings had command of the army and were responsible for certain religious duties, their political role was restricted to their contributions within the aristocratic Council of Elders. The twenty-eight other members of this council, the *Gerousia*, were elected for life and were male citizens over the age of sixty. The council's function was primarily advisory. Its proposals were subsequently passed to the assembly for approval. Membership in the assembly consisted of those Spartan males who at the age of thirty had satisfactorily completed their military studies and were elected citizens. Known as Equals, they approved the proposals offered by the *Gerousia,* but lacked authority to initiate legislation themselves and could be dismissed. The Assembly had the right to decide questions of war and peace and to elect a board of five Ephors, or overseers, for one year terms. This position served as a check on the power of the kings and was an important democratic feature of the Spartan constitution. The Ephors supervised military training, enforced justice, and, as time went on, arrogated more and more political powers to themselves.

Society

All Spartan citizens were deemed essentially equal and Sparta enjoyed a measure of democracy. The vast majority of the Spartan population, however, had no political rights. The *perioikoi,* or "those who dwell nearby," were former Spartan captives who were allowed to live freely in their own villages under the watchful eye of the Spartans as long as they served in the army and paid some dues. The *helots* were descendants of the old residents in Messenia who had been reduced to serfdom by the Spartan conquest. Their lot was an exceptionally hard one, and their lives counted for little in the Spartans' minds.

Training and Education

The life of a Spartan citizen was consumed with military duties and regulated almost completely by the state. At the age of seven, Spartan boys were taken from their families and placed in barracks where they underwent rigorous, often cruel military training. This included walking barefoot in winter and being flogged. Girls also received physical training to place them in top condition for childbirth. Sickly or deformed infants were left on a mountaintop to die from exposure. At thirty a man could finally leave the barracks and marry, but he was required to take one meal per day at his mess until he was sixty. Spartan education stressed physical over mental achievements. Especially after 600 B.C., the extreme militarism of Spartan life as well as its deliberate isolation from outside influences discouraged the arts and stifled creative thinking. As a result, Sparta offered little to Greek civilization. Nonetheless, the ancient Greeks regarded Sparta with awe and admiration for its military strength, political stability, and the courage and devotion of its citizens.

Athens

Athens was the largest and most renowned Greek *polis*. Its contribution to the culture and politics of Western civilization is almost incalculable. In contrast to the conservative Spartans, the Athenians were noted for their forward-looking nature. They recognized the importance of trade and commerce; experimented—sometimes under the pressure of imminent civil war—with a variety of solutions to their economic, social, and political problems; and accepted the necessity of sharing political power with the masses. These attitudes were vital in Athens' establishment of one of the world's greatest democracies.

Early History and Government

The Athenians were slow to develop a *polis*. Early in their history they conquered the large surrounding territory of Attica, but they never enslaved its occupants. At first kings ruled Athens, which escaped Dorian attack, but the great aristocratic families rapidly deprived them of all but their religious functions. The *Areopagus*, a council of nobles drawn from the heads of clans, exercised unchallenged control over affairs until the end of the seventh century. Executive tasks were handled by three—later nine—archons, or magistrates, who were elected by the council for one-year terms, after which they became members of the *Areopagus*. The popular Assembly in Athens was virtually powerless during the period of aristocratic ascendancy.

Draco

In 632 B.C., Athens was shaken by the attempted coup of a young nobleman, Cylon. Perhaps as a result of this, a special commissioner, Draco, was appointed c. 620 B.C. to codify a set of laws, especially those dealing with homicide. So severe were the punishments exacted by Draco's laws, that the word *draconian* has come to mean extremely harsh or cruel. Yet Draco's laws did make possible a more impartial administration of justice.

Solon

Among Draco's code were laws that permitted the sale of a debtor and his family into slavery. Debt slavery became so prevalent that in 594 B.C. the Athenian aristocracy, confronted with a potentially explosive social situation, gave over emergency powers to the archon Solon so that he could arbitrate matters. Solon became one of Athens' greatest statesmen and was the first to express sympathy and seek redress for the suffering of the poor. His reforms are paradigms of moderation and compromise and were effected without violence.

Economic and Political Reforms. Solon first tackled the problem of debt slavery by canceling all debts; then he abolished the practice of debt slavery and framed a new, more humane, law code. He sought to solve Athens' agricultural troubles by promoting commerce and industry. One of these new laws encouraged the intensive cultivation of the more economically profitable olive trees by forbidding the export of grains. Solon also instituted political reforms which set Athens on the road to democracy. In order to weaken the power of the aristocracy, he divided the citizens into four classes according to the income they received from the produce of their lands. Offices were now open to a man based on his class. All four classes were able to sit in the Assembly, vote, and elect the archons, although the latter were drawn only from the first two classes. Thus landed wealth, not noble blood, became the criterion for political participation.

Council of Four Hundred. Solon is credited with founding a new political body, the Council of Four Hundred. It existed alongside the older Council of the *Areopagus* and was composed of one hundred members from each of the four tribes. It was less dominated by the great families than the *Areopagus* and became very important in the management of political affairs. A revived popular assembly also gained in power, thanks to the reforms of Solon. Legislation prepared by the new Council was now set before it for approval. At some point the popular assembly began to assume judicial functions, sitting as a court to pass judgment on certain matters, notably the conduct of retiring archons.

The Tyranny of Pisistratus

The very moderation of Solon's reforms left dissatisfied groups at either end of the political spectrum. The poor farmers, while freed from enslavement, were displeased that they were denied political equality and did not achieve a redistribution of the land. The nobility resented the new qualifications for office-holding as an attack on their political supremacy.

Seizure of Power. Pisistratus, an Athenian general, saw this class discord as an opportunity to establish himself as a tyrant, a course of action which Solon had proudly rejected. In 561 B.C., with the backing of the poor farmers from the hill country and with a bodyguard ironically provided for him by the Assembly, Pisistratus seized power. Exiled several times, he firmly established his control in 546 B.C.

Administrative and Economic Reforms. The tyranny of Pisistratus benefited Athens in many ways. The main organs of government continued to function almost unimpaired, thus affording Athenians uninterrupted experience in self-government. Yet all major offices were held by Pisistratus's men. Nobles who refused to support him were exiled, and some of their lands were redistributed among the poor who had backed the tyrant. Pisistratus improved the lot of the small farmer by making loans available on easy credit terms. He continued, even intensified, Solon's emphasis on commerce. His public works opened more jobs to the lower class. As a patron of the arts, he oversaw the building of several exquisite Athenian temples. Under his sponsorship plays began to be performed about 535 B.C. at the annual festival of Dionysus from which Attic tragedy would originate a few generations later.

The Democratic Reforms of Cleisthenes

Pisistratus died in 528 B.C. and was succeeded by his son, Hippias, who ruled effectively for over a decade. Following a conspiracy, however, he took sterner measures. Four years later, the exiled noble Alcmaeonid family, led by Cleisthenes, returned with the aid of the Spartans and compelled Hippias to flee Athens. Cleisthenes aspired to make himself the undisputed political leader in Athens. To do so, he appealed to the common people for support by offering them a greater role in governing the *polis*. Once in power, Cleisthenes made good his promises in a series of constitutional reforms beginning in 508 B.C. that transformed the structure of Athenian society and introduced a large measure of democracy to its political system.

New Tribes. Cleisthenes perceived that the only way to end internal strife was to make a permanent change in the tribal system. In place of the four old racial tribes, he created ten new tribes whose membership was determined by the *deme*, or village, in which a person resided. By this reordering, he ensured that every tribe would contain members from all classes and from each of the territorial regions: hills, plain, and coast. No longer could one clan dominate the affairs of a tribe.

Council of Five Hundred. Cleisthenes used the new tribes as the basis of representation in his new Council of 500 which replaced the earlier Council of 400. Each tribe contributed fifty councilors chosen by lot from lists of candidates elected in the *demes*. Members of the fourth or lowest property class, the *thetes*, were ineligible to sit in the Council, although as adult male citizens they were able to vote in the Assembly. Councilors were chosen for one-year terms and could serve a maximum of two terms, though only once as chairman. By dividing the year into ten periods, called *prytanies*, each tribe was given its chance to supervise the affairs of the *polis*. The chairmanship was rotated on a daily basis according to lot. This system allowed the widest possible participation of Athenian citizens in the management of their government.

Ostracism

Cleisthenes may also have been responsible for the well-known Athenian practice of ostracism, although it seems more likely that it was devised a few decades later, as the first mention of its use appeared in 487 B.C. Each year the Assembly was asked if there was someone whom members considered a danger to the state. If a quorum of at least 6000 citizens voted on *ostraca*, or pieces of broken pottery, overwhelmingly against a certain individual, then he was sent into exile for ten years, although his family was unharmed and his property left intact.

The Persian Wars

Shortly after Cleisthenes reformed Athens' government, the new democracy was put to the test by an external threat. The Persians, who under Cyrus and Cambyses had forged a great new empire in the Near

East, appeared at the beginning of the fifth century to menace Greece proper.

The Ionian Revolt

War between Greece and Persia originated in Ionia. The Greek cities along the western coast of Asia Minor had fallen under Persian suzerainty in 547 B.C. They were required to pay tribute, furnish soldiers, and accept a Persian governor in each city, but they were left culturally autonomous and well treated. Nevertheless they resented their loss of freedom. In 499 B.C. they revolted against Persia and appealed to mainland Greece for help. Sparta refused aid, but Athens finally agreed to send twenty ships. Despite these reinforcements, the Persian king, Darius the Great, succeeded in putting down the revolt by 493 B.C. and began making plans to attack Athens in retaliation for its assistance to the Ionians. Darius also seemed intent on conquering all of Greece as an ideal natural frontier for the Persian Empire in the west.

The Battle of Marathon

In 490 B.C., a Persian fleet with twenty thousand men landed at Marathon, northeast of Athens. Sparta was in the midst of a religious festival, and thus Athens' forces met the invaders alone. Under the bold leadership of one of their generals, Miltiades, the outnumbered Athenians defeated the Persians and then rushed back to Athens in time to forestall an enemy attack on the city. Darius was forced to sail home with the remains of his army. The great Athenian victory at Marathon, while failing to end the threat of invasion, did symbolize that the last of the great ancient Near Eastern empires was not invincible.

Themistocles' Strategy

Darius died in 486 B.C. before he was able to bring to fruition his plans for revenge. His son and successor, Xerxes, was at first preoccupied with quelling a revolt in Egypt, but by 485 B.C. he began to prepare for a new invasion. In Athens, the decade of the 480s brought renewed quarreling among rival factions, from which the popular leader Themistocles eventually emerged as the most influential figure. He advocated reducing still further the power of the clans and strengthening the Athenian navy in readiness for war. His advice was heeded. Athens built more ships and the jobs thus provided for the common man aided the growth of Athenian democracy.

Xerxes' Invasion

In 480 B.C., Xerxes launched a massive invasion of Greece by land and sea. His army crossed the Hellespont into Europe by means of an ingenious pontoon bridge built specifically for the purpose. A large Persian fleet stocked with supplies accompanied the army as it moved southward along the Aegean coast. This time the Greeks were prepared. Athens had two hundred new ships at its disposal, and in early 480 B.C. most of the *poleis*, including Athens and Corinth, agreed to form a defensive league under Sparta's leadership.

Thermopylae

The Greeks made their first stand against the Persians at the narrow pass of Thermopylae. Greatly outnumbered, three hundred Spartans, led by their king, Leonidas, and supported by several thousand other Greeks, succeeded in holding off repeated Persian attempts to break through the pass, until, after three days, a Greek traitor revealed the existence of a mountain path by which the Persians overwhelmed the Greeks from behind. The Spartans fought valiantly to the last man, an inspiring example of Greek resistance for centuries to come.

The Battle of Salamis

The Persians then marched to Athens and burned the city. Its population had been evacuated in advance, however, and the Athenian fleet lay in the nearby Bay of Salamis, where it planned to make a rigorous defense. Themistocles tricked the Persians into attacking under disadvantageous conditions, resulting in the great Athenian naval victory of Salamis. Xerxes was forced to change his plans and return to Asia Minor.

The Battles of Plataea and Mycale

One year later, in 479 B.C. at Plataea, Sparta spearheaded an army of 100,000 Greeks and decisively defeated the Persian forces which had remained in Greece. Almost simultaneously the Greeks won another stunning victory on the coast of Asia Minor at Mycale by destroying the Persian fleet. Although a formal peace was not concluded until 448 B.C., the war was essentially over by 478 B.C.

Results of Greek Victory

The Greeks had successfully met the greatest challenge so far to their autonomy and demonstrated that in time of dire need they could work together and set rivalries aside. Victory over Persia insured the further maturation of democratic rule in Athens and set the stage for the fullest flowering of Greek culture.

During the second millennium B.C., two Bronze Age civilizations flourished, the Minoan on Crete and the Mycenaean on mainland Greece. Each developed a written language, a thriving maritime trade, and a rich culture. The Minoans were the dominant cultural force in the Aegean until c. 1450 B.C., when they were most likely conquered by the Mycenaeans. The latter were the first Aegean peoples to speak Greek. Mycenaean civilization fell in the wake of the Dorian invasion of the twelfth century B.C. The next three hundred years, Greece's Dark Age, were a time of cultural decline.

Around 800 B.C., Greek civilization entered a period of prosperity and creativity that endured for over four hundred years. These years saw the growth of the characteristic Greek political unit, the polis, *or city-state. These small, autonomous communities were the focal point of Greek life. In most instances, their governments evolved from monarchy to oligarchy to tyranny to democracy and back to oligarchy or one-man rule. Sparta, with its subject peoples and militaristic society, followed its own unique course. In Athens, the reforms of Cleisthenes in 508–507 B.C. created the most outstanding example of ancient democracy. Athenian citizens—although not women, slaves or aliens— enjoyed a degree of political participation almost unheard of until modern times.*

While the Greek poleis *tended to regard each other with suspicion if not outright hostility,their united victory over the Persians demonstrated that they could band together against a common enemy. Success in the Persian Wars bolstered Greek self-confidence and set the stage for the Golden Age of Greece.*

Recommended Reading

Antony Andrewes, *The Greeks* (1973).

Antony Andrewes, *The Greek Tyrants* (1966).

Diana Bowder, ed., *Who Was Who in the Greek World* (1982).

C.M. Bowra, *The Greek Experience* (1957).

Walter Burkert, *Greek Religion* (1985).

A.R. Burn, *Persia and the Greeks: The Defense of the West, 546–478* B.C. (1962).

J.B. Bury and R. Meiggs, *A History of Greece to the Death of Alexander the Great* (1975).

John Chadwick, *The Decipherment of Linear B* (1967).

John Chadwick, *The Mycenaean World* (1976).

V.R. d'A. Desborough, *The Greek Dark Age* (1972).

V. Ehrenberg, *From Solon to Socrates* (1973).

Sir Arthur Evans, *The Palace of Minos* (1921–36).

M.I. Finley, *The Ancient Greeks* (1977).

M.I. Finley, *The World of Odysseus* (1978).

M.I. Finley and H.W. Pleket, *The Olympic Games: The First Thousand Years* (1976).

W.G. Forrest, *The Emergence of Greek Democracy 800–400* B.C. (1970).

Hermann Fränkel, *Early Greek Poetry and Philosophy* (1975).

W.K.C. Guthrie, *The Greeks and Their Gods* (1968).

N.G.L. Hammond, *A History of Greece* (1967),

Herodotus, *The Histories,* de Selincourt trans. (1954).

C. Hignett, *A History of the Athenian Constitution* (1952).

Homer, *The Iliad*, R. Lattimore trans. (1951).

Homer, *The Odyssey*, R. Lattimore trans. (1968).

Jeffrey M. Hurwit, *The Art and Culture of Early Greece 1100–480* B.C. (1985).

R.W. Hutchinson, *Prehistoric Crete* (1962).

Charles H. Kahn, *The Art and Thought of Heraclitus: An Edition of the Fragments with Translation and Commentary* (1982).

H.D.F. Kitto, *The Greeks* (1951).

Albin Lesky, *A History of Greek Literature* (1966).

Geoffrey E.R. Lloyd, *Early Greek Science: Thales to Aristotle* (1974).

H. Mitchell, *Sparta* (1952).

George Mylonas, *Mycenae and the Mycenaean Age* (1966).

Denys L. Page, *History and the Homeric Iliad* (1959).

H.W. Parke, *Greek Oracles* (1967).

Milman Parry, *The Making of Homeric Verse* (1971).

J.D.S. Pendlebury, *The Archaeology of Crete* (1965).

Sarah B. Pomeroy, *Goddesses, Whores, Wives and Slaves: Women in Classical Antiquity* (1975).

Chester Starr, *The Influence of Sea Power on Ancient History* (1988).

Emily Vermeule, *Greece in the Bronze Age* (1972).

CHAPTER 4

Classical and Hellenistic Greece

Time Line

c. 480 B.C.	Transition from archaic to classical style
c. 478 B.C.	Formation of Delian League
462–429 B.C.	Age of Pericles; height of Greek classical culture
454 B.C.	Transfer of Delian League's treasury to Athens
448–432 B.C.	Parthenon built
431–404 B.C.	Peloponnesian War
421 B.C.	Peace of Nicias between Athens and Sparta
415–413 B.C.	Sicilian Expedition

399 B.C.	Death of Socrates
386 B.C.	King's Peace dictated by Persia
371 B.C.	Sparta's supremacy over Greece ends
359 B.C.	Philip II elected King of Macedon
338 B.C.	Macedonians defeat Greeks at battle of Chaeronea
336 B.C.	Philip of Macedon assassinated
335 B.C.	Aristotle founds the Lyceum
331 B.C.	Alexander the Great triumphs over Persians at Gaugamela
330 B.C.	King Darius of Persia murdered
326 B.C.	Alexander reaches Indus River
323 B.C.	Death of Alexander the Great
323–30 B.C.	Hellenistic Age
300 B.C.	Stoic philosophy founded; Euclid establishes school of mathematics in Alexandria

Victory over the mighty Persian Empire marked a turning point in Greek civilization and left the Greeks with renewed confidence and heightened spirits. It represented the triumph of a different kind of society—a small but powerful structure of freemen—over a despotic empire. Intense intellectual activity and an outpouring of creative genius rarely matched in history followed upon the Persian Wars and lasted until approximately the middle of the fourth century B.C., making this the Golden Age of Greek civilization. Athens dominated Greece during most of the Classical Age. Its achievements in art, architecture, literature, philosophy, ethics, history, and self-government represent the zenith of Greek creativity and enriched all later Western civilizations. Athenian supremacy was shattered by the Peloponnesian War in which polis *fought* polis. *Not until the advent of Macedonian rule did Greece regain political stability; it was at the expense, however, of freedom. Alexander the Great created one of the world's greatest empires in a few short years. The Hellenistic Age that succeeded his death spread Greek culture throughout the Mediterranean world and beyond.*

The Classical Age, c. 500 – c. 350 B.C.

The Rise of the Athenian Empire

Athens emerged from the Persian Wars as the leading Greek *polis*. It had the strongest navy, a prosperous maritime trade, healthy democratic institutions, and the most splendid cultural life. After rebuilding its city and walls (against Spartan wishes), Athens was in an excellent position to withstand any future Persian attacks. Sparta relinquished leadership of the Hellenic League after 478 B.C. and returned to its traditional isolationism, leaving Athens to assume command.

Formation of the Delian League

During the winter of 478–477 B.C., numerous Greek city-states met on the island of Delos to form a confederation later known as the Delian League. The League's avowed aim was to liberate Ionian city-states still under Persian control and to maintain military preparedness. Each member *polis* contributed to the common defense. Most chose to pay cash, while Athens supplied its fleet of 200 ships.

Athenian Control of the League

It is easy to see how this system worked to Athens' advantage. The allies' annual dues in effect subsidized the Athenian navy. Once the League had won a crushing victory over the Persian fleet in 467 B.C. and freed most of the Ionian cities, many members questioned the necessity of continuing the alliance. Athens, however, refused to allow any *polis* to leave the League and used force to prevent the secession of Thasos in 465 B.C. The transfer of the League's treasury from Delos to Athens in 454 B.C. confirmed what had already become apparent: that Athens had transformed the Delian League into an empire.

Greece, 431 B.C.

The Age of Pericles

The Age of Pericles, a great Athenian leader, was a brief but extraordinary period in Greek history that spanned the years from his rise to prominence around 462 B.C. to his death in 429 B.C. In this short time the Athenians completely democratized their government, ruled a flourishing naval empire, built unsurpassed monuments to their architectural genius, excelled at writing history and drama, and perfected the art of rational discussion.

Character of Pericles

Pericles graced this age in name and fact. His greatness derived not from his noble birth but from his character. He possessed a clear and farseeing mind, incorruptible morals, and great powers of persuasion. In addition, his loyalty to the Athenian people was never doubted. His position as one of ten generals elected annually from the tribes allowed him to suggest policies to the Council of 500 and through it to the Assembly. Both recognized the wisdom of his views and let themselves be guided accordingly.

Democratic Reforms of Pericles

Initially Pericles convinced the Assembly to reduce even further the authority of the aristocratic Council of the *Areopagus*. As a result complete sovereignty lay with the people as represented in the Assembly, the Council of 500 (also known as the Boule by this point), and the courts. All offices were open to every citizen regardless of class. To enable even the poorest citizens to participate in government, Pericles began the practice of having the *polis* pay jurors and later other officials for their services. The expenditures for these salaries came out of money received from Athens' allies. In 451–450 B.C. Pericles reduced the number of eligible recipients by restricting citizenship to those whose parents were both Athenian citizens. The population of Athenian male citizens has been variously estimated as between 20,000 and 168,000.

Economy

Pericles strove to make Athens great in all fields. He encouraged the economic growth of the Athenian Empire and supported its military actions against the Persians in Egypt and the Spartans and their allies at home. The years between 445 B.C., when peace was concluded with the Spartans, and the outbreak of war in 431 B.C. were those of Athens' greatest prosperity. The strength of its navy made Athens the preeminent commercial power in the Aegean. Tribute money flowed in from around the Empire. Even the poorest citizens shared in this general well-being.

Culture

Much of this wealth went to beautify Athens and patronize the arts. Pericles played an instrumental role in the great building program that transformed the *Acropolis* into an architectural masterpiece. Its Parthenon, Propylaea and other splendid structures were all completed under his supervision. Sculpture and painting thrived. The intellectual brilliance of the age is attested by the long list of thinkers and writers who worked during the era. Aeschylus, Sophocles, and Euripedes composed plays, Herodotus and somewhat later, Thucydides, wrote histories, and Socrates taught the pursuit of self-knowledge during this period.

Athenian Imperialism

After the transfer of the Delian League's treasury to Athens in 454 B.C., Athens' domination of the alliance became outright exploitation. The most obvious example is the use by Athens of the league's funds for purely domestic expenses unrelated to defense. The Parthenon was built from league money and public officials were paid from it. In effect Athens extracted annual tribute from league members. At its high point, Athens collected tribute from approximately 170 city-states.

Control of Allies

Athenian imperialism exerted itself in numerous other ways. Athens forced members to remain in the League and coerced others to join. All allied mints were shut down after 448 B.C. and Athenian coins and standards were used exclusively. Athens interfered directly in the political affairs of league members, suppressing oligarchic factions. The Athenians even confiscated allied territory, which enabled them to keep a close watch over their allies' behavior. Thus to Sparta and its allies the Athenians appeared to have welded together a formidable empire of democratic city-states.

Allied Discontent

The member *poleis* had few means to protest Athens' imperialistic ways. Since their resources had strengthened the Athenian navy at the expense of their own forces, military resistance seemed impossible. Pericles justified the empire because it provided members security from

Persian attack, increased their trade, and supported their democratic governments. The allies did in fact benefit from the enlarged free trade area of the empire and the protection it afforded. Yet Athens treated them as subjects and infringed upon their rights. Resentment built up against Athens' high-handed ways and eventually led to its demise.

The Peloponnesian War, 431–404 B.C.

To many Greeks, war appeared as the inevitable outcome of antagonisms that existed between democratic Athens and oligarchic Sparta. Sparta was suspicious of the aggressive intentions of the Athenian Empire while Athens continued to behave in a greedy, domineering fashion.

Steps to War

When in 433 B.C. Athens took the side of Corcyra in a quarrel with Corinth, partially because of commercial rivalry with the latter, all hopes for a lasting peace vanished. Athens acted belligerently again the next year by besieging the Corinthian colony of Potidaea. Corinth appealed to its Spartan ally to attack Athens for violating the peace. The Spartans deliberated on the charges and voted to go to war if Athens refused to heed their demands. The Athenians responded negatively at Pericles' urging, and after a final incident, war began in 431 B.C.

The First Period of War, 431–421 B.C.

Sparta's strategy in the opening years of the war was to invade Attica in an attempt to involve Athens in a pitched battle. Following Pericles' advice, Athens avoided confrontation with Sparta's superior army and relied instead on its navy for offense. Pericles gathered all the inhabitants of Attica within the city walls. Although Sparta devastated the countryside, Athens remained invulnerable to attack until plague broke out in 430 B.C. Raging on until 426 B.C., the plague killed a third of Athens' population and robbed it of Pericles, who died in 429 B.C.

Despite the demoralizing effects of the plague, Athens held the upper hand during the early years of the war because its sea raids against the Peloponnesus proved very damaging. Neither side, however, was able to score a conclusive victory until 425 B.C., when Athens captured the cream of the Spartan army at Pylos. Sparta immediately sued for peace, but the Athenian Assembly led by Cleon held out for even more favorable terms.

The Peace of Nicias

Finally in 421 B.C., after the war leaders in both *poleis* had been killed and almost everyone was tired of fighting, the Peace of Nicias was signed. For the next six years a tenuous peace prevailed as Sparta and Athens disciplined their unruly allies. In 416 B.C. Athens slaughtered and enslaved the population of Melos for refusing to join the Athenian alliance, an atrocity which blackened Athens' name.

The Sicilian Expedition, 415–413 B.C.

During the interval of peace, a nephew of Pericles, Alcibiades, became head of the popular party in Athens. An intelligent, charming man, Alcibiades was also ambitious for power, morally corrupt, and emotionally unstable. As the major spokesman for war, he vied for the Athenians' support against the elderly, conservative Nicias, who sought to uphold the peace that he had negotiated. When in 415 B.C. the town of Segestra in Sicily appealed to the Athenians for assistance against Syracuse, Alcibiades convinced them to launch a massive naval expedition against Syracuse, Sicily's largest and most important *polis*. The conquest of Sicily would have greatly enriched the Athenian Empire.

Defection of Alcibiades

Alcibiades' enterprise might have succeeded had he not been summoned home once he arrived in Sicily to stand trial on charges of impiety, and had the Athenian fleet attacked sooner. To avoid certain conviction for a trumped-up charge, Alcibiades defected to the Spartans and advised them to send immediate aid to the Syracusans.

Failure of Expedition

Spartan reinforcements enabled Syracuse to thwart the Athenians' attacks. Nicias refused to give up until it was too late. The Syracusans trapped the Athenian fleet within the harbor, forcing the Athenian sailors to seek escape through the interior. Most were captured by enemy cavalry and enslaved. The Sicilian operation was a costly failure.

The Final Years of War, 413–404 B.C.

The great sea expedition against Syracuse marked the end of Athens' political supremacy. Its allies, especially in Ionia, asserted their independence. The appeals of both Sparta and Athens for Persian help allowed the Persians to play a pivotal role in the war's course.

Internal Disruptions

Internally, Athens was racked by anarchy and factional discord. A revolution in 411 B.C. temporarily placed the reins of government in oligarchic hands and established a new constitution. After a naval victory the next year, however, the democratic fleet led the way for a return to popular rule. The opportunistic Alcibiades returned as commander of the Athenian navy and served until 406 B.C.

Defeat of Athens

The Spartans inflicted the final blow against Athens in 405 B.C. when they captured its unattended fleet. Starving, unprotected, and without allies, Athens had no alternative but to surrender. Sparta's terms were surprisingly moderate. Athens was required to relinquish its Empire, do away with its fleet, tear down its walls, and take orders from Sparta in foreign affairs. Sparta did not slaughter or enslave the Athenian populace. Overall, the war left Greece debilitated and in political upheaval.

Classical Greek Civilization

Tragedy

The fifth century was the great age of tragedy and Athens was its center. Greece's greatest dramatists, Aeschylus, Sophocles, and Euripedes, all worked there, and the *polis* provided an environment conducive to artistic achievement.

Origin of Greek Tragedy. Greek tragedy originated in choral songs performed at the Athenian religious festivals of Dionysus. The word tragedy means "goat song" in Greek and refers to a Dionysiac ritual in which a goat, representing the god, was torn apart and its pieces awarded to those with the best song. The lyrics described the mythological exploits of Greek deities and heroes. At some point during the sixth century B.C., one man stood out from the chorus and began to act out some of the events narrated and to engage in a dialogue with the chorus. To this nascent tragedaic form, Aeschylus added a second and Sophocles a third actor, thus greatly increasing the dramatic potential.

Religious and Moral Meaning. Greek tragedy retained its close ties to religion. Its greatness and universality lay in the questions it raised and the moral dilemmas it forced its audience to contemplate. It examined the abiding interests of human fate and suffering, the individual's relationship to the gods, and the nature of right action and justice. As well as entertaining the spectators, it made unprecedented intellectual demands on them.

Dramatic Conventions. At Athens' annual spring festival, the Greater Dionysia, and at other times throughout the year, playwrights submitted four works—a tragic trilogy and a satyr-play—in competition for prizes. These were performed in huge, outdoor theatres before as many as 14,000 spectators. The dramas were produced in conformity with certain formalized conventions. There were never more than four main actors, all of whom were male, and these players frequently assumed more than one part. Supporting actors, the "chorus," performed on a lower stage, the orchestra. All players wore thick-soled boots, padded clothing, and larger-than-life size masks to enhance their stature in keeping with the gods, heroes, and kings they portrayed.

Aeschylus. Aeschylus (c. 525–456 B.C.), Athens' first great dramatist, was an outstanding innovator and master poetic stylist. Only seven of his estimated 90 plays have survived in full. Among them, the *Oresteia, Prometheus Bound,* and the *Persians* are considered most important. They reveal Aeschylus' deep belief in Greek religion and his affirmation after intensive analysis of the fundamental order of things. His characters exemplify great individuals who have been brought low by their overweening pride, or *hubris.*

The *Oresteia,* the only extant trilogy, tells the story of the violent crimes of the House of Pelops. Agamemnon, King of Mycenae, had been forced to sacrifice his daughter, Iphigenia, to insure a fair wind by which to sail to Troy. In the opening play, his wife, Clytemnestra, exacts revenge by murdering him and seizing the throne for herself and her lover. In the second play some years later, Apollo orders Orestes to avenge his father's death by killing his mother and her consort. In punishment for his crime, Orestes is pursued by the Furies, ancient spirits of revenge. The third play addresses the problem of how to end this feuding. Should the primitive law of retribution (the Furies) win out, or should the state (as represented by the new Council of the *Areopagus*) intervene on the side of moderation? The play concludes with Athena casting the tie- breaking vote in Orestes' favor and placating the Furies. Aeschylus thus argues that true justice resides not in blood revenge but in the impartial decisions of the *polis*.

Sophocles. Sophocles (c. 496–406 B.C.) was the most traditional of the Greek dramatists. His best-known tragedies, *Antigone* and *King Oedipus*, suggest that he accepted suffering as an inescapable part of the human condition. Both protagonists are fated to meet terrible ends. Yet Sophocles' plays reflect a profound faith in the dignity and greatness of humans as they struggle to do right and face death honorably.

The plot of *King Oedipus* is well known to all Westerners and has been used by Freud and others to express the incestuous longings in human nature. Oedipus unwittingly killed his father and married his mother as an oracle had predicted before he was born. When as king of Thebes he seeks to root out the moral pollution that is causing a plague in his kingdom, he slowly and horrifyingly discovers his own crime, gouges out his eyes, and wanders off to lead a life of suffering. Oedipus was not a bad man, only somewhat proud and arrogant. His humbling serves as a lesson of the divine inevitability of fate and shows that no life can be judged happy until its end.

Euripedes. Of all Attic drama, the plays of Euripedes (480–406 B.C.) appear most modern because they delve most deeply into their characters' psyches. In an intensely realistic manner, Euripedes describes the overwhelming emotions that gain control over his characters and often lead them to commit cruel and terrible acts.

In *Medea*, for example, when Jason abandons his barbarian mistress in order to marry a Greek princess, the despondent Medea poisons her lover's bride and coldly kills her two children by him. By the end of the play when Medea is allowed to escape, her cruel deeds make it impossible for the audience to sympathize with her. Yet, they have had to think about issues such as the uncontrollable power of human emotions, the place of women in society, and the extent to which her revenge was justified.

In many of his plays, Euripedes employed a piece of equipment which lowered a man dressed as a god onto the stage from on high in order to resolve the plot's complexities in rapid fashion. This device became known by its Latin term, *deus ex machina* ("god from a machine.")

Comedy

Like tragedy, Attic comedy also began as part of a Dionysiac ritual, in this case a fertility rite.

Aristophanes. Attic Old Comedy, as represented by the plays of Aristophanes (c. 445–c. 380 B.C.), was unrestrained in its use of obscene words and lewd gestures. Aristophanes was a genius at deriving hilarious effects from all types of comic devices— salacious *double-entendres*, absurd characters, and slapstick situations. Yet this ribald spirit never totally concealed the more serious nature of the playwright's concerns. Aristophanes was a conservative who viewed much of contemporary Athenian life with disdain. Many of his plays ridicule Athens' political leaders and democratic system. In *Lysistrata* the wives go on a sex strike until their husbands agree to end the Peloponnesian War. Aristophanes opposed the war not from pacifist convictions, but because he believed the democratic element in Athenian society profited from it. His dislike of innovation made him sometimes unfair, as in his biting satires of Socrates in *Clouds* and of Euripides in *Frogs*.

History

The Greeks were the first to write history as we think of it today. In their eyes, the historian's job was to inquire objectively into the causes and consequences of past events. In contrast to the Israelites' God-centered theme, the Greeks viewed the study of history as humanistic in nature with its action directed by individuals. In the late sixth to early fifth centuries B.C., several Greek geographical and navigational accounts in prose anticipated this "scientific" approach to history.

Herodotus. Ethnographic interests are still evident in the writing of Herodotus (c. 484–425 B.C.), who has been called the Father of History. Born in Asia Minor, Herodotus visited or lived in an exceptional number of places for his time, including Egypt, the areas around the Black Sea, Mesopotamia, South Italy, Athens, and elsewhere in Greece. Throughout his travels, Herodotus acquainted himself with native cultures and gathered stories and information about their origins and development. The fruit of this research appears in his masterful history of the Persian Wars.

Herodotus' history is as much a study of the peoples of the ancient world as it is a narrative of the war. It chronicles what in the historian's mind was the victory of Greek freedom over Persian despotism. He digresses frequently to relate myths or extraneous details and shows a keen awareness of the influence of climate and geography on customs and social relations. Because he drew upon mostly oral sources to describe an earlier age, a good deal of what he included was closer to fiction than fact. Yet Herodotus often alerted the reader before presenting data about which he was skeptical. Herodotus' greatness lies in his broad view, intellectual curiosity, and lively, fact-filled prose style.

Thucydides. A generation later Greece produced another of the Western world's outstanding historians. Thucydides (c. 460 – c. 400 B.C.), an Athenian by birth, was intimately acquainted with Athens' political life and took part as a general in its war against Sparta. When he failed to prevent the city of Amphipolis from falling to the enemy, he was exiled for twenty years. This bitter punishment nonetheless freed him to travel throughout Greece in search of information from both sides with which to write a history of the Peloponnesian War. Thucydides' account, which ends in 411 B.C., is a model of impartial, accurate historical analysis.

The historian understood well the deeper causes which underlie great conflicts. He saw the Peloponnesian War as the outcome of Athens' growing appetite for imperial power and the fear it generated in other Greeks. Thucydides reveals his insight into human psychology in his series of set speeches reconstructing what leading political figures might have said in order to expose their characters, lay bare their motives, or convey the mood of the times. These imaginative recreations, such as Pericles' Funeral Oration, display Thucydides' prose at its most artistic and compelling.

Architecture and Art

Greek architecture and art reached their apogee during the Classical Age. In both fields a new, classical style emerged shortly after 500 B.C. This change from the archaic to the classical is characterized by improved technical skills and a more refined sense of harmony and proportion.

Temples. Classical Greek temples varied little from one another in overall plan. Rectangular in shape with gabled roofs, they contained inner rooms, or *cellae,* that housed the statues of patron gods, and porches at both ends that contained two columns each. Important temples were surrounded on all sides by colonnades. Since few people had the right to enter the *cella,* external design and decoration were of paramount importance.

Orders of Architecture. Greek architecture is unique in that all its buildings belong to one of three generalized architectural types, or *orders,* of Greek invention: the Doric, Ionic, and Corinthian. The essential elements of each order are remarkably constant and must always be present.

1. The *Doric* order is the simplest and probably the oldest. It is most easily distinguished by its fluted columns that end in plain capitals. Doric columns have a swelling or bulge in the middle which gives them a sturdy, "muscular" quality and prevents the illusion of concavity that a long row of columns creates.

2. The *Ionic* order features columns that are more slender than Doric ones. Their capitals are more elaborate, terminating in spiral, scroll-shaped ornaments called volutes at each corner. Sometimes Ionic porch columns were sculpted into female figures called caryatids. The Erechtheum on the Athenian *Acropolis* is of this type.

3. The *Corinthian* order is essentially a more ornate adaptation of the Ionic. Its capital has the appearance of an inverted bell covered with acanthus leaves. Little used during the Classical Age except for interiors, the Corinthian order found great favor with the Romans.

The Acropolis. The buildings that Pericles had constructed on the *Acropolis* to replace those destroyed by the Persians represent Greek Classical architecture at its most sublime. Of them, the crown jewel and most perfect example of classical Doric temple architecture is the Parthenon that honors Athena, the founding goddess of Athens. Built between 448 and 432 B.C. by the architects Ictinus and Callicrates with superior white marble, the Parthenon epitomizes the Greek ideal of balanced grace and harmonious proportions. It was originally painted and gilded, as were most other Greek temples and statuary.

Sculpture. Our imperfect knowledge of Greek sculpture is based on written descriptions, Roman copies, and existing fragments. Early Greek sculpture was dependent on Egyptian models that depicted the human form in a stiff, formalized manner. The transition from archaic to classical styles occurred around 480 B.C. During the next thirty years, Greek sculptors mastered the art of representing human movement naturalistically in large free-standing statues.

Classical sculpture attained its maturity during the Age of Pericles and is exemplified by the architectural sculptures of the Parthenon. At the beginning of the nineteenth century, many of these were collected by Lord Elgin and brought to London, where they now constitute a stellar attraction in the British Museum. Architectural sculpture refers to those statues executed in high relief which adorn two principal areas of a temple's exterior: the pediments and the inner and outer friezes. Some credit the sculptor Phidias, who oversaw Pericles' building projects and created the huge ivory and gold statue of Athena that stood in the *cella*, with the design of all the Parthenon's decoration. Quite probably it was an achievement by numerous master craftsmen working together.

Painting. Not enough examples of Greek mural painting have survived to allow one to describe it satisfactorily. Thus knowledge of Greek painting derives from later Roman copies as well as from Greek vase painting. The latter reached its artistic height during the Archaic Age.

Science

For a good part of the Classical Age, the tasks of the scientist and the philosopher remained closely allied. Both sought to apply human logic to deduce the fundamental principles that govern the universe.

Empedocles. Continuing the work of the Milesian school, Empedocles postulated that there were actually four prime substances—earth, air, fire, and water—which combined in various ways to produce all forms of life.

Democritus. Democritus (c. 460–c. 370 B.C.) theorized that all matter was composed of innumerable, indivisible and indestructible particles called "atoms." He was the first to attribute the formation of all things to a purely mechanistic process without supernatural intervention.

Hippocrates. In the field of medicine, the Greeks began to show a greater interest in empirical studies. Hippocrates of Cos (c. 460–377 B.C.), known as the Father of Medicine, founded a school of medicine that stressed the necessity of observation and experimentation. The *Hippocratic Corpus* of writings by Hippocrates and his fellow physicians presents detailed case reports of the outbreak, course, and conclusion of various diseases. An illness was diagnosed scientifically according to its symptoms and often treated by changes in the patient's diet, environment, or hygienic habits. Hippocrates' name is also associated with the Hippocratic Oath which sets forth a high concept of medical ethics.

Limitations of Greek Science. Greek science, while advancing the use of reason to examine natural phenomena, did not develop a scientific methodology based on experimentation. Greek science sought knowledge of the natural world through speculation and logic rather than through theories based on empirically observed facts.

Philosophy

Towards the end of the fifth century, Greek philosophy changed direction. The teachings of the Sophists and especially Socrates turned philosophy away from its preoccupation with the natural world and the origin of things and gave focus to the study of human values and institutions.

The Sophists. The Sophists were not, strictly speaking, philosophers, but rather itinerant teachers who lectured on the arts of rhetoric and composition for a fee. They instructed men in skills, such as persuasive public speaking, which would help them get ahead in life. The Sophists took little interest in the search for pure knowledge. In fact most of them were skeptical about the existence of absolutes including god and truth and thus rejected many traditional values. Protagoras, the best thinker among them, summarized their belief that each individual must analyze the world for himself with his saying that "man is the measure of all things."

Socrates. Socrates (469–399 B.C.), a former Athenian stonemason whose view of knowledge forms the basis of systematic Western philosophy, is often mislabeled a Sophist because he appeared to share the Sophist technique of questioning accepted beliefs and ancient institutions. Socrates' logical criticisms, however, never ended in moral relativism or verbal sophistries, nor was he a teacher paid to transmit skills profitable to worldly success. Socrates' philosophy revolved around the simple premise that "the unexamined life is not worth living." He devoted his entire existence to discussing problems of right action and truth.

The Socratic Method. In his incessant conversations—which have been preserved in the writings of Plato and Xenophon—Socrates urged listeners to subject all their assumptions to the test of reason and to become aware of the real purpose and worth of things. He helped people think clearly by asking questions and then correcting false responses until gradually, after further questioning, the right answers become apparent. This Socratic method remains a highly regarded pedagogical device.

Ethics. Socrates sought by his constant debating to uncover ethical standards that would assist Athenians to live moral and rational lives. For him, knowledge and virtue were one, so that "no one ever does wrong willingly." In regulating his own moral conduct, he claimed he followed the promptings of a divine inner voice, i.e., his conscience.

Trial and Death. Despite Socrates' preoccupation with high moral purpose, he was often misunderstood, especially by those Athenian democrats who disliked him for political reasons because he had tutored such antidemocrats as Alcibiades and Critias. Owing partly to the hysterical atmosphere of post-war Athens, Socrates was brought to trial in 399 B.C. on charges of not believing in the gods and of corrupting the youth. In the *Apology*, Plato recorded Socrates' defense: that he was a faithful citizen of the *polis*, obedient to its laws as well as divine ones. A jury nonetheless found him guilty by a slim margin. Refusing the possibility of exile or a fine, Socrates drank a cup of poisonous hemlock and awaited death serenely and without malice. Ever since, the inspiring example of his life and thought have influenced generation upon generation of individuals concerned with human values, beginning with his most gifted pupil, Plato.

Plato. As a young man, Plato (c. 427–347 B.C.), an Athenian aristocrat by birth, met Socrates and became his disciple and good friend. After Socrates' death, Plato carried on his mentor's search for objective moral standards in numerous philosophical writings. Most of these took the form of dialogues or discussions with Socrates as the principal interlocutor. Plato also founded the first of the great Athenian philosophical schools, the Academy, which remained open until A.D. 529 and helped make Athens the educational center of the Mediterranean world.

Theory of Forms. Plato built his own philosophical system upon Socrates' teaching that there is objectively a good life which is knowable and thus can be rationally attained. In order to live the good life, people must learn to distinguish true knowledge and value from mere appearance, convention, or opinion. This belief led Plato to elaborate his famous theory of Forms. Every object, quality, or virtue has its ideal form or pattern which is eternal and unchangeable. Plato insisted that the Forms have a real existence independent of the physical world and that they can be perceived by the soul only after long study. The Forms are what give the universe its orderly and intelligible nature. The highest among them and the most difficult to perceive is the Form of the Good, which is the source of all wisdom, truth, and right conduct. The philosopher's task is to lead humanity towards a vision of the Good.

The Republic. Plato's theory of Forms is crucial to his portrayal of an ideal state in his best-known work, the *Republic*. According to Plato, the good state can be achieved only when political power is entrusted to those few individuals who, through natural talent and education, have gained a true knowledge of what is good for all human beings. Plato grew up during the Peloponnesian War and harbored for the rest of his life a dislike of democratic government, which he held responsible for Athens' disastrous failure and for the death of his master. Thus Plato's ideal state was fundamentally elitist and anti-democratic.

Influence. A bold and original thinker, Plato posed many of the fundamental questions in a wide range of fields which continue to preoccupy philosophers in the present. His argument for the true reality of a world of Forms apart from the material world constitutes the basis of the philosophical doctrine of Idealism and made his writings congenial to some early Christians as well as to the Renaissance.

Aristotle. The most illustrious of Plato's students at the Academy, Aristotle became the tutor of the young Alexander the Great and went on to found his own school, the Lyceum, in Athens. Son of an Ionian Greek physician at the Macedonian court, Aristotle (384–322 B.C.) equaled if not surpassed his teacher in the comprehensiveness of his philosophical speculations.

Ethics and the Good Life. Following Plato, Aristotle was concerned above all with the good man and the good life. He rejected his mentor's theory of the separate existence of Forms. In the Aristotelian system, all individual objects are made up of both form and matter. Only the Prime Mover, or god, was pure form and caused all else to be. In the realm of ethics, Aristotle counseled basing one's conduct on the Doctrine of the Mean, which holds that every virtue is the mean between two extremes. For example, temperance is the mean between overindulgence and abstinence. Hence Aristotle championed moderation in all things. He believed that the highest human activity is the use of one's reason and, therefore, the happiest life is the contemplative one.

Politics. In his *Politics* Aristotle makes clear that the good life can be realized only within the *polis* because the *polis* provides its citizens with an education, encourages them to use their reason, and furnishes them with laws to guide their actions. Aristotle and his students examined the constitutions of 158 *poleis* and divided them into three basic forms according to where sovereignty resided: (1) in one man, or monarchy, (2) in a few men, or aristocracy, and (3) in the bulk of the citizens, or "polity" (moderate democracy). He recognized that there were also deviant types of each, i.e., tyranny, oligarchy, and democracy (mob rule), respectively, in which power is exercised for the ruler's benefit only. In order to decide which constitution enabled its citizens to live the most satisfying lives, he distinguished between that which was ideally best (rule by one or a few individuals of superior wisdom and virtue) and that which was best for the majority of states and people (moderate democracy because it was most stable). "Polity" was the mean between extremes and thus the best.

Systematization of Knowledge. Much of Aristotle's thought has come down to us in the form of lecture notes taken by his pupils. These touch upon aesthetics, literary criticism, rhetoric, ethics, politics, logic, psychology, astronomy, zoology, mathematics, physics, and metaphysics. In almost every discipline Aristotle's brilliant systematizations of previous knowledge together with his own findings contributed greatly to the advancement of learning. His geocentric theories on the physical universe were finally overturned by the scientific revolution of the seventeenth century, but his work in zoology remains relevant to modern inquiries. Aristotle was fascinated by the material world and examined it methodically. For example, he dissected animals in order to group them and describe their parts in exact detail.

Logic and Criticism. Aristotle's penchant for classification extended to his nonscientific work. In his writings on logic he invented the syllogism as a tool for reasoning. In the *Poetics*, he developed standards by which to judge poetry and drama. His definition of tragedy as purging the audience of pity and fear by their vicarious participation in the action is justly famous.

Influence. Despite the depth and significance of Aristotle's work, the ancient Greeks regarded Plato more highly. Aristotle's greatest influence was felt during the Middle Ages, when much of his thought and methodology was absorbed into Christian theology by St. Thomas Aquinas.

The Era of the Hegemonies

The impressive philosophical accomplishments of the fourth century B.C. took place in an intellectual environment largely detached from the political realities of the day. In matters of state, the period between the end of the Peloponnesian War and the rise of Macedon was one of continual bloodshed and political instability for Greece. Historians refer to this period as the era of the hegemonies (from the Greek word for "to lead"), as several *poleis* held political control over allies and fought wars with each other. The Era of Hegemonies was a period of crisis for the Greeks during which the basic assumptions of their civilization such as the superiority of life in the *polis* were called into question.

Spartan Hegemony

Sparta's victory in the Peloponnesian War placed it in a dominant position that allowed it to set up oligarchic governments favorable to its interests. Even in Athens itself, the Spartans reorganized the government so that control was in the hands of thirty men. "The Thirty" led by Critias instituted a reign of terror and misrule that eventually led to their overthrow by the democratic forces in 403 B.C.

Internecine and Foreign Wars

The numerous wars and shifting alliances of this period are complicated. Between 400 and 387 B.C., the Spartans and other Greeks fought a losing battle against the Persians over the status of the Ionian Greeks. Dictating the terms of the King's Peace in 386 B.C., Persia confirmed its suzerainty over the Greeks in Asia Minor and declared the autonomy of all other Greek *poleis*. During this time the Spartans, who lacked experience in governing other people, were also involved in conflicts at home. Sparta's self-interested and tyrannical ways alienated many Greek *poleis* and condemned its attempts at hegemony to ultimate failure. Sparta's supremacy over Greece ended in 371 B.C. with its defeat by Thebes at the battle of Leuctra.

Athenian Confederacy

At one point during the 370s Athens appeared to have resumed its former position of leadership. In 377 B.C. it formed the Second Athenian Naval Confederacy, as a means to coordinate opposition to Sparta, but the Confederacy never reached the size or importance of the fifth-century naval league.

Theban Hegemony

Thebes assumed the role as dominant *polis* in Greece from 371 to 362 B.C. The Thebans proved no better able than Spartans in putting the interests of Greece as a whole first. When its leader, Epaminondas, was killed in the battle of Mantinea against Athens and Sparta (362 B.C.), Thebes lost sway over Greece.

The Ascendancy of Macedon

The factional struggles of the early fourth century B.C. placed the Greek *poleis* under tremendous strain and exposed them to the danger of foreign conquest. Just such a potential conqueror, Macedon, was gaining in power in the mountainous region north of Greece.

The Macedonians

The Macedonians were a mixture of Anatolian and Hellenic peoples whom the Greeks accepted as relatives, although they couldn't understand their language. The Macedonians did not share the Greek political structure of the *polis*. Instead they were organized into tribes that were ruled by an hereditary king whose power was limited by the nobility and the army. The traditional ancient Greek image of the Macedonians as uncivilized barbarians is being reevaluated in the light of recent excavations at Pella. These excavations reveal that at least some Macedonians lived a wealthier, more cosmopolitan urban life than previously thought. Agriculture and the raising of livestock were nonetheless the primary economic activities, and the Macedonians were quite isolated from Greek culture.

Philip II

Beginning in the fifth century B.C., Hellenic influences increased in Macedon and the country became increasingly involved in Greek affairs. Macedon's emergence as a powerful nation was accomplished almost solely by one man, Philip II. In 359 B.C., as the newly appointed regent for his nephew, the infant king, he contrived to get himself elected king on his own. During his youth, Philip had been a hostage in Thebes. There he learned Theban military tactics, such as the use of the phalanx formation, and came to appreciate Greek culture. Once in power, he sought to develop Macedon into a strong and unified nation that would win the Greeks' admiration. He began by military reforms. He created a corps of highly trained and efficient peasant foot-soldiers who fought alongside the aristocratic cavalry. His concern for and personal leadership of the army molded it into a superior fighting force.

Philip used his new army as well as diplomatic ploys to extend Macedonian control first over much of Thrace, and later over Thessaly and other areas of north central Greece.

Defeat of Athens and Thebes

Philip's expansion alarmed the Greeks, but only Athens was in any position to resist him. The Athenian orator Demosthenes urged his fellow citizens to defend their freedom against the Macedonian threat in a series of famous speeches, the *Philippics*, beginning in 351 B.C. Demosthenes' advice went generally unheeded until it was too late. At the battle of Chaeronea in 338 B.C. the Macedonians decisively defeated the Athenian and Theban forces, thus making themselves masters of Greece. From that date forward, the *poleis* were no longer politically independent.

The League of Corinth

Philip did not destroy Athens as Demosthenes claimed he would. In fact, he found it politically expedient to treat the Greeks—with the exception of Thebes—leniently because he needed their assistance in his projected war against the Persian Empire. He forced all *poleis* except Sparta to join together in a military alliance, the League of Corinth, which was sworn to maintain peace within Greece and ally with Macedon in fighting the Persians. Although the League retained a semblance of autonomy, Philip was named its commander and in effect he directed all its activities.

Philip's Achievements

In 336 B.C., as the invasion of Persia had just gotten under way, Philip was assassinated by one of his officers. The accomplishments of Philip are impressive. He turned a weak and disunited nation into the leading power in Greece and fashioned a strong army which his son Alexander would use effectively in future conquests. He succeeded in uniting the unruly Greeks and brought a degree of peace and security to the mainland. While his brief rule was moderate, the methods he used to gain power were often unscrupulous. Thus the final judgment on Philip is a difficult one.

Alexander the Great

Philip was succeeded by his twenty-year-old son Alexander (356–323 B.C.), who had been groomed since childhood in the arts of warfare and statecraft.

Youth and Early Reign

From Aristotle, one of his tutors, Alexander learned about Greek philosophy and natural science and developed a passionate interest in Greek literature, especially Homer. He demonstrated his capabilities for ruling immediately upon ascending the throne. He saw to it that the League of Corinth elected him to his father's post as commander and acted promptly against those areas of Philip's empire, Thessaly, Thrace and Illyria, which had seen in the king's death an opportunity to reassert their independence. Yet Alexander also displayed early the hard and destructive side of his character. He put down a revolt in Thebes by destroying the city (except for its temples and the home of the poet Pindar), selling the Thebans into slavery, and distributing their land among neighboring *poleis*.

Conquests

By 334 B.C., Alexander was ready to carry out his father's plans to invade Persia. At the head of a combined Macedonian-Greek army, he embarked on what would become an eleven-year march of conquest. Crossing the Hellespont into Asia, he rapidly defeated King Darius III's army at the Granicus River and aided the establishment of democratic governments in the Ionian Greek city- states. After conquering most of Asia Minor, he moved into Syria, where he again triumphed over the Persians at Issus. He then made himself master of the Phoenician cities. Alexander now set his sights on conquering the entire Persian Empire. Rejecting several of Darius's generous offers of peace, in late 332 B.C. he marched into Egypt, where he met no opposition. The Egyptians declared him their pharaoh and accorded him divine honors.

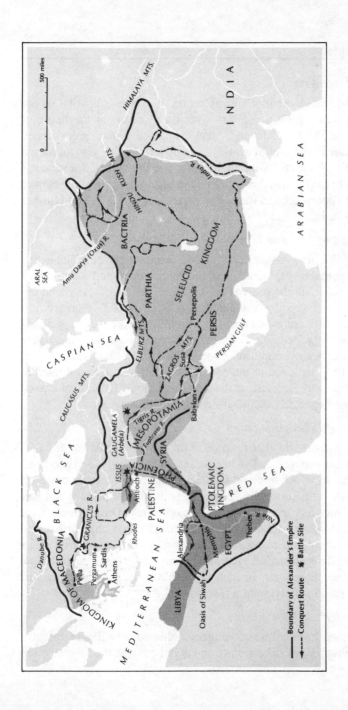

Alexander's Empire, 336-323 B.C.

Thrust into Asia

From Egypt, Alexander's army returned to Mesopotamia, where they won a final, decisive victory over the Persians at the battle of Gaugamela in 331 B.C. Alexander had the palace at Persepolis burned and confiscated the royal treasuries. In 330 B.C. Darius was murdered by one of his own men. Nothing now stood in the way of Alexander's assumption of the Persian throne. Only the eastern portion of the empire had not been occupied, and thus he pressed his army further and further into central Asia.

Blending of East and West

During this time Alexander married a Bactrian princess and began adopting Oriental ways, such as wearing Persian dress and requiring his subjects to prostrate themselves before him. He also encouraged the intermarriage between Persians and Greeks. All of this greatly antagonized his officers, who considered themselves Alexander's equals and superior to the Persians. These orientalizing ways were not solely the product of vanity, ambition, or even shrewd political calculation. Alexander truly believed in the equality of peoples. He continued to use Egyptians and Persians in the administration of their conquered cities, and he eventually included Persians in his army.

Failure of Indian Campaign

By 326 B.C. the army had reached as far as the Indus River. It seems that Alexander thought that if he crossed India he would come to an eastern ocean by which he could sail back to Greece. Thus he continued to march eastward, concluding alliances with several princes and battling others such as Porus, whose use of elephants in battle struck terror in the Macedonians. Finally his men refused to go any further and forced their disappointed leader to turn back. The return trip was a difficult and dangerous one. Alexander was not granted enough time to demonstrate how well, in fact, he would have governed his vast empire; he died in Babylon of a fever in 323 B.C.

Alexander's Achievements

Alexander the Great was courageous, shrewd, a brilliant strategist, and a master of detail. The empire he carved out was the largest yet in the ancient world. He achieved this, nonetheless, with an army already superbly organized by his father and against an enemy that was militarily weak and poorly prepared.

Alexander both destroyed cities (Thebes, Tyre, and Persepolis) and founded them (Alexandria in Egypt, and others). These new cities served as outposts of Greek culture in the East. He could be cruel, especially when in a drunken rage, and executed a number of those who opposed him or were corrupt. Yet, he never slaughtered the population of a conquered city and treated the Persian royal family with respect.

Some scholars hold that Alexander undertook his conquests to realize his vision of the brotherhood of humanity by joining together East and West. Others stress instead the terrible costs his ambition for glory incurred. Regardless of his intentions, Alexander's conquests brought together two very different civilizations. From their meeting emerged a new Hellenistic culture.

The Hellenistic Age, 323–30 B.C.

The years between Alexander's death in 323 B.C. and the suicide of Cleopatra, the last Ptolemaic ruler of Egypt, in 30 B.C. constitute the Hellenistic Age. During this period, the diffusion of Greek culture throughout the Near Eastern and Mediterranean world begun by Alexander's conquests continued as the Age's most important feature.

The Breakup of Alexander's Empire

Alexander's sudden death triggered a fierce struggle for power among his generals. His only two legitimate heirs, a dimwitted half-brother and a posthumous son, were unqualified to rule. They were both soon assassinated. After almost forty years of constant warfare, intrigue and murder, Alexander's empire was divided into three separate kingdoms, each ruled by a Macedonian dynasty: the Ptolemies in Egypt, the Seleucids in Asia, and the Antigonids in Macedon and Greece.

The Ptolemaic Kingdom

Ptolemy, one of Alexander's generals, who also wrote a history of their expedition, founded a dynasty which controlled Egypt according to ancient traditions. The Ptolemies made themselves pharaohs, and ruled for their own benefit by means of a vast bureaucracy staffed mostly by Greeks and Macedonians. Nonetheless, the Ptolemies were able administrators and during their reign Egypt prospered and regained some of its earlier glory. Life thrived within the new cities settled by Greeks, such as Alexandria, which the Ptolemies wisely accorded a measure of autonomy.

The Seleucid Kingdom

Another general, Seleucus, consolidated his hold over most of Syria, Mesopotamia, and Asia Minor. The Seleucids also aspired to be absolute rulers but the vastness of their domains made centralized control impossible. The regions of Bactria, Parthia, and Alexander's Indian holdings soon broke away from Seleucid domination. In Asia Minor, the splendid kingdom of Pergamum was likewise independent. Within the empire itself, revolts and civil disturbances were a constant problem. The Seleucids' solution to governing such a difficult territory was to continue Alexander's policy of founding new cities as secure centers of military and administrative control. The most important of these was Antioch. Greeks and Macedonians were encouraged to settle in the new cities by offers of free land in exchange for their services in the army.

The Antigonid Kingdom

In Macedon, a general named Antipater first exercised control and then it passed on to another general, Antigonus, whose son was finally recognized by the Macedonians as king in 294 B.C. Antigonid rule supposedly extended over all of Macedon and Greece except for Sicily, yet in practice some *poleis*, notably Sparta, were virtually autonomous. The Antigonids allowed the traditional forms of self-government within the *polis* to function undisturbed. Nevertheless, many Greek cities sought to increase their independence by joining one of two leagues, the Aetolian in the north and the Achaean in the Peloponnesus. In the mid-third century B.C. the Achaean League appeared on the verge of freeing all Greece from Macedonian rule, but its members fell to quarreling with Sparta and the Aetolian League. During the second century B.C., the Romans increasingly involved themselves in Greek affairs.

Economic and Social Life

The Hellenistic Age was a period of economic prosperity throughout most of Alexander's former empire. Only the *poleis* of mainland Greece suffered a loss of trade. Elsewhere, commerce and industry expanded and agriculture flourished. The many Greeks and Macedonians who immigrated to the cities founded by Alexander and his successors brought with them new ideas, new methods, and an entrepreneurial spirit. For example, they taught the Egyptians new irrigation methods and introduced the cultivation of grapes for wine.

Economy

Trade and industry increased dramatically under the Hellenistic monarchs who closely regulated the economy. The great influx of Persian wealth which Alexander had seized had a stimulating effect on the economies of Egypt and the Near East, though it contributed to a rampant inflation. In addition, the creation of roads, canals, and standard coinage facilitated economic growth. Above all, Alexander's empire had opened up many new markets between East and West and these were extended during the Hellenistic Age. Alexandria, Antioch, and Rhodes replaced Athens and other Greek *poleis* as great commercial centers. In industry, production was carried out on a larger scale using cheap and abundant labor.

Society

In spite of the general increase in wealth, the lot of the poor did not improve during the Hellenistic period. Wealth went instead to the Hellenistic monarchs and members of the upper classes who were predominantly of Greek or Macedonian birth. The wide gap between rich and poor aggravated social tensions sometimes to the point of conflict.

Rise of Cities

While agriculture remained the single most important component of the economy, most of the new fortunes were urban-based. The rise of great cities as the commercial, intellectual, and governmental centers of the Hellenistic kingdoms is a hallmark of the age. Alexandria, the greatest of them, had a population of perhaps one million inhabitants. Its two harbors, museum, library, and huge lighthouse attracted travelers from all over the Mediterranean world.

Religion and Philosophy

The changed economic, social, and cultural milieu of the Hellenistic Age gave rise to new intellectual developments.

Religion

The decline of the *polis* brought with it a falling away from traditional Greek religious beliefs and the growth of mystical religions. Lack of communal ties in the new and larger Hellenistic world created a sense of isolation which many individuals sought to assuage by joining Near Eastern mystery cults. Most of these cults promised immortality through the ritual worship of a dying and rising god whose rebirth insured the salvation of mankind. The Persian religion of Mithraism was one of the most popular of these cults. Christianity was born into and its development influenced to some extent by this religious climate of mysticism and belief in a cycle of birth, death, and rebirth.

Philosophy

Many educated people turned to philosophy for ethical guidance and emotional support. Plato and Aristotle had both posited that to enjoy the good life it was necessary to be a participating citizen of the *polis*. When the success of Macedon made it evident that the *poleis* were too small and strife-torn to deal with the problems of the new age, philosophers looked elsewhere for the mainstay of human conduct and happiness. Two major schools of philosophy, Epicureanism and Stoicism, expressed disillusionment with public life and sought to make individuals self-sufficient in their own private spheres. This shift in emphasis distinguishes Hellenistic philosophy.

Epicureanism. Epicurus (c. 341–270 B.C.) founded in Athens a school of philosophy that considered individual happiness to be the highest good. He taught that this life on earth, free of supernatural intervention, is what matters. To live a happy life one must seek pleasure. Epicurus defined pleasure not in physical terms, but rather as the avoidance of pain and worry. These were best achieved by leading a serene life devoted to intellectual pursuits and the company of friends.

Stoicism. Stoicism was established by the Cypriot Zeno of Citium (c. 335–263 B.C.) around 300 B.C. It too sought to free the individual from anxiety and fear of death but differed from Epicureanism in how this was to be accomplished. The Stoics believed in a rational and orderly universe governed by divine providence. By using reason, human beings can live in accordance with the divine will. The ideal "Wise Man" resigns himself to his fate, and becomes self-sufficient by doing his duty, living virtuously, and subordinating passion to reason. The Stoics' political theories exerted a tremendous influence on Roman and later Western thought. In place of the *polis*, the Stoics spoke of a world-state in which all men are brothers and in which the principles of tolerance and concord reign supreme. Of all Greek philosophies, Stoicism proved the most congenial to the Romans, many of whom adopted its ideals as revised by the second-century B.C. Stoic Panaetius of Rhodes.

Science

Closer contacts between East and West had a fertilizing effect on Hellenistic science. With Alexandria as its center, the scientific research of the time made important discoveries in geography, astronomy, medicine, physics and mathematics. On the whole, Hellenistic scientists applied more stringent methodologies, stressed the value of experimentation, and became more specialized in their studies. This enabled them to obtain more precise and accurate calculations.

Geography

Erastothenes. Erastothenes, who headed the library at Alexandria around 240 B.C., made one of the most accurate measurements of the earth's circumference until modern times. He also drew, using lines of longitude and latitude, a remarkably exact map of the known world based on travelers' descriptions.

Astronomy

Aristarchus. The mid-third century Greek Aristarchus is credited with being the first to propose that the earth rotates on its axis and revolves around the sun. Most of his contemporaries, however, rejected his heliocentric theory of the universe. They continued to adhere to the Aristotelian notion of the earth as the center of the universe.

Hipparchus. Another important Greek astronomer, Hipparchus, who lived in the second century B.C., calculated the length of the solar year to within minutes and the length of the average lunar month to within one second of the actual number. Many future astronomers were to use his comprehensive charts of the heavens. He also invented the astrolabe and made important contributions to the study of trigonometry.

Medicine

Hellenistic scientists also progressed in the study of medicine. By dissecting the corpses of animals, they gained a greater understanding of the human circulatory, muscular, and nervous systems.

Mathematics

The most distinguished contributions of the Hellenistic Age occurred in the field of mathematics.

Euclid. The great geometrician Euclid established a school in Alexandria around 300 B.C. in which he taught the fundamental principles of arithmetic and plane and solid geometry. His renowned book, the *Elements*, has had a lasting influence because its theorems are models of mathematical reasoning.

Archimedes. Archimedes of Syracuse (287–212 B.C.) was a genius in both theoretical and practical knowledge. He calculated the value of π (pi) and created a mathematical system for expressing very large numbers.

Physics

In physics, Archimedes demonstrated the theory and practical use of the pulley and the lever, discovered the "law of floating bodies," and set down the fundamentals of mechanics and hydrostatics (fluids). Among his numerous inventions are an improved catapult and "Archimedes' screw," a machine used to pump out water from ships, mines, and irrigation systems.

Culture

The culture that issued from intermingling Greek and Oriental forms was urbane, cosmopolitan, and individualistic. The spread of learning and the adoption of Greek as the common language among the educated contributed to this atmosphere. Scholars from all over Greece and the Near East flocked to Alexandria to pursue government-sponsored studies. Persons with expertise in a specific branch of knowledge gradually replaced the amateur scholars of Hellenic times. This trend to professionalism and specialization is another important aspect of Hellenistic culture.

Literature

The greatest achievements of literature occurred in scholarship. Hellenistic scholars wrote literary criticism, compiled anthologies and catalogs, and were responsible for preserving much of earlier Greek literature. In comparison to the masterpieces of classical Greek poetry and drama, the creations of Hellenistic writers appear lacking in energy and originality, but Callimarchus and Theocritus did compose excellent poetry and the historian Polybius wrote an important account of early Rome.

Architecture

Hellenistic architecture reflected the grandeur of a monarchical age in its preference for the elaborate Corinthian capital and the large scale of its buildings. Hellenistic architects made notable advances in urban planning of the many new cities of the period.

Sculpture

Sculpture remained on a high level during the Hellenistic Age. Some of the best known ancient sculptures, such as the Venus de Milo, the Winged Victory of Samothrace, and the Dying Gaul, date from this period. Unlike classical Greek sculptures, Hellenistic works are noted for their intense realism and heightened emotions.

Influence of Hellenistic Culture

Hellenistic culture played a crucial role in the development of Western civilization. Apart from its own achievements, by spreading the classical Greek legacy throughout the ancient Near East and Roman West, it ensured the survival of one of humanity's most productive and original cultures. Roman civilization owed much to what it thus absorbed from the Greeks.

In his famous Funeral Speech, Pericles said of Athens: "Our city is an education to Greece." Athenian pride during the Classical Age was not misplaced, for from c. 500 to c. 350 B.C. Athens evolved a democratic form of government that allowed for the widest possible participation of its citizens in decision-making and office-holding. Within its walls the arts of tragedy and comedy were born and the writing of history as fact, not divine revelation, was begun. Socrates, Plato and Aristotle all lived and worked at some time in Athens. Its classical sculpture and architecture set standards of beauty and proportion that are of continuing influence.

Yet, pride also contributed to Athens' political and economic downfall. It led the polis *to convert the Delian League into its own empire. Imperial ambitions brought Athens into conflict with Sparta. The resulting Peloponnesian War left all of Greece weakened, demoralized, and open to conquest by Macedon to the north over half a century later. Philip II of Macedon imposed peace and unity upon the Greeks but at the expense of their political independence. His son, Alexander the Great, built the largest empire in the world up until his time, but it broke up upon his death a decade after he had begun. The Hellenistic Age that followed diffused Greek culture east and west and made important contributions of its own in mathematics and science.*

Recommended Reading

Aristotle, *The Politics*, T.A. Sinclair, trans. (1962)

Arrian, *Life of Alexander*, A. de Selincourt, trans. (1958).

Peter Bamm, *Alexander the Great* (1968).

Charles Rowan Beige, *Ancient Greek Literature and Society* (1975).

John Boardman, Jaspar Griffin, and Orwyn Murray, *The Oxford History of the Classical World* (1986).

A.R. Burn, *Pericles and Athens* (1949).

Donald W. Engels, *Alexander the Great and the Logistics of the Macedonian Army* (1976).

M.I. Finley, *Ancient Slavery and Modern Ideology* (1983).

Peter Green, *Alexander the Great* (1970).

David Grene and Richard Lattimore, eds., *The Complete Greek Tragedies* (1959).

Erich S. Gruen, *The Hellenistic World and the Coming of Rome* (1986).

W.K. Guthrie, *Greek Philosophers from Thales to Aristotle* (1950).

Edith Hamilton, *The Greek Way* (1930).

W. Jaeger, *Paideia: The Ideals of Greek Culture* (1945).

Donald Kagan, *The Archidamian War* (1974).

Donald Kagan, *The Fall of the Athenian Empire* (1987).

Donald Kagan, *The Outbreak of the Peloponnesian War* (1967).

Donald Kagan, *The Peace of Nicias and the Sicilian Expedition* (1981).

H.D.F. Kitto, *Greek Tragedy: A Literary Study* (1950).

Bernard Knox, *The Heroic Temper* (1964).

Bernard Knox, *Word and Action: Essays on the Ancient Theater* (1979).

Geoffrey E.R. Lloyd, *Greek Science After Aristotle* (1973).

R. Meiggs, *The Athenian Empire* (1980).

Plato, *The Last Days of Socrates*, H. Tredennick, trans. (1959).

Plato, *The Republic*, B. Jowett, trans. (1982).

Plato, *The Symposium*, W. Hamilton, trans. (1951).

Plutarch, *The Rise and Fall of Athens: Nine Greek Lives*, I. Scott-Kilvert, trans. (1960).

John Herman Randall, *Aristotle* (1960).

Mary Renault, *Funeral Games* (1981).

Mary Renault, *The Persian Boy* (1972).

Martin Robertson, *A History of Greek Art* (1976).

W.D. Ross, *Aristotle* (1956).

M. Rostovtzeff, *The Social and Economic History of the Hellenistic World* (1941).

G.E.M. de Ste. Croix, *The Origins of the Peloponnesian War* (1972).

W.W. Tarn, *Hellenistic Civilization* (1952).

A.E. Taylor, *Plato, the Man and His Work* (1966).

Thucydides, *History of the Peloponnesian War*, R. Warner, trans. (1954).

H.D. Westlake, *Essays on the Greek Historians and Greek History* (1969).

Xenophon, *The Persian Expedition*, R. Warner, trans. (1949).

Alfred Zimmern, *The Greek Commonwealth* (1971).

CHAPTER 5

The Roman Republic

Time Line

753 B.C.	Traditional date of founding of Rome
c. 700 B.C.	Flowering of Etruscan civilization
509 B.C.	Traditional date of founding of Roman Republic
494 B.C.	Office of tribune of the *plebs* created
c. 450 B.C.	Law of Twelve Tables issued
338 B.C.	Rome subdues the Latin League
287 B.C.	*Concilium Plebis* recognized as a sovereign legislative body
270 B.C.	Rome in control of Italian peninsula

264 B.C.	First Punic War against Carthage begins
237 B.C.	Rome annexes Sardinia and Corsica
218 B.C.	Second Punic War begins; Hannibal crosses Alps
202 B.C.	Scipio defeats Hannibal at Zama
191–188 B.C.	Syrian War
149 B.C.	Third Punic War begins
c. 146 B.C.	Macedon and Greece added to Roman Empire
133–30 B.C.	The Late Republic
133 B.C.	Land reform of Tiberius Gracchus; Rome gains first province in Asia
121 B.C.	Death of Gaius Gracchus
107–100 B.C.	Marius elected consul six times
88 B.C.	Sulla elected consul
82 B.C.	Sulla becomes dictator
66–62 B.C.	Pompey's conquests in Near East
63 B.C.	Cicero's *Orations Against Catiline*
60 B.C.	Pompey founds first triumvirate with Crassus and Julius Caesar
58–50 B.C.	Caesar's victories in Gallic Wars
49 B.C.	Caesar assumes dictatorship
44 B.C.	Caesar assassinated
43 B.C.	Octavian, Antony, and Lepidus form second triumvirate

| 31 B.C. | Octavian defeats Antony and Cleopatra at Battle of Actium |
| 30 B.C. | Antony and Cleopatra commit suicide |

History offers few more engrossing stories than that of the rise of Rome from a minor agricultural settlement on the banks of the Tiber River to a world empire of awesome proportions and significance. Although they were highly successful as military conquerors, the Romans' true greatness lay in their administrative and legal skills. Modern Europe inherited much of its political structure and framework of laws from the Roman Empire. While lacking the creative genius of the Greeks, the Romans excelled at adapting the accomplishments of other cultures to their own and disseminating them to their polyglot populace. Thus they played a highly important role in preserving and transmitting to the West the heritage of Greek civilization.

The history of ancient Rome covers at least one thousand years from the founding of the Republic around 509 B.C. until the collapse of the Empire in the West in A.D. 476. This remarkable longevity owes much to the character of the Romans themselves. A practical-minded people who recognized the value of compromise and flexibility, they were also deeply respectful of tradition and authority.

Rome Before 509 B.C.

The Founding of Rome

The origins of Rome are shrouded in myth. According to one tradition, the city was founded in 753 B.C. by Romulus on the site where he and his twin brother, Remus, abandoned on the Tiber as infants, had drifted ashore and been suckled by a wolf. A later legend credits Rome's foundation to the Trojan prince Aeneas who supposedly emigrated to Italy after the fall of Troy. In reality, the city's beginnings were humble and offered no suggestion of Rome's future greatness.

The Latins

The Italian peninsula was originally inhabited by a Neolithic population of Mediterranean origin. Sometime between 2000 and 1000 B.C., several waves of Indo-European peoples flowed into Italy bringing with them bronze and, later, iron tools. Among them were the ancestors of the founders of Rome, the Latins, who settled in the area of Latium, a broad alluvial plain to the south of the Tiber River. In the eighth century B.C. or somewhat earlier, the Latins established a small village on the Palatine, one of the famous seven hills of Rome. Archaeologists have uncovered traces of this settlement including a cemetery at the foot of the Palatine on the site of what would become the Roman Forum.

Advantages of Site

Although not located directly on the sea or beside a major water-way, the site of Rome offered several benefits. Its hills provided a good natural defense against invaders and isolation from the malaria-ridden lowlands. Its location at a point on the Tiber where an island afforded easy crossing facilitated Rome's communication with the rest of the peninsula. In addition, the city was near enough to the sea to be able to engage profitably in overseas trade. Once the plain of Latium was drained, it became an invaluable source of food.

Etruscan Supremacy

Despite these advantages, Rome remained for several centuries only one of many small and rather backward settlements of Italic tribes. These were overshadowed on the peninsula by the presence of two great urban civilizations. To the south and in Sicily the Greeks had begun planting colonies around 750 B.C. In the north and center an enigmatic people, the Etruscans, developed a brilliant civilization that during the sixth century B.C. ruled Rome itself.

To judge by their unique language and culture, the Etruscans were most likely from Asia Minor. Settling northwest of the Tiber River in the region which today encompasses Tuscany and Umbria, they founded a number of important city-states such as Tarquinii. These were never politically unified but were joined together in a loose confederation.

Trade

Etruscan civilization burst into flower around 700 B.C. The rich mineral deposits of Etruria and the nearby island of Elba amply satisfied their own needs and enabled them to produce a variety of metal objects, weapons, and pieces of gold and silver jewelry for export. This brisk trade brought Etruscan civilization to the height of its wealth and power during the seventh and sixth centuries B.C.

Etruscan Tombs and Religious Practices

The Etruscans remain a mysterious people to us primarily because their language has not yet been adequately deciphered. Scholars are able to read it since the Etruscan alphabet was derived from the Greek, but the meanings of all but a few words are still unknown. The tongue does not appear to belong to any of the major language classifications. Thus for the present, material sources provide most of our knowledge about Etruscan culture. Archaeologists have unearthed numerous rich Etruscan tombs. Many of these were decorated with lively frescoes and contained pottery urns, bronze or clay statuettes, and sarcophagi shaped like couches with reclining human figures sculpted on their lids. The elaborate nature of these tombs suggests that the Etruscans believed in a cult of the dead as did the Egyptians, with whom they traded. Etruscan religion evidently centered on the worship of a triad of gods and practiced divination or foretelling the future by analyzing the flight of birds, the entrails of sacrificed animals, and other omens.

Etruscan Rule of Rome

As the Etruscans' maritime power increased during the seventh century, they began to expand territorially. By the sixth century they exercised hegemony over much of the land between the lower Po valley in the north and Naples to the south including Rome itself. The legendary Tarquin kings of Rome were of Etruscan birth. The Etruscans transformed Rome from a group of small, disunited villages into a true city. During their century-long rule, they drained and paved the marshy lowland area of the forum, constructed roads and stone structures, and built the first temple on the Capitoline Hill. Rome's trade expanded rapidly thanks to the stimulus of Etruscan commercial ties. Few aspects of Roman life escaped the influence of Etruscan ways.

The Early Republic, 509–133 B.C.

Revolt Against Etruscan Monarchy

Despite the general prosperity afforded by Etruscan rule, the Romans chafed under foreign control. Sometime around 500 B.C. (the traditional date is 509 B.C.) they overthrew their Etruscan monarch and established an independent republic (*res publica*, or "commonwealth"). While the ensuing loss of trade connections plunged Rome into a period of decline, the Roman Republic survived nonetheless and eventually absorbed Etruscan civilization within its folds.

Roman Society in the Early Republic

The main features of Roman society were already well established by the beginning of the fifth century B.C. At its core stood the family.

The Gentes

All Roman families claiming descent from a common ancestor were joined together in a *gens*, or kinship group equivalent to a clan. In early Rome these *gentes* played an important role in political, social, religious, and economic affairs. For example, they administered justice within the group. Later most of these functions were taken over by the state.

The Patricians

Some of the *gentes* were recognized as possessing a higher social status than the rest, essentially because of their members' wealth as large landowners. Such individuals formed a privileged noble class in Roman society known as the patricians. It was they who led the revolt against the Etruscans, and at first only patricians were eligible to hold public office.

The Plebeians

The vast majority of citizens (probably more than 90%) made up the plebeian class. It contained great variations in degree of wealth from prosperous merchants to the urban poor. As Roman citizens, the plebeians served in the army, paid taxes, voted in the assemblies, and came under the protection of Roman law. These latter two privileges of citizenship did not, however, constitute real political power for the plebeians because they were easily turned to patrician advantage. Roman social relations were frequently regulated by a system of clientship (*clientela*) in which poorer citizens would receive financial assistance and legal protection from wealthy patrons in exchange for political and other forms of loyalty. During the early Republic, the plebeians were barred from holding secular or religious offices and lacked full social, political, economic, and legal rights. Roman society included at its bottom a slave population which fluctuated in size.

Political Institutions

The change from monarchy to republic was not as radical or abrupt as Roman tradition depicts it. In both governments aristocratic elements dominated. Rather than inheriting the throne, Etruscan kings were most likely elected by a popular assembly in the hands of the great Roman families. Two of Rome's most important political institutions, the senate and the centuriate assembly, probably already existed at least in rudimentary form under the monarchy. Once the foreign monarchy was done away with, the aristocracy strengthened its political control even more.

Consuls

The king's executive functions and supreme power, or *imperium*, were transferred to two new magistrates (consuls) who at first were exclusively patricians. Elected annually to serve a one-year joint term, each consul was given veto power over the actions of the other. Their primary responsibility was command of the military. In times of war or serious emergency the Romans had the option of appointing a "dictator" who ruled without check for a period of no longer than six months.

The Senate

The senate originated in a council of the heads of great patrician families to advise the king. Under the Republic it grew in power and effectively controlled the government. While the consuls, other magistrates, and the centuriate assembly theoretically served to check and balance the senate, in actuality they were usually subordinate to it. During the early Republic, the senate was composed of 300 members chosen for life. They were almost all ex-magistrates drawn from the same small group of Rome's ruling families.

The Centuriate Assembly

All of Rome's arms-bearing citizens were eligible to sit in the centuriate assembly. Its name derived from the century (the smallest unit of the Roman army) by which its voting groups were organized. The centuriate assembly elected the consuls and other public officials, debated issues of war and peace, passed judgment on legislation placed before it by the consuls and senate, and acted as a court of last appeals in capital cases. Despite these prerogatives it was never as powerful as the senate, and because voting was done by groups according to property qualifications, the interests of the wealthy predominated in it.

Praetors, Quaestors, Aediles, and Censors

During the fifth and fourth centuries B.C., in response to the tremendous growth of Rome, new magistracies were created to relieve the consuls of some of their responsibilities. The praetors, whose number gradually expanded from one to eight, were elected annually to handle judicial functions, assist in commanding the army, and after 277 B.C. to administer several of Rome's provinces. The quaestors were primarily responsible for financial matters. The aediles oversaw municipal affairs such as the water and drainage systems. Two censors were charged with the important task of compiling a census which was used to determine the tax, military, and voting status of the population. In addition, they acted as regulators of public conduct; hence the modern meaning of the word censor.

The Plebeians' Struggle for Equality

Soon after the founding of the Republic the plebeians began to demand a greater share in its government. Although as members of the centuriate assembly they had the right to elect Rome's two patrician consuls, they were excluded from holding religious or civil office and suffered discrimination. In 494 B.C. they expressed their dissatisfaction by threatening to secede from Rome en masse and establish a new city-state. This strategy won for them the privilege of electing their own plebeian magistrate, the tribune of the plebs, who was charged with defending their rights.

The Concilium Plebis

Several decades later the plebeians were granted their own assembly, the *Concilium Plebis* (assembly of the plebs). This assembly was based upon tribal or geographic divisions, thus insuring the preponderance of plebeian interests. It elected the tribunes and with their assistance passed resolutions.

Tribunes

By the mid-fifth century there were ten tribunes. Although they never possessed the power to command troops (*imperium*), they gradually gained prerogatives which made them a formidable political force. For example, they received the right to veto any legislation or official acts which interfered with plebeian rights. To protect the tribunes from violence, their persons were considered sacrosanct, so that it was a capital crime to harm them.

The Law of the Twelve Tables

Around 450 B.C., the plebeians extracted an important legal concession with the codification of the Law of Twelve Tables. Rome's laws, which had heretofore been transmitted orally, were written down on twelve engraved tablets and displayed in the Forum. Thus the plebeians' right to equal treatment before the law was safeguarded against arbitrary legal interpretations by patrician judges.

In 445 B.C. the plebeians came closer to achieving social equality with the patricians when a law was passed allowing marriage between the two classes.

Further Plebeian Gains

Beginning in 421 B.C. with the opening of the quaestorship, the plebeians gradually gained admittance to all of Rome's magistracies and became eligible to sit in the senate. From 367 B.C. forward it was agreed that one of the two consuls elected annually had to be of plebeian origin. By the end of the fourth century B.C., the dictatorship, censorship, praetorship, and important religious positions were all open to plebeians. Final victory came in 287 B.C. when the *Concilium Plebis*, henceforth called the tribal assembly, was empowered to enact legislation that was binding on patricians and plebeians alike.

Results of the Struggle

When summarized in the foregoing fashion, the plebeians' struggle for equality appears to have followed an orderly progression and ended in clear-cut victory. In fact, the outcome was never certain at the time and the concessions did not amount to a transfer of political power from the patricians to the plebeians. On the contrary, while shorn of many legal privileges, the patricians maintained their supremacy in government for the next century and a half on the basis of their birth, wealth, experience, and connections. Most of the political reforms benefited only that small portion of the plebeian class which had sufficient wealth and free time to engage in politics. These individuals were gradually assimilated into a broadened office-holding class referred to in later Roman history as the *nobiles,* and they came to share its conservative outlook and interests. The story of the plebeians' struggle for equality thus illustrates not the triumph of democracy but the ability of the Romans to work out viable solutions based on adaptability and compromise.

Agrarian Reforms

For the rest of the population, economic grievances probably outweighed political ones. The patricians were compelled to make concessions in this area as well. In 367 B.C. a law was enacted which limited the amount of land any one individual could own. In 326 B.C. debt slavery was abolished and the plebeians were permitted to mortgage their land instead of their persons. These agrarian reforms provided some relief at first but were rather laxly enforced as time went by.

The Conquest of Italy

Rome achieved dominion on the Italian peninsula over a period of more than two centuries during which the progress of Roman arms suffered numerous reverses. The waning of Etruscan power in the fifth century B.C. incited a battle for control of Latium. The assertion of later

Roman writers that the Republic's wars were defensive in origin holds most true for this first period.

Early Victories

It is often difficult to separate fact from fiction in accounts of Rome's early wars. We do know for certain that in 439 B.C. the Romans concluded a treaty of alliance with the League of Latin Cities in order to provide for mutual defense. Rome's skillful diplomacy in gaining allies helped it to defeat its rivals in Latium and gain control by the early fourth century of the important Etruscan city of Veii. This key victory made Rome the most powerful city in Latium and opened the way to its eventual conquest of Etruria.

Invasion of Gauls

In 390 B.C., however, Rome suffered a disastrous setback: the sack of the city by the Gauls, a Celtic people who had occupied the Po valley in the sixth century. They withdrew only after the Romans paid a huge ransom.

The Samnite Wars

Beginning in the second half of the fourth century, a recovered Rome waged three lengthy wars against the fierce Samnites to the south. The first won for Rome the fertile area of Campania around Naples but prompted the defection of Rome's Latin allies, who were uneasy over Roman expansion. After several years of fighting, Rome subdued the Latin League in 338 B.C. and arranged separate treaties with each of its members.

Defeat of Greek Colonies

Defeat of the Samnites brought Rome face to face with the Greek colonies in southern Italy. One of them, Tarentum, appealed to King Pyrrhus of Epirus for assistance. Pyrrhus succeeded in defeating the Romans in 280 and 279 B.C. but with such heavy losses that he supposedly said "One more such victory and I am lost" (hence the phrase "Pyrrhic victory"). The stalwart Romans refused to negotiate a peace and Pyrrhus withdrew. Within a decade all of *Magna Graecia* had fallen into Roman hands.

The Roman Army

By 270 B.C., Rome was master of the entire Italian peninsula south of the Rubicon River in the Po valley. The Romans owed their success to a combination of superior military force and wise diplomatic policies. The Roman army was organized by legions, basic units containing approximately 4000 infantry and 300 cavalry soldiers, which made it capable of quick and efficient action. All Roman citizens were eligible for military service. The hearty small farmers of Italy supplied most of the army's manpower and proved to be excellent fighters.

Integration of Subject Peoples

The Romans were as dexterous in converting enemies into allies as they were in conquering them. Through planting colonies in the subdued territories, making treaties of alliance with former foes, and extending full- or part-citizenship rights, the Romans insured the loyalty of the subjugated Italians and were able to expand Rome's conquests to the Mediterranean and beyond.

Rome Against Carthage

Dominion over southern Italy placed the Romans in close proximity to the island of Sicily. For several centuries control of Sicily had been divided between the Carthaginians in the west and Greek city-states such as Syracuse in the east. The ancient Phoenician city of Carthage on the coast of North Africa near modern Tunis was by the third century B.C. the foremost mercantile power in the western Mediterranean. Its great navy and merchant marine monopolized the area's trade and established Carthage's sway over the northern shores of Africa, Sardinia, and parts of Sicily, Corsica, and Spain.

Confrontation in Sicily

Ruled by an oligarchy of nobles and rich merchants, prosperous and powerful Carthage was the logical rival of an expanding Roman state. Yet it is misleading to view the long epic struggle between Rome and Carthage as if it were predestined, as did Virgil and other later Roman writers. Rome's involvement in war came about almost by chance. Responding to an appeal from Messana, a city strategically located in Sicily, the Romans intervened against the interests of Carthage. Thus began the first of three Punic Wars.

The First Punic War

The First Punic War (264–241 B.C.) changed rapidly from a local conflict into a major contest between the Romans and the Carthaginians for supremacy over the entire island. The defeat of Carthage required that Rome also become a rival naval power. Even though the untried Roman navy won several battles, fighting dragged on inconclusively for over twenty years. With Herculean resolve, the Romans rebuilt their storm-wrecked fleet and finally wore down the Carthaginians, who sued for peace in 241 B.C. The Romans required the Carthaginians to pay a huge indemnity and give up all their holdings in Sicily. The western part and later the whole of the island with its rich grain resources became Rome's first province.

Annexation of Sardinia and Corsica

In 237 B.C. Rome took advantage of Carthage's internal weakness to annex the Mediterranean islands of Sardinia and Corsica. These were joined into another province a decade later. In contrast to its allies on the Roman Peninsula, the provinces were ruled by Roman governors rather than their own officials and sent tribute to Rome instead of supplying troops. Thus Rome began on a trial and error basis to develop a system of government which it would later use with great success in governing its burgeoning empire.

The Second Punic War

Beaten but not annihilated, the Carthaginians waited for an opportunity to avenge themselves. For the next twenty years they concentrated on reasserting and augmenting their control in Spain, a populous land rich in mineral resources. Rome too had an interest in Spain, and was alarmed over the rapid expansion there of Carthaginian power. Thus a new area of conflict opened between the two rivals. Tensions mounted when in 221 B.C. a twenty-five-year-old Carthaginian general named Hannibal succeeded to the command in Spain. In 219 B.C. he besieged the Spanish city of Saguntum, which was allied with Rome. This incident provoked the Romans to declare war.

The Second Punic War (218–202 B.C.) was the most dramatic and decisive of the three titanic encounters. In Hannibal, Carthage possessed a military commander whose fearless character and outstanding tactical genius have rarely been equaled.

Hannibal's Invasion of Italy. The young general quickly put into action his bold strategy to invade Italy by land. In the fall of 218 B.C., he crossed the Alps with an army of about 25,000 and a number of elephants to transport needed supplies. Casualties were severe at the first encounter with Roman troops, but once he reached the Po valley Hannibal won several victories against the Roman legions and obtained support from some Gallic tribes there. Moving down the peninsula, he again defeated the Romans at Lake Trasimene. The city of Rome escaped conquest partly because the temporary dictator, Quintus Fabius Maximus Verrucosus, used such delaying tactics as harassing the Carthaginians though never engaging them in pitched battle. This earned Fabius the title of *Cunctator* (the Delayer). Unfortunately the Romans failed to recognize the wisdom of Fabius's policy and replaced him in 216 B.C. with a leader committed to direct confrontational tactics. This new strategy ended disastrously for Rome at Cannae, where Hannibal scored his most overwhelming triumph.

Roman Victory. Despite his supremacy in the field, Hannibal was unable to carry out his plan of conquest. Rome lost the important cities of Capua and Syracuse, but its Italian allies did not flock en masse to the Carthaginian side as Hannibal had calculated. Rome itself proved too well fortified to risk an attack. Thus Hannibal and his undersupplied, outnumbered army were left with the alternative of devastating the countryside. This afforded the Romans time to recoup their strength. Control of the seas and the ability to raise new recruits worked to Rome's favor, and enabled it to mount a counteroffensive. Hannibal was compelled to return to Carthage, where he staged a last-ditch effort to oppose invading Roman forces commanded by the brilliant young general, Publius Cornelius Scipio (the Elder). At Zama in 202 B.C., Scipio defeated Hannibal and was awarded the title of "Africanus" in honor of his triumph. The Carthaginians once more sued for peace. The new treaty imposed even harsher terms than after the first war. Carthage was forced to concede its possessions outside of North Africa, dispense with its navy, pay a large indemnity, and follow Roman dictates in foreign policy.

Results of the War. Rome's gains were enormous. It displaced Carthage as the strongest power in the western Mediterranean. Rome acquired the vast Carthaginian territories in Spain, although it took more than a half-century of brutal guerrilla warfare to subdue the rebellious Spanish tribes and consolidate two provinces there. Internally, victory over the Carthaginians buttressed the cause of those who advocated further Roman expansion. Many patricians grew rich from the war. The small farmers who filled the ranks of Rome's army, on the other hand, often returned home to find their livelihood destroyed by the ravages of Hannibal's men. Politically, the war's successful conclusion further enhanced the power of the senatorial oligarchy, which was largely responsible for the wise and steadfast policies that had won the day.

The Third Punic War

Despite the decisiveness of Rome's victory, the specter of a revived Carthage continued to haunt the Romans, and Carthage did slowly recover commercial prosperity. Regarding this as a threat, a group of fanatical senators led by Cato the Elder clamored for the city's destruction. In 149 B.C. Rome accused the Carthaginians of violating the peace treaty and thus started the Third Punic War (149–146 B.C.). After a three-year siege, Scipio Aemilianus conquered and totally destroyed Carthage. All its buildings were leveled; the ground was plowed over, ceremonially sown with salt, and cursed. The city's territory was incorporated into the Roman province of Africa.

Wars with the East

Roman involvement in the East increased gradually during the latter part of the third century B.C.

The First Macedonian War

To protect Italian trade routes, Roman ships cleared the Adriatic of pirates in 229 and 219 B.C. and established a foothold in Illyria. This won for Rome the friendship of several Greek city-states. The great Hellenistic monarch, Philip V of Macedon, however, viewed these actions as stepping stones to further Roman intervention. Thus during the Second Punic War Philip allied himself with the Carthaginians.

Aided by a group of friendly Greek city-states, Roman forces prevented Philip's navy from crossing the Adriatic. The First Macedonian War (215–205 B.C.) ended inconclusively.

The Second Macedonian War

In addition to Rome's informal affiliations with certain Hellenistic states, many wealthy Romans formed private relationships, the *clientelae*, with foreign communities. They championed the cause of their Spanish, African or Eastern clients in the senate in return for their loyalty and services. This powerful system of contacts and influence helps to explain Rome's willingness to heed the appeals of Rhodes, Athens, and Pergamum, and go to war with Philip V in 200 B.C., only two years after the conclusion of the exhaustive Second Punic War.

Philip's imperialistic ambitions were checked at the battle of Cynoscephalae, where the Roman legions proved for the first time their superiority over the renowned Macedonian phalanx. According to the peace terms of the Second Macedonian War (200–196 B.C.) Philip remained on the throne but was obliged to become an ally of Rome, pay a large indemnity, scale back his armed forces, and relinquish his control over Greece. Rome proclaimed the Greek city-states free and independent and withdrew its troops, but Roman influence remained nonetheless.

The Syrian War

Events conspired to embroil Rome once more in the Greek world. Antiochus III, king of Syria, was ambitious to restore his Seleucid empire to its former glory. He won victories in southern Syria, Asia Minor, Egypt, and Thrace and then unwisely invaded Greece. This triggered a confrontation with Rome. During the Syrian War (191–188 B.C.), Roman legions expelled Antiochus from Greece and pursued him to Asia, where they won their first victory on Asian soil The Romans deprived Antiochus of his holdings in Asia Minor, dividing them between Rhodes and Pergamum, levied reparations, and greatly reduced the Syrian army and navy in size.

The Third and Fourth Macedonian Wars

Once again Rome accepted no territory for itself, but its role as arbiter in Greek affairs made it impossible to avoid ongoing involvement. Thus when Philip V's son, Perseus, tried to reassert Macedonian influence in Greece, Rome again stepped in and defeated him at Pydna in 168 B.C. This time the Romans dealt severely with Macedon. As a result of the Third Macedonian War (171–168 B.C.), Rome abolished the Macedonian monarchy, took Perseus captive, and broke up his kingdom. This solution proved only a temporary one. After putting down several Macedonian uprisings in favor of monarchy (Fourth Macedonian War, 149–148 B.C.), Rome finally annexed Macedon and turned it into its first Hellenistic province by 146 B.C.

Subjection of Greece

During these years, Rome encountered growing difficulties with the Greek city-states, some of which maintained strong anti-Roman feelings. When Sparta called upon Rome's aid in a conflict with the Achaean League, the Romans moved quickly and brutally. They destroyed Corinth, the League's leading city, and sold its women and children into slavery. They then disbanded the League and placed the Greek city-states under the jurisdiction of the governor of Macedon. Greek liberty thus perished in the hands of its supposed defender.

From City-State to Empire

Rome added further to its rapidly expanding empire in 133 B.C. when the King of Pergamum, an ally, died without an heir and willed his kingdom to the Romans. This became Rome's first province in Asia. Thus from the First Punic War until 133 B.C., Rome had grown from a power on the Italian mainland to a major overseas empire that spread across three continents and encompassed the provinces of Sicily, Sardinia, the two Spains, Macedon, Africa, and Asia. Imperial rule brought new challenges that would severely test the Roman Republic in the century to come.

The Late Republic, 133–30 B.C.

Economic and Social Ills

The years between 133 and 30 B.C. were a revolutionary time for Rome during which its old Republican institutions sought to cope with the new problems engendered by more than a century of conquest and expansion. Rome in the mid-second century B.C. was no longer a simple agricultural society dominating the Italian peninsula. The small city-state had transformed itself into a huge empire and a great commercial power. Tribute and profits flowed in from the provinces to swell Rome's treasury and the coffers of its well-to-do. There was a new class of merchants, financiers, and businessmen, the *equites*, whose wealth was derived from imperial trade, government contracts, and lucrative provincial posts. Their business practices were often corrupt.

Growth of Large Estates

While a few Romans were able to amass huge fortunes, the economic situation of the general population declined. The position of the yeoman farmer had long been precarious. Most public lands accumulated during the conquest of the Italian peninsula fell into the hands of patricians or wealthy plebeians by means of leases. Agrarian laws passed in the fourth century to limit the size of estates proved ineffective, and by the second century B.C. many leaseholders of public lands considered these tracts as private property.

For several reasons, war encouraged the trend towards *latifundia* (large estates). New agricultural methods and the gradual depletion of the soil forced a shift from the traditional cultivation of grain to the raising of livestock and the production of wine and olive oil. To be profitable these new enterprises required large tracts of land and long-term capital investments, both of which were beyond the means of the average small farmer. Many of those who had grown rich from the empire's increase in commercial activity invested their profits in land in order to gain further profits. Rome's foreign conquests enhanced the growth of the estates by making available a large supply of cheap labor in the form of enslaved prisoners of war.

Emigration of Dispossessed Farmers

Gradually pressure from the *latifundia* and competition by farmers abroad who exported cheap grain to Rome drove the small farmer off his land. In many cases lengthy military service and other devastating effects of war had already brought him to the brink of ruin. Unable to find employment in the countryside because of the profusion of slave laborers, many dislocated farmers migrated to Rome.

This demographic shift had far-reaching consequences. Rome traditionally depended on the conscription of small landowners for the bulk of its armed forces. Just when its huge empire demanded the expansion of its military, Rome was faced with an acute shortage of manpower. Domestically a strong military was essential in curbing threats to internal order by the large influx of slaves. (This was made glaringly evident when a slave war in Sicily jeopardized Rome's grain supply.) The emigration also caused problems within Rome. Since most displaced people were unable to find jobs, they joined ranks with the urban poor and lived in overcrowded, unsanitary tenements where discontent was rife. Throughout the first century B.C. Rome was periodically disturbed by violent outbursts from the lower class.

Political Tensions

Changes in Rome's economic and social structure created tensions within the senatorial oligarchy as well. The large increase in new voters who were uncommitted to any aristocratic house incited a fierce competition for new clients within the oligarchy; this competition aggravated factional rivalries. In addition, many wealthy provincial governors acted independently of Rome, and this threatened the senate's traditional role as administrator of the empire. The greatest menace to senatorial control in the first century B.C. came from a new breed of ambitious and unscrupulous military commanders who could rely on the exclusive loyalty of their troops to usurp power.

The Gracchi

The first to make a significant attempt to remedy Rome's grave social and economic ills were two brothers, Tiberius and Gaius Gracchus (grandsons of Scipio Africanus, the conqueror of Hannibal).

Tiberius

Tiberius, the elder brother, believed that the solution to many of Rome's problems lay in the transfer of public land to displaced farmers and other urban poor.

Land Reform. Despite his noble birth, Tiberius recognized that the conservative senate would never take the initiative to reform a system which so favored the interests of its members. Thus he stood for the tribunate of the people and upon election in 133 B.C. introduced a land reform plan to the tribal assembly. The bill proposed to re-enact the earlier Agrarian Law of 367 B.C. which had limited the amount of public land any citizen could own to about 320 acres. The state would then confiscate the surplus and parcel it out to the Roman poor in small lots. Three land commissioners were to be appointed to supervise the redistribution.

Although landowners were to receive compensation for confiscated properties and former public lands in their possession were to be legally declared private property, most large landholders vehemently opposed Tiberius's measures. While the tribal assembly adopted the reform, a fellow tribune vetoed the legislation probably at the instigation of the senate. Rather than accept defeat, Tiberius countered with the Greek democratic theory that a tribune who failed to carry out the will of the people could be dismissed. He convinced the assembly to depose his opponent and to pass the agrarian bill. The senate responded by charging that Tiberius's action was contrary to Roman practice and was a violation of the constitution. Nevertheless the bill became law.

Assassination. At the end of his one-year term Tiberius again broke with tradition and sought reelection in order to carry out the details of his reform. Election riots broke out and in the fracas a group of senators murdered the reformer and about three hundred of his followers. Tiberius's death in 133 B.C. marks a turning point in the history of the Republic. From then on, violence became an increasingly accepted means for dealing with internal problems.

Gaius

Tiberius's agrarian law remained in force after his death and under the guidance of the Land Commission, public lands continued to be redistributed until 120 B.C. One of the commissioners was Gaius Gracchus, who took up his brother's mantle of agrarian reform. He became a tribune for the years 123 and 122 B.C. thanks to a new law which legalized reelection. Gaius was more radical than his brother in his perception that the only way to insure land reform was to break up the senate's control over political affairs. Therefore, he proposed a series of measures designed to unite the interests of groups outside the senatorial oligarchy, i.e., the urban poor, the *equites* and the Italian allies.

Reforms. He reenacted Tiberius's agrarian bill and called for the establishment of colonies in southern Italy and North Africa for the resettlement of Rome's landless population. He also initiated legislation which enabled the urban poor to buy grain from the government so that they might be protected from dishonest profiteers. This reform set a precedent for the later free distribution of grain to the poor. To appeal to the *equites,* Gaius introduced bills which allowed them to collect taxes in the rich province of Asia and to sit on the heretofore senate-dominated juries for the extortion courts. This latter privilege was especially important to the *equites,* as the extortion courts had jurisdiction over the conduct of Roman provincial officials. Thus the *equites* were able as jurors to protect their own interests and to deal severely with aristocratic provincial governors who opposed them.

Defeat of Gracchi Reforms. Gaius also won favor from Rome's Italian allies by proposing the extension of Roman citizenship to all Italians. Again the senate strongly disapproved of the Gracchan program, but this time they proceeded more cleverly. By discrediting many of his reforms in the eyes of his supporters they succeeded in preventing Gaius's reelection to the tribuneship for 121 B.C. Rioting ensued nonetheless and Gaius was accused of plotting to overthrow the government. Gaius and three thousand of his partisans were slain. Within a decade after his death all the Gracchi's reforms were abolished. The civil strife they had engendered continued to plague the Republic in its last years.

Marius

A deceptive lull fell over Roman politics for over a decade after Gaius's death, and the senate reasserted its supreme authority. Agrarian reform, the opening of the Po valley, and the creation of a new province in southern Gaul made significant amounts of land available to the poor and eased their plight. Foreign conflicts, however, precipitated new crises which gave rise to the first of Rome's generals whose political power depended totally on support from their armies.

Jugurthine War

In 111 B.C. war broke out with the Numidian prince Jugurtha. While it did not endanger Rome directly, the Jugurthine War (111–105 B.C.) imperiled the commercial interests of the *equites* in North Africa and damaged the senate's reputation for competence in foreign affairs. It also made the fortune of Gaius Marius (c. 157–86 B.C.), a soldier of plebeian origin who had risen within the army and served as a tribune in 119 and praetor in 115 B.C. Frustration over the senate's inept management of the war led the Romans to elect Marius consul in 107 B.C. He was a "new man"; that is, none of his ancestors had ever held a consulship. The tribal assembly then conferred on him command of Rome's legions in Africa, an act that infringed on the senate's jurisdiction over military appointments. Marius defeated Jugurtha and then saved Rome from the even greater threat of barbarian invasion by vanquishing the Teutoni and Cimbri, Germanic peoples from the north.

Reform of the Army

Marius's victories owed a great deal to his reform of the Roman army. In order to raise sufficient troops, he had done away with the property qualification for military service and accepted volunteers from among the Roman poor. In the past Rome's legions had consisted entirely of citizens who returned to their occupations after each campaign. With Marius's reforms, soldiers now served long enlistments of sixteen or more years. Marius also remodeled the army's tactics and introduced new, more standardized weapons. The transformation of the Roman army from a citizen's militia to a professional fighting force was to have profound consequences. Assured employment and land grants upon retirement improved the economic position of the masses while long years of service attached soldiers more closely to their commanders than to the state.

Political Career

Marius himself exemplified the inordinate political power that generals who had the loyalty of their men could command. He held the consulship an unprecedented six times between 107 and 100 B.C., becoming virtually a military dictator. Extremely popular with the masses and full of ambition, Marius unfortunately lacked the political acumen necessary to become a great leader. A few years after his triumph over the Cimbri, his aristocratic opponents outmaneuvered him and cast his political career into eclipse. The senatorial oligarchy resumed its control but showed itself willing to undertake several reforms.

Sulla

Rome's next great military personality, Lucius Cornelius Sulla (138–78 B.C.), also came to prominence as a result of renewed strife.

The Social War

Rome encountered a violent revolt from its Italian allies, who had not been granted the citizenship promised by Gaius Gracchus. In 91 B.C. Marcus Drusus, a tribune, reintroduced legislation to provide the Italians full citizenship, but Roman opposition proved so strong that Drusus was assassinated. As a consequence, the Italian allies seceded and engaged Rome in a bitter civil war, the Social War, between 90 and 88 B.C. (the name came from the word for allies, *socii*.) The Italians fought valiantly and the Romans ended the war by agreeing to extend the rights of full citizenship.

War with Mithridates

Sulla emerged from the war as Rome's most successful general, and he was elected consul in 88 B.C. just when a new threat loomed large. Mithridates VI, ruler of the kingdom of Pontus on the Black Sea, took advantage of Rome's preoccupation with the Italian revolt to enlarge his own empire. In 88 B.C., his army captured the Roman province of Asia and massacred thousands of its inhabitants. The question of who was to command Roman troops against Mithridates triggered a civil war in Rome. The senate chose Sulla, a patrician. His role was challenged by Marius, who gained the backing of the tribal assembly. Sulla won the position in 88 B.C. by moving his soldiers into the capital and expelling his adversaries. This was the first time a Roman army marched against Rome. He then boldly set out with a small contingent of troops to confront Mithridates in Greece. During his absence Marius regained the consulship and instituted a reign of terror against his enemies. After Marius's death in 86 B.C., Rome remained firmly under the control of his supporters.

Sulla's Dictatorship

Sulla defeated Mithridates in 84 B.C. and hurried back to Rome, where the senatorial and popular parties fought another civil war from 83 to 81 B.C. Sulla's forces emerged victorious. In 82 B.C. he revived and occupied the old office of dictator and abolished the traditional six-month limitation of tenure. After legalizing his authority, Sulla launched one of the most ferocious reprisals in Roman history. He ordered the deaths of thousands of political enemies and confiscated the wealth of many innocent people.

Reorganization of Government

Sulla used his enormous powers to restore the senate to its former position of supremacy. He enacted measures that sharply reduced the power of the tribunes and took away the tribal assembly's right to independent legislative action. Other laws safeguarded the Republic from ambitious young politicians and generals and reorganized the judiciary. Secure in the belief that he had established the senate's ascendancy on a permanent basis and that he had restored order, Sulla retired from office in 79 B.C. In fact, his reactionary reforms endured hardly a generation.

Julius Caesar

The Emergence of Pompey

Despite Sulla's accomplishments, a scramble for power resumed shortly after his death in 78 B.C. It took little time for the senate to reveal its fundamental weaknesses and for a new crop of ruthless young men to appear. Among them was Cneius Pompeius Magnus, called Pompey the Great (106–48 B.C.), a Roman general who had won fame during his youth while fighting for Sulla in the civil wars. During the 70s Pompey enhanced his military prestige. Between 77 and 72 B.C. he led Rome's forces in Spain against Sertorius, an exiled follower of Marius who had stirred the Spaniards to revolt.

Returning victorious to Italy in 72 B.C., Pompey assisted in putting down a slave rebellion headed by the Thracian gladiator Spartacus.

Although Pompey always claimed credit for himself, the major role in crushing the Spartacist uprising belonged to Marcus Crassus, a former adherent of Sulla.

Alliance with Crassus. Crassus was one of Rome's wealthiest men thanks to an inheritance and financial acumen—he bought up the confiscated properties of Sulla's foes. In 71 B.C. Crassus and Pompey, their loyal armies intact, were in a position to make themselves masters of Rome. Each elected to march his troops on the capital to forestall the other. Once it became obvious that neither could rule singly, they agreed to be joint candidates for the consulship in 70 B.C. Neither qualified for the office according to the requirements set down by Sulla. Pompey was too young and had not held the customary sequence of magistracies. Both he and Crassus had refused to disband their armies. Nonetheless, they were elected, with support from the popular party. As consuls they reversed many of Sulla's reforms. Tribunes regained their former powers and the senate was forced to share its control over the juries of the extortion courts with the *equites.* To win popular favor, Pompey revived the grain dole that Sulla had abolished. Both Pompey and Crassus amassed great personal power during their year in office, yet neither used it as yet to tear down the Republic. At the end of their term, they left office quietly. Only in retrospect does the Republic's fate appear already sealed by this time.

Expeditions in the East. In 67 B.C. the Romans once more called upon Pompey's military talents to rid the Mediterranean of pirates. Pompey dealt swiftly with the problem and by the next year received an even more important assignment, to conduct a new war in the East. In 74 B.C., Rome's old enemy, Mithridates VI of Pontus, had seized the neighboring kingdom of Bithynia, which the Romans had inherited. The Roman general Lucullus drove Mithridates out of Bithynia and pursued him as far east as Armenia, but his unpopularity in Rome and a mutiny within his army forced Lucullus to relinquish the Eastern command to Pompey in 66 B.C. Pompey completed the conquest of Mithridates, and then he reorganized Rome's vastly expanded Asian empire. He incorporated Pontus into the province of Bithynia, and conferred the status of client-kingdom on Armenia and other Eastern states. Pompey increased the size of the Roman province of Cilicia, added Syria to the provincial system, and conquered Palestine in 63 B.C.

As a result Roman dominion in the East stretched from the south shore of the Black Sea to the borders of Egypt; eastward it extended to the Tigris and Euphrates Rivers.

The First Triumvirate

Pompey returned to Rome in 62 B.C. at the summit of his career. Backed by a large army, rich from the booty of conquest, and possessing extraordinary wartime powers of *imperium,* he could easily have taken Rome. Instead he dismissed his troops and demanded only that the senate ratify the settlements he had made independently in the East and reward his veterans with grants of land. Enemies within the senate, envious of Pompey's great success and apprehensive of his future plans, saw that his fair requests were denied. In 60 B.C. Pompey discovered a way to secure his two demands. He joined secretly with two other dissatisfied politicians, Crassus and Julius Caesar, to form an alliance later named the First Triumvirate. Each participant stood to gain from the coalition they formed.

The Rise of Julius Caesar. The figure of Gaius Julius Caesara (102?–44 B.C.) towers over the history of Rome. For with his dictatorship the Republic expired and the foundations of Empire were laid. By birth Caesar was a member of one of Rome's oldest patrician families, the Julian gens, but his personal sympathies lay with the popular cause. His aunt was wife to Marius, the leader of the popular party, and Caesar himself wed the daughter of one of Marius's lieutenants, with the consequence that he was proscribed by Sulla and had to flee Rome. Upon his return he began to rise in the popular party, whose support he courted. By 60 B.C. Caesar was second in importance only to Pompey within the popular party. His expensive political career, however, had put him deeply in debt to Crassus. Thus he welcomed an alliance with Pompey and Crassus as a means to gain the consulship and afterwards a lucrative provincial office which would enable him to pay off his debts.

With Pompey's military strength, Crassus' wealth, and Caesar's popular appeal, the First Triumvirate wielded tremendous influence. Elected consul in 59 B.C., Caesar confirmed Pompey's arrangements in the East and granted fertile land to Pompey's soldiers, mostly in southern Italy. Caesar satisfied Crassus' demand that tax collectors in

Asia return a reduced portion of their collections to the state. In addition, Caesar secured the passage of another agrarian bill providing land for the urban poor over the resistance of the senate. He was then given command of the provinces of Cisalpine Gaul, Illyricum, and Transalpine Gaul with four legions for a period of five years.

Gallic Wars. Although at first glance this command did not appear especially significant, the governorship of Transalpine Gaul proved the springboard for Caesar's rise to dictatorship. The Gallic Wars brought Caesar the prerequisites for grasping political power in first century B.C. Rome: wealth, military fame, and a devoted army. Most scholars agree that Caesar undertook his conquest of Celtic Gaul (a region now encompassing the nations of France and Belgium) because of personal ambition rather than the need to defend Rome. In a series of brilliant campaigns lasting from 58 to 50 B.C., he vanquished the Helvetti, conquered the Belgae, suppressed the uprisings of numerous other Celtic tribes throughout Gaul, crossed the Rhine into Germany in 55 B.C., and even landed expeditionary forces in Britain in 55 and again in 54 B.C. In 52 B.C. Caesar defeated his most implacable enemy, Vercingetorix, who had roused all of central Gaul in rebellion against the Romans.

Results of Caesar's Victories. Caesar's victories extended Rome's borders to the Rhine and the Atlantic with far-reaching consequences for the future of Europe. The Romans organized the new territory and set out to civilize its barbarian inhabitants. Roman language and culture gained widespread acceptance in Gaul and exerted tremendous influence on the cultural development of modern France. The Gallic wars established Caesar's reputation as one of history's greatest military commanders. He was exceptional not only in tactical matters but above all in winning the loyalty of his troops. He shared with them both the spoils and privations of war, and he took a genuine interest in their concerns. During the nine years of fighting in Gaul, Caesar forged a personal army which made possible his future success.

Renewal of Triumvirate. Despite his long absences from home, Caesar remained abreast of political developments there. He knew of the growing animosity between Pompey and Crassus, and in 56 B.C. he arranged a meeting of the three triumvirs at Lucca to renew their alliance. It was agreed that Pompey and Crassus would become joint consuls for the year 55 B.C. and then receive control over the provinces of Spain and Syria respectively. Caesar had his own command over Gaul extended until 49 B.C. Crassus jumped at the chance to win martial glory by launching a campaign against the Parthians, a powerful new dynasty that had displaced the Seleucids in Persia. To his misfortune Crassus' military prowess did not equal his ambition. At Carrhae in 53 B.C. the Parthians crushed Rome's legions and murdered their commander.

End of Triumvirate. Crassus' death put an end to the triumvirate. Relations between Pompey and Caesar cooled considerably after the death in 54 B.C. of Julia, Caesar's daughter, who was wife to Pompey. Bloody factional quarrels between the followers of Pompey and Caesar in Rome heightened the tensions. In 52 B.C. Pompey, with senatorial backing, became the sole consul. From then on he led the senatorial party in its opposition to Caesar.

Civil War

Caesar's long-range plans and personal aspirations are difficult to assess. What is clear is that senatorial intransigence spurred him to drastic action. Upon completion of his term in Gaul, Caesar sought the consulship of 48 B.C. for himself. The senate, however, was determined to thwart his political advancement. After long and fruitless negotiations, an aggravated senate demanded that Caesar disband his army even before his command had expired. Caesar responded quickly to this attack on himself, and, as he interpreted it, on the army, the populace and their tribunes as well. In January 49 B.C., with the wholehearted support of his soldiers, Caesar crossed the small Rubicon River which divided his province of Cisalpine Gaul from Italy (hence the expression "to cross the Rubicon," meaning to take a decisive and irrevocable step). A widespread and ferocious civil war ensued.

Pompey withdrew the senatorial forces to Greece. In a matter of weeks Caesar was in control of Italy. He eliminated Pompey's lieutenants in Spain and then defeated his rival at Pharsalus in August 48 B.C. Pompey eventually fled to Egypt where he was immediately assassinated. Caesar's supremacy was essentially established although three more years of fighting against Pompey's supporters elapsed before the civil war was finally brought to an end in 45 B.C.

The Dictatorship of Julius Caesar

One of the outstanding features of Caesar's rule was its brevity. Between 49 B.C., when he first assumed the dictatorship, and his death in 44 B.C., Caesar spent less time in Rome than abroad. Only after he crushed the last embers of resistance from Pompey's supporters in Spain in the fall of 45 B.C. did Caesar devote his entire energies to reconstructing Rome. Only six months remained him before the Ides of March.

Control of Government. Caesar's brief rule makes clear his contempt for Republican institutions and his belief in personal autocracy. Caesar held the consulship five times. He had his dictatorship renewed for ten years in 46 B.C. and two years later received the role of dictator for life. His powers were virtually unlimited because he removed the traditional restraints of Roman government. By enlarging the senate to about 900 members and filling it with supporters, many from the provinces, who were loyal to him alone, he nullified the senate's independent authority.   In addition, he controlled most of the magistracies and handed them out to his adherents.

Social and Economic Reforms. Caesar used his dictatorial powers to put through reforms which reflect his aspirations to improve social and economic conditions and to retain the favor of the Roman masses. His measures reduced the debts of the poor, many of whom were resettled in colonies established throughout the empire. His veterans also received grants of land in the provinces. By curtailing slave labor and embarking on vast building and public works projects, he increased the number of available jobs and was thus able to cut back on the free distribution of grain.

Reforms of Provincial Administration. Two of Caesar's reforms were of especially long lasting significance. He advanced the political standing of the provincials within the empire by extending Roman citizenship to Cisalpine Gaul and a few other areas. In general he took steps to ameliorate provincial administration and encourage local self-government within the Italian municipalities.

The Julian Calendar. Even more durable was Caesar's introduction of a new, highly accurate calendar of 365 1/4 days. The Julian calendar was not revised until the sixteenth century, and it is essentially the prototype of our modern one.

Assassination. Practical reforms and conciliatory policies characterized Caesar's short rule. He pardoned his defeated opponents and treated them generously. Yet many senators interpreted his actions and the distinctions bestowed upon him, such as the right to wear a purple robe and mint coins with his image, as indicative of his intention to make himself king in the manner of a divine Eastern monarch. His assumption of the dictatorship for life violated Roman custom and outraged republican feelings. On March 15, 44 B.C. (the Ides of March) a group of conspirators led by two of his friends, Marcus Brutus and Gaius Cassius, stabbed Caesar to death in the senate.

The Contest for Succession

Instead of restoring the senatorial oligarchy and saving the Republic, the assassination of Caesar plunged Rome into a new round of civil war. Brutus and Cassius regarded themselves as "liberators" but had little idea of what to do once they eliminated the "tyrant." In fact, their deed had not met with widespread popular approval. The Caesarian party did not die with its leader. Caesar's army and provincial clientage remained loyal to his name and constituted a powerful base of support for whoever took up his sword.

The Three Claimants

Three aspirants quickly staked their claims. At first Marc Antony (c. 83–30 B.C.), one of Caesar's protégés and the consul for 44 B.C., appeared the most likely successor. In a rousing funeral oration, Antony turned the public against Caesar's murderers and forced them to flee Rome. Another of Caesar's lieutenants, Marcus Lepidus, also sought power for himself but soon allied with Antony. The third contender for Caesar's power was Caesar's own grandnephew, Gaius Octavius (63 B.C.–A.D. 14), whom the dictator had adopted under the name Gaius Julius Caesar Octavianus and made his heir.

The Second Triumvirate

Only nineteen at the time, Octavian at first sided with the republicans, now led by the writer and stateman, Cicero, who attacked Antony for having unlawfully seized the command of Gaul in 43 B.C. Cicero believed he could use the "boy" and then discard him, but Octavian proved to be the most politically astute of them all. He obtained the consulship and in November 43 B.C. he changed allegiances by joining with Antony and Lepidus to form an alliance known as the Second Triumvirate.

Consolidation of Power

The triumvirs marched their armies on Rome and compelled the senate to recognize their political control for a period of five years. Once in power, the three instituted a massive proscription against their enemies. This ultimately claimed the lives and property of thousands, Cicero among them. Antony and Octavian then sailed east where in 42 B.C. at Philippi in Macedon, they defeated the republican forces assembled by Brutus and Cassius, both of whom then committed suicide.

Conflict Between Antony and Octavian

Victory over Caesar's assassins narrowed the struggle for power to within the Caesarean party itself. For about a decade Antony and Octavian engaged in cooperative efforts, but the rivalry between them was intense. Antony's marriage to Octavian's sister in 40 B.C. helped to forestall open hostilities. The triumvirate was extended for another five years in 37 B.C. although shortly thereafter Octavian engineered the removal of Lepidus who had been challenging his command in Sicily. A confrontation between Antony and Octavian was now all but inevitable.

Antony and Cleopatra

While Octavian was strengthening his base of power in the West, Antony remained in the East to engage in a romantic affair with Cleopatra, the last Ptolemaic ruler of Egypt (69–30 B.C.), who bore him two sons. The famous love affair between Antony and Cleopatra had political implications. War with the Parthians had not gone well for Antony and he came to rely increasingly upon Egyptian wealth for his finances. In exchange, he assigned certain Roman territories to Cleopatra and her children. The Romans viewed these arrangements with growing aversion. Octavian fanned the public's hostility by his adroit use of propaganda until he finally gained the senate's approval to wage war against the lovers.

Victory of Octavian

In 31 B.C., Octavian's ships triumphed over those of Antony and Cleopatra in a naval engagement off the northwestern coast of Greece at Actium. Antony followed Cleopatra to Alexandria where they attempted to rally their forces, but Octavian's arrival in 30 B.C. put an end to such hopes. Antony committed suicide as did Cleopatra, supposedly after being rebuffed by the new victor. The decisive battle of Actium made Octavian sole ruler of the Roman empire and marks the beginning of a new era in Roman history.

Roman Values and Culture

Family and Religion

The Romans were sustained in their long years of conquest by a character and set of values that distinguish them from other peoples. Unlike the Greeks, who placed a high premium on individual freedom, creativity and the intellect, the Romans stressed above all the need for discipline, obedience to authority, and self-control. Especially during the early centuries of the Republic, the most important individual attributes were considered to be a sense of duty, honor, morality, courage, loyalty, and serious-mindedness.

The Family

Responsibility for inculcating these Republican virtues lay with the family, above all with its head, the *paterfamilias*. The father's control over every member of his family and all its possessions was total. In the early days of the Republic, women were not allowed to own property, and upon marriage they transferred their submission from father to husband. Children learned to obey paternal commands unquestioningly and defer to ancestral customs. Sons (unless they were emancipated) remained under the father's authority until his death, when they in turn headed their own families. As the state grew in importance, it commanded the same respect and allegiance that Romans showed towards the family. The impact of new influences during the late Republic and the Empire contributed to a loosening of these familial ties and a general breakdown of values.

Religion

The most ancient form of Roman religion developed at the time when the Romans lived in small agricultural communities centered on the family.

Household Spirits

At the heart of this early religion was the animistic belief that spirits, or *numina,* govern all aspects of human life and manifest themselves in natural phenomena. In order to insure a good harvest or to protect their home, the Roman family worshipped a variety of household spirits. For example, Janus guarded the door. As priest within the family, it was the father's duty to win favor and to appease these spirits by performing sacrifices and ritual ceremonies.

State Religion

With the emergence of the Roman state many family spirits assumed communal functions. As a consequence state cults and rituals evolved, and these were supervised and maintained by colleges of priests and priestesses that were subordinate to the *Pontifex Maximus,* the highest priest. Roman state religion also involved the worship of anthropomorphic gods, the foremost being Jupiter. Contact with neighboring civilizations added new gods to Rome's pantheon and their identities were merged with preexisting Roman divinities. Thus the Greek Zeus became Jupiter, Hera became Juno, Athena became Minerva, Aphrodite became Venus, and so on. From the Etruscans the Romans adopted the practice of divination. No political actions were taken without first consulting the augurs, Roman priests who foretold the future by interpreting various signs. Rome's religion expanded further during and after the reign of Julius Caesar, when Rome's rulers were deified, usually after death.

Eastern Cults

Rome's state religion never meant as much to the ordinary Romans as did their household deities. At time went on, the state religion became even more divorced from the people, for it concerned itself exclusively with correct performance of routine rituals by the priestly caste. This helps to explain the popular reception in the early second century B.C. of Near Eastern cults that offered spiritual satisfaction and promise of an afterlife.

Literature Under the Republic

To judge from the few examples that have survived, the early Romans produced no literary masterpieces comparable to the *Iliad* or the *Odyssey*. Latin literature did not evolve until the third century B.C., when writers responded to the fertilizing effects of contact with Hellenistic civilization. The best Roman writers drew inspiration from and adapted Greek forms to create original works that were distinctly Roman in spirit. Latin literature truly came of age during the last century of the Republic. This period witnessed a burst of creative energy in the fields of lyric poetry, history and oratory.

Early Influences

Andronicus.   The introduction of Greek literature by Livius Andronicus, a Greek enslaved after the fall of Tarentum and later freed, stimulated the growth of Latin writing. In 240 B.C. he presented the first Greek play performed in Latin. In addition he translated the *Odyssey* and adapted other Greek dramas for Roman audiences.

Ennius.   The Italian Quintus Ennius (239–169 B.C.) also wrote Latin imitations of Greek tragedies, but he is best remembered for his epic poem, *Annales*, a patriotic history of Rome. Aspiring to be his country's Homer, Ennius greatly polished Latin verse, was the first to use hexameter, and is often considered the father of Latin poetry.

Comedy

Unlike the Greeks, the Romans never cultivated a taste for tragedy. They preferred comedy, and Plautus and Terence catered to their tastes.

Plautus.   Plautus (c. 254–184 B.C.) was the most popular dramatist in Rome and probably the greatest. He filled his hilarious comedies with lively plots, slapstick situations, bawdy language, and such stock comic characters as the slave who outwits his master, the nagging wife, and the star-crossed lovers. Shakespeare, Jonson and Molière found him a valuable resource for their own plots and characters.

Terence.   Terence (195?–159? B.C.) eschewed Plautus's ribaldry and wrote instead in a more refined and subtle vein. His witty comedies were never thoroughly appreciated by his contemporaries, but served as models for the later comedy of manners.

Poetry

Catullus. In the writings of the young Catullus (84–54 B.C.), Roman lyric poetry attained its highest level. Catullus took his inspiration from the poets of Alexandria who were noted for their highly polished, emotional verse. He drew upon his own experiences, especially his disappointed love affair with the faithless Clodia (whom he called Lesbia), to create love lyrics of great beauty and depth of feeling.

Lucretius. The fame of the Republic's other great poet, Lucretius (c. 94–55 B.C.), rests on his long philosophical work, *On the Nature of Things.* In it Lucretius describes in poetic form the Epicurean philosophy that the universe functions according to mechanistic natural laws without need of divine intervention. Though the Romans never developed an original philosophical school, many found Epicureanism, particularly as expressed in Lucretius' touching verse, a congenial world view.

History

Roman historical writing also took shape under Greek influence but never reached the levels of Herodotus and Thucydides.

Polybius. The earliest extant history of Rome was written by a Greek, Polybius (203?–120 B.C.). Polybius was among the Greeks who were deported to Rome in 167 B.C. for advocating the Achaean League's neutrality in the Third Macedonian War. There after being befriended and patronized by some of Rome's leading families he witnessed several significant events in Roman history. His history of the Mediterranean world from the First Punic War until 46 B.C. attempted to explain Rome's rapid rise to world supremacy. Although somewhat pedantic in style, Polybius's work is an important example of well-researched, impartial historical analysis.

Caesar's Commentaries. The turbulent events of the late Republic gave rise to several notable histories by men who were themselves involved in Roman politics. The statesman Julius Caesar (102?–44 B.C.) was an historian of uncommon ability. His surviving works, the

Commentaries on the Gallic Wars and on the Civil War against Pompey, provide detailed information about his military campaigns between 58 and 48 B.C. Although written to justify his own actions, they constitute an excellent source for the study of ancient Rome. In addition they establish Caesar's reputation as a master of lucid and concise Latin prose.

Sallust. Sallust (86–c. 34 B.C.), one of Caesar's adherents, also composed histories of current events that are valuable for their character sketches of Caesar and other leading politicians.

Cicero

Without question the outstanding literary figure of the century was Marcus Tullius Cicero (106–43 B.C.). Cicero impressed his own and later generations by the range of his activities. An urbane lawyer and influential statesman, he was also Rome's greatest orator and prose stylist. His voluminous writings covered a broad sweep of topics from philosophy and political theory to art, literary criticism, and rhetoric. In politics, Cicero was a conservative. He staunchly defended the republican constitution against what he perceived as threats to it by Julius Caesar and later Marc Antony. In his many speeches to the senate and in the law courts Cicero carried the art of persuasive oratory to new heights. The most famous of his speeches are the *Orations against Catiline* in which he denounced the Catiline conspiracy.

Cicero's command of the language was unsurpassed. Students from the Renaissance to the present have studied Ciceronian Latin as a paragon of elegance and clarity. His many letters (some 900 of which are extant) shed light on his character and on the troubled times in which he lived. Cicero was not an original thinker. His philosophical treatises are an eclectic mixture of Greek, especially Platonic and Stoic, thought. They were important, however, in adapting Greek philosophy to the Roman temperament. The widespread appeal of Stoicism within the Empire owed much to Cicero's presentation of its philosophy so that it encompassed the Roman ideals of duty, morality and public service.

The Roman Republic endured from 509 B.C., when its patricians abolished the Etruscan monarchy and established a republic, until 30 B.C., when Octavian defeated his enemies and began one-man rule.

During the Early Republic (509–133 B.C.), Rome was governed by its patrician class. Over time the plebeians demanded and received many political and social rights, among them the granting in 287 B.C. of force of law to the resolutions of the tribal assembly. Yet, the aristocratic senate—expanded to include wealthy plebeians—remained the most politically powerful. This same period also witnessed the foundation of Rome's empire. The Romans first unified the Italian peninsula as a confederation of allies. Then in a series of wars, Rome conquered Sicily, Sardinia, Corsica, Spain, Macedon, Greece, and parts of North Africa and Asia.

The Late Republic (133–30 B.C.) was a time of social and political turbulence that led ultimately to the Republic's demise. Rapid territorial expansion profoundly altered the Republic, above all by widening the gap between the rich and the poor. Two brothers, the Gracchi, sought by agrarian reform to ease the plight of the poor, but they ended in failure. In 107 B.C. Marius, the first of a number of dictators in Rome whose power derived from their military rank, challenged senatorial authority. Civil war erupted between Marius's supporters and those of Sulla, who succeeded in temporarily restoring the senate's preeminence in 82 B.C. In the following decades, ambitious young men jockeyed for control. With the support of the popular party and the loyalty of his army, Julius Caesar defeated Pompey and assumed dictatorial powers. Caesar's antirepublican actions led to his assassination in 44 B.C., yet, ironically, paved the way for the establishment of imperial rule under his grandnephew, Octavian.

Recommended Reading

F.E. Adcock, *Caesar As Man of Letters* (1956).

Peter Arnott, *The Romans and Their World* (1970).

E. Badian, *Foreign Clientelae, 264–70 B.C.* (1958).

E. Badian, *Roman Imperialism in the Late Republic* (1968).

J. Balsdon, *Roman Women: Their History and Habits* (1975).

R. Barrow, *The Romans* (1975).

Arthur E. Boak and William G. Sinnigen, *A History of Rome to A.D. 565* (1965).

Henry C. Boren, *The Gracchi* (1968).

Diana Bowder, *Who Was Who in the Roman World* (1980).

P. Brunt, *Social Conflicts in the Roman Republic* (1974).

Julius Caesar, *The Gallic War and other Writings*, M. Hadas, trans. (1957).

M. Cary and H.H. Scullard, *A History of Rome down to the Reign of Constantine* (1975).

Karl Christ, *The Romans, An Introduction to their History and Civilization* (1984).

Martin L. Clarke, *The Roman Mind: Studies in the History of Thought from Cicero to Marcus Aurelius* (1956).

T.A. Dorey, ed., *Cicero* (1965).

T.A. Dorey and D.R. Dudley, *Rome Against Carthage* (1971).

Donald R. Dudley, *The Civilization of Rome* (1960).

T.J. Dunbabin, *The Western Greeks* (1948).

D.C. Earl, *The Political Thought of Sallust* (1961).

Tenney Frank, *Life and Literature in the Roman Republic* (1930).

Matthias Gelzer, *Caesar: Politician and Statesman* (1968).

Michael Grant, *The Etruscans* (1980).

Michael Grant, *History of Rome* (1979).

Erich S. Gruen, *The Last Generation of the Roman Republic* (1973).

Paul MacKendrick, *The Mute Stones Speak: The Story of Archaeology in Italy* (1960).

Theodor Mommsen, *A History of Rome* (1854–56).

Claude Nicolet, *The World of the Citizen in Republican Rome* (1980).

Massimo Pallottino, *The Etruscans* (1954).

Plutarch, *Fall of the Roman Republic*, R. Warner, trans. (1958).

Beryl Rawson, *The Family in Ancient Rome* (1986).

Emeline Richardson, *The Etruscans: Their Art and Civilization* (1964).

H.J. Rose, *A Handbook of Latin Literature* (1954).

H.J. Rose, *Religion in Greece and Rome* (1959).

E.T. Salmon, *Roman Colonization under the Republic* (1969).

H.H. Scullard, *From the Gracchi to Nero: A History of Rome from 133* B.C. to A.D. 68 (1971).

H.H. Scullard, *History of the Roman World 753–146* B.C. (1980).

David Stockton, *Cicero: A Political Biography* (1971).

Lily R. Taylor, *Party Politics in the Age of Caesar* (1949).

F.W. Walbank, *Polybius* (1972).

CHAPTER 6

Imperial Rome

Time Line

A.D. 14–138	Silver Age of Latin literature
A.D. 43	Claudius invades England
A.D. 64	Great fire of Rome during Nero's reign
A.D. 68	Year of the Four Emperors
A.D. 69–96	Flavian dynasty founded by Vespasian
A.D. 70	Titus captures Jerusalem and destroys Temple
A.D. 79	Eruption of Mount Vesuvius
A.D. 80	Colosseum completed
A.D. 96–180	Age of the Antonines; Empire's greatest territorial extent
A.D. 101–106	Trajan victorious in Dacian Wars
A.D. 192	Commodus assassinated and Empire in West begins to decline
A.D. 284	Diocletian becomes Emperor; divides Empire between himself and a co-emperor in the West
A.D. 324	Constantine the Great reunifies the Empire
A.D. 330	Constantinople founded

There is no fixed date to signal the end of the Republic and the beginning of the Empire. Rome's first emperor, Octavian (Augustus), refused to call himself emperor and never officially proclaimed the Empire's inauguration. Yet once Octavian had eliminated the last of his rivals, he stood as the supreme power in the Roman world. The government he erected, known as the Principate, provided for absolute rule without eradicating basic republican institutions. The Principate endured without significant change for over two hundred years. During this time Roman civilization reached the acme of its cultural splendor, territorial expanse, and political well-being. Rome brought almost all of the civilized world in the West under its dominion.

*The two centuries from the beginning of Augustus' rule in 27 B.C.
until the death of the emperor Marcus Aurelius in A.D. 180 constitute
the Pax Romana, a period when the Empire was essentially at peace,
the provinces were well administered, and the economy prospered. By
the end of the second century A.D., however, serious strains began to
weaken the Empire. A long period of decline ensued as one emperor
replaced another in rapid sequence according to the whim of the army.
Rome's economy languished. Between 284 and 337 A.D., the emperors
Diocletian and Constantine made attempts to halt this downward slide
by reorganizing the imperial structure along even more authoritarian
lines, but their success proved only temporary. Rome slowly succumbed
to external pressures and internal decay until finally in A.D. 476, with
the deposition of Rome's last emperor, the Roman Empire in the West
came to an end.*

Augustus

The Principate

Upon his return to Rome in 29 B.C., Octavian faced the challenge
of creating a new and lasting form of government. As a triumphant
general, a multiterm consul, and the leader of the victorious Caesarean
party with the wealth of Egypt at his personal disposal, Octavian had
virtually unlimited power. The events in Julius Caesar's brief rule had
shown a need for strong central control over the greatly enlarged empire
and had demonstrated Roman aversion to overt autocracy. Octavian
made absolute rule palatable to the Romans by disguising it within
traditional forms. Thus, in 27 B.C., in accordance with what was most
likely a carefully prearranged plan, he handed over all his powers to the
senate and the people of Rome. They in turn begged him not to desert
the Republic and accorded him the title of Augustus ("the Revered"),
hitherto applied solely to Roman deities. With his full powers restored
and legitimized, Octavian devised a new constitution.

Augustus' Absolute Rule

Although the powers of the senate, assemblies, and magistracies were severely curbed, these truncated bodies continued to function as under the Republic. Augustus, as Octavian was henceforth known, transferred those powers to the emperor, the real ruler of the state. Additional powers were added to his office. In 29 B.C. the senate conferred on him the role of *imperator,* or commander of the army, a term from which the modern word "emperor" is derived. In the following year he was granted the old republican title of *princeps,* a term that connoted the first among equals within the state. In addition, Augustus' provincial command gave him legal control of virtually all of Rome's military and essentially removed the threat of any armed resistance to his rule.

In 23 B.C. the senate conferred two new and even more wide-ranging powers on Augustus. He received vast proconsular powers that gave him final authority over all of Rome's provinces, including those governed by the senate. In addition he was invested with the powers of a tribune for life. This cast Augustus as the defender of the Roman people and gave him important prerogatives that allowed him to introduce and veto legislation within the senate. Despite these enormous powers that made his supremacy unassailable, Augustus preferred to be known by his most humble title, *princeps,* and thus historians refer to the government he established as the Principate.

Political and Military Reforms

During his 45-year reign, Augustus substantially accomplished his stated goal "to build firm and lasting foundations for the government of Rome."

Provincial Administration. Augustus' reforms led to the development of an efficient civil service, a more equitable tax system based on regular censuses, and a more honest provincial administration, because the state paid the salaries of all imperial officials. He promoted local autonomy and formed provincial councils to apprise Rome annually of grievances and suggestions. However, none of these reforms enabled provincials to participate in a truly representative government.

Italian and Roman Government. Augustus significantly improved the government of Italy and the city of Rome itself. By the time of his death in A.D. 14, the Roman Empire was a thriving world-state, which enjoyed better and more secure government than under the late Republic.

Military Reforms. Rome's military also benefited from Augustus's outstanding skill for practical reform. In an age of relative peace, he reorganized the army to prepare it for its new role: that of defending the frontiers and maintaining order within the Empire. In contrast to conditions under the Republic, Augustus established a standard sixteen- (later twenty-) year term of service for legionary soldiers and founded a special state retirement fund for pensioning veterans upon discharge. These reforms shifted the soldiers' loyalty from their generals to the state and minimized a problem that had plagued the late Republic.

The military reorganization effected by Augustus included the creation of several new forces. In addition to Rome's legionary army of Roman citizens, Augustus created an auxiliary force whose ranks were composed of provincial recruits. Augustus's auxiliaries not only proved themselves loyal to Rome, but they also played an important part in the Romanization of the Empire. After thirty years of service, the auxiliary and his family received Roman citizenship. As a third force within Rome's military, Augustus founded the elite Praetorian Guard. Incorporating nine thousand men drawn exclusively from Italy, the Guard had responsibility to maintain the security of Rome. The guards were higher paid than other soldiers and received special privileges. In later years, they came to exert a powerful influence on the selection of Rome's emperors and were an unstable element within the Principate. Finally, Augustus reorganized the Roman navy to increase its effectiveness in patrolling the Mediterranean and keeping piracy at bay.

Extension of Territory

Augustus did not reform the army with the intention of adding new territories to the Empire. Instead he opted to pursue a nonaggressive foreign policy geared to pacifying the provinces and safeguarding imperial borders. However, his desire to protect Italy and Gaul from barbarian invasions did force him to engage in expansionary wars. His generals successfully incorporated into the Empire present-day Switzerland and Austria, as well as territories eastward along the Danube in what are today parts of Hungary, Yugoslavia, and Bulgaria. Yet

Augustus' attempt to extend Rome's border northward to the Elbe River, which would have provided an easier line of defense, led to the only major defeat of his reign. In A.D. 9 the German leader Arminius (Hermann), who had learned military tactics during service in the Roman army, headed a rebellion that massacred three Roman legions and ended any hope of creating a Romanized Germany. Under Augustus and his successor the northern frontier of the Roman Empire in Central Europe was stabilized at the Rhine–Danube line.

Augustan Society

The years between Octavian's assumption of the title of Augustus in 27 B.C. and his death in A.D. 14 constituted an age of economic affluence, social and political tranquility, renewed confidence, and creative excellence. The relief from strife afforded by Augustus' lengthy reign proved a boon to almost every aspect of Roman life.

Economic and Social Conditions

Rome's economy flourished in peaceful times. Augustus undertook a massive program of road-building throughout the Empire and established an imperial postal service. Both of these endeavors fostered the growth of commerce in addition to facilitating military control and centralized provincial administration. Economic conditions within the Empire as a whole were healthy.

The major beneficiaries of this prosperity were the businessmen, financiers, and imperial officials of the equestrian order (the *equites*). Augustus advanced their position even further by filling his enlarged civil service almost exclusively with men from their ranks. The senatorial class on the other hand had been hard hit by the long years of war and found its influence and prestige on the wane. The extensive construction projects of the age brought employment and economic well-being to Rome's artisan class. Little was done, however, beyond the palliatives of "bread and circuses," to better the lot of the urban poor. In general, conditions improved slightly for the small farmer, although large estates run by slaves continued to dominate Roman agriculture.

Slavery

The buying and selling of slaves was taken for granted in Roman society, and even freed slaves purchased slaves of their own. Most of the Empire's slaves were prisoners of war captured during Rome's wars of conquest. Some were purchased from barbarian tribes or kidnapped. Slave conditions varied according to location and type of work. In Sicily, for example, where the standard of living for laborers on the great *latifundia* was appalling, slave revolts were numerous and severe. Yet, not all slaves performed servile labor. Greek slaves (mainly captured soldiers) often served as tutors in the best Roman families. Slaves had the very real hope of being freed, either by manumission or by purchase. There was little stigma attached to past bondage, and freed slaves were physically indistinguishable from other Romans.

Family Life

Augustus showed considerable concern over the decline of traditional Roman morals and family life that had begun in the late Republic. In 17 B.C., he put through a series of social laws affecting the upper classes that made adultery a serious offence punishable in some instances by death, penalized bachelors and childless couples, and offered incentives for raising larger families. This attempt to legislate morality met with much ridicule and little success even within Augustus' own family.

Women

By the time of the Late Republic and during the Empire, formal marriage ceremonies were increasingly replaced by "free" marriages in which the wife usually retained the right to own property such as jewelry or slaves. Roman law continued, nonetheless, to protect the male's superior status. Women were excluded from voting or holding public office. Yet the Roman matron had important functions that accorded her respect. She saw to the children's upbringing and education and managed the household. Unlike ancient Greek women who were segregated in women's quarters, she presided over the dinner table with her husband, acted as hostess, and attended public spectacles. Within the imperial family, women often manipulated events from behind the scenes.

Religion

Augustus, who became *Pontifex Maximus* in 12 B.C., also sought to revive Rome's ancient religion. He gave orders to repair scores of old temples and had many new ones built. In order to strengthen provincial ties to the Empire, he allowed himself to be worshipped along the lines of a Hellenistic monarch and encouraged the construction of temples to the cult of Rome and Augustus. Within Italy, however, the practice of worshipping a living ruler did not yet exist, so Augustus's deification, like Julius Caesar's, would occur only after his death. Despite these efforts to promote Rome's ancient religion, oriental mystery cults continued to grow in popularity among the Romans. The birth of Christ during Augustus's reign had little immediate impact on the Roman world.

Improvement of Rome

Augustus' zeal for building and the restoration of the capital changed the face of Rome. During his reign he saw to the construction of temples, theaters, *fora,* and other public and private structures, and to the reconstruction of many historic Roman monuments. His *Ara pacis,* or Altar of Peace, dedicated in 9 B.C. with its magnificently carved reliefs of Augustus, his family, and Rome's senators, epitomizes the civilized spirit of the Augustan Age. Augustus promulgated several municipal reforms that among other accomplishments established Rome's first police force and fire department and improved living conditions in the city.

The Julio-Claudian Emperors

Augustus' decision not to declare himself emperor left the question of succession in doubt. Theoretically, the senate had the right to choose Augustus's successor. In reality, Augustus was able to ensure that his designee would receive senate approval. Augustus was troubled throughout his reign, however, with the problem of finding a suitable male heir. He and his second wife, Livia, had produced no children and every relative he had adopted as heir died young. Finally Augustus chose Livia's son by her first marriage, Tiberius, who at the time was one of Rome's greatest generals. With the accession of Tiberius begins the line of the Julio-Claudians, so-called because they were related to the family of Julius Caesar and Augustus. The five Julio-Claudians who ruled between A.D. 14 and 68 were not equal in character and ability to Augustus, yet they more or less continued his policies and the Empire remained financially sound, politically stable, efficiently administered, and mostly peaceful during their reigns.

Tiberius

Tiberius (ruled A.D. 14–37) was an able administrator who reduced provincial taxes, cut expenses, and improved the Empire's financial liquidity. Yet he allowed himself to become unduly reliant upon Sejanus, the commander of the Praetorian Guard, and he left Rome almost completely in his hands after A.D. 26. Sejanus secretly arranged the murder of the emperor's son and the removal of other rivals. Finally in A.D. 31, Tiberius had him executed for plotting to seize the throne.

Caligula

Tiberius was extremely unpopular and Romans rejoiced when they learned of his death in A.D. 37. Unfortunately his successor, Gaius, proved to be one of Rome's worst rulers. Grandson to Tiberius, Gaius was nicknamed Caligula ("Little Boots") by the army when a child. Undoubtedly insane, Caligula was a cruel tyrant who used his power to wreak havoc during his reign between A.D. 37 and 41. He displayed his contempt for traditional Roman government by making his horse a consul. He was finally assassinated by a member of the Praetorian Guard.

Claudius

Caligula's successor, his uncle Claudius (ruled A.D. 41–54), was the first of many Roman emperors who owed their ascendancy to the ability of the Praetorian Guard to force its choice upon an unwilling senate. The lame, stammering, and sickly Claudius, whom Roman historians portrayed as a man at the mercy of his wives and freedmen, was in fact a scholar and a gifted administrator. During his reign, the Empire resumed its expansionistic course. Mauritania in North Africa and Thrace, Lydia, and Judea to the east all became Roman provinces. In A.D. 43, almost a century after Julius Caesar had led the first expeditions to Britain, Claudius's army invaded the island, conquered most of southeastern England, and made it into the province of Britain. Domestically, Claudius's most important innovations lay in administration. After enlarging Rome's bureaucracy, he divided it into various departments according to function and staffed it with loyal freed slaves who were well trained in handling imperial matters effectively. His generous extension of citizenship rights to provincials made him popular. He undertook numerous public works projects, including the construction of new roads, aqueducts, and port facilities. Claudius's private life was marred by intrigue. He executed his third wife for conspiring against him and was himself most likely poisoned at the hands of his fourth, who sought the throne for her son by a previous marriage.

Nero

The infamous Nero (ruled A.D. 54–68) repaid his mother's efforts by having her killed several years later. The last of the Julio-Claudian emperors was a profligate and murderer. Although his reign began well and the provinces continued to prosper throughout, during its later years Rome was plunged into a bloodbath of crimes and executions. Among those who died at Nero's behest were his first wife, Octavia, Claudius's son, Britannicus, the philosopher Seneca, and the poet Lucan. When suspicion for starting the great fire of Rome in A.D. 64 fell on the emperor, he transferred the blame to a new religious sect, the Christians, and ordered their persecution. Nero committed suicide in A.D. 68 when faced with army mutinies and senatorial censure.

The Flavian Emperors

Nero's death precipitated the first civil warfare in almost a century. Because there was no heir in the Julio-Claudian line, the throne became available to whoever could take it by superior force.

Year of the Four Emperors

For more than a year, four different emperors, all generals backed by rival army factions, struggled to hold onto the succession. Finally the last, Vespasian, who had been in charge of quelling the Jewish uprising of A.D. 66 and who possessed the support of the Eastern legions, succeeded in taking Rome and eliminating his competitor.

Vespasian

Vespasian founded the Flavian dynasty that governed Rome from A.D. 69 to 96. As emperor (ruled A.D. 69–79), his simple tastes and frugal nature helped Rome to recover from the lavish reign of Nero and the costly civil strife. With the money saved, he launched new construction projects, notably Rome's Colosseum.

The Jewish War

In external affairs, Titus, who had replaced his father as commander of Rome's legions in the Jewish War, captured Jerusalem after a long seige and destroyed the Temple in A.D. 70. Roman troops also put down a rebellion in Gaul. From then on Vespasian's reign was one of peace, prosperity, and restored order.

Titus

In A.D. 79 the imperial mantle passed to Titus (ruled A.D. 79–81) whose kindliness and beneficence won for him the love of the Roman people. His short reign was troubled, however, by an epidemic of the plague, a devastating fire in Rome, and the eruption of Mount Vesuvius in A.D. 79.

Domitian

Titus was succeeded by his younger brother, Domitian (ruled A.D. 81–96). The last Flavian was a much-hated autocrat who nonetheless administered the Empire well. During his reign the capable governor of Britain, Agricola, brought most of England and North Wales under Roman dominion. The Emperor met with less success in his campaigns against the Daci along the Danube and was compelled to make peace with them on unfavorable terms. Toward the end of his life, Domitian grew increasingly tyrannical. He began a reign of terror against aristocrats whom he suspected of conspiring against him which raged until he was finally assassinated in A.D. 96.

The Age of the Antonines

The Age of the Antonines was the high-water mark of the Roman Empire. Nerva and his successors, who reigned between A.D. 96 and 180, are known in Roman history as the "five good emperors." Under them the Empire reached its farthest limits. It covered an area of approximately 1,250,000 square miles and contained an estimated 70 million inhabitants. The provinces gained in power and importance as Roman law, language, and culture took root. Empire-wide markets, unhampered by customs barriers, an advanced system of transportation, and the continuation of the *Pax Romana* all contributed to the rapid growth of trade and industry.

Yet amid this general prosperity other developments boded ill for the future. In cultural affairs the age was less creative than that of Augustus although great writers such as Tacitus and Juvenal still abound. Socially, the disparity between rich and poor grew even more pronounced. Italian agriculture remained in the doldrums and the number of tenant farmers, or *coloni*, who cultivated the land of huge estates increased substantially relative to that of the small farmers who owned their plots.

Nerva

The expiration of the Flavian line had once again raised the question of succession in Rome, but this time the senate, rather than the army, seized the initiative in selecting a new emperor. The senators chose Nerva (ruled A.D. 96–98), who governed the Empire even-handedly and established a system of state grants to poor children during his brief reign. Having no progeny of his own and feeling the pressure of the Praetorian Guard, Nerva devised a new method by which to transfer power smoothly from one emperor to the next. He appointed as his successor the man he considered best qualified to rule and adopted him as his son. The principle of succession by adoption gave Rome almost a century of peaceful, uninterrupted rule.

Trajan

Nerva designated as his successor the powerful commander of

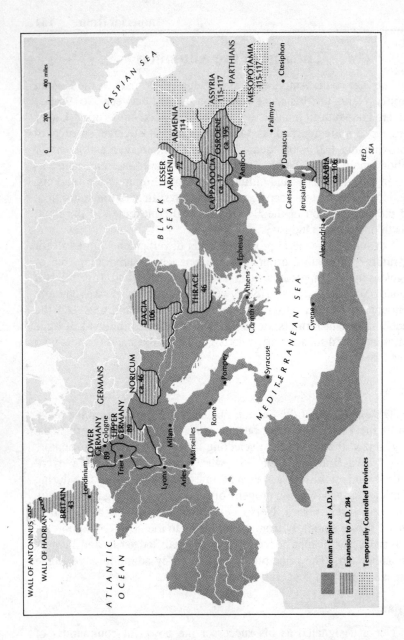

The Roman Empire, A.D. 14–284

Rome's legions in Germany, Trajan (ruled A.D. 98–117). Born in Spain, the new ruler was the first non-Italian to become *princeps*. His enlightened policies and martial exploits won for him the reputation as one of Rome's best emperors and most outstanding military heroes. Trajan continued and augmented the social welfare measures, the *alimenta*, begun by his predecessor in Italy. These were charitable grants to poor children funded by interest paid back on state loans to farmers. He administered the provinces closely and well, urged fair treatment of the Christians, and fostered many new building projects including the huge Forum of Trajan in Rome. Trajan's most spectacular achievements, though, were in the military realm.

Military Victories

Success in the Dacian Wars (A.D. 101–106) added Dacia (modern Rumania) to the provincial system. Defeat of the Parthian Kingdom gained Armenia and Mesopotamia as Roman provinces. Thanks to his victories, Rome reached the farthest point east that the Empire ever attained. Trajan died in A.D. 117.

Hadrian

Trajan had adopted an equally competent individual, his ward and fellow Spaniard Hadrian (ruled A.D. 117–138), to succeed himself. The latter was one of the most dynamic figures in the history of the Roman Empire. He was noted for his intellectual curiosity, command of Greek culture, abundance of energy, and varied talents. Hadrian astutely concluded that Trajan's conquests in the East were too difficult to maintain. Thus he returned the conquered lands east of the Euphrates to the Parthians and concentrated instead on strengthening defensible borders throughout the Empire. The most famous example of this policy was Hadrian's Wall, a system of fortifications that stretched 73.5 miles across the narrow, northern part of Britain and was designed to hold back invasions from the Celtic tribes to the north.

For more than a decade, Hadrian traveled widely throughout the Empire and acquainted himself with local needs, casting a critical eye over Roman provincial administration, instituting reforms, and inspiring the construction of new public works and monuments. Except in Palestine, Hadrian was well liked wherever he went. In Palestine, his harsh suppression of the Jewish uprisings of A.D. 117 and 132 and his efforts at Romanization, such as forbidding circumcision, earned for him the hatred of the Jews. In Rome itself, Hadrian also put his skills to good use and in so doing further concentrated power in the hands of the emperor. He and his advisers adjusted taxes, added to the civil service, and issued laws to improve the conditions of slaves. To satisfy the Roman poor, he spent freely on public amusements and charities and cancelled debts owed to the state. The codification of Roman law progressed during his reign. Finally, like so many of his predecessors, he sought to enhance his own prestige and that of Rome by cultivating the arts and building magnificent structures such as his villa at Tivoli.

Antoninus Pius

Upon his death in A.D. 138 Hadrian was succeeded by his adopted son, Antoninus Pius (ruled A.D. 138–161). A man of sterling qualities, Antoninus governed the Empire ably although with less vigor than Hadrian. In retrospect, his reign appears as the Indian summer of imperial greatness. The Roman world was prosperous and at peace; yet this tranquility would be disturbed shortly thereafter.

Marcus Aurelius

Antoninus was succeeded by his wife's nephew, Marcus Aurelius (ruled A.D. 161–180), perhaps the best educated and most humane of all the Roman emperors. Given more to study than warfare, he was forced nonetheless to do battle with the Parthians in the East and to push back a major invasion of Germanic tribes that had moved into Dacia and threatened the whole northern frontier. The campaign in Syria had horrendous long-term consequences for Rome. Its returning legions brought back with them a vicious epidemic of the plague which would sap the Empire's strength for years to come.

While fighting along the Danube, Marcus found time to write his famous *Meditations*, a work that espoused the Stoic philosophy of calm acceptance of one's fate and humanitarian concern for one's fellow man. After thirteen years of hard combat he finally defeated the invading Marcomanni and might have succeeded in extending Rome's border to the Elbe had not a rebellion in the East called him away.

Commodus

The opportunity for creating a strong defensive line against barbarian tribes to the north was lost forever because Marcus's son and successor, Commodus (ruled A.D.180–192), preferred a life of debauchery at Rome to one of completing his father's work. By choosing his own son as emperor, Marcus Aurelius broke the century-old practice of succession by adoption that had provided the empire with some of its best rulers. Commodus was a cruel and corrupt tyrant who was eventually assassinated in A.D. 192. With his reign the Empire began its slow decline.

Roman Civilization

The Golden Age of Latin Literature

The Golden Age of Latin literature spans the last decades of the Republic and the early years of the Empire. It is usually divided into two parts, with the first half (70–43 B.C.) dominated by Cicero. The second, the Age of Augustus (43 B.C.–A.D.14), was a remarkable period of literary accomplishment, and the phrase "Augustan Age" has been appropriated to classical literary periods in other nations. Latin literature achieved its most sublime expression during the Augustan Age in the works of Virgil, Horace, Ovid, and Livy. Augustus encouraged the arts and letters not only because he appreciated their intrinsic worth but also because he recognized their usefulness in establishing stable government and supporting his own rule. Virgil, Horace, and Livy all counted him as their friend and patron and repaid his generosity with glowing encomiums to his rule. The literature of the period was not, however, debased by this close association between artists and men in power. Rather these authors sincerely shared Augustus' belief in the destiny of Rome and its moral regeneration under his leadership. Their writings benefited from the peace and enthusiasm of the Augustan Age and embody its spirit.

Virgil

The poetry of Virgil (70 B.C.–19 B.C.) is perhaps the best example of a literature in harmony with the aspirations of its age. Raised on a farm in Cisalpine Gaul, Virgil first attained fame with two books of verse in imitation of Greek models: the *Eclogues*, pastoral poems that idealize life in the country, and the *Georgics*, a didactic work that describes with fine poetic feeling various aspects of farming and animal husbandry.   Both accorded with Augustus' subsequent policy of promoting agriculture and a return to simple, rural life.

Virgil's greatest work and one of the masterpieces of world literature, the *Aeneid*, was unabashedly patriotic. In Homeric fashion, Virgil recounted the wanderings of Aeneas after the fall of Troy and his final settlement on the Tiber, where he fought with native rulers and laid the foundations of the Roman state. The poet glorified ancient Roman virtues as epitomized by his hero and prophesied their restoration under the empire. He heralded the dawning of a new age under Augustus, who would "bring back the age of gold" and expand the Empire. While obviously composed to flatter Augustus, these lines convey the poet's firm belief in Rome's mission to rule the world. Virgil's influence on all subsequent Latin literature was immense and continued through the Middle Ages when his poetry was interpreted allegorically as foreshadowing the Christian era. He is appreciated today for his eloquent expression of universal aspects of the human character and its relation to nature.

Horace

Virgil's contemporary and friend, Horace (65 B.C.–8 B.C.), also reflected the spirit of his age in his verse. Son of a slave who had bought his freedom, he wrote in several different veins. His *Satires* and *Epistles* poke fun at the daily life of the Romans in a style of urbane good humor and advocate a philosophy of tolerance and moderation. His *Odes* are masterly crafted lyric poems on a variety of subjects. Horace also made contributions to literary criticism and was often consulted by later writers, especially in England.

Ovid

Ovid (43 B.C.–A.D. 17 or 18), another great poet in the Augustan Age, did not follow Virgil and Horace in praising the new reign. Rather he took pleasure in composing sophisticated, witty, and sometimes erotic elegies on all aspects of love. These were nonetheless equally representative of the brilliant and dissolute nature of the times. His well-known *The Art of Love* counseled men on how to procure and retain a mistress. Augustus considered Ovid's "immoral" verse detrimental to his goal of moral regeneration. In A.D. 8 he exiled the poet to Tomis on the Black Sea. There Ovid lived out the last ten years of his life writing obsequious poems pleading for his return. Apart from his love poetry, Ovid also wrote on mythological subjects. His *Metamorphoses* is a delightful collection of tales about changes of form beginning with the creation of the universe out of chaos and including many stories about legendary Greeks such as Orpheus and Eurydice. A perennially popular work, it was instrumental in passing on classical mythology to medieval Europe.

Livy

The fourth major figure of the age was the historian Livy (59 B.C.–A.D. 17), who devoted forty years of his life to composing a history of Rome from its foundation in 753 B.C. to the death of Drusus in A.D. 9. Livy's *History* is often compared to the *Aeneid* as an epic in prose. Like Virgil, Livy wrote with an eye to the future. He shared the poet's belief in the Empire's high destiny and sought by depicting Rome's heroic past to revive those "antique virtues" necessary for future greatness. As an historian, Livy accepted much as fact, especially about the early days of the Republic, which modern scholarship has shown to be legend. He was aware, however, of the problematic nature of many of his sources. The work's brilliant narrative style and sweeping panorama of Roman history as viewed through the eyes of a patriot compensate for its inaccuracies.

The Silver Age of Latin Literature

The years between Augustus' death in A.D. 14 and that of Hadrian in A.D. 138 constitute the Silver Age of Latin literature. While the period produced several first-rate talents, there was a leveling off of creativity compared with the previous age. Gone was the perfect harmony between the Empire and its artists as personified by the works of Virgil. Writers of the Silver Age proved more critical of Roman society and government as the latter grew more autocratic. A spirit of disillusionment pervades much of the period's literature. This is evident in the writings of the historian Tacitus (A.D. c. 55–A.D. c. 117). The Silver Age's interest in writing history is also attested to by the Greek author Plutarch's *Parallel Lives of the Greeks and Romans* and the Roman official Suetonius's *The Twelve Caesars.*

Tacitus

Tacitus eschewed Livy's monumental undertaking and concentrated instead on works more restricted in scope and design. Yet he also used the study of history to comment on the present era. In his *Germania*, for instance, he depicted the Germans as a simple people whose primitive, heroic ways contrasted sharply with the luxurious, degenerate life style of the Romans. Although a prejudiced picture, Tacitus's brief study is a valuable source of information about the Germanic tribes that would come to play a significant role in the decline of Rome. Tacitus's mature texts, the *Histories*, which covered the years from A.D. 69 to 96 and the *Annals*, which treated the reigns of Rome's emperors from Tiberius to Nero, make transparent the historian's hatred for imperial tyranny and his senatorial bias. Despite his lack of objectivity, Tacitus's high moral purpose, caustic character analysis, and incisive, epigrammatic prose make him perhaps Rome's greatest historian.

Juvenal

Satire was the authentic voice of the Silver Age. Its best mouthpiece, Juvenal (A.D. c. 50–127), attacked in scathing verse the follies, cupidity, boorishness, and despotism of Roman society. His bitter satires, which addressed such topics as the vanity of human wishes and the immorality of women, are well known and became models for later satirists such as Swift and Pope.

Seneca

Roman taste in literature favored the excessive and the rhetorical. Hence the popularity of the dramatist and Stoic philosopher Seneca (c. 3 B.C.–A.D. 65), whose tragedies were filled with bloodshed and bombast. His nine plays were especially appreciated by Elizabethan and Jacobean playwrights, who shared his penchant for horror and melodrama.

Roman Law

One of Rome's greatest legacies to the modern West is its system of laws and jurisprudence. Alone of all the ancient peoples, the Romans created a body of laws based on broad principles of right and extended it throughout its vast empire.

Types of Law

In its advanced form Roman law consisted of essentially three types. The oldest, *ius civile* ("law of the citizen"), derived from ancient customs and religious practices and included those enactments that applied only to Roman citizens. The *ius gentium* ("law of the peoples") was that body of laws that developed in order to handle transactions, often commercial in nature, with noncitizens. Because it tended to be more flexible than the *ius civile*, the *ius gentium* came to be used extensively throughout the empire. The *ius naturale* ("natural law") referred to the Stoic ideal of a universal law of nature that is from God and thus eternal, everywhere the same, and binding on all people.

Development of Law

Rome's vast corpus of laws was created in various ways. Beginning with a core of customary laws, the senate and assemblies added new legislation during the Republic. The praetors, magistrates in charge of legal functions, contributed to Roman jurisprudence when they interpreted old ordinances that they set forth in edicts issued at the start of each term. The decision of judges in cases that went beyond the scope of current law also influenced legal development. In later Roman history, imperial orders and decrees made up a large portion of Rome's laws.

Influence of Roman Law

Roman law underlies the legal systems of most Western European countries and their former colonies as well as international, commercial, and canon law; Great Britain and the United States and their colonies are excepted since they adhere to the rival English common law. Even in the latter, Roman jurisprudence has exerted its influence through its intimate association with the law of equity and its principle that the law belongs to all people. The West owes its inheritance of Roman law to several fortuitous occurrences, including a series of codifications that culminated in the Byzantine emperor Justinian I's exhaustive *Corpus Juris Civilis* (see Chapter 8) and the agency of the Roman Catholic Church whose canon law incorporated much Roman legal matter.

Roman Architecture and Engineering

The visible remains of Roman architecture testify eloquently to the magnificence of the Empire and the skill of the Romans as builders. The innovative qualities of Roman architecture derive from the Romans' development of several new building techniques, including the use of cement, mortar, and fired brick, which enabled them to enclose large areas of interior space without the use of supporting columns.

New Techniques

Although the principle of the arch was known thousands of years earlier in the Near East, the Romans were the first to exploit its potential fully. Roman bridges, aqueducts and domed structures all employed the use of the simple arch and its variant forms. These included the barrel vault, a series of arches set side by side to form a tunnel-like roofed structure. The Romans also devised the more sophisticated groined vault, which allows two barrel vaults to intersect at right angles. This places the thrust on the four corners and allows the sides to be opened up, and was readily used in the construction of stairwells for multistoried buildings. By assembling numerous arches over a circular space meeting at the center, the Romans created impressive domed structures. The extensive use of concrete, a material introduced by the Etruscans, made construction possible on a grandiose scale and also the duplication of their distinctive style throughout the Empire. Cheap, durable, and quick-setting, concrete allowed the Romans to mold desired shapes with unskilled labor.

The Forum

The Romans erected a wide variety of structures to suit their urban way of life. The focal point of Roman commercial, political, and legal activity was the *forum*, an open public square. The original Forum had gradually evolved from a marketplace to a general meeting place surrounded by temples, monuments, shopping arcades, the senate house, law courts, and other government buildings. Beginning with Julius Caesar, emperors built six additional *fora* in Rome to cater to the city's expanding size and to magnify their own prestige.

The Pantheon

Perhaps the most distinguished surviving example of Roman architecture is the Pantheon (early second century A.D.). The huge dome of this awe-inspiring circular temple epitomizes the Romans' success at creating spacious interiors unencumbered by columnar support.

Baths and Amphitheaters

Roman architecture is noted for several unique building types. The huge Roman baths, or *thermae,* with their immense vaulted halls far surpass in size and conception the Greek *gymnasia,* which may have inspired them. This same massiveness appears in Roman amphitheaters where gladitorial games and other violent spectacles were held. The grandest of them all, Rome's Colosseum, completed in A.D. 80, employed simple arches, barrel vaults, and groined vaults to bear the weight of its multilevel stone seating.

The Basilica

Another important Roman contribution to architecture, the *basilica,* also owed its distinctiveness to the use of groined vaults. Although during Roman times the *basilica* housed law courts and other civic offices, Christians (in the early fourth century A.D.) adopted its essential features for churches. Thus some of Europe's greatest cathedrals trace their structural ancestry to a Roman building type.

Private Dwellings

In addition to new public buildings, the Romans invented original private dwelling types. The wealthy resided in luxurious country villas with elaborate gardens. The typical single family home or *domus* was built around an *atrium* or central hall that was open to the sky. The urban poor lived in multistoried apartment houses that gained notoriety as firetraps and as slum dwellings.

Public Works

Underlying the architectural accomplishments of the Romans was their genius as engineers. They excelled at town planning and the new cities they founded benefited from their rational approach to design. The Romans covered the Empire with a network of paved roads. To satisfy the growing needs of urban civilization, they constructed bridges, aqueducts, sewer systems, harbors, tunnels, and dams. Rome's public water supply system, the largest in the ancient world, was unequaled until the nineteenth century. It relied upon fourteen aqueducts that delivered water to the city from great distances by creating an ever-declining slope. Every provincial town of any importance throughout the empire had its own public works.

Roman Art

Roman achievement in art was not as substantial as in other fields. The Romans' great admiration for Greek art stifled their own creativity, and after the conquest of Greece in 146 B.C., Greek art and artists flowed into Rome. Many famous Greek sculptures are known today only by their Roman copies. The Romans valued art more for its use in interior decoration than for its creative originality.

Despite their reputation as imitators, the Romans did evolve a unique style in two types of sculpture: portraiture and narrative relief.

Portraits

Roman portraits have a long history, tracing back to the ancient Republican practice of having a death mask made of the *paterfamilias* and kept in the family shrine. The outstanding characteristic of Roman portrait sculpture is its factual exactitude. It brings the viewer in direct contact with the subject's physiognomy and character. It was customary to commission statues of famous Roman soldiers and statesmen for public display. Under the Empire many imperial portrait busts were executed. Those of Augustus unite a classical Greek idealization of the figure of the emperor with the ancient Roman penchant for realism. In portraits of later emperors, the balance sometimes shifted toward greater idealization or greater expressive realism, but the distinctly Roman factual quality was never lost.

Narrative Relief

In narrative reliefs the Romans struck out in a direction not taken by the Greeks. They adorned their altars, columns, and arches with great episodes from Roman history. For example, Trajan's Column in Rome depicts his victories over the Dacians.

Painting

Of Roman painting less is known because of the limited number and narrow range of surviving examples. Most of these are wall paintings from Pompeii and other towns buried by the eruption of Mt. Vesuvius.

Mosaics

In keeping with their skill as craftsmen and copyists, the Romans excelled in the decorative arts, especially mosaic work. Extremely fine mosaics often of marine life have been found throughout the Empire.

Science

In science, the Romans were inferior to their predecessors and they did little that was original. Their main contribution lay in cataloging and applying previous knowledge. Rome's three greatest scientists, Pliny the Elder, Galen, and Ptolemy all exhibit this encyclopedic trend in their works, and Galen and Ptolemy were accepted as authorities in their respective fields until the sixteenth century. Roman science not only preserved much of ancient learning but also transmitted many of its misconceptions. The great respect and deference accorded Pliny, Galen, and Ptolemy by scientists in succeeding ages actually hindered scientific progress.

Pliny the Elder

Pliny the Elder (A.D. c. 23–79) was an indefatigable observer of natural phenomena. In his vast encyclopedia, the *Natural History,* he gathered together a great deal of the scientific knowledge of antiquity on topics ranging from astronomy and geography to anthropology and botany. Although the work contains much incorrect data, it became the source book of scientific learning until the more advanced Hellenic and Hellenistic treatises were rediscovered in the Middle Ages. Pliny's intellectual curiosity cost him his life. He was asphyxiated while attempting to view the eruption of Mount Vesuvius at close range.

Medicine

Marcus Aurelius's physician, the Greek Galen (A.D. c. 130–c. 200), wrote hundreds of treatises in which he synthesized past medical scholarship and correlated it with his own findings. These derived from his dissection of animals and various other experiments and led Galen to make significant observations concerning the nature of the nervous, respiratory, and circulatory systems. In general, however, advances in medicine during Roman times were more clinical than theoretical. The Romans established hospitals, a public health service, and invented new surgical techniques such as the Caesarian section. Their numerous baths and excellent water supply made for better sanitary conditions than anywhere else in the ancient world.

Ptolemy

The mid-second-century A.D. astronomer, mathematician, and geographer Ptolemy, was a Greek from Alexandria. His large work, the *Almagest,* served as the standard text for medieval astronomers. In it he summarized and augmented the work of his predecessors, especially Aristotle, whose world view was authoritative in that era. Unfortunately the Ptolemaic system posited that the earth was stationary in the center of the universe while the other planets, stars, and sun revolved in circular epicycles around it. This geocentric theory dominated the study of astronomy until overturned by Copernicus in the sixteenth century.

Decline and Recovery

Period of Political Crisis

The third century A.D. was a period of severe crisis in the Roman world, which brought the Empire to the verge of collapse. Confronted with a deepening economic depression and the menace of barbarian invasion, Rome's political leadership broke down.

Septimius Severus

Beginning with the reign of Commodus there occurred a serious deterioration in the quality and competence of Rome's rulers. Following the death of that emperor by strangulation in A.D. 192, a vicious struggle for succession ensued. The eventual winner was Septimius Severus, a military commander from North Africa who gained the throne by marching his troops on Rome. Severus set the pattern for future emperors by catering to the army so that he might retain their crucial support. He rewarded them with higher pay, better living conditions, and what amounted to outright bribes. Foreign campaigns satisfied their lust for booty.

Severus paid for his increased military expenses by extending taxes, debasing the currency, requisitioning certain services, and confiscating the estates of his enemies. In Rome, Severus turned against the senate. He murdered some of its members and stripped the last vestiges of power and prestige from that institution. Subsequently neither the senate nor Rome's other traditional offices could deter the emperor's growing autocracy. Although Severus proved more able than most of his successors and the Empire was secure against invasion, his subservience to the army, his hostility to the senate, his deleterious financial policies, and his use of murder as a political weapon all foreshadowed the worst to come.

Caracalla

Severus left the throne to his two sons, one of whom, Caracalla, murdered his more popular brother to gain sole control. The ruthless Caracalla (ruled A.D. 211–217) heeded his father's advice to enrich his legions above all else. In so doing he weakened the currency even further. During his reign, Roman citizenship was extended to all citizens of cities within the Empire. Whether Caracalla took this action from altruistic or financial motives is unclear. Most likely he saw the measure as a way to raise tax revenues by enlarging the number of those eligible for taxation.

"Soldier Emperors"

Caracalla was followed by a long line of cruel and incompetent emperors. The years from A.D. 235 to 284 were a critical time for Rome, since real political power resided with the legions and the Praetorian Guard, who made and unmade emperors at rapid intervals. Succession by murder was commonplace. Scores of pretenders to the throne fought and killed each other. Of the twenty-six emperors who ruled during this half century, all but one met unnatural deaths. These "soldier emperors" were usually coarse men from the provinces with little administrative or executive expertise.

Beginning of Barbarian Invasions

The weakening of imperial authority in this turbulent age was especially harmful as Rome faced serious external dangers. Germanic tribes raided deep within imperial borders, and the rise of a rejuvenated Persian Empire posed a new threat in the East. During the third century A.D. the size of Rome's empire began to shrink. The province of Dacia that lay north of the Danube was lost to the Goths, the first Germanic tribe to menace the Empire. Another Germanic tribe, the Alemanni, extended their control southward as far as Milan during the reign of Valerian. In A.D. 260, while campaigning against the Persians, Valerian was taken prisoner and died in captivity. Rome's tottering defenses encouraged parts of the Empire, such as the client kingdom of Palmyra in Asia, to assert their independence.

Partial Recovery

With the reign of Claudius II (ruled A.D. 268–270), Rome's fortunes began to improve. Claudius defeated the Goths in the East, and his successor Aurelian (ruled A.D. 270–275) cleared Italy of barbarian invaders. Although he was forced to relinquish Dacia for good, Aurelian regained much lost imperial territory. He also strengthened Rome's borders along the Rhine and the Danube and brought Palmyra to submission. He surrounded Rome with a huge fortifying wall, parts of which still remain standing. The Emperor Probus (ruled A.D. 276–282) cemented Aurelian's gains with victories over the barbarians in Gaul and Illyria. While the immediate external crisis had been circumvented, the Empire had become so debilitated that only a radical solution would allow it to recover.

Economic and Social Decay

The political disorder of the third century was accompanied by domestic decline in both the economic and social spheres. Serious fissures in Rome's economy developed as early as the Age of the Antonines, and were much widened by the calamitous events of the next century. Various factors induced a major economic depression that was accompanied by profound social dislocations. Roman agriculture declined in productivity, as a result of soil exhaustion and inefficient crop methods.

Coloni

Once the Empire ceased to expand, the supply of slaves to work on the *latifundia* diminished. Amid this labor shortage many large land-owners were forced to use tenant farmers, or *coloni*, to cultivate their estates. Although the *coloni* were free men, they were obliged to pay their landlord a percentage of the crop and render certain labor services. The burdens of rent and government taxes in hard times forced many of them into debt. Indebted *coloni* were not allowed to leave their lands until they paid back the sums owed. This in effect made them serfs. The number of *coloni* increased substantially during the third century. Small farmers found it increasingly difficult to hold their lands in the face of rising taxes, unstable political conditions, and frequent pillaging.

Urban Poverty

In the cities a decrease in trade and inflated prices for food and goods caused unemployment and considerable hardship; as a result many urban workers sought work in the countryside. The poor who remained made up about fifty percent of Rome's population, and they depended on government subsidies of free grain and government-sponsored public spectacles. These measures constituted heavy demands on reduced imperial resources. As commerce and industry dwindled in the urban areas in response to lessened productivity, heightened costs, and lack of investment capital, urban prosperity faded and the dynamic character of an empire whose cities were its lifeblood was lost.

Economic Problems

Government measures during most of the third century only exacerbated the problem. In order to finance Rome's mounting defense costs, emperors heavily taxed all segments of the population. When these proved insufficient, emperors resorted to the disastrous measure of debasing the coinage by reducing the amount of silver to alloy. This naturally led to rampant inflation and massive economic disorders. Outside forces such as a terrible plague scourged the Empire for fifteen years during the middle of the century, weakening it still further. While the reigns of Diocletian and Constantine ameliorated conditions somewhat, the decay of Roman social and economic life was already so deeply rooted that it could not be totally reversed.

Diocletian

In A.D. 284, the army placed yet another emperor on the throne. Diocletian was a Dalmatian of humble background who had risen within the military. Astonishingly, his reign was to last for twenty years after which he retired peacefully.

Restructure of Empire

Diocletian's success in ruling so long was due largely to his thorough restructuring of imperial administration. In order to end the repeated military coups and general anarchy of the past half-century, he set out to create a stronger, more efficient central government and an assured method of succession that would eliminate the army's unstabilizing influence. In a series of radical steps, he divided the Empire between himself and a co-emperor, his fellow Illyrian Maximian. Diocletian elected to rule in the East and Maximian took command of the West. These two Augusti in turn chose two Caesars. These assistants shared administrative responsibilities and were groomed to take over the throne on the death or retirement of their Augustus. Two new Caesars would then be selected. Thus Diocletian hoped by this system, known as the Tetrarchy, to ensure the peaceful transfer of power from one emperor to the next.

Administrative Reorganization

Diocletian completely reorganized the administrative structure along lines that increased imperial authority and provided greater regimentation. Rome's provinces were divided into smaller, more numerous units and then regrouped into twelve dioceses, each headed by a vicar. These were assigned to one of four great prefectures overseen by an Augustus or his Caesar. The new administrative system did away with local autonomy and vastly enlarged the imperial bureaucracy. It enabled Diocletian, who retained his supremacy among the four rulers, to supervise the empire more closely and completely.

Military Reforms

Diocletian's reforms encompassed all aspects of Roman life. To bolster the power of the legions in this time of grave external pressures, he increased their size to more than half a million men, raised their pay, effected disciplinary controls, and facilitated promotions. He organized a new, highly mobile fighting force in which the cavalry acquired prominence over the infantry in recognition of its newly won superiority in the field. Responsibility for the Empire's defense was placed more and more in the hands of soldiers recruited from Germany and Illyria. Finally he strictly separated the jurisdiction over military and civil affairs to reduce the likelihood of provincial revolts. The merits of Diocletian's reinvigoration of the army were quickly perceived, for the military quenched several rebellions throughout the Empire, notably that in Britain, and it defeated the Persians and held back the barbarian tide.

Economic Measures

The Empire's economic problems also called for vigorous action. The expense of maintaining an expanded army and the new bureaucracy added substantially to Rome's financial burdens. To raise the needed revenues, Diocletian increased the autocratic powers of the state. He overhauled the tax system by making productivity and labor requirements of units of land the base for taxation. High imposts were also levied on commerce and the professions.

When taxation failed to provide sufficient funds, it became customary to requisition certain goods and services. In order to prevent individuals from shirking their duties to the state, they were forbidden to change professions and sons were compelled to take up their fathers' trade. Likewise, soldiers and *coloni* were tied to their respective occupations, which became hereditary. Diocletian tackled inflation by issuing a new revalued coinage and promulgating a decree that fixed prices and wages for virtually all of the Empire's goods and services. Although violations carried the death penalty, the Edict of Prices (A.D. 301) proved impossible to enforce and it was revoked shortly thereafter.

Despotism

Another facet of the state's augmented authoritarianism was the final transformation of the emperor into an Oriental despot. Diocletian was no longer the *princeps* but rather the *dominus* or absolute ruler. The senate now acted merely as the governing body of the city of Rome. In contrast to earlier emperors, Diocletian magnified rather than concealed his autocratic powers by adopting various marks of royalty such as wearing a diadem and insisting upon elaborate court ritual. Diocletian's purpose in all of this was to raise the status of the throne after decades of degrading civil war. It appears that even his infamous persecution of the Christians was carried out because some Christians had affronted the emperor's authority.

Breakdown of Government

Diocletian retired quietly in A.D. 305 and compelled his co-emperor to follow suit. The position of Augusti then passed on to the two Caesars who appointed new men in their place. Unfortunately without Diocletian's strong presence rivalries quickly came to a head. Hope for a peaceful succession was dashed, and civil war once again shook the Empire.

Constantine the Great

In A.D. 306, the son of one of the Augusti, Constantine, was proclaimed emperor by his soldiers upon the death of his father. Other pretenders also vied for the throne in bloody fighting. Constantine, whose base of power was in Gaul, first sided with one and then the next until in A.D. 312 he defeated his last rival in the West at the battle of the Milvian Bridge near Rome. For over a decade Constantine ruled jointly with Licinius, Emperor in the East. Then in A.D. 324, after a final round of battles, Constantine emerged victorious. The Empire was once again governed by a single head.

Economy and Society

Under Constantine the economic and social structure of the Empire hardened into a rigid mold, which more closely resembled the medieval world to come than the Roman past. Continuing the work of Diocletian, Constantine further subdivided the provinces, expanded the bureaucracy, raised taxes, and completed the transformation of Roman society into a caste system. Taxes and compulsory contributions in kind became so oppressive that individuals abandoned their livelihoods rather than pay them. To counteract this, Constantine issued a series of decrees that prohibited people from changing jobs or leaving their land. Transgressors were severely punished. Thus membership in the great guilds or corporations into which each trade or profession was organized became hereditary. Men were obliged to remain and marry within their guild and their sons after them. In the country, the status of the *coloni* was likewise frozen.

Support of Christianity

Constantine earned the accolade "great" in large part because of his championship of Christianity. His sympathies toward the new sect led him to reverse Diocletian's policy of persecution and grant universal religious tolerance by the Edict of Milan in A.D. 313. Constantine did not, however, make Christianity the official religion of the Empire as is sometimes supposed. Yet he favored Christianity in many ways, including building churches, making donations, and extending tax benefits. Eusebius, Bishop of Caesarea, related that the emperor underwent a genuine mystical conversion before the battle of the Milvian Bridge that transformed him into a devout believer. He was not baptized, however, until near death.

Modern historians have tended to interpret Constantine's behavior toward the Christian Church in the light of political expediency. One-tenth of the Empire had already taken up the new religion and Constantine may have hoped to use the Christians as a bulwark of support and a force for unification. To further this goal, he often interfered in

Church affairs. The Empire's new capital, Constantinople (modern Istanbul), which Constantine founded in A.D. 330 on the site of the ancient Greek settlement of Byzantium, was dedicated to the Virgin Mary. Christianity would flourish there for a thousand years to come. (See Chapter 8.) Irrespective of the sincerity of Constantine's convictions, his aid to the young church had a profound effect on the course of history.

Constantine's Legacy

Constantine's reunification of the Empire did not stem the tide of decline in the West. After his death the Empire was divided among his three sons and other relatives who proceeded to struggle with one another for supremacy. Chaotic conditions returned. Rome's recovery was short-lived. In the East, however, the highly stratified and autocratic system that Diocletian and Constantine had set up lasted for more than a millennium in the form of the Byzantine Empire.

Rome's first emperor, Augustus, fashioned an autocratic government, the Principate, that nonetheless respected the appearance of republican forms. The senate, assemblies, and magistracies remained intact; yet, Augustus's vast military, proconsular, and tribunal powers as well as his immense wealth and prestige made his authority virtually unassailable. Augustus and his Julio-Claudian, Flavian, and Antonine successors for the most part ruled well and expanded the empire to its farthest territorial extent. Their reigns constitute a period in Roman history, the Pax Romana, during which time the benefits of peace and prosperity brought Roman civilization to its apex. The Romans made lasting contributions in law, architecture, engineering, and administration. Their role as synthesizers of Greek culture helped to ensure its preservation and dispersion throughout the Roman world.

From A.D. 192 to 284 a succession of bad emperors, who typically owed their office to the support of the Praetorian Guard, ruled the Empire. They stripped the senate and other bodies of any remaining power, confiscated the lands of their political enemies whom they murdered with impunity, and debased the currency. The Empire began to decrease in size. Diocletian's radical reforms temporarily halted the

decay by totally reorganizing the empire's provincial, economic, and
military structure. Yet his reforms did not endure beyond his lifetime.
As the West declined, the imperial locus of power shifted eastward, a
change symbolized by Constantine's founding of a new capital at
Constantinople in A.D. *330.*

Recommended Reading

Philippe Aries and Georges Duby, eds., *A History of Private Life, vol. I: From Pagan Rome to Byzantium* (1987).

Marcus Aurelius, *Marcus Aurelius and His Times... Meditations* (1945).

J. Carcopino, *Daily Life in Ancient Rome* (1940).

M.P. Charlesworth, *The Roman Empire* (1951).

S. Dill, *Roman Society from Nero to Marcus Aurelius* (1973).

Peter Garnsey and Richard Saller, *The Roman Empire: Economy, Society and Culture* (1987).

Robert Graves, *I, Claudius* (1934).

Edith Hamilton, *The Roman Way* (1932).

A.H. Jones, *Augustus* (1972).

Josephus, *The Jewish War*, G.A. Williamson, trans. (1984).

M.L.W. Laistner, *The Greater Roman Historians* (1947).

Livy, *The History of Rome*, B.O. Foster et al., trans. (1919–1959).

Edward N. Luttwak, *The Grand Strategy of the Roman Empire from the First Century* A.D. to the Third (1977).

Ramsay MacMullen, *Roman Social Relations 50* B.C. to A.D. 284 (1976).

Fergus Millar, *The Emperor in the Roman World* (1977).

H.T. Rowell, *Rome in the Augustan Age* (1962).

Peter Salway, *Roman Britain* (1981).

C.G. Starr, *Civilization and the Caesars: The Intellectual Revolution in the Roman Empire* (1954).

Suetonius, *Lives of the Caesars*, R. Graves, trans. (1972).

Ronald Syme, *The Augustan Aristocracy* (1987).

Ronald Syme, *History in Ovid* (1979).

Ronald Syme, *The Roman Revolution* (1939).

Ronald Syme, *Tacitus* (1958).

Tacitus, *The Annals of Imperial Rome*, M. Grant, trans. (1956).

Virgil, *The Aeneid*, R. Fitzgerald, trans. (1983).

Virgil, *The Eclogues*, G. Lee, trans. (1980).

P.G. Walsh, *Livy: His Historical Aims and Methods* (1961).

Alan Watson, *The Law of the Ancient Romans* (1970).

Graham Webster, *The Roman Invasion of Britain* (1980).

M. Wheeler, *Roman Art and Architecture* (1964).

CHAPTER 7

Early Christianity
and the Fall of Rome

Time Line

63 B.C.	Pompey conquers Jerusalem
4 B.C.	Death of Herod
c. A.D. 30	Crucifixion of Jesus Christ
c. A.D. 48	Conversion of Paul
A.D. 64	First persecutions of Christians under Nero
A.D. 66–70	Jewish War
A.D. 135	Jews expelled from Judea

A.D. 250	Emperor Decius begins systematic persecution of Christians
A.D. 303	Diocletian's edicts against Christians
A.D. 311	Christianity legalized in Roman Empire
A.D. 313	Constantine's Edict of Milan reaffirms tolerance of Christianity
c. A.D. 320	Pachomius organizes first true monastic community
A.D. 325	Council of Nicaea convoked by Constantine
c. A.D. 370	Basil creates monastic rules
A.D. 374	Ambrose chosen Bishop of Milan
A.D. 376	Visigoths enter Empire
A.D. 378	Visigothic victory over Roman legions at Battle of Adrianople
A.D. 381	Emperor Theodosius I convenes second ecumenical council that reaffirms Nicene Creed
A.D. 394	Christianity declared official religion of Empire
A.D. 395	Augustine becomes Bishop of Hippo
A.D. 397	Augustine's *Confessions*
A.D. 410	Visigoths sack Rome
A.D. 453	Death of Attila the Hun
A.D. 455	Vandals sack Rome
A.D. 476	Fall of Western Roman Empire
A.D. 493–554	Ostrogoths rule Italy
A.D. 529	Benedict establishes monastery at Monte Cassino and sets down Benedictine Rule

Christianity evolved within the confines of Roman civilization, and its founder, Jesus, was born during the long and glorious reign of Augustus at a time when Rome led the Western world. Four hundred years later the Empire seemed on the verge of collapse, its defenses overwhelmed by barbarian invaders, while the small sect based on the life and teachings of Jesus Christ had attained the status of a world religion. Rome's eventual fall and Christianity's tremendous success were in many ways interconnected. Christianity filled a void left by the disintegration of Rome's political structure in the West, and for centuries after the fall of Rome in A.D. 476 it provided the greatest force for unity in an otherwise disordered world. Powers once exercised by imperial authorities gradually accrued to the new religious leaders. Christianity absorbed many elements from the Romans: their language, law, administrative hierarchy, and much of their culture. Pagan Europe was converted to Christianity and the heritage of classical civilization was kept alive through the agency of the Church.

The Background to Christianity

Pagan Religions under the Empire

At the time Christianity emerged, the religious climate in Rome allowed the populace a variety of sects and practices. Rome's official religion required simply that people revere the emperor and perform certain rituals in honor of the traditional Roman gods. Beyond this, Romans were free to worship any number of gods, as long as their religious practices did not prove conducive to political opposition or moral depravity. Within the Empire it was standard practice for Celtic, Germanic, and other peoples to incorporate or merge local gods with traditional Roman deities for common worship. This blending of gods, known as Syncretism, illustrates the highly flexible and tolerant nature of Roman beliefs.

Eastern Cults

Since Rome's state religion was more patriotic than spiritual, it offered little solace to those who suffered hardships or sought a more emotionally fulfilling religious experience. As a result, the introduction of numerous Oriental mystery cults in the late Republic proved very popular, and many gained a widespread following. The most important of these were the cults of Isis from Egypt, Cybele from Anatolia, and Mithras from Persia. All three promised personal immortality for initiants through a savior god. Each possessed elaborate ceremonies and rituals. The cult of Mithras, the god of light in the Zoroastrian religion, who mediated between the remote, supreme god Ahura-Mazda and humanity, had the widest following. It required that initiants undergo demanding tests at each of the seven grades of initiation before their souls were conducted to heaven. Since Mithras possessed an invincible, masculine nature and the cult was closed to women, it appealed strongly to Rome's legions. Many soldier-emperors of the third century A.D. adhered to Mithraism.

Christianity's Unique Attributes

Christianity's competition with these rival cults was stiff and by no means was the outcome certain until well into the fourth century. In achieving its ultimate victory, Christianity enjoyed the advantage that it shared many attributes with the other great mystery religions. All had universal appeal, offered hope for salvation, and even partook of similar rites. For example, the sacrament of baptism appears in the cults of Cybele and Mithras. The latter also held sacred banquets akin to the Christian Eucharist. These affinities and the ability to absorb or to adapt actually worked to the advantage of Christianity. By familiarizing the Romans with mystical ideas of sin and redemption, these competitive cults made it easier for Christianity's spiritual content to gain acceptance. Yet Christianity differed from Eastern mystery religions in many important respects. Christians advanced the claim that Christ gave his life to save all humanity, not merely those initiated into cultic secrets. Furthermore, the founder of Christianity, Jesus, was an historical figure whose message was one of love and faith. Christianity was exclusively monotheistic, whereas participation in one pagan cult did not preclude membership in others.

Judaism and Roman Palestine

The story of Jesus' life and teachings is inextricably intertwined with that of the Jews who had been subjected to foreign overlords since their return from the Babylonian Captivity in 538 B.C. As a Jew, Jesus conducted his entire ministry in Palestine. The story of Judaism in the period prior to his birth throws light on Christianity and deepens one's understanding of a period crucial to the future of the Jewish faith.

Jewish Factions

Despite its essential coherence, Judaism was rent with factionalism throughout this time. Class conflicts, opposition to foreign rule, and disagreements over religious beliefs all created unrest. In the second century B.C., when Palestine was ruled by the Seleucid monarchs of Syria, the issue of Hellenization sharply divided the Jews. Many, especially among the upper classes, were attracted to the Hellenistic culture, learned the Greek language, and imitated classical ways. Hellenistic Jews in Alexandria translated the Hebrew Bible into Greek, an important version known as the Septuagint. Conservative Jews regarded this act a profanation of the faith and urged strict adherence to the traditional laws.

Maccabean Revolt

In 168 B.C., Antiochus IV took advantage of this division among the Jews to suppress their faith. As king of Syria he forced them to worship Greek gods and set up an altar to Zeus in the Temple at Jerusalem. This action triggered a rebellion led by a Jewish priestly family, the Maccabees. Judas Maccabeus defeated the Seleucids and rededicated the Temple to Yahweh in 165 B.C. This important victory was subsequently celebrated as Hanukkah, the Jewish Feast of Lights. After his death, Judas's brothers continued the fight. In 142 B.C. the last of them, Simon, won recognition of his supreme authority in Jewish civil as well as religious affairs. The Maccabean Wars won not only religious freedom for the Jews but a great measure of political independence as well. The descendants of the Maccabees monopolized the office of high priest until 37 B.C. and governed much of Palestine until the advent of the Romans.

Herod the Great

Self-rule did not eliminate discord within the Jewish community. After a period of civil war among Jewish factions, the Romans stepped in. Pompey conquered Jerusalem in 63 B.C. and ended the conflict. Rome transformed Judea in southernmost Palestine into a client-kingdom eventually ruled by the Herod dynasty, whose most famous member was Herod the Great. Herod's father was a gentile from a neighboring territory who had been forcibly converted to Judaism. With the aid of Marc Antony, Herod gained the title King of Judea and reigned (37–4 B.C.) at about the time of Christ's birth. To guard against revolt, Herod curried the favor of the Jews by rebuilding the Temple and carefully observing Jewish law. Yet he also greatly promoted Hellenization within his realm and was much hated by the Jews for serving the Romans and brutally suppressing all dissent. (He is remembered for the Biblical story that, fearing the rise of a rival king, he ordered the massacre of male Jewish infants at the time of Christ's birth).

Sadducees and Pharisees

A decade after Herod's death in 4 B.C., Augustus heeded the appeal of the Jews and removed Herod's son from the throne. Judea was made a Roman province administered by a prefect. Nonetheless, factionalism and discontent did not end. Rather, the divisions within Jewish society penetrated even deeper. Two great parties stand out at this time. The Sadducees were drawn primarily from the Jewish upper classes and had close ties to the Temple priesthood. They adhered only to the Mosaic Law and not to the oral traditions that had grown up around it. They disclaimed belief in good and evil spirits, the coming of a Messiah, the resurrection of the dead, and the immortality of the soul. More open to Graeco-Roman influences, they were accused by their enemies of collaborating with the Romans. The other great sect of Jews, the Pharisees, was the more popular party and became the dominant force in Judaism after A.D. 70. They strove to keep traditional Jewish life uncontaminated by Hellenistic ways. Thus they insisted upon the faithful carrying out every detail of Jewish law. Although the New Testament refers to the Pharisees as self-satisfied hypocrites, they were in fact noted for their high ethical standards and erudition. They contributed substantially to the preservation of the Jewish faith.

Jewish Status in the Empire

The Jews occupied a unique status within the Empire and Roman emperors allowed them to practice their strict monotheistic religion. Jews were exempted from worshiping the emperor, although they did offer prayers to him in their synagogues. They were not required to render military service, and they were even permitted to omit from their coins the image of the emperor. They retained their own judicial system, the Sanhedrin, which regulated all aspects of Jewish life. Because of their special privileges and exclusive ways, the Jews were often envied and despised by other imperial subjects. On the local level, however, Roman officials were often less tolerant.

End of the Jewish State

Yet even these prerogatives failed to quench the desire of Jews for independence or calm their dread of persecution. In A.D. 66 the Jewish aristocracy undertook a major rebellion against the Romans and their supporters. Led by the Zealots, the Jewish War raged for four years. It ended in A.D. 70 when Titus, son of the Emperor Vespasian, captured Jerusalem. The Jewish historian Josephus, who sided with the Romans, described this decisive event in his eyewitness account, *The Jewish War*. The fall of Jerusalem marked the end of the ancient Jewish state. But the Hebrew religion held steadfastly to its guiding beliefs and endured.

The Essenes

Of the sects within Judaism, the ascetic and separatist Essenes hold the most interest for modern Christian scholars. Until recently these Jews were known only through references in the writings of Josephus, Philo, and Pliny the Elder. Much new light has been cast on the Essenes thanks to major archaeological discoveries since 1947. In a cave at Qumran above the northwest shore of the Dead Sea, shepherds accidentally uncovered in 1947 several jars that turned out to contain the oldest known fragments of the Hebrew Bible as well as texts by the Essenes. Among the manuscripts were copies of the Book of Isaiah that predated by 1,000 years the oldest previously known biblical text. Differing only slightly from the Book of Isaiah currently in use, these substantiate the essential accuracy of the later version. Numerous other caves in the area have subsequently yielded additional scrolls. Since these discoveries, archaeologists have unearthed the remains of the sect's monastery-like housing and cemetery at Qumran, which they have dated from the second century B.C. and which were destroyed in A.D. 68 by Roman legions during the Jewish War. Its members probably hid their texts during the war to preserve them from destruction.

Beliefs and Practices

These manuscripts, now called the Dead Sea Scrolls, reveal that the Qumran community shared several common aspects with the early Christians although predating them by at least a century. The Qumran community lived in monastic seclusion apart from the regular Temple worship at Jerusalem. They were founded by a Teacher of Righteousness who had suffered at the hands of a Wicked Priest. Like Christians they awaited the coming of the Messiah and the end of the earthly world. Their lives were marked by extreme piety and asceticism, and members were expected to remain celibate. They followed strict rules of ceremonial cleanliness as described in a scroll known as the *Manual of Discipline*.

Comparison with Christianity

Like the early Christians, the Essenes held property in common and maintained high ethical standards. They condemned slavery and prohibited the use of oaths. They engaged in ritual baths and sacred meals somewhat similar to the Christian rites of baptism and the Eucharist, although the former were repeated frequently by the Essenes and in performing the latter they did not allude to the body and blood of a savior.

Because of these common features, some scholars have contended that the Essenes strongly influenced the development of Christianity. Others have correctly noted that sharp differences exist, while most are now convinced that Jesus was probably not a member of the Essene sect. The Essenes restricted salvation to those few who adhered to the sect's demanding ways; by contrast Jesus held out the hope of immortality to all humanity. More importantly, the Essenes had no concept of resurrection, a key factor in convincing Christians of Christ's divinity. Their belief in a battle between the Sons of Light and the Sons of Darkness, while similar in tone to the Biblical Book of Revelations, expressed a dualism more akin to Eastern religions than to Christianity. Nonetheless, the thought and practices of the Essenes are part of the religious climate in which Christianity was nurtured.

Jesus Christ

Conception and Birth

The main outlines of Jesus' life as presented in the first four books of the New Testament are known the world over. The Gospels, or "good news," of Matthew, Mark, Luke, and John together tell of a child conceived by the Holy Spirit and born to Mary, wife of Joseph, in a manger in Bethlehem either around 4 B.C. or A.D. 6–7. (The date A.D. 1, arrived at in the sixth century when the system of reckoning from Christ's birth was developed, is based on an erroneous calculation.) By angelic direction, the parents named the infant Jesus, which means savior. He grew to manhood in Nazareth where Joseph worked as a carpenter.

Ministry

At about the age of thirty, Jesus was baptized by John the Baptist, an itinerant preacher, and soon thereafter commenced his brief ministry of spreading word of God's love and redemption, healing the sick, and performing miracles based on faith. Gathering around himself twelve apostles, Jesus disclosed to them that he was the Messiah and the Son of God and that he would die shortly but would rise again after three days. After teaching for three years throughout Galilee, the thirteen men went to Jerusalem, where large crowds greeted Jesus as the Messiah. There during the Feast of Passover the apostles partook of a meal, the Last Supper, during which Jesus told them to eat the bread, which was his body, and to drink the wine, which was his blood.

Trial and Crucifixion

Jesus' reformist preaching had made many enemies for him among the Jewish hierarchy. In addition, he disappointed those who had expected the Messiah to deliver them from Roman rule. His criticism of the Pharisees for adhering to the letter of the law while ignoring its spirit incurred their wrath, while his ousting of the money-changers from the Temple seemed a direct challenge to the leaders of the Jewish community. Thus they convinced one of his disciples, Judas Iscariot, to betray him. Jesus was arrested and condemned by the Sanhedrin for blasphemy. He was then brought before the Roman governor, Pontius Pilate, on the charge of treason for claiming to be "the King of the Jews." Refusing to come to his own defense, Jesus was deemed guilty and sentenced to be crucified as a common criminal.

Resurrection and Charge to Disciples

Three days after Jesus' death and burial, associates found his tomb empty. Shortly thereafter Jesus appeared before his disciples and commissioned them to preach repentance and forgiveness of sins in his name to all nations. The Resurrection confirmed their belief in the divinity of Christ, a name that means "The Anointed One," or Messiah, in Greek, and they set out to spread his teachings. After a brief period Jesus ascended into heaven.

Historical Evidence

Christians accept the Bible's account of Jesus as a matter of faith. For modern biblical scholars, however, the figure of an historical Jesus poses many intriguing problems. Virtually all the information about Jesus' life must be derived from the four gospels in the New Testament. In fact, non-Christian sources during the first century and a half of the Church's existence are so scanty and unreliable that they are virtually useless. The Gospel narratives are not strictly historical, since they fail to provide an accurate factual record of past events. They were not composed until approximately the last third of the first century A.D., but they did draw upon earlier sources. The Gospels also in some instances contradict each other.

Some scholars today explain these discrepancies and other disputed issues by asserting that the Gospels were composed in the Jewish tradition of *midrash* whereby scribes interpreted Old Testament texts to bring them into line with evolving thought and practice. According to this theory the authors of the Gospels reconstructed Jesus' life to conform with Old Testament prophecies and their belief that he was the Son of God. With the information now available, it is impossible to prove or disprove the events in the New Testament related to the life of Jesus. Their importance lies perhaps less in their historical accuracy than in the deep meaning they assumed for followers of Christ.

Teachings

In large measure Christianity owes its lasting appeal to the universality and timelessness of the teachings of its founder.

The Gospel Message

Jesus' message was a simple yet revolutionary one. His two great commandments were to love God totally and to love one's neighbor as oneself. Jesus widened the Hebrew Yahweh of the Old Testament into a God of fatherly love and forgiveness for all his children. God's compassion was made evident in that he sent his only Son to suffer for the sins of humanity and thus earn human redemption. Jesus taught that God is open to all the people—the poor, the weak, outcasts, prostitutes, all sinners. He called upon them to repent of their sins and lead lives of charity and faith in preparation for the day of final judgment.

The Sermon on the Mount

The essence of Jesus' teachings is found in the Sermon on the Mount as recorded in Matthew. In this moving homily Jesus exhorted his listeners to be humble, love their enemies, do good, give up worldly riches, and trust in God. Jesus conveyed wisdom in part by means of parables, simple stories drawn from everyday life to illustrate spiritual truths. In the famous parable of the mustard seed, for example, Christ likened the Kingdom of Heaven to a grain of mustard seed that is the smallest of all seeds but that grows into a luxuriant tree housing birds.

The Spread of Christianity

The First Christians

Shortly after Jesus' death and Resurrection his disciples took up their Teacher's charge to spread his Word. At first they had only a limited vision of what that mission entailed. As Jews they sought to convince fellow Jews that Jesus was the promised Messiah.

Jewish Christians

Sizable communities of Christian Jews grew up in Jerusalem and throughout Judea and Galilee. These first Christians remained faithful to their Jewish heritage. They continued to follow Mosaic Law, avoiding impure meat and circumcizing their sons. According to the Bible the first Christians lived communally and shared their possessions with one another.

Gentile Converts

As long as Christianity remained a sect within Judaism its potential as a great spiritual movement was severely hampered. A few disciples realized this and at some time during the first decades they began preaching to non-Jews as well. The Bible credits the apostle Peter with being the first to baptize gentiles after receiving a sign from Heaven.

The Compromise on Gentiles

The issue of gentile Christianity posed a serious problem in the early Church. Many Christian Jews insisted that gentiles be circumcised and observe Jewish law in order to be considered Christians. Others argued that Christianity must be universal. Finally a compromise was reached whereby gentile converts were exempted from circumcision and the provisions of the Mosaic Law on condition that they abstain from unchastity and from eating the meat of any sacrificial animal.

Significance of Gentile Inclusion

The significance of this compromise in terms of the history of the early Church cannot be overestimated. Without broadening its audience beyond the Jewish community, Christianity would most likely have suffered a fate similar to that of the Essenes. The Christian Jews never succeeded in winning over the Jewish authorities or the majority of their fellow Jews. With the fall of Jerusalem in A.D. 70 and the near exclusion of Jews from all of Judea in A.D. 135 after a final rebellion, Judaeo-Christianity ceased being an important force within the Church. By this time Christian missionaries had carried their faith throughout the Mediterranean world and founded important churches at Damascus, Antioch, Alexandria, and above all, Rome.

Paul's Mission to the Gentiles

The individual most responsible for bringing Christ's teachings to the Gentiles and thus establishing Christianity as a world religion was a Jew from Tarsus named Saul. Earlier in his life, Saul had worked actively to suppress the fledgling Christian movement. Then one day around the year 48, on the road to Damascus he underwent a mystical conversion. Thereafter Saul, now referred to by his Greek name Paul, proselytized zealously on behalf of his newfound faith. During his long missionary travels he established Christian congregations in Syria, Asia Minor, Greece, and Macedonia. For this reason, he is known as a "Father of the Christian Church." He journeyed also to Rome where tradition holds that he was martyred along with the apostle Peter during the reign of Nero.

In retrospect at least Paul's position in early Christianity stands above even that of the original apostles. Although he had not personally known Christ, Paul played the decisive role in disseminating Christianity to the non-Jewish world. He successfully championed the right of Gentile converts to be considered Christians without observing Jewish practices. Through his travels and letters he kept in close touch with the Christian communities he had founded, supporting them in their work and advising and disciplining them on matters of faith and conduct. The Pauline Epistles, thirteen letters to various local churches, form a substantial part of the New Testament. Paul was well educated, knew Greek, and admired classical learning. In his evangelizing he developed Christian theology in a way that would appeal to the Graeco-Roman world and thus facilitated its conversion. He formulated the idea of the Church as one holy, universal, and apostolic body in which all individuals are joined through baptism and belief in Christ.

Persecution and Acceptance

The Romans generally tolerated all religions provided they manifested loyalty to the Empire. But the early Christians' refusal to recognize pagan gods, perform rites of sacrifice to the emperor, and serve in the army appeared tantamount to political treason in Roman eyes. Christianity never received the special dispensations that Roman officials accorded to Judaism. All Christians were suspect and liable to be blamed for any catastrophe that befell the Empire. Many Romans even believed that the new sect practiced incest and cannibalism at nocturnal meetings.

Early Persecutions

Although the early Christians were often reviled and despised, the first general persecution against them arose from special conditions of the moment rather than from fixed policy. In casting about for a scapegoat to take the blame off of himself for setting Rome aflame in the year 64, Nero turned to the new sect. Christians had early shown themselves willing to die bravely for their faith. The first Christian martyr, Stephen, was stoned to death near Jerusalem after he was falsely accused of blasphemy. Peter and Paul were reportedly martyred under Nero. Nonetheless, until the third century A.D. persecutions were never continuous and usually resulted from the initiative of a local governor rather than from an imperial directive to extirpate the offending sect entirely.

Growth of Christian Communities

In part because of the limited and sporadic nature of these early persecutions and most emperors' unwillingness to take the new religion seriously, Christianity was able to become firmly rooted within imperial society and to spread rapidly throughout the Empire. Large Christian communities grew up in Syria, Asia Minor, and Greece during the first century A.D. By the end of the next century, Christianity flourished in Italy and Egypt as well and missionaries began taking the Gospel to Gaul, Spain, and Britain. At the same time, Christianity expanded socially from a movement drawn primarily from the urban poor and disaffected to one that had penetrated the army, upper ranks of Roman society, and even the imperial household. By the time of Constantine, scholars estimate that one-tenth of the Empire's population had been converted to the new faith.

Systematic Persecutions

Christianity's swift growth and the decaying conditions within the Empire during the third century led to a more concentrated effort to suppress the offending religion. The first systematic, empire-wide persecution was organized by the Emperor Decius in A.D. 250. Many Christians were arrested and many bishops (including the Bishop of Rome) and lay people lost their lives. Later in the same decade the Emperor Valerian instituted another persecution, but his successor, Gallienus, allowed Christians freedom of worship in A.D. 260. The last and most relentless persecution occurred during the reign of Diocletian. Beginning in A.D. 303, Diocletian issued a series of edicts that called for the destruction of all churches and confiscation of church property including all Bibles, liturgical matter, and holy objects. Christians were forbidden to worship together. In A.D. 304 all inhabitants of the Empire were ordered to sacrifice to the gods or face death. The "Great Persecution" raged viciously in the East for ten years while the West escaped its full brunt.

Toleration

How many Christians were killed or renounced their faith as a result of these persecutions is a question that admits of no precise answer. Probably only a few thousand were martyred, but among them were some of Christendom's most prominent members. What is certain is that the persecutions failed dismally in their purpose. Rather than wiping out Christianity, they served to strengthen it. In recognition of this Diocletian's successors ended the persecutions and Galerius legalized Christianity in A.D. 311. Two years later, Constantine's Edict of Milan reaffirmed this law. Christians were free to worship publicly, build churches, and proselytize. Church property confiscated during the persecution of Diocletian was returned. In A.D. 321 the Church received the right to inherit property, and thus began its accumulation of wealth.

Establishment

While Constantine's motives are open to question, the results of his policy of favoritism are clear. With the exception of the emperor who ruled from A.D. 361 to 363 (Julian the Apostate), those from Constantine onward embraced Christianity. In A.D. 394, Theodosius I made it the official religion of the empire. Sacrifices to pagan gods were outlawed and their temples closed. By the end of the fourth century A.D. Christianity had replaced its rivals as the sole religion for the empire's inhabitants.

The Early Church

Doctrines

Christianity developed a body of written doctrine, the New Testament, which incorporated its basic tenets and practices and prevented the accretion of spurious beliefs. A major task for early Christian leaders was to decide which writings about Christ they deemed to be divinely inspired and thus worthy of inclusion in the official Christian canon of sacred texts. By the fifth century A.D., the Church had reached agreement, according that status to twenty-seven canonical books of the New Testament. Those writings that were excluded are known as the Apocrypha.

Sacraments

The early Christians believed that Jesus had instituted certain ritual acts, which they called sacraments, that served as visible signs of God's invisible grace and that gave outward expression to their faith. While the later Roman Catholic Church recognized seven sacraments as means through which a Christian received grace, the early Church consistently practiced only two, baptism and the Eucharist. During the Reformation in the sixteenth century, Protestant churches rejected the sacramental nature of all but these two rites.

Baptism

Baptism or purification by water was an ancient custom. The Christians invested it with new meaning in light of Jesus' own baptism. New converts were baptized by being immersed in a river, stream, or specially designed baptistery or by having water sprinkled on their heads. This ceremony was normally performed by a member of the clergy, who invoked the blessing of the Holy Trinity: the Father, the Son, and the Holy Ghost. Baptism was perceived to cleanse away one's sins by God's grace, and it made the recipient a Christian.

The Eucharist

At the heart of Christian worship is the sacrament of the Eucharist. Its name derives from the Greek word *eucharistos* ("grateful"). The Eucharist is a ritual repetition of Jesus' last supper with his apostles, at which he gave them bread, saying: "Take, eat; this is my body" and wine, saying: "Drink of it, all of you; for this is my blood of the covenant, which is poured out for many for the forgiveness of sins." (Matthew 26:26–28, Revised Standard Version.) In later centuries Christians disagreed as to whether to take these words literally or symbolically. It is clear, however, that the Eucharist was of supreme significance to the early Church.

The Clergy

The first Christian churches were founded by itinerant missionaries and consisted of informal, often secret, gatherings of Christians. Periodically Christian prophets and teachers who traveled from city to city would arrive to preach and confer on problems of dogma and conduct. Eventually the local churches came to have their own resident clergy. At first Christians did not draw a sharp line between the clergy and the laity, or body of worshipers. The important office of deacon was often filled by a layman and in many cases church government and the election of officers were entirely in the hands of the congregation.

Priests and Bishops

As the churches grew in membership the tasks of providing order and doctrinal direction, conducting services, and overseeing church business were assumed more and more by church officials able to devote full time to them. These first clergymen were known as bishops (from the Greek *episkopos* meaning "overseer") and presbyters or priests (from the Greek *presbyteros* meaning "elder"). In the beginning their functions were essentially identical and both terms were often used to refer to the same person. Gradually, however, a distinction arose. Bishops accrued more and more authority to themselves so that by the second century A.D. they were recognized as superior to the priests.

Over the centuries the Church evolved an organization that was hierarchical in nature and based on the preexistent administrative units of the Roman Empire. This structuring made for strong and efficient governance and enabled the Church to absorb and maintain discipline over the masses of new converts who flocked to Christianity. At its lowest level stood the specially trained and ordained priest who was in charge of an individual church and its parish. All of the churches in an area were absorbed into a diocese headed by a bishop whose seat of office was in a Roman *civitas*. Bishops assumed a central role in the administrative hierarchy and their functions were myriad. These included ordaining and supervising priests, judging matters of discipline and ethics, providing charitable relief, and overseeing finances. Councils of bishops met frequently to clarify dogma. With the collapse of the Empire, bishops were forced to exercise numerous secular powers as well, and they handled many legal affairs in their own courts.

Archbishops and Patriarchs

During the third century the bishops of the larger cities within the Empire, including the provincial capitals, acquired an exalted status among their fellow bishops. They came to be referred to as archbishops or metropolitans. They acted as heads of administrative units called provinces that encompassed all the bishoprics within that territory. Finally, by the fourth century the bishops of the greatest cities within the Empire: Rome, Alexandria, Antioch, Constantinople, and somewhat later, Jerusalem, were especially honored with the title of patriarch owing to the antiquity or special location of their dioceses. Such an honor carried no additional power. This was to change in the mid-fifth century when the Bishop of Rome successfully acquired state sanction from Valentinian III to support his assumption of leadership over the Church. Based on the claims that Christ made Peter head of the Church and that Peter founded the diocese of Rome, the Bishop of Rome became the head of the Church in the Western Empire. The Petrine doctrine was rejected outright by the patriarch of Constantinople and the bishops in the Eastern Empire. By the seventh century, however, the Bishop of Rome's position as the leader of the Roman Catholic Church was firmly established. The term "pope" (from *papa* meaning "father") was now used exclusively by him.

Early Heresies

The survival of the Church in its early centuries was jeopardized not only by persecutions from without but by schisms within. Even while Paul was alive some Christians began interpreting Christianity in ways at odds with the apostolic faith. Once the personal authority of the apostles ended, the threat posed by rival ideas increased greatly. If the Church was to remain united and continue to expand, it was essential that matters of doctrine be clearly defined, beliefs and practices made uniform, and disputes resolved. Thus the Church took a strong stance against these variant views and branded them as heresy.

Gnosticism

The first serious challenge to Christian orthodoxy came from Christian Gnosticism. The numerous sects known as Gnostics (from the Greek *gnosis* meaning "knowledge") believed that they alone possessed secret knowledge about the origin of evil and how to become free of it. In contrast to the account in *Genesis*, they held that the natural world had been created not by the supreme God but by an evil creator god. Most Gnostic sects regarded Jesus as the Redeemer who enlightened the elect about their divine nature. After death their souls would ascend to the higher heavenly sphere with the aid of magic formulae.

Gnostics rejected the central Christian belief in the union of divinity and humanity in Christ because in their view Christ could only be pure spirit uncontaminated by evil. Since the material world was wholly evil they acknowledged no responsibility toward it. This led to extreme asceticism on the part of most sects and extreme licentiousness among others. Several of the early Church Fathers strongly refuted these dualistic views.

Manichaeism

In the third century, the Persian Mani founded a widely popular religion, Manichaeism, which took up the Gnostics' belief in the radical separation of matter and spirit. Manichaeism was also vigorously condemned by the Church.

Donatism

Another heresy that gravely troubled the early Church arose from the persecutions under Diocletian. The emperor had demanded that all sacred books and relics be surrendered to the state. Those priests who complied, the *traditores,* were censured by many within the Church but resumed their clerical duties once religious freedom was declared. The Donatists, led by Donatus, Bishop of Carthage, insisted that the *traditores* had forfeited their right to administer valid sacraments and thus began rebaptizing those who doubted the authenticity of their baptism. Donatism raised the important question whether or not the personal character of a priest influenced the operation of sacramental grace. The Council at Arles, summoned by Constantine in A.D. 314, concluded that the validity of the sacraments was independent of its priestly administrator. Donatism continued to flourish for another century in North Africa where it split the church into two rival factions.

Arianism

Perhaps the most serious challenge to orthodox belief involved the nature of Christ. Arius (A.D. c. 256–336), a presbyter of Alexandria, put forth the notion that since Jesus was created by God, he could not be equal or coeternal with him as Christian doctrine maintained. Thus the doctrine of the Trinity was cast into doubt. Arius won a large following, especially in Greece, where the church became embroiled in a debate over whether Christ was of the same substance as God or rather of a similar substance. So divisive was this issue that Emperor Constantine was forced to intervene. In A.D. 325 he convoked at Nicaea in

Asia Minor the Church's first ecumenical council, so-called because of the large number of bishops who attended although they were almost all from the East. The Council of Nicaea determined against Arius and adopted a creed that affirmed a godhead of three parts, each coeternal and of identical substance with the others. Almost all Christian churches still adhere to the statement of belief expressed in the Nicene Creed. Despite condemnation, Arianism did not die out. Constantine's successors on the throne embraced it and numerous councils met to deal with the conflict. Finally, in A.D. 381, the Emperor Theodosius I convened the second ecumenical council at Constantinople, which reaffirmed the Nicene Creed. Thereafter Arianism slowly lost its hold except among the Germanic Goths. One of the significant legacies of the Arian heresy was the increased antagonism it left between the Latin West and the Greek East.

Monasticism

Christianity's victory as the dominant religion of the Empire did not end its problems. A major question was whether the Church could remain spiritually pure and true to the teachings of Jesus as it occupied a position of wealth, status, and influence in the secular world. Many who were dissatisfied with these secular developments felt a need to retreat from worldly preoccupations and to live a life of severe self-denial in order to prepare themselves for the life to come.

The Hermits

From the beginning Christianity had exhibited a strong strain of asceticism. A number of Christians in the Church renounced marriage and worldly goods and devoted themselves instead to prayer and charitable endeavors. In the East it became common by the third century for ascetics to withdraw from civilization and lead a life of solitude and deprivation in the desert. These hermits, who sought to purify their souls by fasting, meditation, and self-flagellation, were held in great respect by ordinary Christians. One such hermit from Syria, Symeon the Stylite, actually confined himself to a small, exposed platform on top of a sixty-foot column for more than thirty years. Such extremes of ascetic behavior, resulting in the notion of an elite of self-mortifiers, were potentially as damaging to the Christian movement as was excessive worldliness.

Development of Monastic Communities

In contrast to the individualism of these early hermits, a new form of communal ascetic life known as monasticism emerged during the fourth century. The Egyptian hermit Anthony is often called the father of monasticism because he gathered a group of hermits who worshiped with him and ate communally. Around A.D. 320 Pachomius, another Egyptian, organized the first truly monastic community. The first rules for these early monastic communities were promulgated by Basil (c. A.D. 330–379), Bishop of Neo-Caesarea in Asia Minor, and these served as the standard in Eastern monasteries. Basil rejected the individualism and self-inflicted suffering of early eremetical monasticism. Instead he stressed the monk's service to society. Although monks lived within a community detached from worldly temptations, they were required to perform charitable works such as founding hospitals, schools, and orphanages, and to undertake manual labor. Basil's rules insisted upon strict obedience to one's superior as well as poverty and celibacy.

The Benedictine Rule

An Italian monk, Benedict of Nursia, accomplished for Western monasticism what Basil had done for the East. Around A.D. 529 Benedict established a great monastery at Monte Cassino in southern Italy and wrote the set of rules under which its monks would live. The routine was one of simplicity, discipline, and frugality experienced in common. The Benedictine Rule prescribed vows of poverty, chastity, and obedience to the head of the monastery, known as the abbot. Within the abbey, life was strictly ordered. During the Middle Ages, Benedictine monks laboring as scribes were responsible for preserving much of the literature of antiquity. Benedictine abbeys became centers of intellectual life and exerted a powerful influence on the development of modern Western culture. The Rule of Saint Benedict has been the primary rule of Western monasticism. Monks who lived under the rule are known as the regular clergy (from the Latin *regula* for "rule") as distinct from the secular clergy, who administer the sacraments and tend to the laity.

The Church Fathers

The process of interpreting Jesus' teachings commenced with the apostles and still continues. The work of the great Christian writers in the first through the sixth centuries A.D., particularly their reflections and commentaries upon theological questions, substantially augmented Christian theology. They are referred to as the Fathers of the Church and their writings are generally accepted as authoritative interpretations of the Christian tradition. Collectively they gave Christianity its philosophical cogency. At first theologians from the Greek East took the lead in explicating points of faith and combating heresy. Toward the end of the fourth century, however, there appeared three outstanding Church Fathers in the Latin West: Ambrose, Jerome, and Augustine.

St. Ambrose

The church statesman Ambrose (A.D. 340?–397) began his career in the Roman civil service. As governor of Liguria and Aemilia headquartered in Milan, his popularity was such that he was chosen bishop of the city in A.D. 374, even though he was not yet a baptized Christian. Ambrose was a powerful preacher, a significant opponent of Arianism, and the author of some of the Church's earliest hymns. One of his most important contributions was as spiritual adviser on religious matters to several Western emperors. By resisting imperial actions deemed detrimental to the Church and Christian ethics, he helped establish the Church's supremacy over secular powers in matters of faith and morals.

St. Jerome

In Jerome (A.D. c. 347–420?) the Western Church possessed one of its greatest biblical scholars and the most erudite and cultivated man of his age. Born in Dalmatia, Jerome was well educated in classical studies in Rome but gave them up to devote himself instead to scriptural exegeses. His biblical commentaries were so highly praised that Pope Damascus commissioned him to produce a new Latin text of the Bible. Drawing upon his knowledge of Hebrew and Greek, Jerome translated the Bible into Latin in a version known as the Vulgate, which is still used in the Roman Catholic Church today. Jerome's translation aided immensely in the diffusion of Christianity throughout the Latin-speaking West and its admirable literary style both improved the quality of Church Latin and left its mark on the developing vernacular literature of the medieval West.

Augustine

The greatest of the Church Fathers was Augustine of Hippo (A.D. 354–430). His brilliant theological writings continue to play a major part in the religious thought of the West. In addition, his *Confessions* (A.D. 397) is the first and arguably the finest spiritual autobiography ever composed.

Early Life

Augustine was born in a small town in North Africa to parents of lower middle class origins. His pious mother raised him a Christian but while a university student at Carthage he abandoned the faith and turned instead to riotous living. As was the custom, he took a concubine who bore him a son. Writing of all this later in his *Confessions*, Augustine repented of his profligate ways.

Departure from and Return to Christianity

At Carthage, Augustine became thoroughly acquainted with Latin literature and fell under the spell of Cicero's seductive prose. Inspired by the latter, the young Augustine proceeded in his quest for truth to reexamine Christianity. He was repelled, however, by what he considered the Bible's irrational tales and crude style in comparison to the classics. Thus he gravitated to Manichaeism. For nine years while he taught classical rhetoric in Carthage and Rome, Augustine remained a Manichee but gradually disillusionment set in. The turning point came in A.D. 384, when he accepted a post as professor of rhetoric in Milan. There he came under the influence of Ambrose, whose eloquent sermons demonstrated to him that Christianity could appeal to the intellect.

For several years Augustine immersed himself in the study of Neoplatonist philosophy. Based on Plato's writings, Neoplatonism seeks the mystical union of the soul with the divine One. This brought him ever closer to Christianity. Finally after a period of intense soul-searching and a mystical experience of conversion, he was baptized by Ambrose on Easter in A.D. 387. A year later he returned to North Africa where he lived at first with friends in monastic retirement.

Bishop of Hippo

In A.D. 391 the Christians at Hippo, a city in modern Algeria, persuaded Augustine against his will to become their priest. Four years later he was named Bishop of Hippo, a position he retained for the rest of his life. As bishop, Augustine became a great defender of the faith. In sermons and scores of books he explained God's message as revealed in the Scriptures and polemicized against various heresies. In the course of these and other writings, he laid the groundwork for much of Christian theology.

The Pelagian Heresy

Toward the end of his life, Augustine became involved in a major theological controversy with a British monk, Pelagius. Pelagians believed that humans could attain salvation on the basis of their own actions. Augustine interpreted Pelagius's teaching as a challenge to God's absolute authority and to the Church's role in dispensing sacramental grace. Augustine's belief in original sin and the necessity of divine grace for salvation triumphed over the Pelagians' attempt to invest humans with freedom of choice in the moral and spiritual realms. Although the Roman Catholic Church did not accept Augustine's extreme statements on grace and predestination, more than a millennium later, during the Reformation, Calvin took them up again as the basis of his revised theology.

The City of God

Augustine lived in an age of profound social and political unrest, and many of his writings are colored by this atmosphere of anxiety. One of his best-known works, *The City of God*, was begun as a response to those pagans who blamed Christianity for the sack of Rome by the Visigoths in A.D. 410. Augustine's real concern was to contrast the ephemeral "earthly city" with the eternal "City of God." The "City of God" includes all those from Abel until the end of time who receive grace, love God, and are saved. The "earthly city," on the other hand is composed of the vast majority of people of all eras who place themselves and the material world above God. In this life, however, it is impossible to distinguish between the two. Both State and Church include both kinds of people. Christians must obey the State unless its demands are contrary to their faith. But on earth no state is safe from disaster or abides forever. At the Last Judgment citizens of the heavenly city will gain eternal life while those of the earthly city will be damned for eternity.

Underlying Augustine's description of the two cities was a new, uniquely Christian philosophy of history. Whereas classical writers often depicted history as cyclical, Augustine held that the world had a beginning, the Creation, and will have an end, the Last Judgment. Between these two points history moves in a linear progression according to God's plan. History's real significance thus resides in the playing out of humanity's sin and redemption through Christ.

The Dissolution of the Roman Empire in the West

Christianity's triumph coincided with the decline and fall of the Western Roman Empire. The century and a half following Constantine's death was a period of almost unremitting disaster for the Empire. Beginning in the last quarter of the fourth century, a great movement of barbarian peoples took place, which would lead to the eventual collapse of Rome's political and economic organization in the West.

The Germans

The barbarian invaders who successfully breached imperial frontiers and occupied Roman lands at this time were predominantly of Germanic descent. An ancient ethnic group, the Germans were originally settled along the shores of the Baltic and North Seas in what is now northern Germany, Denmark, and southern Sweden. At some point early in their history they began to migrate southward as far as the

Rhine and Danube Rivers and the Black Sea in search of richer lands and new sources of plunder. Like the Romans, their language was Indo-European but they lacked the facility to write it. The highest political unit of the Germans was the tribe. Some of the most note-worthy tribes were the Visigoths, Ostrogoths, Vandals, Burgundians, Franks, Alemanni, Angles, Saxons, Jutes, and Lombards.

Kinship Groups

All of the Germanic tribes exhibited certain common charac-teristics. German society was organized according to kindreds, or groups of families related by blood. The chief concern of these kinship groups was to protect their kinsmen and avenge injuries by inflicting the same or even greater punishment upon any of the guilty individual's kin. The endless feuding that arose from this duty of revenge was so disruptive that there gradually evolved a peaceful means of settling disputes through monetary compensation. Wronged kindred agreed to accept a fixed sum of money in lieu of taking bodily revenge. The value of a person's life, his *wergeld,* was set according to his rank in society and the nature of his injuries. Germanic custom also provided for the accused to stand trial. To determine guilt or innocence the accused would call upon the testimony of twelve "oath-helpers" who would swear to his upright character, or he could submit to trial by combat or trial by ordeal. In the latter the accused was required to plunge his hand into boiling water or walk barefoot with his eyes covered over an area strewn with red-hot metals. If he escaped serious injury, his innocence was established.

The Comitatus

Another characteristic German social institution was the *comitatus* or band of followers that gathered around powerful warrior chiefs. These chieftains were usually wealthy lords whose reputation for valor in battle attracted to them a group of young men eager for war. In exchange for the fighting services and personal loyalty of his followers the chieftain took care of their material needs, led them into combat, and shared the plunder with them. So close was the tie between a warrior and his chief that if the latter were slain, all his men joined him in death on the battlefield.

Political Structure

The institution of kingship was not widespread among the Germans at first. With the invasions, however, most tribes elected kings in order to provide for a unified military command. Their functions were essentially military and religious. All important decisions were taken in conjunction with an assembly of the freemen of the tribe. These tribal assemblies injected an element of democracy into German political life and were one of its leading features.

Contacts with Rome

The barbarian world had been pressing in on Rome for centuries. Under the Republic, Marius and Julius Caesar both contended successfully with Germanic foes. Contact between the Romans and the Germans was not limited to warfare. The two peoples carried on a small but significant trade, which exposed the barbarians to the attractions of civilized life. Many Germans first entered the Empire as slaves or prisoners of war. Tacitus wrote admiringly of their courage and virility. Most Germanic tribes (except the Franks) converted first to Arianism owing to the missionary work of Ulfilas.

Peaceful Penetration of Empire

Relations between the Germans and Romans were relatively peaceful throughout the *Pax Romana,* although skirmishes continued to occur beyond the Rhine-Danube frontier. With the reign of Marcus Aurelius, however, Germanic tribes began again to encroach upon imperial borders. They continued to batter Rome's defenses throughout the turbulent third century. At this time Rome adopted a policy whereby certain Germanic tribes were invited to inhabit unoccupied imperial lands usually near the frontiers in order to keep the soil in cultivation and to act as a buffer against further barbarian inroads. These Germanic settlers within the Empire were called *foederati,* or allies. Other individual Germans labored on the great landed estates of wealthy Romans. Rome's emperors came to rely increasingly upon Germans to serve in the imperial army until by the end of the fourth century the Roman legions were composed almost entirely of barbarian mercenaries. Even Rome's generals were now most often of barbarian ancestry. Thus the Germans infiltrated the empire peacefully in various

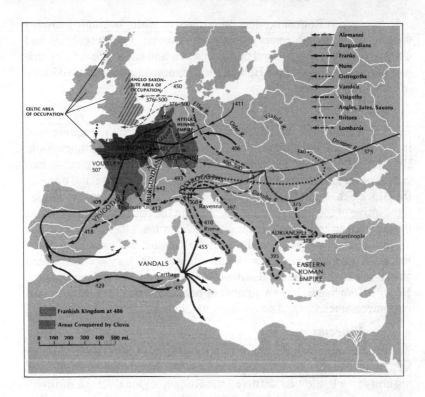

Barbarian Invasions

ways long before the devastating invasions that brought down the
political superstructure in the West.

Barbarian Invasions

Various factors drew the Germans into conflict with the mighty
Empire. Lust for booty and the allure of a richer civilization exerted a
powerful stimulus as did the Germans' love of adventure and combat.
Perhaps most important, the seminomadic Germans were constantly
seeking new, fertile lands because their primitive agricultural methods
made it difficult for them to support their expanding population. The
answer to why after centuries of intermittent combat the Germans were

able to overrun Roman borders on a massive scale, beginning toward the end of the fourth century, lies both in external contingencies and internal weaknesses. Around this time a new and explosive factor came into play in the shape of the Huns, a ruthless nomadic people most likely of Mongolian descent.

The Huns

For reasons still ill-defined, the Huns abandoned their native land in Central Asia and began migrating swiftly westward on horseback. By A.D. 372 they had reached the Volga River where they came into contact with the Germanic Goths who inhabited the steppeland north of the Black Sea. First the Alans and then the Ostrogoths, or East Goths, fell captive to the terrifying hordes. Next in the path of destruction was the western tribe of the Goths, or the Visigoths. Panic-stricken, the Visigoths fled westward to the Danube frontier and appealed to the Eastern Emperor, Valens, for shelter. In A.D. 376 they were admitted en masse into the empire and settled along the south bank of the Danube. Never before had so large a number of barbarians been allowed to cross into imperial territory. The decision would have grave consequences.

The Visigoths

Poor treatment at the hands of corrupt Roman officials incited the Visigoths to rebel. At Adrianople in A.D. 378 they defeated Valens and his army in a battle that shattered the Roman legions' image of invincibility and demonstrated the superiority of cavalry over infantry forces. The Romans, with their army fatally weakened, were forced to accept a Visigoth settlement within the empire and to cede the defense of the Danube to them. The floodgates were now open. For a few years during the reign of Theodosius I, the Visigoths lived peacefully, but after his death in A.D. 395 they raided throughout the Balkans and Greece and then turned on Italy. Led by their chief Alaric they captured the city of Rome in A.D. 410. More than the conventional fall of the Western Roman Empire in A.D. 476, this event sent shock waves throughout the ancient world. In Bethlehem, Jerome wrote that "the whole world perished in one city." Alaric's death shortly thereafter saved Italy from further devastation. The Visigoths moved on to southern Gaul as allies of the Romans and eventually into Spain, where they ruled until A.D. 711.

The Vandals

The Goths were not the only barbarians to pierce imperial defenses around the turn of the fourth century. On the last night of the year A.D. 406, the Rhine froze over and scores of Vandals, Alans, and Suevi rushed into Gaul. The Rhine frontier was irreparably breached. After three years of pillaging Gaul, the Vandals migrated into Spain, where they remained until A.D. 429 when at the request of the Roman governor of North Africa they crossed over into Africa. Within a decade of fighting they had carved out a powerful kingdom for themselves in North Africa. Taking up piracy, the Vandals launched frequent raids against Italy and Sicily and further dislocated the already sagging Mediterranean trade. In A.D. 455 Rome fell once more into barbarian hands. The Vandals sacked the city and carried away many of its treasures.

Invasions of Britain and Gaul

Under repeated barbarian attacks the Empire began to crumble. Territorial losses mounted. Crises elsewhere necessitated the withdrawal of all of Rome's legions from Britain by A.D. 407. In a short time the Angles, Saxons, and Jutes from what are now Denmark and northern Germany overran the island. Other Germanic tribes such as the Franks, Burgundians, and Alemanni occupied parts of Gaul although the Romans maintained better control there for a while. Wherever they settled within the empire, the various barbarian tribes established their own independent kingdoms. Those of the Franks in Gaul and the Angles and Saxons in England were to last the longest and play a tremendous part in the development of their respective countries.

Attila the Hun

By the mid-fifth century an even greater threat to the Empire loomed. The predatory Huns under Attila, "the Scourge of God," swarmed into Gaul in A.D. 451. They were defeated there by a Roman army composed almost entirely of Germanic troops. A year later the Huns invaded Italy. Rome escaped destruction partly through the intercession of Pope Leo I, who appealed to the barbarians to spare the city. Attila was ill prepared to lay siege and accepted a huge ransom instead. With the death of Attila in A.D. 453, the threat subsided and many of the Huns eventually returned to Asia.

End of the Imperial Succession

Throughout the perilous fifth century, imperial leadership was at a low ebb. Almost without exception Rome's last emperors in the West were nullities. Real power resided with the Master of the Soldiers who commanded the army. Toward the end of the Empire, when Germanic mercenaries had become indispensable to Rome's defense, there were eight such Masters all of whom were barbarians. In A.D. 476 Odovacar, king of some of the Germanic tribes in the service of Rome, decided to put an end to the fiction of imperial control in the West by deposing the boy-emperor, Romulus Augustulus, and declaring himself Master of Italy. Odovacar did, however, seek to legitimize his rule by placing himself under the authority of the Eastern emperor, who conferred upon him the title of patrician. Thus came to a close the long line of Roman emperors in the West that had begun with Augustus. The Western Empire fell totally into barbarian hands and was partitioned into various Germanic kingdoms.

Rule of Theodoric

In Italy, Odovacar ruled over his subjects with a measure of success. His relations with the Eastern emperor Zeno, however, deteriorated badly. In A.D. 488 Zeno convinced Theodoric, king of the Ostrogoths, to invade Italy on his behalf. Since their release from Hunnic subjection, the Ostrogoths had been plaguing the Eastern Empire. Zeno hoped that by offering them an opportunity to conquer Italy he could divert their aggressions elsewhere. After prolonged fighting, Theodoric finally defeated Odovacar in A.D. 493 and treacherously murdered him.

Despite its bloody beginnings, Theodoric's rule was a long and prosperous one for Italy. Agriculture and trade revived somewhat. Theodoric had spent his youth in Constantinople as a captive and had developed a deep reverence for classical civilization, which he sought to preserve during his own reign. The arts and letters thrived anew at his capital of Ravenna. While king of his own people, he recognized the sovereignty of the Eastern emperor and ruled over Italy as an imperial official. Romans and Goths were kept strictly separate, each being governed according to their own laws and traditions. Only Goths manned the army while only Romans served in civil posts. One-third of the land was turned over to the Ostrogoths. Despite this mild and enlightened rule, Theodoric was never truly accepted by his Roman subjects. By the time of his death in A.D. 526, he appears to have become embittered and was plotting war against the Eastern Empire. Theodoric's heirs held precarious control over his kingdom until A.D. 554, when the Emperor Justinian reconquered Italy for the Eastern Empire.

Theories on the Fall of the Roman Empire

Students of history have long been fascinated with the problem of why the Roman Empire in the West collapsed in A.D. 476 while its Eastern half survived for almost a millennium thereafter. A myriad of explanations have been proffered, with varying degrees of credibility. But no single, monolithic cause will suffice to explain the disintegration of so complex a structure as that of the Western Empire. In addition, the Empire did not, properly speaking, "fall" without leaving a trace but rather was transformed into something else, which retained many aspects of its former status. Any acceptable theory must take into account both long-term causes and those of more immediate influence.

External Factors

Each age has tended to regard the dissolution of the Western Empire in the light of its own pressing concerns and beliefs. For Augustine the capture of Rome in A.D. 410 was part of God's divine plan for ushering in the heavenly city. In contrast, the eighteenth-century historian Edward Gibbon in his famous study, *The Decline and Fall of the Roman Empire,* attributed Rome's demise to the "triumph of barbarism and religion." Recently historians have delved into the economic and geopolitical roots of the Empire's disintegration. Decline in these areas had set in several centuries before Rome's loss of political power.

Other scholars emphasize the significance of political and military weaknesses. The policy after Marcus Aurelius of catering to the army and enfeebling the senate and other civil offices destroyed the potential for leadership among Rome's upper classes and allowed military commanders to control civil affairs. As the army became progressively barbarized, its leaders, who were themselves barbarians or semibarbarians, came to hold the fate of Rome in their hands. The desire for plunder replaced duty to the state as the motivating force of the Roman soldier. With the transfer of the capital to Constantinople and the weakening of centralized imperial authority in the West, the Empire became even less able to mount effective opposition against invasion.

Internal Decay and Stagnation

In the third century the Western Empire suffered a decrease in population due in part to plague and civil warfare. This depopulation had ominous consequences. Land lay fallow for want of agricultural workers; the army recruited more and more barbarian mercenaries to fulfill its manpower requirements; and taxation fell more heavily upon a smaller number of people. During the late Empire tenant farmers (*coloni*) replaced the small, independent farmers who had been the backbone of the Empire. The growth of large estates (*latifundia*), which could satisfy most of their own needs, contributed to the stagnant economic environment in which little new wealth was being produced. Debasement of the coinage, lack of security, and reduced demand from the provinces led to a sharp reduction in trade. Cities shriveled in size and importance as their economic livelihood diminished. Some scholars point to the failure of the Romans to make significant technological advances as the key to the Empire's eventual breakdown. This lack of inventiveness has been in turn blamed upon the extensive use of cheap slave labor, although from the second century A.D. onward the supply of slaves decreased markedly.   Diocletian's and Constantine's reforms, while lengthening the Empire's life, brought their own pernicious effects. The Roman state became an enormous centralized organization run by compulsion. Individuals were chained to their professions and overburdened by taxes required to support a corrupt, top-heavy bureaucracy and a largely barbarian army. Such conditions discouraged initiative and undermined the citizens' devotion to Rome.

Natural Conditions

Historians also cite natural phenomena such as soil exhaustion, climatic changes, and disease as contributory causes for the Empire's decline. One theory holds that as a result of using lead utensils and drinking water from lead pipes Rome's upper classes contracted lead poisoning, which rendered them infertile.

Loss of Roman Will

Other more amorphous causes also played a role in Rome's disintegration. Some scholars advance psychological theories ranging from the effect of repressive government on the populace's will to defend itself to the debilitating influence of luxurious living among the upper classes and free bread and circuses among the lower. A discredited racial theory attributes this lack of virility to the admixture of foreign peoples (Germans, Greeks, and Slavs) with the native Roman stock. Christianity may have contributed to the fall of Rome as Gibbon suggested. Its promise of an afterlife open to all appealed to the Roman masses and distracted them from worldly concerns. Thus the Empire as a force for loyalty gradually ceased to exist.

A Combination of Causes

The overwhelming influx of barbarian tribes seeking shelter from the Huns proved too great a stress when added to the Empire's own weaknesses. The West's long Rhine–Danube frontier was easier to breach than the mountainous terrain of the Eastern Empire and thus felt the full brunt of the barbarians' attack. Rome fell, the victim of an accumulation of numerous, interacting short- and long-term causes.

Christianity began as a small sect on the fringe of Judaism. Jesus and his apostles were all Jews, and they directed their mission at first towards those of the same faith. Yet Jesus' message was a universal one: all people could attain eternal life by believing in him. Led by the apostle Paul, the first Christians widened their mission to include gentiles, whom they released from the requirements of Mosaic Law.

For its first three centuries, Christianity was only one of a number of competing religions that flourished in the polytheistic atmosphere of the Roman Empire. Yet it possessed a special appeal that fulfilled the spiritual needs of late antiquity. Its savior had actually lived and his death and Resurrection were offered as concrete proof that God would save all who trusted in Christ. Jesus taught that all humans were equal in the eyes of the Lord and that the poor and downtrodden would be rewarded in heaven.

The Early Christians won many converts by their charitable deeds. Likewise, the stalwart faith of martyrs and the proselytizing zeal of early missionaries impressed many with the committed nature of Christianity. Christians carefully preserved their doctrine into a body of sacred writing, the New Testament, that could be referred to for divine guidance. Early Church Fathers such as Ambrose, Jerome, and Augustine clarified its meaning and defended it against heretical beliefs. In A.D. 394, Christianity became the official religion of the Empire and its victory was complete.

Roman civilization did not disappear with the fall of the Empire in the West to barbarian invaders. Rather, it was kept alive within the Eastern Empire and the Church. Even the barbarians were respectful of Roman law and culture. Gradually Germanic and Roman elements blended to form a new civilization: that of Western Europe.

Recommended Reading

A. Alföldi, *The Conversion of Constantine and Pagan Rome* (1948).

Augustine, *Confessions*, J.F. Sheer, trans. (1947).

H.S. Bettenson, ed., *Documents of the Christian Church* (1963).

Peter Brown, *Augustine of Hippo: A Biography* (1967).

Peter Brown, *The Making of Late Antiquity* (1978).

R. Bultman, *Primitive Christianity* (1956).

Henry Chadwick, *The Early Church* (1967).

Mortimer Chambers, ed., *The Fall of Rome—Can it be Explained?* (1970).

Barry Cunliffe, *Greeks, Romans, and Barbarians* (1988).

Herbert A. Deane, *The Political and Social Ideas of St. Augustine* (1963).

Eusebius, *The History of the Church*, G.A. Williamson, trans. (1981).

J. Ferguson, *The Religions of the Roman Empire* (1970).

Robin Lane Fox, *Pagans and Christians* (1987).

W.H.C. Frend, *Martyrdom and Persecution in the Early Church* (1965).

Edward Gibbon, *A History of the Decline and Fall of the Roman Empire* (1776–88).

Walter Goffart, *Barbarians and Romans* A.D. 418–584 (1980).

Michael Grant, *The Fall of the Roman Empire, a Reappraisal* (1976).

Michael Grant, *Jesus: an Historian's Review of the Gospels* (1977).

Michael Grant, *The Jews in the Roman World* (1973).

A.H.M. Jones, *The Decline of the Ancient World* (1975).

A.H.M. Jones, *The Later Roman Empire, 284–602; A Social, Economic and Administrative Survey* (1986).

D. Kagan, ed., *The End of the Roman Empire: Decline or Transformation?* (1978).

H. Kee and F. Young, *Understanding the New Testament* (1983).

William L. Langer, ed., *Perspectives in Western Civilization, Vol. I* (1972).

Ramsay MacMullen, *Christianizing the Roman Empire* A.D. 100–400 (1984).

Ramsay MacMullen, *Enemies of the Roman Order: Treason, Unrest and Alienation in the Empire* (1966).

Ramsay MacMullen, *Soldier and Civilian in the Later Roman Empire* (1963).

R.A. Markus, *Saeculum: History and Society in the Theology of Saint Augustine* (1970).

Robert L. Milburn, *Early Christian Art and Architecture* (1988).

Arthur Darby Nock, *Conversion* (1961).

Arthur Darby Nock, *Saint Paul* (1955).

Elaine Pagels, *The Gnostic Gospels* (1979).

Jaroslav Pelikan, *The Catholic Tradition, Vol. I: The Emergence of the Catholic Tradition (100–600)* (1971).

Jaroslav Pelikan, *The Excellent Empire: The Fall of Rome and The Triumph of the Church* (1987).

M. Rostovtzeff, *The Social and Economic History of the Roman Empire* (1957).

D.S. Russell, *The Jews from Alexander to Herod* (1967).

E.P. Sanders, *Jesus and Judaism* (1985).

Morton Smith, *Jesus the Magician* (1978).

G. Vermes, *The Dead Sea Scrolls in English* (1962).

Lynn White, Jr., ed., *The Transformation of the Roman World: Gibbon's Problem After Two Centuries* (1966).

Robert L. Wilken, *The Christians as the Romans Saw Them* (1984).

Edmund Wilson, *The Dead Sea Scrolls, 1949–1969* (1969).

Herwig Wolfram, *History of the Goths* (1988).

CHAPTER 8

The Byzantine Empire, Kievan Russia, and Islam

395	Roman Empire divided into Eastern and Western segments
528	Work begins on Justinian's Code
553	Justinian rejoins Italy to Empire
568	Lombards invade Italy
c. 570	Muhammad born in Mecca
622	Muhammad's Hegira
632–661	Orthodox Caliphate; Muslims conquer Syria, Palestine, Egypt, Cyprus, Iraq, and Persia
661–750	Umayyad Caliphate; Beginning of schism between Shiites and Sunnites; Muslims conquer North Africa and Spain

717–718	Muslim threat in West contained
732	Charles Martel defeats Arabs at Battle of Tours
750–1258	Abbasid Caliphate
843	Final defeat of iconoclasts
862	Traditional date of migration of "Varangian Russes" to Russia
867–1057	Macedonian dynasty founded by Basil I Highpoint of Byzantine Empire
882	Founding of Kievan state
988	Conversion of Kievan Russia to Orthodox Christianity
1054	Schism between Eastern and Western Christianity
1055	Seljuk Turks capture Baghdad
1071	Victory of Seljuk Turks over Byzantine army at Manzikert; Sultanate of Rum founded
1204	Fourth Crusade sacks Constantinople; establishes Latin Empire of Constantinople
1240	Mongols burn Kiev; end of Kievan supremacy
1258	Mongols destroy Baghdad and conquer much of Islamic Empire
1261–1453	Palaeologus dynasty rules Byzantium

The division of the Roman Empire into eastern and western halves was apparent long before its actual political separation in A.D. *395. The West was essentially Latin in its language and culture while the East was predominantly Greek. Owing largely to its state-controlled economy, powerful military force, and more sheltered frontiers, the Eastern Roman Empire was able to escape the economic decline and barbaric onslaughts that beset the West. With the transfer of the imperial capital to Constantinople early in the fourth century and the collapse of Rome approximately 150 years later, the East fell heir to the traditions, laws, and governmental institutions of the Roman Empire. These endured with modification until 1453 when Constantinople finally succumbed to the Ottoman Turks. As oriental influences superseded the Roman during its long history, the Eastern Roman Empire became known as the Byzantine Empire. Although politically and militarily the Empire went through periods of revival and decline, its brilliant culture and great commercial wealth flourished for centuries. During the early Middle Ages when the West had descended to a lower level of civilization, the East remained literate, cosmopolitan, and cultivated. Byzantine culture and Orthodox Christianity were profound influences on the shaping of the first Russian state.*

The Early Middle Ages witnessed not only the continuation of Graeco-Roman civilization in the East but also the birth of a new, dynamic religion, that of Islam. Founded by Muhammad in the early seventh century, Islam soon spread far beyond its Arabian homeland. During the seventh and eighth centuries its converts, known as Muslims, conquered a great empire that stretched from the Indus River to the Atlantic Ocean and encompassed most of North Africa and the Middle East. While the Islamic Empire broke up into separate, independent Muslim states, Islam gave to vast areas of the world a new sacred language, Arabic, and a new religious unity. Its translations of Greek works into Arabic preserved them for later transmission back to the West.

The Byzantine Empire

"New Rome"

The splendid new capital of the Roman Empire built on the site of the ancient Greek settlement of Byzantium well merited its name of "New Rome." Roman traditions lived on in the "City of Constantine," or Constantinople, as the capital came to be called. Its inhabitants considered themselves "Romans" although they were largely of Greek descent. Its senate, founded by Constantine I, was modeled after that in Rome. Roman laws continued in force.

Eastern Emperors

The Eastern emperor was regarded as the legitimate successor of Augustus and usually followed the Roman custom of choosing or adopting his own heir. Yet as the Empire in the West declined, Constantinople looked increasingly eastward for its inspiration and sustenance. The Eastern emperors furthered the orientalizing tendencies that had begun with Diocletian. Although not themselves deified, now that the Empire was Christian, they reigned as God's divinely appointed agent on earth and defender of the faith. Their power was absolute and their person surrounded by awe-inspiring ritual. Palace officials, frequently eunuchs, took care of most of the minutiae of daily governing. Revolutions and incessant plotting bloodied the Empire's long political history.

Natural Advantages

Constantinople's superb location at the dividing point between Europe and Asia epitomized its dual, east/west orientation. The city occupied a promontory of land on the European side of the Bosporus, a narrow strait that joins the Sea of Marmara with the Black Sea. To the north an inlet of the Bosporus forms the city's protected harbor, the Golden Horn. To the south the Sea of Marmara connects with the Aegean Sea through another famous strait, the Dardanelles. Thus Constantinople's position enabled it to control all military and commercial traffic that passed from the Mediterranean to the Black Sea. The new capital rapidly became the most important trading center of the Empire and a melting pot for the cultures of East and West. Strategically the city's heavily fortified and all-but-impregnable site shielded Europe from aggressors for more than a thousand years.

Justinian and the Expansion of the Empire

Like the West, the Eastern Empire had been subject to repeated raids by a host of barbarian invaders—Visigoths, Huns, Ostrogoths, Vandals, Bulgars, and Slavs—during the fourth, fifth, and early sixth centuries.

Territory

Greater wealth, population, and military strength enabled the East to ward off its attackers and preserve intact its territorial core in the Balkan Peninsula and Asia Minor. Egypt and Syria remained within the imperial fold at this time although religious differences increasingly alienated them from the Empire's Hellenized nucleus. Theoretically Italy, Spain, and Gaul were still under imperial jurisdiction, but in fact barbarian chiefs ruled them as independent kingdoms. Nonetheless, the vision of a reunited Empire did not die with the fall of Rome.

Justinian's Character

Before he died in 565, the Eastern emperor Justinian I (ruled 527–565) had successfully restored the Empire to some of its former extent and grandeur at the cost, however, of ruining its finances and gravely weakening its future fighting capability. All of Justinian's many activities reflected his desire to revive the power and glory of the Roman Empire. His reign was characterized by a thorough-going despotism and headlong pursuit of his goals. Justinian owed much to his ambitious wife, Theodora, an actress and courtesan in her youth. She urged the weak-willed Justinian to remain on the throne when in 532 he was confronted with a rebellion in Constantinople. With the aid of his capable generals, he ruthlessly suppressed the Nika Revolt, thus extinguishing all opposition for decades.

Reconquest of Italy

Justinian began his campaign to win back the lost Western provinces in 533 by dispatching an army under Belisarius to North Africa. With surprising ease, Belisarius defeated the Vandals in 534. The following year he set out to reconquer Italy. The Ostrogoths put up spirited resistance and it was not until 553 that all of Italy south of the Alps rejoined the Empire. What Justinian recovered, however, was not the heartland of the West, but rather a country impoverished beyond immediate recovery. His troops also captured a portion of southern Spain from the Visigoths. The price of reuniting much of the former Roman Empire was high. Justinian's conquests critically depleted the Eastern Empire's resources and weakened its defenses against the Persians to the east and the pillaging Slavs and Bulgars in the Balkans.

Ultimately, the expanded territory proved impossible for his successors to maintain.

Administrative Reforms

More lasting were Justinian's administrative and legal reforms. Spurred by his vision of imperial greatness, he sought to promote good government and a fair and orderly judicial system. To reduce corruption he ended the sale of offices, eliminated profit taking from office revenues and extortion, and commenced to pay salaries from the state treasury. In the interest of more effective provincial government he gradually reversed an earlier practice of dividing the provinces into small units and keeping separate the civil and military authority. In frontier areas and in trouble spots he conferred civil powers upon the military commanders and allowed them to expand their territorial jurisdiction by merging several provinces. Justinian's successors extended this system to Italy and North Africa, both of which were then reorganized into large military domains or exarchates and governed by powerful exarchs.

Reform of the Law

Justinian's greatest achievement as emperor was reform of the Roman law. In 528, he commissioned a number of jurists led by Tribonian to undertake a systematic reorganization of the jumbled and sometimes contradictory body of enactments, imperial decrees, and juristic opinions that had evolved unsystematically over the centuries. The fruit of their labors, the *Corpus Juris Civilis*, summarized the Roman law in a precise, orderly, and accessible form. It consisted of four parts. The *Codex Justinianus* presented in revised and coherent fashion all valid imperial edicts since the reign of Hadrian. The *Digest* reconciled and consolidated the legal opinions of jurists according to subject matter. The *Institutes* served to introduce students to the law. Finally, Justinian's own augmentative laws, written in Greek, not Latin, as was the rest of the work, were collected in the *Novels*. Together these works constitute the Empire's most precious legacy to the West.

Architecture

Justinian made visible his aspiration to restore the Empire to its former glory in the city of Constantinople itself. There and throughout the realm he erected lavish public buildings, churches, palaces, and fortifications. The greatest of them, the domed Church of the Holy Wisdom (*Hagia Sophia*), is still today a marvel of architectural skill and decorative splendor.

Religion

In the East, the emperor was recognized as the supreme authority over both the Church and the state. Thus Justinian became involved in religious issues that clouded his reign. The Monophysites, who were strong in Egypt and Syria, refused to accept the dual nature of Christ as divine and human. Justinian attempted to bring them back to the fold of orthodoxy by alternating policies of tolerance and persecution. His efforts succeeded only in antagonizing the papacy. By the end of his reign Justinian himself had retreated into theological speculation.

External Threats

In the years following Justinian's death, the overstrained Empire had to contend with a number of enemies who succeeded in dismembering most of Justinian's conquests.

Barbarians

In the West the Empire contended unsuccessfully with the Lombards and the Visigoths. After invading northern Italy in 568, the Lombards soon spread themselves throughout the peninsula. Rome remained under papal control, and the imperial exarchate of Ravenna managed to endure until 751, when it fell to the Lombards. In 629, the Visigoths recaptured the territory conquered by Justinian in southern Spain. In the northeast the Empire faced challenges from the Avars and Slavs. The nomadic Avars migrated westward from Central Asia during the sixth century. By 568 they inhabited the Danube plain and Pannonia along with the Slavic tribes that they had enslaved as they moved west. Avars and Slavs raided throughout the Balkans, gradually settled there, and even threatened Constantinople several times.

Persia

At the same time as barbarians annexed imperial territories in Italy, Spain, and the Balkans, the Empire became involved in a lengthy and devastating war with the Persians. By the reign of Phocas (602–610) the situation had become critical. The Persians had managed to absorb parts of Armenia, Mesopotamia, and Syria and were ravaging Asia Minor. The exhaustion of the Byzantine treasury deprived the army of needed provisions and demoralized the troops. In 610, Heraclius (reigned 610–641), son of the exarch of Africa, overthrew the tyrannical Phocas and slowly turned the tide of events. With a loan from the Church he engaged the Persians in three outstanding campaigns between 622 and 628 and defeated them. In the midst of these campaigns the Byzantine navy repulsed an assault on Constantinople by the Avars and Persians in 626. As a result of their defeat the Persians agreed in a treaty signed in 628 to restore most conquered Byzantine territory. The Persians never threatened Byzantium again.

Heraclius's Reforms

Heraclius began a major reform of provincial government that succeeding emperors carried to completion. All of the provinces were eventually reorganized into military divisions known as *themes,* each under the command of a local military governor who assumed civil authority as well. The troops in each of the *themes* were given land in return for their military service and that of their progeny in perpetuity. One of the *themes* was designated to furnish recruits for the navy. Thus a body of free peasant-soldiers was created that supplied the Empire with its military manpower for centuries to come. Heraclius also restructured the bureaucracy and revised the tax system to repay the debt to the Church.

Hellenization

During Heraclius's reign the Empire became thoroughly Hellenized, a change symbolized by the adoption of the Greek word *Basileus* as the emperor's official title. Greek replaced Latin as the official language of the Empire.

Islam

Heraclius's military victories and internal reforms gave the Empire a new lease on life. Unfortunately, by the end of his reign a new peril had arisen in the deserts of Arabia, the conquering faith of Islam. Armies of Arab converts swiftly subjugated vast areas of North Africa, the Near East, and parts of Europe. The Empire permanently lost its possessions in Palestine, Syria, Egypt, North Africa, and elsewhere. Asia Minor was overrun, and Cyprus and Rhodes fell into Arab hands, enabling them to disrupt Byzantine maritime trade. Muslim troops besieged Constantinople annually from 674 to 677, and the threat ended only when a Byzantine naval victory wiped out the Arab fleet.

Barbarian Raids

Barbarian raids added to the dangers. In 679–80, the Hunnish Bulgars crossed the Danube and settled in the Balkan area of Thrace and Moesia, which constitutes present-day Bulgaria. They subjugated the Slavic inhabitants and intermarried with them. By the ninth century they were indistinguishable from the Slavs, having adopted their language and culture. The Bulgar state came to rival the Empire for power in the Balkans.

Renewed Conflict with Islam

Political conditions within Byzantium were anarchic. Frequent revolutions placed a string of military men on the throne between the years 695 and 717. In March 717 yet another general of one of the *themes*, Leo III (reigned 717–741), was made emperor. Four months later the Muslims launched a new, year-long siege of the capital. In its most desperate hour the Empire again displayed the essential strength and resilience of its core. The Byzantine navy severely crippled the Muslim fleet with the aid of its secret invention, Greek fire, a chemical compound that when projected upon enemy ships caused them to burst into flames. The Empire's superiority at sea prevented the invaders from starving Constantinople into submission. In September 718, the Arabs gave up their siege and returned home. Constantinople's perseverance safeguarded Western Christendom from the force of Islam. With Leo III's reign the Empire entered into a period of recuperation.

Byzantine Recovery and Counterattack

The year 717 to 718 marked a turning point in the history of the West. By containing the Muslim threat, Byzantium ensured that Europe would remain Christian.

Leo III

Under the Isaurian dynasty (717–802) founded by Leo III, the Empire slowly began to recover. Leo and his successors instituted important military reforms. In order to reduce the power of ambitious generals they divided some *themes* into smaller units and they implemented military reforms. Until the eleventh century this reformed army was the most professional fighting body in the West: well trained, organized, and equipped. It employed various strategies, each according to the nature of its opponent. Until 1071, its best soldiers were recruited from Asia Minor. Leo also increased taxes to replenish his treasury, and he instituted social legislation to make Roman law more compatible with Christian ideals. In the realm of religion, however, a new and bitter controversy broke out over the use of icons and other devotional aids in churches. Their use was prohibited between 726 and 787 and again between 813 and 843 but they were thereafter restored with directions against misuse by the laity.

Basil I

The Empire attained the summit of its military and cultural greatness under the Macedonian dynasty (867–1057) founded by Basil I. Although he gained the throne by murder, Basil, like many of the other Macedonian emperors, proved himself to be not only a successful general but also an outstanding administrator and patron of the arts. Basil and his successors completed the codification of Byzantine law that had developed since the time of Justinian. In addition he reorganized imperial finances. Under the Macedonians the Empire entered a period of military resurgence that lasted until the mid-eleventh century. Internal dissension within the Muslim world facilitated the reconquest of lost territory.

Nicephorus II Phocas

As general and later emperor, Nicephorus II Phocas recovered Crete from the Arabs in 961 and Cyprus shortly thereafter. Byzantine superiority at sea was thus restored. In 969 his army recaptured the city of Antioch and much of North Syria. Other emperors reaffirmed the Empire's hold over southern Italy.

Basil II

Basil II (reigned 976–1025) extended the Empire's frontiers even farther by subjugating Bulgaria. At the end of his reign the Empire reached from the Danube to the Euphrates and its cultural influence extended as far as the new state of Russia. Domestically Basil took a strong stand against those wealthy landowners who expanded their estates at the expense of the free peasants. Like most other Macedonian emperors, he defended the interests of the small peasant proprietors against the encroachments of "the powerful." However, laws against encroachments proved difficult to enforce. Under the pressure of poor harvests, burdensome taxation, and constant military service, the number of peasants who abandoned or sold their lands continued to increase. This development had ominous repercussions for the state. The transformation of a free peasant-soldier into a tenant-serf who owed allegiance to his lord had serious repercussions on the system of *themes* upon which imperial defense was based. It deprived the Empire of a large share of its revenue and military recruits. In addition, by increasing the military power of local aristocrats it posed a severe threat to centralized government.

The Last Centuries of Decline

After Basil II a series of weak emperors were unable to halt this trend toward a feudal society. The Macedonian dynasty came to an unhappy end in 1057, just three years after the Eastern and Western Churches had split irrevocably. Over the next 400 years Byzantine fortunes slowly decayed.

The story of the last centuries of the Byzantine Empire may be summarized here in brief because it will reappear within the context of Western European affairs.

New Invaders

The decline of the free peasant-soldier reduced the Empire's ability to deal with new invaders. In southern Italy, Norman adventurers conquered the port of Bari in 1071, thus eliminating Byzantine rule on the Italian peninsula. On the eastern frontier, a tribe of nomadic Turks, the Seljuks, descended upon the Empire. In 1071 they crushed a large

Byzantine army at Manzikert and captured the emperor. As a result, a large section of Asia Minor fell into Turkish hands, which became the Sultanate of Rum. This loss deprived the Empire of its most valuable military recruiting ground and led the Byzantines to solicit the aid of the Christian West in repulsing the Turkish infidels, an appeal that contributed to the opening of the First Crusade in 1095.

The Latin Empire

Instead of helping the Empire, the Crusades hastened its downfall. Although Byzantine military and financial strength revived during the reign of the powerful aristocrat Alexius I Comnenus (reigned 1081–1118), the Fourth Crusade dealt the Empire its deathblow as a great power a century later. Encouraged by Venice, Byzantium's commercial rival, the Crusaders turned against their eastern ally and sacked Constantinople in 1204. After dividing the city's treasures among themselves, they established the Latin Empire of Constantinople. The remaining imperial territory was partitioned to form four independent states. In 1261, the Greek Michael Palaeologus of Nicaea reconquered Constantinople, ended the Latin Empire, and founded the Palaeologi dynasty that ruled Byzantium until its fall in 1453.

Byzantine Civilization

The Eastern Orthodox Church

Whereas in the West the papacy had secured a measure of independence from secular control, the Byzantine or Eastern Orthodox Church was headed by the emperor himself and often functioned as a department of state.

"*Caesaropapism.*" The emperor was God's chosen servant who ruled a Christian empire as defender of the faith. He appointed or dismissed the patriarchs and bishops, paid their salaries, enforced Church discipline, and supervised the monasteries. He convened and presided over Church councils that resolved doctrinal issues and embodied their decisions in his laws. At times he even legislated independently on points of dogma. Modern historians refer to this system whereby authority over both the church and the state is vested in the emperor as "caesaropapism," although the absolute power over ecclesiastical affairs that this term connotes is not strictly correct. The emperor could not, for example, abrogate the Nicene Creed or act as a priest.

Religious Split. These opposing notions of the relationship between ecclesiastical and secular power set a wedge between the eastern and western branches of the Church which after centuries of discord finally split them apart. The Byzantines rejected papal claims to supremacy over the whole of Christendom and considered the patriarch of Constantinople to have equal rights with the pope. This fundamental disagreement was at the root of the many quarrels between the Orthodox and Roman churches. During the Iconoclastic controversy of the eighth and ninth centuries, the estrangement deepened. Devotion to holy objects had never been as strong in the West as in the East. Thus the pope permitted it and excommunicated all iconoclasts (i.e. image-breakers) in 731. In the ninth century the conversion of the Bulgars and other Slavs opened up a new area of rivalry.

The final breach came about in 1054. The ambitious new Patriarch of Constantinople, Michael Cerularius, clashed with a papal delegation over old issues. The papal legate excommunicated Cerularius, who in turn convinced the emperor to denounce the Latin church as heretical and anathemize the pope. This formal schism between the Eastern and Western branches of Christendom was not ended until 1965, 911 years later, with the lifting of the mutual excommunications.

The Wealth of Byzantium

Throughout most of its history the Byzantine Empire was fabulously wealthy, and its capital was the premier city of the early Middle Ages. Economic prosperity enabled the Empire to weather its many political crises and survive for more than a millennium. Byzantium derived its wealth from three main sources: land, commerce and industry.

Land Tax. A tax on land provided the Empire with its major source of revenue. Only acreage under cultivation was eligible to be taxed. Thus if the land became vacant or its owner unable to pay his taxes, the state required that a neighboring landowner assume responsibility for the property and its tax burden. While it was to the government's advantage to preserve free peasant ownership of the land, this system of taxation encouraged the growth of large estates and the transformation of peasants into serfs bound to the land. Nevertheless, until the eleventh century Byzantine agriculture generally furnished the Empire with sufficient food and revenue.

Commerce. Constantinople's location favored its development into the most important trading center of the entire Mediterranean during most of the Middle Ages. Ships arrived in the city's great port laden with goods from around the world: furs, hides, amber, beeswax, honey, caviar, and wheat from Russia and other Slavic lands; spices, perfumes, precious stones, and glass from the East; and slaves, iron, and timber from the West. The capital's large colony of foreign merchants purchased some of these wares for resale chiefly to the clergy and wealthy nobles. Other goods were bought directly by rich Byzantines or for use in Byzantine industry. Constantinople and several other manufacturing towns exported large quantities of goods as well. The government levied taxes on imports, exports, sales, and profits.

Sound Coinage. The Empire's maintenance of a sound coinage for eight hundred years, an unparalleled accomplishment, enormously aided Byzantine commerce. Until the reign of Alexius Comnenus, the Byzantine gold *bezant* was never altered or debased. It was the standard of value throughout Europe and the Near East for most of the Middle Ages, and it, along with the Arabic *dinar,* was the only gold coin in use in the West for centuries.

Industry. Another rich source of imperial revenue came from the state's monopoly over the silk industry. During the reign of Justinian, two missionaries smuggled silkworm eggs out of China and began the Empire's lucrative silk industry. Silkworkers as well as other craftsmen, tradesmen, and professionals were organized into hereditary guilds. The government closely regulated all aspects of the Byzantine economy. It fixed the prices of agricultural and manufactured goods; set wages, hours, and working conditions; and even dictated the amount to be produced and to whom it could be sold. Until the eleventh century this system worked well and contributed to the state's prosperity.

Byzantine Culture

The hallmark of Byzantine culture as a whole was its continuity with the Graeco-Roman past. The Byzantines preserved classical art and literary forms and perpetuated them in their own works. Constantinople with its magnificent churches and palaces, cosmopolitan population, and learned culture impressed visitors as the greatest city of its time. This thriving urban life is one of the traits that distinguished Byzantine civilization from that of the medieval West.

The Arts. In the arts their Roman heritage blended with the Greeks' sense of balance, order, and clarity and the Oriental taste for color, splendor, and abstract design to create a new, distinctly Byzantine style.

First Golden Age. Byzantine art and architecture experienced their First Golden Age during the reign of Justinian in the sixth century. The greatest of the many churches and public buildings erected under his patronage and the most superlative example of Byzantine architecture was the *Hagia Sophia*. Completed in the short space of five years, the huge domed structure was so magnificent that Justinian supposedly proclaimed at its dedication: "I have outdone thee, O Solomon." *Hagia Sophia* represents a significant architectural achievement. It was the first to utilize pendentives, spherical triangles that shifted a dome's weight to four corner piers and thus off the walls. This facilitated the building of domes on top of square bases.

A characteristic feature of Byzantine church architecture was its extensive use of mosaics. These depicted Christ, the Virgin Mary, and the Saints. Composed of tiny pieces of colored glass or marble set in plaster, they covered the interior surfaces of domes, half-domes, and walls and created a glittering, illusionary effect. Most mosaics in Constantinople were destroyed during the iconoclastic controversy. Thus the finest specimens of Byzantine mosaic work exist outside the capital in places such as Ravenna on the Adriatic coast of Italy.

Second Golden Age. With the final defeat of the iconoclasts in 843, Byzantine art and architecture entered a Second Golden Age that lasted until the eleventh century. This period witnessed the production of the most exquisite examples of Byzantine decorative arts. Fine mosaics, brilliantly illuminated manuscripts, jewel-encrusted book covers, delicate ivory carvings, and superb gold, silver, and enamel works all attest to the Byzantines' creative powers and love of rich ornamentation. In architecture the outstanding structure of the age was the five-domed Church of St. Mark's in Venice.

Third Golden Age. Although the sacking of Constantinople in 1204 and increasing impoverishment left the Empire politically impotent, its art enjoyed a third period of brilliance in the fourteenth and early fifteenth centuries. Because of the costliness of mosaics, many artists turned to painting wall murals or icons on panels. These magnificent, formalized images had an important influence on Russian and Italian painting of the time.

Literature and Scholarship. In the field of letters, fidelity to the heritage of classical antiquity was even more pronounced. In contrast to the Germanic West, where knowledge of the Greek language virtually disappeared, Greek was the official language in Byzantium. As a result, Byzantine scholars were able to pursue classical studies with no interruption, and many devoted themselves to the recovering, copying, and studying of ancient Greek writings. Many masterpieces of classical literature were passed to the West thanks to the work of Byzantine copiers. Scholarship in Byzantium was not the sole preserve of the clergy as in medieval Europe. Rather it was dominated by imperial civil servants and by a literate upper class. Schools of higher learning at Constantinople offered instruction in theology to monks and priests and prepared men for careers in civil service. The importance of secular subjects such as law, medicine, philosophy, mathematics, and rhetoric was recognized. In their own writings Byzantine scholars usually sacrificed creativity and slavishly imitated classical models. Yet they produced histories of the Empire that reveal a greater understanding of characters and events than any works of their kind in the contemporary West. They also produced important religious writings including saints' lives, biblical commentaries, and hymns.

Kievan Russia

Byzantine commercial connections and the Christian Church played a major role in the development of the first Russian state. The territory that now comprises European Russia had been occupied since Paleolithic times by a succession of different peoples. Between the sixth and the ninth centuries the East Slavs settled in southern and central Russia. Scholars theorize that the Slavs originated in Galicia. From there the South Slavs spread into the Balkans and the West Slavs into the area of present-day Poland and Czechoslovakia, while the East Slavs migrated eastward to become the forebears of today's Russians.

The early history of the East Slavs remains dim. In addition to hunting and farming, they were active traders and founded over 200 towns, among them Novgorod on Lake Ilmen and Kiev on the Dnieper River.

The Origin of the First Russian State

The origin of the first Russian state is the subject of considerable controversy among historians.

The Primary Chronicle

The main original source on Kievan Russia, the *Primary Chronicle*, is a collection of annals composed between approximately 1040 and 1118 by several monks. According to it the Slavic tribes frequently quarreled among themselves. In 862, some of them appealed to a group of Scandinavians whom they referred to as "Varangian Russes" to rule over them and bring order. Under the leadership of three brothers chosen by the Slavs, the Rus migrated en masse from their Scandinavian home. The eldest brother, Rurik, became prince of Novgorod. His successor, Oleg, captured Kiev in 882 and joined it to Novgorod, thus establishing the first Russian state.

The *Primary Chronicle's* account is fraught with difficulties for the historian. Most modern Soviet historians reject outright the contribution of foreigners in the founding of Kievan Russia. They do not accept the Chronicles' foundation date of 862 or the identity given the Rus. Whereas the *Primary Chronicle* states that the area of Novgorod became known as the land of Rus, other references connect the name "Russes" with Kiev to the south. In addition, Byzantine sources note the Rus staged an attack on Constantinople as early as 860. Furthermore, the name Rus does not appear in any contemporary Scandinavian sources, a fact that leads some historians to posit a Slavic origin for the word.

The Varangians

While the *Primary Chronicle* is no longer accepted as completely reliable, it still seems most likely on linguistic grounds that the Varangians were the first rulers of Kievan Russia. They belonged to the larger movement of Scandinavian adventurers and traders known variously as Vikings or Norsemen who raided the periphery of Europe during the ninth century and later. Archaeological findings substantiate that some of them were in Russia at this time and that they carried on a lively trade between Constantinople and Scandinavia by means of the great Russian waterways. In some still obscure fashion, the contact between the Norsemen and the East Slavs gave birth to the Kievan state.

The Kievan Dynasty

Oleg and Igor

The state Oleg founded was a loose union of semiautonomous city-states headed by the prince at Kiev. Oleg and his successor, Igor (reigned 913–945), extended Kievan authority over most of the East Slavic tribes from whom they gathered tribute as a sign of fealty. Common commercial interests bound the Kievan city-states together. In 907, Oleg led a great plundering expedition against Constantinople and succeeded in extracting a highly favorable trade treaty from the Byzantines. Igor also launched a raid against the Byzantine capital in 941, but his fleet was destroyed by Greek fire and he was forced to accept less advantageous trading terms.

Olga and Sviatoslav

Russia and Byzantium strengthened their ties during the reign of Igor's widow, Olga (reigned 945–c. 962), who traveled to Constantinople, converted to Christianity, and was baptized by the Emperor himself into the Orthodox Church. By the end of her reign, the Scandinavian settlers had become completely integrated with the native inhabitants and a form of the name "Russia" came to designate the Kievan state. Olga's son, Sviatoslav (reigned 962–972), was a great warrior-prince. He successfully led campaigns against the Khazar state on the southern steppeland, extended Kievan rule over the whole length of the Volga River, and temporarily gained possession of the Danubian plain. Russian control of the Balkans proved intolerable to the Byzantines, and after bitter fighting they forced Sviatoslav to give up his Balkan lands.

Vladimir

An event of major significance occurred during the reign of Sviatoslav's third son, Vladimir (reigned 978–1015), who seized power from his brothers following a period of civil warfare. Vladimir adopted Orthodox Christianity around 988 and imposed the new faith on his subjects. According to legend, the prince considered several religions before converting to the religion of Byzantium. His choice opened the way to even greater Byzantine influence on Russian life. Vladimir himself married the sister of the Byzantine emperor in exchange for furnishing him with Russian military aid.

Yaroslav the Wise

Upon Vladimir's death, renewed civil strife endangered the Kievan state until one of his sons, known as Yaroslav the Wise, finally consolidated his control. Under Yaroslav (reigned 1019–1054), Kievan Russia reached the pinnacle of its political and cultural development and the Russian state was known and respected among all European ruling houses. Yaroslav extended Russia's borders to the north and southwest. In 1037 his army dealt a crushing blow to the nomadic Pechenegs that menaced Kiev from the steppes north of the Black Sea and disrupted trade along the Dnieper. Yaroslav continued a Kievan policy of concluding advantageous matrimonial alliances between members of his family and those in the royal dynasties of France, Hungary, Norway, Poland, and Byzantium. He allowed Kiev to become a place of refuge for exiled European princes and kings. The erudite monarch fostered cultural growth by encouraging the translation of many Greek religious works into Slavonic. In addition he patronized artists, founded a school and a library at Kiev, and is credited with ordering the first written codification of Russian law. He further advanced the position of Christianity within his realm and built many fine churches and monasteries.

Economy

Prosperity in Kievan Russia at its height rested upon the dual bases of a healthy agriculture and extensive trade. Most Russians lived off the land as free peasants. Serfdom increased over time, however, and slaves existed as well.

The outstanding feature of the Kievan economy was its well-developed foreign commerce. According to a tenth-century chronicler, the Kievan prince and his retinue collected tribute in kind throughout the countryside every winter. When the Dnieper was free of ice in the spring, they took the goods to Kiev, where they constructed boats for the great summer expedition down the river and across the Black Sea to Constantinople. At the Byzantine capital, the Kievan ruler, other nobles, and Russian merchants sold their cargoes of fur, wax, honey, and slaves in exchange for silks, wine, jewels, and spices. Detailed trade treaties regulated every aspect of these transactions. This widespread commercial activity promoted the use of money and created a thriving urban life to a far greater extent than in medieval Europe.

Government

Government in Kievan Russia was a combination of monarchical, aristocratic, and democratic elements. The prince at Kiev possessed judicial, administrative, and military powers. He made most important decisions, however, in collaboration with his retinue and the local aristocrats who collectively were called the *boyars*. These aristocrats formed a council, or *duma*, which advised the prince and even, on rare occasions, opposed his will. In the towns the ancient institution of the *veche*, or town meeting, where all citizens voted on important matters, also served to balance princely power.

Prior to his death in 1054, Yaroslav divided his kingdom into principalities. These he ranked hierarchically under Kiev, the most important, and apportioned them among his sons. When one son died the other sons were expected to move up to the next principality. By this device Yaroslav offered a novel approach to royal succession; the throne passed from brother to brother and no longer from father to son.

Decline

The complex succession system caused much disagreement and led to many civil wars that weakened the state. Kievan decline was hastened in 1061, when a new Turkic tribe, the Polovtsy or Cumans, began their persistent battering of the southern frontier. They blocked the Russians' trade route to the Black Sea, thus severing contact with the West. During a new round of internecine strife, Andrew Bogoliubskii, prince of some of the northern principalities, sacked Kiev in 1169 and replaced it as capital. When Mongol invaders burned the city in 1240,

Kievan supremacy had ended. The future of the Russian state now lay with the new city of Moscow to the north.

Kievan Culture

Under Byzantine influence Kievan culture attained a high level of sophistication and its upper class, at least, was remarkably well educated.

Religious Influences

Conversion to Christianity had a profound effect on the growth of Kievan culture. While the East Slavs were not culturally barren, their acceptance of Christianity from Byzantium at the end of the tenth century gave a powerful stimulus to the flowering of Russian art, architecture, and literature. The Orthodox form of Christianity, with its close association of church and state, rapidly replaced the pagan, animistic faith of the East Slavs. Through Christianity the cultural achievements of Byzantine civilization were made available to the Kievan state. Church Slavonic, the written language created for the Slavs by the missionary Cyril and his followers, became the literary and liturgical language of the Russians. Using its Cyrillic alphabet, they blended Church Slavonic with the Old Russian vernacular to produce the first written Russian.

Literature

At first, Russian literature consisted of translations from the Greek of parts of the Bible, liturgy, and patristic texts borrowed from the Byzantines. Within a century, though, the Russians were producing their own original works. Most of these closely followed Byzantine models. In history and epic poetry, however, the Russians struck out on their own. The *Primary Chronicle* and other historical works reveal a keen sense of realistic detail and served to enhance the notion of Russia's destiny. The brilliant and moving poem, *The Lay of Igor's Campaign*, if authentic, is the only surviving example of the Russian epic tradition.

Art and Architecture

Russian art and architecture were patterned after Byzantine types, but these were modified to suit the Russian environment and taste. Most of the great Russian churches of this period were built and decorated by architects and artists imported from Constantinople. Nevertheless, their distinctive "onion domes" exemplify the adaptation of a basic Byzantine form to new needs and preferences. Likewise, Russian artists carried the Byzantine tradition of icon painting to new heights of splendor and coloration.

Islam

Arabia

In European history the seventh century stands as a period of relative "darkness" and decline. In the Middle East, on the other hand, this century witnessed the birth and spread of a major world religion, Islam. Its founder, the Prophet Muhammad, was a Bedouin and the faith he propagated evolved within the context of the unique geographical, social, and religious climate in the Arabian Peninsula.

Geography

Since most of Arabia is arid desert or steppeland ill-suited to a settled, agricultural existence, nomadism was the principal way of life for most of its inhabitants. The Bedouins eked out a living as graziers and by raids on each other or traveling caravans. Like the Germans, the Arabs were grouped into tribes headed by elected chiefs or sheiks and were bound by ties of blood revenge. Feuding among the tribes was endemic. The rigors of desert life bred in them a fierce sense of pride, great courage, and a keen fighting spirit, traits that would make them implacable conquerors in the name of Islam.

Religion

The traditional religion of the Arabs was animistic. They worshiped many gods who resided in sacred stones, trees, and other elements of nature. The city of Mecca, fifty miles inland from the Red Sea, was the spiritual home of the Arabs even in pre-Islamic days. It contained a famous square-shaped religious building, the Kaaba ("cube"), in which the images of hundreds of local deities were lodged.

All Arabs especially revered a small black stone there which they believed to be of heavenly origin. Many tribes made annual pilgrimages to worship it.

Foreign Influences

Outside influences entered Arabia through its chief cities, Mecca, Yathrib (later Medina), and Jiddah, which were all situated on or near the coast or at the intersection of caravan routes. Urban-dwelling Arabs earned their livelihood by catering to the trade that flowed between the Mediterranean and the East through Arabian ports and byways. Many of those engaged in commerce were Jews who may have immigrated to Arabia after their expulsion from Palestine in the first and second centuries A.D. Communities of Christian converts also existed in Arabia. Thus by the time of Muhammad's birth, Christian and Jewish ideas, especially the belief in one God, had permeated the Arabian Peninsula and would have a profound impact on the shaping of the Islamic faith.

Muhammad

The man whose teachings would alter the course of world history was born in Mecca around 570. Most of what is known about Muhammad is derived from faulty sources, and it is difficult to separate the facts from traditions. But sufficient data are available to sketch the outlines of his life.

Youth and Early Life

Muhammad's parents belonged to a lesser clan of the prominent Kuraish tribe that ruled Mecca. The Kuraishites derived their wealth and power from the caravan trade and from their custodianship of the Kaaba. Orphaned young in life, Muhammad spent his childhood under his uncle's care and learned the caravan trade. At the age of twenty-five he married a wealthy widow, Khadija, who carried on her late husband's successful caravan trade. Subsequently, Muhammad became a prosperous merchant. Yet his true interests were spiritual rather than material. He fasted frequently and spent many hours in solitary meditation.

Religious Revelations

When he was about forty years old Muhammad received the first of a series of revelations that would continue for the rest of his life and provide the essential content of his new faith. Transmitted from God (Allah) through the intermediary of the Archangel Gabriel, these revelations informed Muhammad that he was chosen as a prophet to whom would be revealed a perfect religion. Many religious concepts in the revelations parallel those in the Jewish and Christian religions.

Emigration to Medina

Initially, Muhammad was able to convert only his wife, Khadija, his cousin, Ali, and a prominent Meccan merchant, Abu Bakr. His preaching antagonized many prominent Kuraishites who feared that his attacks on the old pagan religion would jeopardize their revenues from the yearly pilgrimages to the Kaaba. They persecuted him and his small band of Muslims. Only in the town of Yathrib, over two hundred miles north of Mecca, did Muhammad's teachings gain encouraging acceptance. The citizens of Yathrib invited the Prophet to move there and put an end to a feud between rival ruling tribes. In 622 Muhammad and his followers secretly left Mecca for Yathrib. This event, the famous Hegira ("flight"), was so crucial to the future of Islam that its date of 622 became the year one in the Muslim calendar. Muhammad rapidly became both the spiritual and temporal ruler of the city, which he renamed Medina. He put into practice there his ideal of a theocratic state in which social, political, and religious conduct were all prescribed by Islamic law.

Conversion by Conquest

Muhammad's proselytizing brought him into conflict with the large and affluent Jewish community in Medina. Much to his disappointment, the Jews did not accept his new religion as an improvement on their own, and Muhammad began to persecute them. At the same time he endeavored to convert other Arabs. He harassed Meccan caravans as they moved north until war finally broke out. The Muslims first won a spectacular victory against great odds, then lost another and finally gained the right to make pilgrimages to Mecca. Muhammad went there himself in 629 and attracted important new followers. The next year

Mecca surrendered to a Muslim army without a fight. Muhammad cleared the Kaaba of all but the sacred Black Stone and made it the spiritual center of the Islamic faith.

By the time of his death in 632, Muhammad had brought large parts of Arabia under Islamic control. His ambitions for Islam were not, however, limited to an Arabic empire. In 629 he had launched an attack on the Byzantine Empire that proved unsuccessful. He preached the notion of a holy war, or *jihad,* against all unbelievers and promised paradise to those who died in fighting for Islam. Conversion by conquest became an accepted part of the faith.

Islamic Doctrines

The Prophet of Allah

Islam is essentially a simple faith. Its cardinal doctrine is that "there is no God but Allah and Muhammad is His prophet." The name Islam means "submission" and its adherents, Muslims, are "those who submit" to the will of Allah, "the God" in Arabic. Muhammad believed that Allah, one of the Arabs' ancient deities, was the only God and the same God as that worshipped by Christians and Jews. He came to regard himself as the last and foremost of a long line of prophets, beginning with Adam, to whom God had revealed his one, true faith.

Muslims recognize Abraham, Moses, Jesus, and numerous others as divinely chosen prophets. None was in possession of God's complete truth, and after their deaths humanity had gradually fallen away from the will of God. Muhammad, however, was selected as the last prophet and his revelation alone was God's definitive one. As such he was commissioned to preach the need for repentance and submission to these divine commands. After him there would be no further messages from God but rather the coming of the Last Judgment. Paradise awaits the faithful and those who die in defense of Islam, while the torments of hell will consume those who are evil or disbelieving.

The Koran

A few years after his death Muhammad's divine revelations were collected to form the Muslim holy book, the *Koran.* The official version of the *Koran,* established in 651–52, appears disorganized and abstruse to non-Muslim readers. Its 114 chapters follow no chronological or topical order, but are in general arranged according to length. The same fixed prayers to Allah are repeated throughout the work. Nonetheless, the beauty of its Arabic prose, especially when recited, and the force of its message of Allah's kindness and omnipotence make it one of the world's great religious books. The *Koran* is always used in Arabic for worship. Thus Muslims of every nationality are joined in their common knowledge of the Arabic language.

Five Duties of Islam

At Medina, Muhammad laid down five principal religious duties that all Muslims are obliged to carry out. Above all, they must profess with total conviction belief in only one God, Allah, and Muhammad's role as his prophet. Five times every day they must face in the direction of Mecca and recite set prayers of thanksgiving and praise to Allah. They must give alms generously to those in need. For the entire month of Ramadan all who are physically able must keep a strict fast, doing without food, drink, or sexual relations, between dawn and dusk. Finally, if at all possible Muslims must undertake a pilgrimage to Mecca at least once in their lives. These obligations constitute the essence of Islamic worship.

Other Requirements

Other rules were developed for Islam. Muslims who were able were required to fight in holy wars. Muhammad legislated against certain secular practices. For example, Muslims are prohibited from gambling, drinking wine, eating pork, venerating idols, and practicing usury. Other Muslim laws permitted men to have four wives, regulated divorce, and bettered the lot of women and slaves.

Period of Islam's Expansion

A century after the death of Christ, Christianity remained a small, persecuted religious sect. By contrast, within one hundred years of the Hegira, Islam had spread with breathtaking speed throughout the Near East, North Africa, and parts of Europe. Between the seventh and the ninth centuries, Muslim generals conquered vast territories from the western frontier of China to the Iberian peninsula.

Reasons for Islam's Success

Many explanations have been given to account for the tremendous success of Arab conquests. Among them are the universal appeal of Islam's religious message; the disaffection of many Christians, Jews, and Zoroastrians in the Near East with their religious and political status; and the weakness of the Byzantine and Persian Empires after decades of debilitating conflict. History books often depict the Arabs as storming out of the desert with a sword in one hand and the *Koran* in the other to be rewarded for death in a holy war with the assurance of going to paradise. While this image conveys some truth, the Arabs were motivated by other forces as well. These included their appetite for war, the lure of booty, and the need for more fertile lands.

Muhammad's Successors

At the time of Muhammad's death in 632, the future of Islam was in doubt. The Prophet's followers quarreled over who would become the first caliph, the temporal and spiritual leader of the Muslim community. Their choice was Abu Bakr, a close friend of Muhammad and one of his earliest converts. Bakr suppressed a rebellion of Arabic tribes against Islamic control and then set out to forge a great Arab empire on behalf of the new faith. He and his three successors, Umar, Uthman, and Ali, are known as the Orthodox Caliphs (ruled 632–661) and under them Islam entered its first phase of expansion.

Conquests in the East

After inflicting several defeats upon the impoverished Byzantine Empire, the Arabs had added Syria to their domain by 636. Jerusalem surrendered in 638 and all of Palestine fell into Arab hands. Between 639 and 642 the Byzantines lost Egypt, which became the Arabs' chief naval base on the Mediterranean. From there Arab ships captured the island of Cyprus in 649. Simultaneous with their attacks on Byzantine territories, the Arabs set upon the feeble Sassanid dynasty and brought it to an end. First Iraq and then Persia itself were joined to the burgeoning Islamic Empire. During these early conquests, Arab armies encountered little opposition because the Persian and Byzantine Empires were in weakened condition. Heavy taxes and religious persecution estranged the Monophysites in Syria and Egypt from their

250 Chapter 8

Byzantine masters. While the Arabs expected their new subjects to convert to Islam and imposed a special tax on those who did not, in general they treated the conquered peoples well. Jews and Christians received religious toleration as "peoples of the Book." All non-Muslims were prohibited from serving in the new government or military.

Conflict and Schism

Succession to the caliphate created unrest throughout medieval Islamic history. Of the first four caliphs, all but Bakr were murdered. At issue was often the problem of whether the caliph should be a member of Muhammad's family. Ali, the fourth caliph, was a cousin and son-in-law of the Prophet. The powerful Umayyad family, to which the third caliph, Uthmann, had belonged, refused to recognize Ali's right to rule. Their leader Muawiya, governor of Syria, struggled with Ali over control of the government until the latter's assassination in 661. Muawiya became caliph and founded the Umayyad Caliphate (661–750), triggering a major religious schism within Islam. Those who believed that only Ali and his descendants were the legitimate rulers of Islam became known as Shiites. They differed from the main body of Muslims as well in their denigration of the first three caliphs and their rejection of the post-Muhammad *Sunna* traditions about and sayings of Muhammad that supplemented the *Koran*. The majority of Muslims, known as Sunnites, held the caliphs before Ali in high esteem, supported the Umayyad dynasty, and denied the claims of Ali and his progeny to exclusive sovereignty. As the party of orthodoxy, the Sunnites accepted both the *Sunna* and the *Koran* as authoritative guides to proper conduct.

Conquests Under the Umayyads

Muawiya transferred the capital of Islam to Damascus in Syria and made the caliphate hereditary. He created a standing army and molded the Arabs into a unified fighting force. Under the Umayyads further conquests extended Islamic control from the Pyrenees to the Indus River and the western border of China. War continued with the Byzantine Empire. For many years the Muslims staged annual attacks on Constantinople, all of them unsuccessful until 1453. The failure of the siege of 717–718 proved crucial in the struggle to block the Arabs' movement

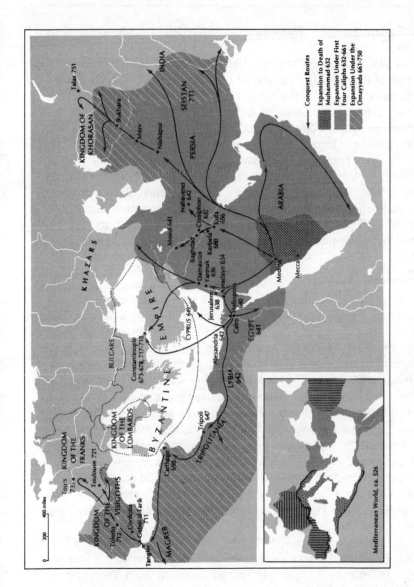

The Expansion of Islam

Conquest Routes

Expansion to Death of
Muhammad 632

Expansion Under First
Four Caliphs 632-661

Expansion Under the
Omayyads 661-750

KINGDOM OF KHORASAN

INDIA

SEISTAN
711

PERSIA

Talas 751

Bukhara

Merv

Nishapur

Nahavend
642

Ctesiphon
637

Kufa
656

Mosul 641

Baghdad

Karbela
680

Damascus

Yarmuk
636

Qadisiyah 634

ARABIA

Medina

Mecca

KHAZARS

BYZANTINE EMPIRE

BULGARS

Constantinople
673-678, 717-718

CYPRUS 649

Jerusalem
638

Heliopolis
640

Cairo

Alexandria
642

EGYPT
641

LYBIA
642

KINGDOM OF THE FRANKS

Tours 732

Toulouse 721

KINGDOM OF THE LOMBARDS

KINGDOM OF THE VISIGOTHS

Toledo
712

Cordoba

Gebel al Tarik
711

Tangier

MAGREB

Carthage
698

Tripoli
647

TRIPOLITANIA

0   200   400 miles

Mediterranean World, ca. 526

into Eastern Europe. Elsewhere, however, Islam made tremendous strides.

In 698, Byzantine Carthage fell and after prolonged resistance on the part of the nomadic Berbers, all of North Africa was brought over to the new faith. From there, in 711, a combined array of Arabs and Berbers crossed the Strait of Gibraltar to conquer the Visigothic kingdom in Spain. Fourteen years later the Muslim army had reached the Pyrenees and began advancing into the realm of the Franks. In 732, near Tours, a Frankish force commanded by Charles Martel won an important victory over the Arabs. The Battle of Tours had momentous consequences for the future of Europe. The weakened Muslim invaders retreated behind the Pyrenees, never again to pose a serious threat to northern Europe from Spain. Islam retained, nonetheless, its foothold on the Iberian peninsula, where a brilliant offshoot of Islamic civilization arose.

Abbasid Caliphate

In general the Umayyads were good rulers and their reigns saw prosperous economic conditions and splendid cultural accomplishments. Their principal support came from the Arab tribes of Syria. Thus the Arabs enjoyed a favored position under the Umayyad Caliphate even though they were now in the minority among the Empire's inhabitants. They received higher wages and more booty as soldiers, paid fewer taxes, and occupied most governmental posts. This Arab bias antagonized many of the various peoples who had been converted to Islam in the wake of a century of conquests.

Revolt Against Umayyad Rule. Opposition to the Umayyads crystallized around the Shiite party whose ranks were now filled with disgruntled non-Arab Muslims. In 750, a descendant of Muhammad's uncle Abbas overthrew the Umayyads in temporary conjunction with the Shiites. Some ninety members of the Umayyad family were massacred.

Persian Dominance. Under the new Abbasid Caliphate (750–1258), Persian influences came to prevail over Arabic and Byzantine ones. In 762, the capital was moved eastward from Damascus to Baghdad in Iraq. Persians and other non-Arabs took over most important positions in the administration and military. The caliph assumed the autocratic powers and lavish ceremonial trappings of a Persian monarch. All religious and civil authority including the power to declare a holy war emanated from him. He was expected, however, to use it in keeping with the provisions of the *Koran* and the *Sunna*. Instead of administering the empire directly themselves as their predecessors had done, the Abassids transferred the responsibility to paid officials. The head of this bureaucracy was the vizier. In times of weak caliphs, he was often the effective chief of state.

Height of Islamic Civilization

During the first century of Abbasid rule, medieval Islamic civilization reached its zenith. The reigns in Baghdad of Harun al-Rashid (ruled 787–809), a contemporary of Charlemagne, and his son, al-Mamun (ruled 813–833), stand out as the summit of Islamic wealth, opulence, and cultural glory. After them the Empire gradually fell into decay.

The Breakup of the Islamic Empire

The Abbasid Caliphate had been troubled by insurrections from the start. Especially after the reign of Harun al-Rashid, assassinations, rebellions in the provinces, and a decline in imperial revenues seriously vitiated the caliph's central control.

Local Rulers

Rural dynasties began challenging the political unity of the Abbasid empire. As early as 755, a member of the deposed Umayyad family had founded an essentially independent state in Spain centered at Cordova. In 929, its rulers awarded themselves the title of caliph. Other local governors established their own kingdoms in Morocco, Tunisia, Egypt, Syria, and eastern Persia during the late eighth and ninth centuries.

Fatimid Dynasty

Most of North Africa as well as Malta, Sardinia, Corsica, Sicily, Palestine, and parts of Syria and Arabia came under the sway of the Shiite dynasty, the Fatimids, in the tenth century. The Fatimids claimed descent from Ali and his wife Fatima, the daughter of Muhammad.

After conquering Egypt in 969, they built the city of Cairo as a rival to Baghdad. Fatimid prosperity was short-lived. A century later, the Fatimid Caliphate had been stripped of its territories and in 1171 Abbasid Sunnite rule was restored at Cairo.

Turkish Encroachment

As their empire broke up around them, the Abbasid caliphs were preoccupied with palace intrigues and voluptuous living. No longer able to support a large standing army from their reduced funds, the caliphs began to grant large tracts of land to those who furnished troops and goods. This fostered the growth of semiautonomous fiefdoms and further undermined centralized authority. Turks replaced Persians in both the army and administration. In 1055, the Seljuk Turks captured Baghdad and eventually controlled most of the Muslim lands in the East as well as Byzantine Asia Minor. Although the Abbasids remained on the throne, apart from spiritual matters they were little more than ciphers.

Fall of the Islamic Empire

Two centuries later, the rise of the Mongols, an obscure nomadic people from inner Asia, brought wholesale destruction to the Islamic world. Baghdad fell in 1258. The conquerors deposed the Abbasids, slew the caliph, and laid waste to the irrigation system upon which civilized life in Iraq had relied. Not until modern times did Iraq regain its economic well-being. One member of the Abbasid family made his way to Cairo where he founded a new line of the Abbasid Caliphate. Real power was in the hands of the Mamluks, non-Arab slaves who formed a warrior caste in Egypt. They successfully repulsed the Mongol attack and ruled Egypt and parts of the Near East until conquered by the Ottoman Turks in 1517. Shortly after that date the last of the Abbasid caliphs died and the line came to an end. The Arab empire ceased to exist. Yet, the rending of Islamic political unity did not disturb the growth and sense of community of Muslim civilization. The Abbasids' Seljuk and Ottoman conquerors embraced the Islamic faith. New converts continued to flock to Islam so that at present approximately one out of every seven human beings is a Muslim.

Islamic Civilization

Medieval Islam was deeply interested in the advancement of learning. Beginning in the ninth-century reign of Harun al-Rashid, Muslim scholars translated into Arabic a great number of ancient Greek, Indian, and Persian writings on philosophy, medicine, mathematics, and astronomy. Harun's son, al-Mamun, founded in Baghdad a "House of Wisdom" in which translators could work and their copies be stored for future reference. Thus the Muslims had access to the wisdom of the classical past that was largely unavailable at the time in medieval Europe. They preserved and eventually passed on this heritage of Greek philosophy and science to the West along with their own contributions. Under the munificent patronage of the Umayyad and the Abbasid caliphs, Islamic literature, philosophy, architecture, and decorative arts all burst into flower.

Economic Basis

Like its Byzantine neighbor, Islam enjoyed a level of prosperity far superior to that of medieval Europe during the eighth through the twelfth centuries. There are numerous reasons for Islam's flourishing and varied economy. The broad extent of the Empire promoted a busy and diversified trade among its various states, while its geographic location made the Muslims natural intermediaries in the trade between north and south and east and west. Silks from China, spices from India, furs from Russia, and ivory from Africa often passed through Muslim traders on their way to Western Europe. Goods produced within the Empire (i.e., steel from Damascus, textiles from Baghdad, and leather from Cordova) were also highly sought after. The use of one language, Arabic, throughout the Empire was a boon to travel and commercial transactions. Mobility within the Empire was also promoted by the religious requirement of a pilgrimage to Mecca.

Importance of Trade. Islam's favorable attitude toward commerce also contributed to the Empire's economic well-being. Muhammad had himself been a trader. Thus the merchant occupied an honorable position within Islamic society. Even non-Muslim merchants were permitted to live within Muslim boundaries in order to trade with their homelands. The heart of the empire lay along the ancient caravan routes of the Near East. These remained an important generator of Muslim riches. In addition, trade by sea became a major source of the Empire's prosperity. Muslim fleets sailed as far as the Indian Ocean.

Cities. The commercial wealth of the Muslim world was concentrated in its great urban centers: Baghdad, Damascus, Cairo, and Cordova. Almost every conceivable product of the known world filled the markets or bazaars of these cities.

Agriculture. An extensive and innovative agriculture sustained this urban affluence and commercial expansion. The Muslims planted new crops such as rice, which they had brought back from Asia. In Iraq they greatly increased the land's yield by the use of irrigation. The agricultural work force consisted of both slave and free labor.

Economic Decline. Until the thirteenth century, most of the Islamic states continued to enjoy a thriving economy. Thereafter, trade dwindled as the Venetians and others supplanted Muslim maritime power on the Mediterranean. The caliph's wealth declined significantly and the growth of large estates and a rural aristocracy undermined urban prosperity.

Islamic Society

Medieval Islamic society displayed an essential uniformity despite the variety of cultures and peoples within the Muslim world, because everywhere social practices were based on the religious laws of Islam.

Status of Non-Muslims. The most unbridgeable gap within Islamic society was that which separated Muslims from nonbelievers. The latter were excluded from any role in governing or protecting the state. Except for Jews, Christians, and Zoroastrians, they were regarded as enemies to be converted or killed.

Sectarian and Class Divisions. Within Islam itself sectarian differences such as those that divided the Sunnites and Shiites created another social chasm. Although Muhammed taught that all Muslims are brothers and equals, national and class distinctions were apparent within the social order of medieval Islamdom. At the top were the caliph, his family, and the highest government and military officials. City-dwellers for the most part ranked above inhabitants of the countryside. Slaves, who were usually non-Muslims, possessed the lowest social status although, if converted, they often occupied important posts within the government, army, or harem.

Status of Women. One of the most prominent features of traditional Islamic society is the secondary status allotted to women. Females lived under a series of religious and social restrictions. They were subservient first to their fathers and then to their husbands, who were able to divorce them with ease. Though their property rights were protected, they were forced to live secluded lives, to pray at home, and to veil their faces in front of all but their husbands. Islamic law sanctioned polygamy, although its practice was never widespread among the whole population.

Islamic Medicine

In the field of medicine the Muslims progressed beyond their Greek and Indian models. Not until the eighteenth century did Europe approach the Muslims in their understanding and treatment of diseases such as smallpox and measles.

Rhazes. Muslim doctors drew their knowledge of medicine from the writings of Galen and Hippocrates and from their own clinical experience. One of the greatest of them was al-Raxi, whom Westerners called Rhazes (c. 860–c. 925). He was head physician at the hospital in Baghdad and the author of more than two hundred works. His treatise *On Smallpox and Measles* contains the first known description of smallpox. He also wrote a textbook and a multivolume encyclopedia of medicine, the *Comprehensive Book*, which collected all available knowledge including his own clinical observations about a wide variety of diseases. His encyclopedia and some other works were translated into Latin in the fifteenth century and became an invaluable source of information for European physicians.

Avicenna. The other outstanding figure in Muslim medicine was the Persian philosopher Avicenna (980–1037). He also wrote an encyclopedic work, the *Canon of Medicine*, in which he systematized ancient Greek and Arabic medical scholarship. From the twelfth to the sixteenth centuries Avicenna's name dominated the study of medicine. The *Canon of Medicine* first appeared in Latin in the 1100s and was reissued dozens of times during the next 400 years.

Islamic Sciences

Muslim scholars added to the store of knowledge in other scientific fields.

Optics and Mathematics. In optics the Muslims surpassed the ancient Greeks in their understanding of vision and the reflection and refraction of light. In mathematics they borrowed the Hindus' numerical system and were most likely responsible for adding the essential notion of zero. These are the "Arabic" numerals of Western usage. Building upon Indian and Greek accomplishments, they made considerable headway in algebra, geometry and trigonometry. The famous Persian poet Omar Khayyám was also a noted mathematician who wrote on cubic equations.

Astronomy. Muslim astronomy remained tied to astrology but it progressed nonetheless. In order to study the heavens the Muslims constructed observatories and took careful measurements of the heavenly bodies over an extended period of time. They devised a more precise astrolabe and revised the astronomical calculations of the ancient Greeks.

Geography. Muslim geographers enriched knowledge of the earth. Because of the empire's great span and the constant travel of merchants and pilgrims, Muslim cartographers were able to make more accurate maps of their lands than any comparable maps to be found in the medieval West.

Islamic Literature

Arabic literature is rooted in the nomadic poetry of the pre-Islamic past. The Bedouins composed odes on love, combat, hunting, and tribal life in a distinctive style that was rich in imagery. With the coming of Islam, the *Koran* replaced poetry as the focus of Arabian literature. Although written in prose, the Koran retained this poetic impulse, perhaps because of the expressiveness of the Arabic language.

Omar Khayyám. Arabic poetry flourished again beginning in the late eighth century. The eleventh-century Persian poet and mathematician, Omar Khayyám, wrote beautiful, melancholy quatrains on the fleeting pleasures of life. His *Rubáiyát* achieved immense popularity in the West as a result of Edward Fitzgerald's free English translation of it in 1859.

Arabian Nights. The other famous classic of Islamic literature is the prose romance, the *Thousand and One Nights*, or *Arabian Nights*. This is a collection of exotic stories of unknown origin from the eighth to the fourteenth centuries. Most of the stories are probably of Indian, Persian, Jewish, or Greek derivation although they have been set in a Muslim framework and the caliph Harun al-Rashid often appears in them. The tales of Ali Baba, Aladdin, and Sinbad the Sailor are familiar to most Westerners.

Philosophy. Islam inspired numerous nonfictional writings. These included Koranic interpretations, theological and philosophical works, legal treatises, biographies of Muhammad, and histories. Of these, Muslim philosophy had the greatest impact on Western culture. The Muslims analyzed the writings of Plato, Aristotle, and the Neoplatonists in order to answer the pressing questions of free will and predestination, faith and reason, and the nature of God and His revelation. The physician Avicenna and others attempted to bring Greek philosophy in accord with Islamic belief. The great Spanish philosopher Averroës (1126–1198) held that philosophic reason and religion did not conflict but operated in separate spheres. His commentaries on Aristotle played a more important role in the development of medieval Christian thought than in that of Islam and were a piquant influence on the great thirteenth-century Western theologian Thomas Aquinas.

Islamic Arts

In the arts, the pre-Islamic Arab heritage was less rich than in literature. The nomadic Arabs had no tradition of monumental building and Muhammad banished their pagan statuary. Thus Islamic art and architecture developed as an eclectic synthesis of Byzantine, Sassanid, and later Chinese forms. The earliest mosques were decorated in the Byzantine mosaic technique by craftsmen imported from Constantinople. When the Abbasids moved their place of residence to Baghdad, Sassanid influences predominated. From the Persians the Muslims acquired their taste for bright colors and highly decorative mythical animals.

Architecture. While Islamic architectural styles varied according to time and place, they had several features in common. For example, Muslim mosques are all aligned toward Mecca. They include a minaret, or tower, from which the *muezzin* (crier) calls the faithful to prayer. Outside of North Africa and Spain, where a distinctive Islamic style known as Moorish prevailed, most mosques were domed structures. Muslim architects also made frequent use of horseshoe-shaped arches. They covered the interior and sometimes the exterior surfaces of Muslim buildings with a wealth of surface ornament. Calligraphic bands of passages from the *Koran* and divine law or the same basic abstract patterns, such as the interlacing arabesque line, are repeated over and over.

Painting and Sculpture. Islam's negative attitude toward the representation of living things stifled the development of Muslim painting and sculpture. Muhammad forbade images that might detract from the direct worship of God. He abominated sculpture but his opinion of painted images was less clear-cut. By the ninth century, however, Islamic law prohibited the representation of human and animal figures because God alone has the power to create. Yet people and animals continued to appear in Islamic art. Their portrayal was tolerated when on a small scale and used as decoration, though they were never allowed in sculptural form. Therefore, Muslim artists tended to concentrate on arts such as metalwork, rugmaking, lusterware, leatherwork, and illuminated manuscripts, which they decorated with rich geometric patterns, abstract flower designs, or sinuous calligraphy.

The two great civilizations, the Byzantine and the Islamic, that flourished in the East for much of the time between the fall of Rome in 476 and the fall of Constantinople in 1453 shared a number of common features. Both were highly prosperous urban cultures in which learning and the arts thrived. Both were major purveyors of the achievements of Indian, Persian, Graeco-Roman, and their own civilizations to the more culturally backward medieval West. Each possessed an empire and was governed by an absolute ruler who held religious as well as secular power. Yet differences outweigh similarities.

Byzantium was the bastion of classical civilization and Orthodox Christianity. Rome's laws, cosmopolitan outlook, and imperial structure lived on in it and blended with Greek, Oriental, and Christian influences to create a uniquely Byzantine culture. The new Kievan state's conversion to Orthodox Christianity in the tenth century brought the benefits of Byzantine civilization to a new people, the Russians. During its long history Byzantium experienced periods of political greatness and decline and was gradually shorn of its extensive territories, many of which fell into Muslim hands. Yet, for a millennium the Byzantine Empire served as a barrier protecting the West from barbarian and Islamic attacks out of Asia.

Byzantium's rival and eventual conqueror, the civilization of Islam, derived its zeal for conquest from its faith. Founded in the early seventh century by Muhammad, the new monotheistic religion of Islam incorporated many Jewish and Christian beliefs. It differed, however, in its view of Muhammad as the final prophet and in its formulation of religious life and duties. Motivated by the desire to attain paradise as well as the need for better land, Arab Muslims conquered a broad segment of the ancient world and converted it with astonishing swiftness to Islam. At its territorial and cultural zenith during the early years of the Abbasid dynasty at Baghdad, the Islamic Empire eclipsed Rome's in size. By the thirteenth century, however, it had disintegrated into separate Muslim states and its culture had declined, yet the Islamic religion has remained a potent force in world affairs up through the present.

Recommended Reading

Philippe Ariès et al., eds., *A History of Private Life, vol. I: From Pagan Rome to Byzantium* (1987).

J.B. Bury, *A History of the Eastern Roman Empire* (1912).

J.B. Bury, *A History of the Later Roman Empire 395–802* (1889).

Patricia Cone and Michael Cook, *Hagarism: The Making of the Islamic World* (1980).

Samuel Hazard Cross, ed., *Russian Primary Chronicle: Laurentian Text* (1953).

Charles Diehl, *Byzantium: Greatness and Decline* (1957).

G.P. Fedotov, *The Russian Religious Mind* (1946).

Deno J. Geanakoplos, *Byzantium: Church, Society and Civilization Seen Through Contemporary Eyes* (1986).

H.A.R. Gibb, *Mohammedism: An Historical Survey* (1953).

Harold Lamb, *Theodora and the Emperor* (1952).

Bernard Lewis, *The Arabs in History* (1966).

Bernard Lewis, *The Muslim Discovery of Europe* (1982).

Bernard Lewis, ed., *Islam and the Arab World* (1976).

Bernard Lewis, ed. & trans., *Islam from the Prophet Mohammed to the Capture of Constantinople* (1987).

Harry J. Magoulias, *Byzantine Christianity: Emperor, Church and the West* (1982).

Dean A. Miller, *The Byzantine Tradition* (1966).

Dean A. Miller, *Imperial Constantinople* (1969).

William Muir, *The Caliphate, Its Rise, Decline and Fall* (1915).

George Ostrogorski, *History of the Byzantine State* (1957).

Jaroslav Pelikan, *The Christian Tradition, vol. II: The Spirit of Eastern Christendom (600–1700)* (1977).

M. Pickthall, trans., *The Meaning of the Glorious Koran* (1948).

Fazlur Rahman, *Islam* (1966).

David T. Rice, *Art of the Byzantine Era* (1985).

Steven Runciman, *Byzantine Style and Civilization* (1975).

Alexander A. Vasiliev, *History of the Byzantine Empire 324–1453* (1952).

George Vernadsky, *Kievan Russia* (1973).

Vladimir Volkoff, *Vladimir the Russian Viking* (1985).

T. Ware, *The Orthodox Church* (1963).

W.M. Watt, *Muhammad: Prophet and Statesman* (1961).

CHAPTER 9

The Early Middle Ages

Time Line

263

756	"Donation of Pepin"
c. 782	Alcuin establishes palace school at Aachen
787	First Viking raid on England
800	Charlemagne crowned "Emperor of the Romans"
843	Treaty of Verdun divides Carolingian Empire
845	Viking army burns Paris
865	Large settlement of Danes in England
871	Alfred the Great becomes first King of all England
878	Peace of Wedmore recognized Danish overlordship in part of England
911	Normandy recognized as independent Norse duchy
c. 1000	Oldest extant manuscript of *Beowulf*
1016–1035	Canute rules over England, Denmark, and Norway

The approximately one thousand years between the collapse of the Western Roman Empire in the fifth century A.D. and the rediscovery of classical culture in fifteenth-century Renaissance Italy are known as the Middle Ages. Until fairly recently, scholars regarded the Middle Ages as an age of darkness and cultural barbarism that fell between two great civilizations. While retaining the term Middle Ages for these years, modern historians no longer consider them as stagnant and unproductive. Rather, their researches have revealed the era to be a dynamic and innovative one.

The descriptive term, "Dark Ages," seems most true for the early Middle Ages, a period from approximately A.D. 500 to 1000. The transition from ancient to medieval civilization did entail substantial losses at first. Above all the central authority of the Empire disappeared and with it the Europeans lost the amenities of imperial administration, postal service, road maintenance, and coinage. Communications during the early Middle Ages were slow and difficult. Trade was greatly reduced. Violence and insecurity were endemic. Much of the classical heritage disappeared. Only the Roman Catholic Church remained as a symbol of universality. Yet it was during this period that a new European civilization evolved out of Roman, Germanic, and Christian elements. Largely because of the Muslims' dominance of the Mediterranean region, its center of gravity shifted farther north and west than in the old Roman Empire.

Most of the barbarian kingdoms founded in the wake of Rome's dissolution survived for only a few centuries. Those of the Anglo-Saxons in Britain and the Franks in Gaul proved, however, of long-lasting significance. Under Charlemagne, the Franks temporarily restored the order and cohesiveness of an imperial structure. The failure of the Carolingian Empire and the chaos wrought by the Viking invasions of the ninth century spurred the creation of new social, political, and legal institutions that afforded a measure of stability in tumultuous times. Historians refer to this new form of government and social structure as feudalism. Its economic counterpart was the manorial system.

Anglo-Saxon England

Roman civilization never penetrated the remote province of Britain as deeply as it had the European continent. Two hundred years after the last Roman troops departed from Britain, at the beginning of the fifth century, few traces of Roman influence remained. Many towns were deserted, Roman villas were abandoned, and the upper strata of educated Romans had practically disappeared.

Anglo-Saxon Invasions

Abandoned to their own defenses by an overburdened Empire, the native Britons, or Celts, as they are called, had been too weak to fend off barbarian invaders from across the North Sea. These invaders—the Angles, Saxons, and Jutes—were part of the great migration of Germanic tribes that swept across Roman borders during the fifth century.

Our picture of them is imperfect because the few written sources for early Anglo-Saxon England are unreliable. However, fresh archaeological discoveries are modifying and gradually filling out this picture.

Origins of Anglo-Saxons

Historians disagree over the exact place of origin of these closely related tribes. It is generally thought that the Angles originated in Schlesweg. The Saxons probably first lived in Germany while the Jutes may have come from Jutland in Denmark. Another people, the Frisians, may also have settled in Britain. Unfortunately, none of this is certain. Wherever their precise homelands, the Anglo-Saxons, as the invaders are traditionally called, were all illiterate pagans barely touched by Roman civilization. They first appeared in Britain as countless small bands of raiders led by warrior chieftains. The indigenous Britons may even have invited some to aid them in fighting the Picts to the north in exchange for land. Eventually the Anglo-Saxons settled down in piecemeal fashion and gradually lost contact with their native lands.

Anglo-Saxon Settlement

Around the middle of the fifth century a full-scale Anglo-Saxon invasion seems to have taken place. Evidence suggests that the Celts were successful for a time in resisting the Anglo-Saxons' advance. But many native Celts were later massacred, while others fled northward and westward into parts of Scotland, Wales, and Ireland ("the Celtic Fringe"), where they preserved intact their language and customs. At a later date English Celts crossed the Channel and settled in the area still known as Brittany. Others remained to work the land as the subjects of their new Anglo-Saxon masters. The process of settlement was a slow one. By the beginning of the seventh century, however, the Anglo-Saxons were firmly in control of most of "Angle-Land," or England.

Religion

Religious unification preceded political unification in England.

The Romans had brought Christianity to Britain. The Anglo-Saxons, however, were heathens, and their conquest destroyed the administrative structure of the Roman Catholic Church. Memory of Christian beliefs faded away among the native Britons.

Celtic Christianity

The Church continued to thrive, however, in Cornwall, Wales, Ireland, and parts of Scotland. Because they were increasingly cut off from contact with the Continent, these Celtic Christians developed certain practices that were at variance with the Roman Church. In the sixth century, both Celtic and Roman missionaries undertook the task of converting pagan England. Celtic Christianity spread to Scotland and northern England from a monastery on the Scottish island of Iona founded by St. Columba in 563.

Roman Christianity

In 597 Pope Gregory sent a Benedictine monk, Augustine, and forty other monks to evangelize at the court of King Ethelbert in southern England. Following the conversion of this kingdom, Gregory named Augustine Archbishop of Canterbury in 601.

The Synod of Whitby

Over the next sixty years, Anglo-Saxon kingdoms embraced the Christian faith. In 663 or 664 a synod at Whitby resolved the major differences between Celtic and Latin Christianity in Rome's favor. Henceforth England joined the mainstream of continental Christianity. Conversion had a tremendous civilizing effect on Anglo-Saxon England. The English Church grew into a strong and vital institution and acted as an important unifying force.

Rise of the Seven Kingdoms

After the conquest, political power rested in the hands of tribal chieftains who had the good luck and military prowess to dominate their neighbors. By the seventh century, the most powerful chieftains had consolidated these petty dynasties into seven territorial states: Northumbria, Mercia, East Anglia, Essex, Sussex, Kent, and Wessex (the Heptarchy), each ruled by its own king. These kingdoms were rivals and often fought each other for land. Supremacy passed from Kent in the early seventh century to Northumbria, and in the eighth century, to Mercia. One of Mercia's kings, Offa (reigned 757–796), called himself *Rex Anglorum*. He built a long dike to mark the border between England and Wales and signed the first English commercial treaty with his contemporary, Charlemagne. Mercia's primacy ended with Offa's death. In the ninth century Wessex emerged under King Egbert (reigned 802–839) as the leading kingdom. His grandson, Alfred the Great, became the first king of a united England.

Development of Government

While political centralization eluded the English for several centuries, they developed governmental institutions, especially at the local level, which greatly enriched England's political heritage.

The Witan

All Anglo-Saxon monarchs ruled with the aid of counselors known as the *witan* ("wise men"), who were drawn from the most powerful families of the realm. The *witan* gave advice, adjudicated cases, helped put royal decisions into effect, and even selected kings in times of crisis when no heir existed.

Earls

There grew up over time and in various ways regional divisions known as shires and subdivisions of them known as hundreds. In late Saxon England there were over fifty shires. Each was headed by a shire lord, or ealdorman, the main administrative and military leader of the district, who was responsible only to the king. Many ealdormen became so powerful that they exercised control over neighboring shires and became hereditary earls.

Sheriffs

To curb the independence of the earls and carry out the king's business in the shires, a new royal official, the "shire reeve," or sheriff, was appointed. As a royal administrator with judicial functions, he presided over the shire court, which met twice yearly to try the most important cases in the shire.

Courts

Local freemen who sat as members of the shire court made known the customary law, but the verdict was reached by the use of oathhelpers or trial by ordeal, a procedure that relied on God's intervention to make known the truth. There were also hundred courts that convened monthly to deal with routine conflicts. These courts brought royal justice to the local level and encouraged both popular participation and a degree of administrative uniformity. By the eleventh century, however, royal grants had transferred most of these courts into the hands of aristocratic landowners.

New Invasions

The rise of Wessex to hegemony over the other Anglo-Saxon kingdoms coincided with a new invasion of England's shores.

The Vikings

In 787, heathen raiders from Scandinavia, called Northmen or Vikings, landed their long ships for the first time on English soil and plundered the surrounding countryside. For the next 150 years the Vikings spread destruction along major waterways in the British Isles and western Europe. They colonized Iceland, conquered Ireland, and took possession of the area of Normandy in northern France that bears their name. Viking leaders from Sweden and Finland gained power in Russia. Their delight in bloodshed and unrestrained violence inspired terror in the settled populations of Europe.

The Danes

In English history these Northmen are usually referred to as Danes because the principal invaders of England at this time came from Denmark. Until the mid-ninth century small bands of warriors raided England each summer for plunder and returned home. However, in 851 a much larger force of Danes sailed up the Thames River, burned London, and wintered near the English coast. Henceforth the Danes began to settle permanently. A great expedition of Danish settlers arrived in 865 and overran almost all of the land.

Alfred the Great

Of the Anglo-Saxon kingdoms in England, only Wessex succeeded in containing the Danes, thanks to the stalwartness and foresight of its king, Alfred the Great (reigned 871–899). In 870 Danish forces launched a major assault upon Wessex. After several years of inconclusive fighting, Alfred negotiated a truce by paying the Danes a large tribute. He raised the money by levying a tax (the *Danegeld*).

Military Reforms

In the five years of peace that followed the truce, Alfred wisely initiated a series of military reforms. To combat seaborne invasions, he ordered the construction of new ships and improved their design. For this he has been called the founder of the English navy. To strengthen Wessex's defenses on land he built large fortifications and refurbished existing ones. He reorganized his peasant infantry, or *fryd*, into two units at the shire level so that while one was away fighting the other could stay home to till the fields. This reduced desertion and made continuous military service possible. These reforms enabled Wessex to hold its own against the Danes and laid the basis for its conquest of England.

Treaty with Danes

In January 878, a group of Danes under the command of Guthrum invaded Wessex by surprise and forced Alfred to take refuge on the Isle of Athelney. However, in the spring Alfred rallied his army and decisively defeated Guthrum at Edington. In the ensuing Peace of Wedmore (878) the Danish chieftain agreed to vacate Wessex permanently and to convert to Christianity. In the treaty, Alfred acknowledged Danish lordship over a broad area to the east and north of the Thames, which included Yorkshire, East Anglia, and a part of eastern Mercia called the Five Boroughs. Collectively known as the Danelaw, this region adopted Danish customs and laws that had a lasting imprint on English culture.

Alfred's Achievements

By the end of his reign Alfred was acclaimed the King of England with authority over all the country except those parts under Danish control. He had reaped further military successes by recapturing London and parts of Mercia from the Danes in 886. Yet his fame lay not solely on his role as soldier-king but also as a scholar. He gave new impetus to vernacular writing. Because the Danish invasions had greatly reduced the number of people who knew Latin, he promoted the reading and writing of Old English among the nobility as well as the clergy. To this end he and his scholars translated some of the most valuable Latin works, including Pope Gregory's *Pastoral Care* and Boethius's *Consolation of Philosophy*, into the English tongue. The unique *Anglo-Saxon Chronicle*, a composite history of England in the vernacular that extended from the time of Christ until the twelfth century, was probably begun at this time. Alfred's sense of justice and his creative mind are also reflected in the code of laws he compiled by selecting and rejecting the laws decreed by his predecessors. These intellectual accomplishments are rendered all the more impressive when set against the insecurity and lawlessness of the age.

Alfred's Successors

Until 975, Alfred's descendants enjoyed fruitful reigns. They gradually reconquered the Danelaw and made themselves kings of a unified England. Their administrative structure attained a degree of centralization far in advance of those on the continent. Trade and towns enjoyed a revival of growth. Church reform restored the English monasteries to strict Benedictine rule and promoted learning and morality among the secular clergy. Unfortunately, with the reign of Ethelred "the Unready" (ruled 978–1016), the quality of royal leadership declined. In 991, a Danish army ravaged southern England until Ethelred levied a *Danegeld* to pay them off. Henceforth the *Danegeld* was collected regularly and continued to furnish the monarchy with income long after it had lost its association with the Danish emergency.

Canute

Recurrent Norse invasions revealed England's weakness and the incompetence of its king. The Anglo-Danes turned disloyal to English rule. Upon Ethelred's death in 1016 a quarrel over the succession arose. Parts of England supported Ethelred's son, Edmund Ironside, while other areas rallied to the Dane, Canute, whose father had conquered most of England three years previously. Canute quickly defeated his rival and ruled England from 1016 until 1035. In addition, he succeeded to the throne of Denmark and conquered Norway, thus amassing a powerful northern empire. A civilized, Christian monarch, Canute reigned fairly and with respect for English laws and customs. He promoted the interests of the church and was generally well regarded by his subjects. His reign marks the end of strife between the English and the Danes. His sons, however, lacked their father's talents. Canute's great northern empire disintegrated rapidly after his death. In 1042 the *witan* selected as king a descendant of Alfred, Edward the Confessor (reigned 1042–1066).

Culture

Some historians have tended to overlook the cultural achievements of the Britons, because they appear as rude barbarians in contrast with the urbane Romans. Anglo-Saxon society was markedly unequal. The majority of the population worked the land to support a relatively small warrior noble class. Yet during the early Middle Ages the Anglo-Saxons and the Celts produced a notable culture. The discovery at Sutton Hoo in 1939 of a seventh-century royal burial ship filled with gold and silver jewelry, arms, and utensils revealed the East Anglian kings to have possessed an unexpected degree of wealth.

Irish Monasteries

As a Roman province, Britain had contributed little to the cultural life of the Empire. With the advent of Christianity, however, Britain began to develop its own distinctive ecclesiastical culture. During the early centuries of Anglo-Saxon occupation Christianity survived only on the Celtic periphery of the island in Cornwall, Devon, Wales, southwestern Scotland, and Ireland. However, despite its isolation the Celtic Church flourished, especially in Ireland, which had been converted to Christianity by the British missionary, St. Patrick, during the first half of the fifth century. Irish monasteries were the most important centers of learning and piety in all of Western Europe during the sixth and seventh centuries. As part of their work in copying and preserving sacred texts, Irish monks created some of the most beautiful illuminated manuscripts of the Middle Ages, including the exquisite eighth-century *Book of Kells.*

The Venerable Bede

The return of Christianity to Anglo-Saxon England led, during the late seventh and early eighth centuries, to a flowering of ecclesiastical culture that is known as the Northumbrian Renaissance. This era represents the high point of Anglo-Saxon culture. Its most celebrated scholar and probably the most learned man of the time in the West was the Benedictine monk, the Venerable Bede (c. 673–735). His famous and enduring work, *A History of the English Church and People*, narrates the growth of Christianity in England from 597 until a few years before Bede's death. Its main theme is the mollifying effect of Christianity on barbarian culture. Bede wrote excellent Latin and took unusual care in the selection and use of his source materials. His history, despite its inclusion of miracles, still remains the best source of information about many aspects of early Anglo-Saxon times.

Influence on the Continent

The brilliance of Northumbrian culture made itself felt even on the Continent. In the late eighth century, English scholars and missionaries traveled throughout France and Germany converting heathen tribes and reforming the Frankish Church. The churchman Alcuin of York spent most of his later life at the court of Charlemagne where he made significant contributions to the Carolingian intellectual revival. By this time in England, however, Viking raiders had sacked the great Northumbrian abbeys and brought their intellectual life to a close.

Beowulf

In addition to creating original works in Latin, the Anglo-Saxons produced a body of writings in the vernacular that was unique in Western Europe at the time. The Anglo-Saxons early developed Old English into a literary language and used it in the construction of their poems, chronicles, laws, and other documents. The oldest extant examples of Germanic literature are in Old English. The great epic *Beowulf* survives in a sole manuscript dating from around the year 1000, but this is certainly a copy of an earlier text. Some scholars suggest it was composed in Northumbria during the eighth century. The poem is based on a much older saga that was transmitted orally for generations. The epic tells how the hero, Beowulf, comes to the aid of the king of the Danes, Hrothgar, whose great hall is being ravaged by the evil monster Grendel. Beowulf does battle with Grendel, slays Grendel's mother, and later kills a dragon. The poem, which ends with Beowulf's funeral, extols the qualities that make a great hero. Simply yet powerfully written, it offers invaluable insights into the still-barbaric world of the early Middle Ages when battle was a way of life, and strength, courage, and loyalty were the paramount virtues.

The Frankish Kingdom

On the Continent a relatively minor Germanic tribe, the Franks, achieved a degree of political unification that for a time surpassed the Anglo-Saxons in extent and duration and that was unique in its age. In the third century A.D., the Franks were settled along the east bank of the lower and middle Rhine. Toward the end of the next century they began to move slowly southward and westward until by 481 they had reached as far as Paris. At that time they were divided into two main groups, the Salian Franks in the north and the Ripuarian Franks in the south.

The Merovingians

Merovech, a chief of the Salian Franks, gave his name to the first Frankish dynasty, the Merovingians, which under his grandson, Clovis I (reigned 481–511), came to rule almost the whole of Gaul.

Clovis

When Clovis became king of the Salian Franks, he reigned over only one of the petty Germanic kingdoms within Gaul.

Conquest of Gaul. Through cleverness, military skill, and treachery, Clovis succeeded in extending his rule over most of Gaul, or France, as it eventually was called after its Frankish conquerors. Clovis first conquered the Gallo-Romans at Soissons in 486, thus eliminating the final traces of Roman authority in Gaul. A decade later his defeat of the Alemanni in a battle near Strasbourg opened the way for Frankish conquests beyond the Rhine in Germany.

Conversion to Christianity. According to Gregory of Tours, a sixth-century bishop who wrote an informative *History of the Franks*, Clovis called upon Christ's aid to gain victory at Strasbourg after his pagan gods failed him. Following the victory, Clovis and 3,000 Franks were baptized into the Catholic Church. This conversion had profound consequences for the future of France, for by choosing Roman rather than Arian Christianity Clovis forged a link between the Frankish kingdom and Rome that proved mutually profitable. Adoption of Christianity guaranteed Clovis support from the Frankish Church and greatly eased the assimilation of the numerically inferior Franks with the native Gallo-Romans. It also gave his later wars against various Arian tribes the nature of a religious mission.

Clovis's Achievements. In 507 the Franks routed the Arian Visigoths at Vouille, drove them into Spain, and absorbed Aquitaine and Gascony. By the time he died in 511, Clovis had reunited the Franks, issued a primitive but forward-looking codification of Salian law, and chosen the strategically located Paris as his capital. Thus in many important ways Clovis set the course of France for centuries to come.

Descendants of Clovis

In the Frankish tradition, Clovis's four sons received almost equal shares of his kingdom. Initially, the heirs banded together to expand the Frankish kingdom. They added Burgundy in 534 and Provence in 536, and by other conquests they extended Frankish authority over a large part of Germany. Clovis's last surviving son, Chlotar, reunited all of France, but his greedy and degenerate sons received their portions after his death in 561, and unity disappeared. Internecine fighting raged until 613 when two dominant individuals put forward Chlotar II (reigned 584–629) as sole king of the Franks.

The Carolingians

During the period of "darkness" following Clovis's death, Dagobert (reigned 629–639) was the last Merovingian to rule the Frankish kingdom in an effective manner. His successors were all *rois fainéants*, or do-nothing kings. Their chief administrators, the mayors of the palace, held the real power of government. One particularly powerful noble family succeeded in making this office hereditary.

Pepin

Pepin of Heristal (ruled as mayor 680–714) controlled almost the entire Frankish kingdom. As sole mayor of the palace he restored a measure of unity and order to the realm. His descendants founded a new dynasty, the Carolingian, whose illustrious member, Charlemagne, would lead the Franks to conquer an impressive empire.

Charles Martel

Pepin of Heristal's death in 714 threatened to plunge the kingdom into renewed anarchy when his young grandsons were named the new mayors of a divided realm. The problem was resolved when Pepin's illegitimate son, Charles (ruled as mayor 714–741), seized control and after some fighting brought the whole kingdom back under a single hand.

Charles's Rule. As mayor of the palace, Charles was in effect a king, save for title. He administered justice, appointed bishops and royal officials, and served as commander of the army. After winning a stunning victory over the Muslims near Tours in 732 he was known as Charles Martel, "the Hammer." It was from his first name (*Carolus* in Latin) that the Carolingian dynasty took its name. During his reign, Christian missionaries made important advances among the heathen Germanic tribes east of the Rhine. With Christianity came civilized culture and Frankish control.

Restructuring of the Army. Charles Martel, in restructuring his army, endowed his mounted warriors with lands taken from the Church to help defray the new, higher costs of war and to retain their loyalty, a development that lay at the root of feudalism. The introduction around this time of two inventions, the stirrup and the horseshoe, had important political and social consequences for France and Europe. The stirrup reduced the fatigue of riding and permitted a mounted warrior to remain firmly in his seat while striking with his weapons. Shoeing enabled horses to traverse rough terrain more quickly and securely. Both these developments contributed to making the cavalry superior to the infantry in battle. Thus warfare became the exclusive profession of the aristocracy, for only they could afford to purchase the necessary horses, arms, and equipment.

Pepin the Short

In 741, Charles Martel was succeeded by his two sons, Carloman and Pepin the Short, each of whom became mayor of the palace for half of the realm. The pious Carloman retreated to a monastery in 747 and left Pepin the Short as sole mayor and as king in all but name. To ensure the permanence of his dynasty, Pepin dispensed with the fiction of Merovingian kingship, with the approval of Pope Zacherias. Late in 751 the Frankish assembly dethroned the last Merovingian monarch and elected Pepin king. In the coronation ceremony the divine sanction of Carolingian rule was symbolized by the anointment of Pepin by Archbishop Boniface.

Relation with Papacy. Pepin's request for papal authorization came at an opportune moment. Earlier that year the Germanic Lombards had seized Ravenna, the Byzantine capital of Italy. Pepin owed the papacy a favor and in 754 Pope Stephen traveled to the Frankish monarch in order to collect it. Pepin promised to send an army across the Alps against the Lombards and to turn over the reconquered territory to the pope. In exchange the pope personally anointed Pepin and his two sons, confirming the earlier sanction. This act provided legitimization to the new dynasty. At the same time, the papacy's claim to authority over temporal affairs was considerably reinforced.

Donation of Pepin. Frankish soldiers battled the Lombards in 754 and conquered Ravenna from them in 756. These lands, subsequently called the Papal States, were presented by Pepin to the pope in the "Donation of Pepin." Until the nineteenth century the papacy held both secular and spiritual authority over this territory which extended across the middle of Italy from Rome to Ravenna. The alliance between France and the papacy became a keystone of medieval politics.

Pepin's Achievements. By the end of his reign, Pepin had advanced the level of religious and cultural life in his land, added conquests in the region of the Pyrenees, and made the Frankish kingdom the protector and ally of the Western Church. This not inconsiderable legacy he left to his still more glorious son, Charlemagne.

Charlemagne

Charles the Great, or Charlemagne (reigned 768–814), lives in legend as well as in history.

Charlemagne's Character. According to his contemporary biographer, Einhard, Charles was a tall, powerfully built man whose tremendous vitality manifested itself in his love for warfare and hunting, intellectual ability, and lust for women. During his long reign he conquered most of Continental Europe with the exception of Muslim Spain, Scandinavia, Southern Italy, and Sicily. He was the first monarch to revive the idea of a universal empire in the West and to proclaim himself emperor. He ruled in the name of Christianity and as guardian of the Church. His fascination with knowledge abetted the revival of learning, a momentous accomplishment that is called the Carolingian Renaissance. In an age when the machinery of government was limited and weak, Charlemagne's achievements are all the more impressive. His empire owed its unity and well-being to his inexhaustible energy, his creative intellect, and the force of his personality.

Seizure of Power. So ingrained was the Germanic custom of dividing the kingdom among all the king's sons that Charlemagne, like his father, had to share his inheritance with his younger brother, Carloman, until the latter's death in 771. Again following in his father's footsteps, Charlemagne seized his brother's domains from its heirs and made himself sole king of the Franks. He then embarked on a long series of victorious wars.

Conquests. In response to the pope's pleas, Charlemagne conquered the Lombards and incorporated the remainder of their kingdom into the Frankish realm. As a Christian monarch, Charlemagne equated conquest with the extension of Christianity. Nowhere is this clearer than in his thirty-two-year struggle with the Saxons, a German tribe that inhabited northern Germany between the Rhine and Elbe rivers. After conquering them, Charlemagne forced the entire population to convert to Roman Christianity, punishing with death those who refused. Charlemagne's attempt to conquer and Christianize Muslim Spain did not succeed, and he was forced to settle with a military buffer zone (the Spanish March) just inside Spain. The famous epic poem the *Song of Roland* is based on the annihilation of Charlemagne's heroic rear-guard at the pass of Roncesvalles during the Franks' retreat across the Pyrenees.

Advances into Eastern Europe. Elsewhere in Eastern Europe, Charlemagne attempted to reduce barbarian attacks and created frontier military buffer zones, or Marches. For example, the land south of the Danube was organized into the East March, which later became the country of Austria. Charlemagne's campaigns resulted in the addition of considerable new territories at the expense of the Slavs and Avars. German missionaries and settlers began to move into their former territory, laying claim to parts of Eastern Europe that would remain a source of trouble into the twentieth century.

"Emperor of the Romans." In 799 hostile groups in Rome threatened to depose the newly elected pope, Leo III, who managed to flee to Germany in quest of Charlemagne's aid. Siding with Leo, Charlemagne traveled to Rome in order to settle matters. While kneeling at the altar of St. Peter's Basilica on Christmas Day 800, Charlemagne was crowned "Emperor of the Romans" by Leo. In his biography Einhard depicts Charlemagne as surprised by the pope's gesture and perturbed by the pope's assumption of the right to designate the emperor. The papal coronation posed the problem of the relationship between the spiritual and temporal authorities, which was to be troublesome throughout most of the Middle Ages. At the time, however, there was no question that Charlemagne was the more powerful of the two men.

Extent of Empire. The title "Emperor of the Romans" possessed tremendous symbolic value. It testified to the great appeal the Roman Empire continued to exert more than 300 years after its demise. Despite his supposed displeasure at the manner of conferring, Charlemagne had earned the honor and sought it for himself. Except for Britain, southern Italy, the greater part of Spain, and North Africa, his Christian empire encompassed all of Rome's former provinces in the West and included as well the whole of Germany south of the Elbe and considerable lands in eastern Europe that had never been under Roman domination. Not until 812, however, did the Eastern Roman Emperor grudgingly recognize the legitimacy of what appeared to the East as a barbarian usurpation of the title. With Charlemagne's coronation the West severed its final ties of submission to the Eastern empire.

Administration. The task of ruling such a large empire was almost impossible given the deteriorated state of communications and the government's inability to tax on a broad scale. Charlemagne attempted to administer the realm personally with the aid of his household staff. For example, the chamberlain, keeper of the royal bedchamber, was in charge of the treasury, and the counts of the palace supervised the royal court. He also consulted with the preeminent nobles of the kingdom, usually at an annual assembly, but was not compelled to follow their advice.

Charlemagne relied essentially on the administrative structure of his predecessors but effected some reforms. The division of the kingdom into counties was retained, as were the supervisory counts who had the duties of maintaining order, dispensing justice, and commanding the mounted troops within their jurisdiction. By Charlemagne's time there were some 300 counties. In the marches, special margraves assumed similar duties. At the local level, dukes had military responsibilities. All freemen in the realm were liable to military service at their own expense, a burden Charlemagne attempted to lighten for the poorest of them. Charlemagne's most significant administrative innovation was his utilization of *missi dominici*, royal experts who acted at the local level. Drawn principally from the ranks of wealthy ecclesiastical and lay nobles, these agents traveled in pairs throughout the empire and attempted to enforce local compliance with royal authority, uphold justice, and ferret out corruption.

Legal Reforms. Charlemagne allowed all conquered people to live under their own laws. However, he did impose on them new laws that were applicable to all subjects. He issued scores of directives on specific subjects, usually administrative or legal in nature. These are called *capitularies* because they were subdivided into chapters. According to Einhard, Charlemagne perceived the confusion created by so many different legal systems—the Franks themselves had two kinds of law—and sought to make them more homogeneous. He ordered that the customary laws of all the peoples within his empire be set down in writing. By the time of his death in 814, Charlemagne had brought the return of a degree of law and order to much of Western Europe.

The Carolingian Renaissance

Between the sixth century and the beginning of Charlemagne's reign, the heritage of Graeco-Roman civilization was gradually lost to memory. Outside of scattered monasteries, the papal states, and Visigothic Spain, knowledge of Latin had grown feeble.

Revival of Classical Learning. A large measure of Charlemagne's greatness lay in his determination to revive classical learning. Charlemagne himself appreciated the value of education. Although not a scholar in the modern sense of the word, he nonetheless spoke and read Latin and acquired some proficiency in Greek. According to Einhard, he never learned to write despite nightly practice at copying letters.

School at Aachen. Charlemagne was troubled by the widespread illiteracy among the clergy. Lack of comprehension threatened the priests' correct interpretation of the Scriptures. Thus, around 782 Charlemagne invited the Anglo-Saxon scholar Alcuin to Aachen to establish a palace school there for the instruction of the sons of the king and his retinue. Encouraged by its achievements, seven years later Charlemagne ordered all bishops and monasteries to set up schools for the education of boys. Alcuin, who had studied at Bede's school, contributed tremendously to the revival of ancient learning. In addition to composing poetry, letters, and important theological works including a corrected version of Jerome's translation of the Bible, Alcuin wrote textbooks that served to clarify and systematize knowledge. Under his guidance, a standardized curriculum was introduced, consisting of the *trivium* (grammar, rhetoric, and logic) and the *quadrivium* (arithmetic, geometry, music, and astronomy). This course of study eventually became the bedrock of medieval education.

Minuscule Writing. Charlemagne encouraged the study and preservation of ancient texts. Many classical works of literature would have been lost had they not been copied at this time. The invention during Charlemagne's reign of a new script, the Carolingian minuscule, aided scribes in their work. Unlike the former writing that consisted entirely of capitals, the new form of handwriting employed small letters as well, allowing scribes to copy books more quickly. The texts were easier to read and contained more words per page, making them less costly to produce. These factors stimulated the production of more texts.

The Arts. Charlemagne's interest in reviving the classical past extended to the arts.   A hallmark of Carolingian architecture and decorative arts is an obvious familiarity with classical models. Both forms incorporated a blend of Celtic and Germanic forms with the classic to create a unique fusion of styles. As befiting his new imperial station, Charlemagne sought to recreate at his capital of Aachen (Aix-la-Chapelle) the splendor of ancient Rome. The most important surviving example of Carolingian architecture, the Palace Chapel at Aachen, is patterned after Justinian's Church of San Vitale in Ravenna. Its emphasis on the facade, however, heralds a new departure in medieval architecture.   Numerous examples attesting to the high quality of Carolingian ivory carving, and enamel- and metalwork have survived. Carolingian artists also produced superb miniatures that radiate energy and movement.

The Viking Invasions

Toward the end of Charlemagne's reign the Frankish empire fell victim to Viking assaults.   There as in Anglo-Saxon England, the Northmen came at first in small warbands. They plundered the rich, largely unprotected monasteries and towns along the coasts and returned home to winter in Scandinavia. Charlemagne and his successor, Louis the Pious, kept these first raids in check and even attempted to convert the Danes to Christianity.

Extent of Viking Inroads

By the mid-ninth century, the Vikings' predatory incursions had increased in scope and intensity. Individual groups banded together to form veritable armies. Improved Viking ships, which employed both oars and sails and were capable of transporting sixty men, journeyed as far as Spain and Morocco to the south, Russia to the east, Iceland and Greenland to the north, and probably even North America to the west. In 845 a Viking army sailed up the Seine and burned Paris. Gradually the Northmen established settlements in Europe.

Motives for Invasions

The reasons for this explosion of Norse activity are difficult to ascertain.   Perhaps the most convincing thesis rests on the idea of overpopulation.   The Germanic invasions of late Roman times had depleted Scandinavia and thus enabled the remaining population to grow unchecked. Around 800 it had outstripped the tenuous agricultural capacities of the frigid North. Because of the shortage of suitable land, defeated tribal chiefs (of which there were many at this point in the consolidation of Scandinavian kingships) or younger sons looked abroad for sustenance. Once the relative ease and lucrativeness of a life of plundering became apparent, more Northmen took up piracy. The practice of polygamy—although never widespread—may have aggravated the already fierce competition for land.

Long a seafaring and trading people, the Northmen knew of the great wealth of the lands to the south. Judging from their poetry and gravestones, the lure of booty and love of war exercised a powerful attraction. Their technical abilities as navigators and the design of their boats had improved just prior to the great era of Nordic migrations and enabled them to carry out raids far from home. Charlemagne's conquest of the Frisians along the North Sea east of the Rhine removed a barrier that had for centuries separated the Scandinavians from their more civilized neighbors. That the Viking age coincided with a period of military and political weakness throughout most of Europe helps to explain the relative ease with which they invaded and ultimately settled Western and Eastern Europe.

Fragmentation of the Carolingian Empire

The Viking marauders both profited from weaknesses in the Carolingian Empire and hastened its breakup. Charlemagne's imperial revival proved premature. The overwhelmingly agrarian economy of the Frankish dominions was unable to sustain the bureaucratic structure necessary to administer and protect it. Powerful nobles endowed with large land grants from the king regularly escaped royal control. Such a vast, unwieldy territory required someone with Charlemagne's all-powerful personality to hold it together. Finally, the Franks never discarded their custom of dividing the kingdom among the king's heirs, even though this practice led to incessant civil wars and fratricidal quarreling.

Struggle for Succession

At the time of his death, Charlemagne left his empire to his only

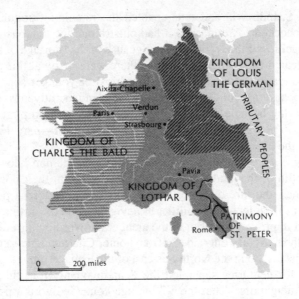

Partition of the Carolingian Empire, 843

heir, Louis the Pious (reigned 814–840). During most of his reign this religious but weak emperor was challenged by his sons, who sought to appropriate for themselves the best part of the Empire. In 833 he was deposed by his eldest son, Lothair, but was restored to the throne a year later by his two younger sons. Upon his death in 840 his three sons fought for shares of the Empire. Louis the German and Charles the Bald successfully defeated their elder brother, Lothair, who was named emperor, at the battle of Fontenoy in 841. The following year Louis and Charles met at Strasbourg and swore an alliance, the famous Strasbourg Oaths, to continue their opposition to Lothair. The historical importance of the Strasbourg Oaths is that they were taken not in Latin but in the two vernaculars that had developed east and west of the Rhine. Louis's vassals in the eastern part of the Empire swore in German while Charles's vassals in the west swore in Romance, an early form of French. The Empire had already begun to break up along linguistic lines.

Division of the Empire

The combined forces of Charles and Louis were insufficient to conquer Lothair; nor did he have the strength to prevail over them. As a consequence the three agreed in 843 to end their conflict by the Treaty of Verdun. In it they partitioned the Empire into three essentially equal portions. Charles the Bald received the western Carolingian lands that today are roughly equivalent to modern France; Louis the German acquired that territory east of the Rhine that subsequently became the heart of the German Empire. The remaining territory that lay between them and extended from the North Sea to central Italy was given to Lothair, who retained his imperial title but was no longer able to impose his will on his brothers. While the kingdoms of East and West Frankland were not national states in the modern sense, they did possess cultural, geographic, and linguistic continuity. Lothair's domains, on the other hand, lacked a common tongue, logical natural frontiers, and a single center. They soon split into three main regions: Lorraine, Burgundy, and Italy. Down into the twentieth century, Germany and France have fought each other for possession of the valuable territory of Lorraine.

Trend toward Decentralization

The Carolingian monarchs after Louis the Pious were an ambitious, greedy, and fractious lot. Although Charles the Fat briefly reunited the Empire in 884, not one monarch was equal to the task of ruling a great realm. Centralism in continental Europe steadily gave way to localism, as smaller units such as duchies and counties increasingly asserted their independence from central authority. This trend was abetted by the fact that the Frankish territories were torn apart by civil wars, quarrels over land, and barbarian invasions.

Muslim and Magyar Invasions

This unstable situation was aggravated by outside attacks. From their bases in North Africa Muslims set out to conquer Sicily and parts of southern Italy in 827. They ravaged the Italian coastline and in 846 despoiled St. Peter's Basilica in Rome to the horror of Western Christendom. After establishing a base on the French Riviera, Spanish

Muslims launched piratical forays against Western ships and even raided caravans in the Alpine passes. The growth of Islamic sea power forced trade between Byzantium and the West almost to a standstill. In eastern Europe a new Asiatic people, the Magyars, migrated into the valley of the Danube in the mid- 890s. Until their shattering defeat by the German Emperor Otto the Great at Lechfeld in 955, they spread destruction throughout Germany, Italy, and parts of France. Thereafter they peacefully settled along the Danube in a region that later became the Hungarian state.

Norman Invasions and Settlements

The depredations of the Vikings were by far the more costly of the barbarian invasions. At first local lords and even the Carolingian kings themselves resorted to buying off the Northmen. An angry nobility dethroned Charles the Fat in 887 because he saved Paris from destruction by paying a ransom and by allowing the Vikings to despoil Burgundy. As his replacement the French magnates selected Eudes (Odo), Marquess of Neustria, who had bravely defended Paris against the Viking attack. Members of his family alternated with rulers of the Carolingian house on the French throne until 987. By 911 a Norse "army" had so solidly entrenched itself in Normandy that King Charles the Simple of France accepted Rollo as a vassal, and recognized the Norse leader's territory as an independent duchy. This new duchy would play a major role in European history. The Viking settlers there, known as Normans, accepted Christianity and quickly absorbed the French language and culture. During the eleventh century they provided Europe with some of its most outstanding soldiers, administrators, and conquerors. With the cession of Normandy to the Vikings, raids slowly tapered off in France.

End of Central Government

In Germany the Carolingian dynasty founded by Louis the German ended in 911. In its place the German magnates elected one of their own to serve as king. Their choice of the Duke of Saxony in 919 proved a fortuitous one and under the house of Saxony Germany became the strongest state in Europe during the tenth century. In France, by contrast, the central authority of the monarch collapsed under the weight of civil strife and external threats. In vying for the loyalty of powerful magnates, the Carolingian kings had bribed them with land and offices and granted their territories immunity from royal control. This contributed to the growth of hereditary local dynasties whose strength permitted them to defy the king. Royal government no longer extended into the provinces. Charlemagne's *missi dominici* ceased to function. Local lords were better able to defend against the lightning Viking raids than the king was, and individuals increasingly gave their land to them in exchange for protection. A new set of social, political, and economic relationships emerged in France during the ninth and tenth centuries. Historians came to term these relationships *feudalism* and the *manorial system*.

Feudalism

Interpretations of Feudalism

Feudalism is one of the most contentious "isms" in the study of European history. Some historians favor a narrow definition, confining the word to its strict legal meaning in connection with the fief, a form of tenure in which real property is granted in return for military service and other obligations. Others, influenced by Marc Bloch's pathbreaking book *Feudal Society*, employ the term to encompass the whole of medieval society. Still others prefer to do away with the label altogether. Most scholars agree that there was no one such thing as feudalism and that in describing its nature historians are in fact speaking of an ideal type.

Meaning of the Term

The term itself in its French form, *feodalité*, was coined by lawyers in the seventeenth century from the medieval Latin word for fief, *feodum* or *feudum*. Since then it has been employed to mean a number of things. In its earliest usage *feodalité* referred specifically to the duties incident to the fief. By the time of the French Revolution, however, the term denoted a broad variety of aristocratic and ecclesiastical privileges and abuses. To Marx in the nineteenth century, feudalism was a mode of production based on the exploitation of serf labor that prevailed during the Middle Ages and was superseded by bourgeois capitalism. Twentieth-century western scholars for the most part reject the simple equation of feudalism with serfdom. They prefer instead to draw a clear distinction between feudalism as a set of social and political institutions that involved only the upper level of society, and the manorial system that regulated the economy and employed the vast majority of the population. Many historians today hold that other societies in other eras, e.g., ancient Egypt or tenth-century Japan, went through phases in their development that may be described as feudal.

General Characteristics

The picture of medieval European feudalism that follows rests on broad generalizations. The chief distinguishing features of feudalism are: (1) the personal bond between a superior (lord) and his inferior (vassal) known as homage; (2) the granting of heritable land (fief) rather than a salary to compensate the vassal for services; and (3) the exercise of governmental authority by private individuals. Not all of Europe was feudalized at the same time or to the same extent. Feudal institutions were largely absent from Scandinavia and Ireland.

Origins

Feudalism first appeared in northern France in the ninth century in response to a need by landowners for protection against the dissolution of the Frankish empire and the barbarian invasions. The territory between the Loire and the Rhine rivers became the most highly feudalized area of Europe. Traditional descriptions of feudalism apply to conditions there during the tenth and eleventh centuries.

Variations

Elsewhere the system showed variations. In Germany strong monarchs such as Otto I retarded the growth of feudal institutions until the twelfth century. The Norman pattern of feudalism was applied in England, southern Italy, and the Latin Kingdom of Jerusalem during the eleventh century as the result of military conquest.

Two "Ages" of Feudalism

Feudal arrangements altered over time. The historian Marc Bloch divided Western feudalism between the ninth and the early thirteenth centuries into two successive "ages." Bloch characterized the "first feudal age" as a period with a declining population, poor communications, scarcity of money, and the dispersion of political power among petty lords. In the "second feudal age," which began around the middle of the eleventh century and lasted until approximately 1250, Europe experienced a surge in population and a revival of commerce and intellectual activities. During this time, European kings and princes made use of the feudal structure to increase the central authority of the state.

The Personal Bond: Lord and Vassal

Feudal society was held together by the reciprocal relationships between lords and their vassals (the word "vassal" is of ancient Celtic origin and initially meant "boy" or "servant.") By the ninth century the social status of the vassal had risen to that of a free armed follower of a lord. These relationships were forged during the chronic unrest and disorder of the ninth and tenth centuries when weak central governments failed to provide security. Many men from the upper levels of society offered their military services to more powerful individuals, especially those who owned castles. Persons of rank, in turn, welcomed this opportunity to increase their retinue of armed warriors. Thus from mutual needs the aristocrats evolved the complex feudal ties of lordship and vassalage. These ties had antecedents from the past and they were strongest whenever the bonds of family, clan, guild, or state were most slack. Ties of dependence between unequal but free individuals were commonly found in the Roman institution of patronage and the German *comitatus,* or band of companions that served a chief.

Homage

In the early Middle Ages the attachments that bound a lord and his vassal were more akin to those that united families and clans than to those defined by law. They were determined by custom and rested upon mutual trust and comradeship. During the first feudal age vassals often lived in the home of their lord and shared his table. When a lord agreed to accept a social inferior as his "man," the union was formalized by the ceremony of homage. The vassal placed his joined hands within those

of his overlord to signify his obeisance. The two then usually exchanged a kiss of friendship. In Carolingian times the swearing of an
oath of fealty or faithfulness to one's superior was added.

Reciprocal Obligations

The act of homage created a feudal contract in which each man
owed certain obligations to the other.

The Lord's Obligations. The lord, also referred to as the suzerain
or overlord, was obliged to protect his vassal from harm and see to his
well-being. He offered the vassal refuge in his castle and the protection
of his armed retainers. He took care of his vassal's material needs either
by feeding and housing him under his own roof or by endowing him
with land. This land, the fief, tended to become hereditary. The lord
also maintained a court of justice and afforded his vassals the right to
be tried only by their peers, i.e., social equals.

The Vassal's Obligations. The duties of the vassal were manifold.
Essentially he pledged to aid and obey his lord. This involved above
all the rendering of military service. The vassal was required to provide
a stipulated number of fully equipped mounted warriors to fight on the
lord's behalf for a prescribed number of days (traditionally 40) each
year. Thereafter the lord had to pay for any additional days of military
service. The vassal also owed the lord the services of his counsel. He
attended the lord's court, which convened periodically, and passed
judgment on his fellow vassals. The lord also consulted him at this time
on all important matters.

Obligations of the Vassal in Special Circumstances. Other obligations placed a heavy pecuniary burden on the vassal. These varied
according to local custom. By the eleventh century he was generally
compelled to expend large sums of money referred to as "aid" on three
specific occasions: the knighting of the lord's eldest son, the marriage
of his eldest daughter, and the payment of ransom in the event of the
lord's capture. In France and elsewhere the lord also demanded aid
from his vassal to cover the cost of going on a crusade. Upon the death
of the vassal, his heir paid something similar to an inheritance tax
known as "relief" to his lord in thanks for the right to succeed to the
property. This tax was at first paid in kind (a horse and/or arms were
customary exactions) but gradually became replaced by a fixed sum of

money. Finally, the vassal had to bear the cost of lodging and feeding his lord whenever he was traveling in the area of the vassal's fief. This right of hospitality could be so financially ruinous to the vassal that over time it became precisely defined and limited by feudal law.

Rights of the Lord in Special Circumstances

In addition to these mutual obligations, the lord also possessed certain other rights concerning the administration of the fiefs under unusual circumstances. When no legitimate heir existed, the fief reverted to the lord upon the vassal's death. If the heir were a minor and thus unable to render military and other services, the lord regained possession of the fief and its revenues according to the right of wardship until the heir reached maturity. The lord had similarly lucrative rights in those parts of Europe where inheritance by a woman was accepted. He received the profits from the estate until the female heir married. The choice of her husband was also in the lord's hands despite her wishes in order to ensure that the man she married would make a courageous and obedient vassal.

Provision for Breaking Ties

If either party to the contract became derelict in performing his duties, the ties of vassalage were considered broken. If the vassal failed in his obligations, his fief reverted to the lord according to the right of forfeiture. If the lord similarly defaulted, the vassal was free to abandon him and even take up arms against him in a private war to force him to observe his obligations. Thus under feudalism a person's political rights and duties were determined not by uniform laws executed by centralized authority emanating from the state but by laws affecting the individual's position in the feudal nexus.

The Fief

The characteristic landholding system employed in feudalism was the fief, a conditional grant of land dependent on the execution of military and other services.

Origins and Development

Traditionally in discordant times power and status accrued to whoever possessed the largest private army. Thus kings and great magnates as well as lesser lords hastened to recruit vassals who would fight for them. To cover the great expense entailed in outfitting an armed horseman, lords endowed their vassals with estates or other income-bearing honors and offices. At first these lands were conferred by lords for the duration of the lives of the parties. The status of the fief was changed over time. In 877 a royal decree confirmed that a son should succeed to his father's land and offices. By the twelfth century the word fief had come to mean a hereditary grant of land charged with the services of vassalage.

Structure of Fiefdom

In theory feudal society was structured as a great pyramid with the king at the apex. Technically he owned all land in the nation and entrusted large tracts of it to those whose support he coveted. In return his vassals, the tenants-in-chief, owed the king military service and provided him mounted warriors, the number of which was based on the size of the fief awarded. To fulfill this military obligation, the vassals of the king surrendered part of their fiefs to men who became their vassals. This practice of subinfeudating estates extended down to vassals who had only a single manor. Each vassal owed obeisance exclusively to his immediate lord within the feudal hierarchy. As a consequence the king, as least in France and elsewhere, could not command the fealty of all his subjects. Fiefs were created in other ways as well. In many cases when weaker men sought protection they turned over their own lands to lords and received them back, after the act of homage, in the form of a fief with traditional feudal obligations. Some landowners escaped the system altogether. Throughout Europe, there continued to exist independent estates known as *allods* that owed no services to a superior lord.

Transmitting of Fiefs

A vassal formally received his fief in a ceremony called investiture that followed the rituals of homage and fealty. In it the lord handed his man a small stick, a piece of earth, or other symbol to indicate actual transfer of property. This act, like homage and fealty, had to be renewed upon the death of either the lord or his vassal by their respective heirs.

To secure their inheritance the new vassals were forced to pay "relief" to their lords.

Place of the Church

Eventually the Church was integrated into the feudal structure, principally because it became a substantial owner of lands held in feudal tenure. Much of this property had been bequeathed to the Church by feudal lords and thus retained its feudal obligations. Because members of the clergy were forbidden to bear arms (a restriction numerous popes and bishops cleverly circumvented), lay substitutes known as *advocati* were recruited to perform requisite military services. A bishop's role as a feudal lord or vassal sometimes clashed with his religious responsibilities. The Church's attempt to free itself from the feudal structure led to conflicts with the state and culminated in the lay investiture issue during the eleventh century.

Feudal Justice

During the Middle Ages a considerable amount of jurisprudence passed from the central government into the hands of private individuals.

Development of Feudal Courts

This phenomenon had antecedents in fourth- and fifth-century Rome and in early Germanic Europe where rulers granted immunity from royal jurisdiction to inhabitants on their own vast estates and to great landowners whose loyalty they hoped to purchase. Public officials, especially the much-hated tax collector, were barred from entering these estates. In Carolingian France rival claimants to the throne extended the privilege of immunity to a substantial number of their noble supporters. In time the state's powers to tax, administer justice, and enforce laws were assumed almost entirely by local aristocrats. These functions included the collection of court fines, and they could be very profitable to the lord. Feudal courts addressed matters that related to lord-vassal and vassal-vassal disputes. It was the vassal's privilege to be tried only by his fellow vassals. In addition to feudal courts, most lords exercised nonfeudal jurisdiction over the inhabitants in their regions.

Manorial Courts

The award of a fief normally included authority for the vassal to exercise control over the peasants who worked it. As a consequence, each fief had its own manorial courts for handling administrative and judicial matters. These were normally presided over by manorial officials appointed by the lord such as seneschals or bailiffs. The peasants within a fief had free access to these courts, but they were permitted to bring action only against other peasants. Most disputes were decided according to local custom. The extent of a court's jurisdiction corresponded to the power and standing of its lord. The court ruled not only on criminal cases but also on disputes over inheritance and the proper rendering of dues and services. It pronounced on "the custom of the manor" by which all its activities were regulated.

The Nobility

At its height, feudal society consisted primarily of three social classes: the nobility, the clergy, and the peasants. The noble's main duty was to fight, the clergy's was to tend to spiritual needs, and the peasant's was to till the fields.

Origins and Development of Military Service

Because warfare was endemic, feudal society accorded its highest value to those who bore arms, a right that had once belonged to all citizens. By the tenth century, however, particularly in France, the obligation to perform military service had devolved upon those who could afford the expense of a horse, armor, and weapons. Gradually there arose a class of nobles set apart from the rest of society whose privileged position derived not only from its wealth in land but also from its monopoly over fighting on horseback. It was not until the twelfth and thirteenth centuries, however, that this class acquired hereditary status and a genuine nobility as defined by law can be said to have existed.

The Profession of Warrior

Vassals were warriors by profession. When not fighting the lord's battles, protecting his castle, and honing his military skills in tournaments, a vassal was essentially idle. He was forbidden to engage in

manual labor. Thus most vassals eagerly received a summons to battle.
They delighted in its physicality, its opportunities for heroism, and its
relief from boredom. This love of combat resounds throughout the
secular poetry of the age such as the famous *Chansons de Geste*.
Everywhere rival lords fought each other in private wars to gain
revenge, expand their territory, or enrich themselves through plunder
and ransom.

Attempts to Restrict Warfare

Incessant warring and despoiling severely disrupted medieval
agriculture. Its ill effects bore most heavily upon the unarmed peasant
whose fields and cottages were often ransacked and whose family was
abused. By the end of the tenth century, there were attempts to impose
restraints upon the nobility's appetite for war. The Church played a
leading role in this movement. It initiated the "Peace of God," by which
nobles within each diocese vowed to abstain from harming all noncom-
batants, including peasants and their property. Such a "peace" proved
difficult to enforce, and in the middle of the eleventh century it was
augmented by a "Truce of God," which attempted to restrict fighting to
specific days of the week and times of the year. However, these efforts
were only partially successful and it was not until strong national
monarchies were restored that private warfare was finally stopped.

Knights

In medieval parlance a knight was a fully armed mounted warrior.
With few exceptions, every vassal under the obligation of military
service was ipso facto a knight. Admission to the ranks of knighthood
followed a prescribed series of steps.

Steps to Knighthood. At the age of seven a vassal's son was sent
to live as a page in the castle of his father's lord or another noble. There
he waited on the family and learned by imitation to hunt, fight, and
conduct himself as a noble. After reaching the age of fourteen he
became the squire of a knight. As such he tended his master's horse
and cleaned his arms. He went into battle at his master's side as servant
and practiced long and hard to perfect his mastery of horsemanship and
the martial arts. He also acquired the rudiments of a literary education
and learned courtly etiquette. If they had not previously been knighted

for bravery on the battlefield, squires became eligible to advance to the title of knight at age twenty-one.

The Knighting Ceremony. The ceremony used in conferring knighthood evolved into one of the most solemn and impressive occasions of medieval life. It also proved costly, and it drained the resources of even the richest of lords. Its essence was the accolade, a light blow upon the shoulder with the flat edge of a sword, imparted by a lord upon the candidate. By the twelfth century this ancient gesture had acquired an overlay of religious rituals. These required the future knight to take a purifying bath and to pass the night in vigil before the chapel altar, where he dedicated himself and his arms to the service of God. The next day a priest blessed his sword. The candidate was then formally presented with his weapons and "dubbed" a knight.

Chivalry. The institution of knighthood developed its own code of ethics known as chivalry. At first chivalric virtues reflected the violence of the times and favored physical strength, courage, and loyalty above all else. These militant virtues were gradually tempered by the influence of women, the Church, and French culture in general. The "perfect knight" became one who was courteous, good, trustworthy, valiant, and faithful to God, his lord, and his chosen lady.

Courtly Love. The love of an unattainable woman played an important part in the ethos of chivalry. Feudal marriages were normally concluded on the basis of economic and family considerations, with no element of romantic love. To fill this void, chivalry developed a new notion of love that exalted the adored one above all others. A knight humbly placed himself at the service of a socially superior woman to whom he dedicated his victories and even wrote love poetry. The union between a knight and his lady, who was almost always already married, was not meant to be consummated. This obstacle lent a poignancy and sense of melancholy to courtly love and is the dominant note in the lyric poetry of the troubadours.

Manor Houses and Castles

The nobility possessed a distinctive way of life as well as a clearly defined code of conduct. Most nobles lived in the country in manor houses that were often fortified or in actual castles, which by the twelfth century were increasingly built of stone. Castle life, while obviously preferable to a peasant's meager existence, was by no means glamorous. Because they served primarily as shelters against attack, castles were cold, dark, and uncomfortable. Their windows were slits from which to attack the enemy. All activity centered on the great hall where the lord and lady of the house took their meals in company with their retainers.

Amusements

For amusement, nobles took part in sports that tested their skill as warriors. Hunting was not only popular but also an important source of food. Falconry and running with the hounds were also keenly pursued. The Middle Ages even invented its own distinctive form of warlike recreation, the tournament. Knights traveled at times great distances to compete in contests held by kings, princes, or other preeminent nobles. Tournaments consisted normally of two types of combat: the joust in which two horsemen charged at each other with lances, and the *mêlée* or mock battle between two groups of opponents in which prisoners were taken for ransom. Victory could mean considerable riches. These contests were so bloody that the Church prohibited them in the twelfth century. In tournaments as well as in battle, knights wore decorative symbols on their shields and armor to identify themselves since their faces were often concealed behind visored helmets. These devices were known as coats of arms and the study of them, heraldry, was engaged in with great seriousness during the Middle Ages and beyond. The herald became indispensable on the battlefield and in settling many inheritance disputes.

The Manorial System

The Manor

The typical economic unit of the Middle Ages was the manor. This was a large, predominantly self-sufficient estate owned by a feudal aristocrat and inhabited mainly by dependent peasants who held rights to utilize small plots of land owned by the lord in exchange for compulsory labor services and fixed payments in money and kind. Manors could be very large, containing as many as 5,000 acres of arable land and fifty peasant households, or quite small with only 350 tillable acres and twelve families. A noble's military fief might encompass one or more manors. The primary economic function of the manor was to provide the medieval population with food and the necessities of life. Free and unfree peasants cultivated its land for the benefit of the manor's noble or ecclesiastical owner. Like feudalism, the manorial system was based on relationships of dependence, but the gap between a noble seigneur and his peasants was vastly greater than that between a lord and his vassals.

Origins and Development

Scholars generally believe that the manor evolved from the Roman *latifundium* and that the majority of its serfs were descended from Roman *coloni*, tenant farmers who were bound to the soil. Yet, the growth of serfdom was more complex than this and there are important differences between the two. Present evidence indicates that *coloni* were not obligated to render compulsory labor services to the manor. It was much easier for serfs to leave their plots than for *coloni* to desert their farms because of the fragmentation of political authority in the early Middle Ages. The Germanic village subordinated to its chief also clearly influenced the structure of the manor.

During the early Middle Ages, when land was readily available and the cost of feeding and housing sufficient agricultural workers was prohibitive, local potentates parceled out sections of their land to dependent farmers in return for labor services on the remainder of their estate. Thus great landowners acquired a continuous source of agricultural manpower without the burden of supporting it. Like feudalism, manorialism spread rapidly during the chaotic conditions of the post-Carolingian era. While it was not common to all of Europe, it proved to be the most suitable form of agricultural organization for southern England, northern France, Denmark, and parts of Germany where abundant rainfall and fertile ground made the growing of large cereal crops possible. Manors could also be found in Spain, Italy, and Eastern Europe, but they were rare in mountainous and wine-growing regions.

Typical Manor

A "typical" manor (there were numerous variations) contained a village community: a cluster of peasant cottages along a road or perhaps by a stream, the village church, and parish priest's residence. The lord's manor house was often situated on the highest point of land and was built to offer protection to the manor's inhabitants in case of attack. Close by were the lord's mill, oven, and winepress. Cultivated and untilled fields, forests, meadows, and wastelands encircled the peasant village. Approximately one-third of the arable land made up the lord's demesne, and it was cultivated by the peasants to provide sustenance and income for the noble household. The remaining two-thirds was partitioned into small holdings, the *mansi*, that the peasants farmed for their own use and for income to pay customary dues and services. In some manors the demesne was set entirely apart from the peasant plots, but more often it was interspersed among them. Most manors employed an open-field system. Land was divided into acre-long, narrow strips separated only by unplowed earth. Because the soil was not uniformly fertile, each tenant was given a number of widely scattered strips to ensure a fair and equitable distribution of good and bad land.

Medieval Agriculture

The medieval economy was overwhelmingly agricultural and was crude and unproductive by modern standards. It was characterized by low yields and frequent periods of scarcity. The methods it employed varied according to geography, and there are sharp differences between those used in northern and southern Europe.

New Techniques

The arid climate and thin soil in the Mediterranean region allowed farmers to cultivate special crops and to use the light plow of the Romans. Despite ample rainfall, the heavier soils in the fertile plains of northern Europe were hard to plow. During the early Middle Ages, farmers in the north devised new methods to increase the productiveness of their land. In the sixth century they developed a heavier plow to cut deep furrows into the ground. Since this heavy plow required as many as eight oxen to drag it, it was costly as well as cumbersome. Technological advances in the ninth century resolved the problem by allowing farmers in the north to exploit the horse as a major source of nonhuman power. An improved, rigid horse-collar prevented the animal from choking itself as it strained in its work. The use of tandem harnessing enabled horses to be hitched in more than one row. The use of horseshoes guarded their sensitive hooves from the rocky soil.

Crop Rotation

The earliest documented instance of the three-field system of crop rotation is found in northern Europe in the eighth century. Earlier the Romans and Germans practiced a method that enabled the soil to restore its fertility; they simply left it uncultivated for a year. Each year they planted only half of their fields, thus creating a two-field system. Plentiful rainfall in northern Europe permitted farmers to grow a spring crop as well as an autumn crop, and this opportunity to increase production induced them to abandon the old system. Instead, each of three fields was planted alternately in winter wheat, a spring crop such as oats, beans, or barley, and then left fallow for a year. Such a system improved soil fertility, increased crop yields, provided more fodder for livestock, and reduced the amount of time spent plowing. While agriculture remained at a subsistence level for most of the Middle Ages, these innovations laid the foundation for future growth.

The Peasants

Apart from the lord, his relatives, and officials, the manor community was composed entirely of the peasantry. As non-nobles, they were not part of the feudal complex. They themselves were generally separated into two classes, the free and the unfree. These categories differed so widely according to time and place, however, that the distinction between the free tenant, usually called a villein, meaning an inhabitant of a manor (from the Latin word *villa*), and the serf or servile tenant gradually became blurred. Freemen were usually exempt from the personal labor services, head tax, and inheritance levy required of serfs and they could leave the manor if they found a new tenant for their land.

Serfs

During the harsh environment of the ninth and tenth centuries many free peasants sank into serfdom. By the twelfth century most peasants were serfs. Slavery was rare on manors. Most European slaves had been freed in the sixth and seventh centuries. Former owners gave them plots of land on their estate and this allowed them to enter the ranks of serfs.

Obligations of Serfs. The obligations of serfs varied considerably from region to region and from period to period. In general a serf owed his lord compulsory labor service and dues in money and kind. Each week one member from each serf household was required to perform three days of *week-work* on the lord's demesne. All members of the family were obliged to do extra *boon-work* during harvest time and in emergencies. A serf could not attend to his own fields until the lord's crop was reaped. A peasant was also obligated for labor services in the repair of manorial roads and bridges and in the maintenance of the lord's castle. Peasant women made cloth and items of clothing for the noble household. In addition to these labor services, a serf ordinarily owed his lord a fixed portion of his own crop as a form of rent.

Other Payments to the Lord. Because the peasant holdings were heritable, heirs paid an inheritance tax called the *heriot.* It customarily consisted of the peasant family's most valuable animal or piece of furniture. Manorial laws forbade the serf and his family to leave their holdings and to marry someone outside the manor without prior seigneurial approval. Consent in both instances usually had to be purchased. The lord also profited from his peasants by his monopoly over most essential services. His judicial rights enabled him to collect all court dues and fines. He had exclusive ownership over such things as the grain mills, winepresses, and baking ovens and charged fees for their use. Peasants had no alternative but to utilize the lord's equipment. The lord also monopolized the right to sell the serfs certain goods, such as salt and iron, that were not produced on the manor. In addition, he collected a small head tax from all serfs as well as customary gifts.

Rights of Serfs. Serfs were thus under heavy obligations to their lord. Yet their lot was not totally grim. Since they were not slaves, these unfree subjects could not be bought or sold. Although they did not own the land they worked, custom recognized their moral right to it. The lord could not dispossess them provided they fulfilled their dues and services. Their children could inherit the land and thus benefit from their parents' hard work. Most of what the serf owed his lord had come to be fixed over time and thus could not be arbitrarily changed. The peasant also had restricted rights to use common lands on the manor. He was allowed to collect fallen wood in the forest and pasture a specified number of livestock on common lands. The manor offered its peasants military protection, a sense of order and stability, and recourse to justice at least in cases involving fellow peasants.

Peasant Life

It was not unusual during the early medieval centuries for a peasant to live his entire life without leaving the confines of his village community or knowing any authority other than that of his lord and the Church. The peasant was both a resident of a local village and a tenant of a manor. The two were frequently but not always coterminous.

Homes. The peasant and his family lived in a small, thatched, one-room cottage that had an adjoining area for livestock. Living conditions were quite primitive. The hut's floor was earthen, windows lacked glass, and a chimney was a rare luxury. The peasant cooked over an open fire and the whole family slept together on a pallet of hay. Meals were bland and monotonous and nutritionally deficient. Black bread, soups, porridge, and beans were staple items. The family garden supplied vegetables in season while farmyard chickens furnished eggs and meat. Most milk was made into cheese.

Daily Routine. During the critical periods of planting and harvesting, peasants labored from sunrise to sunset on their own plot or on the demesne of their lord six days a week. Crude farming implements made their tasks even more exhausting. Peasant life was closely attuned to the vicissitudes and harshness of nature, and the threats of bad weather, a poor harvest, and scarcity were ever present. Insects, rodents, and crop diseases severely restricted yields. Communicable diseases took an incredible toll.

Amusements. Peasant life was not altogether gloomy. Sports such as wrestling and cock-fighting offered escape from toil. Sundays and numerous religious holidays provided welcome rest and occasional festivities. Medieval church records contain many clerical complaints about peasants dancing and singing in their churchyard. The Christianity of the peasants was a thin veneer over pagan superstitions and nature worship inherited from their ancestors.

Supervision. For the peasant, government, justice, social status, and economic well-being all operated on the level of the manor. The lord had little to do with the daily management of the estate. Since he often owned several manors, he left the overseeing of manorial affairs to his agent, the steward, who traveled from manor to manor. Another official, the bailiff, who was customarily of peasant stock, lived on the manor full-time. He directed the work on the estate and collected the lord's profits from his various dues, rents, tolls, and fines. The peasants elected their own representative, the reeve, who brought their concerns to the lord's attention. He worked together with the other officials to see that the peasants performed their services well. What little contact the peasant had with the state also occurred at the manorial level. The lord collected any governmental taxes and recruited his tenants as foot soldiers when needed.

Community. Peasant life was communal by nature. Open fields made it impossible for any tenant to follow a schedule of planting, sowing, and reaping different from that of his neighbor. Peasants labored together on the demesne and on other work projects around the estate. They shared the common lands. Collectivity extended to farm equipment. The lord usually furnished the plow while the peasants owned their own oxen or horses. Common interests and the seemingly unchanging customs of the manor lent stability to the peasant's life and help to explain why for centuries rural areas of Europe remained bastions of conservatism.

The breakdown of Roman political authority in the West during the fifth century A.D. and the gradual disappearance of Roman cultural influences resulted in a decline in the centralized political power, economic prosperity, and intellectual environment of early medieval Europe. None of the Germanic successor kingdoms, with the exception of the Carolingian Empire, were able to control areas anywhere near the size of the former empire nor were they able to administer their territories with the same thoroughness as the Romans. Political power passed into the hands of a great number of often bellicose feudal lords. This fragmentation of authority bred disorder and instability. It made a weakened Europe more vulnerable to the attacks of marauding bands of Muslims, Magyars, and Vikings.

The absence of large-scale political organization had economic repercussions as well. During the early Middle Ages, Roman roads and bridges fell into disrepair. No central authority existed to maintain the Roman postal service. News traveled at an exceedingly slow pace. As communications worsened, international trade all but disappeared and urban life contracted. By the ninth century Muslim ships controlled the Mediterranean. A severe shortage of currency prevailed. This encouraged the trend toward self-sufficiency (autarky) within the manorial system and the exaction of services rather than money as a form of payment. Population declined and much land went out of cultivation.

Yet the early Middle Ages also saw creative solutions to the conditions of political fragmentation and barbarian assaults. Feudalism defined the social and political relationships among the European upper classes while the manorial system regulated economic life by granting peasants the right to cultivate part of the lord's demesne in exchange for various fixed dues and services. Each was based on ties of dependence and provided a certain amount of protection and stability. Also during the early Middle Ages the Anglo-Saxons in England and the Franks in France laid down the roots of the English and French nations. Literacy and ancient learning lived on in the great monasteries, and in the palace schools of King Alfred and Charlemagne.

Recommended Reading

Richard P. Abels, *Lordship and Military Obligation in Anglo-Saxon England* (1988).

Philippe Ariès and Georges Duby, eds., *A History of Private Life, vol. II: Revelations of the Medieval World* (1988).

Geoffrey Barraclough, *The Crucible of Europe: The Ninth and Tenth Centuries in European History* (1976).

Bede, Venerable, *A History of the English Church and People* (1955).

Marc Bloch, *Feudal Society* (1961).

Prosper Boissonnade, *Life and Work in Medieval Europe: Fifth to Fifteenth Century* (1982).

Jacques Boussard, *The Civilization of Charlemagne* (1968).

K.J. Conant, *Carolingian and Romanesque, 800–1200* (1956).

Kevin Crossley-Holland, ed., *The Anglo-Saxon World* (1983).

Kevin Crossley-Holland, trans., *Beowulf* (1968).

A. Dopsch, *The Economic and Social Foundations of European Civilization* (1937).

Georges Duby, *The Chivalrous Society* (1978).

Georges Duby, *The Three Orders: Feudal Society Imagined* (1980).

Einhard, *The Life of Charlemagne (1962)*.

Henri Focillon, *The Year 1000* (1969).

Patrick J. Geary, *Before France and Germany: The Creation and Transformation of the Merovingian World* (1988).

Patrick J. Geary, ed., *Readings in Medieval History* (1989).

James Graham-Campbell, *The Viking World* (1980).

C.H. Haskins, *The Normans in European History* (1915).

David Herlihy, ed., *History of Feudalism* (1979).

David Herlihy, ed., *Medieval Culture and Society* (1968).

David Herlihy, *Medieval Households* (1985).

Maurice Keen, *Chivalry* (1984).

Maurice Keen, *A History of Medieval Europe* (1967).

M.L.W. Laistner, *Thought and Letters in Western Europe A.D. 500–900* (1931).

Jacques Le Goff, *Medieval Civilization 400–1500* (1989).

Jacques Le Goff, *Time, Work and Culture in the Middle Ages* (1980).

Archibald Lewis, *Emerging Medieval Europe A.D. 400–1000* (1967).

F. Donald Logan, *The Vikings in History* (1983).

Henri Pirenne, *Mohammed and Charlemagne* (1939).

C.W. Previté-Orton, ed., *The Shorter Cambridge Medieval History, vol. I* (1952).

Edward K. Rand, *Founders of the Middle Ages* (1928).

P.H. Sawyer, *Kings and Vikings: Scandinavia and Europe A.D. 700–1100* (1982).

Martin Scott, *Medieval Europe* (1964).

Shulamith Shahar, *Fourth Estate, A History of Women in the Middle Ages* (1984).

Frank Stenton, *Anglo-Saxon England* (1971).

Carl Stephenson, *Medieval Feudalism* (1956).

E.A. Thompson, *The Early Germans* (1965).

J.M. Wallace-Hadrill, *The Barbarian West: The Early Middle Ages 400–1000* (1989).

R. Winston, *Charlemagne: From the Hammer to the Cross* (1952).

CHAPTER 10

The High Middle Ages

Time Line

911	German dukes elect Conrad as king
919	Henry I founds Saxon dynasty
951	Otto conquers northern Italy
955	Germans defeat of Magyars at Lechfeld
962	Otto crowned as "Emperor of the Romans"; Beginning of Holy Roman Empire
1000–1350	High Middle Ages
1024	Conrad II founds Salian dynasty
1073	Hildebrand becomes Pope Gregory VII

1075	Pope Gregory VII forbids lay investiture
1077	Henry IV humbles himself before Gregory at Canossa
1095	First Crusade begins
1098	Cistercian Order founded
1122	Concordat of Worms resolves Investiture Controversy
1137	First of Hohenstaufen dynasty chosen German King
1147	Second Crusade begins
1176	Lombard League triumphant over Frederick I at Legnano
1183	Peace of Constance ends war with Lombard League
1189	Third Crusade begins
1194	Henry VI adds Sicily and Southern Italy to German Empire
1198–1216	Height of papal supremacy under Innocent III
1209–1229	Albigensian Crusade
1210	Franciscan Order approved by pope
1215	Fourth Lateran Council
1216	Dominican Order confirmed by pope
1220–1250	Frederick II reigns as Holy Roman Emperor; failed in unification of Italy
1226	Conquest of Sicily by Charles of Anjou
1228	End of Hohenstaufen line

1291   Fall of Acre to Muslims

                             End of Crusades

---

*The dawn of a new millennium ushered in a slow but profound trans-
formation of medieval life. With the cessation of barbarian assaults,
around the year 1000 a large measure of stability returned to the West
and its institutions began to display renewed vigor. During the next
three centuries the economy, social structure, political order, and cultural life of Western Europe all changed significantly. So important
were these changes that some scholars have termed either the whole or
a part of this period a "renaissance."*

*This chapter deals with the economic, social, and religious aspects
of the High, or Central Middle Ages (1000–1350) as well as the history
of the German Empire and its relations with the Papacy. Chapter 11
concentrates on the thought and culture of medieval Europe and the
political developments outside of Germany and Italy during essentially
the same period.*

*During the course of this creative era, medieval civilization
reached its zenith. Europe's population increased substantially, adding
vitality to all areas of medieval life. Hitherto sparsely occupied territories were settled. The revival of trade and industry prompted urban
growth and the rise of a new social class of merchants and town-
dwellers, the bourgeoisie. Despite these secularistic trends, the period
was a consummate "age of faith." A newly reformed and reinvigorated
Catholic Church attained the height of its temporal and spiritual
authority by the thirteenth century. Throughout most of this time the
church contended for supremacy with the other great power of the age,
the German Empire. By the second half of the thirteenth century both
were exhausted from the struggle. The Crusades offer further evidence
of renewed confidence as medieval Europeans set out in 1095 to evict
the Muslims from Jerusalem and to establish a Christian presence in
the Holy Land. The Crusaders continued to battle the Islamic world,
but with diminishing success until their final defeat in 1291.*

Economic Revival

Europe still remained an overwhelmingly agrarian and feudal society. Yet the resurgence of commercial and industrial activity during the Central Middle Ages introduced new forces into the medieval economy that would eventually undermine the old forms.

Population Growth

One of the first signs of the new dynamism of the eleventh century was a dramatic increase in population, a factor that persisted until the end of the thirteenth century. Since late Roman times, Europe's demographic growth had remained static, and the population actually declined. The reasons seem clear. Low fertility rates, famines and malnutrition, inadequate sanitation, the persistence of plagues and other communicable diseases, and wars combined to reduce Europe's population. Death struck early, its easiest victims being women and children. Parents during the early Middle Ages appear to have continued to some extent the Graeco-Roman practice of killing unwanted baby girls, usually by simply letting them starve to death. Peasant families were small. People lived clustered in manors, which were separated from each other by vast desolate spaces. Only a few cities existed.

Reasons for Increase

After the year 1000, however, this demographic decline began to change slowly for reasons that are still not altogether clear. Scholars estimate on the basis of incomplete statistics that the population of England in the mid-fourteenth century was more than three times greater than that of three hundred years earlier. Continental Europe appears to have experienced an upsurge of similar magnitude. The surrender of Normandy to the Vikings in 911 and the defeat of the Magyars at Lechfeld in 955 together mark a turning point in medieval life. Thereafter Europe was safer from foreign attack than it had been for centuries. Greater security clearly contributed to the spurt in population growth as did the absence of major plagues after 767. Domestic peace enabled peasants to leave the confines of the manor and venture into unoccupied territories. The cultivation of virgin soil increased crop yields as did the widespread application of new technology such as the heavy plow and the use of windmills. Even climatic changes resulting in warmer weather are thought to have improved harvests. More food produced heartier and stronger Europeans and allowed the continent to support a larger population.

Results of Population Growth

The expansion of Europe's population had highly significant economic, social, and political repercussions. A larger population necessitated even more intensive farming and additional searches for new arable lands. Thus peasants cut down forests, drained marshes, reclaimed land from the sea, and began settling sparsely inhabited areas within Europe and its periphery.

Economic Growth. All these activities resulted in an increase in agricultural productivity and made possible further economic expansion. Surplus crops could be sold or exchanged for money or goods, thus fostering the growth of trade. Increased numbers gradually put an end to the isolation of the early Middle Ages. Towns grew in size and importance as commerce revived. Peasants founded villages in newly cultivated areas.

Decline of Serfdom. By the thirteenth century serfdom had declined on the Continent. To encourage the clearing of forests and the draining of swamps on his manor, a lord often made special concessions to his serfs that freed them from manorial obligations. Other royal, noble, and ecclesiastical owners offered similar incentives to serfs to bring unoccupied land under the plow. These concessions normally were made in the form of a written charter that allowed the substitution of a money rent for peasant labor services and declared free their new village. Peasants in these free villages did not need permission from the lord to sell the rights to their property or to move. They generally administered their own judicial affairs. Any serf who managed to reside in a town or free village for a year and a day was freed of his servile status. Lords of manors had another reason to emancipate serfs. The availability of a cheap labor supply—comprised mainly of the younger sons of serfs—induced many lords to accept cash payments from some or all of the serfs and to reduce operating costs. Greater profits enabled the lords to buy luxury goods that had become more available with the increase of commerce.

Expansion of States. Europe's growing population had an impact on the political development of its states as well. Many of them expanded their frontiers as a result of peasants pushing into new lands for settlement. During the eleventh and twelfth centuries, Germans colonized the lands east of the Elbe River. By 1212 Christian settlers had driven the Arabs from most of the Iberian peninsula.

Revival of Commerce and Industry

Decline of Trade in Early Middle Ages

The virtual closing of the Mediterranean Sea by the extension of Islamic power caused long distance trade to dry up during the Carolingian Age[1]. What little trade occurred resulted from Venice's enduring ties to Constantinople. Because early feudal Europe possessed few desirable items to exchange for the precious goods of Byzantium and the East, international trade drained the West of its limited supply of gold and silver coinage. Although little money was available for domestic consumption, internal commerce never completely died out. In theory, money and markets were unnecessary to the self-sufficient manorial system. In practice, small local markets persisted where peasants continued to sell or exchange surplus commodities and handicrafts for such necessities as iron and salt. In times of local and regional famines profiteers transported produce from unaffected areas and sold it at high prices to those faced with starvation. This trade was nonetheless severely restricted by poor communications, a shortage of currency, limited demand, and the periodic barbarian disturbances in the age.

---

1   In his book *Medieval Cities* (1925), the Belgian historian Henri Pirenne linked the decline of trade in the Carolingian Period to the expansion of Islam and its revival to the breaking of Muslim control over the Mediterranean. Recently, Pirenne's thesis has come under attack by historians who stress other factors such as the Germanic and Viking invasions as equally important influences on the level of trade.

Renewal of Domestic Trade

The eleventh century again proved a turning point. Higher agricultural productivity induced both lords and peasants to sell surpluses. In addition, the growth of towns stimulated market growth, since expanding urban populations increased demand for manorial crops. Over time many lords and peasants began growing food expressly for towns, a venture that offered considerable profits, and they relied upon trade to satisfy other needs. The larger cities soon outstripped the ability of local manors to provide for them and they increasingly turned to regional producers for their foodstuffs and other goods. All of this contributed to a resurgence of economic activity.

Reopening of Trade with the East

At the same time the reopening of Europe's trade routes to the East provided an even greater impetus to commercial growth. Italians gained Sardinia from the Arabs in 1022 and Corsica in 1091, while Normans conquered the whole of Sicily by the latter date. The removal of Muslim control over the Mediterranean as well as the stimulus of the Crusades renewed commercial contacts that had languished since Roman times.

Maritime Trade

During the tenth and eleventh centuries Italy and Flanders commanded maritime trade activity primarily because they enjoyed favorable geographic locations.

Italy. The Italians dominated trade in the Mediterranean, especially with the Levant. Fleets from the great commercial cities of Venice, Genoa, and Pisa plied the Mediterranean and kept it free from corsairs. They transported Western goods such as raw wool, woolen cloth, iron, salt, wood, grain, weapons, olive oil, and wine to Constantinople and other ports of the eastern Mediterranean. In return they sailed home laden with the highly desired spices, silks, dyes, jewels, ivories, perfumes, and drugs transshipped from the Orient, and sugar, cotton, and finely crafted objets-d'art from Byzantium. Because of the high cost and light weight of most of these luxury items, merchants could reap fortunes from even one voyage. Yet the risk of total loss due to shipwreck, piracy, or other hazards was also high. Many of these early overseas merchants were younger sons of serfs whom the great growth in population had forced to seek their livelihood away from the land. Much akin to adventurers, they injected a spirit of enterprise into European economic life.

Flanders. Merchants from Flanders, a region now part of western Belgium and northern France, assumed the leading position in trade that linked the British Isles and the coastline of the North Sea to Russia, the Baltic region, and the Levant. Using established trade routes along Russia's rivers, Western ships carried spices, silks, and other oriental goods from Constantinople back to northern Europe. From Russia and the Baltic, Flemish traders imported furs, grain, timber, pitch, tar, amber, herring, and honey. In exchange they sold English raw wool, fine Flemish woolen cloth, German minerals and metalworks, and some products from southern Europe. From the twelfth until the fifteenth century the Flemish city of Bruges was the fulcrum of this lucrative northern trade.

Hanseatic League. In the thirteenth century a group of northern European cities joined together as the Hanseatic League. Collective power enabled the League to extract trading privileges and for at least two centuries it dominated the Baltic trade.

Overland Trade

By the twelfth century long-distance trade began to penetrate the interior of Western Europe. Cities such as Barcelona, Marseilles, Cologne, Mainz, London, Florence, and Milan emerged as important commercial or industrial centers. Overland trade routes across Alpine passes and along the great rivers of the Rhone, Rhine, Meuse, Scheldt, Danube, and others connected Italy to Flanders and the rest of Europe. The focal point of this overland trade was the plain of Champagne in northeastern France. For much of each year a series of six fairs at this site attracted merchants from all over Europe.

Caravans of merchants traveled together for greater safety and to enhance their power and resources through cooperation. Since they were not personally subject to any lord, they won exemption from most local laws and forged their own commercial code, the *law merchant*, that was based on common business practices and was everywhere the same. At fairs, merchants operated their own courts, which offered disputants speedy and equitable justice. Nobles such as the Counts of Champagne promoted both fairs and local markets within their territories because they generated money in tolls and court fees.

Use of Money

The revival of commerce increased the amount of money in circulation. New silver mines were opened and coins minted. The creation of a market system and a money economy had profound effects on the nature of feudalism and manorialism. By the late twelfth century feudal lords increasingly commuted military services into cash payments and accepted money in lieu of manorial services from the serfs. Prices rose gradually, and the trend to commutation benefited vassals and serfs alike. The earning of a wage rather than other forms of remuneration became commonplace.

Development of Manufacturing

The revival of commerce stimulated manufacturing and mining and increased the availability of raw materials. This was accompanied by new demands for manufactured goods such as textiles, arms, and armor. The production of woolen cloth offered considerable profits and became the most important medieval industry. It involved a number of complicated steps. Medieval workers labored in their homes, as there were no factories.

Credit and Banking

To finance distant commercial exchanges, medieval merchants invented new and ingenious methods of raising capital to circumvent the Church's prohibition against usury. The Medieval Church held that every commodity had a "just price," an amount that covered the cost of the raw material, the worker's wage at a rate sufficient to allow him a decent standard of living, and a small sum to compensate the seller. Long-distance traders generally eluded this restriction on technicalities associated with the difficulty of determining a just price for foreign luxury goods. Italian merchants were most innovative in evading the usury laws when they borrowed the large sums necessary to purchase and transport a cargo to its destination. One of the first and most widely used means of extending credit at interest was to issue a bill of exchange that stipulated the loan be repaid at another place in another currency.

The currency exchange rates always allowed profits for the lenders. Another method of credit, a rent or annuity, offered the lenders fixed sums of money *per annum* normally for the rest of their lives. The total amount paid naturally far exceeded the original loan. Partnerships increased available funds and reduced risk. These were typically of two types: temporary agreements between a merchant and his silent investors (a *commenda*), or a more permanent association (a *compagnia*) that at first involved members of the same family.

Gradually the Church's strict opposition to the taking of interest weakened, perhaps because the Jews, who had once been the major moneylenders, were expelled from France and England around the year 1300. By the end of the thirteenth century Italian merchants had responded to the emergence of an incipient capitalism by developing an important banking and credit system that enriched many of them.

The Rise of Towns

The growth of trade and the rise of towns were closely related phenomena. By the ninth century, most medieval towns in Europe owed their existence primarily to the fact the bishops resided within their walls. These towns exercised ecclesiastical, administrative, and defensive functions within their dioceses but were of negligible commercial and industrial importance. In general most remained poor and depopulated. With the increase in population and the reappearance of commerce beginning around the year 1000, however, urban life took on renewed meaning.

By the opening of the fourteenth century, medieval towns had emerged as thriving commercial and industrial centers. They were the seat of a new class of people, the bourgeoisie, who championed new ideas and a new, nonfeudal way of life. Because of their growing accumulation of wealth, towns came to play an increasingly active role in the politics of the late Middle Ages.

Location of Cities

Itinerant merchants needed a place to settle and store their wares during the winter season and between travels. They chose sites that were secure from attack and strategically located. The earliest centers of commerce were located along the seacoast, on major rivers, and at the intersection of trade routes. Some of these were old Roman towns, while others grew up around well-situated burgs or fortresses built by local dynasties. Because the walls of the burg limited the number of its inhabitants, merchants settled outside the castle in what was known as the *faubourg*. This too was fortified to provide defense against brigands. By the twelfth century, its walls began to be built of stone.

Living Conditions

Medieval cities served as homes to merchants, and to artisans, day laborers, and runaway serfs who found employment in the industries that concentrated there during the thirteenth century. Except in northern Italy and southern France, few nobles maintained residences in the city after the eleventh century. The Church, by contrast, kept its contact with urban life and the bishops maintained residences in cathedral towns. Most medieval cities were unsanitary, overcrowded, and hazardous places. Nevertheless, to live in the city offered residents advantages not found in the countryside. It offered them greater freedom, security, and a more varied existence. Extremely harsh criminal laws preserved the peace and protected property, and city government and law in general proved more equitable than that in rural areas. Because commercial transactions required reading and reckoning skills, the literacy rate in most towns was higher than in the countryside. Despite these advantages, urban life was difficult. Town dwellers were especially vulnerable to fires and plagues. Social conflicts between the rich and the poor periodically erupted into violence.

The Bourgeoisie

In most European states, town residents were called by names derived from the word burg. A town dweller was known as a *bourgeois* in France, a *burgher* in England, and a *burger* in Germany. Collectively these bourgeoisie constituted a special class in medieval society that was neither noble nor peasant. Their free status derived from their place of residency, and they enjoyed laws and institutions of their own. They earned their living principally from commercial and industrial enterprises, not from agriculture. Although many towns had nominal ties with feudal lords and most remained dependent upon neighboring manors for their food, they were essentially a foreign element within the feudal and manorial structures.

Associations of Townspeople

At first the persistence of feudal obligations, restrictions upon land ownership, and multiple jurisdiction encumbered the economic growth of medieval cities. To increase their bargaining power against the king, prince, or monastery upon whose territory they lived and to whom they owed feudal dues and tolls, townspeople soon learned to act collectively. Wealthy merchants took the lead in representing the interests of the urban population. Having early formed themselves into guilds or corporate unions, they used their collective strength to win concessions. In some towns, known as communes, the inhabitants swore a mutual oath of association and used their collective strength to improve their status in regard to defense and taxation.

Town Charters

By the end of the twelfth century most towns had become largely self-governing. Either by force or by consent, they had won charters from their immediate lords that granted them control over their economic life and guaranteed their personal liberty. The vast majority of charters recognized the city as a distinct legal entity with its own law, its own special tribunal run by the burghers, and its own administrative officials. Charters also commonly exempted burghers from oppressive seignorial rights, dues, and monopolies, and they substituted a fixed yearly sum for the market tolls on merchandise that passed through the city gates. Cities were thus freed from the restrictions of feudalism. Charter concessions varied, but those issued by the king were usually the most generous. Most towns with royal charters were completely autonomous and paid only fixed annual taxes to the king.

Guilds

Medieval economic life was highly regulated. As commerce and industry grew in size and complexity, specialized guilds were founded in most cities. These were of two types. Merchant guilds included all those engaged in commerce within a city while craft guilds encompassed all the workers of a specific industry.

Regulations and Training

Most city governments handed over to the guilds the tasks of admitting members and enforcing strict regulation of their profession. Only guild members were allowed by law to practice its craft or trade. To ensure good workmanship, the craft guilds established a stringent apprenticeship system. Around the age of ten a boy would go to live with and work for a master craftsman in order to learn his skill. After approximately seven years of study, and if his work was deemed acceptable, he became a journeyman and could work for hire in his master's shop. Eventually, if he saved his money and exhibited proof of his ability, he could hope to become a master, own his own shop, and join his industry's guild. Artisans fraternized together in guildhalls and enjoyed a privileged position by virtue of their guild membership.

Rights and Responsibilities

Each guild possessed a monopoly over its craft or trade and its members were protected from competition. Guilds fixed the prices of goods and the wages of workers on the basis of what was supposed best for both producers and consumers. Guild leaders established rigorous standards of quality, determined the volume of goods produced, and set the hours and conditions of labor. Guilds played a social role as well. They provided for the medical needs and burial arrangements of their members and looked after their widows and children.

The German Empire and the Papacy

The German Empire

For most of the tenth, eleventh, and twelfth centuries, Germany was the leading secular power in Western Europe. The East Frankish lands had been the first to revive after the turmoil of the ninth century. Their division into large units, the duchies, that corresponded to the four main Germanic tribes—the Saxons, Bavarians, Swabians, and Franconians—had helped to preserve a degree of cohesiveness. Whereas in France political power had fallen into the hands of numerous petty feudal lords upon the dissolution of the Carolingian Empire, in Germany ancient customs and tribal loyalties militated against the growth of feudalism.

Instead, tribal magnates in each of the four principal or "Stem" duchies (Saxony, Bavaria, Swabia, and Franconia) assumed the title of "duke" and began acting like independent monarchs within their territories. Encountering little opposition from the last German Carolingian, Louis the Child (reigned 899–911), they seized royal estates and asserted the right to control the Church in their duchy.

Despite the strong particularism of the duchies, the Germans felt no need to abandon their monarchical government. Powerful magnates recognized the value of the crown as a unifying agent in the state, but they wanted to limit the monarch's powers. Thus when Louis the Child died in 911 without issue, the four dukes chose the weakest among themselves, Conrad, Duke of Franconia (reigned 911–918) as king.

Henry I

As his electors correctly anticipated, Conrad proved unequal to the tasks of reasserting royal power, warding off the Magyars, and preventing insurrections. Wisely, he named as his successor the powerful Duke of Saxony, Henry "the Fowler" (reigned 919–936). Henry envisioned himself not as the king of a united Germany but as the head of a ducal confederation, and refused to be crowned by the Archbishop of Mainz. Yet by the end of his reign he had won back important royal prerogatives from the dukes and advanced the cause of monarchical authority through his military triumphs.

Military Victories. In 925 Henry succeeded in recovering the duchy of Lorraine (Lotharingia) from the French. To the east he launched a war of conquest against the Slavs that marked the beginning of Germany's centuries-long *Drang nach Osten* ("drive to the East"). The Slavic territory of Brandenburg became a German march while to the south the Czechs of Bohemia were forced to accept Henry's suzerainty. In 933 he won a key victory over the Magyars. Slowly German soldiers and missionaries began to colonize and Christianize the lands east of the Elbe River. Henry established fortified towns or burgs to secure his expanded eastern frontier. His great prestige opened the way to a revived German monarchy under his successors. The Saxon dynasty of strong kings that Henry founded ruled Germany until 1024.

Otto I

Henry I's undisputed successor was his son Otto I, the Great (reigned 936–973). Otto possessed none of his father's ambivalence about the German kingship. He had himself crowned king in Charlemagne's basilica in Aachen and set out immediately to reduce the independent power of the dukes.

Conflict with Duchies. Otto's determination to establish royal supremacy over a united Germany touched off a widespread revolt. In hopes of pacifying the rebellious duchies, Otto replaced their rulers with members of his own family who were then linked by marriage with the ancient ducal houses. In addition, he assumed direct control over the duchy of Franconia in 939. Henceforth Franconia would belong to the German king regardless of his native duchy. When Otto's own kinsmen proved as ambitious and disloyal as the former dukes, he looked to the Church for allies and used the upper clergy as royal administrators. He granted bishops and abbots vast estates from which he received a significant revenue and an assured supply of soldiers. Because of weakness and corruption in the papacy at the time, Otto, as feudal overlord, was able to exercise complete control over the Church within Germany.

Expansion of Territory. Otto's vision of a united Germany was matched by his desire to restore the empire of Charlemagne. He felt himself heir to a great imperial tradition and moral ruler of Western Christendom. He sponsored education and patronized a distinctive revival in the arts. When in 951 the widowed Italian queen, Adelaide, offered her hand in marriage to whoever would free her lands from the grasp of the new king of Lombardy, Otto marched southward. He declared himself king of Italy and married Adelaide, but his conquest of the *Regnum Italicum* in northern Italy was interrupted by rebellion at home. After subduing ducal unrest, Otto was confronted by a major Magyar invasion. His tremendous victory at Lechfeld near Augsburg in 955 finally put an end to a hundred years of depredations. Otto carried on his father's expansion of Germany eastward, founding five new marches in conquered Slavic territory and erecting a large number of burgs. German colonists gradually moved into Eastern Europe. Their settlement among the Slav natives remained a point of friction even into the twentieth century.

Emperor of the Romans. Otto returned to Italy in 961 at the request of Pope John XII and easily reaffirmed his authority over the *Regnum Italicum*. The grateful pope revived the imperial title of the Carolingians and bestowed it upon Otto early in 962. To be called "Emperor of the Romans" greatly strengthened the German king's claim to Lombardy, Burgundy, and Lorraine, lands that had once belonged to the middle kingdom of the Carolingian emperor Lothair. Otto's new empire, later called the Holy Roman Empire, endured until 1806. Unlike the ancient Roman Empire or its Carolingian copy, the German Empire encompassed only Germany, Italy, and the adjoining provinces of Burgundy, Bohemia, and Provence. Even within these lands, the power of local magnates often exceeded that of the emperor. Nor did the new emperor possess the same authority over the Roman Church that Charlemagne had exercised. For succeeding generations, the union of Italy to Germany would prove more a liability than an asset.

Otto II and Otto III

Until the last year of his life Otto was embroiled in Italian affairs. His successors, Otto II (reigned 973–983) and Otto III (reigned 983–1002), preoccupied themselves with Italy to the detriment of centralized authority in Germany. Their frequent absences allowed the forces of feudalism to grow at home.

Henry II

Recognizing this threat to royal authority, Henry II (reigned 1002–1024), the last of the Saxon line, turned his attention more closely to German affairs. To curb the increased authority and defiance of the great nobles, he leaned even more heavily upon ecclesiastical support. He gave generous grants of land to the bishops, and demanded his right to nominate them to ensure their loyalty. This alliance with the Church by Saxon kings enabled them to become the strongest European monarchs of their age, but it contained a fundamental flaw that would eventually lead to the ruin of German central authority.

The Medieval Church

The medieval Church was the one truly universal institution of its age and guardian of Roman Catholicism's divine revelation. As such it possessed tremendous powers. Owing to the far-reaching activity of Roman Catholic missionaries, virtually all Western Europeans belonged to the Christian Church except for a small number of Jews and Muslims.

Beliefs

Medieval beliefs blended pagan myths, magic, and superstition with Christian doctrine. The veneration of saints and worship of relics played a vital part in the religious consciousness. Medieval people viewed life on earth as a transitory existence that had value only insofar as it brought them closer to the eternal rewards of Heaven. All earthly events were interpreted as having supernatural significance. Most Christians believed that the Day of Judgment was imminent: Christ would return and sinners would be condemned to eternal damnation while the saved would attain heavenly bliss. Fear of hell and concern for salvation colored the thoughts, actions, and art of medieval people. All human beings, so they believed, were born with the taint of Adam's original sin. Only through the seven sacraments administered by the Church could an individual be absolved of his sins and receive the grace necessary for salvation.

Excommunication and Interdict

To enforce compliance with the Church's will and conformity with its activities, the pope could threaten an individual with excommunication. This prevented the person from entering a church, taking the sacraments, acting in a legal capacity, or receiving a Christian burial. Another powerful weapon directed against secular rulers was the interdict. The population of lands under interdict were denied all benefits of the Church except baptism and extreme unction (last rites for the dying). Public worship, marriage, and burial services were suspended. Even the most defiant monarch did not take lightly the disastrous consequences of being expelled from the Christian community.

Organization

The great wealth and political influence of the medieval Catholic Church added to its exalted stature. Its highly regularized hierarchy extended from the lowly parish priest to the canons, bishops, and archbishops, and finally the pope in Rome aided by his Curia, or bureaucracy. This organization provided the Church with the most efficient administrative structure in Europe. Many medieval monarchs relied upon churchmen to administer their realms. Clergymen were usually the only literate members of medieval society, and until at least the end of the thirteenth century, the Church monopolized higher education. Evolving for itself a well-defined body of canon law, the Church courts and skilled canon lawyers abetted the growth of the Church's centralizing power by the eleventh century.

Privileges and Wealth. One of the clergy's most coveted privileges was the right to be tried only by the ecclesiastical courts, where punishments were normally more lenient than in their secular counterparts. Church courts also held jurisdiction over many cases involving the laity such as those dealing with heresy, perjury, usury, and marriage. The Church's vast riches stemmed from two main sources: the *tithe*, an obligatory tax of one-tenth of a person's income for the maintenance of the religious establishment, and revenue from land that had, in most instances, been donated to the church by devout laypeople.

Secular Involvement and Moral Decline. Despite its accumulation of immense power and prestige, the Church lapsed into moral decline in the post-Carolingian era. Its very wealth and involvement in secular affairs endangered the purity of its spiritual character and priestly functions. Since much of the land donated to the Church required its owner to perform feudal services, the Church necessarily found itself involved in secular affairs. Lay control over ecclesiastical offices tightened. Nobles took over large Church estates for themselves as fiefs. At the local level many parish churches actually belonged to the lords who endowed them and who retained the right to name the priest. In an age of moral chaos many members of the clergy were corrupt, greedy, and ignorant men. Most bishops and abbots owed their offices and their lands to the king or a great noble. Hence they ordinarily felt a greater sense of loyalty to their patrons than to a distant pope. Many prelates acted more like feudal magnates than religious leaders. The sin of simony, the purchase of offices, was one of the most ubiquitous evils of the age. Bishops and even popes openly bought and sold their offices. Unschooled parish priests unscrupulously charged fees for performing their duties. Because so many individuals entered monasteries for nonreligious reasons, adherence to the rules of monastic life grew lax.

The Cluniac Reform. There remained, nonetheless, those within the Church who viewed with horror the trend toward secularism and the breakdown of clerical devotion, discipline, and morality, but they had generally only a local influence. In 910, however, Duke William I, the Pious, founded a monastery at Cluny in French Burgundy, from which would spread the spirit of reform. Until the late eleventh century, the zealous abbots of Cluny enforced strict adherence to the Rule of Benedict within their "mother" monastery and within the hundreds of "daughter" houses they founded throughout Europe and over which they retained control. From these centers Cluniac reformers demanded that church officials end all forms of simony and reinstitute strict adherence to clerical celibacy. They regarded the abolition of lay control as essential to rid the Church of its abuses. They called for a tightening of the pope's authority over bishops and abbots and demanded that he be independent of imperial domination.

Conflict between Emperors and Popes

Conrad II

When the Saxon dynasty died out in 1024, a descendant of Otto I through the female line, Conrad II of Franconia (reigned 1024–1039), was elected king. He founded the Salian dynasty that ruled until 1125. Conrad II was interested in strengthening the Empire, not reforming the Church. In 1034 he added Burgundy to the imperial domain and marched into Italy two years later. In both Italy and Germany he promoted the interests of the small nobility (the counts) against those of the dukes. He allowed the offices and holdings of the lesser nobility to become hereditary. In order to decrease the Empire's reliance on the Church, he began using men of servile origin as administrators. They formed a unique medieval class, the *ministeriales*, found only in Germany. Although endowed with lands, they were beholden to the king and were not at first members of the feudal nobility. Conrad left to his son a wealthy and powerful empire.

Henry III

In contrast to his father, Henry III (reigned 1039–1056) was an ardent reformer. Whereas Conrad II had bought and sold church offices as it suited his needs, Henry condemned the practice and banned the customary fees paid by new bishops to the king. In 1046 he intervened in papal affairs to depose three rival claimants and to secure the election of his own choice as pope. Later he elevated his cousin Leo IX, an outstanding sponsor of reform. Henry's reign brought the German Empire to the peak of its power. He defeated the Bohemians, fixed the border between Austria and Hungary, and attempted by various means to subdue the chronically rebellious dukes. Yet his policy of looking to a reformed papacy for aid proved an illusion.

Leo IX

Leo IX was the first of a new kind of pope unwilling to remain subservient to imperial control and willing to struggle with the emperor for supremacy of the West. Leo traveled constantly to reestablish the central authority of the papacy within the Western Church and to ferret out corruption. He called for free canonial elections of bishops totally devoid of secular intervention, and he disciplined prelates for simony and other vices. His assertion of papal power contributed to the worsening of relations between the Eastern and Western Churches that culminated in the final schism in 1054. Leo died that same year, and Henry III followed him to the grave two years later. The stage was now set for a test of strength between their successors.

Henry IV

Henry III was succeeded by his six-year-old son, Henry IV (reigned 1056–1105). The papacy, the bishops, and the great nobles all took advantage of Henry's minority to act independently. In 1059 Pope Nicholas II issued a decree that gave the cardinals in the Church the sole power to elect a pope. The papacy then secured military support from the Normans who had begun their conquest of southern Italy in 1016. Within Germany the archbishop of Cologne seized the young king in 1062 and ruled as regent. Four years later, having reached the age of majority, Henry began to assert his own authority over the discordant Empire. His efforts to revive royal power led to a conflict with the

Saxons, who cherished their tribal independence and resented the central control administered by low-born *ministeriales*. In 1073 a tremendous revolt broke out in Saxony and raged for two years. Shortly thereafter a new controversy, this time with the Church, plunged the Empire into further civil war.

The Investiture Controversy

In 1073 Hildebrand, an ardent reformer who had served as assistant and administrator to Leo IX and his successors, became Pope Gregory VII. The devout but combative new pope believed that spiritual authority took precedence over all forms of temporal power. In order to carry out the reformers' goal of freeing the Church from worldly influence and assuring the pope supremacy in the West, he forbade the practice of lay investiture in 1075.

As feudal lords, the German emperors and other medieval monarchs had assumed the right to bestow upon prelates not only the secular authority of their office but their symbols of spiritual authority (i.e., the bishop's ring and staff) as well. This lay investiture in effect gave a layperson control over the selection of church officials. Without such control the German emperor could not be certain of the loyalty of clerical vassals upon whom he had conferred great estates and to whom he looked for administrative and military support.

Gregory's action was a direct challenge to the German emperor's domination of the Church that had formed the bedrock of imperial policy since Otto I.

Henry's Penance. Henry responded to Gregory's decree by summoning a council of his bishops at Worms, which declared the Pope dethroned. In response Gregory excommunicated Henry (the first excommunication of a monarch since the fourth century) and absolved his subjects of allegiance to him. These measures placed Henry's right to the imperial crown in jeopardy. Shortly afterward the great German nobles issued an ultimatum: either Henry gain the Pope's absolution by early 1077 or they would elect a new king in Gregory's presence. Henry had no alternative but to cross the Alps and put himself at the pope's mercy. For three days in January 1077 he waited barefoot in the snow before the gates of the castle of Canossa in the Apennines where Gregory was staying. After this act of contrition, the pope had little choice but to allow Henry to do penance and to remove the sentence of excommunication.

Henry's Political Victory. Although Henry had been forced to humble himself before an omnipotent pope, he accomplished his political purpose. He regained support from the majority of his German subjects. The seditious dukes, however, continued to repudiate Henry's kingship and proceeded to elect Duke Rudolf of Swabia monarch. Civil war erupted anew.

Further Conflict Between Henry and Gregory

In a new quarrel with Henry in 1080, Gregory sided with Rudolf and again excommunicated the emperor. In response Henry backed a new anti-pope. Gregory then appealed to the Normans for military assistance against the emperor. In the struggles that followed, Rudolf was slain in battle and Rome fell to Henry in 1084 after a long siege. Norman troops arrived a year too late, in time only to plunder the ancient capital and carry off the pope. Gregory died in exile in 1085, a sorely disappointed man.

Concordat of Worms

Henry had won an impressive but impermanent victory over the papacy. Gregory's reform of the papal office had raised it to a new, high level of moral and political potency. Simony and clerical marriages were outlawed, and the clergy was more isolated from secular life. A generation after Henry's death in 1106 the issue of lay investiture was resolved. Wearied by the incessant strife, Emperor Henry V (reigned 1106–1125), the German nobles, and the pope all agreed in 1122 to the Concordat of Worms. This famous compromise granted the free canonical election of bishops and abbots and gave to high ecclesiastics the right to confer upon clerics the spiritual symbols of their office. The emperor continued to invest them with their *regalia* of secular jurisdiction, and because this ceremony occurred in Germany before the ecclesiastical consecration, it ensured the priority of their oaths of fealty to the emperor. In addition, the emperor or his representative was allowed to be present at clerical elections, a privilege that was tantamount to influencing them. In Italy and Burgundy the emperor's powers were more circumscribed.

Results of Controversy. The investiture settlement released the clergy from lay control. However, the conflict left in its destructive wake a legacy of civil war and particularism in Germany. The long struggle with the papacy had badly damaged the centralizing authority of the German monarchy. This left the great German nobles, hereafter known as princes, largely free from royal interference. Smaller territorial states built upon feudal relations gradually supplanted the ancient, loosely-organized tribal duchies. Thus, in the long run the investiture controversy ended in victory for the German nobility.

The House of Hohenstaufen

Henry V's death in 1125 ended the line of Salian monarchs. Since the time of Otto the Great, hereditary right had determined the successor to the German kingship. Now the absence of a direct heir to the throne enabled the German princes to reassert their right to elect the king. They selected Lothair, Duke of Saxony (reigned 1125–1137) over his closest rival, Frederick of Hohenstaufen, Duke of Swabia.

Civil Conflict and Growth of Feudalism

Lothair joined the fortunes of his house to that of the powerful Welfs by marrying his only daughter to its head, Henry the Proud. Thus began the turbulent, century-long competition between the Welfs and the Hohenstaufens for possession of the imperial throne.

When Lothair III died in 1137 without an heir, the German nobles chose the Hohenstaufen, Conrad III (reigned 1138–1152) rather than Lothair's son-in-law, the powerful Henry the Proud, whom they viewed as a threat to their own powers. Conrad proved a weak and short-sighted king. His decision to strip Henry the Proud of Saxony and Bavaria engulfed Germany in renewed civil strife. Continued violence fostered feudalism to such an extent that when Frederick I came to the throne his revival of royal authority took place wholly within a feudal context.

Frederick Barbarossa

Welf-Hohenstaufen hostilities subsided briefly during Frederick I's reign (1152–1190) in part because the new king was related to both houses. (Conrad III had persuaded the German princes to elect his nephew Frederick rather than his own six-year-old son.) Known in

Italian as Barbarossa (Red Beard), Frederick I was one of Germany's greatest medieval kings. Under him the German Empire first received its formal title, the Holy Roman Empire.

Pacification of Germany. Frederick understood that the restoration of order in Germany was a precondition for reviving imperial might elsewhere. Thus he returned the duchy of Bavaria to Henry the Proud's son and heir, Henry the Lion, in hope of ending the disastrous feud. He also announced a general peace throughout the land and prohibited private warfare.

Intervention in Italy. Frederick's policy of restoring imperial greatness required that he not only preserve peace and establish his dominion over the German princes as a feudal monarch, but also that he reassert imperial control over Italy. In 1156 he skillfully acquired Burgundy by marriage. Two years later he crossed into Italy a second time to restake his claim to sovereignty over the northern Italian cities whose tax revenues the Empire sorely needed.

Revolt of Italian Cities. After subduing Milan, Frederick held a diet at Roncaglia, where he prohibited private warfare and decreed severe penalties for violations of the peace. Profiting from the recently revived study of Roman law, he declared that he ruled Italy as the legitimate successor to Charlemagne and the Caesars. Thus he reclaimed from the cities the right to collect all tolls and taxes, appoint officials, and mint coins. These rights are known collectively as the *regalia*. Frederick then placed German officials in the Italian cities to oversee imperial administration and end internecine quarreling. The harsh behavior of Frederick's officials and their excessive taxation drove the cities to revolt. Putting aside their traditional rivalries, the northern Italian cities formed an alliance, the Lombard League, in 1167. Pope Alexander III, who had won out over several of the Emperor's candidates, supported the League in its conflict with Frederick.

The Peace of Constance. While the Lombard cities were hastily leaguing together, Frederick was busy to the south. Rome fell to him in July 1167 and the conquest of Sicily appeared imminent. A terrible plague, however, decimated his army and forced him to return home. In 1174, Frederick recrossed the Alps to subjugate the insurrectionary towns. In large part because the Welf Henry the Lion refused to provide troops, the imperial forces sustained a crushing defeat at the hands of the League at Legnano in 1176. This victory, the first triumph in European history of townspeople over an imperial army, frustrated Frederick's efforts to rule Italy directly. At the Peace of Constance in 1183 he recognized the autonomy of the Lombard towns within their own walls and conceded their rights to membership in a league. In exchange, the cities acknowledged Frederick's authority in the countryside, continued to pay a tax for the maintenance of the imperial army, and agreed that their officials owed fealty to the emperor as a feudal lord.

Frederick's Legacy. In the years after Legnano, Frederick turned from force to conciliation in dealing with the northern Italian towns and the papacy. He adroitly brought the disloyal Henry the Lion to trial and stripped him of Bavaria and Saxony, which he divided into smaller principalities. In 1190 while he was in the East on the Third Crusade at the peak of his fame, Barbarossa drowned. His clear vision and superlative talents as a statesman had restored strength to the Empire as much by diplomacy as by conquest. Yet Frederick left his heirs no system of imperial officials and centralized government by which to administer his vast empire. The continued involvement of the House of Hohenstaufen with Italy led to the dynasty's final collapse a little over a half century later.

Henry VI

Thanks to his marriage to the heiress of the Norman Kingdom of Naples and Sicily (Kingdom of the Two Sicilies), Henry VI (reigned 1190–1197) had a chance to accomplish what had eluded his father Frederick I: the union of Sicily and Southern Italy to the German Empire. Only after quelling resistance from the pope, the Sicilians, the Welfs, and their ally, Richard the Lionhearted of England, did Henry in 1194 become master of his inheritance. Like his father, Henry envisioned the creation of a great empire that commanded the Mediterranean as well as Germany. To realize his southern ambitions and his desire to restore heritability to the German monarchy, he granted additional concessions to the great territorial princes. Thus while the German Empire appeared to reach a new summit of power and prestige, it rested dangerously on the shifting sands of papal antipathy and German particularism.

Innocent III: The Height of Papal Authority

German domination of Italy outside the Papal States presaged renewed conflict between the Empire and the papacy. This time the papal throne was occupied by a man whose conception of the power of his office was without earthly limits. Innocent III (reigned 1198–1216) became pope a year after Henry VI's death. Henry's heir was his three-year-old son, Frederick II, who became ward to Innocent after the death of his mother in 1198. As guardian of the Emperor the Pope was in an excellent position to undo the German-Italian connection that hemmed in papal lands on all sides and restricted the papacy's temporal powers in Italy. Soon after Henry's death, Italy rose in revolt against imperial control. Innocent used this opportunity to reassert papal sovereignty over central Italy.

Involvement in European Affairs

Innocent involved himself in the worldly affairs of European states to a greater extent and with greater success than had any of his forerunners. He freely used his powers of excommunication and interdict to achieve his goals. In his quarrel with King John over the appointment of Stephen Langton as archbishop of Canterbury, for example, he laid England under interdict and excommunicated the king in 1209. Threat of war with his enemy, Philip Augustus of France, and pressure from the English barons and people forced John to comply with the pope's will. He handed over England to the pope, receiving it back as a papal fief for which he paid annual tribute. The lands of King Philip Augustus of France were also placed under interdict as punishment for deserting his first wife. Innocent succeeded in compelling Philip to give up his new consort and return to his mistreated queen. The pope also dictated at times to the rulers of Spain, Portugal, and Scandinavia, believing that it was his duty to guide lay rulers and supervise their moral conduct.

Control of Church

Innocent exercised an equally vigilant control over the Church. He was the first pope to assert the papacy's right to fill all vacant ecclesiastical offices by direct appointment. In addition, he levied the first income tax on the clergy and monasteries. He pressed for the unity of Christendom and conformity to Church doctrine. After initial opposition and dismay, he came to regard the sacking of Constantinople by the Crusaders in 1204 as a means to restore the union of Eastern and Western Christianity.

Heresies

During Innocent's reign the Church was troubled by several heresies that first emerged during the eleventh and twelfth centuries. The two most threatening were the Waldensian heresy and the Catharist, or Albigensian, heresy. Both were essentially expressions of urban discontent over the failure of the worldly and powerful priesthood to meet the spiritual needs of the new, overcrowded towns.

The Waldensians. The Waldensians were founded by Peter Waldo, a rich merchant of Lyons who around the year 1170 gave away all his possessions to the poor and began preaching in the streets. His followers, Waldensians, lived exemplary lives of poverty and austerity. They held the view that all human beings are capable of reading and interpreting the Bible, which was the one, true guide to Christian faith. They further believed that sacraments were not needed for salvation and bitterly attacked the church hierarchy. The Church condemned these views as heretical in 1184 and again in 1215, but Waldensians continued to exist and are often considered the spiritual ancestors of Protestanism.

The Catharists. The heresy that posed the greatest threat to Catholic orthodoxy was that of the *Cathari* (Greek for "pure"). They held dualist beliefs akin to the Manicheans of the third century. The heretical movement found its greatest acceptance in southern France, where it was protected by the secular authorities. Its adherents are often called Albigensians after the town of Albi in Languedoc where a large number of them lived. Like the Manicheans, the Catharists believed that the earth was created not by God but by Satan and that all matter including the human body was contaminated by evil. For them Christ was pure spirit. Thus they rejected the Old Testament, the sacraments of the Church, Jesus's bodily resurrection, and the priesthood. Instead they preached an extreme asceticism in order to release the soul from its fleshly prison. Because of the strictness of its tenets, Catharism would have had little appeal had it not divided its followers into two groups: the Perfect Ones who led devout and ascetic lives, and the Believers who were required simply to venerate the Perfect Ones.

The Albigensian Crusade. Catharism was more of a rival religion
than an aberrant branch of Roman Catholicism. Its attacks, that claimed
the clergy and the Church were mired in evil, and its growing popularity
roused the papacy to action by 1184. When Innocent III's attempt to
call the Catharists to obedience peacefully failed, he preached a crusade
against them. From 1209 to 1229 nobles from northern France led by
Simon de Montfort savagely attacked the strongholds of Catharist
support in Languedoc and Provence. In 1233 Pope Gregory IX established the Inquisition, a special clerical court authorized to use torture
and secret denunciations in order to extirpate the remaining heretics.

The Fourth Lateran Council

Innocent III summed up the fruits of his pontificate at the Fourth
Lateran Council of 1215. The council enacted canons that regulated all
aspects of Church doctrine and administration. Among them was the
requirement that all Catholics go to confession and take communion at
least once a year. It formally adopted the dogma of transubstantiation:
that the bread and wine of the Mass were changed into the true body
and blood of Jesus Christ. The council further recognized seven sacraments as necessary for salvation. It dealt a death blow to trial by ordeal
by prohibiting clerics from serving as participants. It declared the
Waldensians heretical and proclaimed a new crusade against the Muslims. Other canons set the standards for admission to the priesthood,
regulated episcopal elections, and sought to improve the religious
quality of monastic life. Few Church councils have had as great an
impact on the governance of the Church and the conduct of its members
as the Fourth Lateran Council. It represented a triumph for Innocent's
ideas of the Church.

Frederick II

Raised in the culturally rich atmosphere of Norman Sicily,
Frederick II was at heart, more Italian than German. A gifted poet,
linguist, and scientist, he was referred to by his contemporaries as the
"wonder of the world" (*stupor mundi*). His book *The Art of Falconry*
is still consulted by ornithologists. He was a generous patron of the arts
and sciences at his Sicilian court. Not the least of Frederick's talents
was his genius for statesmanship. His lifelong ambition became to unite

all of Italy under his own autocratic rule. This obsession triggered the resistance of the northern Italian towns and led to a final confrontation between the papacy and the Empire.

Policies in Germany

As ward of Innocent III, Frederick had appeared to be docile and obedient. Soon after his guardian's death, however, the young ruler of Sicily began to display a cunning disregard for promises he had made. Contrary to Innocent's wishes, he sought to be crowned Holy Roman Emperor without renouncing his Sicilian kingdom. To secure the election of his son Henry as king of Germany, he granted virtual autonomy over their church lands to the ecclesiastical princes. In addition, the ecclesiastical princes assumed royal judicial functions within their fiefs. Frederick relinquished his right to build new towns, issue municipal charters, and levy custom duties within these lands. He purchased support from the princes for his Italian ambitions by giving them all former imperial rights except those involving foreign affairs and disagreements concerning more than one principality.

Sicilian Kingdom

In 1220 Pope Honorius III personally crowned Frederick emperor in exchange for his promise to provide aid to the distressed Fifth Crusade. Frederick cleverly put off fulfilling this pledge for eight years. Instead he occupied himself with establishing the most centralized monarchy of its day in Sicily and Southern Italy. There he dismantled the power of the feudal nobility and introduced an efficient administration run by trained bureaucrats and loyal local officials. In 1224 he founded the University of Naples to train students for government services. Profiting from his knowledge of Roman law, he issued a forward-looking code, the *Liber Augustalis*, that mandated centralized imperial authority in place of feudal law. His economic and military reforms strove to modernize and centralize the kingdom at the expense of feudal custom. As a consequence of these reforms his Sicilian kingdom became the most prosperous and advanced in Western Europe at the time.

Attempt to Control Italy

Once Frederick had pacified Germany and set in motion his

reconstruction in Sicily, he announced his intention to reassert imperial control over Lombardy in 1226. This attempt to unify all of Italy provoked immediate opposition from the northern cities, who joined in a defensive league, the Lombard League. Frederick did not actually attempt to implement his plan until 1236, because of his involvement in the Crusades. Thereafter his conquest of the Lombard cities began in earnest. Despite early successes, warfare soon exhausted his kingdom and brought down the wrath of the papacy at a time when Europe was threatened with a Mongol invasion from Asia. Fearful of being encircled, Gregory excommunicated the emperor for the third time in 1239, but this had little immediate impact and within two years Frederick was in possession of almost all of the Papal States. He failed, however, to fill the vacant throne with a conciliatory pope in 1241. Under Innocent IV, the battle between the papacy and the Empire escalated still further. Innocent called a Church council, which deposed the emperor on charges of suspected heresy. The pope then declared a crusade against him and arranged for German bishops to elect an anti-king. Germany suffered under the interdict and the ensuing civil war. Death overtook the beleaguered Frederick in 1250 before he was able to complete his subjection of the Lombard League.

Results of Frederick's Policies

Frederick's thirty-year struggle to unite Italy ended in total failure but had a profound impact on the future histories of Italy, Germany, and the papacy. Without his presiding genius, the cause of Italian unification was left moribund, not to be revived until the nineteenth century. Northern Italy remained a land of independent and competitive city-states. At the pope's instigation, Sicily was conquered by Charles of Anjou, brother of King Louis IX of France, in 1266. This advanced kingdom slowly sank into poverty and backwardness. Frederick's policies in Germany resulted in the final victory of the princes over imperial rule. Here too, national unification was delayed until the nineteenth century. The Hohenstaufen line ended in 1268 with the beheading of Frederick's young grandson, Conradin, by Charles of Anjou. The papacy also bore deep scars from the long conflict. Its use of ecclesiastical weapons for political purposes badly undermined papal prestige. While on the surface its victory over Frederick II seemed to reaffirm the papacy's supremacy over temporal affairs, a little more than half a century later the pope would become the captive of the French king. Thus the prolonged struggle between the Empire and the papacy came ultimately to a mutually disadvantageous close.

New Monastic Orders

While the papacy was transforming itself into a temporal power on a par with the greatest medieval kings, some members of the Church resisted this trend to worldly power and riches. From the late eleventh until the early thirteenth century, four major new monastic orders along with several minor ones evolved as antisecular responses to restore the Church to its primitive roots. The older orders had become wealthy and comfortable havens for younger sons and daughters of the nobility as well as for orphans and disabled persons. Many of these people entered monastic life without a true vocation for it.

The Carthusians

In reaction to this growing worldliness, Bruno of Cologne founded the isolated monastery of Grande-Chartreuse in 1084. Throughout the Middle Ages Carthusian monks were known for their strict adherence to monastic rule. They lived lives of poverty and devotion totally cut off from society.

The Cistercians

Another order, the Cistercians, founded in 1098 at Cîteaux in Burgundy, sought to abide by the letter of the Benedictine Rule. The new order owed much of its popularity to its greatest adherent, the ardent and spellbinding preacher, Bernard of Clairvaux. Under his charismatic leadership the order grew rapidly. Bernard became as powerful as the pope. He supervised the conduct of kings and nobles and issued the call for the Second Crusade. By 1300, Cistercian monks had founded approximately 700 monasteries primarily in wild and secluded areas of Europe. Cistercian abbeys were preserves of learning and orderly conduct, although with the passage of time, some grew lax.

The Mendicant Orders

In the early thirteenth century two new orders arose that kept alive the ascetic impulse. The Dominicans and the Franciscans differed radically from their predecessors in that they did not require their monks to live apart from society. Instead, friars of the "mendicant," or begging, orders moved among the people seeking alms. Their preaching and saintly example inspired a great revival of religious feeling. Both orders had their greatest impact upon urban populations whose hatred of clerical wealth and intense religious enthusiasm had made them highly receptive to heretical beliefs.

The Dominicans

St. Dominic (1170–1221), founder of the Dominicans, was a Castilian clergyman who received papal permission to preach against the rampant Albigensian heresy in southern France. To increase the efficacy of their message, in 1205 he and his small group of fellow missionaries adopted absolute poverty. Dominic believed that sincere and zealous preaching of orthodox Christian doctrine was the most effective way to combat heresy. The Dominicans were the first to achieve some success in converting the Albigensians. Pope Honorius III officially confirmed the new order in 1216.

The Franciscans

In Italy, Dominic's contemporary, Francis of Assisi (1182?–1226), also founded an order based on the principles of absolute poverty and Christian simplicity. Whereas the Dominicans were for the most part well educated and excellent organizers, the early Franciscans modeled their conduct upon the humble, joyous personality of their founder. St. Francis had been born into a family of wealthy merchants. As a young man, however, he repudiated his riches and gave away all he owned to the poor. Although still a layman, he began preaching to the poor as he wandered from town to town begging for his daily bread. He attracted a band of followers and sometime around 1210 they appealed to Innocent III to approve their new Order of Friars Minor.

St. Francis's message was a simple one: through Jesus Christ to love one's neighbor and all God's creatures on earth. He added a new note of rejoicing and mystical piety into orthodox medieval Christianity. Many consider the "little poor man" of Assisi the greatest saint of the Middle Ages. Two years before his death he became the first Christian allegedly to receive the *stigmata,* replicas of Christ's wounds on the cross, signifying great holiness.

Significance of Mendicant Orders

The Dominican and Franciscan orders grew with extraordinary speed. Their tremendous success brought with it material wealth and an all-but-inevitable decline from the humility and zeal of their original members. Yet as the orders matured and became institutionalized, they continued to play a vital role in the religious life of medieval Europe. Both orders had by the end of the thirteenth century produced the most brilliant philosophers and theologians of the age. The Dominicans also were largely responsible for administering the Inquisition and extirpating heresy. But in sum, the new monastic orders contributed significantly to the spiritual revitalization of the medieval Church by reaching out to the masses with their renewed vision of the simple and austere Christian life.

The Crusades

In November 1095, before a large audience gathered at the Council of Clermont, Pope Urban II preached a rousing sermon in which he exhorted his noble listeners to take up arms against the Muslims who held control of the Holy Land. From that date until the surrender of the last Crusader stronghold in 1291, Westerners poured into the Near East in a steady stream of expeditions that historians have traditionally but somewhat incorrectly grouped together as nine specific Crusades. The crusading movement is yet another expression of the dynamism and religious exuberance of Western society after the year 1000.

Historical Background

The Crusades were part of the European counteroffensive against the Muslims that began in the eleventh century. They were made possible by the political fragmentation of the Islamic world and the growing population and prosperity of the West.

Western Moves against Muslims

By 1087, the Italian city-states of Venice, Genoa, and Pisa had succeeded in ejecting the Muslim fleet from the Western Mediterranean and in opening the sea to Western ships. After three decades of fighting, the Normans cleared Sicily of its Muslim rulers in 1091. The pope lent powerful support to the Christian reconquest of Spain, the *Reconquista*, by granting it the status of a Crusade or holy war in 1063.

Pilgrims

Since the third century Christians had gone on pilgrimages to the East as an act of religious devotion. At first scores of pilgrims, later groups of over one thousand, journeyed to the Holy Land to visit the sites associated with Christ's life and to worship at the Church of the Holy Sepulcher in Jerusalem. These visits were not seriously disturbed by the Islamic conquest of Palestine and Syria in the seventh century. Early in the eleventh century, however, conditions deteriorated significantly during the reign of a mentally unbalanced Egyptian ruler of Palestine, and pilgrims were persecuted. After the Seljuk Turks captured Jerusalem in 1071, travel there became extremely dangerous, and Christians who reached the Holy Land were heavily taxed. Gradually there developed in the West a growing desire to free the holy places from Muslim control. This made the West receptive to Alexius I Comnenus's appeal for military aid to reconquer Asia Minor from the Seljuks.

Motives

Urban II added his own concerns as pope at the time of the Investiture Controversy to the Byzantine plea for assistance and the popular outcry in favor of a crusade.

Advantages to Papacy

The papacy's claim to supreme leadership of the Christian community stood to benefit by initiating this international offensive. Urban II and Pope Gregory VII before him both perceived the Crusades as a means to heal the split between the eastern and western branches of the Church. Reconquest of the Holy Land further offered the opportunity for making new converts.

Advantage to Crusaders

In a sermon at Clermont, Urban touched upon most of the motives that would lead people to take up the cross. The main motive was the religious one.

Remission of Sins. Not unlike the Islamic *jihad*, the pledge of the pope to all who fell fighting the Muslims was direct ascent into Heaven without need to do further penance for sins in Purgatory. Thousands of volunteers responded to this guaranteed remission of past sins by sewing a cross on the front of their clothing as a symbol of their vow to regain the Holy Land.

Material Gains. Participation in the Crusades held out the hope of material rewards as well. Urban recognized the economic motive by noting the opportunities for plunder in a land that "flowed with milk and honey." Even at home the Crusader enjoyed privileged status. For the length of his absence he paid no taxes, his debts were postponed, and the Church protected his home and property.

Opportunities for Nobles. The worldly benefits of going on a Crusade were especially attractive to the noble class. Eleventh-century Europe was filled with restless and bellicose knights who lacked employment or wealth. Urban II correctly saw them as a disruptive element within Western society. The Crusades offered them a chance to use their fighting skills on behalf of a good cause and to seize for themselves vast new lands in Syria and Palestine.

The Response to Urban's Call

Urban's pleas for the recovery of the holy places met with an overwhelming response. For the next several months he traveled around Europe to win support and to plan the expedition. Popular preachers, including the highly successful Peter the Hermit, stirred up emotions in France and Germany. Before the official Crusade had gotten under way, several bands of impoverished peasants set out for the East and plundered villages as they went. One such fanatical group began by murdering Jews in the Rhineland.

The First Crusade

The First Crusade (1095–1099) achieved greater success than any

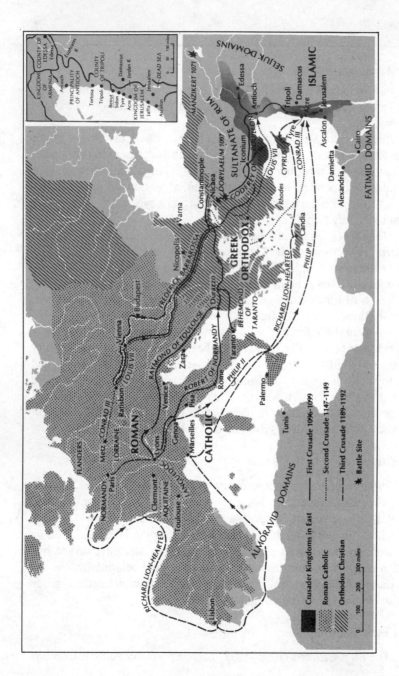

The Crusades

of the subsequent expeditions. Since no European monarch was willing to take part at this time, it was commanded by great nobles.

Baldwin's Conquest

The Crusaders rapidly advanced into the Seljuks' Sultanate of Rum, where they won an important battle at Dorylaeum in 1097. From there one army led by Baldwin, brother of another leading Crusader, Godfrey of Bouillon, Duke of Lower Lorraine, broke off from the main body of knights. The able Baldwin carved out a large principality for himself on both sides of the Euphrates River with its center at the ancient city of Edessa. In 1098 the County of Edessa became the first of four Crusader states to be set up by leaders of the First Crusade.

Conquest of Antioch

While Baldwin was preoccupied to the north, the majority of the crusading forces marched south and laid siege to the valuable city of Antioch. After long resistance the city fell in the summer of 1098 to Bohemond, commander of the Normans from Southern Italy. Bohemond proclaimed himself prince of the second Crusader state around Antioch.

Conquest of Jerusalem

Continuing south the remaining Crusaders captured Jerusalem in July 1099 and massacred its Jewish and Muslim inhabitants—men, women, and children alike. Godfrey of Bouillon was elected by his fellow Crusaders to govern the new Latin Kingdom of Jerusalem as "Defender of the Holy Sepulcher." Upon his death a year later, his brother, Baldwin of Edessa, assumed the title King of Jerusalem that Godfrey had been too modest to accept.

Conquest of Tripoli

With the invaluable assistance of ships from Genoa, Pisa, and Venice, Raymond of Toulouse and his son Bertrand conquered the last Crusader state, the County of Tripoli, in 1109. Established at the peak of European feudalism, the four Latin states were organized along purely feudal lines.

Results of First Crusade

In a little less than fifteen years the Crusaders had gained posses-sion of the entire coastline of the eastern Mediterranean from the Egyptian frontier to beyond the Euphrates River. Every subsequent Crusade began as an attempt to maintain or recover these holdings. Strategically the long, narrow kingdom was difficult to defend, and the Crusaders never captured the nearby Muslim cities of Aleppo or Damascus.

Military Orders

Shortly after the First Crusade, two military orders of knighthood emerged to assume the lion's share of defending the Crusader states. These orders, the Templars and the Hospitalers, combined the strictness of monastic life with the attraction of fighting for a chivalrous cause. They fielded the best-disciplined troops of the Crusades, and were famous for their valor and fervid devotion. Through gifts and conquests they accumulated great wealth and castles in the East as well as extensive lands in the West that gave them tremendous influence. However, ambition and rivalries led the orders to stray far from their original monastic vows.

The Templars

The Templars, or Knights of the Temple of Solomon, were or-ganized around 1119 to protect pilgrims en route to the Holy Land. In time the order was entrusted with the transport and safekeeping of money from the West and came to function as a powerful banking institution.

The Hospitalers

The Hospitalers, or Knights of the Hospital of St. John of Jerusalem, were initially established to minister to the sick and infirm in Jerusalem. By 1130 they had transformed themselves into a fighting order.

The Teutonic Knights

About 1190 a third military order, the Teutonic Knights, was created, made up exclusively of German nobles. During the early thirteenth century this order shifted its concern from the infidel Muslims to the heathen Baltic Coast, where it conquered a large territory. The Teutonic lands formed the core of the later German state of Prussia.

Muslim Recovery

Muslim political disunity allowed most of the Western gains in the First Crusade. Not only had the Seljuk empire splintered into various, virtually independent states, but also its ruler faced competition from the Fatimid caliphs of Egypt in asserting hegemony over Palestine. Resolution of these problems was possible during the twelfth century when Zangi, a strong Muslim ruler in Syria, set out to reunite the Muslims and recover their lost territories.

The Second Crusade

In 1144 the Muslims permanently recaptured the city of Edessa. Its fall roused the West to action. Crowds in Germany and France greeted St. Bernard's call for a new crusade with great enthusiasm. For the first time European monarchs (Louis VII of France and the German emperor Conrad III) joined the undertaking. The Second Crusade (1147–1149) was marred, however, by Western pillaging of Byzantine territory, duplicity on the part of the Eastern emperor, and the half-hearted support of the Latins in Jerusalem. It ended in utter defeat after failing to capture Damascus from its independent Muslim emir. In 1154 the city came under the dominion of Zangi's heir, Nur ad-Din. The Latins now faced a united enemy in Syria.

Saladin

Most responsible for the revival of Muslim fortunes was Saladin (1137?–1193), the nephew of one of Nur ad-Din's generals. In 1169 he succeeded to his uncle's posts of both vizier to the Fatimid Caliph in Cairo and assistant to Nur ad-Din. After the latter's death, Saladin declared himself sultan of Egypt and took over Nur ad-Din's position of dominance in Muslim Syria. From these dual bases Saladin extended his territory westward along the North African coast, southward to Yemen, and against the Christians in Palestine and Syria. In 1187 he and his large Muslim army, all of whom the Christians called Saracens despite their varying Islamic backgrounds, inflicted a calamitous defeat upon the Crusaders. Two of their leaders and a large number of knights were taken prisoner and Jerusalem fell into Muslim hands.

The Third Crusade

With the intention of recapturing Jerusalem, in face of this disaster, the West launched the Third Crusade (1189–1192). It was led by three outstanding and temporarily united medieval monarchs: Richard I, the Lionhearted, of England; Philip II of France; and the Holy Roman Emperor Frederick I, Barbarossa.

Campaigns of the Kings

Frederick's army left first but ran into difficulties while passing through Byzantine territory because Isaac II, the weak and incompetent Eastern emperor, had allied himself with Saladin to protect his throne. Barbarossa finally got his army across to Asia Minor, but the emperor drowned in Cilicia in 1190 before reaching the Holy Land. Philip Augustus and Richard, who continued to act more like rivals than allies, did not arrive until 1191. Richard had stopped along the way to conquer the island of Cyprus from the Byzantines.

Results of the Third Crusade

The principal military action of the Third Crusade revolved around a two-year siege of Acre. The port city finally surrendered to French and English forces in July 1191. Having been taken ill, Philip returned home shortly thereafter, but Richard continued the battle against Saladin. Impressed by Richard's military valor and skill, Saladin agreed to a three-year truce. This provided Christians control of a strip of coastland from Ascalon to Acre, the sole remnant of their Kingdom of Jerusalem. In addition, Christian pilgrims were granted free access to the Holy City, but the Third Crusade had failed in its purpose of recovering Jerusalem. While the Crusaders maintained their hold over Antioch and Tripoli, the Western position in the Holy Land never regained its earlier strength. The Third Crusade received its greatest renown as the backdrop for the epic struggle of two great heroes of chivalry. Richard the Lionhearted proved himself a courageous warrior while Saladin displayed all the qualities of a perfect knight.

The Later Crusades

The later Crusades all exhibit the debasement of the original ideal of a holy war. Self-aggrandizement, material gain, and personal and national rivalries almost completely effaced the religious enthusiasm that had overshadowed base motives in the opening Crusades. By the end of the twelfth century the West had tired of crusading. After repeated military disappointments, fewer recruits flocked to the call. Many Europeans became disillusioned with the idea of holy wars after the papacy had instituted such wars against Christian heretics in southern France and the Holy Roman Emperor Frederick II. Others found that the Church rewarded them with the same spiritual benefits for fighting in Europe against the Albigensians as for combating the Muslims in the East. None of the later Crusades accomplished their goal of liberating the Holy Land from Islamic domination. In 1291, Acre, the last Christian stronghold, fell to the Muslims.

Impact of the Crusades

Despite their failure to achieve their purpose, the impact of the Crusades on medieval Western civilization was significant and manifold. They brought the West in touch with the richer and more sophisticated civilization of Islam.

Economic Effects

New products from the East, primarily sugar, spices, and cotton fabrics, awakened demand and had a quickening effect upon the growth of trade and towns. The Crusades also stimulated the Western economy by bringing into circulation money that had been hoarded away or invested in illiquid assets. Kings and popes began for the first time to tax land and people directly in order to raise the necessary capital to support the crusading enterprise. The Church augmented its revenues at this time also by selling indulgences (the remission of punishment after death for one's sins) to those unable to achieve this by going on crusade. The complexities of handling financial transactions over such a great distance spurred the development of new business methods such as letters of credit and bills of exchange.

Effects on Italian Cities

The great Italian maritime cities profited tremendously from this heightened commercial and financial activity. Their control of the eastern Mediterranean ensured that money and provisions from the West would reach the Crusaders' new states in the East. They provided almost all the ships used to transport the Crusaders to the Levant. In almost every important Eastern port they set up merchant colonies with special trading privileges.

Intellectual Influence

The Crusades had an impact on the intellectual life of the West as well. Although much of Islamic learning had already begun to make its way to the West from Spain and Sicily, the Crusaders' centuries-long contact with the Muslims in Syria and Palestine increased the flow of information. The drama of the Crusades resounds in the Western poetry and history of the age and gave concrete expression to the medieval ideal of chivalry. By whetting people's appetite for travel and greatly enlarging Western knowledge of the Near East, the Crusades contributed significantly to the fledgling science of geography.

Political Repercussions

In the realm of politics the Crusades influenced the shifting balance of power among the monarchy, nobility, and papacy. Many historians believe that the Crusades favored the rise of national monarchies by draining off the nobles' energies and providing the king with instruments of central control such as the ability to impose direct taxes. By the end of the thirteenth century, European monarchs also appeared to have strengthened their hand against the pope. Although in the first Crusades the papacy gained in power and prestige by its assumption of leadership, as the religious zeal of the later Crusades waned and the political motives behind the Church's use of holy wars came clearly into view, many Christians lost respect for the papacy. The Crusades also had a destabilizing effect upon the Byzantine Empire, which was gravely weakened by the fall of Constantinople to the Crusaders in 1204.

The *High Middle Ages were a time of growth and increased economic activity in Western Europe. As barbarian invasions tapered off after 1000 and the Mediterranean was reopened to Western ships, trade revived. An expanding population enlarged agricultural productivity. People were able to sell surplus crops at market, and demand grew. As trade prospered, urban life quickened and many new towns were founded. Town dwellers gained charters from the king, bishop, or lord upon whose territory they resided. These typically granted them self-government and freedom from feudal services and dues in exchange for fixed sums of money. Inhabitants of towns composed a new class, the bourgeoisie, that occupied a middle position between the nobility and the peasants. The revitalization of trade and urban life also contributed to the gradual disappearance of serfdom. Lords willingly commuted labor services and other feudal dues into cash payments to buy luxury items, which were becoming more readily available.*

The two strongest powers of the age were the papacy and the German Empire. Otto the Great's restoration of the Roman Empire in 962 linked their fortunes. For a time, the German emperor dominated the Church and employed its clergy as imperial administrators. In the eleventh century, however, reformers gradually restored piety and discipline to the Church. New monastic orders were founded. In the Investiture Controversy a reformed papacy challenged the right of monarchs to control ecclesiastical appointments. With supreme confidence, Pope Urban II summoned in 1095 the first of nine Crusades that ultimately failed to rid the Holy Land of Muslim domination. Under Innocent III in the thirteenth century the papacy attained the height of its power and influence over temporal affairs. His equally mighty successors thwarted Frederick II's ambition to make a united Italy the center of his empire. The papacy's victory over the Hohenstaufens gravely weakened monarchical authority in Germany. Instead of devoting their energies to reining in the rebellious nobles, the German monarchs' preoccupation with Italy drove them to grant far-reaching concessions to the hereditary rights of the princes within their own territories. The triumph of particularism would keep Italy and Germany disunited for centuries to come.

Recommended Reading

Aziz S. Atiya, *Crusade, Commerce and Culture* (1962)

Frank Barlow, *Thomas Becket* (1986)

Geoffrey Barraclough, *The Origins of Modern Germany* (1946)

Christopher Brooke, *Europe in the Central Middle Ages, 962–1154* (1987)

Robert Chazan, *Church, State and Jew in the Middle Ages* (1979)

Margaret Deanesly, *History of the Medieval Church 590–1500* (1969)

Georges Duby, *Rural Economy and Country Life in the Medieval West* (1968)

Georges Duby, *William Marshal: The Flower of Chivalry* (1985)

Andrew S. Ehrenkreutz, *Saladin* (1972)

Jean Gimpel, *Medieval Machine: The Industrial Revolution of the Middle Ages* (1977)

R. Herzstein, ed., *The Holy Roman Empire in the Middle Ages: Universal State or German Catastrophe?* (1966)

J. K. Hyde, *Society and Politics in Medieval Italy* (1973)

Ernest H. Kantorowicz, *Frederick II* (1957)

Robert S. Lopez, *The Commercial Revolution of the Middle Ages, 950–1350* (1971)

Michel Mollat, *The Poor in the Middle Ages: An Essay in Social History* (1986)

P. Munz, *Frederick Barbarossa: A Study in Medieval Politics* (1969)

Charles W. Oman, ed., *The Art of War in the Middle Ages A.D. 378–1515* (1960)

Sidney Painter, *Medieval Society* (1951)

Henri Pirenne, *Economic and Social History of Medieval Europe* (1937)

Henri Pirenne, *Medieval Cities* (1924)

M. M. Postan, *The Medieval Economy and Society* (1975)

M. M. Postan and Edward Miller, eds., *The Cambridge Economic History of Europe, vol. II: Trade and Industry in the Middle Ages* (1987)

J.M. Powell, ed., *Innocent III, Vicar of Christ or Lord of the World?* (1963)

Eileen Power, *Medieval People* (1924)

C.W. Previté-Orton, *The Shorter Cambridge Medieval History, vol. II* (1952)

Steven Runciman, *History of the Crusades* (1987)

Kenneth M. Setton, ed., *History of the Crusades* (1955–1985)

R. W. Southern, *Western Society and the Church in the Middle Ages* (1970)

Joseph R. Strayer, *The Albigensian Crusade* (1971)

Joseph R. Strayer, *Western Europe in the Middle Ages* (1982)

Gerd Tellenbach, *Church, State and Christian Society at the Time of the Investiture Controversy* (1948)

James W. Thompson, *Feudal Germany* (1928)

Walter Ullmann, *A Short History of the Papacy in the Middle Ages* (1974)

CHAPTER 11

Medieval Culture and the Foundation of National Monarchies

Time Line

987	Hugh Capet founds Capetian dynasty
1050–1200	Height of Romanesque art and architecture
1066	Norman Conquest of England
1085	Castile conquers Toledo from Muslims
1086	William I orders compilation of *Domesday Book*

1144	Abbey of Saint Denis rebuilt as first example of Gothic style
	First King of Portugal recognized
1152	Marriage of Henry Plantagenet to Eleanor, Duchess of Aquitaine
1154	Henry II founds Plantagenet (Angevin) line
1170	Murder of Thomas à Becket at Canterbury Cathedral
1214	Philip Augustus's victory over England at Bouvines
1215	Magna Carta signed
1226	Parlement of Paris now exists apart from *Curia Regis*
1249	Portugal defeats Muslims and establishes national borders
1258	Provisions of Oxford
1265	First time Parliament includes knights of the shire and burgesses together
1267–1268	Roger Bacon writes *Opus Maius*
1274	Death of Thomas Aquinas
c. 1283	Edward I conquers Wales
1290	Jews expelled from England
1295	"Model" Parliament meets
1296	Papal bull, *Clericis laicos*
1297	Parliament granted right to assent to all new taxation
1302	Papal bull, *Unam sanctam*

1302	Philip the Fair summons first Estates General
	Dante exiled from Florence, conceives of *Divine Comedy*
1311	Ordinances of 1311 expand Parliament's power
1328	Philip VI begins Valois dynasty
1387	Year in which *Canterbury Tales* take place
1415	Portugal takes Ceuta from Moors

The central years of the Middle Ages (1000–1350) produced important changes in the cultural and political life of the West. There occurred a reawakening of Europe's artistic and intellectual energies. The years after 1000 witnessed a broadening of communications, the spread of learning and the rise of universities. Medieval artists built magnificent Romanesque and Gothic cathedrals and created outstanding literary masterpieces in the vernacular. The great philosophers and theologians of the age sought to reconcile faith and reason within an ordered synthesis that epitomized the optimism of medieval civilization at its height.

In the realm of politics, the period from the eleventh to the mid-fourteenth century saw the growth of unified national states ruled by monarchs. Monarchs frequently advanced their own interests by disguising them in feudal garb, thus ultimately weakening the feudal power structure. Nowhere, however, were kings able to rule successfully for long in complete disregard of their subjects. Throughout Europe the king's need for financial aid and advice took on institutionalized form during the thirteenth century. Representative assemblies of nobles, clergy, and townsmen emerged in England, France, Spain, Portugal, and other countries. In their struggle to curb noble and ecclesiastical privileges, monarchs often found allies among the increasingly prosperous burghers of the medieval town.

Medieval Culture

During the eleventh and twelfth centuries the curtain of semi-barbarism that had hung over European life since the fall of Rome was slowly lifted. As the population grew, trade and towns expanded, travel increased, and people's desire for knowledge revived.

The Rise of Universities

One of the clearest and most enduring indications of the rebirth of intellectual curiosity was the appearance of a new institution of higher learning, the university. Education during the early Middle Ages had been almost exclusively the prerogative of the Church. Literacy had declined precipitously and even within most monasteries, monks lost the ability to reason logically and write correct Latin. The Church frowned upon most pagan literature. In the late eighth century Charlemagne's educational reforms began gradually to reverse this trend. He charged abbots and bishops to provide at least rudimentary instruction within their monasteries and cathedral towns to those destined for the clergy.

Monastic and Cathedral Schools

Until the mid-eleventh century monastic schools were the most important centers of intellectual activity, and they were responsible for the preservation of much ancient literature. Their isolation and preoccupation with the spirit made them ill-suited, however, to lead a general revival of learning. In this they were eventually supplanted by the cathedral schools, whose urban setting and greater openness to the world fostered a more creative and inquiring outlook. Most of the teaching at these schools was done by scholars who traveled from town to town giving lectures for a fee. Students, too, moved around in search of the best education.

The First Universities

Against this background of monastic and cathedral schools there arose in the twelfth century a new institution, the university. Its name derives from the Latin word *universitas* ("entire"), which was employed to address any association of persons such as a guild. The university itself began as a form of a guild. It was a corporate body of students and masters formed to protect and regulate their common interests.

The Italian Universities. Secular schools for training doctors, lawyers, and notaries never entirely disappeared south of the Alps. At Salerno there already existed during the early Middle Ages a famous school of medicine, making it arguably the oldest university in Europe. In northern Italy the city of Bologna began to attract students from around the Continent because of its school of law founded in the late eleventh century by the great legal scholar, Irnerius. At Bologna students grouped together to assume government of the university. Since medieval universities at first owned no buildings and little other property, the students could easily threaten to move to another location if the townspeople overcharged them for room and board. The Bolognese students also held the upper hand over their professors. They had the power to hire them, set lecture fees, and even fine a professor who was late to class, failed to cover the assigned curriculum, or ran overtime. They boycotted the lectures of unpopular teachers, forcing them to go elsewhere to earn their fees. New universities south of the Alps modeled themselves after Bologna.

The University of Paris. In northern Europe the university grew out of the cathedral schools and was run by the masters, not the students. The University of Paris (c. 1200) is the oldest of the northern European universities. It specialized in humanistic and theological studies and for most of the Middle Ages dominated the intellectual life of Europe. It inspired the growth of many other universities, notably Oxford in England.

Courses of Study

Student life in the central Middle Ages bore many resemblances to modern times. As the thirst for knowledge grew, students thronged to universities in ever-increasing numbers. Education became an avenue by which to advance in Church and State. The seven liberal arts (grammar, rhetoric, logic, arithmetic, geometry, music, and astronomy) remained the basis of the medieval curriculum. Because there were few manuscript texts, students copied their professors' lectures verbatim and committed long passages of them to memory. Public discussion was a lively and important part of the learning process. After studying and being examined, the student received his degree of Bachelor. To earn one's license to teach and be admitted as a Master of the Faculty (also called "Doctor") required further years of study within the fields of law, medicine, or theology. Relatively few individuals were able to devote long, arduous years of preparation to attain the highest degree.

The College System

Students were chronically short of funds to pay for their tuition and their lodging in private homes, since there were no dormitories. Beginning in the thirteenth century, however, wealthy patrons set up residences or "colleges" where poor students could live without paying. Robert de Sorbon endowed the first such "college" in Paris, hence the modern University of Paris's epithet, the Sorbonne. Although the collegiate system was eventually abolished at Paris, Oxford, and Cambridge in England have continued to house and teach their students within separate colleges.

Student Life

In northern universities such as Paris, all students were clerics and as such possessed privileged status. They were exempt from military service and subject only to the jurisdiction of their bishops or masters. This immunity from local justice was a source of irritation to the permanent residents of the town in which the university was located. Quarrels between "town and gown" were frequent and sometimes bloody. Because of the early prominence of their schools of law and medicine, Italian universities admitted both lay and clerical students. Despite their clerical profession, students in the Middle Ages enjoyed their share of drinking, brawling, and wenching.

Contribution to Classical Learning

The great international universities of Paris, Chartres, Oxford, Cambridge, and Bologna contributed significantly to the restoration of interest in classical knowledge. The new learning of the High Middle Ages was founded on a deeper understanding of and appreciation for classical texts. Greater awareness of Latin culture inspired a flowering of medieval artistic and intellectual activity that some modern historians have termed the "Twelfth Century Renaissance."

Scholasticism

Medieval cathedral schools and universities were the seat of most of the important philosophical speculation that occurred after the year 1000. Their teachers, called "Schoolmen" (*Scholastici*), provided the name for the great movement of medieval Christian thought, Scholasticism, which attempted to reconcile reason and revelation. Because the vast majority of medieval thinkers were clerics and were interested above all in such religious concerns as the nature of God and man, the means to attain salvation, and the divine order of the universe, philosophy and theology were virtually indistinguishable.

Anselm

Renewed confidence in the power of the human intellect and its essential compatibility with Christian faith are the hallmarks of Scholastic thought. For this reason, Anselm, Archbishop of Canterbury (1033–1109), is often considered the founder of Scholasticism. He employed logical analysis to substantiate the existence of God and other fundamental tenets of Christianity. Yet, while he held that reason could clarify and deepen one's understanding of what one believed on faith, it was not, he said, sufficient unto itself: "I do not seek to understand that I may believe, but I believe in order that I may understand."

Scholastic Reasoning

Scholastic thought in general rested upon the premise that knowledge already existed. God had revealed truth to humanity and it was the task of medieval thinkers to apply deductive reasoning to ancient texts, both sacred and profane, in order to recover it. The Bible, the writings of the Church Fathers, and classical literature were the authorities to whom Scholastics looked for enlightenment. When these authorities were in conflict, as they often were, the Scholastics used a method of reasoning, the dialectic, borrowed from the ancient Greeks, that sought to demonstrate the logical connections between opposing statements.

Universals

Medieval philosophers were fascinated by the problem of "universals." They were divided over whether universals, i.e., general notions or categories, had an existence independent from individual things. For example, was there such a thing as humanity or were human beings the only real entities? Those who, following Plato, believed that universals existed in reality apart from people's minds were called Realists. Nominalists, by contrast, regarded universals as simply names (*nomina*) that the human mind uses to categorize similar objects. They had no real existence. Many Scholastics held views between the two extremes. The debate over universals had important implications for medieval social and political thought. The widespread acceptance of a modified form of Realism helps to explain why medieval people often placed the needs of corporate bodies (i.e., the Church, the guilds, the manors) above those of individuals.

Abelard

The vogue for applying the dialectic to all manner of subjects threatened to engulf it in trivial or fatuous questions that were barren of meaning. Such, for example, was the famous problem of how many angels could dance on the head of a pin. One of those who inveighed against this misuse of logic was Peter Abelard (1079–1142). Abelard held a moderate position in the Nominalist-Realist controversy and his solution, known as Conceptualism, formed the basis of the modified Realism of Thomas Aquinas.

Dialectical Reasoning. Abelard gained fame as a brilliant though argumentative teacher at the Notre Dame school. He attracted outstanding pupils such as John of Salisbury, and, most likely, Peter Lombard, who contributed to the growth and intellectual renown of the emerging University of Paris. Abelard championed the use of reason to bear out the truths of faith. He taught the value of subjecting all beliefs to rational scrutiny. His most famous work, *Sic et non* ("*Yes and No*"), was a clever appeal for use of the dialectic in matters of religion. In it he posed more than 150 theological questions followed by passages from the Bible and Church Fathers that could be used to defend either side of the argument. He thus adroitly made his point that without the dialectical method to resolve contradictory statements, Christian doctrine was riddled with inconsistencies. Abelard's reliance upon reason infuriated St. Bernard of Clairvaux and other prominent mystics who insisted upon the primacy of faith. Two separate Church councils declared Abelard's writings heretical.

Abelard and Heloise. Abelard's personal life is as well known as his philosophic career. His autobiographical *Historia calamitatum* (*"The Story of My Misfortunes"*) tells of his tragic love for a young woman whom he tutored, Heloise, niece of the canon of Notre Dame. After the birth of a son, the two were secretly married, but Heloise's uncle paid assailants to attack the young scholar and emasculate him. Abelard fled to a monastery, thus putting a premature end to his teaching career in Paris. Heloise became a nun. Their love letters have retained their poignancy through the centuries.

Recovery of Aristotle's Works

The first Scholastics had based their knowledge of classical authors upon only a limited number of ancient texts. This situation changed dramatically during the second half of the twelfth century as Western translators, working predominantly in Spain and Sicily, brought to light a multitude of important classical Greek and Hellenistic works on mathematics, science, and philosophy. By the early thirteenth century virtually all of Aristotle's extant writings along with Arabic commentaries upon them had been translated into Latin. The recovery of Aristotle's full works presented Western scholars with a body of systematic thought founded entirely upon reason. Aristotle's reputation rose above all other ancient philosophers. The study of his works dominated the University of Paris and elsewhere throughout the thirteenth century.

The Scholastic Synthesis: Aquinas

Western acceptance of Aristotle raised a new dilemma for Christianity. Aristotle's philosophy was essentially naturalistic and appeared in many places to conflict with Christian doctrine. His most famous Arabic commentator, Averroës, had concluded, for example, that Aristotle's writings denied the immortality of the soul. The Church attempted to ban the study of some of his works in 1210 and again in 1215. Many Scholastics who wished to remain faithful to both Aristotelian philosophy and the Scriptures found it necessary to assert that each had its own truths that were not always harmonious and therefore had to be kept separate. This uneasy solution was superseded by two great Dominican scholars, the German Albertus Magnus (1193–1280) and his still more talented Italian pupil, Thomas Aquinas (1225?–1274). Both were for a time celebrated teachers of theology at the University of Paris. They sought to demonstrate in their extensive works the fundamental compatibility of faith and reason. Their efforts at intellectual synthesis represent the summit of Scholastic thought.

Influence of Aristotle on Aquinas. St. Thomas Aquinas stands out as an intellectual giant. His clearly reasoned and wide-ranging writings constitute a complete philosophical system, Thomism, that continues to attract adherents today. Aquinas was deeply influenced by Aristotelian thought. Following Aristotle he held that human beings operate by reason, not instinct. It was proper that individuals use their God-given gift of reason to extend their knowledge of the world of the senses and to offer rational proof for the articles of faith. Yet reason was incapable of knowing all that God intended people to know. It must bow down before the superior truths presented by divine revelation. Aquinas ascribed all contradictions between philosophy and Church dogma to errors in human reasoning.

Writings of Aquinas. Aquinas applied his mind to practical issues of politics, justice, and social relations as well as to problems of religion and philosophy. His numerous writings—commentaries on Aristotle and the Scriptures, philosophical essays and treatises—examine logically such varied questions as the essence of law, the best form of government, and whether or not lending money is ever lawful. In his most famous work, the *Summa theologica,* which was left incomplete at the time of his death, he attempted to construct a towering synthesis of all knowledge, pagan as well as Christian. Beginning with a rational proof of God's existence, the work takes up in systematic fashion every important point of orthodox Christian theology and ethics and explains it with the aid of reason.

Challenges to Scholasticism

By the fourteenth century, Aquinas's masterly synthesis had come under attack from several directions. The eventual collapse of this synthesis of faith and reason marked the end of Scholasticism as a creative body of thought.

Roger Bacon. In England, the Franciscan scientist and philosopher Roger Bacon (c. 1214–1294?) opposed Aquinas's reliance upon deductive reasoning and stressed instead the importance of basing knowledge of the world upon experience.

Duns Scotus. The Franciscan John Duns Scotus (c. 1266–1308) formulated a rival philosophical system, Scotism, that challenged many of Aquinas's views. Duns believed in the priority of faith over reason.

William of Ockham. William of Ockham (c. 1285–c. 1349) denied the existence of ideal forms or essences outside of the human mind. He therefore limited the use of reason to the examination of individual things. The existence of God and other metaphysical beliefs are outside the scope of human reason and must be objects of faith. Ockham's philosophy triumphed in the universities. He became especially famous for his principle of economy in logic known as "Ockham's razor." It held essentially that simple assumptions and proofs are almost always better than complicated, lengthy ones.

Vernacular Literature

Latin was the language of learned culture throughout the Middle Ages. Students debated and composed in it. Scholastics wrote their *summae* and governments issued their decrees in it. The Church communicated exclusively in it. Even contracts between individuals were frequently drawn up in Latin. Yet, knowledge of the ancient tongue was limited to the small percentage of the medieval population who received a clerical education. The peasantry and most nobles were largely ignorant of it. The mass of people spoke their own local languages. If these derived from Latin, as in France, Spain, Portugal and Italy, they are known as Romance languages. English, German, and the Scandinavian tongues, on the other hand, evolved from a common Germanic origin. Other European vernaculars stemmed from Celtic or Slavic roots.

Beginning of Vernacular Writings

As early as perhaps the eighth century in Britain the vernacular served as a medium of poetic expression and produced its first extant literary masterpiece, *Beowulf.* The arrival of the French-speaking Normans in 1066, however, retarded the growth of the English tongue for over a century. Elsewhere in Europe, above all in France, there came into being in the eleventh and twelfth centuries a sizable body of literature in the vernacular. Its flowering represents yet another aspect of the cultural renaissance of the Central Middle Ages. The new vernacular literature was written primarily for the amusement of the noble class and closely reflected its chivalrous ideals and warrior ethos. Nevertheless, since much of it was sung or recited orally by wandering minstrels, or *jongleurs,* at provincial courts, fairs, and pilgrimage sites, it reached a fairly widespread audience.

Epic Poetry

Medieval vernacular literature developed along several lines. In northern France where a French dialect, the *langue d'oïl,* was spoken, the tradition of epic poetry flourished. These poems of war and heroism, known as *chansons de geste* ("songs of deeds"), were composed by *trouvères* who drew from legends and history for their subject matter. Many of the songs recounted events in the life of a great central figure such as Charlemagne and were thus grouped together in cycles. The oldest and greatest of the poems about Charlemagne is the *Song of Roland.* Composed in the eleventh century, its main action is based on an earlier historical event: the ambush of Charlemagne's rear guard at Roncesvalles in 778. Its tale of conflicting loyalties, treachery, and hatred of the infidel mirrored the values of French feudal society. The medieval epic thrived in other countries as well. The German *Nibelungenlied* ("Song of the Nibelungen") and the Spanish poem "El Cid" are two other illustrious examples of the heroic epic.

Lyric Poetry and the Courtly Romance

The older *chansons de geste* were gradually replaced by new poetic forms, lyric poetry and the courtly romance, in which love and romantic adventure rather than war and carnage predominated. Both display a keener awareness of individual feelings. Their world is that of the chivalrous knight, not the feudal warrior. Lyric poetry sprang from the wealthy and cultured soil of southern France. The social environment of twelfth-century Provence was more sophisticated and leisurely than in the north. Noblewomen played an important role at court. They were frequently called upon to administer their estates in the absence of their husbands, fathers, or sons. Female tastes are clearly reflected in the gentler poetry of the south. Courtly love became its chief theme.

The Troubadours. Poets called troubadours, many of whom were aristocrats, sang of their love for their ladies, who were typically married women of higher social status. They wooed her with extravagant praise and humble devotion, expecting only a word of encouragement in return. Their verses, composed in the *langue d'oc* of the south, record the shifting emotions of love from elation to despair. With its intricate rhyme schemes and calculated nuances of style, troubadour lyric poetry ran the risk of artificiality when inspiration flagged. After a century of flowering it grew stale in southern France and perished along with most of Provençal culture in the repressive environment of the Albigensian Crusade. By this time, however, it had spread the conventions of courtly love throughout feudal Europe. Poets such as the German *Minnesinger* continued to produce excellent verse in its spirit.

The Romance. The vogue for courtly love also expressed itself in a new narrative form, the medieval romance, during the twelfth century. It blended the troubadour's fascination with women and love with the concern for heroism of the older epics. Northern poets invented new, purely imaginary story materials in which chivalrous knights set off on adventures and encounter mythological creatures all for the sake of their lady. The most famous story cycle in this new mode centers on the legendary British king Arthur and the Knights of the Round Table.

Italian and English Vernacular Poetry

The triumph of vernacular poetry encouraged prose writers to begin penning their histories, biographies, and other texts in the popular tongue. Use of the vernacular had become widespread by the thirteenth century. In Italy and England, however, literature in everyday language took longer to establish itself. In Italy historical ties to ancient Rome and the presence of the papacy gave to Latin a prestige beyond all other tongues. At the English court, Norman French remained the spoken language from the eleventh until the fourteenth century. Despite this slow development, the Italian and English vernaculars produced at the end of the Middle Ages two of the greatest Medieval masterpieces: Dante's *Divine Comedy* and Chaucer's *Canterbury Tales*. Thus, by the end of the fourteenth century, everywhere in Europe the vernacular had become an accepted, sometimes even the preferred, vehicle for artistic expression.

Dante. At its most literal, the *Divine Comedy* is the story of the poet's own experiences. A Florentine by birth, Dante Alighieri (1265–1321) was banished from his native city in 1302 as a result of a political squabble. He spent the rest of his life moving from city to city in northern Italy. The *Divine Comedy* was born during these years of exile. Its opening reflects the poet's embittered and dispirited state of mind at the time. He finds himself at the middle of his life lost in a dark wood of doubt and confusion. His attempt to escape from misery by climbing a mountain is blocked by three wild animals that symbolize the poet's sins. Then the figure of Virgil appears and offers to conduct Dante down the nine circles of Hell and up the seven terraces of Purgatory. In his journey the poet learns by examining the fearful punishments of others how to atone for his own failings. The pagan Virgil can lead Dante no farther than the earthly Garden of Eden. To find ultimate peace in Heaven, Dante finds a new guide, Beatrice, a woman whom he has loved from afar since he was nine. She accompanies him through the heavens until he attains a vision of God and is left joyful and at peace at the poem's end.

As most great medieval works, the *Divine Comedy* functions on an allegorical level as well. Dante is every human being and his journey becomes an allegory of Christian progress from sin through suffering and penance to redemption and peace in the presence of God. Virgil symbolizes worldly wisdom while Beatrice incarnates divine love and revelation. In its moral idealization of women and high esteem for reason, the *Divine Comedy* is a superlative yet typical product of high medieval culture.

Chaucer. Wholly different in spirit yet no less characteristic of the medieval mind are the *Canterbury Tales* of Geoffrey Chaucer (c. 1340–1400). Chaucer spent most of his life in government service and little is known about him. In his preeminent work, the *Canterbury Tales*, Chaucer cast an amiable yet satirical eye upon the behavior of a group of pilgrims bound for the shrine of St. Thomas à Becket at Canterbury. In the Prologue the narrator sets the stage by describing his fellow travelers gathered at an inn on the road to Canterbury in the spring of

1387. Then each pilgrim presents a story. These range in substance from the Miller's bawdy tale of adultery, to the Knight's romance of courtly love, and the Parson's story of Christian piety. Chaucer wrote the *Canterbury Tales* in Middle English, an early form of English speech. Their fame did much to gain respect for the English tongue as a literary language.

Art and Architecture

Medieval art and architecture were overwhelmingly religious in nature and inspiration. They were animated by an authentic faith that gave them tremendous power and vitality. Their sheer richness of design and execution still impresses us today. The Church remained the most important patron of the arts throughout the Middle Ages. It had both the wealth and the desire for beautiful things for the glorification of God that were needed to support a flourishing artistic community. Contemporaries regarded medieval artists as craftsmen, although some architects attained positions of authority and great respect.

The Romanesque

The same forces in eleventh-century Europe that were at work to revitalize the medieval economy, fan religious enthusiasm, and stimulate intellectual life, also made themselves felt in the arts. This reawakening of creative activity was signaled by a great wave of church building in stone. Not since late Roman times had large stone structures been erected with vaulted roofs and monumental sculpture decorating the exterior.

Stylistic Elements. Later ages used the somewhat inaccurate term "Romanesque" to describe the common Roman elements in the art and architecture produced between approximately 1050 and 1200. These included use of the Roman basilica, vault, and semicircular arch. In fact, Romanesque was an international style that encompassed many regional variations and drew upon early Christian, Carolingian, Ottonian, Byzantine, and even Islamic architectural styles as well as Roman.

Churches. The Cluniac revival and the growth of new monastic orders such as the Carthusians and the Cistercians created a demand for new abbeys in the Romanesque style. Other Romanesque churches were built along the great pilgrimage routes to Santiago de Compostela in northwestern Spain, to Rome, and ultimately to the Holy Land. Pilgrimage churches served the needs of a larger population than that of a monastery and were accordingly of more ample proportions. Romanesque architects used masonry barrel and cross vaults. The weight of these vaulted ceilings bore heavily upon internal piers and thick walls. It was structurally impossible to cut large windows in load-bearing walls. Thus Romanesque churches were typically massive and dark.

Sculpture. The preference for the Romanesque style directly affected the sculpture of the period. Carolingian and Ottonian churches had lacked large-scale sculptural decoration. By contrast the Romanesque style required the adornment of capitals, columns, portals, and the *tympanum,* or space over the main portal. Such employment typically subordinated sculpture to the overall architectural design and required it to be executed in relief rather than in the full round. Nonetheless, Romanesque statues exhibit a tremendous vitality. Most sculptors depicted figures from the Bible although many merged these with plants, devils, and allegorical beasts.

Painting and Tapestry. What little has survived of Romanesque painting indicates that, while exhibiting greater continuity with earlier styles, it too flourished. A unique product of Romanesque skill is the Bayeux tapestry (more correctly an embroidery), which depicts events in the life of William the Conqueror.

The Gothic

In their efforts to resolve the technical limitations imposed by the round arch and the barrel vault, Romanesque architects experimented with new engineering devices.

Stylistic Elements. The main elements of the later Gothic style: the pointed arch, the ribbed groin vault, and the flying buttress, were all first used in tentative form in Romanesque structures. From around the middle of the twelfth century, builders in the Île-de-France began to incorporate these innovative features into a fully articulated style characterized by tremendous height, luminosity, and gracefulness. Writers in the sixteenth century, disturbed by the unclassical appearance of these magnificent medieval buildings, derisively called them "Gothic" after the barbarian Goths.

Use of the pointed arch allowed the Gothic architect to vault over almost any shaped bay and to build the structure higher. The ribbed groin vault concentrated the thrust of the vault on a few points rather than on the entire wall as in Romanesque architecture. External, arch-shaped supports known as flying buttresses carried the weight of the roof down to the ground. Relieved of much of their load-bearing function, walls could be pierced by large windows. Medieval artists decorated these with splendid stained glass that gave Gothic cathedrals their shimmering translucence.

Gothic Cathedrals. Art historians consider the Abbey of St. Denis outside Paris to be the first example of the Gothic style. It was rebuilt from an older church by Louis VI's powerful adviser, Abbot Suger, in 1144. The greatest of the French Gothic cathedrals: Chartres, Notre Dame in Paris, Amiens, and Reims, were all begun within approximately a century of this date. During the thirteenth century the northern French style spread rapidly to other parts of Europe and took on a variety of local aspects. In England, for example, early Gothic cathedrals such as Salisbury were characterized by their great length and their isolation from the surrounding towns. By contrast, their French counterparts rose to soaring heights and were constructed in the heart of the town. Italian Gothic is almost unrecognizable from its northern progenitor. Often lacking ribbed groin vaulting, flying buttresses, and external sculptural decoration, it gave preference to wooden ceilings and colored marble facades. The Gothic cathedral was essentially an urban achievement testifying to the wealth and pride of the medieval town as well as the Church.

Later Gothic Architecture. By the late thirteenth century the pure Gothic style gave way to excessive ornamentation that culminated in the fifteenth century Flamboyant style. In fifteenth- and sixteenth-century England, the Gothic evolved into the unique perpendicular style characterized by its amazing vertical emphasis and decorative fan-vaulted ceilings. The Gothic style was also employed in numerous secular structures, notably castles, urban mansions, town halls, guild halls, and warehouses.

Gothic Sculpture. In keeping with the systematic and well-proportioned design of Gothic cathedrals, the statuary that decorated them displayed a sense of order and clarity of arrangement absent from Romanesque models. It was now created almost in the round and was highly realistic. Gothic statues present a new solidity of form and gentleness of expression that makes them seem alive.

Gothic Painting. Stained glass and manuscript illumination, the two most prevalent forms of Gothic painting outside of Italy, were strongly influenced by the Gothic artist's concern for gracefulness and symmetry.

Science

The contributions of medieval science were of minor significance.

Restraints on Science

Medieval scientists labored in the shadow of Christian dogma and abstract habits of reasoning. All higher education in the Middle Ages (except for professional schools that trained doctors, lawyers, and notaries) was designed to educate men for the clergy. The Church expected even those clerics who studied science to use their knowledge in order to demonstrate the divine order of the natural world. In the schools, Scholasticism emphasized the use of deductive reasoning to arrive at truth, not the study of empirical facts that is at the heart of the modern scientific method. The supremacy throughout most of the Middle Ages of philosophical Realism with its belief in the abstract essences of things, discouraged even further the observation and study of the world of concrete objects. Erroneous ideas of the ancients, such as Ptolemy's belief that all celestial bodies revolved around the earth, Aristotle's theory of the four elements, and Hippocrates' theory of disease, possessed such weight that they retarded progress in astronomy, physics, and medicine for centuries.

Scientific Advances

Despite these inhibiting factors, scientific inquiry did make some headway in the medieval period, principally because of the introduction of major Greek and Arabic scientific and mathematical works in Latin translations. These greatly expanded the West's stock of scientific knowledge but led to few major advances. From the Arabs the West acquired the advanced mathematics of the Middle East as well as the Hindu numerical system and the Arabic concept of zero. The writings of Euclid further enriched western mathematics. In medicine acquaintance with the work of Hippocrates and Galen led to more sanitary operating conditions and greater familiarity with human anatomy. On a practical level, the latter half of the Middle Ages continued to improve upon its methods of agriculture, mining, measuring, and telling time. The compass, a Chinese invention, is first mentioned in European sources in the twelfth century. Two Englishmen, Robert Grosseteste (c. 1175–1253) and his Franciscan pupil, Roger Bacon (c. 1214–1294?), stand out as being far ahead of their age in their interest in experimentation.

Grosseteste. Grosseteste was well versed in ancient learning. In addition to his religious writings, he composed treatises on mathematics, physics, astronomy, optics, and other scientific subjects. In these works he stressed the importance of inductive reasoning.

Bacon. Bacon continued his teacher's interest in scientific investigation and experimentation. Like Grosseteste, he believed that the physical universe functioned according to laws that could be expressed in mathematical terms. In his *Opus maius,* he argued against the Scholastics' reliance upon deductive logic. While they never doubted the ultimate authority of the Church, Grosseteste and Bacon's writings contributed to the establishment of the modern scientific method.

The Foundation of National Monarchies

In England, France, Spain, Portugal, and elsewhere during the High Middle Ages, kings fought to enlarge their royal domains and extend the arm of centralized royal control over rival groups in society.

England

The Norman invasion of England in 1066 was one of those pivotal events in European history that altered the complexion of a nation's development. William the Conqueror imported the highly organized concepts of Norman feudalism into England and used them to strengthen the power of the monarch. Yet he also preserved many

Anglo-Saxon institutions and traditions that gave England a stability and national cohesiveness that contrasted sharply with conditions on the continent.

Edward the Confessor

The last king of the house of Alfred, Edward the Confessor (ruled 1042–1066), preferred the tasks of religious devotion to those of governing. Having spent most of his young life in exile in Normandy he introduced French customs to the English court and appointed Norman friends to important offices. This angered the great English earls over whom Edward had failed to assert his control.

Harold

Contemporary documents describe the Anglo-Saxon noble, Harold, as *dux anglorum*, leader or duke of the English. His landholdings were nearly as large as the king's. When Edward died childless in January 1066, Harold was regarded in many quarters as the rightful heir although he was not of royal lineage. Some sources relate that, on the verge of death, Edward named Harold his successor. A gathering of the *witan* on the day after the king's death approved of the nomination.

Three other claimants immediately challenged Harold's accession to the throne. The first and weakest challenge was offered by Harold's brother, Tostig, whom he had alienated in a quarrel over Tostig's misrule in Northumbria. From exile, Tostig carried out raids on the English coast in May 1066, but his attacks were easily repelled. Harold Hardrada, a second claimant to the throne and the mighty Viking king of Norway, was a more serious adversary because of his great prowess in war, but he lacked support from the English earls.

William the Conqueror

The most formidable threat to Harold's rule came from William, Duke of Normandy (1027?–1087), illegitimate son of Duke Robert I and a tanner's daughter. William had succeeded to his father's dukedom in 1035 but he was forced to spend much of youth in hiding. It was not until 1047 that he succeeded in imposing his authority over the rebellious Norman magnates. By 1066, however, Normandy had become a highly centralized feudal state under William's strict control.

Claim to English Throne. With his courage and tremendous energy, William was a man capable of turning his ambitious dreams to become king of England into reality. He believed that he had a solid claim to the English throne, although the grounds upon which he based it were difficult to substantiate. He was distantly related to Edward, and, according to William, the English king had designated him heir during a visit to the island kingdom in 1051. Furthermore, Harold had been compelled to promise William support in his quest for the English throne. There are as many as nine different versions of the rather unusual circumstances under which this promise was exacted. Essentially, Harold had been shipwrecked and taken prisoner by the count of Ponthieu who turned him over to the Duke. Although William treated Harold cordially, he appears to have made Harold's pledge a condition of his release. By assuming the English crown, Harold thus broke his sacred oath, a serious offense in feudal times.

Norman Invasion of England. William began planning his bold assault upon England as soon as he heard of Harold's coronation, but adverse winds forced him to postpone sailing. Meanwhile, in September 1066, an army led by Tostig and Harold Hardrada landed in Yorkshire. Hastily reassembling his troops, the English king rushed to the scene and on September 25 inflicted a stunning defeat on the invaders at Stamford Bridge. Harold had no time, however, to savor the greatness of his military triumph. Two days later the Channel winds changed direction and William set sail with approximately 10,000 men and 3,000 horses. His expedition carried the blessing of the pope, who was at odds with Harold at the time over the choice of Archbishop of Canterbury.

William's Victory. William's easy victory in the Battle of Hastings has tended to obscure the riskiness of his venture. Eleventh-century England possessed considerable wealth and a skillful citizens' army, the *fyrd*. In retrospect, Harold erred in moving directly south to counter William's invasion with an army that was exhausted and undermanned. The Norman forces engaged the English near Hastings on October 14 in a fierce all-day encounter. Only by nightfall when the English king lay dead on the battlefield was the outcome certain. Anglo-Saxon England had ceased to exist.

Crowning as King of England. William moved quickly to capitalize on his victory. With no central authority, resistance to the invaders was haphazard. The Normans entered London without a struggle and on Christmas Day 1066, William the Conqueror (ruled 1066–1087) was crowned King of England. It took him five years, however, to consolidate his rule in the face of incessant English rebellions. These he suppressed with a fierceness and cruelty that left large areas of England wasted, and blackened his otherwise exemplary character.

Redistribution of Estates. If William had at first appeared willing to leave the Anglo-Saxon nobility intact, their resistance left him little choice but to secure their extinction as a powerful landholding class. By 1076 he had confiscated their estates entirely and placed them in the hands of his Norman followers who came to form a new, French-speaking aristocracy. Because they were beholden to William for their good fortune, the Norman nobles were much more compliant to royal authority than their Anglo-Saxon predecessors had been. William further strengthened his control by appropriating approximately one-fifth of the conquered territory for his own royal demesne. He distributed the remaining estates so that most of his Norman lords held parcels of land that were widely scattered from one another, thereby reducing their value as a power base. He erected castles throughout the countryside to serve as strategic bastions of royal power.

Centralization of Feudal System. The consequences of William's actions have long been a subject of controversy among medieval historians. Most scholars now agree that various aspects of the feudal system such as private justice and commendation to a lord had already taken root in Anglo-Saxon times. What was missing was the landed element, the fief. The division of England into feudal estates owing dues and services was largely a result of the Norman Conquest. William regarded all of England as his by right of conquest. The lands that he then redistributed even to the Church were thus held from him on feudal terms. William gave to English feudalism a highly centralized and regularized character. In contrast to the decentralized role of continental monarchs, William used feudal ties to increase his royal authority. By the famous Salisbury Oath of 1086, he required all vassals to swear primary allegiance to the king above and beyond loyalty to their immediate lord. The condition of the vast majority of Englishmen worsened as a result of this transfer of lands. Many freemen lost their status and peasants now became tied to the soil in hereditary subjection.

Relations with Church. In his relations with the English Church, the new king displayed his genius for political and administrative affairs. He capably supported the cause of Church reform while zealously guarding the English monarch's control over ecclesiastical appointments. He filled most important vacancies with Norman supporters, reinforced Church discipline, and revived clerical learning. To expedite reform, he set up a system of separate ecclesiastical courts to try cases in canon law apart from secular jurisdiction. At the same time he refused to pay fealty to the pope or allow papal letters or decrees of excommunication to be enforced without royal consent. Church building gathered speed during William's reign.

Government. William kept much of the character of English government and law. He retained most Anglo-Saxon institutions and traditions, continued to levy the *Danegeld* and required military service of all freemen. The shire and hundred courts remained as seats of royal justice. Even the ancient Anglo-Saxon *witan* continued to function in somewhat altered form as the Norman *Curia Regis* or Great Council of William's tenants-in-chief. It met briefly three times a year to render counsel and try important cases. For the rest of the year William governed with the aid of a smaller permanent council, whose members were drawn from royal household offices and a few from the highest ranks of society and the Church. From this body evolved separate governmental departments that gradually assumed control of the administration of royal government.

The Domesday Book. The outstanding administrative achievement of William's later years was the *Domesday Book*, a comprehensive survey of his subjects and their property, even including the number of their oxen. William ordered the work compiled in 1086 for the purpose of assessing his kingdom's taxable resources. That it was carried out with such speed and thoroughness testifies to the fact that Norman England had attained a degree of centralized control and financial expertise to be found nowhere else in medieval Europe. The *Domesday Book* has provided modern scholars rich insight into the physical components of post-Conquest England.

William's Achievements. William died of an injury in 1087. The great events of his reign all bear the stamp of his personal genius. A daring fighter, he was an adroit statesman, administrator, and financier as well. He molded England into a powerful and united kingdom under the direction of a strong central monarchy. Stern by nature, he could be unmercifully cruel to his enemies. Nevertheless, William's accomplishments were genuine and long-lived.

Division of William's Kingdom. One of the great disappointments of William's last years was the inferior quality of his heirs. So soured were his relations with his rebellious elder son, Robert Curthose, that he refused to pass his kingdom to Robert intact. When the king died in 1087, Robert inherited the Duchy of Normandy by right of primogeniture while his younger brother, William Rufus, became King William II (ruled 1087–1100) of England. A third son, Henry, received money and land. For the next twenty years the brothers contended for mastery of their father's kingdom.

William Rufus

William Rufus proved a harsh and despised ruler. He taxed the common people excessively, extorted large sums of money from the nobility whenever they wished to marry or inherit an estate, and left Church offices vacant for years in order to collect personally their revenues. Having failed to conquer Normandy by force, he arranged a deal with his brother in 1095 whereby he received control of the duchy for three years in return for a large sum that Duke Robert needed in order to go on crusade. Rufus's reign was cut short in 1100 when he was killed in a hunting accident. For centuries suspicion has focused on his brother Henry, but no solid evidence of murder has ever been found.

Henry I

Rufus's death left the English throne vacant. The king had no sons and his brother Robert had not yet returned from the Holy Land. Seizing the opportunity, Henry quickly gained acceptance as king. In order to strengthen his position among the English, he issued a coronation oath in which he enumerated the abuses of his predecessors and promised to desist from them. In fact, Henry I (ruled 1100–1135) used many of the same oppressive tactics to raise revenues as had his brother. Yet, because he was a much more astute administrator who saw that justice was done and orderly procedure followed, his reign proved peaceful and stable.

Conquest of Normandy. Henry's first task was to stave off the threat of an invasion from Normandy. This he accomplished in 1101 through negotiation rather than force. Five years later, he conquered Normandy by defeating his brother Robert at the battle of Tinchebrai.

Relations with Church. Henry's Norman campaigns and other military projects required a steady flow of funds. These he acquired in part by selling church offices and refusing to fill unoccupied bishoprics and abbacies for several years. Despite this cavalier treatment, the Church won an important concession from the English monarchy during Henry's reign. As a result of a dispute with the renowned Anselm, Archbishop of Canterbury, the king relinquished his right to lay investiture. He retained, nonetheless, a decisive influence over clerical elections.

Administration. Henry I left his greatest mark on the future of English government in the realm of royal administration. Perhaps because he realized more efficient and all-encompassing administrative institutions would be more profitable to the king as well, Henry broadened the reach and centralized the administration of his government. He chose one of his most able advisers to act as chief justiciar charged with assisting the king in overseeing the realm. He also began the practice of sending itinerant justices around the countryside to try important cases in the name of royal justice. The handling of royal finances was also greatly improved in response to a large increase in royal revenues. This augmented income flowed in from sources such as the new custom of allowing the king's vassals to make money payments, "scutage," in lieu of military service. Other revenues came in from the many prosperous towns that were under royal control. A small group of men began to take on the function of a central accounting office, which became known as the Exchequer after the table upon which the royal administrators worked. The Exchequer kept permanent records of royal revenues known as pipe rolls. It thereby served as a check upon the sheriffs, the king's tax collectors in the shires.

Stephen

For thirty-five years Henry provided England with a strong government in the tradition of his father. Upon his death in 1135, however, England collapsed into anarchy. Having no son, Henry had won acknowledgment of his daughter Matilda's right to the crown. The English barons, however, distrusted Matilda's husband, Count Geoffrey of Anjou. They soon rallied to Henry's nephew, Stephen of Blois (ruled 1135–1154), who seized the throne. Faced with civil war and baronial unrest, Stephen allowed Henry's powerful governmental machinery to weaken. He battled Matilda for control of the country until 1148 when she finally admitted defeat. Normandy had, however, by this time fallen to her husband. Matilda's and Geoffrey's eldest son, the future Henry II, would shortly realize his parents' aspirations.

Henry II

Henry Plantagenet, whose family name derived from Geoffrey of Anjou's habit of decorating his helmet with a sprig of broom, was raised to be a king. He received an unusually thorough education and was a robust and quick-witted youth.

French Territory. In 1150 at the age of seventeen, Henry inherited Normandy from his parents. Upon his father's death a year later he became Count of Anjou and Maine. With his marriage in 1152 to Eleanor, the divorced wife of Louis VII of France and heiress in her own right to the prized duchy of Aquitaine, he gained control over territory that stretched from the Loire to the Pyrenees. Nearly the entire western half of modern-day France was now in "Angevin" (from "Anjou") hands.

Accession to the Throne. Through his mother Matilda, Henry laid claim to England as well as his French domain. The main obstacle to this ambition was removed in 1153 when King Stephen's son choked to death. The despondent monarch agreed that upon his demise Henry would succeed to the throne. Nine months later and without bloodshed, the Duke of Normandy became Henry II of England (ruled 1154–1189) the first of the Plantagenet line of kings.

Government. Henry II acted quickly to rein in the anarchic barons. He destroyed or took hold of the many unlicensed castles that had been hastily assembled during Stephen's weak rule. Then he began systematically to revive and expand the administrative and judicial reforms of his grandfather, Henry I. Henry II's contributions to the growth of

England's legal and governmental institutions have led many historians to judge him one of England's greatest monarchs. He provided England a strong, centralized government without resort to the unjust practices of his forebears. The reforms that he instituted gave his kingdom the most orderly and efficient government in medieval Europe.

Legal Reforms. Henry's keen legal mind perceived the extension of royal justice as a means to reduce disorder. He issued a series of important assizes (edicts) that, while operative within the framework of existing institutions, in fact introduced many innovative changes to England's legal machinery. These edicts increased the effectiveness of his rule and brought speedier and more equitable justice to his subjects. The purchase of royal writs necessary for initiating law suits and the payment of court fines generated a lucrative flow of income to the crown.

Inquest Juries. By the Assize of 1166, Henry II empowered royal commissioners, or itinerant justices, to summon periodically to the shire court twelve men from each hundred, and four men from each village. These were required under oath to report all crimes committed within the district since the justices had last been there and to name all whom they suspected of wrongdoing. While these accusing "juries" furnished evidence they did not decide upon guilt or innocence. Until 1215 this was still determined by ordeal. Henry's inquest juries are the ancestors of the modern grand jury that brings indictments based on its findings but does not try cases.

Development of Common Law. Henry applied the use of juries to civil as well as criminal cases, and he created a national system of justice by sending royal judges to local courts on a regular basis and by creating the permanent central courts of King's Bench, Common Pleas, and Exchequer. This had several significant results. The growing popularity of royal justice gradually undermined the jurisdiction of the baronial courts. Local laws, customs, and traditions came to be replaced by a law common to all of England because it was founded upon the judgments of royal justices. These formed precedents by which later cases were decided. For this reason Henry II has sometimes been called the "Father of English Common Law." The use of juries placed greater weight on the importance of evidence in English legal practice and severely curbed abuses associated with trial by battle or by ordeal. Reason came to be held in higher regard than violence and/or divine intervention as a means of settling conflicts.

Conflict with Becket. In all he did Henry was driven by a prodigious, restless energy, which at times exploded into violent fits of temper. Nowhere was his rage more costly to him than in his long struggle with his erstwhile friend Thomas à Becket. Becket had been Henry's intimate companion and served him brilliantly as chancellor for eight years before the king decided to appoint him Archbishop of Canterbury in 1162. Henry no doubt believed that through Becket he could control the ecclesiastical administration in England as tightly as he watched over secular affairs. Events quickly proved otherwise.

Becket's Assertion of Church Authority. Much has been written about Becket's character. Whether he was an ambitious actor able to perform superbly in whatever role he was cast, or whether he truly underwent a religious conversion that compelled him to protect Church interests above all else, clearly he suffered for his intransigent adherence to principle. Within a year after his appointment, he and Henry were already at loggerheads over state interference in the Church. The quarrel between the two escalated in 1164 when Henry issued the Constitutions of Clarendon, which restored ancient customs that curbed clerical independence. Becket refused to consent to them and, after appealing to the pope, fled to France. Although he supported Becket in principle, Pope Alexander III was anxious to effect a reconciliation. In 1170 the king and his archbishop met and attempted to come to terms. Becket was free to return to England but none of the old issues was truly resolved. Instead, Becket promptly excommunicated those bishops who in his absence and contrary to tradition had crowned Henry's eldest son the future king.

Becket's Martyrdom. When news of Becket's final outrage reached the king, he erupted into a tirade, allegedly cursing the barons gathered round him "who leave me thus exposed to the insolence of a fellow that came to my court on a lame sumpter mule and now sits without hindrance upon the throne itself." Immediately four nobles set off without Henry's authorization to carry out the king's implied threat. They confronted Thomas on the steps of the altar of Canterbury Cathedral on December 29, 1170, and struck him down with their swords.

Becket's martyrdom cost Henry dearly. He never regained the popularity and prestige of his early years. The grief-stricken king wore sackcloth and swore before God that he was innocent of Thomas's murder. He was compelled, nonetheless, to do penance and agree that the English clergy would remain subject only to ecclesiastical jurisdiction. The right to appeal to Rome without royal permission was firmly established, provided that litigants underwent an oath that their case made no infringements on royal rights. Nevertheless, Henry successfully prevented the pope from imposing a direct tax on the English churchmen. Becket's tomb at Canterbury quickly became a popular pilgrimage site and miracles were reported to have occurred there. Within three years after his death the Church proclaimed Thomas a saint.

Foreign Affairs. England was never the exclusive focus of Henry's interest. It served largely to finance his ambitions beyond the Channel. Especially during the later years of his reign, he was preoccupied with defending his continental empire from the Capetian monarchy, the anarchic French nobles, and his own disgruntled offspring.

Family Conflicts. Henry dealt with his family with a mixture of harshness and forbearance. He confined his queen to a castle for fifteen years in punishment for her part in the rebellion of his three eldest sons in 1173–74. At the time of his death in 1189, his two surviving sons, Richard and John, had joined forces with Philip Augustus, the French king, in order to strip Henry of his continental possessions. According to tradition, Henry's dying words were: "Shame, shame on a conquered king."

Richard I

Richard I, the Lionhearted (ruled 1189–1199), succeeded to his father's throne without opposition.

Military Campaigns. Little known in England, Richard devoted most of his ten-year reign to fighting the Muslims in the Holy Land and Philip II (Augustus) in France. As the real leader of the Third Crusade, he negotiated a treaty with Saladin that reopened Jerusalem to Christian pilgrims. To his contemporaries, Richard epitomized the essence of chivalry. Returning from the East, he fell captive to the German emperor, who extorted a huge ransom for his release.

Absence from England. After a brief visit to England, Richard devoted his remaining years to defending his continental domains against the machinations of the French king. More soldier than monarch, he spent less than six months in England, and entrusted the tasks of government to loyal officials. To finance his military campaigns, the king ordered offices confiscated and resold, imposed heavy new taxes, and sold many charters of self-government to towns. So solid was the administrative foundation constructed by Henry II, however, that England remained ably governed and at peace despite an absentee king.

John

John Lackland (reigned 1199–1216), the youngest son of Henry II, was as ambitious and grasping as his brother, but he lacked Richard's redeeming virtues. John's moody and changeable personality made him capable of excessive cruelty to his enemies, and in combat he was often indecisive and fearful. Although he devoted considerable talent to royal administration, his lack of scruples and capriciousness provoked the suspicion and hatred of his subjects. His reign was dominated by three fateful struggles: with Philip Augustus, with the papacy, and with the English barons. The outcome of each altered the course of English history.

Conflict with France. John inherited his brother's quarrel with Philip II over England's continental domains. In 1202 the French king declared his vassal John to be in violation of feudal law and proceeded to confiscate his French fiefs. After two years of fighting, the Angevin empire crumbled with the loss of nearly all possessions in France except Aquitaine and part of Poitou.

Conflict with the Pope. John suffered another humiliating defeat at the hands of Innocent III. Traditionally the English king had named his own Archbishop of Canterbury. When John refused to accept the pope's choice, however, Innocent placed England under interdict and excommunicated the king. In 1213 John finally acquiesced to the pope's demands in order to gain his aid in stemming a French invasion. John agreed to become the pope's vassal and to accept England from him as a papal fief.

Defeat by Philip of France. At peace with the papacy, John again took up the offensive against France. He allied with his nephew, Otto of Brunswick, a contender for the Imperial German throne, as well as with the Count of Flanders, and set out to attack Philip Augustus from Poitou. John's hope of restoring the empire built by the Angevin kings to its former extent was quickly dashed. At Bouvines in 1214 Philip Augustus scored a complete victory over England's allies.

Magna Carta. Throughout his reign John had placed heavy taxes on the English people and committed flagrant breaches of feudal custom that created great resentment against him. His costly alliances and disastrous final expedition further estranged the monarch from his subjects. When, to replenish his depleted treasury after the defeat at Bouvines, he demanded a scutage payment from those nobles who had failed to aid him against the French, he was met with widespread refusal. Approximately one-third of the English barons rose in revolt. They drew up a list of grievances and demands, the Great Charter or Magna Carta, and presented it to the king. To forestall further insurrection, John set his seal to it at Runnymede on June 15, 1215. Essentially a feudal document, the Magna Carta's sixty-three clauses reflected the interests of only a small portion of the English people. It forbade the king from levying any new taxes or feudal aids without the consent of the Great Council of the realm. It stipulated that "no free man may be arrested or imprisoned or deprived of his land . . . except by the legal judgment of his peers or by the law of the land." It made little mention of the rights of serfs who comprised the vast majority of the population. Yet, succeeding generations discerned beneath its highly specific demands several general principles upon which subsequent notions of constitutional monarchy and government by law have rested. These were that the king was obliged to rule according to the law of the land and that the king himself was under the law.

Henry III

Shortly after Runnymede, John repudiated the terms of Magna Carta on the grounds that he had been coerced to sign it. He appealed to the now-friendly pope, who absolved him of his oath. The barons rebelled anew and offered the English throne to Philip Augustus's son, Louis. Louis actually landed on English soil but John's death in 1216 united his subjects against foreign rule. A large number of barons threw their support behind John's nine-year-old son, who was crowned Henry III (reigned 1216–1272).

The Development of Parliament. The Magna Carta expressed the belief that royal authority was limited by the laws and customs of the land. It lacked, however, an effective means of carrying out these restraints. The thirteenth century saw the birth of a political institution, Parliament, that gradually assumed the role of checking the king. The English monarchy traditionally ruled with the advice of the great nobles of the realm. Yet, both the Anglo-Saxon *witan* and the Norman and Angevin Great Council existed only at the king's pleasure and possessed neither a fixed membership nor the power to coerce the king. The word "parliament" derives from the French word *parler* ("to speak") and in twelfth-century England was applied indiscriminately to any important deliberative assembly. After 1265, however, the term was generally reserved for meetings of the Great Council.

For most of the thirteenth century, parliament remained a loosely defined body whose composition fluctuated and whose functions included rendering political advice, assenting to new taxes, and acting as England's highest court. It met only sporadically when the king needed it. The key to its growing power, however, lay in its control of the purse strings. By the end of the century, parliament had accrued to itself the right to approve all extraordinary taxation. Several important milestones occurred during the long reign of Henry III.

Provisions of Oxford. Upon declaring himself of age to rule in 1227, Henry displayed little talent for governing. He quickly lost favor with the nobility by appointing Italian and French friends to important posts. He avoided consulting the Great Council. In foreign affairs, Henry, at the pope's invitation, embarked upon a foolhardy quest to place his son on the Sicilian throne. Henry promised to pay the pope an immense sum of money. In 1258 the barons finally balked at Henry's request for one-third of the kingdom's revenues for that year. They agreed to the necessary funds only upon the expulsion of Henry's foreign officials and the election of 24 men charged with reforming the kingdom. Their demands were set down in the Provisions of Oxford (1258) that virtually stripped the king of his political independence. It stipulated that the Great Council, which it called a parliament, must meet at least three times a year. Among its members must be men chosen by the barons and empowered to act for the community.

Simon de Montfort. Discord among the barons put a temporary end to their scheme to limit monarchical authority and by 1262 Henry resumed full control. He rapidly alienated the barons, and in 1263 they resorted to arms. Their leader was the king's brother-in-law, Simon de Montfort. To stave off full-scale civil war, the king and his barons set their quarrel before the saintly Louis IX of France, who in the Mise of Amiens (1264) decided in Henry's favor. The barons refused to accept the verdict and opened battle. At Lewes in May 1264, they won a resounding victory, took Henry and his son prisoner, and forced the king to accede to a revised version of the Provisions.

Parliament of 1265. Although Henry retained the throne, Montfort was the *de facto* ruler of England for nearly fifteen months. The evolution of Parliament made significant strides during his brief rule. Montfort consulted parliament regularly; moreover, in 1265 he summoned a meeting of the Great Council that included not only the great barons and prelates but also two knights from every shire and two burgesses from every town. Montfort's Parliament of 1265 was the first time in which burgesses and shire knights appeared together and is considered the first true ancestor of England's modern, bicameral Parliament.

Edward I

Henry's son, Edward, escaped from prison and defeated the baronial party at the battle of Evesham in August 1265. Montfort was killed, and, after two more years of fighting, internal peace was restored. Having directed affairs from behind the scenes during the last seven years of Henry's reign, Edward I (ruled 1272–1307) succeeded to his father's throne in 1272. One of England's pre-eminent monarchs, Edward left the stamp of his strong personality and systematizing genius upon English law and institutions for generations to come. Parliament broadened its representation and increased in importance during his reign. Two great tasks commanded Edward's attention during his thirty-two years as king; the reordering and extension of English common law and the union of all of Britain.

Extension of Common Law. Edward has been called "the English

Justinian." Unlike the sixth-century Byzantine emperor, however, he did not codify a great body of law but rather issued a series of statutes that rendered English common law more consistent, clearer, and less open to individual interpretation. This was a significant step because it marked the transformation of the medieval concept that held law to be inherited and unchangeable to one that recognized that laws could be made and if necessary amended. Edward's statutes worked ultimately to strengthen central government and reduce feudal privileges. After 1290 only those feudal courts that had received explicit royal approval were allowed to exist. Grantors had to obtain the permission of their suzerain before donating lands to the Church and subinfeudation was ended.

Specialized Courts. The machinery of local and central government functioned in a more orderly and regularized manner under Edward's close supervision. By the time of his reign, in addition to the king and his Great Council, three specialized courts—Common Pleas, King's Bench, and the Exchequer, located at Westminster—handled most of the important judicial work of the realm.

Finances. Edward augmented the crown's revenues by collecting a tax on exported English wool. To pay for his expensive wars, he turned for loans to Italian merchants rather than the usual Jewish moneylenders. In 1290 he expelled all Jews from England and confiscated their property.

Professional Army. By the late thirteenth century, feudalism was losing its *raison d'être* as a military system. Edward's need for a large army serving for long stretches at a time compelled him to pay his knights wages and hire mercenaries.

Conquest of Wales. Edward I's great ambition was to unite all of Britain under one rule. He invaded Wales in 1277 and again in 1282. By the following year his authority extended over all of the formerly independent land. Although the Welsh held onto their language and culture, they were thenceforth governed according to English law and administrative procedure. Since 1301, the heir to the English throne has borne the title "Prince of Wales" in deference to Welsh sentiment.

Failure to Conquer Scotland. Despite several victories in the field, Edward failed to conquer Scotland. Scottish nationalism flared under the leadership of William Wallace, and later Robert Bruce. The Scots decisively defeated Edward's son at Bannockburn in 1314. Until the seventeenth century, England faced an independent and at times hostile neighbor to the north.

The Model Parliament. The need to win both moral and financial support for his foreign policy also moved Edward to continue the practice of inviting shire knights and burgesses to some of his parliaments. His famous Parliament of 1295 is traditionally but somewhat misleadingly referred to as the "Model Parliament" because it included the great nobles and prelates of the realm as well as representatives of the shires and towns and members of the lower clergy. In fact, the Parliament of 1295 did not serve as an example for future gatherings because it was grouped in three orders—barons and knights, burghers, and clergy—that met separately. The characteristic division of Parliament into a House of Commons and a House of Lords did not occur until later in the fourteenth century. The lower clergy opted out of Parliament at this time as well. Edward's willingness to experiment with broadening parliamentary membership marks another crucial step in the evolution of Parliament as a truly representative institution. Likewise his explicit granting to the "community of the realm" in 1297 the right to assent to all new taxation gave Parliament a powerful means to control the king.

Edward II

In its struggles with Edward I's weak son, Edward II (reigned 1307–1327), Parliament consolidated its position as a necessary adjunct to monarchical rule. Edward's refusal to listen to his noble advisers turned them against him. They forced Edward to expel his favorite counselor, the ambitious Piers Gaveston, and agree to the Ordinances of 1311 that stipulated among other things that Parliament was to meet at least twice a year and that it possessed the power to approve or veto the king's choice of important administrative and household officials. In addition, the Ordinances forbade Edward from declaring war without parliamentary ratification. Subsequent parliaments, however, were unable to enforce these provisions. By 1327, when a baronial faction called upon Parliament to depose the king, it was clear that Parliament was now recognized as an organ through which the community voiced its assent.

France

In France as in England, the central years of the Middle Ages witnessed the growth of a strong monarchy and the expansion of royal administration. In France, these developments are associated with the rise of a new dynasty, the Capetians. Between the late tenth and the early fourteenth centuries the Capetian kings slowly but skillfully built up the power of the French throne and reasserted its control over the great nobles.

Decline of Royal Authority

The task of restoring royal authority was a herculean one. By the beginning of the ninth century the central powers of the French monarchy had virtually ceased to function. France had collapsed into a collection of semi-independent and warring territories ruled by provincial nobles who paid scant attention to royal commands. By the time of Louis IV d'Outremer (ruled 936-954), the royal demesne consisted of only one town. One of the greatest of the king's mighty vassals, Hugh the Great, Duke of the French, had wealth and holdings in the center of France that made him more powerful than the king. When Louis V died childless in 987, the great nobles and prelates looked to Hugh the Great's son, Hugh Capet. Hugh Capet (reigned 987-996) owed his election primarily to the bishops, who were loyal to him. Although his lands were less extensive than his father's, the new king added to the royal demesne a compact, centrally located domain known as the Île-de-France, which contained the important cities of Paris and Orléans and their surrounding territories. From this base the Capetians gradually imposed their direct rule over much of France.

Capetian Hereditary Rule

During the first years of his reign, Hugh Capet was preoccupied with subduing a Carolingian claimant to the throne. It seemed unlikely that the new dynasty would have any better luck than the last of the Carolingians in putting a stop to lawlessness and fragmentation. Yet the early Capetians possessed one great advantage in addition to the desirable location of their lands. This was the good fortune of producing male direct heirs without fail for more than three hundred years. Until the time of Philip Augustus in the late twelfth century, the Capetian monarchs assured the unbroken succession of their line by crowning the heir apparent during his father's lifetime. The establishment of their hereditary right to rule was the most important legacy of the early Capetians.

Louis VI

For the first century of their rule, the Capetian monarchs worked simply to prevent the further decay of royal authority. Commencing with the reign of Louis VI ("the Fat") (ruled 1108–1137), however, the Capetian dynasty began to assert itself. Louis undertook the tasks of government with energy and wisdom.

Restoration of Order and Justice. The king moved first against the unruly barons within his own domain who preyed upon travelers crossing their lands, mistreated the peasantry, and flagrantly disobeyed the king's commands. For years, he besieged the castles of his most contentious vassals until finally he had put an end to brigandry and brought equitable justice to the whole of the royal domain. So favorable was the reputation of royal justice that vassals from other provinces began to petition the king to adjudicate their grievances. By consolidating Capetian power within the Île-de-France, Louis bequeathed his successors a sure foundation upon which to build their territorial gains.

Support of Middle Class. Louis eliminated the noble monopoly of officeholding and assumed personal control over the *Curia Regis*. He left some administrative posts vacant and filled others with "new men" from the lesser ranks of the nobility, clergy, and the middle classes. Totally committed to advancing royal authority, these officers provided the nucleus of a reliable and effective central administrative system. In addition, Louis VI cultivated the good will of the middle classes by issuing them charters for their new towns. Their support would prove invaluable to later Capetian monarchs.

Louis's Legacy. Louis VI's reign was also instructive of things to come with regard to England, whose king after 1106 was again their vassal the Duke of Normandy. At his death, Louis VI left to his son a well-ordered kingdom whose potential for greatness was now clear.

Louis VII

Louis VII possessed his father's strengths except in the sphere of

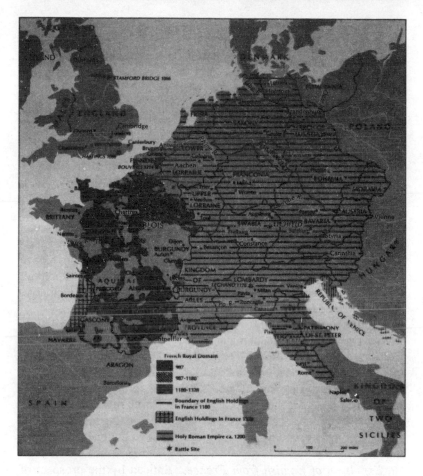

Medieval England, France, and the Holy Roman Empire

political judgment. He governed his own small realm in the same spirit of fairness and harmony, and he continued to uphold the Church and favor the middle classes. An honest, upright king whose reputation for Christian piety increased with age, Louis nonetheless found himself outdistanced by his political adversaries.

Eleanor of Aquitaine. When his marriage to Eleanor, heiress of the wealthy province of Aquitaine, was followed by rumors of her infidelity and failed to produce a male heir, Louis unwisely had the marriage annulled in 1152. Two months later his queen became wife to Henry II of England and she eventually bore him five sons. By 1158, the English territories abroad encompassed Normandy, Anjou, Maine, Touraine, Brittany, Poitou, Gascony, and Aquitaine, or more than half of France.

Philip II

At the age of forty-five, Louis's wish for a male heir was finally granted. He called his son, the future Philip II (ruled 1180–1223), *Dieudonné* meaning "given by God." From his youth Philip was determined to avenge his father's territorial losses and rid France of the English threat. His successes against England earned him the style "Augustus."

Territorial Gains. Philip's lust for territorial gain brought him in conflict with the Count of Flanders. Pressing hereditary and nuptial claims, Philip succeeded in acquiring Artois, Amiens, and Vermandois. This extended the Capetian domain as far north as the Channel.

Intervention in England. Next, Philip set his sights on expelling his Angevin foe. He encouraged Henry II's sons in their rebellion against their father. After Henry's death, Philip turned against his boyhood companion and fellow crusader, Richard the Lionhearted, but made little headway against Richard's military genius. When Richard's younger brother, John, became king in 1199, Philip saw an opportunity to realize his designs. He backed a rival claimant to the English throne, Arthur of Brittany, and bided his time while John engineered his own undoing.

Expulsion of English from France. Enticed by the prospect of adding to his continental lands, in 1200 John married Isabella, heiress to the county of Angoulême in southern France. His action was a foolhardy breach of feudal law, for his wife had already been engaged to a French lord. As feudal overlord, Philip ordered John to appear before him. When the monarch failed to present himself, Philip declared his French fiefs forfeit and invaded them with the support of Arthur of Brittany. In defense of his territories, John captured Arthur and probably had him murdered in the spring of 1203. This act alienated

John's supporters in France, and his empire north of the Loire River soon lay in ruins. Only Aquitaine to the south remained in British hands by 1205. Philip assured the permanence of his conquest of Normandy, Anjou, Maine, and Touraine by defeating John and his allies, Otto of Brunswick and the Count of Flanders, at the decisive battle of Bouvines in 1214. Capetian France emerged as a major European power. So complete was the victory at Bouvines that more than a century passed before England's kings attempted to win back their former French lands.

Government. After Bouvines, Philip II concentrated his energy on the governance of his greatly expanded realm. As early as 1190, Philip had seen the need for reforming his administration in the interests of stronger monarchical control. He transferred royal archives to Paris, fostered growth of specialized departments such as a financial court of audit akin to the English Exchequer, and summoned his great vassals to sessions of the *Curia Regis* to adjudicate feudal laws, using these periodic assemblies as a means to assert his feudal rights. To handle the details of government on a daily basis he relied upon lesser officials, clerks, and knights. In time these formed an expert and loyal bureaucracy.

Philip created a new class of officials in the provinces, the *baillis,* who were beholden to the king alone. Similar to the English itinerant justices, the *baillis* traveled around France performing administrative, judicial, and financial tasks.

Wherever possible, Philip strengthened the monarchy by weakening its main competitor, the French nobility. Thus he allied with the growing towns against their noble lords. In Paris, Philip oversaw the construction of the first Louvre, encircled the city with fortifications, and paved its principal roads.

Louis VIII

At his death in 1223, Philip II bequeathed his son a vastly enlarged realm that was, nonetheless, governed closely from the center owing to the king's administrative innovations.

Territorial Expansion. Reigning a scant three years, Louis VIII carried on his father's work of royal expansion so that by Louis's death the Capetian kingdom spanned the length of France from the English

Channel to the Mediterranean Sea. He conquered Poitou from the English in 1224 and led a crusade against the Albigensians that subjugated most of Languedoc.

Dynastic Provisions. Two important internal developments occurred during Louis VIII's reign. He was the first Capetian king to succeed to the throne without having been crowned prior to his father's death. By now the dynasty's hereditary right to rule was incontrovertible. In his will Louis directed his son and heir to provide for his younger brothers by granting them large, newly conquered territories called *appanages.* By so doing, Louis hoped to smooth the assimilation of formerly independent fiefs into the royal domain. Under successor monarchs, however, this practice encouraged the growth of rival princely houses and injected an unstabilizing element into royal politics.

Louis IX

Philip Augustus had transformed the French monarchy into one of the most powerful in Europe. His grandson, Louis IX (reigned 1226–1270), turned it into one of the most respected and best loved.

Character. By his perfect honor and fairness, simple ways and heartfelt piety, Louis elevated the office of kingship into one befitting God's Anointed and won for it the devotion of his subjects. In all his actions, Louis epitomized the medieval image of the ideal Christian monarch. His subjects adored him. Kings of other nations called upon him to mediate their disputes. Less than thirty years after his death the Church canonized him as Saint Louis.

Suppression of Revolts. For the first eight years of his reign, Louis's mother, Queen Blanche of Castile, ruled as regent. It was she who instilled in her son his ascetic tastes and piety. A wise and able woman who advised her son even after he had come of age, she successfully suppressed a number of revolts by the great magnates during her regency. Louis himself put down uprisings by the nobles of southern France and repelled an invasion by Henry III of England in 1243.

Government. Louis IX took seriously his kingly duty of bringing peace and justice to the land. To this end he forbade private warfare, abolished trial by combat, and negotiated treaties with two of his neighbors. By the Treaty of Paris (1259), Henry III formally acquiesced to the loss of Normandy, Anjou, Maine, Touraine, and Poitou, and agreed to pay homage to his French suzerain for the duchy of Aquitaine and Gascony. In return Louis yielded several territories along the borders of Gascony to England for the sake of future peace. In the administration of his royal domain, Louis carried on the reforming spirit of Philip Augustus. The growth of specialized departments of government staffed by trained bureaucrats continued apace.

Justice. During Louis's reign, the Parlement of Paris, the highest court of the land, can be said to have existed apart from the *Curia Regis.* Not to be confused with the English Parliament, whose counterpart in French history is the Estates General, the medieval Parlement possessed only judicial powers. Under Louis IX it received sole jurisdiction in matters of treason and certain other crimes. The king extended its range by allowing appeals to Parlement from the lower feudal courts. Thus he made available to all of his subjects the benefits of speedy and equitable royal justice. The king himself periodically judged cases. He would sit under an old oak tree in the forest of Vincennes near Paris and hear the complaints of even his most humble subjects. These he dealt with as fairly and equally as with his greatest vassals. Louis also created a new official, the *enquêteur,* who was charged with investigating the oppressive conduct of royal agents in the provinces.

Royal Authority. Louis was a true Capetian in his solicitude for advancing royal power. A devoted servant of the Church, he nonetheless defended royal interests against those of the papacy whenever the rights of monarchy appeared threatened. The degree to which the French throne could now act independently of its great vassals is evident in another of Louis's innovations, the royal *ordonnance.* The king now felt powerful enough to issue commands that were binding upon the whole of his kingdom without obtaining the prior consent of all of his vassals.

Religious Zeal. In his rigorous persecution of infidels, Louis's peace-loving nature gave way to the dogmatism of his faith. He encouraged the use of the Inquisition to extinguish heresy and embraced the crusading cause with the zeal of a fanatic. He personally led the Seventh (1248–54) and Eighth Crusades (1270). By the second half of the thirteenth century, however, the crusading enterprise had largely outworn its usefulness and Louis's expeditions must be counted as failures. Louis died in Tunis in 1270.

Philip IV

Conflict, not conciliation, marked the reign of Louis IX's grandson, Philip IV (ruled 1285–1314), who was nicknamed "the Fair" because of his good looks. By marriage Philip added Navarre and Champagne to the royal domain. Despite a languid and indolent nature, his reign witnessed the ruthless extension of royal power at the expense of his subjects' feudal rights.

Strengthening of Royal Authority. Philip chose middle-class men drawn principally from the ranks of lawyers from the south who would serve him unfailingly and whom he could dismiss at will. He then rewarded them with opportunities to advance themselves socially and economically. These "king's men" proved unscrupulously dedicated to the task of strengthening royal authority, and they used propaganda and deception to achieve that end. Their defense of Philip's unlimited powers laid the groundwork for the absolutism of later French monarchs.

Conflicts with England and Flanders. Philip's resolve to press to their fullest his rights as feudal suzerain brought him into conflict with his two most powerful vassals, the King of England and the Count of Flanders. Philip failed, however, to annex either Gascony or Flanders. These struggles and the pressing need for funds they engendered form the backdrop to an even greater confrontation with Rome.

Conflict with the Papacy. Conflict with the papacy centered upon the claims of the clergy that they were immune from royal taxation except for customary feudal dues and extraordinary levies approved by the pope, for example, to finance a crusade.

Taxation of Clergy. Philip repudiated these claims and he and his rival, Edward I of England, taxed their clerical subjects to raise money for their warfare with one another. Pope Boniface VIII, an ill-tempered and sickly old man, opposed these measures as a violation of papal prerogative. In 1296 he issued a papal document, *Clericis laicos,* which prohibited kings from taxing their clergy without prior papal consent. (Such papal letters are known as bulls, after the papal seal, or *bulla,* affixed to them.) Edward I responded by branding as outlaws all clerics who refused to pay, while Philip IV halted export of bullion from France, thus curbing papal revenues from that realm. Under pressure from his Italian bankers who were consequently strapped for funds, Boniface retreated. He agreed that monarchs could ask for voluntary grants from the clergy in times of dire need even without papal permission.

Unam Sanctam. Boniface VIII held on, nonetheless, to his claim that spiritual authority was superior to secular authority. In 1301 he was prepared to lock horns again with the French king. The new dispute commenced when Philip arrested and condemned a troublesome French bishop, Bernard Saisset, on largely unproved charges. Boniface retaliated with the bull, *Unam sanctam* (1302), which represents the strongest medieval statement of a pope's unlimited sovereignty over lay rulers.

Attack on Pope. By threatening Philip with excommunication, Boniface misjudged the spirit of the times. Popular sentiment and political realities had changed since the days of Gregory VII and Innocent III. In France loyalty to the king and the nation-state now ran high. Sensing his strong position, Philip counterattacked, accusing Boniface of numerous crimes and plotting his capture. In September, 1303, French and Italian forces besieged the pope at his residence in Anagni. Boniface escaped with aid from his supporters but died in humiliation a month later.

Transfer of Papacy to Avignon. In its centuries-long struggle to dominate the secular policies of states, the papacy had frequently engaged in measures that damaged its own prestige and spiritual authority. So general was the disapproval of the Church's misuse of its powers that the degradation of Boniface roused no new lay champion to the papal cause. Philip was thus emboldened to go even further. In 1305 he engineered the papal election of the French cardinal, Clement V, who refused to settle in Rome. After residing for four years within Capetian territory, the French pope transferred the papacy to the imperial city of Avignon in southern France, where it became essentially a puppet of the French monarch.

Suppression of the Knights Templar. Philip IV was deeply in debt to the Order of the Knights Templar, and in 1307 he conceived a plan to refill his treasury by confiscating its wealth. The affluence, power, and secretive behavior of the Templars in France had made them widely unpopular. Thus it was easy for Philip's ministers to raise false charges of vice and heresy against the order and to arrest all of its French members. These were subsequently put on trial and the Inquisition used torture to extract confessions from many of them. Philip prodded Pope Clement V to continue the persecution and secured abolition of the order in 1312 from the tractable pope.

Revenue-Raising Devices. The insufficiency of feudal revenues motivated Philip to lash out against other crown creditors and to seek new sources of income. In 1306 he confiscated property owned by the Jews and drove them from France. Five years later he expelled his Italian bankers and appropriated their wealth. On several occasions he resorted to the ruinous practice of debasing coinage.

Summoning of the Estates General. Lack of money was also a contributing factor in the most significant constitutional development of Philip's reign, the summoning of the Estates General. French kings in need of funds customarily consulted with the higher ranks of society that constituted the royal court. Philip the Fair, however, sought wider approval for his actions. At the height of his conflict with the pope in 1302, he assembled in one place for the first time in French history not only the clergy and nobility but also representatives from the towns. The idea of appealing to the nation in a representative assembly, in France called the Estates General, had thus taken root. Philip convoked the Estates General again in 1308 and 1314 to obtain support for his actions.

Succession to the Throne: The Valois Monarchs

Philip the Fair was the last of the great Capetian monarchs. He was succeeded in rapid order by his three sons, none of whom produced a male heir. The decision at this point to exclude women from the succession established a precedent that shortly thereafter was embodied in the "Salic Law" that forbade women from reigning in France. Thus, in 1328 the crown passed to a cousin, Philip Count of Valois, who ruled as Philip VI (reigned 1328–1350). With him begins the line of Valois monarchs who occupied the French throne until 1589.

Spain

The history of the Iberian peninsula during the central years of the Middle Ages revolves around two major themes: the expulsion of the Moors (Muslims) and the gradual unification of the land south of the Pyrenees into two nation-states, Spain and Portugal. Neither goal was fully realized until the latter half of the fifteenth century.

The Reconquista

The Christian reconquest of Muslim Spain, the *Reconquista*, was a slow and discontinuous process. For many years it was confined to a small pocket of Christian resistance in the northern mountains that had escaped the Muslim invasion of 711. By the end of the eighth century, the small Christian enclave included Asturias, all that remained of Visigothic Spain in the northwest; Charlemagne's Spanish March that developed into the county of Barcelona (i.e., Catalonia) in the northeast; and between them, the Basque-speaking kingdom of Navarre.

The Spanish Offensive. Asturias took the lead in expanding its borders southward into Muslim Spain. By 900 it had conquered the land north of the Douro River and changed its name to the kingdom of Léon. A new county, Castile, won independence from the king of Léon during the mid-tenth century. Rivalries among the Christian states perennially hampered the progress of the *Reconquista*, and the resurgence of Muslim strength in the tenth century all but halted its course. The dissolution of the Spanish branch of the Umayyad Caliphate into numerous warring states in 1031 offered Spanish Christians a favorable opportunity. This time Castile seized the initiative. United with Léon in 1037, the mighty kingdom pushed farther down the peninsula. In 1085 its forces captured the Muslim stronghold of Toledo in central Spain, thus securing for Castile the Tagus River as its southernmost border.

Defeat of Muslims. The quickening pace of the *Reconquista* in the mid-eleventh century was part of a larger Christian offensive against Islam. More than thirty years before the first Crusade to the East, the pope endowed the Spanish struggle with all the spiritual benefits of a holy war. Warfare and disunion among the Christian kingdoms impeded the progress of reconquest for much of the twelfth century. In 1212 at Las Navas de Tolosa, however, a Christian army led by the king of Castile inflicted a shattering blow upon Berber forces from North Africa. This victory was a turning point and the Christians went on to capture Cordova and then Seville. Although the Muslims retained a toehold at Granada until 1492, they never again posed a serious threat to Christian Spain.

Legacy of Muslim Occupation

The national characteristics of Spain and Portugal were profoundly influenced by the unique circumstances of their unification whereby the process of forging a nation involved first expelling foreign infidels. Union was achieved through militancy and propelled by a fanatical religious zeal that legitimized its conquests in the eyes of Spanish Christians. However, because Muslims in Spain had long shown tolerance to other religions, they in turn were treated with respect by their Christian conquerors until the late fifteenth century. Muslim Spain left its conquerors a rich heritage of cultural, commercial, agricultural, and scientific advances from which Spain and Europe would benefit.

Castile

The two preeminent states of what would become a united Spain, Castile and Aragón, followed slightly different courses during the thirteenth and fourteenth centuries. Castile had borne the greatest burden of expelling the Moors, and once this task was near completion, its kings concentrated on consolidating their hold over the highly fractionalized and anarchic groups within Castilian society. The nobility was particularly strong and held large tracts of land as *allodia*, free of feudal obligations. The Church was another rich and overly-powerful body in Castilian society. Many towns had grown up during the resettling of Muslim territory and they too clung to their chartered rights. Constant warfare and the availability of reconquered land put an end to personal serfdom in Castile by 1300.

Cortes

Throughout the Iberian peninsula, Christian kings sought to deal with their truculent subjects through representative assemblies known as *Cortes*. These evolved from the king's councils of nobles and clergy. In some territories, delegates from the towns were invited to attend as early as the twelfth century. In the thirteenth century, these Cortes were more powerful than their English and French equivalents. Yet, except in Aragón and Catalonia, they never obtained the right to consent to new legislation and by the fifteenth century had lost most of their influence.

Aragón

Aragón rose to prominence during the eleventh century. From a small, ancient region ruled by Navarre, it grew into a powerful kingdom encompassing Aragón, Navarre, Saragossa, and Catalonia. The latter retained its own Cortes and in language and customs was more closely bound to France than to Spain. Aragón played a lesser role in the *Reconquista* but was able to wrest Valencia and the Balearic Islands from the Moors. Because of its location on the Mediterranean, Aragón prospered commercially and aspired to become a major sea power. Beginning in the thirteenth century, various members of the royal House of Aragón controlled the Balearic Islands, Sicily, Sardinia, Athens, and other parts of Greece. The Aragónese king also struggled for supremacy against a powerful nobility.

Portugal

Portugal emerged as an independent nation-state during the twelfth century. Previously it was part of the kingdom of Castile, whose king had recaptured much of the area from the Moors a century earlier. The Castilians had been aided in their conquest by knights from north of the Pyrenees. In 1095 the Castilian king gave one such knight, Henry of Burgundy, his younger daughter in marriage and the county of Portugal as his wife's dowry. Their son, Afonso Henriques, rebelled against his family and the king to assert independence of his lands from Castilian overlordship.

Afonso I

After an important victory over the Muslims, Afonso Henriques defiantly declared himself "King of Portugal" in 1139. With intercession by the pope, Alfonso VII of Castile agreed in 1144 to recognize the new title, but assumed technical overlordship by declaring himself Emperor. The Portuguese monarch by these arrangements became vassal to the pope. Afonso I further secured his position by additional gains against the Muslims. In 1147 Portuguese forces, assisted by a fleet of crusaders on their way to the Holy Land, captured the port city of Lisbon at the mouth of the Tagus River.

Consolidation of Territory

Afonso's successors completed the recovery of Muslim-held territory a century later. In 1249 Portuguese troops captured the remaining Moorish territory to the south, the Algarve. This victory fixed Portugal's national boundaries almost 250 years before those of Spain. The new kingdom gradually developed a separate cultural identity and its dialect evolved into a rich and distinctive literary language. Unification speeded the process of resettlement that had gone on simultaneously with the reconquest. Liberal town charters and ample unoccupied land encouraged serfs and migrants from Spain and elsewhere in Europe to settle in sparsely populated areas. Portuguese monarchs such as Sancho I (reigned 1185–1211) took an active part in rebuilding areas ravaged by war and establishing new towns.

Challenges to the Monarchy

Throughout the thirteenth century, the power of the Portuguese monarchy was challenged on all sides. Rival claimants to the throne threatened political stability while the nobility and the Church increased their landholdings and safeguarded their extensive privileges from royal encroachment. Towns too used their municipal charters to evade outside control. Their burgeoning commercial wealth gave them a growing voice in royal affairs. As in Spain, the Portuguese monarch sought out the aid and advice of his mightier subjects by summoning them to a Cortes. The first assembly to merit such a name was held in 1211. It resulted in a victory for the Church. Canon law was given superiority over secular law and the clergy received exemption from most taxes. The attendance of town dwellers at a Cortes appears in the records for the first time in 1254.

John I

During the second half of the fourteenth century, Portugal fought long wars with neighboring Castile in order to maintain its independence. The decisive battle of Aljubarotta in 1385 finally resolved the conflict in Portugal's favor and assured its existence as a separate nation. To gain victory and secure his throne, John I (reigned 1385–1433) called upon English help. In 1386 he concluded a formal alliance with England that has endured to the present, making it the oldest of its kind still in force. With peace at hand, John I set his country on a course of overseas exploration that would propel it to greatness. In 1415 his ships took Ceuta in North Africa from the Moors. His famous son, Prince Henry the Navigator, inspired Portugal's fifteenth-century quest to circumnavigate Africa.

The High Middle Ages were a confident, fertile age in which medieval culture achieved its greatest expression. Renewed interest in learning after 1000 contributed to the rise of universities and the development of Scholastic thought. St. Thomas Aquinas's masterful synthesis of faith and reason dominated medieval philosophy until the fourteenth century and epitomized the age's optimism. Writing in the vernacular also blossomed and in Dante and Chaucer found its richest voice. Medieval architects developed new methods of building in stone that enabled them to produce one of the age's most enduring creations: the Gothic cathedral. It embodied the medieval vision of the universe as an ordered, divinely ordained, and intelligible whole.

The period from 1000 to 1350 was also one of important political developments. In England and France increasingly powerful royal dynasties consolidated and enlarged their kingdoms and extended central authority. While part of the feudal structure, these national monarchs began to employ bureaucrats to run the government and dispense royal justice throughout the land. Spanish Christians succeeded in recapturing most of the Iberian peninsula from the Muslims by 1212, laying the foundations of the Spanish and Portuguese nations.

As the power of the monarchy grew, it became clear that to govern effectively, kings needed a means of summoning a broader range of support for their policies. The key development in the transformation of royal councils into representative assemblies (i.e., Parliament, the Estates General, the Cortes) occurred during the thirteenth and early fourteenth centuries when delegates from the towns were invited to attend. The most pressing reason for summoning the three estates together was the king's dire need for funds. In England, by 1297, Parliament had gained the right to approve all new taxation. The failure of the Estates General and most of the Cortes to win this "power of the purse strings" gravely weakened their ability to limit the growth of royal absolutism.

Recommended Reading

Dante Alighieri, *The Divine Comedy*, Louis Biancolli, trans. (1966)

Thomas Aquinas, *The Political Ideas of St. Thomas Aquinas* (1966)

Thomas Aquinas, *Treatise on Law* (1965)

Frederick B. Artz, *The Mind of the Middle Ages: An Historical Survey, 200–1500* (1954)

Jean Bony, *French Gothic Architecture of the Twelfth and Thirteenth Centuries* (1982)

Christopher Brooke, *The Twelfth Century Renaissance* (1969)

R. Allen Brown, *The Normans and the Norman Conquest* (1970)

Geoffrey Chaucer, *The Portable Chaucer* (1949)

M. D. Chenu, *Nature, Man and Society in the Twelfth Century* (1968)

M. D. Chenu, *Toward Understanding St. Thomas* (1964)

Alan B. Cobban, *The Medieval English Universities: Oxford and Cambridge to c. 1500* (1988)

David C. Douglas, *William the Conqueror, The Norman Impact Upon England* (1964)

Georges Duby, *The Age of the Cathedrals, Art and Society 980–1420* (1981)

Robert Fawtier, *The Capetian Kings of France: Monarch and Nation 987–1328* (1962)

Etienne Gilson, *History of Christian Philosophy in the Middle Ages* (1955)

Etienne Gilson, *The Philosophy of St. Thomas Aquinas* (1987)

Edward Grant, *Studies in Medieval Science and Natural Philosophy* (1981)

Charles H. Haskins, *The Renaissance of the Twelfth Century* (1927)

Charles H. Haskins, *The Rise of Universities (1957)*

Charles H. Haskins, *The Growth of English Representative Government* (1948)

C. Warren Hollister, *The Making of England, 55 B.C. to 1399* (1966)

J.C. Holt, *Magna Carta and Medieval Government* (1985)

Donald R. Howard, *Chaucer, His Life, His Work, His World* (1987)

David Howarth, *1066: The Year of the Conquest* (1981)

W.H. Jackson, *The Literature of the Middle Ages* (1960)

T.M. Jones, ed., *The Becket Controversy* (1970)

Amy Kelly, *Eleanor of Aquitaine and the Four Kings* (1950)

David Knowles, *The Evolution of Medieval Thought* (1964)

M.W. Labarge, *Saint Louis* (1968)

David L. Lindberg, *Science in the Middle Ages* (1978)

Frederic W. Maitland, *Constitutional History of England* (1908)

Emile Male, *The Gothic Image: Religious Art in France of the Thirteenth Century* (1973)

Joseph F. O'Callaghan, *A History of Medieval Spain* (1983)

Erwin Panofsky, *Gothic Architecture and Scholasticism* (1966)

Jaroslav Pelikan, *The Christian Tradition, vol. III: The Growth of Medieval Theology (600–1300)* (1978)

A. Pollard, *The Evolution of Parliament* (1926)

Michael Prestwich, *Edward I* (1988)

Betty Radice, trans., *The Letters of Abelard and Heloise* (1974)

H. G. Richardson and G. O. Sayles, *The English Parliament in the Middle Ages* (1981)

Joseph R. Strayer, *On the Medieval Origins of the Modern State* (1970)

W. L. Warren, *Henry II* (1973)

W. L. Warren, *King John* (1978)

CHAPTER 12

The Close of the Middle Ages

Time Line

1237	Mongols sack Moscow
1273	First Habsburg elected German King
1291	Swiss Oath of Eternal Alliance
1300	Beginning of rise of Ottoman Turks
1305–1377	Babylonian Captivity
1337–1453	Hundred Years' War
1346	English victory over French at Crécy
1347–1351	Black Death decimates Europe

1351	English parliament passes first in a series of Statutes of Labourers
1356	Emperor Charles IV issues Golden Bull
	English defeat French at Poitiers
1358	*Jacquerie* descends upon the Île-de-France
1370	Hanseatic League gains monopoly over Scandinavian trade
1378	Great Schism begins
	Uprising of *Ciompi* in Florence
1380	Russians defeat Mongols at the Battle of Kulikovo
1381	Peasants' Revolt in England
1399	Henry IV takes crown from Richard II
1414–1418	Council of Constance ends Great Schism
1415	Battle of Agincourt returns Normandy to English
	Hus burned as heretic
1429	Joan of Arc leads French forces to victory over the English at Orleans
1431	Joan of Arc burned at the stake
1438	Pragmatic Sanction of Bourges
1453	Fall of Constantinople
1455–1485	Wars of the Roses
1462–1505	Ivan the Great expands Muscovite realm
1483	Richard III deposes boy king, Edward V
1485	Henry VII begins Tudor dynasty after winning the battle of Bosworth Field

1520–1566	Apex of Ottoman Empire under Sulayman the Magnificent
1525	Peasants' War of 1525 in Germany
1529	Ottomans fail to capture Vienna

No age is free from woe, but the late Middle Ages were uncommonly afflicted by misery, death, and destruction. Climatic changes, famine, and the horrific Black Death that reduced Europe's population dramatically between 1300 and 1450 all had profound social, economic, political, and psychological consequences. Chronic warfare, recession, brigandage, and social unrest increased still further the Age's sense of insecurity.

In this era of crisis, familiar institutions lost their cohesiveness. The Great Schism split Christendom into rival camps, and a demoralized Church floundered in corruption as heresy flourished. The aristocracy paid lip service to the ideals of chivalry and feudal ties but conducted itself according to individual ambition, greed, and lust. Monarchs fought to consolidate their authority. A new peril, the Ottoman Turks, threatened to engulf Christian Europe from the east.

The fourteenth and early fifteenth centuries are best understood as a time of transition between an old, decaying civilization and a new world struggling to be born. This change occurred at different rates throughout Europe. In Italy, new forms had already taken root by this time, prompting historians to dub this period the Early Renaissance (see Chapter 13). Elsewhere in Europe signs of recovery and rebirth become evident beginning in the middle of the fifteenth century.

Economic and Social Dislocations

Depopulation

After three centuries of steady growth, Europe's population fell precipitously between 1300 and 1450. This decline relieved Europe's overpopulation and substantially increased per capita wealth. Historians estimate that during these one hundred and fifty years Europe lost more than half, perhaps even as much as three-quarters, of its inhabitants. Most areas did not regain previous levels of population until the sixteenth century, and some towns never recovered.

Factors in Population Decline

The chief cause of this depopulation was the devastating bubonic plague. Following the initial epidemic of 1347–1351, the "Black Death" periodically struck parts of Europe for the next 150 years. Changing weather patterns contributed to depopulation as well. A "Little Ice Age" emerged at the beginning of the fourteenth century and lasted until the end of the seventeenth century. Temperatures dropped and rainfall increased. As a result European farmers had to contend with shorter growing seasons, smaller harvests, and crop failures.

Famines

Since Europe's population in 1300 was close to exceeding its food supply, any decline in food productivity had disastrous consequences. In the winter of 1315–16 unseasonably cold and stormy weather caused crop failures throughout northern Europe. The Great Famine of 1315–17 claimed the lives of the weak and left the remaining population malnourished and highly susceptible to disease. It proved the first of a cycle of famines, because starving people consumed surplus grain they had stored for the next season's planting. Subsequent harvests rarely sufficed to feed the populace and still have enough left over for planting.

Warfare

Human destructiveness also took its toll on Europe's population during the late Middle Ages. The Hundred Years' War between Britain and France was particularly devastating because it was fought out not so much in pitched battles but rather by unpredictable raids upon castles and towns by combatants who lived off the countryside. Human life came cheap in this age of despair.

Effects of Depopulation

The impact of demographic change was felt in all aspects of life. The face of the land itself was transformed. Fields lay untilled, villages and churches were deserted, roads and bridges were devoid of maintenance. Elementary schools were closed for want of pupils.

Economic Consequences. Reduced populations left the depressed economy in disarray. Production and trade fell and labor grew scarce. Rulers were faced with the problem of securing needed revenues from a smaller tax base to conduct their lengthy wars. Their calls for higher taxes frequently led them into conflict with representative institutions.

Psychological Consequences. Drastic depopulation left its mark on the collective mentality of the age. Outside of Italy, a sense of loss and decay pervades late medieval culture. Art and literature are steeped in images of the leveling power of death, now realistically portrayed in all its most gruesome aspects—putrefying corpses, worms, and skulls and bones. A new image appeared in Western culture at the end of the fourteenth century, the *Danse Macabre*, or Dance of Death. It depicts a procession of people of all classes led by a skeleton or corpse, and probably evolved from a morality play danced in the streets at the time of the Black Death. Its lesson was clear—all human beings meet the same ignoble fate. People at the close of the Middle Ages regarded their lives with a profound pessimism that even the solace of religion did little to abate. This view of the late medieval epoch not as a prelude to the Renaissance but as a time of fading and decline was given currency by Johann Huizinga in his *The Waning of the Middle Ages* (1924). Not all historians share this perception of fourteenth- and fifteenth-century France and the Netherlands, however.

Plague

The dominant event of the fourteenth century was the appearance of the Great Plague. The disease, which most scholars identify as the bubonic plague, first appeared on European soil in October 1347 when trading ships from Caffa in the Crimea docked at the Sicilian port of Messina with a fatally stricken crew. Plague soon raged in Messina. From there it spread rapidly so that most of Europe was infected by 1350.

Mortality Figures

After the disastrous first assault of 1347-51, the plague returned frequently between 1361 and 1480 to claim new victims. Had the Black Death been limited to its initial epidemic, Europe's population would most likely have recovered its pre-plague level by 1380. Instead, the recurrence of plague three to five times per generation for the next hundred years ensured further depopulation. Governments sought to limit the plague's spread by passing laws concerning burial practices and public health care and by imposing quarantines, but none of these actions were truly effective. The disease eventually lost much of its virulence after 1480 for reasons that are not yet clear. Localized epidemics of the plague occurred, nonetheless, until late in the seventeenth century. Estimates of the death toll range from twenty million to fifty million Europeans.

Victims

The "Black Death," as it was later called, was a bacillus transmitted by infected fleas. It typically killed from twenty to fifty per cent of the inhabitants wherever it struck. In isolated places, such as in a cloister, it was not uncommon for all to die. In general, the plague had a greater impact in the crowded and unsanitary cities than in the countryside. Likewise the urban poor succumbed in greater numbers than did rich townsmen who were able to take refuge in the country. Years of malnutrition lowered the ability of Europe's poor to resist the disease.

Attribution of Causes

Devoid of theories for the causes and control of infectious diseases, fourteenth-century Europeans ineffectively combated the disease. Some blamed polluted air, while others claimed divine retribution for humanity's sins. In response some sought seclusion by fleeing to mountain retreats, while others quested for divine assistance by engaging in extreme ascetic exercises such as flagellation. As is often the case in troubled times, people sought scapegoats on whom they could blame their misery. Popular hysteria vented its rage against Jews, lepers, and sorcerers.

Labor Shortages and the Movement of Prices

The demographic upheaval of the fourteenth century had an immediate effect upon the late medieval structure of prices and wages. Whereas prior to the Great Plague land revenues generally exceeded the cost of labor, after 1348 this ratio was for a time reversed. The principal cause of this inversion was the severe shortage of labor following the

Black Death and subsequent plague pandemics. With fewer laborers to work the fields, production declined and food prices rose sharply. Income from land rent fell as decimated families were unable to cultivate normal acreages.

Consequences of Labor Shortage

The consequences of scarcity of labor were manifold. For the rural economy, it meant the demise of the traditional manorial system. Earlier the increasing role of money in the medieval economy had served to undermine the manorial structure of dues and services. Many landowners had found it more lucrative and convenient to lease (alienate) parts of their demesne to their serfs, and to hire laborers at cheap wages to perform duties demanded of serfs. Gradually the ties of mutual dependence that characterized the old manorial system disappeared. The Black Death and its accompanying drop in population greatly accelerated these trends. Landowners desperate to keep their fields cultivated were everywhere forced to make concessions to their peasants.

National Differences

Transition to an agrarian economy of wages and rents took place under somewhat varying circumstances in different countries. In France, for example, the lord alienated most of his lands but retained many of his former jurisdictional powers. In England, by contrast, the disappearance of labor services and its replacement with a cash relationship between the lord and his tenants was essentially complete by 1450. In Italy, the notion of regarding land primarily as an investment developed early in connection with the expansion of the city-state's control over its surrounding countryside.

Changes in Land Usage

The combination of high wages and the scarcity of labor encouraged farmers to shift from grain production or to convert lands to other uses requiring less labor or fetching a higher price. Sheep-raising became increasingly popular, especially in England, because it was less labor-intensive than farming and its products were much sought after. Italian landowners had already in the thirteenth century begun to plant olive trees, grapevines, and even rice, instead of grain to increase the land's profitability.

Advantages to Peasants

The peasantry were able to use the scarcity of labor to improve their social, economic, and legal status. Serfdom all but died out in Western Europe. Fearful that their peasants would run away to vacant lands or seek higher wages elsewhere, lords enfranchised serfs in exchange for a yearly or one-time payment. Commutation of labor services enabled the peasants to become masters of their own plot, deciding what plants to grow and how best to utilize the land. Inflation rendered their fixed rents less of a financial burden.

Disadvantages

Peasants too poor to purchase the leases of their own lands sunk to the level of hired workers. Inflationary conditions worked to the detriment of the nobility. Many nobles, particularly in France, were gradually impoverished by a long-term decline in the value of their fixed rents.

Urban Dislocations

The shortage of labor caused dislocations in the urban economy as well. Competition for the reduced number of artisans, craftsmen, and laborers substantially increased their bargaining power. Profits declined as the rise in wages outpaced that of the price of goods. Wages soared throughout Europe.

Attempts to Regulate Wages and Prices

In England, France, and elsewhere, governments stepped in to protect the interests of the ruling class by freezing wages and prices. To halt what appeared to them to be a revolutionary breakdown in the established order of things, the English Parliament passed the first Statute of Labourers that attempted to hold wages at pre-plague levels. It required that every able-bodied person under sixty without other means of support must accept whatever employment was offered. Changing jobs to seek better wages was forbidden. Employers and employees alike were penalized for giving or accepting higher pay. The French enacted a somewhat less stringent system of price control for the area around Paris. In the long run, however, these measures proved unsuccessful. In addition, the workers' sense of injustice at having their wages artificially held down contributed to the social unrest of the period.

Improved Production Methods

Other, more fruitful means were employed in order to deal with the crisis of the late medieval economy. The high cost of labor encouraged employers to organize their production methods along more rational and efficient lines. Another way to increase production with the same number of workers was to provide better tools or whenever possible to replace human with animal labor. Thus, the late Middle Ages witnessed the growth of capital investment in labor-saving devices.

Social Unrest

Social discord added to the misery of the declining Middle Ages. Until the end of the thirteenth century, open social revolt had been rare in medieval Europe. During the fourteenth and fifteenth centuries, however, antagonisms between social classes erupted into violence with alarming frequency.

Causes

Each of the uprisings—whether rural or urban in origin—bore a distinctly local character. Yet they also exhibited numerous traits in common that reflect the period's unusually severe conjunction of economic, political, and demographic conditions. Europe as a whole suffered under the combined weight of famine, war, pestilence, and crushing taxes. On the Continent, mercenary companies lived off the land, doing incalculable damage.

While every class was to some degree affected by these disasters, it was the poor who were least able to cope with them. Ironically, while the scarcity of labor and the breakdown of the manorial system worked to the advantage of the lower classes, this promise of better days ahead rendered the remaining social and economic inequities all the more intolerable. Resentment at unequal treatment was at the core of most of the social uprisings. With few exceptions (notably the Ciompi in Italy), they support the theory that rising expectations are more conducive to revolt than is abject poverty. Peasants and urban workers were willing to fight to retain the social and economic gains they had achieved in an age of rapid change.

Flanders

The disturbances inherent in the shift from a feudal to a capitalist economy made the small county of Flanders on the North Sea a hotbed of revolt for much of the fourteenth century. One of the most drawn-out and violent of the peasant revolts occurred there from 1323 to 1328. It began as a protest against the heavy taxes imposed upon the Flemish peasants following their country's defeat in a war with France. Wool workers from the cities of Bruges and Ypres joined the generally prosperous peasants of western Flanders in their battle against those who owned the land and industry. After five bloody years, the armed forces of the King of France finally suppressed the rebellion.

Relations between workers and employers were especially bitter in the great Flemish weaving cities of Bruges, Ypres, and Ghent because of the early introduction there of capitalist methods of industry. While the wool-workers had won the privilege of organizing in guilds, nothing could protect them from unemployment. Nor had they any real independence, given the economic power of their employers. Their sense of frustration exploded into revolt five times between 1348 and 1379 when a mass insurrection swept the land for three years. After 1384, with the coming to power of the dukes of Burgundy in Flanders and the decline of the Flemish wool industry, open rebellion ceased.

England—The Peasants' Revolt

The most famous instance of fourteenth-century rural discontent took place in England in 1381. The English Peasants' Revolt was directed as much against the national government as it was against the landowners. Its immediate cause was the imposition of new and heavy poll taxes upon every adult in 1377, 1379, and 1380. The government's attempt to collect the 1380 tax a second time because of insufficient funds triggered widespread resistance. Peasants in Essex and neighboring counties refused to pay. The confrontation rapidly escalated into violence.

Peasant Discontent. Underlying the peasants' antagonism was the persistent attempt of the English governing class to hold down wages by means of a series of Statutes of Labourers, beginning in 1351. Peasants who had prospered under the changing conditions of the age bitterly resented the efforts of government and landlords to limit wages, dredge up forgotten feudal dues, and levy excessive taxes. Other less fortunate peasants saw in rebellion a way to free themselves from the bonds of villeinage. The English peasants were motivated as well by a sense of the religious righteousness of their cause. One of their leaders, an itinerant priest named John Ball, had preached for two decades a radical version of Christian egalitarianism that condemned the rich.

March on London. The revolt culminated in a mass march by 20,000 rebels to London in June 1381. Sympathetic townspeople opened the city's gates to the invaders. A band of rebels laid waste to the homes of important officials, destroyed government records, and executed the two ministers most responsible for the hated poll tax. The killing and plundering continued for two days.

End of Revolt. Only the fourteen-year-old king, Richard II, seemed to have any influence over the mob. He bravely appeared before them several times and accepted their demands for the abolition of work services on the lord's demesne and the substitution of low rents as well as removal of the poll tax. When the rebel spokesman Wat Tyler was slain, Richard calmed the crowd by proclaiming himself their leader and then asked them to disperse. Amazingly, the peasants agreed to leave London. Once they did, their cause was lost. Richard reneged on his promises and all further acts of rebellion were quickly repressed.

Consequences of Revolt. The Peasants' Revolt failed to improve the conditions of the poor, although it did lay to rest the idea of taxing the entire English population directly. As with most such factional struggles, the absence of discipline and long-range programs from the beginning doomed the chances of the peasants.

France

In France, social unrest, though less organized than in England, proved equally bloody. In 1320 a mass of starving peasants in northern France, led by a monk and a defrocked priest, spread terror as they moved southward on an imagined crusade. Arriving in the Midi, the Pastoureaux, as they were called, slaughtered Jews there. When the movement threatened to undermine ecclesiastical authority, the pope had it suppressed.

In 1358, an even larger outbreak of peasant rage, the *Jacquerie*, descended upon the Île-de-France. Roused by hatred of the antiquated seigneurial jurisdiction and the various dues and monopolies still demanded by lords from their tenants, the French peasants lashed out with pillage and murder. The rural poor were especially resentful that the nobility did nothing to protect them from roving bands of mercenaries. The *Jacquerie* was savagely put down.

Italy

In the urban communes of northern Italy the sharpening of class conflicts was particularly acute. There, large textile industries using capitalistic methods of production had appeared early. These created a class of proletarian workers who lacked such advantages as guild membership and political participation. Historians cite the uprising of the Ciompi in Florence in 1378 as an early example of the savage class hatred generated by the rise of modern, capitalist society.

The Ciompi Revolt. The Ciompi, or wool carders, were the poorest workers in the great Florentine wool industry. They and other workmen were totally at the mercy of their employers for sustenance. When hard times hit the wool industry in the mid-fourteenth century, many thousands of workers lost their jobs. Because the merchants and entrepreneurs of the all-powerful wool merchants' guild controlled the government of Florence for much of the fourteenth century, they were able to pass legislation that regulated wages, prevented workers from forming guilds, and bound them to their jobs. A Florentine political crisis paved the way for general insurrection. Advancing upon city hall, the wool-workers demanded and received from frightened officials the right to form three new guilds and to have their leader participate in the new government. These reforms failed, however, to solve the problem of unemployment and the poorest workers remained disaffected. When they resorted to further violence, even the new proletarian government moved against them and abolished the guild of the Ciompi. Such divisiveness among the workers and the lack of effective leadership contributed to the fall of the new government after only forty-one days.

By 1382 Florence's ruling oligarchy had reestablished their hold and dissolved the remaining two wool-workers' guilds.

Germany

Elsewhere in Europe the revolts were less serious. In Germany outbursts of rural discontent culminated in the great Peasants' War of 1525.

Undermining of Authority

The widespread social unrest of the fourteenth century suggests another feature of the late Middle Ages—the weakening of accepted authority. Years of war, hardship, disease, and oppression had bred in the lower classes an aversion to the established orders of society and a willingness to fight to preserve gains made possible for them by the fluctuating economic and social climate. While none of the fourteenth century revolts accomplished any substantial change, they demonstrate the people's growing awareness that the inequalities and injustices of medieval society could be called into question.

Political Developments

The Hundred Years' War

Warfare was yet another scourge of the turbulent late Middle Ages. The most significant and prolonged of the many armed conflicts of the period was the Hundred Years' War. It pitted Europe's two strongest monarchies, France and England, against each other in a struggle to resolve the fundamental and longstanding issue of England's continental possessions. Ever since William the Conqueror created an empire that spanned both sides of the Channel, the English presence on the continent had bedeviled Anglo-French relations. At the opening of the fourteenth century, England held the large Duchy of Gascony (most of the old duchy of Aquitaine) in southwestern France as a fief of the French king.

Characteristics of the War

The Hundred Years' War is something of a misnomer, despite the fact that the conflict lasted for well over a century (1337 to 1453).

Unlike modern total wars, this one was frequently interrupted by long stretches of inactivity and periods of truce. Only occasionally did the participants engage in conventional pitched battles. After several initial disastrous defeats, the French typically avoided battle, while the English resorted to a combat tactic of *chevauchée*, or raid, in which towns were pillaged and inhabitants slain.

Causes of the War

A long list of grievances against the French as well as his own chivalric nature disposed England's young king, Edward III (reigned 1327–1377) to war. He resented France's support of Scotland in the wars he fought against his northern neighbor. Above all he sought to protect English economic interests in Flanders against French interference. The county of Flanders, a fief of the French crown, was an essential link in England's economic system. When the Flemish cloth workers revolted against their pro-French count in 1337, they looked to England for support. That same year the French king declared Gascony forfeit because of England's refusal to abide by the judicial decisions of its French overlord. Both of these circumstances propelled Edward III to assert his claim to the French throne, the declared cause of the hostilities that followed.

The last three Capetian kings had died without a surviving male issue. In 1328 an assembly of French barons handed the crown to a cousin of the last Capetians, Philip of Valois, who ruled as Philip VI (reigned 1328–1350). As a grandson of Philip the Fair, Edward III was in fact the nearest living male heir, but his inheritance had been passed through his mother. The Parlement of Paris invoked the supposedly ancient "Salic Law" to forbid inheritance through the female line. Edward's claim was substantial enough to serve as a pretext for war and to elevate a struggle of lord and vassal to one between rival claimants to the throne.

Initial English Victories

In 1338 Edward III easily invaded France through the Low Countries. A naval victory at Sluys in 1340 gave England control of the Channel for the next thirty-two years and ensured that all battles would be on French soil. In 1346 at Crécy and ten years later at Poitiers, a smaller English army equipped with accurate and rapid firing longbows won resounding victories over heavily armored French knights. These triumphs demonstrated the tactical superiority of the well-paid and well-drilled English army that relied upon a balance of mounted nobles and yeoman foot soldiers. Yet, the stout defenses raised by France's towns and the primitive state of English siege tactics ensured that the struggle would be a protracted one. In 1360 the French agreed to the Peace of Brétigny on terms favorable to the English.

French Counterattack

During the ensuing years of peace, the French king, Charles V (reigned 1364–1380), placed his considerable intellect at the service of his country. He transformed the French army into a paid and better-trained fighting force and obtained from the Estates General a much-needed tax on every French hearth. When war broke out again in 1369, a revitalized France won victories on land and at sea. At Charles V's death in 1380 England possessed only Calais and a narrow coastal segment from Bordeaux to Bayonne.

Civil Strife

The emergence in both countries of powerful factions that posed the threat of civil war complicated the final stages of the war.

England. In England, Richard II's (reigned 1377–1399) cousin, Henry of Bolingbroke, heir to the duchy of Lancaster, led a baronial rebellion that forced Richard to abdicate and awarded Henry the crown. Having succeeded by force, Henry IV's (reigned 1399–1413) own claim to the throne was open to attacks by rival noble houses. Parliament, however, was instrumental in winning support for the king's policies. It became the arena in which ambitious baronial factions grappled for power.

France. France too entered a long period of civil strife following Charles V's death. The new king, Charles VI (ruled 1380–1422), was only a youth when he ascended the throne. For much of his long reign, the powerful dukes of Burgundy and Orléans contended for control. Open civil warfare erupted in 1411. Thenceforth, the conflict between the Armagnacs and the Burgundians played an important role in shaping the course of events of the last phase of the Hundred Years' War.

English Victory at Agincourt

During the reign of Henry V (ruled 1413–1422), England regained sufficient strength to press again her claim to the French crown. Henry skillfully took advantage of the anarchic conditions in France to launch a large-scale invasion that met with resounding success at the battle of Agincourt in 1415. Once again the flower of French chivalry was cut down by a smaller army of English archers. Normandy once more fell into English hands.

Treaty of Troyes

In the name of Charles VI, who suffered intermittent fits of insanity, Philip the Good of Burgundy concluded the Treaty of Troyes with Henry V in 1420. It stipulated the marriage of Henry with Catherine, daughter of Charles VI, and declared Henry the rightful heir to the French throne. By its provisions the Dauphin (eldest son of a French king) was completely disinherited and doubt was implied of his legitimacy. Until Charles VI's death, Henry was to rule as regent with assistance from Philip of Burgundy. The provisions of the treaty would have meant the extinction of a separate French royal house had Henry V lived to complete his conquest of France.

Joan of Arc

The Treaty of Troyes did not, however, signal the end of the war. Territories south of the Loire, except for Gascony, remained loyal to the Dauphin. The bleak prospects of France and the Dauphin were soon altered by two significant events. In 1422 Charles VI and Henry V both died, leaving a nine-month-old baby, Henry VI (ruled 1422–1461), to inherit the thrones of both countries according to the Treaty of Troyes. For seven years the Dauphin tried unsuccessfully to get himself crowned since both Paris and Rheims lay in English hands. This situation was changed in 1429 by a peasant girl from Domrémy, on the border between France and the Duchy of Lorraine, who rekindled the French national spirit.

The story of Joan of Arc (Jeanne D'Arc) is one of the most enigmatic and inspiring tales of history. The slight biographical data on this complex heroine add to her mystery.

Joan's Victories. Convinced that she heard the voices of St. Margaret, St. Catherine, and the Archangel Michael, Joan believed that she was instructed by God to have the Dauphin crowned king. In 1428 she convinced the Dauphin Charles of his legitimacy and persuaded him to furnish her with an army. In May 1429 her army defeated the English at Orleans. Victory there was a turning point that galvanized French resistance.

Crowning of the Dauphin. Two months later, Joan accompanied the Dauphin through enemy territory to Rheims, the traditional French coronation site, and he was ceremonially crowned King of France (Charles VII).

Trial and Execution. Shortly after the coronation, Joan's misfortunes began. Failing to liberate Paris, she fell captive to the Burgundians in May 1430. They then sold her to the English, who turned her over to French church authorities sympathetic to England for trial as a witch and heretic. Towards the end of her long trial, Joan momentarily recanted but then reaffirmed the authenticity of her mystical visions. The judges were thus able to declare her a relapsed heretic, and they condemned her to death. Joan of Arc was burned at the stake in Rouen on May 10, 1431. Charles VII made no effort to save her, but twenty-five years later a royal court, at his behest, exonerated her of all charges of heresy and witchcraft.

Joan's Legacy. That a peasant girl could assume the guise of a knight and assert the truth of her visions without the intermediation of the Church was profoundly unsettling to established authority. Clearly, however, the phenomenon of Joan of Arc set in motion a gradual revival of French national energies that coupled feelings of patriotism with loyalty to the Valois monarchy.

Defeat of the English

Still the war dragged on, but the tide had definitely turned in France's favor. In 1435, the Duke of Burgundy deserted his English allies in exchange for cessions of French land and release from his oath of homage to Charles. A year later Paris was recaptured for the French king. Brutal fighting continued in the provinces. Between 1449 and 1451 the French regained Normandy. Victory in Bordeaux followed. By 1453 only Calais remained of England's once-extensive continental possessions. The Hundred Years' War had ended, although no formal treaty of peace marked its close.

Rule of Charles VII

Although desultory in youth, Charles VII (reigned 1422–1461) matured into an excellent administrator whose choice of able ministers earned him the sobriquet, "the Well Served." Under the king's guidance, these men instituted wide-ranging reforms that contributed to France's ultimate success in war and hastened its postwar recovery.

Military Reforms. In a series of ordinances issued between 1439 and 1451, Charles rebuilt the French military, thus freeing himself from reliance upon military service from his vassals. The new companies of 1,200 mounted men formed a standing army ever at the king's disposal to maintain order and put down revolt. This greatly strengthened the power of the French monarchy. Other military reforms recognized the tactical superiority of trained archers and improved France's artillery.

Financial Reforms. Charles's ministers worked to extend the monarchy's control over royal administration and to subordinate competing feudal sources of authority to the crown. Fundamental to this objective was securing the right to tax subjects without having to obtain approval from the Estates General each time. This was secured in 1439, when the Estates General voted to allow the king to levy a property tax, the *taille*, on a permanent basis. The clergy and nobility were exempt from the *taille*. Other taxes, such the *gabelle*, or salt tax, also became fixed royal levies at this time.

Religious Reforms. Another of Charles's reforms made him master of the French Church. The Pragmatic Sanction of Bourges of 1438 severely curtailed the pope's right to make ecclesiastical appointments and levy taxes in France. It enunciated a policy of virtual autonomy for the French Church known as Gallicanism.

Effects of the Hundred Years' War

The Hundred Years' War had a decisive effect on both England and France.

Effects on France. In France a century of warfare worked to the advantage of royal authority. Traditional feudal ties and localism gave way to an incipient nationalism and loyalty to the king. By war's end the French king enjoyed a standing army, a regular and permanent flow of taxes, and considerable freedom to operate without interference by the Estates General.

Effects on England. In England, by contrast, Parliament's role in funding the war helped it to grow in stature and influence. Because Parliament had earlier won the right to consent to all new taxes, the king was obliged to summon its members regularly in order to finance his wartime operations. At these frequent sessions the knights of the shire and representatives from the towns began to sit together separately from the nobles and high clergy in order to discuss money matters more freely. Thus originated the unique division of Parliament into the House of Lords and the House of Commons. From their meeting together the knights and burghers developed a cohesiveness and sense of common interest that gave the English Commons far greater powers than any other European lower house. In the future, England, shorn of its continental possessions, was free to cast her glance across the ocean. The great era of overseas exploration was about to dawn.

The Wars of the Roses

One of the most damaging legacies of over a hundred years of war was the growth of factionalism. In England peace abroad did not translate into peace at home. Instead, an internal power struggle for the throne between the noble houses of Lancaster and York plunged the country into civil war only two years after the end of the Anglo-French conflict.

Motives of Combatants

Fought ostensibly over a dynastic issue, the Wars of the Roses (1455–1485) were ennobled by no high purpose. They were an expression of the baronial age at its most morally bankrupt. The most powerful nobles all had their own bands of hired retainers who wore their lord's "livery" or uniform and who came to his aid in any quarrel. In return the lord "maintained" their interests in any legal dispute and paid them a fee. This system of "Livery and Maintenance" increased aristocratic power and contributed to the lawlessness of the age. The English baronage chose either the red rose of Lancaster or the white rose of York for reasons of personal greed, ambition, or desire for revenge. Allegiances changed rapidly. Death was often the price paid for being on the wrong side, and in thirty years of intermittent fighting, the English nobility came close to extinguishing itself. All semblance of good government was lost in the process.

Richard, Duke of York

The seeds of imminent civil war were sown in 1453 when Henry VI lapsed into a period of mental incoherence and Richard, Duke of York, became Protector of the Realm. As grandson of Edward III's third son, Richard's hereditary claim to the throne was even more direct, although through the female line, than that of the Lancastrians and he stood to inherit the crown at Henry's death. His role as Protector was short-lived, for in October of the same year, Henry VI's queen, Margaret of Anjou, gave birth to a son, Edward, and a year later the king regained his senses.

Displaced as Protector, Richard resorted to arms. At the Battle of St. Albans in 1455, the Yorkists recovered their predominance in the royal council. In 1460 Richard captured the king and declared himself the lawful heir to the throne, but shortly thereafter he was ambushed and killed by the Queen's forces.

Edward IV

Early in 1461, Richard's nineteen-year-old son defeated the Lancastrians and marched into London where he was acclaimed King Edward IV (reigned 1461–1470, 1471–1483). A month later he secured his title with another victory, and the ailing Henry VI fled to Scotland with his wife and child. Four years later Henry was taken prisoner and placed in the Tower of London.

Conflict with Warwick. Edward IV owed much of his success to his cousin, Richard Neville, Earl of Warwick. During the early years of his reign, Edward lived an indolent and dissipated life. He allowed Warwick ("the Kingmaker") a free hand to manage royal affairs. By 1464, however, Edward sought to free himself from Warwick's control. He earned the enmity of his benefactor by a secret marriage to Lady Elizabeth Woodville, a widow of no great distinction apart from her beauty. Edward further estranged himself from Warwick by bestowing favors and gratuities upon his wife's numerous kin.

Warwick's Alliance with French. In 1469 Warwick leagued with Edward's brother, George, Duke of Clarence, to oppose the king, and the two escaped to France. With support from France and the Lancastrians, Warwick invaded England in 1470 and restored Henry VI to the throne.

Edward's Return to Rule. Six months later, Edward returned as head of a small army which defeated Warwick. The "Kingmaker" lay dead on the field. Victory over the Queen's forces at Tewkesbury followed in early May 1471. The young Prince of Wales died in battle, and a few weeks later, Henry VI was murdered in the Tower of London. No obstacles remained to Edward IV's kingship. For the next twelve years, Edward IV ruled England with a firm hand. Royal ministers enforced justice throughout the realm and promoted a return to prosperity.

Richard III

Edward's untimely death at forty in 1483 exposed the crown to new attempts at usurpation. Edward's twelve-year-old heir and namesake, Edward V (ruled April 9–July 6, 1483), proved no match for his scheming uncle, Richard, Duke of Gloucester, who wrested control of the regency from the boy's mother and her Woodville clan.

Usurpation of Throne. After declaring the young King illegitimate, Richard deposed Edward V and incarcerated him and his brother in the Tower. He then assumed the throne as Richard III (reigned 1483–1485).

Character. Richard was neither the hunchback monster of evil that Shakespeare portrayed nor the unblemished, misunderstood king depicted by his apologists. Richard had loyally served his brother, Edward IV, and was an excellent soldier. Nonetheless, his cruel and ruthless temperament led him to use any means in order to accomplish his designs.

The Princes in the Tower. When the two young Princes in the Tower disappeared, rumors that they had been murdered were not answered, and it is highly probable that Richard did in fact order their deaths. What he did not calculate, however, was the cost to him in terms of popular support his action entailed.

Henry VII

A new pretender of Lancastrian descent, Henry Tudor, Earl of Richmond, was already searching out allies for his own reach for the crown. Henry Tudor's hereditary claim as a legitimate successor to the English throne was weak, since his sole right lay in his mother, who was a descendant of Edward III's son, John of Gaunt, by his mistress, Catherine Swinford. Parliamentary legislation legitimized the couple's offspring, but specifically excluded them from royal succession. The deaths of Henry VI and his son in 1471, however, had placed Henry Tudor at the head of the Lancastrian faction. He was thus the obvious leader of the opposition to Richard III. Four depositions between 1227 and 1483 had shown how easily one could get rid of an unpopular or inept king.

Battle of Bosworth

After an earlier, abortive attempt, Henry Tudor landed in Wales in August 1485 with a small army. All those who had come to despise Richard III rallied to the invader. Other magnates refused to fight for either side. At the decisive battle of Bosworth Field, Henry's Lancastrian forces defeated the last of the Yorkist kings. Richard was slain in combat. Henry then advanced to London where he was formally crowned.

End of the Wars of the Roses—Beginning of Tudor Dynasty

Parliament added its sanction to what was considered God's judgment, as rendered in battle, in regard to Henry's right to rule. His marriage to a daughter of Edward IV united the warring houses of Lancaster and York to form a new dynasty—the Tudors. The victory ended the civil wars, restored national unity, and heralded a new age.

German Particularism

The development of strong national monarchies, so apparent in France, England, and Spain at the close of the Middle Ages, never manifested itself in medieval Germany. For a number of reasons Germany's monarchs failed to consolidate their power on a national scale.

A Weak Monarchy

The elective kingship left ultimate control in the hands of the German princes who could easily shift alliances in return for promises of money or preference. French or papal interference often influenced the electors' choice. In 1273 the princes bestowed the throne upon a relatively obscure count, Rudolf of Habsburg (ruled 1273–1291), whose family held lands mostly in Switzerland. The German monarch could not levy taxes or demand military service outside his own lands and thus posed little threat to the princes' independence.

The imperial post held one prerogative, however, which made it personally lucrative for its occupant: the right to confer any vacant or confiscated fief upon whomever he wished. Thus Rudolf and subsequent emperors used this imperial privilege to enrich their own families. With the acquisition of the duchy of Austria, the locus of the Habsburg domain began to shift eastward. Rudolf built the Habsburgs into a powerful princely house by judicious acquisition of lands. At his death the Electors chose a non-Habsburg, Adolf of Nassau (ruled 1292–1298), as king. In 1298, the crown passed again into Habsburg hands when Rudolf's son, Duke Albert of Austria, deposed Adolf. The Habsburgs were unable, however, to gain permanent possession of the imperial title until 140 years later.

The Golden Bull

The German princes cemented their victory over the elected emperors in 1356 by an agreement called the Golden Bull. Issued by Emperor Charles IV, it laid the foundations of an imperial structure that endured until 1806. By creating a seven-member electoral college, it ended disputed imperial elections. The Golden Bull further recognized the territorial independence of the German princes and balanced their rights against those reserved to the emperor.

In their own territories the princes enjoyed virtual sovereign powers, but the Bull stipulated that no territory could be subdivided. Succession in the domains of the lay princes was determined by primogeniture to prevent further fragmentation. The Golden Bull confirmed the actual shift in power from the emperor to the electoral princes that had occurred since the death of Frederick II.

Centralization Within States

Political power in Germany was thus held by particularistic groups. The movement to consolidate sovereign authority occurred not on the national level but rather within the territorial states. It was the Electors and other great princes who benefited from the social and economic trends of the later Middle Ages that favored centralization. In their struggle to increase their territorial power, the princes frequently encountered resistance from both the free towns within their jurisdiction and from a new class of "knights" (*Ritter*).

The Ritter

The rise of a knightly class from the old, unfree *ministeriales* was a development unique to Germany. Originally bound to their lords, the *ministeriales*' service as officials or armed retainers was so in demand that they were gradually able to win personal freedom and grants of land. By the end of the thirteenth century they had melded with the old German nobility to form a new aristocracy. The strong influence of the *Ritter* within their own localities frequently obstructed the princes' attempts to raise armies, levy new taxes, and centralize their control.

Town Leagues

The German towns exerted considerable financial weight to further their own interests and safeguard civic rights from princely interference.

Reasons for Uniting. As centers of vitality and commercial wealth within an ailing empire, towns were a lucrative source of funds for the emperor or lord upon whose land they were situated. Yet, without the protective shield of a strong national government, towns were forced to fend for themselves. Thus they banded together in leagues for mutual defense and used their collective wealth to acquire trading privileges.

The Hanseatic League. The most famous league of towns was the Hanse of the north German trading cities. Formed in the mid-thirteenth century by a small nucleus of Baltic towns, the Hanseatic League evolved into a powerful mercantile association of around seventy members and had its own fleet. Headed by Lübeck, the Hanse negotiated with foreign governments to acquire exclusive trading rights, and it established trading posts as far distant as London and Bruges and at

Bergen in Norway and Novgorod in Russia. With its victory over the King of Denmark in 1370, the League held a virtual monopoly of the Scandinavian trade. The League maintained its hegemony over Baltic and north-Atlantic trade until the sixteenth century. Competition from English and Dutch merchants as well as political and economic changes within Germany brought about its decline.

Swiss Independence

While the princely territories and self-governing towns remained quasi-autonomous bodies within the loose imperial structure, segments of the tottering Empire broke away completely.

The Swiss Confederation. The rise of Switzerland as an independent state dates to the thirteenth century when fear of Habsburg domination compelled the Forest Cantons (i.e., districts) of Uri, Schwyz, and Unterwalden to league together for mutual defense. Their famous Oath of Eternal Alliance *(Bund)* of 1291, provided the foundation of the Swiss Confederation. The cantons of Lucerne, Zurich, Glarus, and Berne joined the Confederation by 1353. A common geography, hatred of Habsburg interference, and a mutual interest in profiting from Alpine trade helped the league to maintain its unity. In 1499 Switzerland was formally released from imperial jurisdiction.

Canton Government. The cantons evolved a unique form of government that left most political power in the hands of each state in the confederation. This stymied the growth of centralized administration and led to frequent quarrels among the cantons. Yet, subject to no king or titled aristocracy, the Swiss stood alone among Europeans at the close of the Middle Ages as founders of a loose union of free states. Warfare honed the Swiss into superb soldiers and for the next three hundred years many earned their living as mercenaries.

German Conquests

For the German Empire, the loss of Switzerland was partially compensated by new territorial gains in Prussia. Since the early thirteenth century the military order of the Teutonic Knights had steadily extended the Empire's eastern frontier along the Baltic coast. Conquering and then forcibly converting the Slavic Prussians, most of whom were enserfed, the Teutonic Knights built castles and founded new towns. They then encouraged German settlers to move into the area as far north as the Gulf of Finland. A rich trade developed as the new Baltic towns joined the Hanseatic League.

Poland and Lithuania

The Teutonic Knights' merciless expansion brought them into conflict with the neighboring lands of Poland and Lithuania to the south and east. In 1386 hatred of a common enemy motivated the two nations to unite their crowns by marriage. The new Polish-Lithuanian Commonwealth became the largest state in Europe at the time. At the Battle of Tannenberg (Grunwald) in 1410, Polish and Lithuanian forces disastrously defeated the Teutonic Order. In 1466 its conquests in West Prussia were ceded to Poland while East Prussia became a Polish vassal.

Ottoman Expansion

While the Teutonic Knights were bringing Christianity to the Slavs along the Baltic shore, a new wave of Turkish invaders penetrated the Balkan peninsula under the banner of Islam.

Early Conquests

As one of many small, nomadic tribes on the Eurasian steppelands, the Ottoman Turks were pushed westward by the expansion of the Mongols. Settling within the Seljuk empire in the northwest corner of Anatolia, the Ottomans gradually absorbed other Turkish clans. Led by a masterful chief, Osman I, from whom the tribe took its name, they broke free from Seljuk overlordship in 1300. A year later they won their first important battle against Byzantine forces near the city of Nicomedia. By mid-century large tracts of Seljuk and Byzantine territory in Asia Minor had fallen under Ottoman control.

Gains in the Balkans

Following their defeat at the hands of the Turks, the Bulgarian Tsar and the Byzantine Emperor became vassals of Sultan Murad I (reigned 1359–1389) in 1371. Defeat at the Battle of Kossovo in 1389 reduced the king of Serbia to vassal as well. Four years later Sultan Beyazid I (reigned 1389–1402) captured the Bulgarian fortress city of Nicopolis and acquired control of the lower Danube.

Of the Eastern European states, only Hungary proved capable of resisting the Ottoman tide. Its king sounded new appeals to the West for aid. France responded with a crusading army composed of knights from all over Europe. Overly confident, licentious, and unable to agree upon a unified command, the French knights and their allies were cut down by Beyazid's forces at Nicopolis in 1396.

Decline and Fall of Constantinople

Substantial as this Turkish victory was, its cost kept Beyazid from marching into Hungary. Instead, the Ottomans pressed their assault upon Constantinople. In 1402 the city was saved from the Ottomans by the arrival of yet another wave of nomadic invaders from the east. A revived Mongol-Turkic empire led by Tamerlane defeated the Ottomans at Ankara and imprisoned Beyazid in the summer of that year.

Lack of Support from West. This timely intervention merely postponed the day of reckoning for the once-great Eastern Empire. Reduced now to little more than its capital city and hemmed in by Ottoman territory on three sides, Byzantium's only outlet was by the sea. For the next fifty years it clung to a precarious independence at the pleasure of the sultan. Efforts to rally support from the West went largely unheeded. The western nations were too embroiled in their own conflicts to take full advantage of the Ottomans' temporarily weakened condition.

Conquest by Muhammad II. With the accession of Sultan Muhammad II (reigned 1451–1481), who craved conquest, the Eastern Empire's days were numbered. On April 11, 1453, Muhammad bombarded Constantinople with the largest cannon then in use. Eight thousand stalwart defenders faced an army of approximately one hundred thousand men and a huge Ottoman fleet. For seven weeks the forces stood firm behind the city's ramparts. Finally, Muhammad devised a way to slip some boats into the city's protected harbor, the Golden Horn, by transporting them overland on wood rollers. In the early morning of May 29, after hours of desperate battle, Turkish soldiers forced their way into the city through an entry that had been mistakenly left open. By midday Constantinople had fallen, its last emperor, Constantine XI, slain while bravely defending the walls. Amid slaughter and looting Muhammad II transformed the great Christian church of Hagia Sophia into a mosque. The capital of a thousand-year-old empire became the Turkish city of Istanbul.

Significance of Byzantine Collapse. Contemporaries regarded the fall of Constantinople as a catastrophe of unmitigated proportions. It marked the end of an almost 1500-year tradition of imperial rule. Because the event had tremendous symbolism, scholars have long viewed the dissolution of the Byzantine Empire as a turning point in the history of the West. In practical terms, however, historians no longer believe that the Empire's collapse was a necessary precondition for the rebirth of classical humanism in Renaissance Italy or for the launching of the great age of exploration.

Causes of the Empire's Long Survival. Of particular interest to modern historians is the related question of why the Byzantine Empire survived for as long as it did. As a political and economic entity, the Byzantine Empire suffered from disintegrating forces for over three hundred years before its final fall. The palace intrigues, assassinations, and full-scale revolts that characterized Byzantine political history from the start became even more damaging as the empire's financial and military strength slowly waned. Greatly reduced in size, the Empire nonetheless clung to its existence thanks to a number of factors. Foremost among them was the continuity of rule provided by the empire's well-trained and centralized bureaucracy. The largely homogeneous Greek population of the later empire added to its cohesiveness, as did a prosperous economy. The powerful Orthodox Church was a strong defender of imperial institutions. Finally, the awe and reverence accorded to the successor state of Rome gave the Eastern Empire an aura of permanence that worked to its advantage for many years.

Continuity in Eastern Empire. While the inauguration of Ottoman rule in 1453 imposed many immediate changes upon the former empire's population, it nonetheless preserved important continuities with Byzantine tradition. The conquerors tolerated the orthodox Christianity of their Greek subjects as well as their Graeco-Roman law, so long as they paid tribute and furnished men for the Ottoman army and civil service. The Sultan assumed the role of protector of the Orthodox Church, and Muhammad II regarded himself heir to an imperial legacy that reached back to ancient Rome. Istanbul emerged as a great cosmopolitan city with Christians and Jews playing a large part in its flourishing commerce and trade.

Factors in Ottoman Success

The Ottomans' success in building an empire stemmed partly from the weakness and disunity of their enemies and partly from their own skills as fighters and organizers of conquered territory. The Turkish invaders were particularly adept at assimilating native talent into their system either by forced levies of men or by the incentive of tax-free status accorded to Muslim converts. In their conquest of the Balkans, the Turks did enslave large numbers of Christians who refused to convert, although there were usually opportunities to purchase one's freedom. A combination of ruthlessness and tolerance served the Ottomans well in creating a new state.

Government

Byzantine as well as Oriental and Islamic influences shaped the Ottoman theory of state. Theoretically the sultan was answerable only to God, but in practice his conduct was guided by his council of state, the Divan, and by Muslim sacred law. To reduce the threat of sedition, it was customary for each new sultan to slay all his brothers. Gradually the sultan became aloof and withdrawn from daily affairs of state and left them to his highest civil servant, the grand vizier. All civil servants owed absolute loyalty to the sultan and were considered slaves.

The Ottomans developed a unique system of recruiting to fill their bureaucracy. They converted some of their prisoners of war to Islam and enlisted them in a new infantry corps, the Janissaries ("new troops"). Trained as professional fighters and given special privileges, they became an elite body within Turkish society. Fanatically attached to the sultan, they later became rivals for his power. During the fifteenth century the Ottoman practice of levying Christian boys to become Janissaries (known as the *devshirme*) was regularized and extended to civil government. The boys were removed from their families, taught Turkish, and forced to accept the Muslim faith. The ablest of them could rise high in the Ottoman ruling class.

Muhammad II

The Ottoman Empire expanded dramatically during the century

after the fall of Constantinople. Muhammad II consolidated his rule over all of Asia Minor and most of the Balkans. This area remained the historic nucleus of Ottoman strength into the nineteenth century. Venice fought a long and disappointing war (1463–1479) against Ottoman expansion and lost several important possessions in the Aegean. Muhammad II expelled the Genoese from their colonies in the Crimea and made the Tartar khan his vassal. In Europe, however, Ottoman progress was checked by Christian victories at Belgrade and on the island of Rhodes.

Beyazid II

Pressure against the West eased during the reigns of the next two sultans. Beyazid II (ruled 1481–1512) faced civil wars at the beginning and end of his reign and failed in most of his attempts to increase Ottoman holdings.

Selim I

Beyazid's son, Selim I (reigned 1512–1520) enlarged the empire to nearly double its size.

Conquests of Arab Lands. Turning eastward Selim defeated the Persians in 1514 and annexed a large segment of territory. Two years later Ottoman troops overran Egypt and Syria, putting an end to Mameluke rule there. Henceforth the Ottoman sultans bore the title and spiritual responsibilities of the Caliphate.

Extent of Empire. Selim's conquests changed the complexion of the empire. Its western borders now ringed the entire eastern end of the Mediterranean and included large numbers of Arabic Muslims. The empire became a sea power and permitted pirates or corsairs to sail the Mediterranean under its auspices.

Sulayman I

Selim's son and successor, Sulayman I (ruled 1520–1566), the Magnificent, brought the empire to its apex of strength and splendor. The sultan was a generous patron of the arts and instituted important legal, military, administrative, and educational reforms as well. Ottoman architecture reached its peak.

Threat to Europe. Europe quaked as Ottoman troops conquered Belgrade in 1521 and seized Rhodes from the Knights Hospitalers the

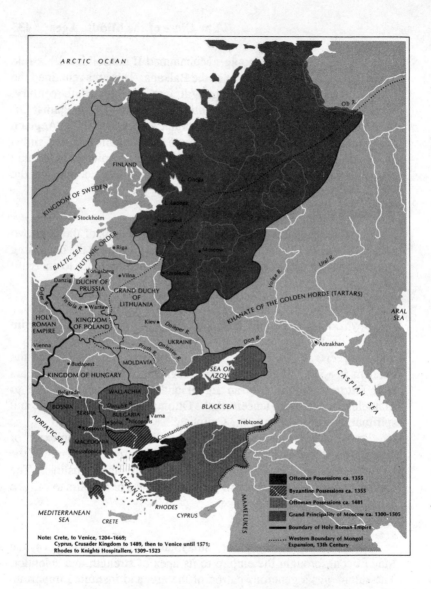

ARCTIC OCEAN

FINLAND

KINGDOM OF SWEDEN

• Stockholm

BALTIC SEA

TEUTONIC ORDER

Riga

Königsberg

Danzig

DUCHY OF PRUSSIA

Vilna •

GRAND DUCHY OF LITHUANIA

• Warsaw

Oder R.

Vistula R.

KINGDOM OF POLAND

HOLY ROMAN EMPIRE

Vienna

• Budapest

KINGDOM OF HUNGARY

Belgrade

BOSNIA

SERBIA

Danube R.

WALLACHIA

BULGARIA

Sofia • Nicopolis • Varna

Kossovo

MACEDONIA

Thessalonica •

ADRIATIC SEA

AEGEAN SEA

MEDITERRANEAN SEA

CRETE

RHODES

CYPRUS

Kiev •

Dnieper R.

UKRAINE

Pruth R.

Dniester R.

MOLDAVIA

SEA OF AZOV

Constantinople

BLACK SEA

Trebizond

MAMELUKES

Smolensk •

L. Onega

L. Ladoga

Novgorod •

• Moscow

Don R.

Volga R.

KHANATE OF THE GOLDEN HORDE (TARTARS)

Ob R.

Ural R.

• Astrakhan

ARAL SEA

CASPIAN SEA

Ottoman Possessions ca. 1355

Byzantine Possessions ca. 1355

Ottoman Possessions ca. 1481

Grand Principality of Moscow ca. 1300–1505

Boundary of Holy Roman Empire

Western Boundary of Mongol Expansion, 13th Century

Note: Crete, to Venice, 1204–1669;
Cyprus, Crusader Kingdom to 1489, then to Venice until 1571;
Rhodes to Knights Hospitallers, 1309–1523

The Ottoman Empire and Russia to 1505

following year. An annihilating defeat of the Hungarians at Mohács in 1526 led to the eventual annexation of most of Hungary.

Failure to Take Vienna. By 1529 the Turkish army was outside the gates of Vienna. Sulayman, however, had underestimated the strength of Viennese resistance and with winter near and supplies running out, the Ottomans were compelled to withdraw. The failure of the Ottomans to take Vienna counts as one of history's turning points. Although the city was periodically menaced by Turkish invaders until 1683, the Ottoman state was never again as formidable as it was under Sulayman the Magnificent.

Diplomatic Affairs. A diplomatic as well as military genius, Sulayman recognized other ways to influence the balance of power in Europe. Thus in 1536 he made common cause with the French king, Francis I, against their mutual Habsburg enemy. This alliance remained the keystone of Franco-Turkish affairs for three hundred years. Sulayman's court became a center of lavish diplomatic activity.

Beginning of Ottoman Decline

At the end of his long life, Sulayman's fortunes began to change. A quarrel over the succession eliminated his most competent heirs. His army won and then lost the island of Malta. To compensate for this loss, the Sultan set out for Hungary, where he died during an inconclusive campaign. The Ottoman Empire had passed its summit. Ahead were centuries of slow decline brightened by brief periods of Turkish strength.

Appanage Russia and the Rise of Moscow

The thirteenth, fourteenth, and first half of the fifteenth centuries were a period of division and decline in Russian history. The disintegration of the Kievan state and the Mongol invasion left Russia devastated and without a focus for political unity. The country broke into a number of independent principalities each with its own unique problems and development. Historians use the term "appanage," which refers to the territory of an individual prince, to describe Russia of this period. In contrast to the active commerce of the Kievan state, appanage Russia was primarily agricultural. It displayed some but not all of the characteristics of Western feudalism. In general the bonds of vassalage were weaker, military service less important, the institution of chivalry absent, and the peasantry freer than in the West. Scholars are thus divided over whether or not the concept of feudalism applies at all to this phase of Russian development.

Mongol Rule

A key aspect of the appanage period was the dominance of non-Russian over Russian peoples.

Genghis Khan. Early in the thirteenth century a supremely gifted leader, Genghis Khan, united the nomadic Mongol tribes and led them on a wave of conquest. Russia tasted defeat at the hands of the Tartars, as Europeans called Mongols, in 1223.

Batu. In 1237, a Mongol army led by Genghis Khan's grandson, Batu, returned for more permanent conquests. The Russian princes were unable to mount a united defense. Batu's army stormed across Russia, burning cities and slaughtering entire populations. It reached deep into Europe, defeating Germans, Poles, and Hungarians before the death of Ogedai in 1241 compelled Batu to return for the election of a new Great Khan. At its height, the Mongol empire was the largest ever assembled.

Effects of Mongol Occupation. Batu's successful campaign placed all of Russia under Mongol sway. His Russian lands became part of the khanate of the Golden Horde (the Kipchak Khanate) with its capital at Sarai. After the initial destructiveness of conquest, the Mongols withdrew from active participation in Russian affairs. They exacted tribute, required obeisance, and gave each prince a *yarlyk,* or charter, confirming his right to rule. The degree to which more than two centuries of Mongol dominion retarded Russian development is a hotly debated issue in Russian history today. Some claim it caused a complete break between Russia and Western civilization, while enhancing Asian cultural influences. Most scholars think that Russia suffered a cultural decline under the Mongols. In two areas, however, native wooden architecture and icon painting, appanage Russia produced superlative results.

Western Russia

Lithuanian and Polish influences played an important part in the history of western Russia. The people of the region, who evolved into the Ukrainians (Little Russians) and the Byelorussians (White Russians) differed ethnically and linguistically from the Great Russians of the north and northeast. The Mongols' march of destruction through western Russia left it weakened and prey to the expansionary designs of Poland and Lithuania. During the fourteenth century Volynia became a part of the growing Lithuanian state while Galicia fell under Polish rule. After the dynastic union of Poland and Lithuania in 1386, Polish culture and Roman Catholicism made themselves felt, especially among the upper classes. As in neighboring Poland and Hungary, the noble class in western Russia was extremely strong and frequently disregarded princely authority. Until the end of the fifteenth century the Polish-Lithuanian state presented a serious challenge to Moscow's drive to unite the Russian people.

Novgorod

After the ninth century the northern city of Novgorod became a leading commercial center, and its status improved dramatically with the decline of the Kievan state. The city was capital of a vast princely territory that came to include most of northern Russia, stretching from the Arctic Ocean to the Ural Mountains. Its sparse soil, however, was unable to maintain a large population.

Trade. Located near the eastern Baltic Sea, Novgorod controlled the northern trade. It exported such materials as fur, wax, and honey, derived from the great Russian forests in exchange for western manufactured goods and metals.

Prince Nevskii. Novgorod also acted as a bastion against western encroachments. Its most famous prince, Alexander Nevskii (ruled 1246–1263), won major battles against the Swedes and the Teutonic knights. Apart from paying tribute, Novgorod suffered little from the Mongol overlordship thanks largely to Nevskii's astute recognition of the futility of resistance in this case.

Aristocratic Rule. Princely authority did not develop to its fullest extent in Novgorod. Beginning in 1136, the city made contracts with its princes that strictly limited their sphere of action. Instead Novgorod was ruled by a group of wealthy patrician families who exercised their power through the *veche*, or town council of all free householders. The government grew more oligarchical during the fourteenth and fifteenth centuries, reflecting wide disparities between the rich and the poor. Class antagonisms undermined Novgorod's chance to lead in the unification of Russia.

Moscow

The mantle of leadership passed to a new and relatively unknown city. Moscow first emerged as a walled town in the mid-twelfth century. It lay in the Russian northeast near the older settlements of Rostov and Suzdal, which had been important under the Kievan state.

Natural Advantages. Despite its early obscurity, Moscow possessed certain advantages that help explain its rapid rise to preeminence. The task of uniting Russia was made easier by Moscow's location in the geographic and ethnic heart of European Russia. Surrounded by Russian territory, it did not have to face constant attacks, especially from the West. Further, its position on the Moscow River near the headwaters of the Oka, Volga, Don, and Dnieper Rivers afforded the city a fluvial network along which to conduct trade and to expand politically. Its soil, though not as rich as that of the southeast, was productive enough to support a growing population. Dense forests provided shelter and a wide variety of goods.

Strong Princely Government. The fact that Moscow was situated in a frontier area had an important influence on the growth of princely power there. Because the city and surrounding countryside were newly settled, there was little time for a boyar or merchant class to entrench itself in city politics. The new settlers looked to the prince for protection and aid. Moscow was blessed with a long line of able and practical princes descended from Daniel, the youngest son of Alexander Nevskii. The princes took advantage of every opportunity—marriage, inheritance, service agreement, purchase, foreclosure, conquest, and colonization—to expand and consolidate their holdings. Moscow broke with the Kievan tradition of dividing inheritances and rotating the succession among brothers. Instead, the eldest son inherited the lion's share of the principality and passed it down to his son. This arrangement reduced civil conflict, provided continuity of leadership, and maintained the integrity of the Muscovite domain.

Aggrandizement Under Mongols. The emergence of a strong

prince played a decisive role in enabling Moscow to take the lead in the "gathering of Russia," as the process of reunification is called. This is clearly evident in Moscow's relations with the Golden Horde. The Mongol invasion had severely battered the northeast. Moscow itself was sacked in 1237. Yet, the shrewd Muscovite princes turned Mongol domination to their advantage. By obedient behavior and heavy bribes, Ivan I (reigned 1328–1341) won for himself and his successors the right to be called "grand prince" and to collect tribute for the Mongols from the other Russian princes. The Khans even awarded Moscow with entire principalities that had fallen in arrears on their tribute payments.

Battle of Kulikovo. Content to remain subservient while the Mongols held the upper hand, Moscow was the first to attack once signs of weakness appeared. A coalition of princes headed by Moscow defeated the Mongols at the battle of Kulikovo in 1380. While foreign rule endured for another century, the Russian victory greatly added to Moscow's prestige as a national leader.

Alliance with Orthodox Church. Moscow's special link with the Russian Orthodox Church proved extremely helpful in enhancing the principality's stature. The head of the Russian church, the metropolitan, had traditionally resided in Kiev. With the breakup of the Kievan state, the metropolitan lacked a fixed see and traveled instead from city to city. In 1328 Ivan convinced the metropolitan to settle permanently in Moscow. During the appanage period the Russian Church was one of the few remaining symbols of Russian national unity. By making Moscow the ecclesiastical capital of the land, the Church lent the weight of its authority to that city's quest for political unification.

Ivan the Great. Ivan I's successors continued his work of patiently enlarging the Muscovite domain. This task was nearly completed during the long reign of Ivan III (ruled 1462–1505). Known as "the Great" for his shrewd statesmanship, Ivan III succeeded in absorbing two of Moscow's most serious rivals, Novgorod and Tver, as well as a host of smaller principalities and towns. Even the once-powerful Mongol empire bowed before Moscow's rising tide. After 1480 all Russian obligations to the Tartar Khan were ended. In 1500 Moscow's victorious army reclaimed large segments of former Kievan lands from their Lithuanian overlord.

Byzantine Alliance. As architect of a newly unified Russian state, Ivan III sought to provide it with an ideology befitting its heightened stature. His marriage to Sophia Palaeologus, a niece of the last Byzantine emperor, made him heir to a wealth of Byzantine ceremonies and symbols. He adapted the Byzantine two-headed eagle and began using the titles "*tzar*" (from the Latin, *Caesar*) and "autocrat" (from the Greek, *autokrator*).

Autocratic Rule. Ivan elevated the role of the grand prince to one of imperial majesty and detachment. Under his direction Italian artists transformed Moscow's ancient fortress, the Kremlin, into a splendid residence for the new "tzar of all Russia," as he termed himself. As such, Ivan promulgated in 1497 a new law code, the first since the eleventh century to apply to the whole land.

With Ivan III's reign, the appanage period of Russian history drew to a close. The Muscovite princes had accomplished the "gathering of Russia" unaided and at the expense of local political authority. Moscow's methods of conquest and centralized rule set Russia on a path of autocracy.

Decline of Papal Power

The Babylonian Captivity and the Great Schism

Profoundly disquieting changes in the nature and influence of the late medieval church cast a pall upon the fourteenth century. Philip IV's humiliating arrest of Boniface VIII in 1303 marked the beginning of a new era in church-state relations.

Trend Toward Secularization

Rising national monarchies increasingly challenged the medieval ideal of a universal Church headed by an omnipotent pope. To keep pace with the growing powers of the secular states, the late medieval papacy adopted their methods. It centralized its administration and devised means to maximize its financial gain. It used its powers of excommunication and interdict more freely to enforce compliance. Thereby it gravely undermined the Church's moral authority.

The Papacy at Avignon

The decline of the papacy accelerated after Boniface's death. To assure its docility, Philip IV drew the papacy even tighter into the French fold by securing the election of a French archbishop as pope in 1305. Clement V (served 1305–1314) abandoned Rome, where factional strife imperiled his safety. Instead, he gathered around himself a predominantly French curia, and established papal headquarters at Avignon in Provence. While not technically a French possession, the city lay within Philip's sphere of influence. From 1309 to 1377, seven French popes resided at Avignon. This era is generally called the Babylonian Captivity, suggesting that like the ancient Jews held captive in Babylon, the Church was unable to escape French control.

Loss of Papal Prestige

During its years at Avignon, the papacy suffered a troubling loss of prestige. Too close association with the interests of one nation-state jeopardized the Church's claim to universality. England, Germany, and Italy resented conforming to the fiscal demands and autocratic pronouncements of popes who were clearly subservient to French policies.

Money-Raising Devices

French interference in papal affairs, however, was not the only reason for the burgeoning anticlericalism of the time. The Avignon popes were sorely in need of funds to support their luxurious court and pay for an enlarged bureaucracy. Turbulent conditions within the Papal States, a traditional source of income, meant that popes had to spend more money supporting mercenary troops in Italy than they received in revenue from the land. Thus the Avignon popes sought new revenues and effected administrative reforms for efficiency. Building on the foundations laid by their predecessors, they reorganized the judicial, financial, and administrative structure of the Church.

Exploitation of the powers of the Church for financial gain led to many abuses and heightened discontent. Taxes such as "tenths," one-tenth of ecclesiastical income, that had originally been designated for a specific purpose such as a crusade, were converted into a permanent source of papal income. Simony, or the sale of offices, and plural holding of benefices by clerics were rampant. During the years at

Avignon, the popes greatly expanded their right to provide candidates for a majority of vacant benefices. Prior to the fourteenth century many church offices had remained elective or were filled by the secular ruler or local patron. Broadening its right of provision added enormously to the papal treasury. Office-seekers often had to pay the pope to gain appointment and then again as much as one- third to a full year's income (annates) upon assuming office. Failure to pay subjected one to the fullest extent of Church discipline.

Attempts to Return to Rome

These developments appalled many devout people within the Church, who called for the swift restoration of Rome as papal head-quarters. However, Italy was plagued with political turmoil and some questioned whether a pope would be safe from his enemies there. In response to intense public pressure, Urban V essayed a return in 1367, but he withdrew to the more hospitable Avignon after three years of residence. In January 1377 Gregory XI made his way to Rome at the urging of the mystic, Catherine of Siena. His death there fifteen months later resulted in a disputed election that further undermined the prestige of the papacy.

Disputed Papal Election

Controversy erupted over a successor. The French cardinals broke into two camps over their choice while the Roman populace called for an Italian, if not a Roman pope. For centuries Rome's prosperity and importance had been allied with that of the Church. The removal of the papacy to Avignon had deprived the city of its most important source of revenue and the Roman people were determined to prevent its recurrence. The college of cardinals had little choice but to elect a compromise candidate, the Italian Archbishop of Bari, as the new pope. Urban VI (served 1378–1389) turned out to be an unfortunate selection. His vituperative language and violent temper alienated many cardinals, especially the French. When he refused to return with them to Avignon, they schemed to depose him.

The Great Schism

In August 1378, the cardinals declared the election of Urban invalid on the grounds that they had voted under duress. The Roman crowd had clearly appeared threatening. Yet, the cardinals first raised this charge of intimidation four months after the actual event in response to Urban's subsequent behavior.

Two Popes. In September 1378, the cardinals elected Robert, the French bishop of Geneva, to the papal office. His selection was another ill-advised one. Robert was hated throughout Italy for participating in the massacre of thousands of Italians at Cesena a year earlier. As Clement VII (served 1378–1394), he reestablished his papacy at Avignon in 1379 but failed in his attempts to dislodge Urban VI at Rome. As a consequence, two popes contended for the allegiance of Western Christians. For nearly forty years, Catholic Europe suffered the divisive effects of the Great Schism. Each pope claimed to be the genuine one and excommunicated his rival as the Anti-Christ. Each had his own college of cardinals and filled vacant benefices with his own appointees. Each depended on the support of secular allies who accorded recognition along nationalistic lines.

Confusion and Disarray. The existence of two popes not only created confusion about the state of humanity's salvation, but also threw the finances of the Church into disarray. With his tax base cut in half, each pope made increasingly severe fiscal demands upon his constituents. Antipapal sentiment reached a high point during the years of schism. Even the pious were demoralized by the situation, for the legal positions of the two popes were nearly equal and neither would agree to step down. Various suggestions were offered as possible means to end the schism. One of the most promising was the idea of convening a General Council.

The Conciliar Movement

The notion that a General Council of prelates and laymen should play an active role in the governance of the Church antedated the Great Schism.

Conciliar Theory

In 1324 Marsilius of Padua, an Italian physician and political theorist, published his great work, the *Defensor Pacis*. According to Marsilius, all authority derived from the people; the people were empowered to make laws while the ruler was responsible only for their execution. As applied to the Church, Marsilius's theory held that the clergy was merely one class within the community and that secular government was superior to papal authority. He contended that true authority to decide upon matters of faith and doctrine resided with the whole body of believers as expressed in a General Council. Marsilius's contemporary, William of Ockham, also advocated the conciliar theory as a means of checking a tyrannical pope.

Calls for a Council

As the Great Schism wore on, people became convinced that the popes were incapable by themselves of resolving the crisis and cleansing the Church of its fiscal and other abuses. Scholars at the University of Paris took the lead in providing theoretical justification for convening a General Council to heal the schism even without papal sanction. In 1409, the College of Cardinals of each pope agreed to meet together at Pisa in an attempt to restore unity. The Council of Pisa, however, only further complicated matters by electing a new pope without successfully deposing his rivals. Western Christendom was now headed by three claimants. At this juncture, a new and convincing leader emerged in the person of the Holy Roman Emperor Sigismund (ruled 1433–1437). He persuaded John XXIII (Baldassarre Cossa), who had been elected pope at Pisa after the death of the Council's first choice, to summon a council.

The Council of Constance

The Council of Constance remained in session from 1414 to 1418 amid great pomp and ceremony. It addressed first an issue upon which there was the greatest unanimity, the extirpation of heresy. The Council voted to execute the reformer Jan Hus of Bohemia as a heretic despite the safe-conduct pass he had received from the Emperor himself. It then moved on to the question of membership and organization. Unlike earlier councils, it decided to include lay representatives and divide the

Council along national lines, with each nation receiving one vote. This reduced the influence of the numerous Italian delegates. After much behind-the-scenes activity in which the lay princes played a significant part, the Council succeeded in ending the triple schism and restored the papacy to Rome. It tried John XXIII on charges that included murder, incest, and sodomy, and deposed him in 1415. Gregory XII abdicated and finally in 1417 the Avignon pope, Benedict XIII, was shorn of his remaining supporters and deposed. The Council then elected a new pope, Martin V (served 1417–1431), of Roman origin.

The Post-Council Church

The Council of Constance represented a triumph for the conciliar movement. It asserted its supremacy over all earthly authority including that of the pope. By the decree, *Frequens*, it resolved that new councils should meet periodically to address issues of faith and church policy.

Obstacles to Conciliar Supremacy

In retrospect, however, the Council was not an unqualified success. The martyrdom of Hus served to spread rather than to extinguish the flames of heresy. Conflicting national interests prevented the Council from dealing in a truly effective way with the fiscal and moral corruption of the Church. Finally, Martin V and his successors gradually repudiated the conciliar theory and reasserted the supremacy of the papal office. Martin V shrewdly exploited national rivalries and negotiated separate agreements with the rulers of several nation-states in order to forestall a joint attack upon the pope's broad fiscal and other powers.

Gains and Losses for Papacy

The trend of the times in both secular and ecclesiastical politics was toward greater centralization. This favored the growth of papal autocracy over the broader representation of government by General Council. Thus, by the mid-fifteenth century, the papacy had reconsolidated its position of supremacy within the Church. A century of turmoil had, however, irreversibly eroded the medieval papacy's claim to superiority over temporal affairs. Growing in wealth and power, secular governments were now ready to challenge the pope on a broad range of issues.

Precursors of the Protestant Reformation: Wycliffe and Hus

In certain quarters resentment against the abuses of the Church spilled over into heresy during the fourteenth and early fifteenth century. The moral corruption, financial avarice, and spiritual confusion engendered by the Babylonian Captivity and the Great Schism contributed to a general questioning of the fundamental doctrines of the Catholic faith. Two figures, John Wycliffe and Jan Hus, stand out among the many minor heretical groups and mystical sects that flourished in the fourteenth century. Their unorthodox ideas were pregnant with meaning for the future of the Church.

Wycliffe

John Wycliffe (c.1328–1384) was an Oxford theologian, Scholastic philosopher, and popular preacher. His writings and sermons gave voice to the growing mood of anticlericalism within England during the second half of the fourteenth century. In the 1360s, Wycliffe served as the king's chaplain and won a reputation for his attacks upon English clerics for venality, absenteeism, immunity from civil justice, and immoral behavior. He represented the English crown at Bruges in its negotiations with the papacy in 1374 over the issue of papal taxes. This was a time when war with France drained the English treasury, making taxes to a foreign pope all the more onerous. In fashioning his defense of the superiority of secular over spiritual authority in temporal affairs, Wycliffe's line of reasoning led him to ever more heretical conclusions.

Wycliffe's Teachings. Wycliffe's two most important treatises, *On Civil Dominion* and *On Divine Dominion*, redefined the notion of dominion. He used this new concept to dismantle many of the basic ideas and practices of the late medieval Church. He denied the need for priestly administration of the sacraments and held that no intermediary was needed between God and the individual saved by his grace. He came to reject the Catholic dogma of transubstantiation, which holds that the bread and wine of the Eucharist are miraculously and entirely transformed into Christ's body and blood. To purify the Church, Wycliffe proposed the abolition of confession, excommunication, pilgrimages, indulgences, and the veneration of relics. Since, according to Wycliffe, the entire Church hierarchy from the pope on down is not needed for one's salvation, he called for the disestablishment of the priesthood in England. This would encompass the return to secular hands of property formerly endowed to the Church, and the exclusion of clerics from temporal office-holding. In Wycliffe's view, God granted power over earthly affairs entirely to the state.

Later Life. Wycliffe's ideas proved too radical for his times. Threatened with arrest by the pope in 1377, Wycliffe escaped conviction as a heretic for several reasons. The English climate of opinion at the time was antagonistic to papal interference. Wycliffe enjoyed for many years the protection of John of Gaunt, the powerful Duke of Lancaster. Finally, Wycliffe's theories were cast in abstract, metaphysical terms that somewhat obscured the extremity of their import. By the end of 1378, however, his increasingly subversive pronouncements clearly exceeded the anticlericalism of his supporters among the English nobility. He and his followers were removed from Oxford in 1382 and many of their theological arguments condemned. Nonetheless, Wycliffe was allowed to spend the remaining two years of his life in peaceful retirement

The Lollards. Wycliffe's teachings did not die with him. During his lifetime he had attracted the support of a group of "poor priests" who went from village to village preaching to the people in the vernacular. His followers came to be known as Lollards. It was they and not Wycliffe alone whom historians now credit with producing the first complete translations of the Bible into English. Wycliffe may have contributed to it in part and this version bears his name. At any rate, he believed that the Bible was authoritative and should be accessible to all.

Influence of Wycliffe and Lollards. During its early years, Lollardy seems to have appealed to members of the English upper classes as well as to the common people, who responded especially to its doctrine of clerical poverty. The majority of the English were not ready, however, to embrace its rejection of so much of the traditional church. In 1401, Parliament enacted a statute condemning heretics to death. The Lollard movement lost most of its supporters among the landed classes thereafter and persecution drove it underground. Because of the scarcity of evidence, historians are at odds over whether Lollardy did in fact survive until the sixteenth century to form a bridge between Wycliffe's doctrine and the English Reformation. Nonetheless, Wycliffe's belief in the individual's direct accountability to God alone was a key notion in all later Protestant thought.

Hus

On the Continent the direct influence of Wycliffe's ideas can be more easily traced. The Czech reformer, Jan Hus (1369?–1415), was familiar with Wycliffe's writings and espoused many of his ideas. He shared Wycliffe's view of the Church not as a priestly hierarchy but as a body of all those who were predestined to be saved. Likewise he believed in the supremacy of the Bible as an infallible guide to a good Christian life. He probably did not go as far as Wycliffe, however, in denying transubstantiation.

Like Wycliffe, Hus denounced the vices of the clergy in his homeland. At Prague, his simple but effective sermons won him a devoted following. Hus's religious message contained a strong nationalistic element. After years of German domination, the Czechs within Bohemia were awakening to a sense of their own national identity. Thus when the Archbishop of Prague attempted to prevent Hus from preaching in 1409 because of his defense of Wycliffe, many Czechs interpreted the ban as a challenge to their national aspirations.

Excommunication and Martyrdom. In 1412 the schismatic Pope John XXIII excommunicated Hus for his attacks upon the sale of indulgences to finance the pope's war with the King of Naples. Hus left Prague in order to spare the city from the threatened interdict. For the next two years, he traveled around Bohemia and wrote his most important theological works.

The emperor, Sigismund, urged Hus to appear before the Council of Constance to defend his views and even gave him a safe-conduct pass. Sigismund's brother Wenceslas, as King of Bohemia, had been Hus's protector, but the emperor himself was determined to rid the land of heresy. The Council, in one of its initial actions, had condemned all of Wycliffe's writings. Thus, when Hus refused to renounce his belief in some of Wycliffe's doctrines, the Council found him guilty of heresy, and in 1415 he was burned at the stake.

Influence of Hus and Hussites. Hus's martyrdom as well as that a year later of his friend, Jerome of Prague, enraged his Czech followers. Violence broke out between the Hussites and the Catholic Church in 1419. Shortly thereafter Wenceslas died. The Hussites refused to recognize Sigismund as heir to his brother's throne unless he accepted their Four Articles of Prague (1420) that called for free preaching, allowing laymen to partake of wine as well as bread in communion, confiscating excess church property, and prosecuting such clerical sins as simony in the civil courts. Sigismund responded by declaring a crusade against the Hussites. The Hussites rallied an army led by Jan Žižka, which repeatedly turned back far larger forces of mounted soldiers for over a decade. They employed the tactic of drawing their wagons into a circle from which they shot at their enemy with the relatively new weapon of guns. From being a defensive war, the Hussites began raiding forth as far away as the Baltic.

Hussite Split. Despite victory, the Hussites found themselves at odds. The moderate wing, the Utraquists, was centered at Prague and held to the Four Articles of Prague. The more radical Taborites at the town of Tabor denounced property-holding and serfdom and rejected the doctrine of transubstantiation. They believed in the Second Coming of Christ and the imminent end of the world. Mostly peasants, they formed the mainstay of the Hussite army.

In 1431 the Council of Basel invited the Hussites to work out a peaceful settlement of their conflict with the Church. The Utraquists were reunited with the Catholics and together they defeated the Taborites at the Battle of Lipany in 1434. Discord soon broke out between Catholics and Utraquists, however, and Hussite views continued to flourish in Bohemia until they were incorporated within the Protestant Reformation less than a century later.

The late Middle Ages were undeniably a period of economic, social, political, and religious distress for most of Europe. Severe weather conditions resulted in widespread crop failures. Many of the young and infirm died, while malnutrition lowered the remaining populace's resistance to disease. The Black Death killed an estimated one-third to one-half of the population. Depopulation had disruptive effects on the economy. Without adequate labor to till the fields, food prices rose. Chronic violence added to the perilous nature of the age. For much of the time, England and France were engaged in the Hundred Years' War over the issue of England's continental possessions. The civilian population suffered greatly from enemy raids and attacks by lawless brigands. Social unrest, as exemplified by the English Peasants' Revolt or the rising of the Ciompi in Italy, broke out with greater frequency than in the past. Even in religion, the period was a troubled one. Rising national monarchies challenged the Catholic Church's claim to supremacy over temporal affairs. Its position as a universal institution was gravely compromised by the move of the papacy to Avignon under French influence and by the subsequent Great Schism. Unable to cleanse itself of corruption, simony, and other abuses, papal prestige declined substantially.

Yet, this focus on the negative aspects of the age obscures its more creative side. Especially in Italy, as is shown in the next chapter, the period from 1350 to 1500 coincided with the flowering of the Renaissance. In addition some of the long-term consequences of the age's calamities were ultimately beneficial. For example, scarcity of labor improved the condition of the peasants, and serfdom all but disappeared in Europe. In this transitional time, old forms coexisted with new ones.

Recommended Reading

Philippe Ariès, *Western Attitudes Towards Death: From the Middle Ages to the Present* (1974)

Jerome Blum, *Lord and Peasant in Russia from the Ninth to the Nineteenth Century* (1967)

A.R. Bridbury, *Economic Growth, England in the Later Middle Ages* (1962)

Norman F. Cantor, *Medieval History: The Life and Death of a Civilization* (1969)

E.P. Cheyney, *The Dawn of a New Era, 1250–1453* (1936)

P. Coles, *The Ottoman Impact on Europe* (1968)

F. Dvornik, *The Slavs in European History and Civilization* (1975)

L. Elliot-Binns, *History of the Decline and Fall of the Medieval Papacy* (1967)

J. L. I. Fennell, *Ivan the Great of Moscow* (1961)

Wallace K. Ferguson, *Europe in Transition* (1962)

Jean Froissart, *The Chronicles of England, France, and Spain* (1961)

H. A. R. Gibb and H. Bowen, *Islamic Society and the West* (1950)

Frances Gies, *Joan of Arc: The Legend and the Reality* (1981)

Robert S. Gottfried, *The Black Death: Natural and Human Disaster in Medieval Europe* (1983)

I. Grey, *Ivan III and the Unification of Russia* (1964)

Denys Hay, *Europe in the Fourteenth and Fifteenth Centuries* (1966)

Johann Huizinga, *The Waning of the Middle Ages* (1924)

E. F. Jacob, *Henry V and the Invasion of France* (1947)

G. Leff, *Heresy in the Later Middle Ages* (1967)

Emmanuel Le Roy Ladurie, *Montaillou: The Promised Land of Error* (1978)

Bernard Lewis, *Istanbul and the Civilization of the Ottoman Empire* (1973)

P. S. Lewis, *Later Medieval France: The Polity* (1968)

Philip Lindsay and Reg Groves, *The Peasants' Revolt, 1381* (1950)

William H. McNeill, *Plagues and Peoples* (1976)

Millard Meiss, *Painting in Florence and Siena after the Black Death* (1951)

Roger B. Merriman, *Suleiman the Magnificent, 1520–1566* (1966)

M. Mullett, *Popular Culture and Popular Protest in Medieval and Early Modern Europe* (1987)

A.R. Myers, *England in the Late Middle Ages* (1952)

E. Pears, *The Destruction of the Greek Empire and the Story of the Capture of Constantinople by the Turks* (1903)

Edouard Perroy, *The Hundred Years' War* (1965)

Michael Prawdin, *The Mongol Empire, Its Rise and Legacy* (1940)

N. Riasanovsky, *History of Russia* (1969)

Charles Ross, *Richard III* (1982)

Charles Ross, *The Wars of the Roses: A Concise History* (1976)

Steven Runciman, *The Fall of Constantinople, 1453* (1969)

M. Spinka, *John Hus: A Biography* (1968)

Barbara W. Tuchman, *A Distant Mirror: The Calamitous Fourteenth Century* (1978)

G. Vernadsky, *The Mongols and Russia* (1953)

Marina Warner, *Joan of Arc: The Image of Female Heroism* (1981)

B. Wilkinson, *The Constitutional History of Medieval England 1216–1485* (1948–1964)

P. Wittek, *The Rise of the Ottoman Empire* (1938)

Philip Ziegler, *The Black Death: A Study of the Plague in Fourteenth Century Europe* (1969)

CHAPTER 13

The Renaissance

Time Line

c. 1428	Masaccio leaves frescoes in Brancacci Chapel unfinished at his death
1434	Rise to power of Medici in Florence
1450–1535	Sforzas rule Milan
1454–1456	Gutenberg publishes his *Bible*
1469–1492	Florentine culture flourishes under Lorenzo de' Medici
c. 1475	Venetians begin to paint in oils
1494	French troops invade Italy
1498	Savonarola burned as heretic
1490s–1520s	High Renaissance
1498	Da Vinci completes fresco of *Last Supper* in Milan
1508–1512	Michelangelo paints frescoes in Sistine Chapel
	Raphael decorates the *Stanze* in Vatican
1509	Erasmus's *Praise of Folly*
1516	Thomas More's *Utopia*
1527	Rome sacked by Emperor Charles V's army
1532	Machiavelli's *The Prince* published
c. 1533	Rabelais writes first of books on Gargantua and Pantagruel
1543	*Concerning the Revolutions of Heavenly Bodies,* by Copernicus, published
	Vesalius's *Concerning the Structure of the Human Body* published

| 1595 | First complete edition of Montaigne's *Essays* |
| 1626 | St. Peter's Cathedral completed |

Perhaps no other period in European history save the twentieth century holds greater fascination for the general public than does the Renaissance. From the early fourteenth century until the late sixteenth century, first in Italy and later north of the Alps, there occurred a quickening of interest in the classical civilizations of Greece and Rome. This was accompanied by a burst of creative energy and self-confidence.

The term "renaissance," a French word for rebirth, is applied to this epoch. First used by the sixteenth-century Italian art historian Giorgio Vasari to describe changes in the fine arts, the term "rebirth" was subsequently applied to developments in other fields. It was only in the nineteenth century, however, that historians began to refer to "The Renaissance" as a distinct historical period. In an influential study, The Civilization of the Renaissance in Italy, *the nineteenth-century Swiss scholar Jacob Burckhardt drew a sharp contrast between the cultural darkness of the Middle Ages and the awakened knowledge of self and nature of the Renaissance. In this idea he was following the Renaissance's own perception of its cultural superiority over the medieval past.*

Today historical research tends to downplay Burckhardt's notions of the uniqueness and separateness of the Renaissance. Scholars have employed the title "renaissance" for other historical epochs, and they have sought the foundations of the Italian Renaissance in the develop ments of an earlier period. Renaissance culture is no longer viewed in isolation from its social, political, and economic context. This search for continuity and roots in the flow of history has even led some scholars to deny that there was a Renaissance. However, few historians are willing to go this far.

Renaissance artists and writers were aware themselves that they were participants in a new and distinctive cultural era. While knowledge of its classical heritage never truly disappeared in the West, Renaissance scholars brought new concerns and interest to ancient Latin and Greek texts and discovered in them new values and meaning.

Harking back to the examples of classical civilization, Renaissance culture esteemed the individual's actions in this world and people's ability to shape their environment to meet their needs. This affirmation of human power sets the Renaissance apart from its medieval predecessor and allies it with the modern age.

Many different currents and countercurrents were at work in Europe during the fourteenth, fifteenth, and sixteenth centuries. This chapter explores the growth of new ideas, the revival of classical learning, and the explosion of creative activity that began first in Italy and spread throughout Europe after 1450. Subsequent chapters will focus on the Protestant Reformation and Europe's overseas expansion, events that owe some of their character to Renaissance individualism, but that also ultimately brought Renaissance culture to an end.

The Political, Social, and Economic Background

The Italian Renaissance took place against a very specific political, social, and economic background.

Italian Political Divisions

The most salient feature of the political landscape of Italy in 1300 was its division into small, self-governing city-states. This was especially true of northern Italy. Italy had been first among European nations to experience a revival of trade and growth of towns after the economic stagnation of the early Middle Ages. These free cities, or communes, advanced their autonomous status by gaining charters and written constitutions during the long struggle between the papacy and the German emperors. The failure of the Hohenstaufen empire to unify Italy in the mid-thirteenth century determined the fragmented nature of Italian political life thereafter.

Republican Government

Until the end of the thirteenth century, most Italian city-states enjoyed a form of republican government. Unlike their northern peers, Italian nobles were not excluded from commerce and maintained urban as well as country residences. Republican government was incapable, however, of curtailing factional strife. Most cities were divided into antagonistic groups. At the top of the social hierarchy were the feudal nobles and merchants (the *grandi*). The majority of the population (the *popolo*, or people) were artisans and shopkeepers and belonged to the guilds. Below them were the industrial workers (the *popolo minuto*), who were excluded from guild membership. Typically, if the *popolo* succeeded in wresting power from the *grandi*, internal divisiveness prevented them from holding onto it.

Rule of Despots

Beginning in the late thirteenth century, many Italian communes entrusted unlimited authority to a single individual in their attempts to restore the peaceful conditions necessary for doing business. A number of despots governed in a brutal, unscrupulous manner. While some had been invited to assume control by one or another of the factions within the commune, others gained power through murder, payment, or military conquest. Many despots succeeded in making their rule hereditary and some acquired legal recognition by purchasing imperial titles. To cast an aura of legitimacy over their rule, despots employed scholars and artists. Renaissance artists have left us a number of revealing portraits of these powerful, violent men.

War Among Cities

Warfare between the city-states and factional conflicts within their walls characterized Renaissance Italian political life. At first, city-state rivalries hinged on old Guelph (pro-papal) or Ghibelline (pro-imperial) sympathies, or on trade. By the fifteenth century a new pattern emerged that involved the conquest and complete submission of many of the smaller city-states by the larger ones. By 1450 Italy was dominated by five territorial states: the Duchy of Milan, the Republics of Venice and Florence, the Papal States, and the Kingdom of the Two Sicilies. A key factor in the creation of these large territorial states was the use of mercenary soldiers. Fear of popular revolution led many Italian city-states to transfer responsibility for defense from their citizen militia to hired mercenaries. These were commanded by soldiers of fortune called *condottieri* whose sole motive for fighting was monetary profit.

Milan

Milan offers the clearest illustration of the movement from

republican government to despotic rule that characterized many smaller Italian city-states.

Strategic Location. Situated on the fertile Lombard plain, Milan grew rich because of its strategic location on the crossroads of transalpine trade. Milan's influence extended over a number of cities in the Po valley.

Republican Rule. Republican government there had always rested on a delicate balance of aristocratic and democratic elements, and these were easily disrupted by feuds and Guelph-Ghibelline clashes. Beginning in the middle of the thirteenth century, both the popular and noble parties turned to despotic leadership to end civil strife.

Visconti Rule. In 1277, the pro-Ghibelline magnates successfully contrived to place a member of the Visconti family in power. From that date until 1447, with one brief interruption, Visconti despots ruled Milan. They systematically transformed the city into a large and wealthy territorial state with control over Lombardy, half of Tuscany, and several cities in the Papal States. Under the shrewd Gian Galeazzo Visconti, the Duchy became one of Italy's most powerful states and seemed on the verge of uniting the north of Italy. His sudden death in 1402 prevented the latter and many of his conquests were lost.

Sforza Rule. When the Visconti line ran out in 1447, Milan attempted to restore republican government. Social and political chaos again necessitated the rule of a strong man. This time the city turned to a family of *condottiere*, the Sforzas. For the most part the Sforzas provided the city-state with able rule. Crafty, ruthless, and arbitrary, they nonetheless encouraged the arts and letters and promoted public works. Ludovico Sforza (ruled 1494–1499) became the patron of da Vinci. During his reign French troops invaded Italy in 1494. He was expelled in 1499 and the Duchy of Milan fell into Spanish hands in 1535.

Florence

Florence, the cradle of Renaissance culture, held onto the pretense of republican government long after power had actually passed into the hands of the city's wealthiest and most powerful family, the Medici. Florence emerged as a self-governing commune in the twelfth century.

In the next century the city grew rich as an important center of banking, trade, and the wool industry.

Guelph Rule. Politics in the city-state was turbulent from the start. The struggles for control between the Guelph and Ghibelline parties were particularly venomous. Although both parties were essentially aristocratic, the Guelphs were more willing to include wealthy merchants and other rich non-nobles. By the last quarter of the thirteenth century, the Guelphs were solidly in control and their opponents had been banished and their properties confiscated. To cement their victory, the Guelphs revised the Florentine Constitution. Through their memberships in the seven greater guilds of merchants and bankers, the Guelphs elected the city's chief executive officers from their own ranks. The fourteen lesser guilds could hold only minor offices. The Ordinances of Justice, as Florence's new constitution was called, created a tangle of conflicting councils, short-term office holders, and unrealistic demands for near unanimity in decision making. Its weakened central authority left Florence prey to further political turmoil and ultimately to one-man rule.

Political Factions. By the opening of the fourteenth century, the Guelph party had divided into warring camps, the Blacks and the Whites. The poet Dante was among those who were exiled from the city for their pro-White sympathies after the Blacks seized power in 1302. For the next 132 years Florentine rule oscillated between a merchant oligarchy and the more democratic rule of the lesser guilds.

Cosimo de' Medici. Eventually, financial and military losses left the oligarchy vulnerable. Exploiting this opportunity, Cosimo de' Medici rose to power in 1434. The Medici were probably the wealthiest family in Italy with their own bank and large interests in the woolen industry. Although Cosimo ruled Florence virtually unopposed for thirty years, like a political boss he exercised power behind the scenes without substantially altering Florence's republican structure. His policy of heavily taxing his wealthy political opponents won him popular support as did his building programs and munificence toward such artists as Donatello, Ghiberti, and Brunelleschi.

Lorenzo de' Medici. The great cultural flowering in Florence under the Medicis has been compared to the Golden Age of Periclean Athens. The Medicis' genuine interest in and financial support of learning and the arts clearly contributed to Florentine culture. No member of the family typifies devotion to the arts and letters better than does Lorenzo de' Medici (ruled 1469–1492). Called *il Magnifico* (the Magnificent), Lorenzo was himself a laudable scholar, poet, and musician as well as statesman. He became patron to an important group of thinkers, including Marsilio Ficino and Pico della Mirandola, and was friend to a number of the finest painters and sculptors of the Renaissance. He supported many building activities as well. His youthful charm and extravagant public festivals and parades gained for him the affection of the people. His diplomatic skills helped maintain a balance of power that kept Italy relatively peaceful. Lorenzo's greatest weakness was demonstrated in the sphere of business, the rock upon which the Medicis' success had been built. His inattention to financial matters and his lavish spending led his banking empire to the brink of insolvency.

Republican Rule. In 1494, two years after Lorenzo's death at 43, an invading army of Charles VIII of France swept down the Italian peninsula. Lorenzo's son was compelled to hand over the city-state's most important fortresses, including Pisa. This action infuriated the Florentines and they expelled the Medici and reestablished republican rule.

Savonarola. For four years the Florentine government was dominated by Savonarola, a Dominican friar who had inveighed against the Medicis' worldly corruption and vices. Holding no political office, Savonarola used his spiritual influence over the populace to convince the republican government to pass stricter laws and to enforce morality. His extreme puritanism and attacks against the papacy, however, soon turned people against him. Excommunicated by the pope, he was burned at the stake in 1498 as a heretic. The Medici swiftly reasserted their hegemony and maintained it, with one short republican interlude, until the eighteenth century.

Medici Influence. The influence of the Medici family extended far beyond Tuscany. The line produced three popes (Leo X, Clement VII, and Leo XI) and two queens of France (Catherine de' Medici and Marie de' Medici). In 1569 the title of Grand Duke of Tuscany was bestowed upon the Medici. By this time, however, Florence's political power and artistic glory were past.

Venice

Of the three great territorial states in north Italy, the Republic of Venice was an exception to the Renaissance trend of one-man rule. In this lovely city of 118 islets on the Adriatic Sea, a powerful merchant oligarchy retained political control for centuries. They exercised power through the Great Council, which was limited in the thirteenth century to the descendants of approximately 200 families. This patrician class was able to provide Venice with a strong and efficient government conducive to trade.

Trade. Situated at a commercial crossroads between East and West, Venice began in the tenth century to secure trading privileges in a number of ports along the Mediterranean. Trade with the Levant enriched Venice. Venetian ships were built in a state-owned arsenal (founded in 1104) and even sailing schedules were determined by the government. After the defeat of Genoa, its major commercial rival, Venice was in undisputed control of the lucrative Mediterranean trade by 1380.

Expansion. Venice then embarked on a policy of conquest on the Italian mainland to safeguard the flow of trade over the alpine passes. At the expense of Milan it extended its territorial confines to include Padua, Verona, Vicenza, and the province of Friuli. Yet the conquest of an Italian empire proved a drain on Venetian resources. It embroiled the formerly neutral Republic in Italian power struggles and diverted the city's attention from the far greater threat of the Ottoman Turks. The fall of Constantinople in 1453 curbed Levantine trade, and Venice entered a period of slow decline.

The Papal States

The pope's temporal possessions in central Italy, the Papal States, derived from a legacy of the year 756 called the Donation of Pepin. For most of the Middle Ages, the popes maintained a loose sovereignty over the free communes and feudal fiefdoms that made up the papal domain. The transfer of the papacy to Avignon and the subsequent Great Schism virtually eliminated papal control over its territories for a century. Rome was ruled by its noble families and experienced a constant state of lawlessness. The other cities of the Papal State fell into the hands of local despots such as the Montefeltros in Urbino. Milan, Venice,

Florence, and the Kingdom of Naples all sought to pry territory away
from the weakened States of the Church.

Renaissance Popes. The papacy was unable to reassert hegemony
over the Papal States until the middle of the fifteenth century. Between
1447 and 1521 a succession of popes totally preoccupied themselves
with recovering fiscal and administrative powers in their territories and
with advancing family interests. The Borgia pope Alexander VI had
seven children whom he used to further his ambitions. These powerful,
crafty popes were increasingly perceived as Italian princes because of
their secular concerns and neglect of spiritual matters. Most patronized
the greatest artists of the Renaissance for self-glorification as much as
to enhance the lordship of the church. Renaissance Rome was a center
of great art and magnificent architecture. The secular activities of the
popes involved them in international politics, with ultimately damaging
results.

The Kingdom of the Two Sicilies

South of the Papal States lay the large Kingdom of the Two Sicilies,
a territory encompassing the southern Italian peninsula and the island
of Sicily. Since the eleventh century this kingdom had been ruled
successively by the Byzantines, the Normans, and the Hohenstaufens.
From the thirteenth to the fifteenth century the French Angevin and
Spanish Aragón Houses contended for control. The impoverished
region never experienced the rapid growth of cities and trade that set
the stage for cultural rejuvenation in north and central Italy. Thus
Renaissance culture failed to take root in the Two Sicilies apart from
the city of Naples, which enjoyed a brief artistic flowering under
Alfonso V of Aragón (ruled 1416–1458).

Urban Society

Historians have attempted to determine those facets distinctive to
Italy that allowed it to give birth to the Renaissance. For Burckhardt,
the main reason the Renaissance began in Italy was the vigorous Italian
civic life. For nearly 200 years Italy was free of feudal and monarchical
forces and foreign intervention. Thus freed, the Italian city-states
devoted their energies to inter- and intra-city power struggles, which
magnified individual talents. Scholars now regard Burckhardt's ex-

planations as too narrowly political and neglectful of social and economic factors. While the impact of the latter factors is difficult to gauge, scholars today see them as having played a significant role in the development of Renaissance culture.

Rise of the Bourgeoisie

One of the hardest tasks for the historian is to assess what social factors contributed to the "collective mentality" or unstated assumptions and common beliefs of an age. Regarding the Renaissance, several factors stand out. Renaissance culture bloomed within the nurturing environment of Italy's many cities. It reflected to a large degree the interests of a relatively new class of society—the bourgeoisie, especially its upper ranks. These "new men" were not noble, although they might later purchase or receive titles of nobility. Renaissance Italy offers numerous examples of men of humble origin such as Francesco Sforza who ended up as princes by means of their own abilities and determination. In order to legitimize their newly risen position in society, they built palatial residences, endowed churches and libraries, and commissioned works of art.

Political and Educational Opportunities

People who lived in Italy's cities tended to be more literate and politically involved than did their rural counterparts. Reading and simple mathematics were essential skills for anyone running a shop or engaged in commerce. City governments fostered the growth of schools. Although women were excluded from the guilds and thus from active political participation in Renaissance Italy, they were generally accorded at least an elementary education.

Respect for Individual Attainments

Increased social mobility and greater economic opportunities contributed to another characteristically Renaissance concept: the notion of *virtù*. The word was applied to a person of great natural talent and energy. The Renaissance valued individual achievement above noble birth. The growth of capitalist industry and new forms of investment afforded greater leisure time for the cultivation of personal interests. The ideal figure of the Renaissance was *l' uomo universale*, the universal man, who like da Vinci or Michelangelo excelled at a wide range of activities.

Courtly Manners

Appreciation for the multifaceted potential of the individual is found in the social manuals of the day. People came into closer contact with one another in the city and thus manners became even more important as a regulator of social behavior. The most famous of the many Renaissance books on manners was *The Courtier*, published by Count Baldassare Castiglione in 1528. In it Castiglione describes the ideal courtier as one possessed not only of bravery and skill at arms, but also of grace, social refinement, goodness, and intellectual accomplishment. While the aristocratic author found these qualities most often in those of noble birth, he left open the possibility that non-nobles could also attain them.

A Society of Young Males

Because of high mortality rates, individuals died at an earlier age. The average life expectancy at birth in fifteenth-century Tuscany was about twenty-nine. This meant that most Renaissance leaders were young men, full of energy and willing to take risks. They preferred action to reflection, and were quick to resort to violence. These traits are echoed in the aggressive, competitive tenor of Renaissance society.

The Growth of Banking and Trade

The economy of early Renaissance Europe was depressed. The combination of wars and disease led to depopulation, and the resulting labor shortage proved disruptive in its immediate effects. Ultimately, however, it accelerated a decline of serfdom and facilitated the transition to a money economy. After 1450 Europe entered a period of recovery marked by population growth, expanding trade, and renewed prosperity. This allowed for a gradual transformation of Europe's economic structure from feudal to early modern capitalism. The earliest signs of these momentous changes occurred in the Italian city-states. Capitalist methods of production and the reinvestment of profits were first evident in certain key industries such as wool-weaving. An expanding trade and the rise of banking generated great wealth for a small percentage of the population and provided an economic underpinning to the cultural blooming of the age.

Growth of Italian Trade

Because it occupied a central position in the Mediterranean world, Italy was a natural conduit for East-West trade. The port cities of Venice and Genoa especially profited from the increased contact afforded by the Crusades. Italian ships exchanged the wool and woolen goods of England, Italy, and Flanders for silk, sugar, spices, cotton, alum, and dyestuffs from the Levant. The introduction of larger, square-rigged ships and other improvements in navigation (such as the use of a stern rudder) during the fourteenth century enabled these products to be transported entirely by sea. The new Atlantic coastal sea route was safer, quicker, and hence cheaper than the older, overland routes across the Alps.

New Methods of Commerce

Overseas trade was a risky business that required substantial outlays of money. As early as the twelfth century, some Italian merchants formed temporary partnerships (*commenda*) in which a silent partner invested his capital in exchange for a percentage of the profits, while the merchant or active partner carried out the trade. With safer routes, merchants no longer had to travel with their cargo but rather began to rely on agents at various foreign ports. Sometimes these agents were hired on a commission basis. As time went on they frequently became partners with the merchant. Large family firms such as the Medici placed family members at the head of legally separate branch offices in the most important European cities such as Venice, Milan, Rome, London, and Bruges so that failure of one branch did not result in the collapse of the entire firm. As another means of reducing risk, the Italians devised the concept of maritime insurance in the fourteenth century.

Double-Entry Bookkeeping

New forms of business association necessitated the keeping of detailed, written records. Here again the Italians were the first, in the fourteenth century to develop an accounting method, double-entry bookkeeping, which greatly clarified and facilitated calculation of profit and loss. This involved entering all transactions twice, as a debit to one account and a credit to another so that total debits equaled total credits. By the fifteenth century double-entry bookkeeping was commonplace in Europe's largest cities, and firms employing it were able to handle even greater volumes of trade.

Italian Bankers

Expanded trade generated greater profits and with them the desire to reinvest capital. Some of Italy's most successful business firms took up banking and lent money to other merchants as well as to heads of government. In the late thirteenth century, the papacy appointed Italian bankers as its fiscal agents because their network of contacts expedited the transfer of ecclesiastical income to Rome. For many years the Medici family enriched its coffers in this capacity. Kings and other rulers financed their wars by pressing Italian banking houses for loans. Many such debts were never repaid. The tremendously wealthy Fugger family of Germany replaced the Medici as the pope's banker after the collapse of the Medici bank in 1494.

Banking Practices

The rise of banking houses allowed the transfer of funds quickly and safely from one individual to another, especially over long distances. Banks reinvested a percentage of the deposits left with them, thus further expanding the amount of credit available. Although church law prohibited usury, there were a number of ways to earn what amounted to interest without violating the letter of the law.

Bills of Exchange

As trading grew in scope and complexity, the appearance of a new business instrument known as a bill of exchange facilitated this extension of credit. Similar to modern checks, these pieces of paper transferred credits from one account to another. Because of the length of time it took for bills of exchange to reach their destinations, a merchant in one city might receive a short-term loan by drawing a bill of exchange on his partner in another city. This partner would not have to pay back the sum until he actually received the bill of exchange several months later. Banks turned a profit from these activities by taking advantage of the fluctuating rate of currency exchange.

Coinage

Banks also functioned as money-changers. In Renaissance Europe, cities and even feudal domains could issue coins, and only someone skilled in handling a variety of coins could accurately determine their equivalent worth. As active commercial and banking centers, Florence and Venice recognized as early as the thirteenth century the need for reliable coinage that held its value. The Florentine florin and the Venetian ducat became international standards of value whose gold content remained remarkably stable for many years.

Early Capitalism

The Renaissance period witnessed the growth of a few large capitalist industries. These were predominantly involved in the production of silk and woolen cloth, both of which enjoyed extensive markets and employed unskilled labor. Many steps in the manufacturing process remained in private homes, however, and factories were unknown.

The Italian Renaissance

Petrarch and the Early Renaissance

Many of the characteristics that historians have come to regard as typical of Renaissance thought and culture found their earliest expression in the writings of Francesco Petrarch (1304–1374). A native of Arezzo, most of Petrarch's formative years were spent in Avignon during the tenure there of the papal court. Years of legal study at his father's behest developed in him a distaste for lawyers and scholastic argument. He embarked instead on a literary career. As a professional man of letters, he garnered an international reputation that far surpassed that of any of his medieval predecessors. Petrarch's talents and accomplishments were twofold: as a classical scholar and as a lyrical poet.

Classical Scholarship

Petrarch read the ancients with a new eye so that they spoke to his own concerns about how to live a moral life in a sophisticated urban setting. He found in Cicero especially a most congenial adviser and friend. Petrarch conveyed his love and veneration for the ancients to his wide circle of acquaintances. He encouraged them to search out and copy ancient manuscripts as he did and to model their Latin prose style after the elegant simplicity of classical expression. He pinned his own hopes for immortality on his epic poem, *Africa*, written along the lines of the *Aeneid*.

Vernacular Love Poetry

It is a paradox befitting this complicated, life-affirming individual that his fame today rests not with the Latin works he and his contemporaries esteemed so highly, but rather with the songs and poems he composed in the vernacular. The greater part of his poetry is dedicated to Laura, a married lady from Avignon. While his poems of unconsummated love evolved from the idealizing tradition of troubadour poetry, Laura emerges in them as a real person and Petrarch's feelings ring true in their emotional complexity. The beauty of the lyrics derives not simply from their content, but also from their style. Petrarch transformed the sonnet from a simple folk song into a highly polished literary form.

Individualism

Petrarch lived in a time of cultural transition, which is reflected in his life and work. Petrarch the individual with very real joys and interests in this physical world is constantly at odds with Petrarch the product of a medieval system of belief focused on the afterlife. In a volume of confessions entitled the *Secret*, Petrarch's dialogue with Augustine reveals the anguished cry of a man caught between the medieval renunciation of things of this world and the modern glorification of human dignity and free will. It is this penchant for self-examination, for "turn[ing] my inward eye upon myself," as he put it, that makes Petrarch a signpost in Western culture.

Humanism

The word "humanism" has acquired a broad range of meanings since it was first coined in the nineteenth century. In its most common sense, the term connotes a secular attitude toward life that emphasizes human dignity and worth. For the student of Renaissance history, however, the term more appropriately applies to the revival of interest in classical letters and devotion to the *studia humanitatis* (humane studies). Humanism developed outside the universities, which remained conservative strongholds for medieval culture. The humanists were for the most part laymen. They earned their living as itinerant tutors, state historians, or secretaries at various Renaissance courts.

Recovery of Classical Texts

Renaissance humanists focused their concerns on the recovery and study of ancient Latin and Greek literature. In their quest to recover ancient manuscripts and to secure the best copies, they faced serious problems, but resolved these by developing new critical tools: philology, grammars, textual and historical criticism, dictionaries, and handbooks of classical mythology, geography, and history. The humanists' edited versions of classical texts were subsequently widely disseminated. Many important libraries such as that of the Vatican and the Medici Library in Florence were founded at this time to house the growing collection of ancient literature available in the West.

Emulation of Classical Latin

The humanists believed that clarity of expression and eloquence of speech helped people to understand one another and thus to achieve human progress. As they weeded errors and inconsistencies from ancient copies, humanist scholars became increasingly aware of the nuances of Latin usage and perceived medieval Latin as a corruption of the ancient language. Ciceronian Latin became for them the standard against which to measure all other Latin prose. In their own writings they incorporated classical phrases and emulated its simple, elegant style. At times their reverence for classical form lapsed into pedantry.

Valla's Textual Criticisms

The work of Lorenzo Valla (1407–1457), the founder of modern historical method, offers a good example of humanism's critical spirit. Living mostly in Rome and Naples, where he worked as a court secretary, Valla had one of the sharpest minds of his time. Employing humanistic techniques, he analyzed Jerome's *Vulgate* translation of Greek and Hebrew texts of the Bible into Latin and found that it contained errors and mistranslations. Valla's most outstanding achievement in textual criticism was his demonstration that the Donation of Constantine, upon which the papacy based its claims to temporal supremacy in the West, was actually a later forgery. He convincingly pointed out that the Latin phrases and grammar used in the document were characteristic of the eighth century, not the time of Constantine four centuries earlier.

Civic Humanism

In the late fourteenth century, Florentine humanists such as Coluccio Salutati and Leonardo Bruni called for active participation in public affairs as integral to leading a virtuous life. These "civic humanists" cited classical texts in praise of the active life to rouse the Florentine public in defense of republican government.

Impact on Education

Humanist scholarship had a tremendous impact upon education. It advocated strengthening the body through exercise and the mind through study of edifying examples from ancient history and literature. The goal was to shape one's character and become a well-rounded individual. In the 1400s secondary schools were founded in Mantua and Ferrara that put into practical use the humanists' philosophy of education. This new curriculum of the "humanities" gradually spread throughout Europe and served almost until the present as the basis of a liberal arts education in the West.

Broadening of Learning

Humanism's emphasis on recognizing the worth of the individual and on reading classical authors as guides to moral behavior has often been misinterpreted as the equivalent of paganism or atheism. On the contrary, the humanists did not perceive their work of scholarship as a threat to established religion. Nor did they believe that classical moral philosophy and Christian ethics were in conflict. Most of them were sincere Christians. But their interest in classical antiquity contributed to the increasing secularization of early modern society by extending the breadth of human interests beyond solely religious concerns.

Revival of Classical Greek

A crucial step in the recovery of the classical past occurred in 1397 when Florence invited the Byzantine scholar and diplomat Manual Chrysoloras to lecture there in Greek. Because of the difficulty of the language and the lack of teachers, few early humanists had mastered Greek. Chrysoloras's stay in Italy sparked a true revival of interest in the Greek language. For the next fifty years, emigrés from Byzantium further increased Italian exposure to the language and a steady stream of Greek manuscripts made their way from east to west. This impetus quickened even more after the fall of Constantinople in 1453, so that by the opening of the sixteenth century, almost all the masterpieces of classical Greek had become accessible to Western culture.

Ficino

Armed with increased knowledge of Greek language and literature, a new generation of philosopher-humanists came to maturity in Florence during the second half of the fifteenth century. They were especially attracted to the writings of Plato. Revived interest in Plato centered on the figure of Marsilio Ficino (1433–1499).

Translation of Plato's Works. At a young age Ficino's brilliance brought him to the attention of Cosimo de' Medici, who endowed him with a lifetime stipend, a villa near Florence, and a collection of Greek manuscripts. Ficino rewarded his patron's faith in him by producing a complete translation of Plato's writings into Latin as well as a translation of a number of Neoplatonic texts.

The Platonic Academy. Scholars and dilettantes alike congregated at Ficino's villa to study with and learn from the master. They formed what was later referred to as the Platonic, or Florentine, Academy. Ficino and his circle found in Platonic and Neoplatonic philosophy a recognition of the mystical dimension of human existence that accorded well with Christian belief. Plato had argued that things of this world are merely reflections of ideal reality. The supreme Idea is the Idea of the Good. For Ficino, God embodies these highest Ideas of goodness, beauty, and truth. Man is endowed by nature with the ability to comprehend these Ideas and hence to know God. Thus Ficino used Greek philosophy to buttress Christian religious belief. He coined the term "Platonic love" to portray a pure, spiritualized love that leads one to God.

Pico

Ficino's most accomplished student was Giovanni Pico, Count of Mirandola (1463–1494). An accomplished linguist, Pico knew Hebrew and Arabic as well as Latin and Greek. He set out in his short life to demonstrate the unity of truth that exists at the core of all religion and philosophy. His views prompted Pope Innocent VIII to place him under house arrest for a time. His most influential work, *Oration on the Dignity of Man*, epitomized the Renaissance belief in humanity's potential for good.

Decline of Humanism

By the beginning of the sixteenth century, Italian humanism had become less important in European culture. With their objectives successfully achieved, humanists increasingly produced slavish imitations of the ancients and ceased to be creative. They had, however, accomplished their main goal: the *studia humanitatis* were accepted as essential to becoming an educated person.

Vernacular Literature

It is one of the ironies of history that most masterpieces of Renaissance literature were penned in the "lowly" vernacular, not in the refined tongues of Latin and Greek that the humanists had worked so diligently to revive. The main reason was that humanist authors placed imitation of correct Latin style above creativity of expression, whereas the more fluid and popular vernaculars allowed for greater originality.

Humanism is often blamed for temporarily retarding the growth of vernacular literature, especially in Italy. In fact, Italy had little in the way of medieval literature in the vernacular prior to Dante. His choice of writing *The Divine Comedy* in his native (Tuscan) dialect demonstrated the poetic beauty of which the language was capable. A generation later Petrarch also used the Tuscan dialect to compose lyric poems of unsurpassed perfection of form. Petrarch then turned away from the vernacular to devote himself to his Latin works. He also influenced his friend and pupil Giovanni Boccaccio (1313–1375) to give up writing in the vernacular, but not before Boccaccio had completed the first great prose work in Italian, the *Decameron*.

Boccaccio

Boccaccio's earliest writings in prose and verse focused on romantic love. They were inspired by his affair with a young, married woman, Fiammetta (Maria), whom he first encountered in a Neapolitan church in 1336. Unlike Dante and Petrarch, Boccaccio's feelings were sensual and physically expressed. His writings reflect his passionate, down-to-earth nature. His masterpiece, the *Decameron* (composed c. 1348–1353), revealed him as one of the greatest storytellers of all time. He set the story during the Black Death in a country villa outside of Florence where ten young Florentines have retreated in hopes of escaping the plague. To pass the time, each person recounts a story on each of the ten days they are together. While the tales in the *Decameron* often derived from earlier literature, they sound a new note in their desire to entertain, not instruct. They humorously expose the corruption and hypocrisy of the clergy, poke fun at standard medieval ideals such as the gallant knight, and portray relations between the sexes in a ribald, sometimes licentious way. In later life, Boccaccio devoted himself wholly to the collection and study of ancient manuscripts. He tried to learn Greek, and wrote an encyclopedia of classical mythology. To his aging eyes, the brilliant, witty *Decameron* appeared an embarrassing indiscretion of his younger years.

Later Vernacular Writing

For almost one hundred years after the *Decameron*, writers in the Italian vernacular produced little of distinction. The humanists' success in renewing appreciation for the stylistic refinements of Latin made it, not Italian, the preferred medium of literary expression. By the middle of the fifteenth century, however, Italian authors turned again to the vernacular and infused it with a classical sense of form. Writing poetry in the "vulgar" tongue became the fashion among those who gathered around Lorenzo de' Medici. Epic poems in the vernacular, especially those based on the medieval French legend of Roland, proved popular at the courts of Florence and Ferrara. The vernacular was particularly well suited for use in contemporary writings on history, politics, and society. Niccolò Machiavelli (1469–1527) composed *The Prince* and *The Discourses on the First Ten Books of Livy* in the vernacular, while Castiglione set down his requirements for the perfect courtier in excellent Italian.

Writings on History and Statecraft

Important humanistic contributions to the intellectual history of the modern West were new directions in writings on history and statecraft. Medieval history had largely been an affair of men and battles played out along a predetermined course set by Divine Providence. The Renaissance liberated history from its theological underpinnings and allowed it to focus on human motivations and earthly causes for events.

Bruni

One of the first historians to write history from a secular point of view was the humanist Leonardo Bruni. Bruni's study of ancient Roman history illumined his *History of the Florentine People*.

Machiavelli

Nearly a century later another Florentine politician, Machiavelli, employed realism to transform the history of political thought. Machiavelli, a practical observer, failed to create a systematic political theory, but he is commonly associated with the modern concept of amoral statecraft that advances the objectives of the state by any necessary means. Born to a poor but noble family, Machiavelli entered politics four years after the Medici had been expelled from power. He served as secretary to the Florentine Republic during a time of grave danger to Italy. Charles VIII's invasion of Italy in 1494 was only the first stage in a long struggle among Europe's rulers for domination of Italy, a struggle characterized by deceit, treachery, and greed. In 1512, the Republic fell and the Medici were returned to power with the help of foreign troops. Machiavelli was retired to the countryside where he began writing on a number of subjects. The following year he was accused of plotting against the Medici and was briefly imprisoned and tortured. He never again held public office, and died a bitter and disillusioned man.

The Prince. Machiavelli's most famous work, *The Prince*, was written in 1513 although it was not published until five years after the author's death in 1527. It was designed as a guide on how to be a successful ruler. Sweeping aside divine, moral, or natural considerations, Machiavelli declared the successful exercise of power to be its own justification. The "ideal" Prince uses whatever means are necessary to accomplish his goal of gaining and holding onto effective political control. While the Prince does not have to be guided by religion, law, or morality, it is useful if he appears to be, for people are more swayed by appearances than reality. Machiavelli believed that critical situations such as those Florence faced justified employing any means—murder, tyranny, force—necessary to preserve the state. In *The Prince* he explicitly states that he is concerned not with how things ought to be, but with how they are. It is not surprising that to later generations the term "Machiavellian" became synonymous with cunning and deceit.

Discourses. To comprehend Machiavelli's political thought one must consult his less popular masterpiece, the *Discourses on the First Ten Books of Livy*. There he expands on many of his concepts and seems to contradict the low opinion of human nature and blatant disregard for laws and morality presented in *The Prince*. In *The Discourses* he concludes that a democratic republic is superior to every other political form. He saw in history a cyclical rise and fall of civilizations. A republic's original goodness is corrupted over time. Eventually the government declines into tyranny unless it is renovated by going back to its original principles.

Interpretations of Works. Few figures in the history of Renaissance thought have generated as many differing interpretations as Machiavelli. Scholars continue to debate whether or not the views espoused in *The Prince* and *The Discourses* are in conflict, and if so, which comes closest to expressing the author's final thoughts. In both books Machiavelli is a realist. He asks what can be done, not what should be done, and praises force, audacity, and decisiveness as vital to accomplishing his ultimate goal of civic glory and greatness. He had little use for Christianity, whose virtues of humility and contemplation he saw as hindering people from engaging in a vigorous civic life. He sought above all to teach rulers the political actions they must take in order to confront difficult times and to establish stable and effective governments.

Guicciardini

As an historian, Machiavelli used examples from the past to illustrate his maxims of political conduct. His fellow Florentine Francesco Guicciardini (1483–1540), by contrast, came to regard history on its own terms as a unique narrative of human actions rather than for the universal lessons it could teach. In his critique of *The Discourses* he judged Machiavelli's maxims to be too absolute and unnecessarily belligerent. Guicciardini focused instead on the problem of causation. His *History of Italy* revealed the base motives of greed, egotism, and desire for power that he found at work in Renaissance Italy. As an historian of his own time, he made use of archival evidence to a greater extent than had ever been done before. His concern for factual accuracy and willingness to look for causes beyond the city-state to encompass Italy and all of Europe set new standards for the writing of history.

Science and Technology

Renaissance Italy made no major scientific breakthroughs comparable to the discoveries of Galileo and Newton in the seventeenth century. But despite the paucity of empirical science, which some attribute to the humanists' reverence for classical authority, the Renaissance is no longer perceived as barren of scientific knowledge.

Analysis and Criticism of Classical Works

Among the humanists' most important contributions to the rise of science were the retrieval of virtually all extant classical writings on science and mathematics and the subjecting of those texts to the rigors of textual criticism. Far from unquestioning adherence to classical authority, humanists came to regard the ancients as offering advice whose validity should be tested by practical application. Because the views of the cosmos advanced by the Aristotelian Nominalists and the Neoplatonists conflicted, no one ancient author was regarded by the humanists as authoritative.

Vesalius

By the mid-sixteenth century, the time was ripe for new scientific theories that challenged the supremacy of the ancients. The Flemish anatomist, Andreas Vesalius (1514–1564) used information derived from his dissections of human cadavers to question a number of Galen's theories considered sacrosanct by Western physicians. Vesalius published his most important work, *Concerning the Structure of the Human Body*, in 1543 while a professor of anatomy at the University of Padua. Criticized in his own day for disputing Galen, some of Vesalius's own findings were later discredited. However, his use of empirical evidence to substantiate his conclusions was a milestone in the development of modern science.

Copernicus

The publication also in 1543 of *Concerning the Revolutions of Heavenly Bodies* overturned the accepted wisdom of the ancients in the field of astronomy. Its author, Nicholas Copernicus (1473–1543), was born and educated in Poland and then spent a number of years studying in Padua and elsewhere in Italy. Employing information from ancient astronomical records as well as his own observations of planetary motions, he concluded that the ancient astronomer, Ptolemy, had been incorrect in positing the earth as the center of the universe with the sun and planets revolving around it. Copernicus offered a heliocentric (sun-centered) alternative. This revolutionary hypothesis encountered considerable resistance over the next century because it conflicted with a world view embraced by the Catholic Church. Furthermore it contained a number of errors, including the theory that planets move in circular orbits. It was not until the discoveries of Galileo, Newton, and Kepler in the seventeenth century that the heliocentric universe could be empirically verified by use of the newly invented telescope and the elliptical movement of its planets accurately described.

Practical Applications of Science

Science and mathematics in the Renaissance made great strides in the realm of practical application. Renaissance Italy was a seedbed of new technologies. The most significant were Brunelleschi's techniques for constructing a dome without a wooden armature, Leonardo's many experiments and inventions in the field of engineering, the discovery of the crank, the use of energy from expanding gasses, and the application of mathematics to the art of fortification. Elsewhere technological advances were made in mining and metallurgy, firearms and ballistics, navigation, and printing. Of these new technologies, the invention of the printing press in Germany during the middle of the fifteenth century had the most far-reaching consequences.

The Arts

In the fine arts, the creative genius of the Italian Renaissance shone forth most brightly in painting and sculpture. The fourteenth and fifteenth centuries witnessed a distinct break with earlier periods in the treatment of subjects as well as in the employment of new techniques and aesthetic principles.

Painting

The period's achievements in painting especially became the standard by which art was measured until the nineteenth century. The painting of the High Renaissance (c. 1490s–1520s) represented the culmination of two centuries of increasing technical achievement. In the work of Leonardo, Michelangelo, and Raphael it attained a sublimity of expression and harmony of ideal form that could have no superior.

Medieval Tradition. In Italy, Gothic art and architecture failed to take hold as in the North. Medieval Italian art was Byzantine in derivation. The Italo-Byzantine tradition in fresco and panel painting was characterized by its two-dimensionality, gold backgrounds, and stylized poses. There was little attempt to suggest spatial depth and to convey individual feelings. Its goal was not to manifest the artist's skills but to clarify lessons of Christian theology to a largely illiterate audience.

Fourteenth-Century Environment. The fourteenth century signaled a new phase in Italian painting. In part its developments were responses to changes in the economic, social, and cultural environment of early Renaissance Italy. Rich and sophisticated laymen patronized artists and exploited art to glorify themselves. Revived interest in the classics also encouraged some artists to turn to secular themes and to imitate nature. Most continued to depict religious themes but they handled these in a new way to evoke stronger emotional responses from their viewers. During this period the social status of artists rose from that of anonymous craftsmen to distinct personalities possessing sought-after intellectual as well as artistic gifts. For the first time in European art, one is able to identify scores of individual artists by name and style. In response to the tremendous demand for artistic works, the artists produced a prodigious number of masterpieces.

Giotto. The key stylistic change in this new Italian art was the trend to "naturalism." Beginning with Giotto (c. 1267–1337) in the early 1300s, Italian art steadily moved toward accurate representations of the natural world. In the attempt to convey the illusion of three-dimensional space, Renaissance artists developed techniques for suggesting spatial depth. Giotto's art imperfectly achieved this goal, but he did place religious figures in natural or recreated settings and humanized his subject matter. Giotto also introduced the concept of *chiaroscuro*, the use of contrasting light and shade within a painting to create the illusion of depth.

Giotto's greatest work was done in fresco, the characteristic medium of Italian painting in which watercolor is applied quickly to wet plaster. The colors seep into the plaster, becoming part of the wall once it dries. In his glorious series of frescoes on the life of Christ in the Scrovegni (Arena) Chapel at Padua, completed around 1306, his figures appear lifelike. They are invested with weight, dignity, and true religious emotion. Giotto even included in his scene of the *Adoration of the Magi* a realistic depiction of Halley's Comet, which he most likely saw in 1301.

Masaccio. The true founder of Renaissance painting, Masaccio (1401–1428), lived in Florence a century after Giotto. He gave Giotto's attempts at creating the illusion of three-dimensional space a scientific basis by utilizing the mathematical laws of linear perspective worked out by Brunelleschi a few years earlier. Linear perspective in painting refers to the creation of spatial depth by means of a vanishing point, a central point at the viewer's eye level at which all parallel lines running into space at right angles to the picture plane will appear to converge. Masaccio also used *chiaroscuro* to create a convincing plasticity in his frescoes in the Brancacci Chapel in Florence. His human beings possess naturalistic bodies that move through a unified space. They convince on an emotional level as well. In the *Expulsion from Paradise*, for example, the viewer empathizes with Adam and Eve's intense shame and anguish.

Fifteenth-Century Environment. Quattrocento painting, as Italians call the art of the fifteenth century, embraced a wide variety of individual styles that revealed the imprint of the artist's own personality as well as the tastes and requirements of his patrons. There was increasing demand for classical scenes as well as for portraits, an art form that had all but died out during the Middle Ages. With their greater technical proficiency, Renaissance artists were now able to produce convincing likenesses of their subjects. Fifteenth-century Italian painting abounds in profile portraits of the new men of Renaissance society—merchants, despots, and *condottieri*—and their wives.

Other Florentine Painters. Artistic styles ranged from the otherworldly canvasses of Fra Angelico (1387–1455), who appeared to turn back from the advances of his day to a more spiritual art, to the timeless elegance, pale coloration, and pure geometric form of Piero della Francesca's (c. 1420–1492) frescoes in Arezzo, Monterchi, Sansepolcro, and elsewhere. Sandro Botticelli (c. 1445–1510), a protégé of Lorenzo de' Medici, painted scenes from classical mythology on a scale previously reserved for religious paintings. While the meaning of his two most famous canvasses, *The Birth of Venus* and *Primavera*, remains elusive, they were most probably inspired by the Neoplatonic theories of the Florentine Academy. Their graceful, linear beauty has retained visual appeal over the centuries.

Venetian Painters. In Venice, artists created their own unique school of painting, which assimilated the innovations of the Florentines but put them to use in paintings that glow with rich color and light. The Venetians were also the first in Italy to adopt (around 1475) the new Flemish technique of oil painting that allowed for greater luminosity. They began to paint on canvas and produced easel-size paintings to hang in the homes of wealthy Venetians. Giovanni Bellini (c. 1427–1516), Giorgione (1477–1510), Tintoretto (1518–1594), and Veronese (1528–1588) are but a few of the outstanding talents that Venice nurtured well into the sixteenth century, long after Florentine creativity had passed its prime. The greatest of them was Titian (c. 1490–1576). Through his works, Venetian colorism and fluid brushwork went on to influence such diverse artists as Rubens, Velásquez, and El Greco.

Leonardo da Vinci. Leonardo da Vinci (1452–1519) best exemplifies the Renaissance notion of a "universal man." The illegitimate son of a Florentine notary, Leonardo grew up in the Tuscan countryside where from an early age his artistic genius and scientific curiosity were apparent.

Scientific Studies. Painter, sculptor, architect, scientist, inventor, engineer, and musician, Leonardo turned his inquiring mind to the empirical study of all natural phenomena from the movement of water, to the flight of birds, to human anatomy. He recorded his thoughts and observations in notebooks containing thousands of pages, and filled them with detailed drawings and secret, mirror writing. Some of his entries anticipated such modern inventions as the airplane, submarine, and tank. Yet his myriad occupations, preference for experimentation, and lack of formal mathematical studies prevented him from completing most of his projects.

The Last Supper. It was as a painter that the Florentine had his greatest impact on posterity, though he finished only a small number of works. Leonardo placed his great technical mastery at the service of an art that was at once mysterious and psychologically penetrating. His large fresco of the *Last Supper* on the wall of a Milan refectory depicts the emotionally heightened moment when Christ declares that one of his disciples will betray him. Unlike earlier renditions of the scene that depended on inscriptions or a physically isolated Judas, Leonardo allows the disciples to reveal themselves by facial expressions and gestures alone. It is difficult for modern viewers to appreciate fully Leonardo's achievement in the *Last Supper* because the fresco is seriously damaged. Leonardo's decision to execute the work in a new and experimental medium is partially responsible, for the fresco began to deteriorate even in his own lifetime.

Other Works. Leonardo's innovative handling of group compositions is evident in one of his finest canvases, *Virgin and Child with Saint Anne,* in which his figures form a balanced triangle. Here too one finds the subtle use of *chiaroscuro* and the soft, misty blending of colors known as *sfumato* that lent an air of mystery to his art. This same enigmatic quality is found in his best-known work, the *Mona Lisa,* a portrait of an unknown woman, which the artist worked on over the years until it became an image of idealized beauty.

Michelangelo. Michelangelo Buonarroti's (1472–1564) towering abilities and volatile, ambitious temperament established a new image of the artist as a brooding "man of genius" even in his own day. Born in Tuscany, he spent the years between 1490 and 1492 in the household of Lorenzo de' Medici. Poet, painter, sculptor, and architect, Michelangelo's tremendous energy animated everything he did throughout his life.

Sistine Chapel. Although Michelangelo found sculpture more congenial to his gift for three-dimensional form, he would be ranked among the greatest artists of all time had he left only one work, the frescoes on the ceiling of the Sistine Chapel in the Vatican. Perched on a scaffold and with only one or two assistants, he covered with frescoes in four years of intermittent work (1508–1512) an area of 133 x 43 feet. The frescoes culminate in nine scenes from the Book of Genesis. Of them, the "Creation of Adam" is one of the most celebrated images in Western painting. God the creator-patriarch invests Adam with the spark of life by the touching of fingertips, a gesture that epitomized the Renaissance's belief in the divinely inspired individual.

Raphael. At the time Michelangelo painted the ceiling of the Sistine Chapel, the third of the triumvirate of great High Renaissance painters, Raphael (1483–1520), was also employed by Pope Julius II to decorate the pope's private apartments (*le stanze*) in the Vatican. By the early sixteenth century Rome had displaced Florence as the creative center of Renaissance art. Renaissance popes such as Julius II and Leo X avidly patronized Italy's leading artists and commissioned works of a magnitude commensurate with the exceptional talents of the age and the glory of their office.

In contrast to Leonardo's encyclopedic mind and Michelangelo's multitalented originality, Raphael's artistry expressed itself largely in a painting style that assimilated the accomplishments of others. An affable, easy-going man, Raphael painted works of great serenity and spaciousness of composition that invested Christian art with deep empathy. His Madonnas are striking in their beauty and tender regard for the Christ child. Raphael possessed an unerring sense of harmony through balanced proportions and could arrange large numbers of figures on a canvas without making them appear crowded. This is evident in his famous frescoes of *The School of Athens* and the *Disputa* in the Vatican.

Sculpture

Of the visual arts in the Renaissance, sculpture was affected most directly by the influence of classical art. While examples of Greek and Roman painting were scarce, a considerable amount of classical statuary had survived and was made easily accessible. Because they depicted pagan subject matter and nudes, most pieces were disregarded and even scorned prior to the early Renaissance.

Pisano. The first Italian sculptor to display familiarity with classical sculpture was Nicola Pisano (c. 1220–1278). Pisano had lived in southern Italy and Sicily where he saw numerous examples of ancient sculpture. Upon his return to Tuscany, he copied figures he had seen on Roman sarcophagi in his reliefs for the pulpits of churches in Pisa and Sienna. However, his literal imitation of classical art came too early to have a direct impact on Renaissance sculpture.

Ghiberti. By the late fourteenth century, Italian sculpture had gradually incorporated the new ideas of naturalistic space introduced by Giotto. The relief carvings by Lorenzo Ghiberti (1378–1455) for the bronze doors of the Baptistery in Florence offer a magnificent example. Ghiberti won the commission for the first pair of doors in 1401, in what was probably the first public competition in the history of art. In them he incorporated the advances in linear perspective made by painters to achieve clarity and a realistic setting. His figures are grouped naturally and set in a convincingly three-dimensional space that includes buildings and landscape.

Donatello. Prior to the fifteenth century, sculpture was generally viewed as an adjunct to architecture, but beginning with the work of Donatello (c. 1386–1466), the ties that bound the two were severed. A prolific and original artist, Donatello created with his bronze *David* the first free-standing nude sculpture since antiquity. The statue reveals not only an understanding of human anatomy, but also a new perception of the human body as the most perfect creation of God. Donatello had traveled to Rome and was enthralled with ancient art. His famous equestrian statue of the *condottiere* Gattamelata, in Padua, was also the first of its kind since Roman times. Yet Donatello sought to improve upon antiquity, making stylistic changes that gave his work a sense of controlled energy and expressiveness that was entirely his own.

Michelangelo. After Donatello, Renaissance sculpture developed along several lines. As in painting, however, it was the genius of Michelangelo that carried Renaissance sculpture to its inimitable heights. Like Donatello, Michelangelo's best-known sculpture is of *David*, a subject whose theme focuses on the power of the individual to triumph over seemingly insurmountable odds. That theme enjoyed wide appeal in Renaissance Italy. In sharp contrast to Donatello's slightly effeminate *David*, Michelangelo depicted a muscular young man with oversize hands and feet. Eliminating almost all references to the story except David's slingshot, Michelangelo created an idealized image of perfect masculine beauty. In this, Michelangelo was strongly influenced by Neoplatonic ideas of man's exalted place in the universe and of the body as the prison of the soul. Many of his greatest pieces, such as the figures of *Night* and *Day* in the Medici Chapel in Florence, were left unfinished.

Architecture

Prior to the fifteenth century, Italian architecture incorporated a blend of Romanesque, Byzantine, and Gothic elements.

Brunelleschi. The innovations of Filippo Brunelleschi (1377–1446), a Florentine goldsmith, sculptor, and architect, enabled architecture to enter a distinctly new phase. Brunelleschi acquired an appreciation of Roman architecture after a visit to Rome in the company of Donatello. There he carefully measured and studied ancient buildings to determine their mathematical proportions. Returning to Florence, he designed structures that incorporated antique forms and won a commission to build a dome on the cathedral at Florence. This massive undertaking, the first since antiquity, required sixteen years of intensive, innovative work. An extraordinary feat of engineering, the dome dominated the city and was more than twice as tall as that of the ancient Roman Pantheon. To construct such a huge stone structure Brunelleschi invented new machines and an unprecedented vaulting technique.

Bramante and Michelangelo. Unlike Gothic architecture, that of the Italian Renaissance was based on simple, static, geometric forms whose mathematical relationships were taken to reflect the perfection of God's divinely ordered universe. This restraint and harmony of proportions are evident in the work of two other great Renaissance architects, Donato Bramante (1444–1514) and Michelangelo, who were in large part responsible for the design of St. Peter's Church in the Vatican. Bramante had been placed in charge of the rebuilding in the early sixteenth century, but he died before his design for St. Peter's could be carried out. In 1546, the task was turned over to Michelangelo. He made changes in Bramante's original design, especially with regard to the dome. He too died before St. Peter's was completed in 1626 and later architects abandoned Bramante's original Greek cross plan for a longitudinal one. The great dome, however, was erected essentially according to Michelangelo's specifications. Its immense size dwarfed even Brunelleschi's dome in Florence.

Domestic Buildings. The Renaissance made notable contributions to domestic architecture and to urban planning (notably *piazze* [squares] or groups of buildings). Wealthy merchants and princes commissioned architects to build them impressive residences in town (*palazzos*) and in the country (*villas*) to accommodate their new desire for a more lavish style of living. Architecture became recognized as an independent profession as the tasks of the architect and the builder became separate. Renaissance classicism in building attained its purest form in the work of Andrea Palladio (1508–1580), whose dignified, graceful villas and churches in and around Venice exerted a profound influence on the development of a later classical style of architecture in Britain and France.

The Northern Renaissance

North of the Alps, the fourteenth and fifteenth centuries were a time of cultural decline rather than rebirth. The serenity and confidence of medieval culture at its height were being undermined from a number of positions. The loss of vitality and meaning within the late medieval chivalric and Scholastic traditions left the transalpine lands open to the winds of cultural change that were blowing from the south.

Italian humanist thought first made itself known beyond the Alps during the last decades of the fifteenth century. Itinerant scholars spread interest in the study and imitation of the Greek and Roman classics. Greek began to be offered at northern universities. By 1520, most courts hired men trained in the classics to carry on correspondence and write treatises in correct Latin.

Contacts with Italy

Knowledge of the artistic and philological achievements of the Italian Renaissance spread first to those lands most closely linked to Italy commercially, the Netherlands, the Rhineland, and South Germany. By the end of the fifteenth century these more urban areas of northern Europe came under the influence of the new humanist values. It was ultimately at the courts of princes and kings, such as Francis I of France, Elizabeth I of England, and Philip II of Spain, that northern Renaissance artists and humanists found their most significant patrons. By the sixteenth century, northern humanists such as Erasmus were attempting through their far-flung correspondence and travels to make the Renaissance international in scope. Likewise, northern artists went south to assimilate classical and Renaissance ideas while Italian artists were imported to work at northern courts.

Divergences from Italian Renaissance

What scholars term the Northern, or Transalpine, Renaissance was never a carbon copy of its Italian forebear. The absence of direct visual, linguistic, and historical links to the classical past as well as the greater strength of religious emotions created a distinct cultural atmosphere. The Northern Renaissance never made as clean a break with the Gothic past as did the south. Nor did northern humanism abjure social and religious issues as was the tendency south of the Alps. More humanists in the north were clerics than in Italy, a fact that partly explains the greater emphasis they placed on religious concerns. In addition, the Northern Renaissance witnessed a resurgence of literature in the vernacular, a development that had been somewhat hampered in the south by the Italian humanists' greater devotion to Ciceronian Latin. The cultural flowering of northern Europe manifested itself along national lines as a taste for classical civilization blended with indigenous cultural traits within each nation.

Lay Piety

The Northern Renaissance's distinctive religious component owed much to the growth of lay piety. Unlike traditional practices such as fasting, penance, pilgrimage, and the worship of relics, lay piety stressed the individual's personal experience of God's presence and love. The new movement of lay piety opened what had hitherto been a monastic experience to laymen who remained within the secular world. It emphasized the individual's ability to feel God's grace through prayer and in the purity of one's personal life. By implication, it undermined the traditional importance of the sacraments as the only path to salvation.

Lay piety's preoccupation with inner religious feelings presaged a shift away from the hierarchical authority of medieval Catholicism and towards a more personal, noninstitutional form of Christianity. Yet its rejuvenation of spiritual emotions made itself felt in the Christian Humanism of the North as well as among both Protestants and Catholics in the sixteenth century. Lay religion was strongest in Germany and the Netherlands. Its origins can be traced to a resurgence of mysticism among Dominican friars along the Rhine.

Eckhart and Groote

The most famous of these mystics was the German theologian, Meister Eckhart (1260–1327), who preached a message of union of the soul with Christ. A half a century later, lay piety received new impetus in Holland where a Dutch lay preacher, Gerard Groote (1340–1384), founded a religious movement known as the *Devotio Moderna* ("modern devotion"). Groote traveled around Holland calling upon his listeners to nourish the inner life of their souls. To do so, they must not only meditate on God's indwelling spirit, but also purify their lives in imitation of Christ. Shortly after his death in 1384, a number of his followers established the Brethren of the Common Life. Although they did not take religious vows, they lived communally in self-supporting groups according to set rules. Groups of Brethren and Sisters sponsored schools which, in addition to teaching academic skills, instilled the values of humility, simplicity, kindness, duty, and love of one's neighbor in their pupils.

Thomas à Kempis

The movement of lay piety produced a quantity of devotional books in the vernacular. The most influential of these, *The Imitation of Christ*, was written by a member of the Brethren of the Common Life, Thomas à Kempis, around 1425 and is still popular.

Christian Humanism

Northern humanists were most interested in the recovery and study of ancient texts pertaining to the primitive Church. They applied the techniques of textual criticism and philology to the Scriptures and writings of the early Church Fathers as well as to canon law and conciliar decrees in order to eliminate medieval errors and accretions and to produce "perfect" texts in their original language as well as in Latin. Animating their work was a reformist desire to return the Church to its earlier purity. This religiously based humanism of the north is referred to as Christian Humanism.

Reuchlin

One such Christian humanist was Johann Reuchlin (1455–1522), a German scholar who had studied with Pico in Florence. Reuchlin recognized the importance of Hebrew for understanding the Scriptures. He became the foremost Hebrew scholar of his day, although he had to spend six years defending his Hebrew studies in ecclesiastical courts against charges that they were a threat to Christianity.

Erasmus

Christian humanism's most eloquent spokesman and perhaps the most appealing and original figure of the entire movement was the Dutchman, Desiderius Erasmus (1466?–1536). Born in Rotterdam, Erasmus received a sound classical education at a school run by the Brethren of the Common Life. From them he assimilated the ideals of Christian love, brotherhood, and high moral conduct. As a scholar and man of letters, Erasmus traveled widely, corresponded with many of the great men of his time, and enjoyed a high international reputation.

Biblical Scholarship. Erasmus devoted much of his life to preparing editions of the Greek and Latin classics as well as of the writings of the Church Fathers. His greatest work of scholarship was his heavily annotated edition of the original Greek text of the New Testament along with his own Latin translation of it. In applying humanist techniques to ancient sources, Erasmus sought to achieve a clearer understanding of the nature of early Christianity and thus a better idea of how to reform the present Church.

In Praise of Folly. In his many letters as well as his original writings, composed in an elegant and witty Latin style, Erasmus expressed a philosophy of tolerance, moderation, reason, piety, and humility. His best-known work, the *Praise of Folly* (1509), satirizes the foolishness and self-pretensions of individuals from various walks of life. Erasmus reserved his sharpest barbs for the Church, believing that it had lost touch with the true spirit of Christ.

Desire for Peaceful Reform. By the opening of the Protestant Reformation, many already looked to Erasmus as the leader of peaceful church reform. His concern for inner piety more than conformity to Church dogma and ritual, as well as his assertion that the Bible was open to interpretation by all people, not just the clergy, made him appear to side with Luther. Erasmus never accepted Luther's notion of salvation through faith alone, however. He remained within the Catholic Church, advocating that reform evolve slowly through education and a renewal of spiritual life.

More

A friend and admirer of Erasmus was the English humanist, Sir Thomas More (1478–1535). As an exponent of the new learning, More combined his literary and philological work with an active political career, serving as lawyer, judge, Speaker of the House of Commons, royal secretary, ambassador, and finally from 1529 to 1532 as Lord Chancellor. It was in this last capacity that his loyalty to the traditional Church forced him into irreconcilable conflict with his sovereign, Henry VIII. More was beheaded for refusing to acknowledge Henry's supremacy over the English Church. Approximately 400 years later, the Catholic Church declared him a saint.

Utopia. In his most acclaimed work, *Utopia*, written in 1516, More extols the virtues of religious freedom as well as social and economic equality. His ideal community on the imaginary island of Utopia has no poverty or status based on wealth and lineage because all inhabitants share things equally and there is no private property or money. Yet, the society is so structured and regimented that there is little room for individual expression. Scholars debate whether More intended his Utopia to be an actual model for reform or merely a humorous way of denouncing social and economic ills in the England of his day. From More's book, the word "utopian" entered the English language as an adjective describing something impossibly ideal.

Printing

One of the most significant events to occur in northern Europe during the Renaissance period was the invention of printing. Most technology necessary for book printing had evolved in China as early as the tenth century, and movable type was in use in Korea fifty years before it first appeared in Germany. Paper was used in China as early as the second century A.D., and was introduced to the Europeans through the intermediary of the Muslims, who established a papermaking facility at Játiva, Spain in 1085. Paper was much less expensive than the parchment or vellum of which medieval manuscripts were made. Most such Chinese discoveries that proved essential to printing were gradually introduced to the West.

Gutenberg

The mass production of relatively inexpensive books became a reality with the invention of movable type. Credit for assembling its necessary components is attributed to Johannes Gutenberg (c. 1397–1468), a goldsmith from Mainz, Germany, who invented an adjustable mold to accommodate matrices of varying widths. Gutenberg published many notable works, including his famous Bible, of which forty-eight copies are extant. They are prized not only for their rarity and historical significance but also for the fine quality of their printing.

Spread of Printing

Printing spread rapidly from Germany throughout Europe. By 1500 there were 1,700 presses in nearly 300 towns that had published almost 40,000 editions. Nearly one-third of the presses were concentrated in Italy. The finest of them, the Aldine Press of Venice, made available at reasonable cost beautiful and accurate editions of the classics in a new, clearer typeface upon which modern italics is based.

Influence of Printing

The shift from script to print dramatically changed the nature of society. The availability of books in quantity at a lower price made possible the spread of literacy to the masses so that the ability to read was no longer the exclusive prerogative of churchmen, scholars, and aristocrats. The printing press also contributed to the preservation and diffusion of classical knowledge. Humanists corrected medieval errors of translation and transcription to produce standardized printed editions of ancient texts. The printing press also greatly facilitated the transmission of contemporary ideas. Luther's use of printed materials, for example, was crucial to the spread of Reformation faith. The ease with which books could be printed created an international market for writers.

Vernacular Literature

A full flowering of national literature in the vernacular north of the Alps occurred in the sixteenth century after the printing presses expanded demand for such works. Many literary masterpieces of Western culture were created at this time.

England

By the end of the fourteenth century, English had achieved recognition as the official language of England. Its use as a literary language had begun with Chaucer and attained a new height of expressive force and beauty in the works of William Shakespeare, Edmund Spencer, and Christopher Marlowe. (See Chapter 15.)

Spain

Spain reached its literary Golden Age at approximately the same time with the dramatic plays of Lope de Vega and Cervantes' *Don Quixote.* (See Chapter 15.)

France

France also produced masterpieces in the vernacular during the sixteenth century. In his thoughtful and clear-eyed musings on a wide range of subjects from the nature of friendship to the meaning of a true education, Michel de Montaigne (1533–1592) created a new literary form, the essay. His near contemporary, François Rabelais (c. 1490–1553), was a comic genius whose five books on the upbringing and adventures of two amiable giants, Gargantua and Pantagruel, sparkle with brilliant word plays, witty *bon mots*, and salacious humor. At times monk, doctor, and humanist, Rabelais wrote novels that mixed serious passages such as defense of a humanist education with pages of sheer nonsense in a fashion that delights and confounds readers to this day.

The Fine Arts

Northern Europe produced its own rich tradition in the fine arts during this period. Flemish painting in particular enjoyed an outpouring of creative energies in the fifteenth century.

Flemish Art

Although too closely linked to the medieval past to be considered classical in inspiration, Flemish art produced innovations of extreme importance to the history of art. While Renaissance Italian artists studied scientific laws of perspective and anatomy, Flemish artists arrived at human figures convincingly articulated in real space by trying out different solutions within the workshop. They discovered the use of aerial perspective, which creates a sense of distance by a subtle gradation of tones and by painting far-away objects as if blurred by the haze of the atmosphere. They strove for realism by depicting objects as exactly as possible and with fine detail. Although their figures do not move through space as naturalistically as do those on Italian Renaissance canvasses, they impress viewers by their richness of details and brilliant coloration.

Oil Painting

These hallmarks of northern painting were made possible by the Flemish invention of oil paints by blending pigments (the colors) with linseed oil, in the fifteenth century. Since oil paints took longer to dry, canvasses could be painted over and corrected. They produced rich, glowing colors and gave artists the option of either a translucent or an opaque surface, depending upon how thickly they applied their paints.

Van Eyck and Van der Weyden

The first great Flemish master to take full advantage of the new medium was Jan van Eyck (c. 1390–1441). His religious scenes are often placed in a contemporary Flemish setting in which the architecture, fabrics, jewelry, and other elements are all rendered with almost microscopic precision. The works of another great Flemish master, Rogier van der Weyden (1400–1464), convey an intense emotion that heightens the realism of the detailed scene.

Dürer

One of the first northern artists to articulate the Renaissance ideals of classical proportion and noble restraint in his own work was the German painter Albrecht Dürer (1471–1528). Dürer traveled to Italy several times and shared the Italian artists' fascination with anatomy and other scientific interests. One of the first artists to paint his own portrait, Dürer excelled not only in painting but also in drawing, woodcuts, and copper engraving. His art reveals a depth of insight and profundity of religious emotion that in its noble simplicity is both powerful and direct.

Holbein

Another northern master of the art of portraiture was Hans Holbein the Younger (1497–1543). Born in Augsburg, Holbein spent many years in England where he painted realistic portraits of Henry VIII, Erasmus, More, and other notables. His paintings often include classical motifs and focus on the individual personality, typical Renaissance traits. Sixteenth-century Northern painting remained true to its own native traditions, however, despite Italian influences.

Bosch and Bruegel

Two of the most original artists of the period were the Netherlandish painters, Hieronymus Bosch (c. 1450–1516) and Pieter Bruegel the Elder (1525–1569). Bosch's phantasmagorical creatures and horrify-

ing scenes of violence and evil bear witness to the northern preoccupation with sin, death, and hell. Bruegel shared Bosch's fascination with
the grotesque in human nature. His greatest achievement, however, was
in legitimizing genre painting (scenes from daily life) and landscape
painting as valid subjects for art.

Sculpture

Northern sculpture and architecture remained Gothic in inspiration
until the sixteenth century, when kings and princes began importing
Italian artists to build and decorate their palaces.

Music

Music in the fourteenth, fifteenth, and sixteenth centuries shared in
the creative and innovative spirit of the Renaissance. It was a time that
saw the creation of new instruments—the lute, violin, double bass,
harpsichord, organ, and kettledrum—and the development of new musical techniques. Music had always been an integral part of religious life.
During the Renaissance it became an important ingredient in most social
gatherings as well. Beginning in the fifteenth century, the level of
performance improved as churches and secular rulers hired professional
musicians. As lay patronage grew, especially in Italy, music became
increasingly secular in nature. Such were madrigal and carnival songs.

Polyphony. During the 1420s at the Burgundian court in the
Netherlands, a new style of music developed in which a number of
voices sang together in complex harmony. This choral polyphony
increasingly replaced the single voice of the Gregorian chant as the
preferred form of sacred music. The greatest composer of the age was
Josquin des Prez (c. 1450–1521). Flemish by birth, he wrote many of
his best works for Italian patrons. His preference for vocal music made
him one of the founders of the *a cappella* style of music in which the
voice is unaccompanied by any instrument.

*The Renaissance was an age of extraordinary brilliance in litera-
ture, learning, and the fine arts. Its vivifying principle was an increased
knowledge and appreciation of the classical world. These new cultural
currents first appeared in Italy in the fourteenth century. There, a
burgeoning commercial economy, active urban life, and large number*

of lay patrons created conditions favorable to the growth of new ideas and artistic accomplishments. Italian humanists recovered lost or forgotten Latin and Greek manuscripts and subjected them to rigorous textual criticism. Contact with the Arab and Byzantine worlds provided the West with a steady supply of hitherto unknown works. Whereas medieval scholars used classical authors piecemeal and made them conform to Christian belief, the humanists confronted classical writings on their own terms and looked to them for wisdom relevant to their own increasingly secular lives. The humanists founded a system of education that stressed human dignity and the pleasures and problems of this world. This concentration on human affairs encouraged the writing of more objective works of history. The Renaissance valued individual expression and nowhere was this more evident than in the art of the period. A broadened awareness of the Graeco-Roman past stimulated artistic developments. Italian Renaissance painters and sculptors depicted the human body and emotions with greater naturalism and set their figures in more convincingly three- dimensional space.

During the second half of the fifteenth century, Italian humanism began to penetrate north of the Alps. The invention of the printing press greatly facilitated the transmission of humanist and other literature. In northern Europe, interest in classical culture joined with religious concerns to produce a movement known as Christian Humanism. Its ultimate goal was to reform the Church by bringing it more in line with primitive Christianity. Thus northern humanists used the linguistic and critical tools of their Italian predecessors to achieve accurate versions of biblical, patristic, and other Christian writings. The Northern Renaissance flourished from the fifteenth until the mid-seventeenth century and was strongly influenced by local cultural traits. The period witnessed new techniques and greater realism in the fine arts as well as the blossoming of vernacular literature in England, France, and Spain.

Recommended Reading

Cecil M. Ady, *Lorenzo dei Medici and Renaissance Italy* (1972)

Frederick B. Artz, *From the Renaissance to Romanticism* (1962)

Hans Baron, *The Crisis of the Early Italian Renaissance* (1955)

Marvin B. Becker, *Florence in Transition* (1967)

Otto Benesch, *The Art of the Renaissance in Northern Europe* (1945)

Bernard Berenson, *The Italian Painters of the Renaissance* (1957)

Vespasiano da Bisticci, *Renaissance Princes, Popes and Prelates* (1963)

Marie Boas, *The Scientific Renaissance 1450–1630* (1962)

Giovanni Boccaccio, *The Decameron*, G. H. McWilliam, trans. (1972)

Gene Brucker, *Giovanni and Lusanna: Love and Marriage in Renaissance Florence* (1986)

Jacob Burckhardt, *The Civilization of the Renaissance in Italy* (1958)

Peter Burke, *The Italian Renaissance: Culture and Society in Italy* (1987)

Ernst Cassirer et al, eds., *The Renaissance Philosophy of Man* (1948)

Benvenuto Cellini, *An Autobiography of Benvenuto Cellini*, J. A. Symonds, trans. (1985)

Michel de Montaigne, *Montaigne's Essays and Selected Writings*, D. M. Frame, trans. (1963)

Raymond De Roover, *The Rise and Decline of the Medici Bank 1397–1494* (1963)

R. Ehrenberg, *Capital and Finance in the Renaissance: A Study of the Fuggers and their Connections* (1928)

Elizabeth L. Eisenstein, *The Printing Press as an Agent of Change: Communications and Cultural Transformations in Early Modern Europe* (1979)

W. K. Ferguson, *The Renaissance in Historical Thought: Five Centuries of Interpretation* (1948)

Eugenio Garin, *Italian Humanism: Philosophy and Civic Life in the Renaissance* (1965)

C. Gilbert, *History of Renaissance Art Throughout Europe* (1973)

Felix Gilbert, *Machiavelli and Guicciardini* (1965)

Myron P. Gilmore, *The World of Humanism 1453–1517* (1952)

Richard A. Goldthwaite, *The Building of Renaissance Florence: An Economic and Social History* (1981)

Ernst Gombrich, *Norm and Form: Studies in the Art of the Renaissance I* (1966)

Ernst Gombrich, *Symbolic Images: Studies in the Art of the Renaissance II* (1972)

Francesco Guicciardini, *History of Italy and Other Selected Writings*, C. Grayson, trans. (1964)

J. R. Hale, *Machiavelli and Renaissance Italy* (1963)

Arnold Hauser, *A Social History of Art, Vol. II: Renaissance to Baroque* (1957)

Denys Hay, *The Italian Renaissance in its Historical Background* (1977)

Denys Hay, *The Renaissance Debate* (1976)

David Herlihy and Christiane Klapisch-Zuber, *Tuscans and Their Families: A Study of the Florentine Catasto of 1427* (1986)

J. H. Hexter, *More's Utopia: The Biography of an Idea* (1952)

Johann Huizinga, *Erasmus of Rotterdam* (1952)

Christiane Klapisch-Zuber, *Women, Family and Ritual in Renaissance Italy* (1985)

Paul Oscar Kristeller, *Renaissance Thought: The Classic, Scholastic and Humanist Strains* (1961)

Leonardo da Vinci, *Notebooks* (1960)

Niccolò Machiavelli, *The Prince and the Discourses*, Luigi Ricci, trans. (1950)

Richard Marius, *Thomas More: A Biography* (1984)

Lauro Martines, *Power and Imagination: City-States in Renaissance Italy* (1979)

Lauro Martines, *The Social World of the Florentine Humanists* (1963)

Garrett Mattingly, *Renaissance Diplomacy* (1964)

Thomas More, *Utopia*, P. Turner, trans. (1965)

Peter Murray, *The Architecture of the Italian Renaissance* (1963)

John J. Norwich, *A History of Venice* (1982)

E. Panofsky, *Renaissance and Renascences in Western Art* (1972)

Margaret M. Phillips, *Erasmus and the Northern Renaissance* (1981)

Donald E. Queller, *The Venetian Patriciate: Reality versus Myth* (1987)

François Rabelais, *Gargantua and Pantagruel*, J. M. Cohen, trans. (1955)

G. Reese, *Music in the Renaissance* (1959)

J. B. Ross and Mary McLaughlin, eds., *The Portable Renaissance Reader* (1953)

Ferdinand Schevill, *A History of Florence from the Founding of the City Through the Renaissance* (1936)

Hugh Trevor-Roper, *Renaissance Essays* (1985)

John H. Whitfield, *Petrarch and the Renaissance* (1969)

Rudolf Wittkower, *Architectural Principles in the Age of Humanism* (1971)

Heinrich Wölfflin, *Classical Art: An Introduction to the Italian Renaissance* (1980)

CHAPTER 14

The Protestant and Catholic Reformations

Time Line

1520	Luther publishes his *Address to the German Nobility, The Babylonian Captivity,* and *Freedom of the Christian Man*
	Leo X excommunicates Luther
1521	Diet of Worms; Edict of Worms places Luther under imperial ban; Luther in hiding at Wartburg Castle
1522	Knights' War
1524	Theatine Order established
1524–1526	German Peasants' War
1529	First use of term "Protestant"
1530	Melanchthon writes *Augsburg Confession*
1534	Loyola founds Jesuits
	Anabaptists set up "New Jerusalem" at Münster
	Act of Supremacy formalizes Henry VIII's break with Rome
1535	Henry VIII begins confiscation of monastic properties
1536	John Calvin publishes *Institutes of the Christian Religion*
1542	Pope Paul III revives Roman Inquisition
1545	Council of Trent convened
1547	Charles V defeats Schmalkaldic League
1555	Peace of Augsburg
1563	Thirty-Nine Articles establishes creed of Anglican Church
1564	Papacy publishes Index of Prohibited Books

1667   Milton publishes *Paradise Lost*

The Protestant Reformation began in 1517 as one man's call for religious reform. Within a decade, however, Martin Luther's attack on the medieval church had accelerated into full-scale revolt. By the time of Luther's death in 1546, Protestantism had established itself as a separate religion. Other religious reformers, notably Ulrich Zwingli and John Calvin, formulated their own variations of Protestant doctrine. The spread of Protestantism created social and political tensions that sparked a century of bitter strife.

Beginning in the fourteenth century with the "Babylonian Captivity" of the papacy at Avignon and the subsequent Great Schism, the medieval church had slipped into decline. Reformist movements such as those inspired by Wycliffe and Hus had preached doctrines that foreshadowed to some extent Luther's own. Erasmus, Thomas More, Rabelais, and others used irony and erudition to goad the Church into purifying itself. Movements of lay piety abounded in fifteenth-century Europe. The time was ripe for a solution to the moral laxness and empty ritualism of the late medieval church. Yet Luther's ideas went beyond an attack on church abuses to encompass a reinterpretation of Christian doctrine. Luther's use of the printing press and the vernacular as well as the support of the German princes contributed to the spread of his ideas and the permanency of his revolt.

In response to the Protestant challenge, the Catholic Church reformed itself. A new clerical order, the Jesuits, spearheaded a revitalization within Catholicism itself. The Council of Trent defined Catholic dogma for centuries to come. By the mid-sixteenth century, all chances for a reconciliation between Protestantism and Catholicism were lost.

Martin Luther and Lutheranism

Martin Luther (1483–1546) was born on November 10, 1483, in the obscure village of Eisleben in what is now East Germany. Of peasant stock, his father had risen by dint of hard work from a mine worker to become owner of several mines and foundries. He held high hopes for his intelligent son, sending him first to Latin School and later to the University of Erfurt to pursue a legal career.

Spiritual Crisis and Doubt

Scarcely six months after receiving his Master of Arts degree in January 1505, Luther experienced a spiritual crisis. As he returned to Erfurt to continue his legal studies, he was hurled to the ground by a lightning bolt. This brush with death left him determined to become a monk. Intensely religious, he entered a strict Augustinian order in Erfurt against his father's wishes, and was ordained on February 27, 1507.

The monastic vocation did not allay Luther's fear for his soul. Upon saying his first Mass in 1507, he was overwhelmed by his own unworthiness and terrified by God's infinite power and majesty. Despite steadfast prayer, fasting, vigils, and self-flagellation, he became even more engulfed in a sense of sinfulness. A pilgrimage to Rome in 1510 left him disillusioned with the Italian clergy and racked with doubt. He began to question whether good works—fasting, prayers, relics, confession, pilgrimages, and the like—sufficed to attain salvation. Upon returning from Rome, he was sent to the newly founded University of Wittenberg in Saxony, where he completed his doctorate in theology in October 1512 and was appointed professor of scriptural theology. As an academician, Luther continued to experience doubts about his own salvation.

The "Tower Experience"

The answer to Luther's spiritual malaise came to him sometime between 1512 and 1516. While meditating most likely in his tower study, he remembered the words of the Apostle Paul to the Romans: "The just shall live by his faith." He came to realize that the sacraments and works of the Church would never of themselves be sufficient for salvation because human beings were by nature corrupt. What tradition calls his "Tower Experience" revealed to him a new, more merciful God than the stern, unconditional figure of his youth. Study of the Bible opened Luther's eyes to a God who, through the sacrifice of his son,

Jesus, took up the sins of the world. People must have faith that God, through his "sheer mercy," will save them.

The Indulgence Controversy

The resolution of his own personal crisis of faith did not inexorably set Luther on the path of revolt. His involvement in a controversy over the merits and sale of indulgences, however, placed him more at odds with the Church.

The Catholic Doctrine of Indulgences

According to Catholic dogma, a contrite sinner could confess his wrongdoings and receive forgiveness from God through the sacrament of penance. This did not, however, absolve him of punishment. The repentant sinner must do some form of penance on earth and/or spend time after death in purgatory where the soul was made pure to enter heaven. An indulgence was a remission of part or all of this punishment. It was justified theologically on the grounds that Christ and his saints, through their infinite goodness, had built up a "treasury of merit" from which the pope could dispense transfers of grace to sinners in exchange for some good work. The practice of granting indulgences had begun during the Crusades, first to reward those who had fought and later to those who contributed money in lieu of participating.

Abuse of Indulgences

Indulgences proved a highly lucrative source of funds for the Church. The pope not only dispensed indulgences for the papacy at Rome, but also granted the privilege to other ecclesiastical and secular authorities. To the uneducated masses, indulgences appeared an easy way to purchase forgiveness of sins or shorten the time in purgatory for those on whose behalf they were bought.

Pope Leo X (served 1513–1521) needed money to complete the rebuilding of St. Peter's Basilica in Rome and had authorized a huge fund-raising campaign that included the sale of indulgences. By papal agreement, half the proceeds of the sale of the new St. Peter's indulgences in Germany went to repay the induction expenses of Albert of Brandenburg as Archbishop of Mainz. Not only was Albert underage, he held two other sees as well. In Luther's mind, the sale of indulgences replaced genuine contrition with a false assurance of pardon that only God could give. It led to avarice and corrupted the true meaning of charity. Luther was especially troubled by the indulgence-hawking activities of a Dominican friar, Johann Tetzel, who acted as papal representative in nearby Brandenburg.

The 95 Theses

On October 31, 1517, Luther posted a list of 95 Theses against indulgences on the north portal of the Castle Church in Wittenberg. This was not in itself a revolutionary act. The posting of notices was an accepted means of calling for scholastic debate on an issue. Written in Latin for an audience of scholars, the 95 Theses were subsequently translated into German and printed without Luther's permission. Within weeks knowledge of them had spread throughout the Holy Roman Empire.

Reasons for Luther's Success

Luther's attack on indulgences raised an immediate and widespread storm of interest in Germany because it reflected the resentment many Germans felt against the Roman Church's seemingly insatiable demand for funds. Their distance from Rome, lack of a central political authority to mediate between the Church and people, and long-standing tradition of pietism all predisposed the Germans to be highly critical of church abuses and responsive to Luther's call for reform. Had Leo X been inclined from the start to take the threat of an unknown friar in a remote German town seriously, or if Luther had lived in the territory of a more devoutly Catholic ruler, matters might have developed quite differently.

Diet of Augsburg

Leo initially left others to deal with Luther. The Dominican Order came to the defense of their fellow monk, Tetzel, and fiercely attacked Luther's views, while the rival Augustinians championed reform. In October 1518, Luther was summoned for a hearing in Augsburg before the general of the Dominican Order, Cardinal Cajetan. Luther refused to change his opposition to the doctrine of indulgences and went so far as to state that the pope could err in matters of faith.

The Break with Rome

Protection of Frederick the Wise

After the interview with Cajetan failed to elicit a recantation, the next logical step would have been to send Luther to Rome for trial. At this point, however, Frederick the Wise, elector of Saxony, intervened and refused to banish Luther from his homeland. The pope did not press the issue because he hoped for Frederick's support in the papacy's attempt (that proved unsuccessful) to prevent the election of the Habsburg Charles of Spain as Holy Roman Emperor in 1519.

Radicalization of Luther's Views

Under the pressure of mounting attacks, Luther's views grew ever more radical.

Debate with Eck. Debating with the German theologian Eck at Leipzig in July 1519, Luther denied the divine origin of the papacy and defended the martyr Hus. The debate at Leipzig attracted even greater attention to the rebellious monk as did the broad dissemination of his writings made possible by the printing press. Between 1518 and 1520 Luther penned a number of pamphlets in which he refined his thoughts on the doctrine of justification by faith and explored what changes it meant for the structure and practice of the Church.

Reformation Treatises. During the year 1520 Luther buttressed his doctrines with several works that have been called Reformation Treatises. In his *Address to the German Nobility*, Luther appealed to the German nobility to end the worldly abuses of the Church and create a reformed German Church. The most radical of his works, *The Babylonian Captivity*, demanded the reduction of the number of sacraments from seven to two. In it he denied the validity of many Catholic practices including the veneration of saints, indulgences, interdicts, and the requirement for priestly celibacy. In another work published that year, *Freedom of the Christian Man,* Luther recognized the value of good works but insisted that faith led to good works and not vice versa. In this treatise Luther proclaimed that the ministry of the Word (the Bible) was supreme.

Excommunication of Luther

Luther's rejection of papal authority at Leipzig spurred Leo into action. In June 1520, a papal bull denounced Luther's teachings and gave him sixty days to recant or be excommunicated. Luther's response was to burn the bull as his own writings had been burned by Rome. Then, with Frederick the Wise's backing, he appealed to the new Holy Roman Emperor, Charles V, to hear his case for reform before a secular tribunal, the German Diet.

The Diet of Worms

Charles agreed and in April 1521, Luther was summoned to appear before the Diet of Worms, an assembly of Germany's emperor, nobility, and prelates. There he refused to modify his views, supposedly declaring: "Here I stand. I cannot do otherwise." In reply, the electors passed the Edict of Worms declaring Luther a heretic and placing him under imperial ban.

Translation of the Bible

Luther escaped a martyr's death thanks again to Frederick the Wise. Having traveled to Worms under a safe conduct pass, Luther was allowed to depart freely. As he left the city, he was "abducted" by Frederick's men and hidden at Wartburg Castle. There he remained for almost a year. During this time he completed a translation of the New Testament from Greek into the German vernacular. Later he translated the Old Testament. Luther's vernacular Bible played a formative role in creating a standard German language.

Life and Work at Wittenberg

The Reformation rapidly gathered speed despite the seclusion of its creator. Luther's followers at the University of Wittenberg, led by the humanist scholar Philip Melanchthon, quickly implemented Luther's ideas. In late 1521, Luther returned to Wittenberg to stem the rising tide of religious radicals who carried his reforms further than he was willing to go. He was to spend the remainder of his life there building his new church. Luther was not only a prolific pamphlet writer but also wrote hymns, devotions, and statements of belief for the nascent church. In 1524, he abandoned his monk's vocation and a year later married Katherine von Bora, a former nun. The marriage was a contented one and gave issue to six beloved children.

Luther's Religious Beliefs

Luther's emphasis on faith rather than good works was not in and of itself contrary to Catholic doctrine. The early Church Fathers, especially Augustine, had spoken of the importance of faith in God's redemptive powers. During the fourteenth and fifteenth centuries Nominalist philosophy asserted that God was too majestic and powerful to be comprehended by human reason and could be approached only through faith. Luther's thoughts on faith evolved, however, to a point where he rejected much of the hierarchical, sacramental, and sacerdotal foundations of the Catholic Church.

Justification by Faith Alone

The basic tenet of Luther's belief was that God bestowed forgiveness of sins through an act of unmerited grace. Individuals did not deserve God's forgiveness nor could they do anything to assure their own salvation. God's grace alone, made possible through Christ's resurrection, saves sinful human beings by giving them faith. This led Luther to deny that sacraments and good works were necessary for salvation.

The Lord's Supper

Luther declared Baptism and the Eucharist, which he renamed Communion or the Lord's Supper, as essential to the Christian faith, because they alone were mentioned in the Bible as instituted by Christ. In addition, Luther redefined the meaning of the Lord's Supper. For Catholics, the bread and wine of the Eucharist are transformed during the Mass into the body and blood of Christ. This miracle of transubstantiation can only be performed by ordained priests. Luther held that no miraculous transformation occurred, but that Christ was present nonetheless in the natural substance of the bread and wine (consubstantiation). Contrary to Catholic practice, Luther allowed the congregation to partake of the wine as well as the bread.

The "Priesthood of All Believers"

If the sacraments were no longer the exclusive channels of God's grace, then they no longer required a special priesthood to administer them. Instead, every person must confront God on a personal level, above all by reading the Scriptures. All are capable of finding salvation without the intervention of clergy. Luther rejected papal primacy and the episcopal form of Church government and substituted his notion of a "priesthood of all believers." He abolished the hearing of confession, allowed priests to marry, and called for the abolition of monasticism.

The Bible as Sole Authority

Because the Bible alone contained the authentic word of God, it—not papal bulls, conciliar decrees, or the writings of the Church Fathers–was the sole authority in matters of religious faith. People are capable of interpreting the Bible for themselves. For this reason Luther emphasized the importance of translating the Bible into native tongues.

The Lutheran Church

Luther was not ready to follow his views to their extreme, anarchical conclusion as some of his followers did. He preserved the institutional church with an ordained ministry and was willing to make it subordinate to the state, provided it retained independence in doctrinal matters. For his new church he simplified ritual and the vernacular replaced Latin as the language of worship. Services in the reformed church centered on prayer, Bible reading, and congregational singing. The main focus was the sermon, an explication of God's word. Music played an important role in Lutheran worship. Luther even composed hymns, of which "A Mighty Fortress Is Our God" is the best known. In 1530, Luther's colleague and ally, Philip Melanchthon, gave systematic expression to Luther's doctrine in the Augsburg Confession, which Lutherans still subscribe to as their statement of belief.

Social and Political Consequences of Lutheranism

Despite the vehemence of his language, Luther proved a most reluctant revolutionary. On religious issues he held out the slight hope until the end of his life that the Catholic Church would accept his ideas on faith and thus preserve religious unity. On social and political matters he came down firmly on the side of law and established authority. He held conservative views on the position of women and the hierarchical nature of society. Luther was largely concerned with issues of the soul, not with things of the world. Yet his concept of the equality of people before God had implications that extended to worldly affairs.

Threats to Established Authority

As early as December 1521, radical reformers in Wittenberg incited the populace to riot. Religious images were smashed and priests threatened. In the days that followed, preachers began implementing Luther's reforms with such breakneck speed that Frederick the Wise acted to slow the wholesale dismantling of Catholic rites. Luther himself preached a series of sermons in 1522 against the use of violence. He counseled patience and concern for those who struggled to decide where they stood on the issue of reform. But such was not to be the reality.

The Knights' War. The first group to use Luther's revolutionary religious concepts for nonreligious purposes was the German knights. As minor noble landowners who owed sole allegiance to the Holy Roman Emperor, the knights resented the expanding power and influence of the German princes and towns. A number of them perceived in Lutheranism a means to reverse their declining status by seizing Catholic territories. Led by Franz von Sickingen, they joined together in 1522 to attack the powerful territorial prince, the archbishop of Trier. The Knights' War provided ammunition to those who accused Luther of fomenting social and political rebellion.

The Peasants' War. In 1524, a particularly bloody Peasants' War broke out in south and southwestern Germany. Its leaders relied upon the Lutheran doctrine of the equality of all people before God to support social change. This reliance is evident in the *Twelve Articles*, a list of grievances drawn up in 1525 by Swabian peasant rebels that called for sweeping alterations in the social structure. Their demands included an end to serfdom, reduction of excessive feudal dues and services, abolition of the death tax, reduction of the church tithe, and the right of every community to choose its own pastor who could preach directly from the Gospel.

At first Luther was inclined to support the disunited bands of peasants in their religious demands but he totally rejected the use of violent means in attaining them. In a ferocious pamphlet, *Against the Murderous and Thieving Hordes of Peasants* (1525), he lambasted the peasants for resorting to robbery, murder, and bloodshed. Fear of chaos led Luther to appeal to the nobles and ecclesiastical lords to suppress the rebellion with every weapon at hand. The revolt was put down within a year.

Increased Support for Luther

The Peasants' War proved a turning point in Lutheranism. Luther's stance lost him the support of much of the peasantry. The Peasants' War also forged an alliance between the Lutheran Church and the German princes that ultimately accounted for the Reformation's success.

Support from German Princes. A number of lay rulers, particularly in northern Germany, converted to Lutheranism and began to pressure their subjects to do likewise. In 1525 the head of the Teutonic Knights espoused the new faith, abolished the order, and declared Prussia a secular duchy with himself as duke. Lutheranism soon displaced Catholicism as the established religion in many German principalities. Later it received state approval as the sole religion in Sweden, Denmark, Norway, Iceland, and Finland.

Few German princes or other rulers embraced Lutheranism from purely religious convictions. For many the new religion offered economic and political advantages. Converting to Protestantism placed the German princes at the head of their own territorial churches. It provided them with real economic gain from the confiscation of monastic properties and the control of church revenues, and it augmented their power at the expense of the Catholic emperor.

Support from the German Cities. Luther's message of a priesthood of all believers found a receptive audience among German townspeople, particularly guild members. In most German cities, the rich bourgeoisie tended to remain Catholic and the poorest workers favored more radical Protestant sects. The remaining middle class inhabitants favored Luther.

Hostility of Pope and Emperor

Despite the increasing number of adherents, conversion to Lutheranism was laden with dangers. New converts were labeled heretics by pope and emperor alike. By 1530, the staunchly Catholic

Charles V had determined to use military force against the new faith. Had he not been faced with other more pressing crises vis-à-vis France and the Turks, his suppression of Lutheranism might have succeeded. The papacy, for its part, refused to make any concessions to Lutheranism. Still fearful of conciliarism, it put off for a number of years Charles V's request that it convene a church council to rectify the worst abuses. Within the German Diet, Catholics outnumbered Lutherans and effectively blocked compromise during Luther's lifetime. The term Protestant originated from a *Protestatio* delivered by the Lutheran minority at the Diet of Speyer (1529) against its refusal to grant religious liberty to the new faith in Catholic territories.

The Schmalkaldic League

In 1531 the Lutheran princes and cities formed the Schmalkaldic League to protect themselves against Charles V. Hostilities did not break out, however, until 1546. Charles's Spanish troops won a decisive victory over the League in 1547, but Lutheranism was too entrenched to be crushed by a single military defeat. By that time nearly half the Empire's population had converted to the new faith. Neither the pope nor the German Catholic princes favored the reassertion of imperial power that Charles's victory seemed to presage. Lacking fiscal and military resources, Charles abandoned his quest to unify Germany under imperial rule and summoned the German Diet to treat religious affairs.

The Peace of Augsburg (1555)

In 1555, Charles V accepted the religious compromise proposed by the German Diet and known as the Peace of Augsburg. It recognized the personal right of each territorial prince to choose either Lutheranism or Catholicism as the exclusive religion of their state, but allowed subjects opportunity to move elsewhere should the ruler's choice prove unacceptable. No accommodation was allowed for adherents to other Protestant sects. The agreement awarded Lutherans legal title to all properties confiscated from the Catholic Church prior to 1552 and assured the permanence of the new religion.

The Spread of Protestantism

As Luther's ideas spread rapidly throughout Europe, they encouraged others to examine their faith. This was especially true because of Luther's emphasis on the Bible as the sole authority in religious matters. Once the Bible was open to all to read and interpret, its many ambiguities and shades of meaning generated a variety of sometimes conflicting viewpoints. The Protestant movement eventually came to encompass not only the views of Luther, but those of Zwingli and Calvin, radical sects, and the national Church of England.

Ulrich Zwingli and Zwinglianism

Chronologically, the first Protestant alternative to Luther's reform ideology was produced by an early Lutheran convert, Ulrich Zwingli (1484–1531), a Swiss humanist and theologian. Zwingli began to preach the reformed faith in Zürich in 1519. He embraced the Lutheran tenets of justification by faith alone and the Bible as the sole source of religious truth. Like Luther, he denied the need for clerical intervention in interpreting the Bible or in administering the sacraments. Again, like Luther, he recognized only two sacraments—baptism and the Lord's Supper—but disagreed with Luther on the theological meaning of the latter sacrament.

Interpretation of Lord's Supper

While Luther preserved the notion of Christ's actual presence in the sacrament, Zwingli interpreted the Biblical passage upon which the Lord's Supper is based as having only symbolic meaning. Communion did not confer grace; rather it was a commemorative ceremony of Christ's death and resurrection.

Simplification of Worship

Zwingli also differed from Luther in his attitude toward church ritual and design. Zwingli favored a simplified, more puritanical form of worship eschewing music and art. Reformed churches based on his views sprang up in various Swiss cities in the 1520s. They were characterized by simple appointments and had the communion table on a level with the congregation rather than an elevated altar. Like Luther,

Zwingli set the sermon at the heart of the worship service. Clergymen and magistrates were together responsible for watching over and enforcing moral conduct.

Religious Warfare and Zwingli's Death

Not all the Swiss cantons accepted Zwingli's reformed faith. Catholic and Protestant cantons formed themselves into hostile aggressive leagues, and in 1531 they resorted to open warfare. Zwingli was killed that year at the Battle of Kappel. Soon thereafter peace was established and the cantons agreed to recognize each other's right to follow the religious doctrine of their choice. Following Zwingli's death, the reform impetus moved from Zürich to Geneva, where John Calvin would create an even more comprehensive theological system.

John Calvin and Calvinism

John Calvin (1509–1564) was second son to the secretary of the Bishop of Noyon in France. In pursuit of an ecclesiastical career he attended the University of Paris, but left that institution for Orléans to undertake the study of law. After receiving a law degree in 1531 he returned to Paris to study the classics, but was forced to flee that university for Angoulême once he embraced the Lutheran ideology. Arrested twice for heresy he took refuge in Basel, Switzerland, where in 1536 he published the first edition of his great theological masterpiece, the *Institutes of the Christian Religion*. In that work Calvin gave Protestantism its systematic theology by using his great skills as an organizer and synthesizer of reformed belief. Calvin not only assimilated Luther's basic doctrines and Zwingli's emphasis on ritual simplicity and moral discipline but also added his own ideas on the Christian government of church and state and the doctrine of predestination.

Institutes of the Christian Religion

Calvin devoted the rest of his life to perfecting his masterpiece so that it might provide an authoritative statement of Calvinism. A work of erudite and careful reasoning, it stands as the most systematic and influential expression of the Protestant religion. In it Calvin restated Luther's and Zwingli's fundamental positions on the primacy of faith over good works, the substitution of Biblical for papal authority, and the rejection of ecclesiastical intermediation as well as much of the sacramental and priestly structure of the Catholic Church. He defined Christ's spiritual presence in the Lord's Supper in terms that eventually enabled the Calvinists and Zwinglians to unite. Moreover, Calvin's logical mind probed to the heart of an issue that had occupied Christian thought since Augustine—the problem of free will versus predestination.

Predestination

For Calvin, the doctrine of predestination, or God's foreknowledge and preordaining of events, was a logical outcome of God's omnipotence. Believing in justification by faith alone, Calvin emphasized the great gulf that separated God and man. To avoid the philosophical dilemma of how a good God allows evil in the world and to preserve the individual's moral responsibility for his actions, Calvin argued that no one can know with certainty that what he is doing is what God would have him do. The individual has the free will to make moral choices in living his life. Yet nothing one does can alter one's predestined fate.

The Elect

Because people can never be absolutely sure that what they are doing is pleasing to God, only faith, not good works, can bring salvation. Individuals do not merit the grace God bestows upon them. It is a free gift and, according to Calvin, not all receive it. Only a portion, the elect, are predestined to receive God's forgiveness and attain eternal life. The rest are foreordained to damnation. Calvin justified this seemingly harsh doctrine by stressing that human reasoning powers are inadequate to comprehend God's plan for the world and for the individual.

Moral Duties

According to Calvin, individuals should act as if they were among the elect even though it is impossible to know or influence one's fate. It is one's Christian duty to honor God and benefit humanity. To this end, Calvin formulated strict moral standards to be enforced by the community of the faithful. Calvinism mandated regular church attendance and an austere, puritanical outlook on life. Swearing, card playing, dancing, and theater going were forbidden.

Calvin's Leadership in Geneva

In late 1536, the Protestant reformer Guillaume Farel invited Calvin to help with the reformation of the Swiss canton of Geneva. Calvin accepted and save for a brief exile in Strasbourg (1538–1541), he remained there for the rest of his life as spiritual leader and as head of a theocratic state.

Church Constitution. Calvin's constitution for the Genevan Church was ratified in 1542. It decreed the law of the Bible the law of the State, assigned the clergy the task of interpreting the law, and formulated a hierarchical ministry of pastors, teachers, lay elders, and deacons to govern the church. Unlike Luther, Calvin believed the State should be subservient to the Church.

The Consistory. Most important in the administration of church/state affairs was the Consistory, a body of ministers and lay elders chosen by the city council whose duty was the enforcement of moral discipline. Other responsibilities included press censorship, supervision over schools, and overseeing of charities. In its zeal to ferret out heresy and immorality, the Consistory resorted to fines and to exile, and even to the death penalty for second offenders in such crimes as adultery, blasphemy, and heresy. The Spanish physician, Michael Servetus, who sought refuge in Geneva from the Inquisition, was nonetheless burned at the stake there in 1553 for disbelieving in the Trinity. The notion of religious toleration was alien to the sixteenth-century mentality.

The Spread of Calvinism

Calvin's clearly propounded and well-organized faith proved a dynamic force in the religious life of the second half of the sixteenth century and beyond. Many flocked to Geneva's newly founded Academy (1559) to receive a Calvinist education and then returned to their homelands taking with them Calvin's organized Protestant faith. Books, pamphlets, and missionaries also spread the word. In Scotland, following a revolt against the Catholic Queen Mary, the Presbyterian Church headed by John Knox was established along Calvinist lines. In Elizabethan England, a small activist group of Calvinist clerics and university professors formed the "Puritan" movement and unsuccessfully attempted to displace the episcopal form of church government with presbyterianism. In France, Calvinists, called Huguenots, became a powerful presence within the Catholic state. In the Low Countries, the rapid spread of Calvinism (Dutch Reformed Church) merged with political grievances to propel the Netherlanders into revolt against their Spanish Catholic overlord, Philip II. Despite the fact that Calvinism was not recognized as a legal religion by the Peace of Augsburg, Calvinism won converts in the Rhineland. Sizable communities of Calvinists formed in Hungary, Bohemia, and Poland as well.

The English Reformation

The establishment of Protestantism in England followed a different course from that on the continent. In England, the Reformation was initiated by the king to allow him to remarry without papal sanction.

Henry VIII

Throughout his life Henry VIII (reigned 1509–1547) considered himself a true Catholic. He had even written a *Defense of the Seven Sacraments* in 1521 against Lutheranism and earned the papal title "Defender of the Faith." However, personal and dynastic concerns propelled Henry into conflict with Rome.

Henry's Desire for an Annulment. Henry's queen, Catherine of Aragon, was daughter of Ferdinand and Isabella of Spain. Although she bore him six children in their eighteen years of marriage, only Mary was to survive childhood. As Henry grew older, he became increasingly preoccupied with the question of a male heir to the throne. In 1527, he appealed to the pope to annul his "barren" marriage on the grounds that he had violated canon law by marrying the widow of his deceased brother Arthur. This pretext of a guilty conscience was an excuse to allow him to marry Anne Boleyn, a lady of the court with whom he had become enamored. Whether succession, sexual infatuation, or other concerns motivated Henry, it is clear that he wanted an annulment badly enough to break with Rome.

Opposition of the Pope. Although Catholic law did not recognize divorce, it was not unusual for popes to accommodate their mightiest subjects by granting annulments. Henry's request put Pope Clement VII in an embarrassing position. To oblige Henry not only would have reversed the decision of an earlier pope who had granted dispensation for the marriage, but would also have antagonized the Holy Roman Emperor Charles V, who was Catherine's nephew. Charles's victorious army had sacked Rome in 1527 and Clement was his political prisoner. As a consequence the pope temporized and bided for time.

Approval of Henry's Annulment by the English Church. By 1529, Henry had grown tired of waiting. He dismissed his Chancellor, Cardinal Wolsey, who had been negotiating with the pope, and began to act on his own. The king summoned the Parliament of 1529 and carried out his religious revolution. In 1531, he compelled the English clergy to acknowledge him as their "singular protector, only and supreme lord, and as far as the law of Christ allows, even supreme head." When the pope still refused to grant his consent, Henry secretly married Anne in early 1533. Parliament passed a number of antipapal statutes, the most important of which denied an Englishman's right of judicial appeal to Rome. By this act, Henry gave his English Church Courts the authority to adjudicate all spiritual cases, including his own annulment. Henry named Thomas Cranmer, a scholarly clergyman sympathetic to the king's dilemma, to be Archbishop of Canterbury. Cranmer proclaimed Henry's marriage to Catherine against divine law and legitimized his union with the by-now pregnant Boleyn. Infuriated by Henry's impudence, Clement excommunicated him and declared his first marriage still valid.

The Act of Supremacy (1534). Henry again turned to Parliament for national approval of his break with Rome. In 1534, it passed the Act of Supremacy that declared Henry to be "the only supreme head in earth of the Church of England." The proviso "as the law of Christ allows," inserted by the clergy in the 1531 act, was omitted. Other parliamentary acts gave the king power to make all ecclesiastical appointments, ended financial payments to Rome, recognized the legitimacy of Anne's offspring, and made it treason to deny the king's supreme authority over the English Church.

Confiscation of Monastic Properties. The Act of Supremacy in effect created a national church in England, the Anglican Church. While Henry's motives in founding it were largely personal and dynastic, he was not alone in its creation. Anticlericalism was widespread, and many Englishmen welcomed the change. As head Henry made no substantive reforms in the church structure and liturgy although he used his new powers to divest it of considerable property. The most substantial losses were encountered when he dissolved the monasteries and confiscated their properties. The crown gained immensely from the former church lands (almost one-tenth of the property in England). Although some lands were given as rewards for service, most were sold, often to affluent non-noble families. The new landowners formed the basis of a new landed gentry that remained loyal to the Tudors and had a financial stake in preserving the Church of England.

Protestantism Under Edward VI

Despite his rejection of papal authority, Henry never considered himself a heretic. The church he founded remained essentially Catholic in dogma and ceremony as prescribed in the Six Articles of 1539 that defined the doctrinal substance of the English Church. Under his successor, however, Anglicanism was brought more in line with Zwinglian and Calvinist tenets. The frail, nine-year-old Edward VI (ruled 1547–1553), son of Henry's third wife, Jane Seymour, inherited a kingdom beset with religious differences. Authority was exercised for the young king, first by his uncle Edward Seymour (duke of Somerset) and after 1549 by his rival John Dudley (duke of Northumberland). During Edward's reign, worship was simplified, priests were allowed to marry, and uniform services were conducted in English as set down in the new *Book of Common Prayer* written largely by Cranmer.

Reestablishment of Catholicism Under Mary Tudor

Edward's untimely death at age sixteen brought to the throne his elder half-sister, Mary Tudor (reigned 1553–1558), daughter of Catherine of Aragon. A devout Catholic, Mary reversed Henry and Edward's Reformation legislation and even persuaded Parliament to repeal the Act of Supremacy. No attempt was made to restore sold church properties. During her reign Protestants were persecuted as heretics and 273 died martyrs deaths, including Archbishop Cranmer. "Bloody Mary's" religious intolerance and her marriage to Philip II of Spain made her vastly unpopular by the time of her death in 1558.

Elizabeth I's Religious Settlement

As the daughter of Anne Boleyn, Elizabeth I (ruled 1558–1603) had to be Protestant in order to be England's legitimate queen. In the

Catholic view she was illegitimate, and thus Mary Queen of Scots was heir to the throne. Whatever her personal religious views, Elizabeth found it politically expedient to define the Anglican Church in broadly Protestant terms. In 1559, an Act of Supremacy recognized her as "Supreme Governor" of the Church and an Act of Uniformity reinstated a revised, Protestant *Book of Common Prayer*. Four years later the creed of the Anglican Church was set down in the Thirty-Nine Articles. They accepted the Bible as sufficient authority for salvation, recognized only the two sacraments of baptism and the Lord's Supper, rejected the requirement for clerical celibacy, and replaced Latin with English in church services. Yet the articles were vague enough to embrace a broad spectrum of belief. The Anglican Church, in effect, offered a *via media* or middle way between Catholicism and more puritanical forms of Protestantism.

Radical Reformers

Protestantism allowed for greater elasticity in the interpretation of spiritual matters than had Catholicism. But the Lutheran, Calvinist, and Anglican churches took some of the personal responsibility from individuals by defining what they should believe within the confines of an organized church. The churches were essentially conservative in their attempts to preserve the social and political status quo. Other reformers, however, gleaned a more radical message from their reading of the Bible.

Anabaptists

Historians sometimes refer to all radical reformers as Anabaptists, but scholars today focus attention on the differences that separate the various Anabaptist sects.

Adult Baptism. The term Anabaptist, which means "Rebaptizer" in Greek, refers to the practice of baptizing individuals as adults so that their commitment to Christ would be an informed one. Upon joining an Anabaptist sect, those who had been baptized as children would be rebaptized by total immersion of their bodies in water as described in the Bible.

Separation from the World. Anabaptists in general read the Bible more literally than did the established churches. They used it as a guide to questions of faith and to the way one lives. This often led them to separate from the world and form communities of those considered to be true believers. Most Anabaptists refused to bear arms, swear oaths, go to court, or use violence. They rejected the authority of the state and declined to serve it in any way. Some Anabaptists lived and worked together in a form of Christian communism. Many held a millenarian belief in the imminent coming of Christ and the end of the world. Anabaptists were therefore often persecuted and exiled by secular as well as religious authorities. Still, a number of sects did survive by espousing nonviolence and by moving from place to place.

The Swiss Brethren. The earliest of the Anabaptist sects was founded in Zürich by Conrad Grebel in 1525. Impatient with the slowness of Zwingli's reforms, Grebel wanted to eliminate all rituals and doctrines not specifically mentioned in the Bible. He named his followers Brethren but they were soon dubbed Anabaptists by their enemies to highlight their practice of rebaptism. Despite severe persecution, Anabaptism survived. It was given a more permanent organization and creed by Menno Simons (1496–1561), a former Dutch priest. Small groups of Mennonites, along with other Anabaptist sects, formed into communities scattered widely across Europe. Some even made their way to America. The Amish people, or "Pennsylvania Dutch," hold Anabaptist beliefs. Under Mennonite influence, the first English Baptist congregation was founded by John Smyth around 1508 and English Baptists were among the early settlers of New England.

Münster. Anabaptism in the sixteenth century frequently provided a haven for those who felt dispossessed or disappointed by established society. Such appears to have been true of the most famous instance of extreme Anabaptism, the Melchiorites. In 1534, they forcibly seized control of the German city of Münster and set up a "New Jerusalem." Led by John of Leiden, a Dutch tailor who declared himself king, they proclaimed the reign of saints, abolished private property, authorized polygamy, forbade all books except the Bible, and disregarded established law and order. They believed they were preparing the way for the Second Coming of Christ. Protestant and Catholic forces joined together to suppress the rebellion. The city was besieged and fell in 1535. Many Melchiorites were killed or fled. John of Leiden and other leaders were savagely tortured and executed. The example of Münster discredited Anabaptism in the eyes of many.

The Catholic Reformation

Whereas Protestant reformers had recast in revolutionary terms the role and nature of the Church and the meaning of faith, a similar desire to get back to its essence led Catholics in the mid-sixteenth century to reform and revitalize their traditional faith. This movement within the Catholic Church is usually called the Counter Reformation by Protestants, but Roman Catholics prefer the term Catholic Reformation. Many historians favor the latter term because it implies that the revival of the Catholic Church occurred not simply as a reaction to the growth of Protestantism but also as the result of dynamic currents within the Church itself, some of which antedated Luther.

Spain

The revitalization of the Catholic faith first made itself felt in Spain, a country which had resisted many of the secularizing effects of the Renaissance. Under the pious monarchs, Ferdinand and Isabella, the Spanish church experienced a spiritual resurgence. The Archbishop of Toledo, Jiménez de Cisneros, abolished many of the worst abuses, patronized Biblical scholarship, founded the University of Alcalá, and fostered a strain of mysticism among the Spanish people. In 1480, Ferdinand and Isabella received papal permission to institute an independent Spanish Inquisition in order to quell heresy. It used torture to extract confessions from converted Jews and Muslims and from others suspected of heretical beliefs. Large numbers perished at the stake, giving the Spanish Inquisition its notorious reputation.

New Monastic Orders

Another sign of the renewal of spiritual life within Catholicism was the founding of a number of new monastic orders to minister to the needs of the people and encourage their spiritual development.

Theatines and Capuchins

The Theatines were established in 1524 with the aim of educating and purifying the clergy. Four years later a new order evolved from the Franciscans. It sought to return to the original spirit of St. Francis. Known as the Capuchins after the four-cornered hood they wore, they lived selfless lives and cared for the poor and sick.

Ignatius Loyola and the Jesuits

By far the best-known and most important of the new clerical orders was the Society of Jesus, or Jesuits. The Society played a crucial role in winning Protestant converts back to the Catholic faith. The founder of the Jesuits, Ignatius Loyola (1491–1556), was a Basque nobleman and soldier. Severely wounded at the siege of Pamplona in 1521, he began to read popular lives of the saints and other works of Christian mysticism during his convalescence. These inspired him to devote his life to doing God's work. He determined to become a soldier of Christ. First Loyola entered a monastery to confess his sins and receive absolution. While there he foresaw the establishment of a new order and began to formulate its rules.

Founding of Jesuit Order. In 1523 Loyola embarked on a pilgrimage to Jerusalem. Returning to Europe a year later, he dedicated himself to improving his education first in Spain and later in Paris. During this time he attracted a number of followers who joined with him in 1534 to form the Society of Jesus. They took vows of poverty, chastity, and obedience, and worked to help the poor and needy. Eventually Pope Pius III gave his formal approval to their preaching and teaching, and Loyola was elected its general in 1541. Loyola imposed a military structure upon his new order. To become a Jesuit, a man had to undergo a long, strict training designed to break all ties with his past and teach him complete submission to his superiors. Jesuits took a special vow of obedience to the pope.

The Spiritual Exercises. Loyola's *Spiritual Exercises* was a devotional tract of immense influence. Its cardinal rule, the suppression of individual desires to the greater good of the Church, allowed for no doubt in matters of Catholic doctrine or papal supremacy. It advocated prayer and self-discipline as the means to achieve a mystical union with God.

Jesuit Influence. Because of their self-control and the certainty of their beliefs, the Jesuits proved to be very effective in halting the growth of Protestantism and winning back large areas of France, Germany, Hungary, Bohemia, and Poland to the Catholic fold. The Jesuits founded a large number of schools and colleges for boys that became noted not only for their doctrinal orthodoxy but also for the rigor and excellence of their training. As missionaries, the Jesuits won converts in India, China, Japan, and the New World. Persuasive preachers, they became confessors and advisers to many of the courts of Europe. As such, their ability to influence the powerful to combat heresy sometimes led to charges of ruthlessness and manipulation. Much of the credit, however, for bringing new converts to the Catholic Church and attracting back former ones justifiably belongs to them.

The Reform Movement

In the early stages of the Reformation, the papacy seemed to turn a blind eye to Luther's revolt and to the need for correcting abuses in the Church. Nevertheless a reforming party gradually gained strength in Rome. Its nucleus was a group of laymen and priests, the Oratory of Divine Love, whose members began to institute reforms on a local scale.

Paul III

In 1534, reformist cardinals elected Pope Paul III (served 1534-1549), who was definitely committed to reform of the church. Paul replaced the moral laxity of the papacy with a new religious strictness. He worked to eliminate financial corruption and immoral conduct in the face of strong opposition from many of Rome's most powerful families. In 1542, Paul revived the medieval Inquisition, as a means of addressing the Lutheran threat in Italy. This Roman or papal Inquisition was separate from the Spanish one. Never as severe as its Spanish counterpart, it nonetheless used torture and burned its victims at the stake. It was only truly active in Italy where it was used to suppress all traces of heretical belief by such means as its famous condemnation of Galileo's theories.

Need for a Church Council

By Paul's time it had become increasingly evident that the only entirely effective way to reform the Catholic Church and stem the tide of Protestantism would be to convene an ecumenical council of prelates. The Holy Roman Emperor Charles V strongly favored its summoning, but Francis I of France and other rulers urged the pope not to resort to a general council for fear that it would strengthen Charles's already impressive power. This advice reinforced the papacy's own worries that a revived conciliar movement would succeed in declaring the Church Council superior to the pope. The calling of a council got off to a number of false starts until it was finally convened in 1545.

The Council of Trent

The Council of Trent was conducted in three sessions, 1545–1547, 1551–1552, and 1562–1563. Unlike most important earlier councils, it was attended on average by only about fifty voting members. Since the majority of its participants were from Italy, and papal legates controlled its agenda, the papacy was safeguarded against conciliar threats to its sovereignty. The Council of Trent was so successful in defining the traditional dogmas of the Catholic Church that they remained virtually unchanged for the next 400 years. Catholicism emerged from its reformation clarified and strengthened but also more rigid and opposed to change.

Preservation of Catholic Doctrines

The Council of Trent's first action was to define the Catholic Church's position on a number of doctrinal issues. The Council offered no compromise with Protestantism. It reaffirmed papal supremacy, the divinely ordained role of the clergy, the efficacy of both faith and good works, and the validity of all seven sacraments as channels of grace. It upheld the doctrine of transubstantiation, the necessity of clerical celibacy, and reliance upon the traditions of the Church as well as the Bible as sources of spiritual authority. Monasticism received renewed approval and the existence of Purgatory was maintained. The council declared Latin the language of worship and recognized the fourth century A.D. Vulgate translation of the Bible as the only authoritative text. The right of individuals to interpret the Bible for themselves was disallowed. Many other traditional precepts received the Council's approval.

Reform of Abuses

The Council also took action to reform the Church. It forbade pluralism and required bishops to reside in their dioceses. In addition, it increased the bishops' jurisdiction over all clergy within their territories. It eliminated abuses in the granting of indulgences and tightened monastic discipline. One of its most far-sighted reforms was a requirement that theological seminaries be established in each diocese for the training of priests.

Papal Supremacy

By the Council's end, the pope's supremacy over the whole Church had been clearly asserted. The Council even voted that none of its resolutions were valid without papal consent. Pius IV (served 1559–1565) issued a papal bull confirming the Council's work and declared that only he had the right to interpret its decrees. One of the papacy's first actions after Trent was to publish an *Index of Prohibited Books* in 1564. This listed all works the papacy considered dangerous to one's faith and were thus forbidden to be read. Many of the greatest works of European literature and learning since the sixteenth century have appeared on the *Index*. The papacy also decreed that religious art be carefully scrutinized to make certain that it was theologically correct.

The Impact of the Reformations

The task of assessing the impact of the Protestant and Catholic Reformations on European history is an arduous one. However, certain general observations do stand out. The Protestant Reformation and its Catholic counterpart both kindled a revival of spiritual energy. Both stressed morality and adherence to church doctrine; yet each church's certainty that it alone possessed the spiritual truth led to persecution and a general temper of intolerance.

Division of European Christendom

Protestantism destroyed forever the medieval notion of the unity of Western Christendom. As a result of the Reformation, European religious life was divided into a large number of national or territorial churches. Monarchs gained in power and prestige by extension of their authority over the religious realm. The division of Europe into Protestant and Catholic states intensified pre-existing hostilities and was a contributing factor in the political struggles of the next hundred years.

Influences on Education

Both the Protestant and Catholic religions contributed to a rise in the level of education of the European populace. Protestantism's emphasis on individual interpretation of the Bible induced people to learn to read while its use of the vernacular stimulated the development of literature. In England, for example, the beauty of the King James version of the Bible (1611) made it a standard to which English writers have aspired ever since. Recognition of the value of learning the dogmas of the Church at a young age prompted Catholics, especially the Jesuits, to establish schools and universities.

Influence on the Arts

The Reformation left its mark on the creative arts of its age. Puritanism received eloquent expression in the writings of two of England's greatest seventeenth-century authors, John Milton (1608–1674) and John Bunyan (1628–1688).

Milton

Milton was a prolific writer. In addition to poetry and masques, he penned pamphlets in defense of Presbyterian reform, the Cromwellian regime, freedom of the press (*Areopagitica*) and the people's right to depose a tyrannical king. His most famous work, *Paradise Lost* (1667), grappled movingly with the problem of the existence of evil.

Bunyon

Bunyon, a Baptist lay preacher, created in his masterpiece, *The Pilgrim's Progress* (1678), a Christian allegory of life as a journey from the City of Destruction to the Celestial City. It was widely read and of substantial influence.

Visual Arts

Because of its desire to simplify worship, Protestantism exerted less influence on the visual arts of the period, although a number of talented artists were of the Protestant faith. Catholicism, on the other hand, invested Baroque art of the seventeenth century with an exuberant spirituality.

Protestantism and the Modern State

In evaluating the long-term consequences of the Reformation, many people have associated Protestantism with modern liberalism, democracy, and capitalism. Looking ahead at the course of European history, they observed that those countries which became most prosperous and scientifically oriented were largely Protestant. Was there something in Protestantism conducive to wealth, progress, and political leadership? It is, however, important to remember that six-teenth-century Protestants were in fact no more tolerant, rational, or democratic than their Catholic peers. If Protestantism did lend itself to the development of democratic government and capitalist industry in the countries in which it predominated, its contribution was probably indirect and a matter of subtle encouragement rather than overt espousal.

Weber's Theory of Protestant-Capitalist Connection

The theory that Protestantism stimulated the growth of capitalism was first stated by the German sociologist Max Weber in 1904. In his book, *The Protestant Ethic and the Spirit of Capitalism*, Weber argued that the Calvinist virtues of hard work, thrift, and simple living were instrumental in creating an environment in which capitalism could flourish. This "Protestant work ethic" encouraged people to be in-dustrious, accumulate capital, and reinvest profits rather than spending them on luxury goods. All these characteristics are essential to a thriving capitalist economy. Protestants believed in the dignity of one's "calling," i.e., that all work no matter how humble was of value in God's eyes. This attitude helped to counteract the medieval prejudice against business. In addition, unlike Catholicism, Protestantism did not place restrictions on the lending of money at interest and it greatly reduced the number of holy days during which work was prohibited.

Opponents of Weber's Theory

Many scholars disagree with Weber's thesis. They cite the fact that the roots of capitalist development were laid down before the Reformation in lands such as Italy that never turned Protestant. In addition, not all Protestant countries (e.g., Scotland) experienced rapid economic growth, whereas certain Catholic lands (e.g., Belgium) developed prosperous capitalist economies. Clearly the rise of capitalism and democratic government are too complicated to be explained by any one factor. Nevertheless, the Protestant Reformation introduced new ideas and emphases to Western civilization which made themselves felt beyond the sphere of religion.

During the first half of the sixteenth century Europe experienced a revolution in the realm of ideas that left the unity of medieval Christendom forever shattered. As shaped by Luther, Zwingli, and Calvin, Protestantism called upon believers to trust in God's saving grace irrespective of their own actions. It opened the Bible to individual interpretations and called for a "priesthood of all believers."

Prompted by internal attempts at reform as well as the immediate threat of the loss of half its adherents, Catholicism responded with a renewed sense of its spiritual purpose. The Council of Trent abolished the most flagrant abuses and redefined Catholic dogma along strictly traditional lines. This made any compromise with Protestantism an impossibility. Headed by a line of reforming popes and armed with a devoted body of spiritual soldiers, the Jesuits, the Catholic Church moved against the Protestant cause. By 1560, the religious realignment of Europe was essentially complete. England, Scotland, northern Ireland, Holland, northern Germany, parts of Switzerland, and Scandinavia were overwhelmingly Protestant while Italy, Spain, southern Germany, and eastern Europe were solidly Catholic. This division along religious lines boded ill for the peace of Europe.

Recommended Reading

Roland H. Bainton, *Here I Stand: A Life of Martin Luther* (1950)

Roland H. Bainton, *The Reformation in the Sixteenth Century* (1952)

William J. Bouwsma, *John Calvin, A Sixteenth Century Portrait* (1987)

Edward M. Burns, *The Counter Reformation* (1964)

John Calvin, *Calvin: Institutes of the Christian Religion*, John T. McNeill, ed. (1961)

John Calvin, *John Calvin on God and Political Duty*, John T. McNeill, ed. (1950)

O. Chadwick, *The Reformation* (1963)

Norman Cohn, *The Pursuit of the Millennium* (1964)

A. G. Dickens, *The Counter Reformation* (1969)

A. G. Dickens, *The English Reformation* (1964)

A. G. Dickens, *Reformation and Society in Sixteenth-Century Europe* (1966)

G. R. Elton, *Reform and Reformation, England 1509–1558* (1978)

G. R. Elton, *Reformation Europe 1517–1559* (1963)

Erik H. Erikson, *Young Man Luther: A Study in Psychoanalysis* (1958)

Oskar Farner, *Zwingli the Reformer: His Life and Work* (1952)

René Fùlop-Miller, *Jesuits: A History of the Society of Jesus* (1963)

Robert W. Green, ed., *Protestantism and Capitalism* (1959)

Hajo Holborn, *A History of Modern Germany*, vol. I, The Reformation (1959)

C. Hollis, *The Jesuits* (1968)

Johan Huizinga, *Erasmus and the Age of Reformation* (1957)

Hubert Jedin, *A History of the Council of Trent* (1957–1961)

Ignatius Loyola, *The Spiritual Exercises of St. Ignatius* (1964)

Martin Luther, *Martin Luther: Selections from His Writings*, John Dillenberger, ed. (1961)

John T. McNeill, *The History and Character of Calvinism* (1954)

John C. Olin, *The Catholic Reformation: Savonarola to Ignatius Loyola: Reform in the Church* (1969)

Lewis W. Spitz, *The Protestant Reformation 1517–1559* (1985)

Lewis W. Spitz, ed., *The Reformation: Material or Spiritual?* (1962)

R. H. Tawney, *Religion and the Rise of Capitalism* (1947)

John M. Todd, *Luther: A Life* (1983)

Max Weber, *The Protestant Ethic and the Spirit of Capitalism* (1930)

George H. Williams, *The Radical Reformation* (1962)

CHAPTER 15

Overseas Expansion;
The Commercial Revolution;
Dynastic and Religious Struggles

Time Line

1419	Prince Henry the Navigator founds school and observatory
1492–1504	Christopher Columbus makes four voyages of discovery to the New World
1494–1559	Italian Wars
1494	Papal Line of Demarcation divides unexplored world between Portugal and Spain

1488	Bartolomeu Dias rounds Cape of Good Hope
1497	John Cabot lays English claim to North America
1498	Vasco da Gama reaches India
1513	Vasco de Balboa crosses Isthmus of Panama and sees Pacific Ocean
1519–1522	Ferdinand Magellan's fleet circumnavigates the globe
1519	Hernán Cortés conquers Aztecs
1521	Francis I begins first war against Charles V
1532	Francisco Pizarro conquers Incas
1534	Jacques Cartier explores Gulf of St. Lawrence for French
1545	Discovery of rich silver deposits at Potosí
1547	Ivan the Terrible crowned tzar of Russia
1556–1598	Reign of Philip II of Spain
1558–1603	Reign of Elizabeth I of England
1572	St. Bartholomew's Day Massacre
1588	Defeat of the Spanish Armada
1589	Henry of Navarre crowned Henry IV; founds Bourbon dynasty
1592	Luis Vaz de Camões' *The Lusiads* published
1598	Edict of Nantes
1603	Shakespeare's *Hamlet* published
1605	Cervantes first publishes *Don Quixote*
1609	Henry Hudson discovers Hudson River for Dutch

	Truce between Spain and Netherlands recognizes independent Dutch Republic
1618–1648	Thirty Years' War
1648	Peace of Westphalia

The Protestant and Catholic Reformations occurred within the broader context of social, economic, and political developments that ushered Europe into the modern age. While Luther and other religious reformers were engaged in a spiritual struggle for the soul of humanity, the Western world was undergoing momentous changes that would dramatically alter the lives of Europeans and non-Europeans alike. Explorers discovered vast new territories, most of which were ultimately brought under Western influence. New monarchies in France, England, and Spain consolidated royal authority to an even greater degree than before and established strong central rule. Encouraged by the centralized monarchies, buoyed by silver and gold from the New World, and propelled by a rapidly increasing population, Europe's economy underwent a remarkable upsurgence.

The period extending from the last quarter of the fifteenth century to the beginning of the seventeenth century was one of unparalleled prosperity and growth. Rising prices created opportunities for advancement for some, while displacing others from their centuries-long contact with the land. Religious issues intertwined with political and dynastic concerns to make the wars of the period particularly bitter ones. In the first half of the seventeenth century all of Europe was engaged in a prolonged conflict, the Thirty Years' War, that left the continent economically depressed, politically altered, and longing for stability.

Overseas Expansion

Beginning with Portuguese voyages in the fifteenth century, European nations and explorers launched an era of discovery that eventually unveiled many of the globe's myriad geographical mysteries. A number of interrelated factors underlay this era of expansion. Traditional explanations of God, gold, and glory were certainly a part of the story, but so too were other considerations such as curiosity, political rivalry, and an expansive spirit that came from the Renaissance ethos.

The Portuguese Empire

The country that opened the doors on exploration of the world was Portugal. Small and insignificant politically, Portugal might have seemed a most unlikely player on the stage of Renaissance exploration. Yet the combination of an ideal geographical location—looking out upon the Atlantic and Africa—together with several generations of exceptionally able mariners, gave Portugal pre-eminence at the dawn of the age of discovery.

Henry the Navigator

Prince Henry the Navigator (1394–1460), son of John I, King of Portugal, was a key figure in his country's leadership in the exploration of the overseas world. Henry was not himself a navigator, but through his keen interest in navigation and his royal influence, he served as a catalyst for Portuguese efforts. In 1419 he founded a famous observatory and school of geography in Sagres in southwest Portugal. Mariners under his authority explored the west coast of Africa, bringing back a lucrative cargo of ivory, gold, and slaves. Their ultimate goal was to open a sea route to the riches of the East that had been cut off from the West by Muslim control of the overland caravan route.

Portuguese Explorers

Driven by varying impulses, including a desire to join with Prester John, the legendary Christian ruler of Ethiopia, in a crusade against the Muslims, and hopes of profiting from the treasure chest of spices, silks, and other goods from the Orient, Portuguese explorers gradually eased their way southward along the African coast. In the process, they discovered the Madeira, Canary, and Cape Verde Islands. Eventually Bartolomeu Dias (c. 1450–1500) rounded the Cape of Good Hope at the southernmost tip of Africa in 1488. A decade later Vasco da Gama (c. 1469–1524) sailed around Africa and succeeded in reaching India. Thereafter Portuguese fighting vessels engaged Arab merchant ships in a fierce war for control of the eastern trade. Eventually Portuguese explorers discovered the Spice Islands (or Moluccas) in the east; westward voyages led to their discovery of Brazil.

Height and Decline of the Empire

During the late fifteenth and sixteenth centuries Portugal controlled a sizable overseas empire. Portugal's early success owed much to its superior sea power. Its ships were designed for both speed and maneuverability and were the first to be armed with cannon. The Portuguese established trading posts throughout Africa, Brazil, Indonesia, Japan, and China but rarely attempted to colonize their empire. Jesuit missionaries were active within Portuguese territories, however. Portugal's conquests are celebrated in one of the great classics of exploration literature, *The Lusiads* (1592) of Luis Vaz de Camões, an adventurer who had personal experience in some of the faraway lands he described. Portugal's far-flung dominions ultimately proved more than this tiny country and its small population could effectively control.

Rivalry with Spain

Neighboring Spain gradually supplanted Portugal as leader of the exploration movement. As early as 1494 the pope intervened to prevent the growing imperial rivalry from erupting into warfare. He divided the unexplored portions of the globe with a north-south Line of Demarcation intended to give Spain lands in the Western Hemisphere while leaving those to the East to Portugal. That same year the two nations signed the Treaty of Tordesillas that reaffirmed the pope's proclamation although moving the line farther west. By this change Portugal's area included Brazil but little else in the New World.

The Spanish Empire

Initially neighboring Spain watched Portugal with growing envy. The marriage of Isabella I of Castile to Ferdinand II of Aragon in 1469 led to their joint rule over a united Spanish nation. In 1492, with the fall of the last Muslim stronghold at Granada, the unification was complete and Spain turned its abundant energies in new directions. One of these was overseas exploration, with a particular focus on opening up a sea route to allow Spain to tap the wealth of the East.

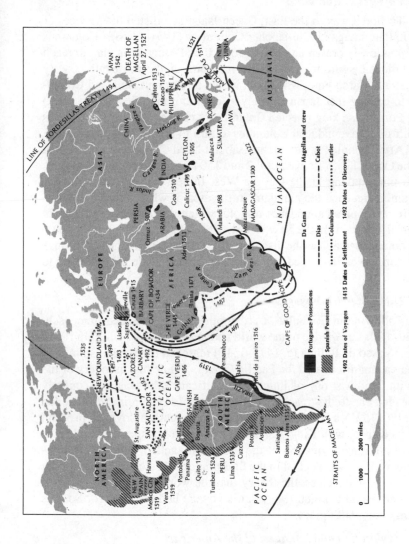

Exploration and Conquest in the 15th and 16th Centuries

Voyages of Columbus

To find a way to the East, Queen Isabella enlisted the services of the Italian navigator Christopher Columbus (1451–1506). Columbus had previously presented to King John II of Portugal his plan to reach the Orient by sailing west. (The memoirs of the thirteenth-century Venetian, Marco Polo, who had traveled throughout Asia, led Columbus to believe that Japan lay only a few thousand miles to the west.) The Portuguese king rejected Columbus's project and his pique at this rebuff may have induced Columbus to turn to Spain for backing.

After complex negotiations, Isabella hired Columbus as "Admiral of the Ocean Sea." Between 1492 and 1504 he undertook four voyages, each time making landfall in the West Indies. On his final journey Columbus reached the mainland in the area of what is today Panama. There he found an abundance of gold, which would be a key factor in Spanish dominion in the New World. Yet Columbus, for all his renown and popular acclaim as the discoverer of America (although the Vikings had done so earlier), died believing that he had made four voyages to Asia.

Other Spanish Voyages

Following in Columbus's wake, other mariners added immensely to Europe's knowledge of the world and to Spain's growing empire. In 1513, Vasco de Balboa (c. 1475–1519) marched across the Isthmus of Panama and discovered the Pacific Ocean. While his discovery of the "South Sea" was one of immense significance, he was subsequently beheaded due to the treachery of a rival. In 1519 Ferdinand Magellan (c. 1480–1521), a Portuguese mariner who sought employment in Spain after a dispute with King Manuel, set out on a voyage that resulted in the first circumnavigation of the globe. Magellan, killed by natives while his fleet was docked in the Philippines, was not able to savor the triumph. Nonetheless, the theory that the world was round had been proven beyond a doubt. Magellan's voyage laid the basis for Spain's claim to the Philippines.

Exploration and Conquest of the Americas

Meanwhile, on land, the Spanish *conquistadores* busily set about carving out an empire in the Americas. Noted for their cruelty and greed, these "conquerors" were typically landless younger sons of Spanish nobles who sought riches and adventure in the New World. Hernán Cortés (1485–1547) conquered the vast lands controlled by the Aztecs in Mexico while Francisco Pizarro (ca. 1478–1541) did the same in the territories of the Incas in Peru and Ecuador. In time Spain's control over large parts of Central and South America yielded enormous riches in the form of gold, silver, and Indian slaves.

Other Spanish explorers on land, including Hernando de Soto, Juan Ponce de León, and Francisco de Coronado expanded Spanish influence over extensive areas in both North and South America. Spain governed her empire through viceroys sent by the Spanish throne who instituted strong centralized rule. Much of the conquered land was divided into *encomiendas*, or large estates on which the native population was enserfed. Because the occupied regions contained vast wealth, the Spanish soon displaced Portugal as the leader in the age of exploration.

English, French, and Dutch Explorers

Other European nations were loath to stand aside while Spain and Portugal reaped overseas riches, and after 1600 the English, French, and Dutch sent their own explorers in search of fame and fortune. Political considerations stimulated rivalries between emerging national monarchies, and in time competition between Protestant and Catholic countries further fueled the fires of imperial competition.

Although England, France, and the Netherlands came to the era of exploration rather late, all made an appreciable impact. Their explorers reoriented European trade routes from the Mediterranean to the Atlantic while at the same time laying the groundwork for major imperial struggles among the European powers. As Spain had gradually supplanted Portugal's overseas preeminence, so would these nations eventually push Spain into the background. A turning point came in 1588 when England defeated the Spanish Armada. This event both heralded England's coming of age as a great sea power and signaled to other European nations the vulnerability of Spain. By 1650 the Dutch had replaced the Portuguese as the major commercial power in southern Asia, West Africa, and Brazil, and had supplanted Spain in the Caribbean.

Emphasis on Settlement

While explorers from England, France, and the Netherlands, including John Cabot, Jacques Cartier, and Henry Hudson, respectively, made noteworthy contributions to the ever-growing European knowledge of the seas, what was perhaps of greater long- range significance is that these countries, unlike either Spain or Portugal, placed considerable emphasis on settlement. Thus the English opened various colonies along the Atlantic seaboard; the Dutch founded New Netherlands along the mouth of the Hudson River (today's New York); and the French settled along the St. Lawrence River in New France (today's Canada).

Motives for Settlements

The trend to settled colonies resulted from a number of considerations. First, overseas territory provided an outlet for the energetic or ambitious who sought new horizons. Second, it was a convenient dumping ground for the disadvantaged and law-breaking elements in society. Third, persecuted religious and political minorities sought refuge in the New World. These varying motivations that underlay the peopling of the North American continent by Europeans would eventually loom large in the shaping of both the United States and Canada.

Impact of European Presence on Native Peoples

The growing European presence had a major cultural impact on the New World and the coastal regions in Africa and Southeast Asia. For native peoples, especially in the great Mesoamerican civilizations, the European presence often resulted in trauma and tragedy. Native cultures were destroyed and the people reduced to servitude. Populations were decimated by imported diseases such as smallpox, measles, syphilis, and gonorrhea. Christianity replaced traditional religions, and customs deemed repugnant by the Europeans were forbidden. Despite attempts by some sympathetic Catholic missionaries to secure humane treatment for the natives, the status and condition of indigenous peoples declined precipitously. On the other hand, Europe introduced its technology and culture, and the Americas gradually became Europeanized.

Elsewhere around the world European culture had little effect on native populations, save those that fell prey to the extensive slave trade.

Impact of Colonization on Europeans

The age of exploration changed Europe almost as dramatically as it did the Americas and other parts of the wider world. All sorts of new food products such as potatoes, tomatoes, various legumes, squash, pumpkins, and maize, added immensely to the variety of European diet. Sugar became more available. The importation of spices, including pepper, cinnamon, and cloves, made foodstuffs easier to preserve. Many spices were also used as medicines. Cotton fibers, silks, and furs meant changed dress habits. The introduction of tobacco (King James I railed against it as a "foul and stinking weed," but to no avail) created an addictive use that remains strong today. Success at conquest and colonization infused Europeans with a general sense of superiority, which colored their actions well into the twentieth century.

The Commercial Revolution

Perhaps the most dramatic effect of exploration, however, was an economic one. The vast influx of gold, silver, precious stones, and other valuable products from newly discovered or conquered lands (especially the discovery of fabulously rich silver deposits at Potosí in Peru in 1545) contributed to a substantial and chronic inflation. Between roughly 1500 and 1650, prices tripled and the economy changed rapidly. Europe's population grew as well. Even in countries that had little direct connection with overseas empires, these changes were significant. The advent of new global markets and the greater availability of money for reinvestment in expanding industries such as shipbuilding, clothmaking, mining, printing, and armaments stimulated the growth of capitalism and the decline of the guild system. These developments are usually termed the Commercial Revolution, although they took place over several centuries. They gave rise to new, markedly different conditions, ultimately affecting virtually every aspect of people's lives.

The Price Revolution

The price inflation that raged throughout Europe in the sixteenth and seventeenth centuries had a profound impact on the fabric of society.

Effects on Income

Those on fixed income suffered severely, while individuals who were able to adjust readily (and frequently) to the changing economic conditions tended to fare quite well. Significant proportions of the royalty, the nobility, and the landed gentry derived most of their income from rents on land that were set through long-term leases. As the purchasing power of this income declined, these groups found the economic foundation upon which their political strength had been based crumbling away.

Challenges to Aristocracy

The aristocracy faced growing challenges from those who benefited from inflation. Merchants, bankers, lawyers, and others profited considerably. These *nouveaux riches* used some of their wealth to acquire property and became a new landed class. In turn, they understandably expected a greater say in the affairs of state. Across much of Western Europe all of this resulted in what historians label a "crisis of the aristocracy." Old ways and established patterns of rule were being challenged by new forces, most of which had their roots in economic change.

Dislocations of Labor

While the impact of what could be termed a real economic revolution was perhaps most visible among the upper tiers of society, everyone was affected. In England, large landowners fenced in the common lands (the enclosure movement) and used them increasingly to raise livestock, which was less labor intensive than agriculture. Socially conscious preachers regularly used their pulpits to decry "sheep eating up men" as rural workers were displaced from the land. Wages failed to keep up with rising prices almost everywhere. The unemployed often became drifters, and an underclass of vagrants emerged, representing a tenth of the population in some countries. Rootless and gypsylike, they wandered from city to city, and many survived through petty crime.

Social Mobility

Numerous other dramatic changes resulted from the price revolution. Western Europe became more urbanized as peasants left the land and moved to towns and cities in search of work and a better life style. What had been a generally static society throughout the Middle Ages now became quite fluid. Social mobility was a hallmark of the times, with shrewd, hard-working individuals facing opportunities to improve their economic status and their standing in society. Indeed, monetary wealth increasingly replaced land ownership as a measure of social status or class.

Differences Between West and East

Those Western European nations that led in overseas expansion felt the primary impact of change. Rising prices tended to favor the western peasantry because most of their dues and fees were fixed by custom. Serfdom gradually disappeared in the West. While all of Europe experienced the repercussions of inflation, lands east of the Elbe River changed less. There, serfdom continued to be the standard lot in life of most people and the landowning class remained powerful and well-to-do. In Russia, serfdom retained its legal status until 1861. This inflexibility and resistance to social change explains, in large measure, why the eastern portion of the continent was rapidly outpaced by the West in terms of wealth and political progress during this period.

Growth of Colonialism

As Western European countries expanded overseas and made immense profits from newly opened areas of the world in the sixteenth and seventeenth centuries, governments began to seek ways to make their windfalls permanent. To this end, they established colonies to serve a number of purposes. Colonies were useful outlets for pressures from overpopulation or for release of domestic social and religious tensions. The settling of convicts in Georgia and later, in Australia, and the landing of the Pilgrim religious refugees are two examples.

Mercantilism. In addition, colonies were perceived as existing for the good of the mother country. They were potential markets for its products and suppliers of the raw materials from which such products could be made. This general economic concept, that envisioned a self-sufficient national economy, a favorable balance of trade, the accumulation of bullion, and exclusive colonial trade was known as mercantilism. It would be the dominating European economic philosophy until late in the eighteenth century. To accomplish these goals, governments passed mercantilist regulations that reduced the power of the guilds, encouraged new industries, passed Poor Laws that forced poor people to work, negotiated favorable commercial treaties with other lands, and raised tariff barriers against foreign imports. Thus government policy controlled much of the economy and contributed to the growing prosperity of merchants and industrialists.

The New Monarchies

Toward the end of the fifteenth century, France, England, and Spain experienced a growth of royal power that some historians describe as the "New Monarchies." Rulers in these countries expanded the bureaucratic reach of the state, made headway against competing powers within society, especially the nobility and the Church, and benefited from overseas expansion. In Russia social and economic conditions differed from those in the West, but powerful tsars also extended their autocratic control.

Valois France

The Valois dynasty founded by Philip VI in 1328 endured until 1589. Its last hundred years were marked by religious and political upheaval.

Louis XI and Charles VIII

Under Louis XI (ruled 1461–1483) France recovered from the Hundred Years' War and its monarchy gained in stature and authority. Louis filled the treasury and added significantly to the royal domain by annexing the Duchy of Burgundy and inheriting Anjou, Maine, and Provence. His son, Charles VIII (ruled 1483–1498), also enlarged the French realm by marrying the heiress to the Duchy of Brittany.

Charles's Italian Wars against the Habsburgs for dominion in Italy, however, proved disastrous for France. Lasting sixty-five years, they drained the French monarchy of funds and ended in defeat. Succeeding Valois monarchs financed the wars and other rising expenses by borrowing heavily, increasing taxes, selling offices (and the titles of nobility that went with some of them), and enlarging the centralized bureaucracy.

Francis I

A significant Valois monarch was Francis I (ruled 1515–1547). He expanded royal power and made the growing royal bureaucracy more manageable and efficient. In 1516 the pope reestablished the French monarch's control over the Gallican Church. Francis viewed the nascent Calvinist faith in France as a threat to the national church under royal authority but his suppression of it was sporadic. While Francis met with little success against the Habsburgs, he did give his country a larger role in European affairs as well as in overseas acquisitions. As a Renaissance monarch, he patronized French humanists and the arts flourished during his reign. Leonardo da Vinci spent time at his court.

Henry II and Catherine de' Medici

Francis's son, Henry II (ruled 1547–1559), signed the humiliating Treaty of Cateau Cambresis (1559) that recognized Habsburg claims to Italy and the Netherlands. Defeat eroded royal prestige, although it was somewhat compensated by the seizure of Calais from the English a year earlier. Henry's reign witnessed the beginning of systematic persecutions of the Huguenots (French Calvinists).

Henry was killed accidentally in a tournament. His widow, Catherine de' Medici, was a woman of exceptional ability and drive. She exerted great influence during the reigns of their ineffectual sons, Francis II, Charles IX, and Henry III. Different factions attempted to control the weak monarchs. Among them were the Huguenots, whose numbers included approximately one-third of the French nobility.

St. Bartholomew's Day Massacre

Religious differences erupted into open war in 1561 with bitter fighting that destroyed much of the French countryside. The Huguenots grew in strength and number. Finally, the Catholic faction, led by the

Queen and her supporters, determined to destroy the Huguenots in one fell blow. This came in the form of the St. Bartholomew's Day massacre of 1572. In this premeditated day of violence and its aftermath, an estimated 10,000 Protestants were murdered.

Henry IV and the Edict of Nantes

The Huguenots endured this adversity, however, and the religious wars dragged on until their leader, Henry of Navarre (Henry IV, reigned 1589–1610), inherited the throne in 1589. He founded the Bourbon dynasty that ruled until the French Revolution. Henry was one of a growing number who believed that the restoration of civil order under a strong monarch was more important than the extinction of one's religious rival. Thus as King, to promote peace and national unity, he converted from Protestantism to Catholicism, the majority faith, saying "Paris is well worth a Mass." Thereby he ended the threat he had faced from a Catholic League led by Philip II of Spain. However, Henry continued limited toleration of the Huguenots. This took concrete form in the 1598 Edict of Nantes, which granted them freedom of public worship in specified places, along with freedom of conscience and equal legal rights. Protestants were allowed to hold one hundred fortified towns, thus providing the Huguenots with a means of defense. This landmark document remained in effect for almost a century, offering official recognition to the possibility of Protestant and Catholic faiths coexisting within a state. It also marked an end to much of the internal strife that dominated France in the sixteenth century. Henry thereby laid the groundwork for France's emergence as the main continental power in the seventeenth century.

Tudor England

Prior to 1485, when Henry VII took the throne as the first of England's Tudor dynasty, the country was torn asunder by the Wars of the Roses. That he won his throne by battle at Bosworth suggested a continuation of factional strife, but this cold, calculating ruler founded what history usually views as England's greatest dynasty. During his reign, which lasted from 1485 to 1509, Henry VII strengthened the Tudor hold on the throne by placing the monarchy on a sound financial footing, instituting political and legal stability in the country, producing heirs, and implementing a shrewd diplomacy. One prominent feature of this diplomacy was the arrangement of a marriage between his eldest son, Arthur, and Catherine of Aragon, daughter of Ferdinand and Isabella of Spain. When the juvenile Arthur died shortly after the marriage, the first Tudor managed to rescue his policy from seeming shambles by arranging a marriage between Catherine and his second son, Henry.

Henry VIII

The antithesis of his father in many ways, Henry VIII (ruled 1509–1547) was a fun-loving, lavish spending monarch who reveled in the role of Renaissance prince. He deserves much of the credit for bringing England into the modern era, but unquestionably the central event of his reign was the break with Roman Catholicism (See Chapter 14.)

Despite his six wives and somewhat ruthless nature, Henry was immensely popular and adept at dealing with people. He worked through Parliament to implement most of his goals, including the creation of an English Church separate from Rome and the raising of funds for his wars. The Tudor Parliament was not yet a democratic one, but it had come to be regarded as speaking for the national interest. The House of Lords was filled with many new nobles who owed their lands and titles to the Tudors and were thus indebted to the king. Desire for royal and noble patronage also inclined the burghers and knights of the shire in the House of Commons to support the monarch. Henry cared little for administrative detail and left it to his able chief minister, Cardinal Thomas Wolsey, and his equally astute successor, Thomas Cromwell. Their work consolidated royal authority and enlarged and reorganized the bureaucracy. Both ultimately fell out of favor with the king.

Edward VI and Mary I

During the reign of Henry's only son, the young Edward VI, England was ruled by regents who made the English Church more Protestant in worship. Henry's religious reform had left a Catholic minority in England, especially in the North, who bitterly opposed Protestantism. When his eldest daughter, the Catholic-born Mary I, ascended the throne in 1553, Catholic interests predominated. (See Chapter 14). Protestants were persecuted and many of them rose in revolt against their unpopular queen. Mary's betrothal to Philip II of Spain further antagonized the nation.

Elizabeth I

Mary's marriage failed to produce heirs, and upon her death in 1558 the throne went to the last and greatest of the Tudors, Elizabeth I (reigned 1558–1603).

Domestic Policies. Under Elizabeth, England returned to Protestant ways, although the queen was quite tolerant of other religious views so long as those following them conformed publicly and remained loyal subjects. When they refused or entered into conspiracies against the crown, Elizabeth responded with harsh corrective measures. She faced continuous threats from Catholic conspirators who attempted to assassinate her. One such conspiracy involved Mary Queen of Scots, who suffered death for her involvement. Elizabeth also suppressed Puritans who were pressing for further religious reforms and the adoption of a presbyterian form of church government.

Like her father, Elizabeth ruled with a strong hand. She reduced even further the independent power of the nobility, involving them instead in elaborate court ritual.

Foreign Affairs. Elizabeth was concerned primarily with the strength and security of the state. She avoided costly wars. Never marrying, she ultimately chose to be "wedded to England," although she used her single status to good diplomatic advantage. Under her leadership England became prominent in European and world affairs. Overseas ventures begun under her predecessors expanded greatly, and several Elizabethan "sea dogs," including Sir Francis Drake and Sir Walter Raleigh, made significant marks as explorers and navigators. Such adventurers loomed large in England's great struggle against Spain, which featured repeated raids on Spanish holdings in the New World and quasi-piratical harassment of Spain's treasure fleet. This conflict reached a climax in 1588, with a grand Spanish design for an invasion of England. However, the swifter English fleet and inclement weather destroyed the Spanish Armada in the English Channel, an event that both signaled England's ascendancy as a world power and marked the beginning of the decline of Spain.

Tudor Achievements. With Elizabeth's death in 1603, "falling gently, like a ripe apple from the tree," as one commentator remarked, the Tudor dynasty came to an end. It had been a remarkable one not only in allowing religious change and the assumption by England of a prominent role in European affairs but also in other ways. During the Tudor era the foundation of what would become the mighty British Empire was laid thanks to the explorations of Cabot, Drake, Raleigh, and others. Elizabeth ruled over a population characterized by extraordinary vigor and a zest for life exemplified by one of the most creative periods in Western literature.

The Elizabethan Renaissance

The Elizabethan Renaissance (which actually encompassed the reigns of Henry VIII to James I) was marked by extraordinary literary achievement. Giants such as Ben Jonson, Edmund Spenser, Christopher Marlowe, and William Shakespeare towered over an age that was productive of many minor talents as well. Elizabethan writing sounded a note of exuberant self-confidence and patriotic ardor, and often lacked restraint. It was replete with allusions to Graeco-Roman mythology. These characteristics are found in abundance in the writings of the greatest of them all, William Shakespeare (1564–1616).

Shakespeare. So slim is the documentary evidence about Shakespeare's life that some have questioned his authorship of the thirty-seven plays that bear his name. Born in Stratford-upon-Avon, Shakespeare had little formal education. By the 1590s he had become involved in the theater and had begun to write plays. With them, modern secular drama in the West came of age. His range was remarkable—from comedy to history to tragedy—as was his breadth of knowledge. The beauty of his language and his great skill at portraying human nature have influenced writers to the present. His peerless tragedies, among them *Hamlet, Macbeth, King Lear,* and *Othello,* unveil their main character's weakness or fatal flaw that leads to his destruction.

Spain and the Netherlands

Thanks to its discoveries and conquests in the New World, Spain underwent a Golden Age in the late-fifteenth and the sixteenth century. Gold and silver poured into royal coffers, although much of it flowed out almost as rapidly as payment for seemingly endless military conflicts.

Charles V

Under the Habsburg Emperor Charles V (ruled 1516–1556) Spain was intimately involved in the wider affairs of the Holy Roman Empire. As emperor, he ruled over Germany, Italy, Austria, Hungary, Bohemia, the Netherlands, and Spain. (The latter came to him through his mother, a daughter of Ferdinand and Isabella.) Although his sage policies of allowing considerable self-government while at the same time expanding royal bureaucracy held a rather polyglot political unit together, Charles V expended much energy and money in policies of aggrandizement. He fought the French over Italy, countered the Protestants in Germany, and defended the Empire against the Ottoman Turks. The Spaniards especially resented the use of their overseas wealth for foreign wars. Two years before his death, Charles V divided the Habsburg dominions between Spain and Austria and retired to a monastery in 1556.

Philip II

Charles V's son Philip II (ruled 1556–1598) ascended the Spanish throne with views differing markedly from those of his father. A Spaniard by birth and preference, he viewed the rest of his Empire (the Netherlands, and holdings in Italy and overseas) as a resource to exploit for the pursuit of royal goals. Among them were the extinction of Protestantism, the advancement of Spanish interests, and the implementation of efficient, centralized rule. His policies led to outright revolt in the Netherlands, where religion blended with nationalistic aspirations in the conflict.

Revolt of the Netherlands. Leaders of the resistance to the Spanish yoke, most notably William of Orange (William the Silent), converted to Calvinism as the Protestant revolt spread. The tyranny of the Duke of Alba, Philip's commandant in the Low Countries from 1567 to 1573, added fuel to the fire. The struggle was a long and complex one, with religious differences in the 17 provinces of the Netherlands often hampering a united front against Spain. A truce in 1609 tacitly recognized an independent Dutch Republic in the northern portion of the Netherlands. The south, later Belgium, remained Spanish and predominantly Catholic.

Decline of Spanish Power. Other reverses in the late sixteenth century, particularly England's defeat of the Spanish Armada, heralded the end of Spain's overseas ascendance. In much the same way it had supplanted Portugal, Spain in turn yielded center stage to England, France, and the Netherlands. Spain's domestic economy and social structure remained backward and the monarchy debt-ridden. The decline was gradual, however, and Spain remained a major power both in Europe and on wider international fronts for another century. Yet clearly its star was declining by the time of Philip II's death in 1598.

Golden Age

Spain's Golden Age nurtured a number of unique creative talents.

El Greco. Arguably Spain's greatest painter of the age, El Greco (c. 1541–1614), was born in Greece but lived most of his adult life in Toledo. He epitomized the Catholic Reformation's fervent religiosity in a highly idiosyncratic style characterized by elongated figures, rapid, flickering brushstrokes, and cool, silvery tones.

Cervantes. Spain's outstanding literary figure, Miguel de Cervantes (1547–1616), lived a colorful but ultimately disillusioning life. He fought in the Battle of Lepanto, was captured and sold as a slave by pirates, and was imprisoned several times for debt. His masterpiece, *Don Quixote de la Mancha* (1605 and 1615), is a novel about the misadventures of an idealistic knight. In it Cervantes satirized the popular chivalric romances of his day as well as the cruelties, hypocrisies, and intolerances of Spanish society. The figure of Don Quixote has come to symbolize in Western culture a romantic dreamer out-of-tune with his times while his squire, Sancho Panza, represents peasant common sense and unheroic pragmatism. Yet Cervantes portrayed his "knight of the woeful countenance" with great pathos and empathy.

Russia

During the period when Western Europe was looking to the overseas world and consequently reaping great economic benefits, conditions were quite different in the East. The Russian Empire was solidly in place, but it was little affected by the religious transformations, economic changes, and Renaissance impulses felt elsewhere. The "Westernization" of Russia would not come until much later.

Ivan IV

For much of the sixteenth century, Russia was dominated by the dread character of Ivan IV, appropriately named "the Terrible" (ruled 1547–1584). Ivan strengthened Russia's military might and added territory in eastern Russia to the Muscovite state. He tightened the tsar's autocratic hold by ruthlessly suppressing the old nobility, the boyars. In addition, he kept the new landholding class founded by his grandfather, Ivan III, subservient to the throne. Russia remained overwhelmingly agricultural and its peasantry enserfed. Serfs had few legal rights while the landlords of the vast estates that characterized the country had almost unlimited powers. Enduring serfdom and a feudal-like system of agriculture remained the heart of Russian economic life well into the nineteenth century.

The Thirty Years' War

The internal and international religious struggles of the sixteenth century waned in the latter part of the century, thanks to the Edict of Nantes, the triumph of Protestantism in England, and the 1609 truce in the Netherlands. Tensions remained high, however, and during the early decades of the seventeenth century Europe experienced economic depression with falling prices and declining trade. This brief period of uneasy calm was shattered in 1618 by the eruption of a major war that was ultimately more widespread, devastating, and lengthy than any of the religious conflicts of the previous century had been. This conflict, which raged its way through three decades of unceasing turmoil, is known as the Thirty Years' War. It involved most of Europe, but England took little part owing to its own civil war.

The Causes of the War

A complex conflict, the Thirty Years' War intertwined secular and religious themes indiscriminately. Passions ran high on both fronts and contributed to the war's bitter and devastating nature. At heart it was a matter of Catholic versus Protestant, but as time passed and the war intensified, religious issues were almost submerged in matters such as German political concerns, the ambitions of various monarchs, and international diplomacy. Through it all, Germany suffered most as the primary battleground.

The Course of the War

By 1618, while Calvinism had spread throughout many parts of Germany, the basic balance between Lutherans and Catholics established by the Peace of Augsburg in 1555 was largely unaltered. The Thirty Years' War began when Calvinists in Bohemia revolted against Habsburg Catholic rule and Ferdinand II of Austria, who soon became Holy Roman Emperor, counterattacked. Ferdinand was bent on eradicating Protestantism in Germany, and he was also motivated by a desire to revive the declining Holy Roman Empire.

For the first decade of the war, Catholic forces decidedly had the upper hand. So certain was Ferdinand of success that he issued an Edict of Restitution in 1629, returning to the Catholic Church all properties secularized since 1552. A year later, however, the balance swung when Sweden's Lutheran king, Gustavus Adolphus, entered the fray. Even some German Catholic princes welcomed his entry as being preferable to complete subjection to Ferdinand II, and ironically, France's Catholic Cardinal Richelieu secretly helped finance the Lutheran king at the outset. Richelieu feared that a decisive victory by Ferdinand II would make Habsburg rule too strong and upset the balance of power on the European continent.

While he lived, Gustavus Adolphus was more than a match for Catholic forces in the field, but with his death in 1632 the tide once more turned. Eventually matters reached such a perilous state that France actively entered the war on the Swedish side, and for its final decade the struggle saw these countries (as well as the German Protestant princes and the Dutch Republic) arrayed against Spain, Austria, and

Europe, 1648

Bavaria. Germany was little more than a battleground where they carried out brutal assaults on one another. Add to this situation mindless actions by mercenaries, the ravages of plague, butchery, and starvation, and the sum was a terrible disaster for Germany. Some historians have estimated that as much as forty per cent of the German population died during the war.

The Peace of Westphalia

Peace negotiations began in the mid–1640s, though the wholesale destruction of life and property within Germany continued unabated as delegates from all the states pursued points of minutiae and debated minor clauses endlessly. Finally, in 1648, the Peace of Westphalia brought the Thirty Years' War to an end. With its signing, certain landmarks appeared in European history. Perhaps most notable is the emergence of France as the predominant power on the continent. The terms of the treaty provided that the more than 300 German states remain intact as sovereign states. France expanded its domains by the acquisition of Alsace. The Austrian Habsburgs lost territory they had gained in Germany, and the Holy Roman Empire existed in name only. The Peace of Augsburg was reaffirmed and its provisions extended to Calvinists. Church territories in Germany were to belong to whoever held them in 1624. The Dutch Republic and the Swiss Confederation were formally recognized. The Dutch received trading rights in Brazil and Indonesia from the Portuguese as well as territory it had conquered along the river Scheldt. Sweden made territorial gains on the Baltic. In many ways a singularly unredeeming conflict, the war nonetheless set the stage for a new, different Europe of independent sovereign states and for a worldwide territorial struggle between England and France that would last until 1815.

For most of the period from roughly the end of the fifteenth to the middle of the seventeenth century, Europe was in an expansionary phase. First Portuguese and shortly afterward Spanish explorers claimed immense territories around the globe whose mineral wealth and trade would enrich their mother countries. For a century the two nations monopolized overseas exploration. Portugal proved too small to control her vast empire, however, and Spain used up her imperial riches in fruitless wars. By 1600 the English, French, and Dutch had begun to challenge Iberian colonial supremacy. Colonization imposed Western language, religion, and culture on native populations and reduced many to servitude. European efforts to work some of the new land led eventually to the importation of slaves. The most dramatic effect of the opening of global markets for Europe was the tremendous influx of new wealth and the inflation it created.

Religious issues engendered by the Protestant Reformation caused much turmoil during this period. France, Spain, and the Netherlands were engaged in religious warfare during the second half of the six-teenth century. Habsburg attempts to eradicate Protestantism led to the Thirty Years' War. Its conclusion put an end to the idea that either Protestantism or Catholicism could destroy the other. The Peace of Westphalia (1648) redrew the map of Europe and reduced the Holy Roman Empire to a shadow of its former self. Europe emerged as a collection of independent sovereign states. France supplanted the Habsburgs as the dominant power on the continent and Holland replaced Spain as the leading maritime nation. Warfare and overseas expansion contributed to the growth of centralized authority and the increasingly secular nature of politics, hallmarks of the modern world.

Recommended Reading

Eric Alexson, *Congo to Cape* (1973)

Trevor Henry Aston, ed., *Crisis in Europe, 1560–1660* (1974)

S. T. Bindoff, *Tudor England* (1950)

Robert Bireley, *Religion and Politics in the Age of the Counter-Reformation* (1981)

Charles R. Boxer, *The Dutch Seaborne Empire 1600–1800* (1965)

Charles R. Boxer, *The Portuguese Seaborne Empire 1415–1825* (1970)

Karl Brandi, *The Emperor Charles V* (1939)

Fernand Braudel, *The Mediterranean and the Mediterranean World in the Age of Philip II* (1972)

Renate Bridenthal et al., eds., *Becoming Visible, Women in European History* (1987)

M. Chute, *Shakespeare of London* (1957)

Natalie Zemon Davis, *The Return of Martin Guerre* (1983)

Richard S. Dunn, *The Age of Religious Wars 1559–1660* (1974)

John H. Elliott, *Europe Divided 1559–1598* (1969)

John H. Elliott, *Imperial Spain 1469–1716* (1964)

G. R. Elton, *England Under the Tudors* (1974)

G. R. Elton, *The Tudor Revolution in Government* (1959)

Carolly Erickson, *The First Elizabeth* (1983)

J. D. Fage, *A History of Africa* (1978)

F. Fernandez-Arnesto, *Ferdinand and Isabella* (1975)

Carl J. Friedrich, *The Age of the Baroque 1610–1660* (1952)

Pieter Geyl, *The Revolt of the Netherlands 1555–1609* (1958)

Carlo Ginzburg, *The Cheese and the Worms: The Cosmos of a Sixteenth Century Miller* (1980)

S. J. Greenblatt, *Sir Walter Raleigh: The Renaissance Man and His Roles* (1973)

E. J. Hamilton, *American Treasure and the Price Revolution in Spain 1501–1650* (1934)

C. H. Haring, *The Spanish Empire in America* (n.d.)

H. H. Hart, *Sea Road to the Indies* (1950)

Hajo Holborn, *A History of Modern Germany, vol I: The Reformation* (1959)

Frederick A. Kirkpatrick, *The Spanish Conquistadores* (1962)

Helmut G. Koenigsberger and George L. Mosse, *Europe in the Sixteenth Century (1973)*

A. W. Lovett, *Early Habsburg Spain 1517–1598* (1986)

John Lynch, *Spain Under the Habsburgs* (1981)

J. D. Mackie, *The Earlier Tudors 1485–1558* (1952)

Garrett Mattingly, *The Defeat of the Spanish Armada* (1970)

Samuel Eliot Morison, *Admiral of the Ocean Sea: A Life of Christopher Columbus* (1974)

Samuel Eliot Morison, *The European Discovery of America: The Southern Voyages* (1974)

Samuel Eliot Morison, *The European Discovery of America: The Northern Voyages* (1971)

Samuel Eliot Morison, *The Great Explorers* (1978)

John E. Neale, *The Age of Catherine de' Medici* (1962)

John E. Neale, *The Elizabethan House of Commons* (1949)

John E. Neale, *Queen Elizabeth I* (1967)

Charles E. Nowell, *The Great Discoveries and the First Colonial Empires* (1954)

Geoffrey Parker, *The Thirty Years' War* (1985)

John H. Parry, *The Age of Reconnaissance: Discovery, Exploration and Settlement 1450–1550* (1963)

John H. Parry, *The Establishment of the European Hegemony 1415–1715* (1966)

John H. Parry, *The Spanish Seaborne Empire* (1966)

W. H. Prescott, *The Conquest of Mexico* (1964)

W. H. Prescott, *The Conquest of Peru* (1961)

David B. Quinn and A. N. Ryan, *England's Sea Empire, 1550–1642* (1983)

E. E. Rich and C. H. Wilson, eds., *The Cambridge Economic History of Europe, Vol. IV: The Economy of Expanding Europe in the Sixteenth and Seventeenth Centuries* (1967)

Michael Roberts, *Sweden's Age of Greatness* (1973)

A. L. Rowse, *The Elizabethan Renaissance: The Life of the Society* (1971)

J. J. Scarisbrick, *Henry VIII* (1968)

Simon Schama, *The Embarrassment of Riches: An Interpretation of Dutch Culture in the Golden Age* (1987)

Lacey Baldwin Smith, *The Realm of Henry VII* (1968)

Stanley J. and Barbara H. Stein, *The Colonial Heritage of Latin America* (1970)

R. L. Storey, *The Reign of Henry VII* (1968)

H. Trevor-Roper, ed., *The Age of Expansion: Europe and the World 1559–1660* (1968)

C. V. Wedgewood, *The Thirty Years' War* (1981)

Richard B. Wernham, *After the Armada: Elizabethan England and the Struggle for Western Europe* (1984)

Richard B. Wernham, *Before the Armada: The Emergence of the English Nation, 1485–1588* (1972)

Charles Wilson, *The Dutch Republic* (1968)

Yves F. Zoltvany, *The French Tradition in America* (1969)

Index